D1071588

Collaboration in Belgium

Collaboration in Belgium

Léon Degrelle and the Rexist Movement
1940–1944

Martin Conway

Yale University Press
New Haven & London
1993

Copyright © 1993 by Yale University

Photographs: Copyright © Centre de recherches et d'études
historiques de la seconde guerre mondiale, Brussels

All rights reserved. This book may not be reproduced in
whole or in part, in any form (beyond that copying permitted
by Sections 107 and 108 of the U.S. Copyright Law and except
by reviewers for the public press), without permission from
the publishers.

Designed by Stephanie Hallin

Set in Linotron Bembo by Best-set Typesetter Ltd, Hong Kong
Printed in Great Britain by St Edmundsbury Press

ISBN 0–300–05500–5

Library of Congress Catalog Number 93–10870

LIBRARY
ALMA COLLEGE
ALMA, MICHIGAN

Contents

Preface

THIS BOOK could not have been completed without the generous assistance of a number of people and institutions. It was originally a doctoral thesis and I am grateful to Wadham College and Christ Church, Oxford, the British Academy, the Commissariat for International Relations of the Belgian *Ministère de l'Education Nationale* and the Institute for Historical Research of the University of London for their financial assistance. The supervisor of my doctoral thesis, Richard Cobb, has been throughout my research a source of academic advice and personal inspiration. A.F. Thompson and Colin Lucas both offered advice and encouragement at important times while Balliol College, Oxford has provided me with an ideal environment in which to revise and complete the manuscript.

In Belgium I have benefited from the guidance of those who have helped an all too ignorant foreigner to understand something of their country's complex history. The staff of the *Auditorat Général près la Cour Militaire* of the Palais de Justice in Brussels generously allowed me to consult the documents in their possession, and I am especially grateful to Colonel Maes and his colleagues for making my visits to their archives such a pleasure. Jean Stengers of the University of Brussels, Francis Balace of the University of Liège, Paul Jamin and Pablo and Sara Layson have all helped my work in important ways. The *Centre de recherches et d'études historiques de la seconde guerre mondiale* in Brussels has provided me with innumerable forms of assistance and I am especially grateful to Albert De Jonghe, Alain Dantoing, José Gotovitch, Rudi Van Doorslaer and Lut Van Daele of the *Centre* for their advice. Madame Hepp of Jemeppe-sur-Meuse kindly allowed me to consult documentary material belonging to her late husband José Streel, while Léon Degrelle in Spain gave generously of his time and hospitality to assist me with my research. John Nicoll of Yale University Press has been the most sympathetic and encouraging of editors.

Throughout my work on the Rexists I have received the support of a wide range of friends and colleagues who have tolerated my interest in the peculiarities of Belgian history. I owe an especial debt to my parents and to Tom Buchanan, Katya Andreyev, Anna Evans, Richard Hering and Robin Gable. Above all, I am indebted to Denise Cripps who has endured the presence of the Rexists in her life for far too long.

Nobody can study the Second World War without being conscious of the profound passions which the events of the war continue to stimulate. This is intended to be a book without heroes or villains. It is dedicated to the memory of all the victims of the tragic events which form its subject.

List of Abbreviations

ACJB	*Association Catholique de la Jeunesse Belge*
AGRA	*Amis du Grand Reich Allemand*
Aud. Gen.	*Auditorat Général près la Cour Militaire*, Brussels
BDC	Berlin Document Center
BIRD	*Bureau d'information, de renseignements et de documentation*
Cahiers	*Cahiers d'histoire de la seconde guerre mondiale*
CCW	*Communauté Culturelle Wallonne*
CERE	*Centre pour la Réforme de l'Etat*
CW	*Cercle Wallon*
C2GM	*Centre de recherches et d'études historiques de la seconde guerre mondiale*, Brussels
DeVlag	*Duits-Vlaamse Arbeidsgemeenschap*
DeWag	*Deutschwallonische Arbeitsgemeinschaft*
Doct.	Document
Doss.	Dossier
DSI	*Département de Sécurité et d'Information*
EM	*Etat-Major*
EMF	*Etat-Major Fédéral*
FC	*Formations de Combat*
GRMA	German Records Microfilmed at Alexandria (USA)
HSSPF	*Höherer SS- und Polizeiführer*
Info.	Information
Inst.	Instruction
JS	José Streel
KK	*Kreiskommandantur*
LC	Louis Collard
LD	Léon Degrelle
Le PR	*Le Pays Réel*
MNPW	*Mouvement National Populaire Wallon*
NSKK	*Nationalsozialistisches Kraftfahrer Korps*
OFK	*Oberfeldkommandantur*
OKH	*Oberkommando des Heeres*
PA	*Partisans Armés*

PPF	*Parti Populaire Français*
Pro Just.	*Pro Justicia*
POB	*Parti Ouvrier Belge*
RuSHA	*Rasse- und Siedlungshauptamt*
Sipo-SD	*Sicherheitspolizei-Sicherheitsdienst*
SVTW	*Service des Volontaires du Travail pour la Wallonie*
UTMI	*Union des Travailleurs Manuels et Intellectuels*
TB	*Tätigkeitsbericht*
VM	Victor Matthys
VNV	*Vlaams Nationaal Verbond*

FLANDERS

WEST
FLANDERS

Bruges •

• Gent

EAST
FLANDERS

Antwerp

ANTWERP

LIMBURG

Hasselt

Brussels

BRABANT

Tournai

HAINAUT

La Louvière

Mons •

Charleroi •

Namur

Huy •

Liège

Verviers

LIEGE

WALLONIA

NAMUR

LUXEMBOURG

Arlon

MAP OF BELGIUM

Introduction

The Origins of Collaboration

THIS BOOK is intended as an examination of the phenomenon of collaboration in German-occupied Europe during the Second World War. Collaboration is a ghost which has haunted the history of twentieth-century Europe. The men and women who for reasons of idealism or self-interest (or, perhaps more frequently, a combination of the two) chose to cast off loyalty to their nation and to their compatriots in order to serve the invader has remained a central memory of the Second World War and has also become an image which expresses the pessimistic spirit of an age all too aware of the profound conflicts of ideology, ethnicity and social class which lie beneath the surface in all nations. If the nineteenth century was dominated by a spirit of common endeavour, of the creation of new nations and empires, it is in this century that attention has come to focus instead on the seeds of division which lurk at the heart of national communities. Collaboration is the revelation of this division and the collaborator has become the symbol not merely of the failings of human nature – pride, cowardice, avarice, lust – to which all men and women are vulnerable but of the enemy within who, more than the external foe, has come to be seen as the real danger to the nation.

Treason is in no sense a modern creation. From the wars of Ancient Greece to those of the 1790s, European history has abounded with examples of individuals and groups who have rejected their community to serve a foreign power. But it is only in the twentieth century that the eternal theme of betrayal has taken on a new significance and a new name. This distinctly modern phenomenon of collaboration is a product both of the era of the modern nation-state inaugurated by the French Revolution and of the internal tensions which have threatened those nation-states during the last hundred years. In times of peace such conflicts are muted. The trappings of modern nationalism – flags, anthems, monarchs and armies – conjure up a comforting image of a people who, whatever their other differences, share an overriding loyalty to the nation. But the mass warfare of the twentieth century has made unprecedented demands on the populations of Europe. No longer have they been passive bystanders in limited conflicts pursued by their leaders out of dynastic or diplomatic ambition. Instead, as conscripted soldiers or citizens, they have been obliged to demonstrate their willingness to place their *lives* at the service of their nation.

In the killing fields of the First World War this commitment to nation reached its apotheosis, but it was a spirit which could never be rekindled with the same intensity. Despite the horror of the battles, nationalism emerged from the conflict of 1914–18 with much of its potency undiminished. The 1920s and 1930s were suffused with a patriotic spirit in which most Europeans readily identified with their nation. But there were also new tensions at work. Social conflicts exacerbated by the economic upheavals of the inter-war years undermined the optimistic image of a nation united by a common purpose. New ideologies arose – communism to the left, fascism to the right – which claimed to transcend national boundaries. Ethnic groups – the Slovaks, Croats and Flemish among others – came of age and challenged existing nation-states in the name of new nationalisms. Buttressed by mass education and law codes, loyalty to the nation-state retained its privileged status but, as Europe moved again towards war at the end of the 1930s, the absence of a patriotic fervour akin to that of 1914 bore witness to an awareness not merely of the horrors of modern war but also of the divisions which lurked behind the gestures of national unity.

It was the complex amalgam of national, social and ideological conflicts conveniently, if somewhat inadequately, described as the Second World War which brought these tensions to the fore. In a war in which there was rarely a clear-cut front-line and where legitimacy within states was often contested by competing regimes, civilians were called upon to make stark choices. As collaboration and its mirror image resistance demonstrated, this was a war in which all were participants and in which even the actions of daily life were invested with a new significance. The private realm had been invaded by political concerns and, though the radical options of collaboration or resistance were only ever embraced by small minorities, few were able to avoid entirely the choices imposed by the conflict. The unemployed worker who volunteered for work in Germany, the woman who crossed the street to avoid (or to meet) German soldiers, or the family which offered food to a fugitive who called at their door were all making choices which – though they rarely lacked a certain human ambivalence – possessed a significance which extended beyond the personal sphere.

Collaboration during the Second World War with the Nazi armies or those of their allies took myriad forms. Some of these had a long tradition in European history. Relationships of women with foreign soldiers, the denunciation of compatriots or trading with the Occupying forces are all actions which, though they too clearly represent choices, form an inherent element of almost any military conflict. What was almost entirely novel in

Europe between 1939 and 1945 was the emergence of movements of political collaboration. During the previous conflict there had been some faint
precursors of this phenomenon but it was only in the Second World War
that political collaboration became a mass movement. From Quisling's
Norwegian regime in the North to the Greek fascist groups in the South
and from Vichy France in the West to Vlassov's pro-German Russian
forces in the East, all of the diverse territories of Axis-occupied Europe –
with the exception of Poland – produced a collaborationist movement of
some importance. Apart from a shared commitment to the German cause,
these groups had little in common. While some were nationalist, others
claimed allegiance to a European fascist cause. Some were clearly reactionary and sought to restore a former era of order and harmony while many
were aggressively modern and revolutionary. Some claimed a religious
inspiration but others were secular and emphatically anti-clerical. Mostly,
they were a confused amalgam of all of these elements. Forged in the
chaotic circumstances of Occupation, collaborationist movements rarely
achieved great coherence and often shared little beyond support for the
German cause and a belief in the need for a vaguely defined 'New Order'.

This study seeks to contribute towards the analysis of political collaboration through exploring the history of the Rexist movement. This was the
principal francophone collaborationist grouping in Belgium during the
German Occupation of May 1940 to September 1944. The case of the
Rexists demonstrates well the diversity of collaboration. Rex was originally a movement of Catholic students and intellectuals led by a young
journalist, Léon Degrelle, which in the mid-1930s had briefly won support
for its populist message of authoritarian political reform from a population
dissatisfied by the failure of the governing parties to respond effectively to
Belgium's economic and social difficulties. Within a few years Rex had
declined to a marginal political force but it was saved from extinction by
the German invasion of 1940. Initially one of many advocates within
Belgium of a peace settlement with Nazi Germany in the wake of the
latter's apparently decisive military victory in continental Europe, Rex
moved gradually towards an explicitly pro-Nazi stance which culminated
in Degrelle's open declaration of support in January 1941. This espousal of
the Nazi cause brought the Rexists few rewards. A large majority of
their compatriots opposed their views while the *Wehrmacht* authorities
responsible for the administration of Occupied Belgium showed little
inclination to work with the movement, preferring to favour those Flemish
Nationalists who had also opted to support the Nazi cause. However, the
German attack on the Soviet Union in June 1941 gave the Rexists the
opportunity to form a volunteer military unit, the *Légion Wallonie*, which
fought with some distinction alongside the German armies on the Eastern
Front. Moreover, within Belgium the increasingly hostile attitude of the
population obliged the German authorities to rely more directly on the

assistance of the Rexists whom they appointed to posts of responsibility within local and provincial government. Differences remained within Rex as to how closely it should identify with the Nazi cause but, as the military conflict turned to the disadvantage of the Axis forces, Degrelle chose to push forward with collaboration, announcing in January 1943 his support for the integration of the francophone Belgians – now deemed by him to be a Germanic race – into an expanded German empire.

Collaboration had become a blind alley from which there was to be no escape. Degrelle spent much of the latter war years in Berlin or with the *Légion Wallonie* on the Eastern Front while his Rexist followers within Belgium became the targets of a ruthless campaign of assassinations by the Resistance forces. The *Wehrmacht* administrators in Brussels still refused to grant the Rexists substantial political power but Degrelle did gradually win support for his cause within the higher reaches of the Nazi elite. The Rexist leader was decorated by Hitler with the Iron Cross with Oak Leaves in 1944 for his military feats on the Eastern Front and became not only a hero of the Reich propaganda machine but also won the all-important support of Himmler's SS. These successes did, nonetheless, provide only modest compensation for the difficulties faced by Degrelle's diminishing band of supporters within Belgium. As the Allied liberation approached, the Resistance stepped up its attacks on Rexist militants, prompting a violent campaign of 'counter-terrorism' by the beleaguered Rexists in the summer of 1944. This final act of blind fury merely served to underline the political and moral bankruptcy of their cause and with the arrival of the Allied armies in September many Rexists fled into exile in Germany. The Reich provided only a temporary haven and, although amidst the chaos of the final German military collapse in May 1945 some Rexists – including Degrelle – escaped to begin new lives beyond the reach of the Belgian judicial authorities, most were ultimately apprehended and returned to Belgium where they faced imprisonment, trial and, in some cases, execution.

The historical significance of the Rexists does not, however, lie solely in their espousal of collaboration. They also provide an important example of the wide variety of anti-democratic currents which were active within inter-war Europe and which are all too readily subsumed under the con-venient label of 'fascism'. At different stages in their political evolution, the Rexists were Catholic authoritarians, Poujadist populists and National Socialists. It is doubtful whether they were ever fascist. Fascism is of course a term which evades easy definition. Despite efforts by historians and others to give it a more specific meaning, it has come to be applied indiscriminately to almost all movements of the inter-war political right which rejected the structures of parliamentary democracy. This is clearly unsatisfactory and has resulted in the grouping together of such diverse forces as the Catholic military dictatorships of the Iberian peninsula, the nostalgic anti-modernists of Vichy France, the nationalist technocrats of Mussolini's Italy, and the racist ideologues of the Third Reich. Such similarities as did exist between these groups arose from their shared antipathy to the liberal, parliamentary structures which had emerged in much of Europe during the later nineteenth century. But their intellectual inspiration, social composition and ideological goals all varied markedly and, rather than seeking to force them within the constraints of a supposedly unitary 'fascism', it would seem more worthwhile to accept that inter-war Europe gave rise to a number of anti-democratic movements of the right, each possessed of its own origins and character.

Rex is one of these movements which needs to be considered on its own terms rather than as a Belgian 'variant' on some standard fascist model. Its origins in the Catholic student world of the University of Louvain place it at the heart of the revival of a more militant form of political Catholicism which took place in many areas of Europe during the inter-war years. This revival was led by young Catholic intellectuals who proclaimed that the solution to the problems of the modern era lay not in the atheistic doctrines of liberalism or Soviet Communism but in a political and social structure modelled on distinctly Catholic ideals. Drawing their inspiration from the series of encyclicals issued by the papacy from the late nineteenth century, Catholic radicals from countries as diverse as Austria, Italy, Spain, Portugal, Poland and Lithuania sought to found political movements which, by defining themselves as against both liberal democracy and modern totalitarianisms, advocated a 'third way' of strong central government combined with a devolved structure of guilds and corporations. It was in the early 1930s that this current of Catholic radicalism reached its peak. The regimes of Salazar in Portugal and of Dollfuss in Austria drew much of their inspiration from these ideas and in turn served as an example which other movements sought to emulate. Rex formed part of this European trend and its subsequent failure reflected the difficulties which faced all of these Catholic political movements at the end of the 1930s. As diplomatic events forced Europe towards a military conflict between nazism and the western democracies, so their hopes of a distinctive 'third way' evaporated and they were forced to choose between two alternatives, neither of which substantially reflected their political ideals.[1]

Rex was also a product of the highly distinctive politics of Belgium. The history of Belgium has been remarkably neglected by historians of modern Europe. Its origins in a diplomatic compromise of 1830, unremarkable geography and seemingly placid political culture have conspired to create an impression of a country hardly worthy of serious attention alongside its larger – and more volatile – neighbours. This neglect is unjustified. The development of Belgium since its creation in 1830 provides an important example of the complex process of nation-building in western Europe. As the Austrian Netherlands in the eighteenth century, and subsequently as part of the Napoleonic Empire and after 1815 of the Dutch monarchy, its peoples had long enjoyed a common destiny. But aside from a shared loyalty to the Catholic faith, the diverse populations of Belgium possessed little natural homogeneity. To the underlying ethnic division between the francophone Walloons of the southern provinces of the country and the Dutch-speaking populations of Flanders were added the long-standing commercial and political rivalries between the different cities of Antwerp, Gent, Bruges, Brussels and Liège. In addition, rapid industrialisation during the nineteenth century – notably in the francophone provinces of the Hainaut and Liège as well as in East Flanders – produced new, stark divisions of social class between a working class which endured some of the harshest living conditions in western Europe and a self-confident, predominantly francophone bourgeoisie.

Despite these obstacles, the new Belgian state initially proved highly successful. The constitutional monarchy and parliamentary system established in 1831 provided the foundations for a bourgeois political culture based on a limited electoral franchise while the conventional trappings of nineteenth-century statehood – a monarch, law code, army and, through the personal initiative of King Léopold II, even a colony in the Congo – contributed to the creation of a distinctive Belgian national identity. Tensions did remain. Fierce electoral rivalries between the Catholic Party and their anti-clerical Liberal opponents culminated in a decisive victory for the Catholics in the elections of 1884 which inaugurated an uninterrupted period of Catholic Party government until 1914. The growth of the industrial proletariat gave birth to a powerful Socialist Party, the *Parti Ouvrier Belge (POB)*, which through electoral campaigns and a series of general strikes campaigned strenuously but unsuccessfully for universal manhood suffrage. The Flemish population, disadvantaged by their poor, largely rural character and by the dominance even in much of Flanders of a francophone middle class, struggled to achieve educational and legal rights for the Dutch language. Nevertheless, the forces for integration remained stronger than those of disunity and, when Belgian neutrality was abruptly violated by the German invasion of August 1914, it was in a mood of genuine patriotism that the Belgian armies rallied under the personal leadership of King Albert to the defence of their nation.[2]

The First World War was Belgium's finest hour and also the source of many of its subsequent discontents. Belgium in the inter-war years was a complex society in which the transition from the nineteenth-century hegemony of a francophone bourgeoisie had not yet produced a new, viable structure of political consensus. The bonds of unity remained strong. The harsh German Occupation of much of the country from 1914 to 1918, combined with the military resistance sustained throughout the conflict by the Belgian armies in a small salient of territory in West Flanders, reinforced a strong sense of Belgian nationhood as well as exalting King Albert to an almost universal veneration. The Allied victory in 1918 and Albert's triumphant return to Brussels was accompanied by an attempt to bring about a new *modus vivendi* in Belgian political life. At the King's insistence, universal manhood suffrage was introduced, social reforms inaugurated and measures introduced to meet Flemish demands. The new electoral system destroyed the overall majority formerly enjoyed by the Catholic Party and instead obliged the three principal parties – the Catholics, Socialists and Liberals – to share power in coalition governments. Composed of ministers drawn from two or, on occasions, all three of these parties, the governments of the inter-war years were on the whole short-lived and their transitory character contributed to a widespread feeling that the political system was failing to meet the needs of the nation.

It was in the 1930s that this discontent began to threaten the established political parties and the *de facto* system of power-sharing which they represented. Though young radicals called for a more confrontational stance, the *Parti Ouvrier Belge* remained firmly rooted within the parliamentary regime but a small Communist Party did emerge, notably in the industrial regions of Wallonia where it drew support from workers hard hit by the world economic depression. In addition, a series of middle-class protest movements, many of them nationalist or Catholic in inspiration, capitalised on popular hostility to the political elite and called for economic reforms and a more authoritarian system of government. Finally, and most significantly, Flemish nationalism emerged for the first time as a movement with mass support. The events of the First World War had given a new momentum to the demands of the Flemish population. The troops who had maintained the military struggle against the German armies after 1914 had been predominantly Flemish in origin and the feeling that they had not received their due reward in post-war Belgium was reinforced by the punitive judicial sentences passed on those few Flemish intellectuals who had chosen during the war to support the German cause. The limited concessions made in the 1920s – notably the transformation of Gent University into a Dutch-language institution – were insufficient to defuse Flemish grievances and, though only a small minority supported the cause of an independent Flemish state, this popular discontent encouraged the creation of a nationalist political party, the *Vlaams Nationaal Verbond* (*VNV*), which in the 1939 elections won almost 8 per cent of the national vote.[3]

Rex formed part of this amalgam of discontents. When it was founded in the early 1930s, it was merely the latest in a long series of Catholic protest movements which had emerged in francophone Belgium since the First World War. Though the overwhelming majority of Belgians were nominally Catholic, large sections of the population – especially in the industrial heartlands of Wallonia – had abandoned the faith during the nineteenth century and religious practice was markedly higher in Flanders and the rural areas of Wallonia than in the major urban and industrial centres. Electoral support for the Catholic Party reflected this imbalance. In contrast to the broad range of support which it enjoyed in Flanders, the electorate of the Catholic Party in francophone Belgium was composed principally of the peasantry of the rural Ardennes and the Catholic bourgeoisie. It was among the latter group that discontent was most marked. The constitutional reforms introduced after the First World War had destroyed their monopoly over political power while the post-war economic difficulties created a much more uncertain environment for small businessmen and members of the professional classes.

Despite still enjoying almost 40 per cent of the popular vote and participating in all of Belgium's many short-lived governments, the Catholic Party lacked any clear sense of purpose in the 1920s and 1930s. Divided between its Flemish and francophone factions as well as between Christian Democrat worker groups and more conservative elements, it could agree on little beyond the defence of the interests of the Church and antipathy to the twin historic adversaries of atheistic liberalism and Marxist socialism.[4] In the immediate post-war years, a number of small nationalist leagues, such as the *Jeunesses Nationales* and *L'Autorité*, had already been established which drew much of their support from francophone Catholics[5] but at the end of the 1920s a more substantial challenge to the hold of the party over Catholic political loyalties began to emerge. It was among the offspring of the bourgeoisie that this trend away from the Catholic Party was most evident. Educated in the substantial network of Catholic secondary schools (*collèges*) and the Catholic University of Louvain, these younger Catholics had come of age during or after the First World War and they shared little of their elders' respect for the established leaders of the party. In their opinion, the party was an outmoded institution still rooted in the clerical-anticlerical battles of the nineteenth century and unable to articulate a new form of Catholic politics for the modern era.

These predominantly middle-class radicals were the driving-force behind the *Association Catholique de la Jeunesse Belge* (*ACJB*). This organisation had been established by the Church in 1921 and it expanded rapidly during the subsequent years into a mass movement which acted as a focus for the enthusiasm of many younger Catholics. The *ACJB* was dominated by a mood of religious exuberance and, although it remained aloof from politics, it forged a new generation of committed Catholic militants who spurned the worldly manoeuvrings and compromises of the Catholic Party.[6] Their quest for a more radical political alternative led some to embrace the ideas of the French journalist Charles Maurras whose anti-parliamentary *Action Française* movement enjoyed considerable support among the Catholic middle class in Belgium during the 1920s.[7] However Maurras' authoritarian nationalism lacked an explicitly Catholic inspiration and, after the papal condemnation of *Action Française* in 1926, it lost much of its appeal. Instead, these Catholic idealists formed their own movements and periodicals which, as titles such as *La Cîté Chrétienne* and *L'Esprit Nouveau* demonstrated, sought to combine the spiritual ideals of the *ACJB* with a radical political programme.

The aims of these various groups were broadly similar. All sought to replace the liberal parliamentary system with a new political order based on the natural communities of region, profession and family. Inspired by the examples of Austria and Portugal as well as by the papal teachings contained in encyclicals such as *Quadragesimo Anno* issued in May 1931, they claimed that only Catholic political ideals could provide a solution to the problems of modern Belgium. Despite their evidently simplistic and naïve policies, these groups attracted considerable support from a young Catholic bourgeoisie whose alienation from the existing political regime was reinforced by events both within Belgium and beyond. The impact of the world economic depression and the consequent rise in mass unemployment caused difficulties even for students well blessed with educational qualifications while developments elsewhere in Europe such as the establishment of the Spanish Republic and, closer to home, the rise of 'pagan' nazism within Germany made the need for an authentic Catholic politics seem ever more urgent.[8]

Rex was one of these groups of young Catholic militants. Its leader, Léon Degrelle, was the son of a prosperous brewer from the small town of Bouillon in the Belgian Ardennes where his father was active in local Catholic Party politics. Like many sons of the Catholic bourgeoisie, Léon attended the University of Louvain where he was active in student politics and journalism. His energy and journalistic talents soon attracted the attention of the Catholic hierarchy and in 1930 the head of the *ACJB*, Monseigneur Picard, invited him to take over the direction of a small Catholic publishing house called 'Christus Rex'.[9] The title of the enterprise was in itself significant. The cult of Christ the King had been encouraged by Pius XI in his encyclical *Quas Primas* of 1925 and it received an enthusiastic response from many younger Catholics who saw in the image of Christ reigning in majesty over the world a symbol of their aspiration for a more aggressive, intransigent Catholicism.[10] Degrelle shared these beliefs but his aims were also more commercial. He recognised that a substantial audience existed for popular Catholic periodicals which was not being reached by the existing, rather pious titles. Thus, he used Christus Rex to launch a series of mass-circulation magazines which combined popular articles and short stories with Catholic homilies. Due in no small measure to Degrelle's talents as a publicist, the venture flourished and the young publisher soon diversified into the production of pamphlets on major news events as well as cheap editions of Catholic novels.

By 1933 Degrelle had assumed sole control of the publishing house and his ambitions began to expand. At the offices of Christus Rex in Louvain, he surrounded himself with young men who had been active in student journalism and who shared his enthusiasm for a more militant Catholic faith. The Rexist periodicals began to take on a political character and Degrelle started to hold public meetings at which he perfected the direct, powerful style of oratory which would be his hallmark throughout his political career. Rex was clearly becoming more than simply a publishing house and, although many within the Catholic hierarchy would continue to look with sympathy on Degrelle's actions, the Catholic Church and the *ACJB* withdrew from all official involvement in the affairs of the organisation. Despite serious financial difficulties, Rex survived and Degrelle organised a series of rallies and banquets during 1934 at which his general calls for a spiritual renaissance in Belgium came to focus more specifically on the failings of the Catholic Party. Amidst the prolonged economic recession of the early 1930s, this was a popular message and Rex gradually began to take on the character of a political movement with local groups and, of course, its own press. Finally, the Rexist leader decided to challenge the leaders of the Catholic Party directly. In November 1935, accompanied by a group of his young supporters, he burst into a meeting in Courtrai of the national leaders of the party and harangued them on their complacency and alleged corruption.[11]

This *coup de Courtrai*, as it became popularly known, was a publicity stunt which brought Degrelle wide attention but it did not mark a decisive break with the Catholic Party. Rex remained essentially a dissident movement *within* the Catholic world and its support was drawn almost exclusively from young francophone Catholics who hoped to force the party to purge itself of discredited leaders and adopt a more militant programme. Nor was Degrelle certain as to his own aims. The success of the Rexist campaigns had taken him very much by surprise and he remained unsure whether to press forward with the creation of his own movement or accept a position within the Catholic Party. The decisive break with the Catholic political elite only took place during the subsequent months. Pierlot, the newly-appointed President of the Catholic Party, refused to enter into negotiations with the young rebels and, although at a local level there were many examples of Rexists continuing to receive encouragement from priests and Catholic politicians alike, no national compromise between Rex and the party proved possible. Thus, with a general election imminent in May 1936, Degrelle – still only 29 years old – belatedly decided that Rex would contest these elections as an independent political force.[12]

This decision brought about a substantial transformation in the movement. Though most of its leaders at a national and local level were still young Catholic militants, the emergence of Rex as an autonomous party led it to become a rallying-point for a diverse coalition of elements unhappy with the status quo. Former soldiers of the 1914–18 conflict, members of right-wing patriotic leagues and discontented tradesmen and shopkeepers were all attracted to a movement which rapidly became, rather in the manner of Boulangism in France in the 1880s or Poujadism in the 1950s, an all-purpose vehicle of protest. Rex no longer remained within the confines of internal Catholic politics and, although the influx of these new men created predictable tensions and resentments, Degrelle's charismatic personality and populist oratory was sufficient at least in the short-term to ensure the movement retained a somewhat precarious unity.[13]

The ideas espoused by the Rexists during the election campaign of 1936 reflected the movement's improvised character. They had few policies of substance and the central theme of the campaign was Degrelle's energetic exploitation of a series of financial scandals in which a number of prominent politicians were implicated. Using the electoral symbol of a broom to indicate his intention of sweeping the guilty men from power, the Rexist leader capitalised on these revelations of corruption to launch a wide-ranging attack on the political elite. At public rallies and in the columns of the hastily-launched Rexist daily newspaper, Le Pays Réel, he continually lambasted the leaders of all the major parties as self-serving and ineffectual men who were responsible for the ills of the country. It was a message with a simple, direct appeal but the Rexists were much vaguer when it came to putting forward their proposals for an alternative political structure. For all the fury of their attacks on the politicians, they were not revolutionaries seeking to overturn the existing political order and they had little to suggest beyond the creation of a network of socio-economic corporations and a modest reinforcement of the powers of the executive.[14]

In the context of the 1930s when almost everybody seemed to be advancing proposals for constitutional reform, these were hardly radical ideas and Rexist policies on social and economic issues were on the whole similarly ill-defined. Apart from presenting the devaluation of the Belgian franc in 1935 as a plot concocted by the politicians, Degrelle had no economic programme and he merely talked in grandiloquent terms of replacing the competitive spirit of liberalism with Catholic values of solidarity and community. It was this moral language which also prevailed in Rexist social policies. One of Degrelle's earliest journalistic pamphlets had been an investigation of slum housing in industrial areas and the Rexists made much of their concern for the sufferings of the Belgian working class. It was, however, a sympathy which was based on little comprehension of the real needs of the proletariat and, although Rex expressed its support for the demands of those workers involved in the wave of strikes which spread across Belgium during June 1936, their attitude towards the working class always remained rooted in the paternalist attitudes of late nineteenth-century social Catholicism. The real focus of Rexist concerns were the middle classes. Not surprisingly, given the social background of many of their supporters, Degrelle and his followers posed as the defenders of the interests of the Belgian middle class. Rex, they insisted, would defend the traditional small enterprises against the evils of 'hypercapitalism' as represented by the financial trusts and economic conglomerates, and promised to act against the rapacious practices of American-style department stores and supermarkets.[15]

Despite the manifold incoherences of its electoral platform with its awkward fusion of Catholic moralism and Poujadist demagoguery, the appeal of Rex in the troubled circumstances of the 1930s was considerable. Degrelle's youthful dynamism combined with his denunciations of an unpopular political elite made a major impact on the election campaign. Nobody, least of all the Rexists, anticipated the extent of their success. After a hectic often chaotic campaign, Degrelle's movement won 11.49 per cent of the popular vote and gained 21 out of 202 seats in the Chamber of Deputies. In the largely static world of Belgian electoral politics, this result was nothing less than a revolution. Though the level of its support in many areas of Flanders was minimal, the Rexist vote in much of southern Belgium – notably the rural Luxembourg province – as well as in certain *quartiers* of Brussels was well in excess of 20 per cent. All of the major parties lost votes to the Rexists but there was no doubt as to the principal source of its votes. Support for the Catholic party slumped from 38.5 per cent in the election of 1932 to only 27.6 per cent in 1936. These disaffected Catholic voters were drawn from all sections of the party's electorate and included not only the young radicals but also many peasant farmers, shopkeepers and members of the professional middle class. The depth of these voters' commitment to the new party should not, however, be exaggerated. Many had voted for Rex not out of any great confidence in its policies or its inexperienced leader but out of anger and frustration. A vote for Rex in 1936 was, as many Rexists subsequently admitted, essentially a protest vote against the political elite and, more especially, against the perceived failure of the Catholic Party to protect the interests of its middle-class and rural francophone constituency.[16]

During the summer and autumn of 1936, the Rexists attempted to capitalise upon their unexpected success. They hastily established a central bureaucracy for their movement, brought some order into the network of local branches which had sprung up over the previous months and launched a 'Rex ou Moscou' campaign intended to present Rex as the only viable alternative to communism. Nevertheless, the sense of momentum so essential to any radical political grouping soon began to disappear. This was in part due to Degrelle's impulsive leadership. In October 1936 the Rexist leader announced a 'March on Brussels' modelled on the March on Rome which had brought Mussolini to power in 1922. This was a typical piece of Degrellian effrontery. It was not intended as a serious challenge to the government but was supposed to demonstrate the extent of popular support for the Rexist cause. It turned, however, into a fiasco when only a few militants braved the government's ban on demonstrations to appear on the streets of the capital. Moreover, by making the Rexists appear as rowdy trouble-makers, it alienated many of those who had voted for the movement in May but who now began to look on Rex as a dangerous, disruptive force.[17]

This negative impression was confirmed by revelations of contacts between Rex and foreign political movements. Despite the insistence of Rexist propagandists that their movement had little in common with authoritarian regimes elsewhere in Europe, Degrelle visited Italy in 1936 and Rex received substantial financial assistance from the Italian fascist regime. Contacts also developed between Rex and Nazi Germany. Neither Degrelle nor his followers felt any great affinity with the Third Reich which, in common with other European Catholics, they tended to regard as a combination of Prussian militarism and pagan racism. But Degrelle was flattered by the attention of the Nazis and in the summer of 1936 he made a private visit to Germany and had a meeting with Hitler. The two men discussed little of substance, but Degrelle remained in intermittent contact with the German leaders and also received a limited amount of material support from them.[18] Nor was it merely their choice of foreign allies which caused problems for the Rexists. In October 1936, Rex concluded an alliance with the Flemish nationalist movement, the *VNV*. This union of outsiders possessed a certain logic, especially as both parties advocated somewhat similar policies of authoritarian political reform. However it had an overwhelmingly negative impact on the largely francophone Rexist electorate who feared that any alliance with Flemish extremists might threaten the already fragile unity of the Belgian state.[19]

The difficulties of Rex deepened during the winter of 1936–7 as the 'union nationale' government of Socialists, Catholics and Liberals under the leadership of the Prime Minister Paul Van Zeeland moved to counter the Rexist challenge. There were a number of right-wing Catholic politicians sympathetic to Degrelle who privately advocated an alliance between the Catholic Party and Rex;[20] but the majority of their colleagues were convinced that the party's best interests were served by remaining loyal to the Van Zeeland government which since its formation in 1935 had begun to address the economic and social problems of the country with some determination. The members of the coalition government were far from united on many matters but they found a convenient point of consensus in their shared hostility to the Rexist trouble-makers who disrupted parliamentary proceedings and noisily declared their determination to destroy the powers of the political parties. Thus, from the autumn of 1936, the government enacted a series of measures to combat Rex, including banning it from the radio, outlawing uniformed militias and initiating modest constitutional reforms intended to appease popular dis-satisfaction with the parliamentary system.[21]

In the spring of 1937, Degrelle attempted to recapture the politi-cal initiative by instigating a by-election in Brussels. One of the Rexist deputies resigned and Degrelle (who had not stood for parliament in 1936) put himself forward as the Rexist candidate. Unfortunately for him, the three governmental parties decided to present a single candidate: the Catholic Prime Minister Paul Van Zeeland. The outcome of the keenly fought and often stormy by-election campaign seemed in doubt until its final days when the Rexist leader made the error of declaring at a rally that the silence of Cardinal Van Roey, the head of the Catholic Church in Belgium, indicated the Church's sympathy for the Rexist cause. In fact, Van Roey had always been reluctant to condemn Rex and, despite issuing a series of warnings to the Catholic faithful to keep their distance from the movement, he had consistently sought to effect a reconciliation between the Catholic Party and the Rexists. But Degrelle's public assertion went too far and the Cardinal issued a statement warning that Rex constituted a danger to the Church and to the country and calling on the Catholic faithful to vote for Van Zeeland. This categorical declaration may well have influenced many Catholic waverers and, when the result of the election on 11 April was declared, Degrelle had obtained only 19 per cent of the vote.[22]

This defeat marked the decisive turning-point in the fortunes of Rex. It exacerbated the personal and ideological tensions within the movement and, perhaps most importantly, it destroyed all hope of an alliance between Rex and the Catholic Party. The Rexists no longer inspired the same fear and a final private attempt by Van Roey and conservative Catholic politicians to achieve a *rapprochement* between the two parties came to nothing.[23] Henceforth, Rex was in the political wilderness. As its member-ship and financial resources slumped, only its unconditional supporters remained loyal to the cause and the movement drifted rapidly towards the extreme right of the political spectrum. Its initial Catholic inspiration disappeared almost entirely and gave way instead to a banal imitation of the policies and gestures of authoritarian movements elsewhere in Europe. Uniforms and salutes became an increasingly prominent feature of Rexist rallies and the movement's former rather ambivalent stance was replaced by categorical opposition to the democratic regime. This extremist stance ensured that electoral support for Rex declined markedly. In the April 1939 general election it received a mere 4.43 per cent of the national vote and its parliamentary representation was reduced to only four deputies (one of whom was Degrelle). In Flanders support for the movement evaporated almost entirely, leaving Rex largely confined to the southern provinces of Wallonia, where it still won 7.58 per cent in Liège and 12.74 per cent in the Luxembourg.[24]

Thus, through a combination of its own errors and the pressure of domestic and international events, Rex had become by the end of the 1930s a fringe grouping which posed no significant challenge to the political status quo. The reasons for its failure are instructive and provide a valuable reminder that not all movements of the radical right were successful in inter-war Europe. But the defeat of the Rexists was anything but a victory for the parliamentary system. The mood of popular dissatisfaction with the political system did not disappear and even appeared to deepen during the immediate pre-war years. It also gained the support of influential voices within the political elite. Especially among younger politicians, such as the Socialist Paul-Henri Spaak who himself became Prime Minister for a few months in 1938, there was a widespread feeling that the parliamentary regime inherited from the nineteenth century needed to be adapted to meet Belgium's modern needs. It was the lack of stable, effective government which was most criticised. The absence of a durable parliamentary majority and the consequent reliance on short-lived coalitions of interest stimulated a wide range of proposals for constitutional reforms, the common feature of which was a reduction in the powers of parliament and of the political parties and a strengthening of the autonomy of the executive. Men such as Van Zeeland and Spaak lent their support to these ideas and, although significant differences remained as to the scope and character of any changes, there were by the end of the 1930s few politicians who did not accept the need for some reform of the political system.[25]

Proposals for change received strong encouragement from King Léopold III. Despite their constitutional status, monarchs of Belgium had always enjoyed substantial formal and informal powers and, when Léopold III succeeded his father after Albert's sudden death in a climbing accident in February 1934, he was determined to use his authority to the full. A young man with a strong sense of duty, Léopold shared the desire for reform of the parliamentary system. This was reinforced by a more personal antipathy towards much of the political elite. Rather like Edward VIII in Britain, he had little time for what he regarded as the petty squabbles of politicians and Léopold made no secret of his wish to see the executive power of the state liberated from the control of the political parties. Only a strong central authority combined with the devolution of some responsibilities to socio-economic corporations could, he felt, provide the effective leadership which the problems facing Belgium required.[26]

It is all too easy in retrospect to exaggerate the importance of these trends. Political fashions change rapidly and the experience of the Occupation would demonstrate the resilience of many Belgians' commitment to their traditional liberties. But it seems probable that, had not the German invasion intervened, some measure of constitutional reform would have been introduced. Belgium was, of course, far from unique in this respect.

The resurgence in liberal democracy after 1945 has disguised the extent to which during the previous twenty years the tide had run in the opposite direction. The views expressed by the Belgian elite were shared by many others throughout Europe who believed that nineteenth-century parliaments were no longer appropriate to the needs of complex, modern societies. A 'crisis of authority' was widely felt to exist and, even in those countries such as France, Belgium and the Netherlands where movements of the radical right failed to achieve power, there were many seeking to change the political system from within in order to create more effective and 'depoliticised' structures of government.[27]

For the Rexists there was no escape from the marginal position which they had come to adopt and they appeared doomed to disappear into history as a short-lived and unsuccessful movement of political protest. Their isolation increased as attention moved remorselessly at the end of the 1930s from problems of domestic politics to the international diplomatic crisis. In 1936, Belgium had terminated the defensive alliance with France which it had signed in 1920 and had reverted to its pre-1914 neutral status. This change in policy enjoyed wide domestic support and there were many during the immediate pre-war years, including Léopold III, who hoped that the new 'policy of independence' (as it was termed) would spare Belgium from becoming embroiled in a second disastrous military conflict.[28] It was this fear of the consequences of war which dominated Belgian diplomacy. Apart from the status of the small German-speaking territories of Eupen, Malmédy and Saint Vith which had been annexed by Belgium from Germany under the terms of the Versailles Treaty, Belgium had no grievances of substance with any of the major European powers and when war broke out in September 1939 the tripartite government of Catholics, Socialists and Liberals led by the Prime Minister Hubert Pierlot hastened to reiterate Belgium's independence. The army was mobilised but there was little patriotic fervour. Memories of the sufferings of the German Occupation of 1914–18 remained fresh and it was still hoped that a compromise peace between the belligerent powers would prove possible.

During the winter of 1939–40, the Belgian population waited anxiously to see if the 'phoney war' between Germany and the western powers would develop into a large-scale military conflict. Neutrality did not exclude sympathy and it was clear that the sympathies of most Belgians lay firmly with France and Britain. However, hopes that the policy of independence might preserve Belgium from becoming once again the battlefield of western Europe soon faded. Intelligence reports from Berlin warned of German military preparations and these were confirmed in January 1940 by the chance capture – in a German military plane forced to land on Belgian soil – of Nazi plans for an invasion of the Low Countries. In response, the majority of the army was deployed on Belgium's eastern frontier and the King and the government redoubled their diplomatic efforts to protect the country against attack.[29]

Throughout these nervous months, the Rexists remained an isolated and largely irrelevant group. Their press was noisy in its support for the policy of independence and the members of Rex in no sense formed a pro-Nazi 'fifth column' within Belgium. Nevertheless, behind their protestations of support for the King and government, there were limits to Rexist neutrality. Degrelle, the *Chef de Rex*, accepted that it had been Hitler who had precipitated the declaration of hostilities but he placed almost entire responsibility for the origins of the war on France and Britain and, more especially, on the occult forces of freemasonry and Jewish finance which, he claimed, had orchestrated their bellicose behaviour. This image of the war as a conspiracy forced upon the peoples of Europe dominated the *Chef de Rex*'s declarations during the winter of 1939–40 and the Rexists devoted much of their energies to unmasking those evil-minded individuals and groups who, they claimed, were now seeking to draw Belgium into the conflict on the Allied side.[30]

Hostility to the Allies did not imply support for the Nazi cause and at least in public Degrelle was careful to avoid making any statement which might suggest sympathy for German ambitions. It was clear, however, that the radicalisation of the movement which had taken place since 1937 had led some within Rex – including Degrelle himself – to abandon much of their initial suspicion of Nazi Germany. Contact between Rex and the Nazis remained limited and the Rexists had little comprehension of the nature of the Nazi regime. But, if nothing else, their insistence that the diplomatic crisis was merely a reflection of a broader conflict within Europe between the forces of decadence and those of regeneration almost unconsciously led many Rexists to look on the Third Reich as the lesser evil.[31] This attitude was certainly not shared by all Rexist militants and Degrelle's rather one-sided neutrality caused a steady stream of departures from the movement during the winter of 1939–40. The *Chef de Rex* appeared unconcerned by these defections and in January 1940 he secretly approached the German embassy in Brussels to seek finance for a new newspaper which, he claimed, would defend the policy of independence against its pro-Allied critics. This request was rebuffed but it seems only to have encouraged Degrelle to move further towards the German camp. In the spring of 1940 he continued to present Nazi actions in a sympathetic light and even claimed that the German invasion of Denmark and Norway in April was a justified response to English provocations. This in turn prompted a further wave of resignations from Rex and served to reinforce the political isolation of Degrelle and his largely moribund movement.[32]

The development of Rex in the years before the German invasion clearly played a major part in determining its subsequent decision to opt for the Nazi cause. Collaboration was not merely an exceptional product of exceptional times and, though the war years were indeed in many respects unique, the course of European history did not end in 1939 to be resumed in 1945. Collaboration therefore has to be seen as a product of Europe's pre-war history.[33] In the case of Rex, this is perhaps especially important. Its subsequent single-minded pursuit of collaboration has created the impression of a movement of crude opportunists blinded by self-interest and devoid of political purpose. That some Rexists were indeed corrupt, brutal men who revelled in the opportunities which the German Occupation provided to enrich themselves and exploit their fellow citizens is beyond question, but the reasons for Rexist collaboration go beyond individual failings of character. It was the product of a series of factors in the pre-war history of the movement which, taken together, help to explain – though not excuse – its espousal of the German cause.

The first of these was Rex's marginal position in the Belgian political system. By a mutually reinforcing process of radicalisation and exclusion, the Rexists had become by the end of the 1930s a movement which defined itself primarily by its opposition to the established order. It gloried in the hostility which its actions inspired and saw in its exclusion from power proof of its ideological rectitude. This marginalisation was more than simply a consequence of electoral failure. It was also a product of the structure of Belgian political life. The three principal political traditions – the Catholics, Socialists and Liberals – each formed a largely self-contained world or 'pillar' composed not merely of their respective parties but also of an extensive network of associated organisations including trade unions, welfare funds, youth and women's movements and cultural institutions. Though it would be wrong to caricature the extent of this 'pillarisation',[34] most Belgians in the inter-war years did define themselves within one of these three political communities. The casting of a vote for the appropriate political party was merely the most tangible expression of an identification which was continually reinforced in daily life by participation in a series of politically affiliated social organisations.

The Rexists developed within and initially formed part of the Catholic 'pillar': but after 1937 they were gradually expelled from the Catholic world and ceased to have access to the sources of influence, patronage and support which it provided. This process of exclusion not merely placed Rex on the margins of parliamentary politics but also turned the Rexists themselves into marginal figures. The social bonds between them and their fellow citizens were weakened and the Rexists became much more clearly defined as a minority apart from the rest of society. This isolation was in turn welcomed by the Rexists. Instances of discrimination against their supporters were seized upon as proof of the sufferings they were obliged to endure and the Rexist image of themselves as a dissident group at odds with a fundamentally hostile society was reinforced. This marginalisation prepared the way for collaboration. Though the Rexists remained members of the national community, they were no longer an integral part of it and, when the military defeat of 1940 occurred, they were inclined to see in it a vindication of their radical opposition to the pre-war order. Psychologically too, the marginal position of the Rexists in pre-war Belgian society prepared them for the isolation which they would experience during the Occupation. Collaboration was in many respects the continuation of their former oppositionist stance and the hostility their pro-German actions aroused among the majority of the population merely seemed to provide further proof of the correctness of their views.

A further factor propelling the Rexists towards collaboration was the connection which they perceived between their domestic political actions and developments elsewhere in Europe. By the late 1930s, the Rexists had come to see events in Belgium as forming part of a wider struggle taking place throughout Europe between decadent democratic elites and those authoritarian, nationalist movements – including Rex – which were seeking to bring about fundamental political change. This 'European civil war' transcended national boundaries and made it impossible to divorce events within individual countries from those elsewhere in Europe. A narrow nationalism which placed a patriotic loyalty to the nation above all other allegiances therefore seemed to the Rexists, as to a number of other movements of the radical right in Europe during the 1930s, to be outmoded. They remained patriots but, rather like many European communists of the same generation, they sought to balance their loyalty to their country with a broader commitment to their Europe-wide political cause.

When war was declared between the western powers and Nazi Germany, the Rexists initially found it easy to combine these twin loyalties: by supporting the policy of independence, they were helping to keep Belgium aloof from those reactionary forces which had provoked the military conflict in the hope of destroying Nazi Germany and its allies. The German invasion did, however, totally change the situation. In the heat of battle few Rexists had any hesitation in giving priority to their national loyalties and they participated actively in the struggle against the Nazi aggressor. However the overwhelming and apparently definitive German military victory reinforced their conviction that the war was not a purely 'international' conflict between nations but also a continuation of the ideological struggle between democracy and its opponents. Thus, although far from welcoming the German armies as liberators, the Rexists found it impossible to avoid heralding the Nazi victory as to some extent also their victory. Memories of German oppression during the previous Occupation of 1914–18 remained strong even within Rexist ranks but it did seem to many Rexists that the German blitzkrieg of 1940 marked a decisive triumph for those forces which had long struggled against the corrupt democratic order. In these circumstances, it was all too easy for them to reach the fatal conclusion that they should collaborate in building the New European Order promised by the leaders of the Third Reich.

The final factor which influenced the Rexist choice of collaboration was the personal character of Léon Degrelle. Ever since its beginnings, Degrelle had been the uncontested leader of Rex and he inspired an unquestioning adoration in many of his followers. Just 30 years old in the summer of 1936, his personal energy and youthful good looks contrasted markedly with the somewhat more staid character of most Belgian politicians. The French writer Robert Brasillach, who met Degrelle in the summer of 1936, hailed him as the incarnation of the spirit of the New Europe, and the *Chef de Rex* did indeed seem to possess all of the attributes required of a successful modern leader. In private he was a man of great charm and conviviality whose personal magnetism often disarmed even the most suspicious of opponents. On the public stage Degrelle was without doubt one of the most effective political orators of his generation in Europe. At the mass rallies he held throughout Belgium during the election campaign of 1936, he mesmerised audiences with his impassioned denunciations of the failings of the political elite, combining a romantic, even poetic, vocabulary with an earthy colloquial language rich in specifically Belgian slang. It was a talent which never deserted him and, even in Rex's darkest days, Degrelle's major public speeches retained an emotional force which restored the morale of the Rexist faithful and even won a few rare converts to his cause.[35]

The Faustian pact which had given the *Chef de Rex* these talents did have a darker side. Degrelle was in many ways a skilful tactician with a shrewd sense of political realities, but this ability was combined with an incorrigible tendency to fantasise about his own importance. Almost from the outset of his political career, he had found it impossible to conceive of the interests of his country separately from his own and, with time, this Messianic sense of his own destiny lost all sense of proportion. Always a volatile, impulsive man, he became ever more rash in his actions and was convinced that success came to the leader who seized ruthlessly upon political opportunities. These were dangerous illusions and, after his Cassandra-like isolation in the late 1930s, it was perhaps inevitable that in the aftermath of the defeat of 1940 he would grasp the chance which the German Occupation offered to return to the centre of the political stage. His self-appointed role as architect of a historic understanding between Belgium and Nazi Germany was one which matched both Degrelle's personal vanity and his ideological ambitions and it was one which he would embrace with rash enthusiasm.[36]

Chapter One

May–December 1940

The Quest For Power

IT WAS at dawn on the morning of 10 May 1940 that the German offensive in the West, so long anticipated and so long dreaded, eventually occurred. Striking simultaneously at Belgium and the Netherlands, the German armies launched a heavily motorised assault similar to that which had already conquered Poland. The Belgian army, composed of some 600,000 men and relatively well-equipped, was no easy challenge for the German forces. Though air-borne attack soon overwhelmed the initial Belgian defences, the bulk of the army was able to withdraw to a fortified defensive line east of Brussels between Antwerp and Namur where it was reinforced by French and British troops. This strategy was, however, rendered redundant by the audacious German motorised advance through the Ardennes which, by striking to the south of the defensive line, threatened to encircle the Allied and Belgian forces. Disoriented by these blitzkrieg tactics, the Belgian armies had little choice but to begin a demoralising retreat. On 17 May the Germans entered Brussels and the remaining Belgian forces were soon confined to a small area of north-west Flanders. King Léopold III who, like his father in the 1914–18 conflict, had assumed direct command of the armed forces, was forced to accept the impossibility of continuing the conflict and after a brief final stand on the Lys river he surrendered to the German commanders. Thus, on 28 May, a mere 18 days after the declaration of hostilities, the exhausted Belgian troops laid down their arms.[1] The war, it seemed, was over almost before it had begun but, in fact, the campaign of May 1940 proved to be merely the prelude to a German Occupation which was to last more than four years.

The mood of the population in the weeks following the capitulation was one of confusion and disorientation.[2] For most Belgians, foreign occupation was not a new experience and they retained vivid memories of the sufferings of the German Occupation of 1914–18. But on this occasion the circumstances seemed very different. During the First World War the Belgian armies had been able to fight on from a small salient of Belgian territory but in 1940 the remorseless speed of the military defeat followed shortly afterwards by the collapse of France and the inglorious evacuation

of the remnants of the British forces at Dunkirk convinced almost every-
one that this time there could be no hope of recovery.

In addition, the military campaign had brought to a head the long latent
tensions between King Léopold III and the coalition government headed
by the Prime Minister Hubert Pierlot. Relations between the King and his
ministers had occasionally been strained before the war, but during May
1940 they deteriorated rapidly. The King, as head of the armed forces,
was reluctant to allow the ministers any role in the conduct of military
operations and preferred to rely instead on his own circle of personal
advisers. Above all, however, Léopold and the government disagreed
fundamentally as to what should happen if it proved impossible to continue the military struggle on Belgian territory. In the opinion of the
ministers, the King should emulate the example of the Dutch Queen
and continue the struggle from abroad alongside France and Britain; but
Léopold, who like his father Albert during the First World War was an
ardent defender of his country's diplomatic independence, had no wish to
become the pawn of the Western allies. For him, a defeat on Belgian soil
would mark the end of the conflict and he was determined to remain
within Belgium and share the fate of his troops. As the German forces
advanced, this issue became ever more urgent and at a last dramatic
meeting at the Château of Wynendaele at dawn on 25 May, the King
and his principal ministers proved unable to resolve their differences.
Thus, while the King surrendered to the German armies and subsequently
returned as a self-proclaimed prisoner to his palace at Laeken outside
Brussels, the ministers fled to France intending to continue the struggle.
On 28 May they announced that, by virtue of his capture by the Germans,
Léopold III was no longer able to act as monarch and at an improvised
meeting of the Belgian parliament in the French town of Limoges on 31
May the ministers and deputies echoed the condemnations of the King
already voiced by the Allied governments.

The resolve of the government to continue the military struggle did,
however, prove to be short-lived. The French capitulation in June led
Pierlot and his fellow ministers to believe that all hope of continuing the
war was impossible and from their exile at Bordeaux and subsequently at
Vichy they attempted to effect a reconciliation with the King and the
German victors. But Léopold III, angered by what he considered to be
their treachery during May, repulsed their advances. He wished to keep
his hands free to pursue his own negotiations with the Nazi regime and
hoped eventually to replace the Pierlot government by ministers loyal to
his own policies. Thus, throughout the summer of 1940, the Pierlot
government remained isolated in France, unable to return to Belgium
and yet unwilling to continue the military struggle. Two ministers had,
however, already made their way to London and, at the end of August,
Pierlot and his Foreign Minister Paul-Henri Spaak decided – more out of

resignation than with any great hope of success – to join them. They escaped from France and, after a difficult journey via Spain, arrived in London where in December they established the nucleus of a government-in-exile. They soon received the recognition of the Allies but their conflict with the King remained unresolved. While the ministers considered themselves to be the legitimate Belgian authorities, they were regarded as traitors by Léopold III who not only ignored their existence but continued with his efforts to reach an understanding with the German authorities. Thus, the events of 1940 had laid the basis for a bitter constitutional and political dispute which was to endure throughout the war and would overshadow much of post-war Belgian history.[3]

For most Belgians such political problems were, however, very remote from their more immediate material difficulties. Not only had much of the country been devastated by the military campaign but as many as two million Belgians, more than one fifth of the total population, had fled to France.[4] The repatriation of these evacuees as well as the restoration of food supplies and means of communication were all problems which had to be confronted urgently. Moreover, many local councils had ceased to operate and, in their absence, ad hoc committees of notables were established in many towns to accomplish the many urgent tasks.[5]

Yet, despite these obstacles, a semblance of normality was gradually restored throughout the country. And, as the Belgian population returned to their homes, families and jobs, so they attempted to adjust to the circumstances of the German Occupation and to assess the position of their country. In doing so, almost all Belgians – regardless of their linguistic or political background – were agreed on one point: namely that the German military victory on the European continent was incontrovertible. While many hoped that Britain would fight off the expected German assault, only a very few rather foolhardy spirits were willing to predict that the British would prove able to challenge the Nazi hegemony on the European continent. For most Belgians, the overriding priority was therefore to preserve Belgian unity within a German-dominated Europe. It was the King who appeared as the most likely guarantor of this national union. The spectacle of the French collapse as well as the accusation made by the French Prime Minister, Paul Reynaud, in a radio broadcast that by capitulating the Belgian armies had betrayed the Western Allies provoked an instinctive patriotic reaction within Belgium of which the King was the principal beneficiary. Thus, while the members of the Pierlot government were almost universally condemned for having deserted the country in its moment of need, Léopold III in his palace at Laeken was inundated with expressions of loyalty.[6]

These spontaneous and unprecedented declarations of support were much less an expression of positive support for the King's political views than a gesture of loyalty to the monarchy as a symbol of national unity.

Nevertheless, there were few Belgians at this time who felt any great affection for their former democratic political system. Though it was not – as in France – held directly responsible for the military defeat, the parliamentary regime was generally deemed to have been discredited.[7] At the root of this short-lived but profound transformation in political attitudes was the widespread belief that the events of May had vindicated the criticisms voiced by many during the 1930s of the parliamentary system. The defeat of Third Republic France and the victory of Nazi Germany appeared to demonstrate that authoritarian states were better equipped to confront the needs of the modern age and many Belgians anticipated that an integral element of their country's adaptation to the German hegemony in Europe would be the replacement of the 1831 constitution by a political system which drew on the authoritarian reforms already instituted in many other European countries during the previous twenty years. Thus, as was also the case in the Netherlands,[8] the military defeat gave a great impetus to those manifold projects for constitutional reform which had long been fashionable in certain intellectual and political circles but which suddenly in 1940 found a more general resonance and became an integral element of *l'air du temps*.

At a national level, the disorder evident in the aftermath of the military defeat soon gave way to a new network of German and Belgian administrative institutions which, although intended to be only temporary, would in fact remain in place largely unaltered throughout the Occupation. For Hitler Belgium's importance in 1940 was principally as a potential base for an invasion of England as well as a source of much-needed industrial resources and his decision to entrust the country to a *Wehrmacht* administration reflected these economic and military priorities. On 1 June a German decree announced the creation of a military administration (*Militärverwaltung*) in Brussels to administer both Belgium as well as the neighbouring French *départements* of the Nord and Pas-de-Calais which by virtue of their heavy industry and proximity to England were also regarded as of particular strategic importance.[9] To preside over this *Wehrmacht* administration, Hitler appointed an aristocratic, anti-Nazi officer, General von Falkenhausen, but he proved to be little more than a ceremonial figurehead and it was his head of administration (*Militärverwaltungschef*), Eggert Reeder, who assumed responsibility for most matters of policy. Also a senior *Wehrmacht* officer, Reeder was both a skilled administrator and an adept manoeuvrer in the power politics of the Third Reich and he became the *de facto* ruler of Belgium for the subsequent four years.

The fact that Belgium, unlike most of the territories conquered by the German armies, was placed under the control of the *Wehrmacht* rather than of a civilian German administration would prove of great importance for the future development of Nazi policies within the country. Yet, when it was created, Hitler intended that the *Militärverwaltung* should be a purely temporary body which would administer the country until the conclusion of military operations. Despite its transitional character, Hitler did issue the *Militärverwaltung* with a number of political guide-lines and, with the continuation of the war, these remained the principal determinants of German policies in Belgium for much of the Occupation. They made clear that the *Führer* had taken no decision regarding the future of the Belgian state and that it was not the purpose of the *Militärverwaltung* to anticipate any such political decisions. Thus, the major task of the *Wehrmacht* officials was – and would remain – the administration of the country as efficiently as possible with the minimum deployment of German manpower, while ensuring that the Belgian economy operated to the maximum benefit of the German war effort. But von Falkenhausen and Reeder were in no sense apolitical administrators. They were to execute all instructions received from Berlin even though these might prejudice the efficient administration of the country. Most importantly, Hitler, like many other Nazi leaders, believed that the Flemish were a 'lost' Germanic nation and he therefore ordered that they should be assisted in every possible way. The francophone Belgians of Brussels and Wallonia on the other hand, as a Latin race, were to be accorded no such favours. This so-called '*Flamen-politik*' ensured that from the outset the *Wehrmacht* officials in Brussels were forced to pursue what was in effect a twin policy. While seeking to maintain the existing administrative and economic structures intact, they were nevertheless also obliged to try to remodel the relations of power within Belgium in favour of the Flemish population.[10]

While German officials were responsible for the direction of policy, it was always intended that much of the day-to-day administration of the country would remain in Belgian hands and a working relationship soon developed between the Occupying forces and Belgian officials. Under the terms of a law hastily passed by the Belgian parliament on 10 May, it had been foreseen that, in the event of a German Occupation, the civil service would remain in place to protect the material interests of the population. The conduct of this enforced partnership with the German authorities was the responsibility of the *secrétaires-généraux*. They were the permanent civil servants who headed each of the ministerial departments and during the Occupation they acted collectively as a cabinet, assuming many of the powers formerly exercised by their political superiors. Their rule, like that of the *Militärverwaltung*, was originally intended to be a temporary phenomenon but the continuation of the war ensured that the *secrétaires-généraux* were to pursue their difficult dual role as the executors of German orders and the guardians of the interests of the Belgian population until the liberation of 1944.[11] Nor were they the only element of continuity during the Occupation. Though the national politicians had been excluded from power, many of the other established forces of Belgian society remained in place. The judiciary, the financial and industrial elite and the Catholic

Church all rapidly established their own form of *modus vivendi* with the Occupying forces and were in turn treated with considerable respect by Reeder and his colleagues.

The King was, however, conspicuously absent from this nascent institutional framework. Since his capture in May, he had remained confined to his palace at Laeken outside Brussels and, under the terms of Hitler's orders of July 1940, he was forbidden from engaging in any form of political activity.[12] Léopold III was, nevertheless, anything but idle. He was able to receive a number of select visitors and his entourage of advisers were an active presence in the life of the Belgian capital. Like so many of his compatriots, he believed that the German military victory in Europe was assured and he was therefore anxious to reach an understanding with the leaders of the Third Reich which would enable Belgium to recover some form of independence within a German-dominated Europe. Therefore, throughout the summer and autumn of 1940, the King made a series of efforts to enter into a dialogue with the Nazi leaders. All of these met with failure until his sister Princess Marie-José, the wife of Crown Prince Umberto of Italy, intervened directly with Hitler. As a consequence of her efforts, Léopold was invited to Berchtesgaden where he was received by the *Führer* on 19 November. Much of their conversation was dominated by the King's efforts to ensure the release of Belgian prisoners of war as well as other humanitarian issues but Léopold also pressed the *Führer* for assurances as to the future unity and independence of Belgium. Hitler, however, refused to commit himself. He possessed no master-plan for the reorganisation of Europe and, apart from reassuring the King that the royal family would be protected, the German leader avoided making any promises as to the future of Belgium. Thus, the interview ended inconclusively and Léopold returned to Brussels where he was to remain until the summer of 1944 in genteel detention in the palace of Laeken.[13] The subsequent evolution of military events caused the chances of any political agreement with Germany to recede still further, but the King remained obstinately committed to the stance he had adopted in 1940. He continued to rebuff all advances from both the Allies and the Pierlot government-in-exile and for the remainder of the Occupation his very presence within Belgium would have a major influence on the political life of the country.

The final element in the institutional structure of Belgium in 1940 was the Flemish nationalist movement, the *Vlaams Nationaal Verbond (VNV)*. Flemish nationalist attitudes towards Germany were dominated by memories of the assistance which some Nationalist intellectuals had given to the German authorities during the First World War in the expectation that the Germans would in turn assist the Flemish to achieve self-determination. Such hopes proved, however, to be misplaced. The Germans did little to favour the Flemish cause and this so-called 'activism' led to the prosecution of a number of Flemish Nationalists by the Belgian authorities after

1918. These events cast a long shadow over Flemish nationalism during the inter-war years. A strenuous campaign was conducted for the release of the imprisoned 'activists' but many Flemish Nationalists subsequently came to regard their wartime activities as a mistake which they themselves were in no hurry to repeat. Nevertheless, at least in intellectual circles, many Flemish did continue to consider themselves to be a Germanic nation and inevitably some still looked to Germany as a historical ally in their struggle for independence. This ethnic solidarity was reinforced by political affinities. Though there were many in the *VNV* who were willing to work within the democratic structures of the Belgian state, the Flemish nationalist movement as a whole drifted towards the right of the political spectrum during the 1930s. A small radical fringe made no secret of its admiration for the Nazi regime and the stance of the movement reflected the widespread popularity of authoritarian political ideas.

In the summer of 1940, the leaders of the *VNV* appeared to be the great beneficiaries of the new political situation. They were energetically courted from all sides and, although mindful of the mistakes of the first Occupation, the dramatic military events of 1940 were sufficient to convince even the more cautious amongst them of the benefits of co-operating with the German authorities. Thus, the head of the *VNV*, Staf de Clercq, met German officials in June 1940 and members of his movement were subsequently appointed by the Germans to key posts within the Belgian administration. Such actions did not amount to a formal policy of collaboration, but they did set the *VNV* on a course which would lead it to emerge before the end of the year as the principal partner of the *Militärverwaltung* in its administration of Occupied Belgium.[14]

Rex was almost entirely absent from this political structure. The Rexist organisation had been decimated by the invasion and, during these first crucial weeks of the Occupation, the movement gave few signs of life. Hardly any of its principal leaders were in the country at this time. Rex had always been dominated by young men and their mobilisation into the armed forces during the previous winter had deprived the movement of many of its most experienced local and national figures. After the defeat, they remained scattered over a wide area, many having been captured by the German armies and deported to prisoner-of-war camps in the Reich, where, despite the subsequent efforts made on their behalf, most would remain for the entire duration of the war.[15]

In addition, a number of those Rexist leaders who were not serving in the army – including Léon Degrelle – had been arrested by the Belgian authorities on 10 May. The long period of anxious vigil as well as the role allegedly played by Quisling and his supporters during the German attack on Norway had led the government to fear that a fifth column of pro-German sympathisers was present within Belgium ready to assist the enemy. Thus, in April 1940, the Minister of Justice, Paul-Emile Janson, ordered that lists be drawn up of all such suspects and on 10 May the order was given that these fifth columnists be arrested. Amidst the general disorder, there was inevitably little logic to these arrests. Amongst those taken into custody were many German and Jewish refugees from Nazism, Trotskyists, anarchists, Flemish Nationalists and a considerable number of Communist militants faithful to the Soviet Union's policy of neutrality. In all, some 2,000 to 3,000 Belgians as well as an equivalent number of foreigners appear to have been arrested.[16] The Rexists constituted only a small minority of this total but they did include some of the most important figures in the movement. Apart from Léon Degrelle, others arrested included the journalists Victor Matthys and Serge Doring and some of the former Rexist parliamentary deputies as well as ordinary rank-and-file militants who were merely swept up in the panic of the time.[17]

The suspicion that these Rexists would have assisted the German armies was in fact largely unjustified. Despite Degrelle's expressions of sympathy for the Nazi cause, for most Rexists Nazi Germany remained a distant land of which they knew little. Thus, during the campaign of May 1940, those Rexists who served in the Belgian army seem to have accomplished their patriotic duty to the full and any isolated incidents of treachery or 'defeatism' have gone unrecorded.[18] A number of those suspects arrested on 10 May were soon released but the majority – including the Rexist detainees – were kept in custody and, as the Germans advanced, they were transferred first to prisons in western Belgium and subsequently to France.[19] Amidst the panic engendered by the German successes, the Belgian prisoners were considered by their French captors to be German agents and on 20 May 1940 at Abbeville in northern France, 21 of their number – including Joris Van Severen, the leader of the Flemish New Order movement, *Verdinaso*, as well as an elderly Rexist – were executed by French soldiers.[20] The remainder escaped such summary treatment but they endured both beatings and unpleasant physical conditions as they were hastily moved from prison to prison throughout France in order to evade the German armies. Indeed, both during and after the war, Degrelle made much of these hardships telling and retelling exaggerated stories of his sufferings at the hands of the democratic authorities with the intention of justifying his subsequent espousal of collaboration.[21]

The Belgian detainees were eventually interned in camps in the south of France but news of their whereabouts was slow to reach Belgium and for a time it was widely believed, even by the German leaders, that Degrelle had been among those suspects killed by their French guards.[22] His dynamic and impulsive personality had always dominated Rex to such an extent that – like, for example, Doriot's *Parti Populaire Français* (PPF) in France – it seemed almost impossible to conceive of a future for Rex without his leadership. Nevertheless, those few militants who had remained in Brussels did what they could to rebuild the movement. This responsibility fell principally upon the *Conseil Général* of Rex which during the winter of 1939–40 had already been in charge of what remained of the national and local structures of Rex. An administrative body of no great political importance, its most influential members were François De Meester de Heyndonck, the Rexist treasurer Maurice Vandevelde, an architect Camille Damman and the prosperous Brussels *notaire* Léon Brunet. The *Conseil Général* met for the first time on 29 May, the day after the Belgian surrender to the German forces, and, assisted by a *comité consultatif provisoire* composed of prominent pro-Rexist figures, it met at least twice a week during the subsequent two months.[23]

For these men, there was no question of launching Rex upon a policy of instant collaboration with the Germans, as occurred in certain other occupied countries.[24] They were reluctant to take any decisions prior to the hoped-for return of Degrelle and, together with members of the Degrelle family, they devoted much of their energies to discovering the fate of their leader.[25] But the *Conseil Général* did take the first steps towards defining the political stance of the movement. Despite the German Occupation, they – like many others at this time – had no doubt that it was necessary to resume their political activities and the *Conseil Général* called on all Rexists to assist in the rebuilding of Rex.[26] In addition, they gave their unconditional support to Léopold III. A letter addressed to the King expressed their 'sentiments de dévouement résolu et de fidélité totale' as well as restating their long-standing belief that only through an increase in the King's legal and political powers could a durable reconstruction of Belgium be achieved.[27] Pro-royalist sentiments suffused all aspects of Rexist activities during these first months of the Occupation and, in the absence of Degrelle, the King, with his supposed authoritarian tendencies, became the principal focus for Rexist hopes. Conversely, a press release issued by the *Conseil Général* accused Pierlot and his fellow ministers of having betrayed the nation and called for the punishment of those responsible for the arrests carried out on 10 May.[28]

There is no doubt that these statements were greeted enthusiastically by most members of Rex. They took no pleasure in the national defeat but, despite the occupation of their country by German forces, Rexist militants did feel that the ignominious demise of the Belgian and French armies had vindicated their past criticisms of the democratic political regime. The German victory was, they argued, a tragedy which could have been avoided had not Belgium been led by corrupt, ineffectual politicians intent upon embroiling the country in an unnecessary conflict. Moreover, they were optimistic that the Occupation would provide the long-awaited opportunity to enact the Rexist revolution. There was an undeniably exultant air to the behaviour of many Rexists during the summer of 1940. They acted with the arrogant confidence of men who believed that their hour had come, daubing the walls of Brussels with slogans declaring that 'Degrelle avait raison' and urging the *Conseil Général* to relaunch the movement without awaiting the return of their leader.[29] It was imperative, declared the Liège branch of Rex on 19 June, that the Rexists should 'sortir de notre réserve et savoir prendre nos responsabilités'. The people, they claimed, were ready to rally to the movement and a propaganda campaign exploiting the mood of the population would meet with unprecedented success.[30]

Although anxious to exercise a controlling hand over these enthusiasts,[31] the *Conseil Général* was also well aware of the need for action. The Flemish nationalist movement, the *VNV*, had, as we have seen, already begun to build links with the German authorities. Meanwhile, two other smaller right-wing groups, the late Joris Van Severen's largely Flemish *Verdinaso* movement and the francophone paramilitary league, the *Légion Nationale*, signed an agreement in July which they hoped would form the basis of a new official political movement.[32] Finally, and perhaps most importantly, Henri De Man, who was both the President of the *Parti Ouvrier Belge* (*POB*) and one of the King's closest advisers, issued a manifesto dated 28 June in which he declared unambivalently that 'pour les classes laborieuses et pour le socialisme, cet effondrement d'un monde décrépi, loin d'être un désastre est une délivrance'. The democratic era, De Man claimed, was at an end and he too advocated the creation of an authoritarian political movement loyal to the King.[33]

Confronted by these various groups and individuals anxious to exploit the apparent political vacuum, the Rexist leaders were already concerned that they were being left behind.[34] Hence, on 9 July the *Conseil Général* decided to create a new paramilitary grouping to be called the *Formations de Combat*[35] which they hoped would constitute the militia of any future official single party. In addition, the Rexists were keen to ensure that they would be represented in the new government which it was widely believed the King would soon create, and the names of potential ministers reputed to be favourably disposed towards Rex were circulating within the movement.[36]

These initiatives gathered pace with the return on 11 July from detention in France of two of Degrelle's closest colleagues, Victor Matthys and Serge Doring. While expressing their support for the *Conseil Général*, the two men gave new impetus to the resurrection of the movement.[37] In particular, they seem to have lent their support to those advocating the reappearance of the Rexist daily newspaper, *Le Pays Réel*. One of the most remarkable features of the first weeks of the German Occupation of Belgium was the rapid re-emergence of a substantial local and national press. Some such newspapers were – or claimed to be – the successors of pre-war titles while others were no more than ephemeral creations of opportunists. All were subjected to German censorship and depended on

German approval for access to supplies of paper but, despite such conditions, many Rexists were enthusiastic that *Le Pays Réel* should reappear in order to act as a mouthpiece for their views.[38] In fact, soon after arriving in Belgium, the Germans had apparently approached Raty, the administrator of the Rexist press, to invite him to relaunch the newspaper. At this stage the Rexists thought it best to await the return of Degrelle but, though the details remain unclear, it seems that their attitude subsequently changed and that negotiations with the Germans took place during July, with the result that on 30 July approval was granted for *Le Pays Réel* to reappear in francophone Belgium.[39]

By the end of July, two months after the arrival of the German armies, the Rexist leaders had already taken the first steps towards defining the future stance of their movement. Although in no sense collaborationist, Rex had emerged as one of the groups advocating some form of understanding with the German forces. In addition, in common with many others, the Rexists had voiced their support for a reform of the constitution which would replace an outmoded parliamentarism with a more authoritarian political structure in which the King would play a prominent role. None of these ideas could be said to have placed Rex on the extremes of Belgian life. Indeed, most Belgians in the summer of 1940 believed in the need to adapt to the German presence and to carry out political reforms. Nevertheless, there was already in the manner of the Rexist espousal of these ideas, some of the germs of their future extremism. While most who advocated such policies did so in the belief that they were the best means of salvaging some hope from the disaster of the military defeat, the Rexists were enthusiasts for change – sparing hardly a thought for the past and glorying in the possibilities of the future.

In this respect, the Rexists might be said to have been already divided from the majority of the Belgian population. But, if Degrelle had indeed perished in France in the summer of 1940, it is impossible to know how the Rexists would have subsequently acted during the Occupation. Though their enthusiasm for New Order ideas might already have defined them to a certain extent as 'proto-collaborationists', there were many other groups in Belgium and elsewhere in Europe who in the early months of the Occupation appeared committed to an understanding with the Third Reich but who, as it emerged that the victory of Germany was not in fact assured, subsequently withdrew into an '*attentiste*' or even pro-Allied stance. Thus, it seems likely that, had Degrelle not returned, the Rexists would have fragmented into several pro-German and neutralist factions. Only loyalty to Degrelle enabled the movement to retain its unity and coherence and it would seem highly improbable that without his leadership Rex would have strayed so far and so dramatically into the mire of collaboration.

Everything, therefore, still depended on the return of Degrelle and several initiatives were taken during the summer to try and locate him. Finally, in July, a group of Degrelle's friends, including Pierre Daye a journalist and the former head of the Rexist group in the Chamber of Deputies, set out to search for him, eventually discovering the *Chef de Rex* in the south of France where amidst the general chaos of the French defeat he had remained imprisoned in a detention camp. His release was obtained and the *Chef de Rex* returned with his friends to Paris.[40] *En route*, the party paused briefly at Vichy where Pierre Daye contacted the Belgian government which, after many wanderings, had established itself in the capital of the new *Pétainist* regime. The morale of Pierlot and his colleagues was at this time very low. After the capitulation of France, few of the ministers saw any purpose in continuing the war against Germany and they had attempted in vain to submit their resignation to the King in Brussels and to contact the German authorities who, unknown to them, had been ordered by Hitler to rebuff their advances. Thus, it was in some desperation that the ministers seized upon this opportunity for contact with Degrelle's supporters. Ironically, it was Paul-Emile Janson, who as Minister for Justice had been responsible only two months earlier for Degrelle's arrest, who met Pierre Daye on 25 July. Clearly anxious to curry favour, Janson expressed his pleasure at the release of the *Chef de Rex* and urged Daye to convey to Brussels and Paris the government's willingness to resign and to retire from all political activity.[41]

For Degrelle, this contact with the Pierlot government could only have confirmed his belief that, having survived the rigours of detention, he was well placed to profit from the new political situation. Although he had lost weight and was suffering from various ailments contracted in prison, the *Chef de Rex* was in a characteristically euphoric mood. Immediately after his release, he began planning the composition of the government he hoped to form, boasting to his colleagues that Hitler, whom he had met briefly in 1936, would be willing to support his ambitions.[42]

When Degrelle reached Paris on the evening of 25 July, he was promptly invited to the German embassy where he dined with Otto Abetz, the representative of the German Foreign Minister von Ribbentrop. It was this meeting which more than any other would serve to determine the pattern of Degrelle's activities during the following months. Abetz in many ways personified the strange character of the summer of 1940. Only 37 years old, he had been active since before the Nazi seizure of power in organisations for Franco-German reconciliation. He spoke almost perfect French and had married the secretary of Jean Luchaire, the future press baron of German-occupied Paris. As a prominent member of von Ribbentrop's unofficial foreign affairs group, the so-called '*Dienstelle Ribbentrop*', Abetz spent much time in Paris during the 1930s and, when his patron was appointed as Foreign Minister, he became a member of the German diplomatic service. Abetz arrived in Paris in June 1940 as the representative of the Foreign Ministry and on 3 August Hitler appointed him as the German ambassador in Occupied France. This was in many ways a bizarre and anomalous position. Much of France remained under military occupation and Abetz's embassy was in a city which had ceased to be the capital. Yet, in the summer of 1940, he became a focus for those who hoped that a New Europe could emerge from the ashes of the military conflict. A firm supporter of the reconstruction of a strong France which would leave Germany a free hand to expand towards the East, Abetz seemed to represent the new spirit of German comprehension for French interests. Thus, the young ambassador was courted enthusiastically by all those keen to play a role in the New Europe and his embassy in the rue de Lille immediately became the centre of innumerable political intrigues.[43]

The wives of Abetz and Degrelle were apparently childhood friends but the two men met for the first time in September 1936 during the *Chef de Rex's* visit to Berlin.[44] Abetz was a frequent visitor to Brussels during the following years and in the winter of 1939–40 he was to be seen at the salon of Madame Didier which was attended by many of those Belgians who inclined towards sympathy for the German cause.[45] Thus, when the two men met in July 1940, Abetz seemed ideally suited to act as an intermediary between Degrelle and the leaders of the Third Reich. The young diplomat stood then at the zenith of his prestige. Sedulously fostering the impression – in reality largely unfounded – that he was a confidant of the German *Führer*, Abetz had already lent his support to the ambitions of Pierre Laval[46] and Degrelle now became the second of his protégés.

Little is known of the detail of their conversation other than that Degrelle seized the opportunity to expound to Abetz his fanciful dream of a Greater Belgium based on the former Burgundian Empire of the fifteenth and sixteenth centuries.[47] This vision of a reconstituted empire, incorporating large areas of both the Netherlands and northern France, was to become a consistent feature of Degrelle's wartime rhetoric. The idea of some form of territorial revision was not unprecedented. After the First World War some fringe right-wing groups had hoped for the territorial expansion of Belgium and there had subsequently been some support among intellectuals for the 'Thiois' idea of a united Low Countries espoused by certain Flemish figures, such as Joris Van Severen.[48] In contrast Degrelle's ideas were merely a personal fantasy. Though he had long been fascinated by Belgian history, such Burgundian ideas had played no role in pre-war Rexist propaganda and his sudden espousal of them at this time was little more than a bizarre product of his euphoric self-confidence. In the strange summer of 1940 everything seemed possible and Degrelle returned to Brussels after his encounter with Abetz apparently even more convinced that he was destined to play a major role in the New Europe.

Degrelle reached the Belgian capital on 30 July and immediately threw himself into a hectic series of political initiatives. In the many accounts of his activities published since the war, the *Chef de Rex* has constructed a substantial mythology surrounding his wartime career. A central element of this has always been his claim that after his return to Brussels he waited several weeks before resuming his political activities and that he only did so after having received approval from figures such as King Léopold III.[49] In fact, the opposite was true. Determined to make up for lost time, Degrelle sought no advice before immediately plunging into the political fray. The entire pace of Rexist activities was transformed as the caution of the *Conseil Général* gave way to the rash enthusiasms of Degrelle.[50] Even for those close to the *Chef de Rex*, it was frequently difficult to keep abreast of his initiatives during these weeks.[51] However, underlying the appearance of chaos, Degrelle did have at least two consistent aims. In the first place, he was determined to make contact with the leaders of the Third Reich including, if possible, Hitler himself. Whilst others such as the Flemish Nationalists were cultivating the German administrators in Brussels, the *Chef de Rex* wanted to go directly to the centre of political power and was confident that in Abetz he had found the perfect means of doing so.[52] Secondly, Degrelle wished to establish himself as the key political figure within Belgium. Thus he sought to reconstruct Rex as a mass political movement as well as entering into negotiations with those other figures, including the King, who also had ambitions to participate in the political life of Occupied Belgium.

Paris seemed to Degrelle to be the gateway to power in 1940 and he spent only a few days in Brussels before returning to the former French capital. On 7 August, he was able to meet Laval, who had arrived from Vichy also in search of German support for his ambitions. Their discussion at the Hôtel Matignon gave the *Chef de Rex* an opportunity to relate once again the horrors of his imprisonment and to demand French action against the Pierlot government still resident in Vichy. But little of consequence was discussed by the two men and the principal purpose of Degrelle's visit was to consolidate his alliance with Abetz.[53]

In the event, Degrelle's second meeting (on 10 or 11 August) with the newly-appointed German ambassador in Occupied France proved both comical and important.[54] The *Chef de Rex* arrived at the German embassy laden with old maps and atlases with which he hoped to demonstrate the historical basis for his vision of a resuscitated Burgundian empire.[55] To his surprise, he found that he was not the only guest. Abetz had also invited the President of the Belgian Socialist Party, Henri De Man, who, as his manifesto welcoming the German victory had demonstrated, had ambitions of his own. Degrelle and De Man hardly knew each other and both in character and political beliefs they could hardly have been more different. Degrelle was an extrovert instinctive demagogue while De Man was an academic, rather awkward figure who – after a number of years spent teaching in Germany – had come to prominence in his native country in the early 1930s through his advocacy of an economic Plan as the means of overcoming the Great Depression. Unlike Degrelle, who revelled in social and political intrigue, De Man had always been something of an outsider in the shifting coalitions of Belgian politics. Though his views had been seized on enthusiastically by a Socialist Party desperate for an alternative to the economic fatalism of orthodox Marxism, he had few firm allies within the party and his experience of ministerial office during the 1930s had left him with a deep distaste for the democratic political process. With the benefit of hindsight, De Man has been hailed by many as a major socialist theoretician whose ideas broke with the rigid orthodoxies of the late nineteenth century and offered a mid-course between the alternatives of revolution and reformism. However, although he was appointed as President of the Socialist Party in 1939 after the death of Emile Vandervelde, De Man had become an isolated figure in the Belgian political world and during the winter of 1939–40 he emerged instead as one of the principal advisers to King Léopold III, whose neutralist and somewhat authoritarian views he had come to share.[56]

Abetz, encouraged probably by von Ribbentrop, seems to have been anxious to exert an influence over political developments in Belgium and he hoped to effect an alliance between Degrelle and De Man, believing that their complementary talents would form the basis of a pro-German regime in Belgium.[57] This would, however, be no easy task. Degrelle, supremely self-confident and ambitious, was reluctant to share power with anybody; while De Man was arrogantly dismissive of the volatile Rexist leader. Nevertheless, neither man was anxious to alienate the German ambassador and with some reluctance De Man agreed a joint political programme with the *Chef de Rex*. Delighted with this outcome, Abetz then telephoned Berlin with the news of the accord, apparently hinting to Degrelle – entirely erroneously – that he could expect to receive a summons from von Ribbentrop or even Hitler.[58]

Thus, the *Chef de Rex* returned to Brussels reinforced in his conviction that he would soon be invested with substantial political power.[59] This confidence was, however, not for the first time largely misplaced. Though Abetz clearly had some respect for Degrelle, he had neither the desire nor the power to invest the *Chef de Rex* with sole power and his purpose in summoning De Man to Paris seems to have been partly to moderate Degrelle's ambitions. Nor was De Man reconciled to an alliance with the Rexist leader. In post-war accounts of his actions, the Socialist Party President was understandably anxious to minimise the importance of his dealings with Degrelle, insisting that his aim had only been to convince him to follow the King's leadership.[60] In fact, matters were more complicated. Though De Man had close links with the King as well as with influential figures in the Reich and seemed well placed to play a major role in a New Order Europe, his meeting with Abetz had apparently convinced him that the Germans intended Degrelle to have some position of power in Belgium and he was therefore anxious to associate the *Chef de Rex* with his plans.[61] On 18 August the two men met again in Brussels and signed a more formal agreement. This text (preserved in the private archives of Léopold III) makes no mention of Degrelle's more fanciful dreams and merely sketches out the political structures of a future New Order state in which parties would be abolished and all power invested in a royal government which would integrate Belgium in 'une Europe unifiée et régénérée par la victoire du Reich'.[62] Though Degrelle hoped that it would form the basis of a government led by the two men, this largely vacuous document in fact amounted to much less than an alliance between the Socialist President and the *Chef de Rex*. It was only one of many such texts which De Man signed during the summer and, though anxious to placate the Rexist leader, he continued to look on Degrelle as a marginal figure of no great value.[63]

Degrelle's dealings with De Man clearly demonstrated the underlying weakness of his position. Despite the German invasion, he remained an isolated figure who desperately needed to prove his political importance. He was therefore willing to meet anybody whom he felt might assist his ambitions and during August, after his return from Paris, he engaged in a ceaseless round of private meetings. There was, moreover, for once no shortage of people anxious to meet the *Chef de Rex*. In Brussels, it was a summer of intrigues, of accords between unlikely partners and of meetings between former adversaries. The events of 1940 had lifted the lid on many frustrated personal ambitions and during the summer Degrelle was inundated with approaches from individuals who all believed that they were destined to act as the saviours of Belgium.[64]

The *Chef de Rex* entered enthusiastically into this manoeuvring. The powerful, the self-important, the naïve and the simply comical were all received by him at his villa in the drève de Lorraine. Among them were the businessman Raymond Delhaye, administrator of the department store *Au Bon Marché* who in May had temporarily taken over the direction of the Ministry of Public Health and Albert Devèze, a former minister, who apparently discussed his plans for a royal government with Degrelle.[65] Devèze was one of a number of right-wing politicians who had flirted somewhat cautiously with projects for constitutional reform before the war but who now advanced their ideas more openly. A central figure in such discussions was Comte Maurice Lippens. A member of one of the most powerful Belgian families, he was a Liberal senator and Minister of State who directed a private study-group, the *Centre pour la Réforme de l'Etat (CERE)*. After the invasion, Lippens energetically advocated the creation of a new government loyal to the King and, believing that the democratic era was at an end, his *CERE* resumed its work with the intention of devising a more authoritarian constitution for Belgium. Like

De Man, Lippens had no great respect for Degrelle but he was anxious to associate groups such as the Rexists with the *CERE* and he approached Degrelle to invite him to participate in its deliberations.[66]

The *Chef de Rex* refused, however, to do so. Although keen to be part of the political initiatives of the time, he had no wish to become the pawn of these establishment figures. His meetings with Abetz had convinced him that he was well placed to emerge as the leader of Occupied Belgium and he saw his meetings with Lippens and others as the prelude to the creation of his own government.[67] If this ambition was, however, to come to fruition, Degrelle was well aware that he would require not just the support of the Germans but also at least the passive acquiescence of Léopold III. The manoeuvrings of the summer of 1940 were all based on the not inaccurate assumption that, if constitutional problems could be resolved, the King would wish to see created a government which would preside over the creation of a new Belgian state. But contact with the self-proclaimed prisoner in the palace of Laeken was difficult. To the many who sought an audience with him during the summer, his entourage invariably replied that, as a prisoner, the King could not receive political figures. In fact, as we have seen, Léopold III was engaged in his own efforts to reach an understanding with the German authorities and met regularly with men such as Henri De Man who enjoyed his confidence. But lesser figures had to content themselves with meeting members of the King's entourage who, under the guise of keeping themselves informed, played an active role throughout the Occupation in the social and political life of the Belgian capital.

Therefore when Degrelle sent his ally Pierre Daye to the palace to request an audience with the King he was disappointed. In his reply, the King's secretary, Comte Capelle, did, however, avoid appearing to rule out any contact with the Rexist leader. Although he reiterated that the King was a prisoner and could not engage in political discussions, he apparently implied to Daye that the King would not necessarily disapprove of the creation of an 'unofficial' government headed by Degrelle.[68] Quite what the King's secretary intended by this ambiguous phraseology remains unclear. Degrelle was not well regarded by Léopold III and his entourage, and a premature initiative by the *Chef de Rex* would only have hindered the King's own attempts to reach an agreement with the Germans. It seems likely therefore that in his anxiety not to alienate the Rexists, Capelle went further than he had intended in his comments. Indeed, the next day he wrote to Daye 'clarifying' the sense of his remarks and stressing that the King would remain entirely aloof from all political initiatives.[69]

Capelle's remarks undoubtedly encouraged Degrelle to believe that royal support for his ambitions remained a possibility. He therefore repeated his request to be received by Léopold III and, although this was once again rebuffed, Comte Capelle did agree to meet the *Chef de Rex* discreetly at Daye's home on 21 August.[70] This was the only meeting between Degrelle and a representative of the King during the Occupation and it has played an important role in his post-war justifications of his actions. According to the Degrellian account, the King's secretary, speaking in the name of Léopold III, gave his full backing to Degrelle's political actions.[71] In truth, the details of the meeting appear to have been much less dramatic. Degrelle described in some detail his sufferings at the hands of his French gaolers and, according to Daye, seemed anxious to discover the King's personal opinion of him. But Capelle was more concerned to learn what the *Chef de Rex* knew of German intentions towards Belgium and, although the two men found it easy to agree on denouncing the behaviour of the Pierlot government, they reached no agreement on future political initiatives. Degrelle enthusiastically recounted his meetings with Abetz and, claiming that he imminently expected a summons from the Nazi leaders, he sought the King's support for the formation of a Rexist government in Occupied Belgium. Capelle, however, avoided expressing approval for the Rexist leader's plans and went no further than merely agreeing with Degrelle that a resumption of political life in Belgium was a patriotic necessity.[72]

Such modest encouragement was in itself significant but the meeting demonstrated how Degrelle's lack of credibility still hindered his attempts to profit from the confused political situation. Though Léopold III and his entourage remained committed to reaching an accommodation with the Nazi regime, they intended that any new government should be dominated by political and military figures drawn from within the traditional elites and Degrelle would only have been accorded at most a very subsidiary role within such an administration. Therefore it was inconceivable that the King would have lent his support to a government headed by the *Chef de Rex*.[73] Only if Degrelle had been able to demonstrate clear Nazi support for his candidature might Léopold's attitude have been different.

This lack of plausibility as a contender for power similarly undermined Degrelle's efforts to reach an agreement with the Belgian Catholic Church. The history of relations between the Rexists and the Church was long and tortuous. In origin, Rex had been a movement for Catholic spiritual renewal and, though Degrelle's ambitions to transform it into a political party had led the Church hierarchy to distance itself from the movement, there had been no sudden or total rupture between the Church and Rex. For a long time Rex remained essentially a dissident movement within the Catholic community and, even after Cardinal Van Roey had publicly condemned Rex during the Brussels by-election of April 1937, the Rexists retained close links with some elements within the Church.[74] By 1940 such ties had, however, become much looser. The decline in Rexist fortunes and the movement's evolution in the pre-war years towards an explicitly fascist stance had ended all hope of a reconciliation with the Church and, although many Rexists still regarded themselves as faithful Catholics, Rexist propaganda had become much more strident in its attacks on the Church hierarchy.

The stance of the Catholic Church after the German invasion was dominated by two factors. On the one hand, the Cardinal and the majority of the bishops gave their full support to the King. Van Roey was a regular visitor to the royal palace and the pastoral letters issued by the Church in 1940 called on the population, in tones reminiscent of Pétain's pronouncements in France, to accept the German military victory and rally behind the King. On the other hand, the Cardinal always saw his principal responsibility as the defence of the spiritual and material interests of the Church. Indeed, in this respect, the German invasion had had remarkably little impact on the Cardinal. Before, during and long after the Occupation, Van Roey's guiding principle would remain the protection of the Church and the faithful against what he regarded as the decadent, modern world. Hence, to the disappointment of many Belgians who recalled the more combative stance adopted by his predecessor, Cardinal Mercier, during the German Occupation of 1914–18, Van Roey refused to confront the German authorities. He certainly felt no sympathy for the pagan doctrines of nazism, but he could see little purpose in courting conflict with the German forces and preferred instead to build a working relationship with the *Wehrmacht* representatives in Brussels.[75]

It was this cautious stance which explains Van Roey's decision to agree to Degrelle's request, conveyed by a priest sympathetic to Rex, for an audience with the Cardinal. Only a few months previously any such request would have been dismissed out of hand: but Van Roey was reluctant to alienate those who appeared to be the beneficiaries of the new political situation and, though the *Chef de Rex* twice postponed their meeting, he was eventually received by Van Roey on 6 September at the episcopal palace in Malines. This encounter between the cautious, uncommunicative Cardinal and the ebullient Rexist leader was not a success. The Cardinal listened sympathetically to the *Chef de Rex*'s declarations of his personal faith and wish to defend Catholic interests but, although Degrelle boasted of his contacts with German and Belgian figures, Van Roey prudently avoided all attempts by the Rexist leader to involve him in his political ambitions. Van Roey refused to give his approval to the newly-relaunched Rexist newspaper *Le Pays Réel*, and was similarly unimpressed by Degrelle's plans to create a new unified youth movement operating under the aegis of Rex. This was an idea hardly inclined to appeal to Van Roey. The Cardinal was undoubtedly anxious that Catholic social organisations should continue to operate without German interference but he had no wish to see the substantial Catholic youth movement pass under the control of those Rexists who before 1940 had done so much to lure young Catholics away from loyalty to the Church.[76]

Thus, as Degrelle has subsequently admitted, his efforts to commit Van Roey to some form of support for his activities was entirely unsuccessful. Though the Cardinal and the Rexist leader were agreed on the need to adapt to the German victory, the temperamental and ideological differences between the two men remained great. In particular, Van Roey had no reason to support the political goals of the Rexists which, if successful, would have led to the dismantling of the formidable network of Catholic social and political institutions which had long been a prominent feature of Belgian society. Degrelle and his colleagues insisted that such a transformation would liberate the Church from its defensive mentality and would enable the Catholic religion to exert its influence over the whole of society. But Van Roey saw in these ideas only a threat to the established position of the Church and, although individual priests might occasionally look indulgently on the Rexists, at an institutional level there would remain throughout the Occupation a complete divergence of interests between the Church and those who had originally been its most enthusiastic apostles.[77]

His meeting with Van Roey once again illustrated Degrelle's failure to emerge as a central political figure in Occupied Belgium. Despite boasting to the press of his meeting with Laval and spreading extravagant rumours about how he enjoyed the support of the Nazi leaders and of Léopold III,[78] the *Chef de Rex* remained an isolated figure ignored by the predominantly conservative German diplomats and *Wehrmacht* officers in Brussels as well as by most of the Belgian political and social elite. The summons to Berlin promised by Abetz never came and by the end of August Degrelle already appeared to have lost much of the prestige which he had enjoyed on his initial return to Brussels. His name never seems to have featured on the lists of potential prime ministers circulating amongst the King's advisers while his attempts to woo the Flemish Nationalists of the *VNV* proved similarly unfruitful.[79] Therefore, unlike the *VNV*, whose gains from the German invasion had been swift and dramatic, Degrelle and the Rexists seemed doomed to remain a noisy, heretical force on the margins of the political stage.

One reason for this failure was simply that Degrelle had returned too late to Belgium. By the time of his release from detention, others – such as the *VNV* and De Man – had already established themselves and there was little that Degrelle could do to dislodge them. However his failure was also the consequence of his personal lack of credibility. Despite the German invasion, the *Chef de Rex* was powerless to change the popular perception of him as a turbulent extremist unsuited for political office. Thus, even amongst those sympathetic to New Order ideas, there were many who regarded Degrelle and his followers with great distrust. In the words of one of the King's advisers, Degrelle was 'une outre gonflée de vanité' whose pretensions were in inverse proportion to his abilities.[80]

Unable to impose himself on his rivals, Degrelle decided at the end of August to turn away from high-level intrigues in the salons and offices of Paris and Brussels in favour of trying to win mass support for his cause within Belgium. The press was central to this new strategy. Degrelle remained a journalist first and foremost and he was well aware that, if he was to succeed, he must control a mass circulation newspaper. Here again, his lack of influential German and Belgian support proved to be an obstacle. Despite some abortive negotiations, his grandiose plans for taking control of major titles such as Het Laatste Nieuws or Le Soir, the most influential pre-war newspaper in Belgium, came to nothing[81] and the Chef de Rex had to be satisfied with relaunching the former Rexist daily Le Pays Réel which reappeared for the first time on 25 August. After an initial succès de scandale in 1936, this newspaper had rapidly declined to become by 1940 a mouthpiece for Rexist campaigns and Degrelle recognised that it would be necessary for it to break with its former sectarian image. Thus, despite modest financial resources and a circulation limited by the Germans to francophone Belgium, Degrelle sought to present the new Le Pays Réel as a 'national' newspaper which, unlike a number of other titles launched in the immediate aftermath of the German victory, would reflect the real sentiments of the population.[82]

The second facet to Degrelle's new strategy was to rebuild Rex as a political party. If he could not acquire power through private negotiations, Degrelle hoped to establish Rex as a mass movement which would provide him with a power-base as well as forming the basis of the future parti unique of a New Order Belgium. Therefore Degrelle toured Belgium in September inspecting local Rexist groups and encouraging his militants to hasten the reconstruction of the movement.[83] He also selected the key personnel to direct this revivified Rexist movement. Although appreciative of the work accomplished by the Conseil Général, he demoted it to a purely consultative body which rapidly lost all importance.[84] In its place, Degrelle characteristically established a much more flexible structure, gathering around him a somewhat motley group of friends and advisers to whom he delegated particular tasks. Some of these, such as Serge Doring who was appointed to the new post of Secrétaire-Général,[85] were veterans of the Rexist struggle, but others were new men who had formerly played no significant role in the movement or who had joined Rex as recently as the summer of 1940.

One such newcomer was Félix Francq. A member of a prominent Brussels family as well as a long-standing personal friend of Degrelle's, Francq acted as his personal secretary and aide-de-camp throughout the Occupation.[86] Another important new figure was Rutger Simoens who was appointed as the *Commandant Général* of the newly-founded Rexist militia, the *Formations de Combat*.[87] Under his leadership, the *Formations* expanded rapidly and Simoens became one of the few Flemish figures to acquire a position of national importance in Rex. He claimed to be a former Communist who had attended a training-school for party cadres in Moscow as well as having participated in the riots in Rotterdam in the mid-1930s. But no evidence exists to substantiate these claims and it seems that by 1937 Simoens had already become active in right-wing organisations. He was a violent and controversial figure and was among those who consistently advocated direct action by the Rexist forces against their many enemies.[88]

However, indisputably the most significant of these new entrants was Fernand Rouleau who in the summer of 1940 was appointed to the new post of *Lieutenant du Chef de Rex* and soon became Degrelle's most influential adviser.[89] Despite his importance, Rouleau always remained a rather mysterious figure. Aged 36 in 1940, he was an engineer who lived in some style at Uccle just outside Brussels with servants, horses and a Bentley car.[90] In the words of one Rexist veteran, Rouleau 'est tombé de la lune' in 1940. No Rexist could recall having met him before the war and he seems to have only become involved in the movement as a result of a chance encounter with Degrelle shortly after the *Chef de Rex's* return from detention in France.[91] Rouleau's pre-war activities remain cloaked in some mystery. Some German documents – possibly confusing him with Simoens – state that he had been a Communist, a claim strenuously denied by one of Rouleau's surviving relatives.[92] It does seem, however, that he was in Spain during the Civil War where he claimed to have fought for Franco's Nationalist cause.[93] Others allege that Rouleau sold arms to the Nationalists or that he was an intermediary between the Germans and Franco's forces. Yet Rouleau was heartily distrusted by the representative of Nationalist Spain in Brussels and it seems that he may in fact have sold weapons to the Spanish Republicans, possibly while also working as a Nazi agent.[94] Whatever the truth, Rouleau's appearance and character appear to have been in sympathy with his murky past. He struck those who knew him as an immoral 'aventurier de grande envergure' and appears to have been motivated only by a ruthless desire for personal advancement.[95]

Despite or perhaps because of his past, Rouleau rapidly established himself as Degrelle's principal political adviser, ousting those others – notably the journalist and former Rexist parliamentary deputy Pierre Daye[96] – who also had ambitions to play such a role. As early as August, Rouleau seems to have become an almost continual presence at the *Chef de Rex's* home and was frequently to be seen at Degrelle's side at public events.[97] Quite why Degrelle had such confidence in Rouleau aroused considerable speculation among other Rexists. Some alleged that he was supplying Rex with money or that he acted as a secret intermediary between the Germans and Degrelle. Degrelle has denied such allegations and the truth appears to have been somewhat more prosaic. Rouleau's fluent command of German and his apparent familiarity with the Nazi world as well as his personal energy appears to have impressed Degrelle who was only too aware of his almost total ignorance of the workings of the Nazi regime.[98]

Aided by this network of assistants, Degrelle devoted himself to the re-establishment of Rex. The pre-war movement had always been a rather chaotic organisation and in 1940 much emphasis was placed on the need for it to renounce this heritage. Henceforth, so Degrelle and his assistants repeatedly declared, Rex must adopt the principles of order, authority and discipline symbolised by its new slogan 'Croire, Obéir, Combattre'.[99] In order to facilitate this transformation, a new organisational structure was introduced. The Secrétaire-Général, Serge Doring, presided over the movement, assisted by three Chefs de Région (Louis Vanderveken in Brussels, Antoine Leclercq in Wallonia and Odiel Daem in Flanders) who administered secretariats based in Brussels, Liège and Antwerp.[100] These in turn directed a local hierarchy of provinces, arrondissements and sections. It was the arrondissements which soon emerged as the principal focus for the political activities of Rex but the sections remained the basic unit of local organisation. The total number of such sections is difficult to assess but a list compiled by the Walloon secretariat of Rex in February 1941 listed some 132 chefs de section in Wallonia alone.[101] In addition, the Rexist militia, the Formations de Combat, established its own hierarchy. Its commander, Rutger Simoens, was nominally responsible to the Secrétaire-Général but in practice the Formations jealously guarded their autonomy and relations between militia units and local civilian Rexist officials were often strained.[102]

The fulfilment of all ambitions for Rex depended, however, on attracting new recruits to its cause. The movement of the immediate pre-war years had been little more than a rump, dependent upon the loyalty of a small group of unconditional supporters. It was therefore essential that Rex should not only win back many of those who had initially supported the movement in the euphoric years of the mid-1930s but also reach out to other groups in the Belgian population who had hitherto proved resistant to the Rexist message. The principal vehicle for this propaganda campaign was the newly-relaunched Le Pays Réel. In a movement so dominated by journalists, the Rexist newspaper had always enjoyed an important role and at no time was this more so than during the early months of the Occupation when it was almost the only means of making their views known. Largely fruitless attempts were made to attract new staff to the paper including Hergé, the creator of Tintin, who instead chose to work for another German-censored title, Le Soir.[103] But the existing staff did their best to give the relaunched paper an air of authority. Its early issues were dominated by calls for realism and national unity. The past, Degrelle declared in his first contribution, was dead and all Belgians must now turn their attention to a future which would inevitably be dominated by Nazi Germany. To place any hope in England was, the Rexist leader insisted, unrealistic and the Rexists confidently predicted that peace would be declared within a matter of a few weeks or months.[104]

This German military victory was not, however, Rexist journalists were at pains to stress, merely an accident of battle. It marked a decisive turning-point in history as important as the French Revolution of 1789. In common with many others throughout Europe who in the summer of 1940 were beginning to move towards categorical support for the German cause, the Rexists insisted that the outcome of the war signified the end of the era of liberal nation-states and the beginning of an immense revolution which would transform both Europe and the entire world.[105] The challenge for Belgium, the Rexist newspaper repeatedly proclaimed, was to exploit the enormous possibilities which these events offered. As José Streel, the principal leader writer of Le Pays Réel and one of the more persuasive exponents of Rexist views, declared: 'S'il fut jamais un temps où les événements parlaient avec la clarté des évidences, c'est bien celui que nous vivons. Le livre est ouvert; nous n'avons qu'à lire. Le sens de ce qui se passe est très clair.'[106] If the Belgian population shook off their old nationalistic prejudices, they could participate in the new unified Europe which would emerge in the wake of the German victories. Standing at the commercial and cultural crossroads of Europe, their country was well placed to benefit from this European integration. A new Renaissance, Degrelle declared with characteristic hyperbole, was in the making and Belgium would recover, in a German-dominated Europe, the prosperity and splendour which it had enjoyed during the fifteenth and sixteenth centuries.[107]

However, in order to participate in this brave, new world, the Belgians must first accomplish their own revolution. As the first edition of the relaunched Le Pays Réel declared: 'C'est l'heure de la révolution, de la vraie Révolution, de celle qui exige non pas la violence extérieure mais la violence intime, rigoureuse, sereine.'[108] This need for a wide-ranging internal transformation of Belgium was the other major theme of Rexist propagandists during 1940. Their rhetoric was frequently violent and never more so than in the case of Degrelle who thundered with his usual verve that his movement would sweep away those cliques – notably the freemasons, Jews, and financiers – who had for so long corrupted and perverted the country for their own ends.[109] But the journalists of Le Pays Réel reserved their greatest ire for the political elite. The events of May, when many civic dignitaries had abandoned their responsibilities and fled to France, had seemed to vindicate the long-standing Rexist denunciations of the self-serving party leaders. These politicians, *Le Pays Réel* never tired of proclaiming, had deserted the people in their moment of need, placing their personal security above the interests of the country. There could be no place for such 'venin politicien' in the New Order Belgium of tomorrow and the Rexist press was quick to denounce efforts by those whom it described dismissively as the *ancien régime* elite to recover their former positions of authority.[110]

Yet, although it was this violent tone which predominated in their propaganda, the Rexists were not devoid of a positive vision of the new society which they were seeking to achieve. At the heart of their ideology remained, as always, a simplistic, somewhat nostalgic vision of a 'pur, fier et propre' Belgium cleansed of the alien cosmopolitan influences of the modern era.[111] The anarchy of individualism and materialistic class conflict would give way to a rationalised, federal state in which power would be devolved to each of the linguistic communities as well as to self-governing economic and social corporations.[112] Material reforms and a vaguely defined commitment to social justice formed part of this Rexist programme[113] but they always took second place to moral priorities. For all of Degrelle's crude demagogy and the undoubted radicalisation which had taken place in the movement during the pre-war years, there remained much in Rexist propaganda in 1940 which recalled their origins in the Catholic intellectual world of the inter-war years. An explicit commitment to the Catholic faith was now absent but it was still what Degrelle termed a 'révolution des âmes' which remained at the heart of their political crusade. Over and above all material changes, it was a transformation in the moral spirit of the country which they were seeking to achieve and it was once again José Streel, writing in *Le Pays Réel*, who best expressed this ideal: 'La révolution de l'ordre nouveau recrée les possibilités d'une humanisation authentique en restituant à l'homme son unité et sa dignité, en lui rendant le goût du travail et de l'effort, en le remplaçant dans les cadres naturels de la famille, de la profession, de la région et de la communauté populaire. C'est un remembrement de la société qui s'opère, c'est l'ordre et la hiérarchie qui sont réintroduits, c'est la discipline de l'esprit et de l'action qui s'impose.'[114]

This Rexist propaganda enjoyed modest success in 1940. It did to some extent match the mood of many Belgians who believed that their country must adapt to the reality of the German military victory and build a new political system more appropriate to the needs of the future. These new recruits to Rexism were of diverse origins. Some were merely prodigals who had deserted the movement in the hard times before the war and who, often to the annoyance of the movement's veterans, now returned to the fold.[115] Many others were patriotic conservatives anxious to express their loyalty to the King and to the political views which he was believed to hold, but a few – if Rexist propagandists are to be believed – were also former supporters of left-wing groups who rallied to the Rexist cause in the belief that it now offered the best hope of achieving their revolutionary goals.[116] More significantly, a number of local political notables – from all ideological camps – decided to ally themselves with Rex after the German invasion. A few may have been true converts but most seem to have been no more than opportunists who hoped that Rexist support would enable them to maintain their positions of authority.[117]

Thus, there was a confident, exultant air to Rexist activities during these first months. They boasted of the large crowds attending their meetings and the columns of *Le Pays Réel* were filled with reports of the creation of new sections and the enrolment of new recruits.[118] Indisputably the most striking example of Rexist success at this time was the *Formations de Combat*. Since its establishment by the *Conseil Général* in July, the *Formations* expanded rapidly and as early as the end of September Degrelle attended an inspection of more than 500 militiamen in Brussels.[119] The *Formations* featured prominently in accounts of local Rexist activities throughout Belgium during 1940 and, according to estimates which for once seem fairly reliable, its total membership had reached approximately 4,000 by the end of 1940.[120] The extent of Rexist success must not, however, be exaggerated. Though it was reaching out to previously hostile sections of the community, the movement did not achieve its ambition of establishing itself as a mass movement at the centre of Belgian political life. It is impossible to assess with any certainty the total membership of Rex in 1940. There are no surviving membership lists and the Rexists were always reluctant to reveal to those outside the movement the number of their supporters. It is, nevertheless, clear that it always remained a relatively small organisation and the major national rally held at Liège in January 1941 was attended by only 5,000 or so supporters.[121] One estimate is that Rexist membership totalled approximately 15,000 to 20,000 in 1940[122] and, although based on no more than supposition, this figure would seem to be roughly correct as an indication of the number of committed, active members of Rex. In addition, there were a roughly equivalent number of sympathisers and members of organisations affiliated either directly or indirectly to the movement.

Rex always remained a political force of limited importance and, even within the ranks of New Order organisations, it was never able to rival the strength of the Flemish *VNV* which increased its membership from 25,000 in May 1940 to 70,000 one year later.[123] The readership of *Le Pays Réel* similarly reflected this failure to reach a mass audience. When it was launched in August, it had a circulation of 65,000 but this had declined to some 23,000 by the autumn of 1940 and, although this figure was still substantially higher than its circulation before the German invasion, it constituted only a very small fraction of the total readership of the francophone press within Occupied Belgium. Thus, far from emerging as

Degrelle had hoped as a national newspaper, *Le Pays Réel* remained in effect a propaganda sheet read only by those already sympathetic to Rex.[124]

Examples elsewhere in German-occupied Europe, such as the Netherlands, Slovakia and France, demonstrate that it was possible in these early months of the German Occupation to attract mass support for political movements which rejected democratic structures in favour of a vaguely defined commitment to a New Order.[125] The failure of Degrelle and the Rexists to capitalise in the same way on the popular mood in Belgium seems to have been due largely to their past. Both the Dutch *Nederlandse Unie* and the Vichy regime of Pétain in France were able to emerge as symbols of national unity in 1940 because they were untainted by association with the political conflicts and failures of the past. Léopold III, if he had chosen to do so, might well have been able to play a similar role within Belgium but the Rexists, as a marginal extremist group, could not do so. Despite the profound changes in popular attitudes provoked by the German invasion, relatively few Belgians were willing to abandon their distrust for a movement which in many respects seemed to typify the divisive conflicts of the old parliamentary regime.

This failure to attract a mass audience within Belgium was compounded by Degrelle's continued inability to convince the Germans that he was the figure best equipped to lead Belgium within the New Europe. Despite his boasts of his special relationship with the Nazis, Degrelle found himself treated as a 'non-person', ignored – on Goebbels' orders – by the Nazi press[126] and shunned by those few German officials with whom he came into contact. The sole exception was, of course, Otto Abetz. The support of the German ambassador in Paris was Degrelle's only significant asset in 1940 and the *Chef de Rex* remained optimistic that Abetz's supposed influence within the Reich would eventually bring him success. Thus, in October, Degrelle travelled again to Paris[127] and it was during this visit that on 20 October he addressed a long report to Abetz which provides the clearest statement of his ambitions at this time. In this private document, the *Chef de Rex* posed unambivalently as a friend of Nazi Germany, offering advice with his customary self-confidence as to how the German leadership should set about building a European New Order. An expanded Belgium allied to Germany could, he declared, play a decisive role in this process. If reinforced by the addition of the north of France and the Dutch west bank of the Scheldt, this Grande-Belgique would become one of the 'plaques tournantes' of the New Europe acting as a point of political, cultural and economic interchange as it had in the era of Charles V. But, for all of his bravura and bluster, a strong undercurrent of anxiety was also evident in Degrelle's report. His greatest fear was that the Germans might suddenly withdraw from the Occupied territories, leading to what he declared would be a recrudescence of the 'vieilles oligarchies parlementaires, ploutocratiques et maçonniques'. Even if the German forces remained, a major change in Nazi policy was required. Degrelle deplored the cautious policies introduced by the German rulers in France and Belgium. Rather than fostering a New Order revolution, they had chosen to work with the personnel and institutions of the pre-war world, thereby creating what Degrelle termed a 'national-socialisme bâtard'. Instead, the Rexist leader called on the Nazi leaders to ally themselves with the true revolutionaries of the New Order Europe: 'L'Europe nouvelle devra être dirigée durement. La guerre ne doit pas se terminer par une transaction idéologique qui pourrirait le National-Socialisme, mais par la victoire totale, sans concessions stériles, du National-Socialisme et de Mouvements identiques de la nouvelle Europe.'[128] Rex, Degrelle stressed, was the only such ally of National Socialism in Belgium. The King was the prisoner of his detestable entourage of reactionary masonic and plutocratic elements, De Man was a mere technocrat while the Flemish Nationalists of the *VNV* remained constrained by their democratic origins and narrowly regionalist outlook. Therefore, Degrelle insisted, the Nazis must turn to Rex which under the leadership of its uncontested leader had, he claimed somewhat extravagantly, proven its ability to win 'foules immenses' to its cause.[129]

This document, with its characteristically Degrellian combination of fantasy and vituperation, brought its author no benefits. There is some evidence that Abetz did suggest to his superiors in the Foreign Ministry that they should support the *Chef de Rex*'s ambitions[130] but it seems unlikely that he did so with any great hope of success. The young ambassador was largely absorbed by his activities in France and in reality there was little that he could do to assist Degrelle. Indeed, his modest efforts would probably have passed unnoticed had they not come to the attention of the officials of the *Militärverwaltung* in Brussels. They were intensely annoyed that Abetz was meddling in their area of responsibility. *Militärverwaltungschef* Reeder wasted no time in explaining to his superiors the foolishness of supporting the Rexists and, according to Degrelle, summoned Abetz to Brussels to warn him not to interfere in matters outside of his domain.[131]

This intervention by the *Militärverwaltung* consolidated the political isolation of Degrelle. Though the *Chef de Rex* apparently made a further visit to Paris in November, Abetz would henceforth be much more circumspect in his actions and Degrelle's subsequent assertion that a meeting between himself and Hitler in the autumn of 1940 was only postponed at the last minute is no more than one of the *Chef de Rex*'s many post-war fantasies.[132] The most formidable obstacle faced by Degrelle was the powerful position of the *Militärverwaltung*. With no end in sight to the military conflict, the *Wehrmacht* administrators in Brussels had emerged as the sole determinants of German policies in Belgium and the policies pursued by Reeder and von Falkenhausen left little room for Degrelle and the Rexists. By the autumn of 1940, the *Militärverwaltung* was working closely with the Flemish Nationalists of the *VNV* but, in accordance with Hitler's orders of July, German activities in Brussels and Wallonia were limited to the maintenance of public order and the integration of the industrial resources of the region into the German war effort.[133] These goals required the German officials to work with the pre-war elite and on several occasions Reeder made significant concessions on matters of policy in order to ensure the continued co-operation of Belgian civil servants and industrialists. The turbulent activities of Degrelle and his followers could only prejudice this partnership and, though the *Militärverwaltung* did apparently give some limited material assistance to Rex in 1940, there was – as Degrelle recognised – no question of it supporting the Rexist ambition of a political revolution.[134] These policy considerations were reinforced by the low esteem in which the German officials held the Rexists. The *Wehrmacht* officers of the *Militärverwaltung* looked with disdain or even repugnance on Degrelle and his followers as political opportunists whose crude demagogic style and 'clerico-fascist' views made them unworthy of German support. A gulf of linguistic and political incomprehension divided the Rexists from these German officials who, despite their role as the agents of Hitler's orders, remained rooted for the most part in the conservative assumptions of a pre-Nazi era. For Reeder and his colleagues, the Rexists were at best an irrelevance and, at worst, a hinderance and the *Militärverwaltung* played little or no part in encouraging the gradual evolution of Rex towards an explicitly pro-Nazi stance. Political collaboration in francophone Belgium was emphatically not a German creation.

As 1940 drew to a close, Degrelle appeared to have reached an impasse. The optimism which he had initially felt in July had evaporated as he had failed to win the support either of the new German authorities or of the established Belgian elite. These reverses were especially galling in view of developments taking place elsewhere in German-occupied Europe. In Norway in September, Quisling and his supporters had formed a pro-German government while in France Hitler had met Laval and Pétain at Montoire in October and had initiated a policy of collaboration with the Vichy regime.[135] Observing these events, Degrelle felt with some justification that he was falling behind in the race to participate in the New Europe. His Rexist supporters, absorbed in their efforts to rebuild their movement, retained a boisterous, confident air which belied their failure to win German favour; but Degrelle and his close advisers did not share this optimism. The doors which had opened to him in the summer were already closing and by the end of October the Rexist leader had become profoundly demoralised by his failure to make any progress towards gaining power.[136]

The fundamental problem facing Degrelle was the continuation of the war. Once Hitler had postponed the invasion of England in order to concentrate first on a peripheral war of attrition against the British and, subsequently, on the attack on the Soviet Union, the imminent end to hostilities which had been so widely predicted in the summer of 1940 disappeared into an uncertain and distant future. Belgium, as the obvious springboard for any assault on Britain, was obviously of much too great strategic importance for Hitler to contemplate allowing control of the country to pass out of German military control. Thus, as Léopold III's fruitless visit to Berchtesgaden in November demonstrated, no political initiative within Belgium could be expected prior to the end of the war. Degrelle was forced to accept this unpalatable truth and on several occasions during the autumn of 1940 he warned his supporters against hoping for political success until after the military conflict had been resolved.[137]

Given this combination of unfavourable factors, Degrelle might have been expected to have stepped back from his attempts to woo the Nazi leaders. Instead, the opposite proved to be the case. Failure merely served to radicalise Degrelle and during the final weeks of 1940 he redoubled his efforts to win German support. This lurch towards collaboration was neither sudden nor dramatic. Indeed, the very concepts of collaboration and resistance were in many respects inapplicable to the political situation which existed in Belgium throughout 1940. These two terms would only gain their full significance once opinion within the country had become polarised between a pro-Allied patriotic majority and a pro-German collaborationist minority. This, however, only took place gradually during the winter of 1940–1. In late 1940 political attitudes remained more complicated. Though feelings towards Germany had hardened significantly since the summer, the broad consensus that Belgium must accept the reality of the German victory remained largely intact and what divisions there were largely concerned the form which this new political order should take. Small groups on the extremes positively welcomed the Nazi invasion or sought clandestinely to continue the fight against the Nazi invaders but most Belgians – including many Rexists – occupied a middle ground which can be categorised as neither resistance nor collaboration. Only once popular opinion realised that the military struggle might not in fact be over would this three-dimensional political situation be replaced by a single overwhelming division between those who supported and those who opposed the Nazi military cause.

Unlike some extremist Flemish Nationalists and the very small anti-semitic organisation, La Défense du Peuple,[138] the Rexists were in no sense instant collaborationists. Despite Degrelle's private efforts to present himself to Abetz as a sincere friend of Nazi Germany, much ambivalence continued to surround the public stance of the Rexists. Though already distinguished from much of the population by the depth of their hostility to any return to the pre-war political order, they remained within the broad centre-ground which accepted the German presence and sought to adapt to it. From October onwards, however, Rex gradually broke with the mainstream of Belgian public opinion and moved significantly closer to what might be termed a proto-collaborationist stance. Even at the end of the year, this evolution would be far from complete but it had nevertheless ensured that a wedge had been firmly driven between the Rexists and a majority of their compatriots.

The first issue on which the Rexists parted company with popular opinion concerned England. With Degrelle to the fore, the Rexist press adopted an ever more virulently anti-English tone ridiculing the naïvety of those who retained any confidence in British military power. Britain, they claimed, was a decadent, imperialistic nation whose power had always been based on the exploitation and enslavement of other peoples.[139] Rexist use of such themes may well have been a consequence of Degrelle's visits to France where a number of radical groups – such as Doriot's *PPF* – were trying to exploit popular antipathy to England fostered by the military disasters of May and June 1940.[140] In Belgium, however, there was little basis for such a campaign. Despite the precipitous retreat of the British forces from Belgium in May, a traditional anglophile sentiment remained strong and most Belgians continued to hope that Britain would prove able to repulse the anticipated German invasion. Rexist insistence on the perfidious, selfish character of England found little echo among the population and merely reinforced their popular image as an extremist group who were all too willing to dance to the tunes of the German propaganda machine.[141]

The increasing radicalism of the Rexists was also reflected in a hardening of their attitudes towards the established political and social elite. Abandoning any pretensions to be a serious national newspaper, *Le Pays Réel* launched a vitriolic campaign against those pre-war politicians who, they claimed, were trying to sabotage the emergence of a genuine New Order in Belgium. Already, *Le Pays Réel* warned, these discredited politicians of the democratic *ancien régime* had succeeded in infiltrating a number of public institutions where they had reintroduced the corrupt practices of the past. Decisive action, Degrelle ranted in the Rexist daily as early as 29 September, must be taken against such men: 'Nous les vomissons. Nous serrons les poings devant cette recrudescence des pires moeurs politiciennes. Mais ces poings, que la colère aura contractés, ne se planteront qu'avec plus de force en plein le but, au jour prochain où la Belgique nouvelle déblayera le terrain pour toujours . . . de la pestilence démocratique.'[142]

The small Jewish community in Belgium also became a frequent target of abuse in the columns of *Le Pays Réel*. The German administrators in Brussels did not give a high priority to anti-Jewish measures but in

October 1940 they did issue a number of decrees intended to control Jewish influence in public life. *Le Pays Réel* welcomed these limited measures and during the autumn of 1940 anti-semitic articles featured prominently in the Rexist press.[143] Anti-semitism was, of course, not a novelty in Rexist propaganda. Ever since 1936, Rexists had, rather in the manner of many French extreme-right groups of the same time, used the Jewish origins of certain prominent politicians and businessmen as a means of attacking the alleged corruption of the political and financial elite. There was, however, a novel virulence to Rexist attacks on the Jews in 1940. Crude anti-semitic stereotypes, dire threats and, increasingly, violent direct action against Jewish property become prominent features of Rex during the autumn. In part, this campaign was no doubt a rather crude attempt to curry favour with the German authorities but it also reflected a genuine enthusiasm for anti-semitic actions among some elements within Rex. A number of Rexist journalists – including on occasions Degrelle[144] – appeared embarrassed by the prominent role given to anti-semitism in the Rexist press and stressed that the danger presented by the Jewish community was less significant than that posed by, for example, the freemasons or the former political elite. Nevertheless these half-hearted appeals to moderation went unheeded by those – especially from the *Formations de Combat* – who saw in attacks on all too vulnerable Jewish-owned businesses in Antwerp and Brussels an opportunity to vent their frustrations. Anti-semitism, thus, became an integral element of Rexist rhetoric and a further indication of the radicalisation taking place within the movement.[145]

The Catholic Church was another prominent target of Rexist ire in the autumn of 1940. Only a few weeks after Degrelle's meeting with Cardinal Van Roey, *Le Pays Réel* was launching intemperate attacks on the self-interest and conservatism of the Catholic hierarchy. It is easy to make too much of these attacks. The Church – unlike the freemasons, politicians or Jews – was not regarded by the Rexists as an irreconcilable opponent of the New Order. But Van Roey's refusal to assist Degrelle's political ambitions led the Church to become for the Rexists a symbol of the more general unwillingness of the institutions of pre-war Belgium to recognise the need for a radical political transformation of the country.

This animosity became more marked as a consequence of a letter addressed by Degrelle to a large number of Catholic priests in francophone Belgium on 23 November. For a number of weeks prior to the despatch of this letter, Rex had been sending free copies of *Le Pays Réel* to many members of the clergy and he now invited them to join those 'Belges lucides et audacieux' who had subscribed to the Rexist newspaper, adding, in an apparent reference to his meeting with Van Roey, that the Church authorities had been consulted and had raised no objection to the newspaper being read by the Catholic faithful.[146] This last flourish was a typical piece of Degrellian effrontery. In a pastoral letter issued on 10 October Cardinal Van Roey had already condemned in cautious terms those opportunists who he alleged were seeking to exploit the German presence by engaging in political adventurism. Rex was not named but the inference of Van Roey's message was clear and thus, when a number of worried priests wrote to the Cardinal to ask whether *Le Pays Réel* did indeed enjoy the approval of the Church, his response was forthright. Degrelle's remarks, he informed them, were 'un vrai abus et une duperie' and the Church in no sense approved of the Rexist newspaper.[147]

Degrelle soon learned of Van Roey's comments and in *Le Pays Réel* on 8 December he made an outspoken attack on the Catholic hierarchy. No longer seeking to woo the Church, the *Chef de Rex* castigated 'le chantage politicien d'un certain clergé' who behaved as if they were agents of Churchill.[148] This intemperate article drew wide attention but it would be wrong to exaggerate its significance. For all of the fury of their attacks on the hierarchy of the Church, the Rexists remained sympathetic towards the Catholic faith. Rexist journalists such as José Streel were at pains to stress that any regime in Belgium would be obliged to build upon the spiritual and moral traditions of the Catholic faith and that the behaviour of certain anglophile priests should not be allowed to disguise the fundamental convergence of interests and beliefs between the Church and the advocates of a New Order.[149] Even Degrelle remained willing to accept the spiritual role of the Church, declaring in December 1940: 'Que l'Eglise s'occupe de sauver les âmes, elle a suffisamment de travail dans ce domaine.'[150] Compromise with the ecclesiastical hierarchy of the Church was, however, now impossible and Rexist militants took up Degrelle's lead by enthusiastically denouncing those representatives of the Church who they claimed were to the fore in rallying support for the English cause. Verbal and even on occasions physical conflict between Rexist Catholics and their fellow parishioners became increasingly common and, as Rex moved towards a more explicitly pro-German stance, so relations between the movement and the Church rapidly deteriorated still further.[151]

The verbal attacks made by the Rexists on those whom they regarded as the enemies of the New Order revolution were soon supplemented by acts of physical violence. Over a number of days in early October 1940, militants in Brussels, Antwerp, Liège, Namur, the Borinage and probably elsewhere launched what the leadership admitted was a concerted campaign of violence against national and local politicians. Instigated apparently by the *Lieutenant du Chef*, Fernand Rouleau, these attacks were much more extensive than the few isolated incidents which had been reported during the summer.[152] In Brussels, one politician was attacked and 'debagged' in the street while in several towns hostile crowds of Rexists gathered outside the homes of politicians to break windows, daub slogans or assault their victims. In the most substantial incident, a large squad of Rexist militiamen who besieged a meeting of the *Conseil Communal* in the Brussels suburb of Schaerbeek had to be dispersed by the local police.[153] Though direct action of this kind enjoyed a long tradition within the Rexist movement, a more novel and sinister feature of the violence in October was the attacks on Jewish businesses. In Brussels, Antwerp and Liège units of the *Formations de Combat* sacked Jewish shops and daubed slogans. In Brussels, the police were once again obliged to intervene and a number of Rexists were arrested.[154]

Degrelle gloried in these various forms of direct action. Declaring 'Ce sont des comptes à régler entre Belges!', he portrayed the violence as acts of vengeance by a population exasperated by the failings of its leaders.[155] In reality, though, they revealed the mood of frustration pervading Rex. Faced with an immobile political situation, the Rexists were forced to resort to acts of this kind which, though they achieved little, satisfied their need for action as well as reminding the German authorities of their existence. If they had hoped that such actions would win them German favour, they were, however, disappointed. The *Militärverwaltung* summoned representatives of Rex and ordered that all actions prejudicial to public order must cease forthwith.[156]

Although Degrelle had boasted that these attacks were merely the opening salvoes in a prolonged campaign against the enemies of the New Order, Rex had little choice but to bow to the German order and no further attacks were launched during the remaining weeks of 1940. This short-lived flurry of Rexist violence served, nevertheless, to confirm the popular image of Rex as an extremist movement. This was an impression which the Rexists themselves did much to foster. The talk of national reconciliation which had featured prominently in Rexist propaganda during the first months of the Occupation was soon replaced by a much greater emphasis on the stark divisions within Belgium between the forces of reaction and those of the New Order.[157] Hence, when Robert Poulet the editor of the pro-New Order newspaper *Le Nouveau Journal* proposed during the autumn the creation of a broadly-based single party which could rally support for the King and for political reforms, the Rexists noisily rejected his project, declaring that they were not interested in a 'révolution de carnaval' which would merely enable the old elite to retain the real power.[158]

Thus, the language, actions and self-image of Rex all demonstrated its evolution away from the centre ground of Belgian opinion. The stance adopted towards the Germans also reflected this change. There was no single moment during these months when the Rexists opted unambiguously for the German cause but their comments did become progressively less cautious. The seeds of this radicalisation had, of course, been present from the outset. Already in late August *Le Pays Réel* had been anxious to present the events of 1940 as a European revolution and had made no secret of its support for the New Order forces throughout Europe, be they French, Italian, Spanish or German.[159] But it was Degrelle who in the autumn of 1940 seized upon this same theme and gave to it a much more explicitly pro-German character. The revolutionaries of the New Europe were, he declared, a single unified political force, of which Rex was the Belgian component. Vague expressions of sympathy were now replaced by a much more categorical commitment to an alliance of European revolutionaries and, speaking at a Rexist dinner in Mons in November, he declared proudly 'Je bois à la Révolution Européenne'. Laudatory references to the Nazi regime, the German people and to Hitler, the 'benefactor' of Europe, increasingly punctuated his rhetoric and in another speech at Huy in December he came close to making an open declaration of support: 'Nous, Rexistes, ne sommes pas des convertis d'aujourd'hui. La jeunesse d'Allemagne, comme toutes les jeunesses qui sont en train de faire l'Europe nouvelle, reçoit notre salut le plus fraternel.'[160]

This evolution towards explicit support for the ideological goals of the Nazis was matched by an ever greater insistence on the patriotic need to work with Germany. This was an argument advanced by many in Belgium in 1940 but Degrelle and his Rexist colleagues gave to it a much more clear-cut form. For them, an association with Germany was not merely a prosaic necessity but a patriotic obligation. Only by working closely with the Nazi regime could Belgium ensure its survival and Degrelle called on his compatriots to respond positively to Goebbels' call for a spirit of collaboration amongst the European nations: 'Le patriotisme le plus élémentaire nous enseigne que, les faits étant ce qu'ils sont . . . seule une attitude correcte, sans aplatissement, mais aussi sans hargne, tendue vers une collaboration entière et loyale, peut encore permettre le redressement de notre pays.'[161] None of this amounted to a formal policy of collaboration in the sense which it was subsequently to acquire. The empty phrases of Degrelle were not supplemented by concrete actions and a strong nationalist tone continued to pervade much of Rexist propaganda;[162] but already the basic facts of hostility to England and sympathy towards Germany had been established. A path towards collaboration had already been defined and, when in January 1941 Degrelle went much further in his support for the Nazi regime, he would only be building on the arguments he had advanced during the previous autumn.

Degrelle was well aware of the disquiet which his comments aroused even within Rex and, in private, he was frequently more cautious, reassuring worried supporters that he had no wish to become one of the 'lécheurs des bottes des Allemands'.[163] Despite the failure of his dealings with Abetz, Degrelle continued with his attempts to win the support of the Germans. For example, if a subsequent statement by Degrelle is to be believed, he proposed to the Germans in October – quite possibly in imitation of similar moves in France – that the Rexists should be allowed to create a corps of Belgian aviators and regiments of colonial troops who would fight to liberate the Belgian Congo from English control. Like so many of Degrelle's advances to the Germans, this fanciful suggestion was ignored.[164]

Despite Degrelle's assurances, not all Rexist militants were happy at the evolution of their movement. Rex had always been an unstable coalition of conflicting groups and personalities and the failure to make the expected advances towards power brought such conflicts to the fore. Many long-standing militants resented the arrival of new men such as Rouleau and Simoens and the influence which they appeared to exercise over Degrelle, while others deplored the radicalisation which had taken place within the movement since the summer.[165] By far the most vocal of these mal-contents was José Streel. As a young Catholic journalist and writer of some repute, Streel represented the opinions within Rex of that younger Catholic intelligentsia which had provided the movement with so many of its first recruits. Though he had always avoided political responsibilities, he had long been an influential and articulate defender of the Rexist cause and was one of the very few members of the movement to enjoy the respect of those outside of Rex. After initially hesitating over what he should do in the summer of 1940, Streel had rejoined the staff of *Le Pays Réel* and, as the principal leader-writer of the paper, he used his powerful position to make known his disquiet at Degrelle's initiatives. Streel had no sympathy with the British but he was firmly opposed to Degrelle's efforts to stress the affinities between Rex and the Nazis and in a number of articles published during the autumn of 1940 he warned his readers that the movement should remain faithful to the ideas which had served it well through more than five years of struggle. Each country, he insisted, had to carry out its own New Order revolution in accordance with its political culture and no purpose could be served by seeking to imitate alien Nazi models.[166]

The climax of Streel's defensive campaign was the forthright article 'Gare aux Déraillements' which he published in the internal bulletin for Rexist militants on 20 December 1940. Once again, his main theme was the need for Rex to retain its distinctiveness. Certainly, he admitted, the movement must adapt to the new political realities but the fashion for borrowing the policies, style and even the language of Germany could only prejudice the success of the New Order cause within Belgium. If Rex was to achieve victory, Streel argued, it must respect the historical traditions of Belgium: 'Dans tous les domaines, restons fidèles à nous-mêmes, à notre passé dans ce qu'il a d'essentiel; ne perdons jamais de vue que notre révolution ne doit pas se faire dans la lune mais dans la Belgique telle que nous la trouvons, oeuvre des siècles avec ses lois et ses constantes.

Nous avons à *faire notre révolution* et non pas n'importe laquelle.'[167] Streel undoubtedly represented the views of many Rexists of long standing and he was a popular speaker at local meetings[168] but the importance of his views should not be exaggerated. Despite the failure to acquire power, most Rexists remained content to place their trust in the judgement of Degrelle and his control of the ideological and political direction of the movement remained unquestioned.

The effect of the hardening in the stance of Rex directed by Degrelle was to create by the end of the year a clear division between the views espoused by the Rexists and those held by the majority of the population. Rexist antipathy to the reluctance of their compatriots to adopt whole-heartedly the New European Order was matched by the hostility with which the actions of Degrelle and his colleagues were regarded by a large majority of the population.[169] The responsibility for this clear division did not, however, lie solely with the Rexists. It also reflected the changes which had taken place in the attitudes of much of the Belgian population during the autumn of 1940. Public opinion in the circumstances of a foreign occupation is of course difficult to assess with any certainty but the reports of both Belgian and German observers were agreed on what, in his reports to his superiors, *Militärverwaltungschef* Reeder described as the deplorable transformation which had taken place in the mood of the people since his arrival. While in June, Reeder commented, most Belgians had seemed favourably disposed towards the Germans, that attitude had changed within a few months to one of scarcely concealed hostility.[170] This was – as Reeder recognised – partly the consequence of military events. Thanks to the radio, the population was well informed about the progress of the war and even in 1940 the broadcasts of the BBC – and from September those of *Radio-Belgique* based in London – were followed avidly. Support for England grew rapidly and the German failure to invade Britain as well as the subsequent Italian debacle in Greece seem to have convinced many Belgians that the war was not over and that the British might eventually prove able to defeat the Axis powers.[171]

The result was a resurgence in patriotic and anti-German sentiments. During the autumn, numerous spontaneous acts of sabotage, a flourishing underground press and the demonstrations which took place at war memorials throughout Belgium on the Armistice Day of 11 November bore witness to the new mood.[172] The change appears to have been especially marked in bourgeois circles such as among students, but the working class of the industrial regions was far from immune to this change in opinion. The food shortages of the first winter of the Occupation caused widespread hardship and there were numerous strikes as workers attempted to protect their living standards.[173] Thus, the German Occupation came to be seen as a temporary phenomenon which was to be endured rather than accepted. Contrary to first appearances, the war had proved to be a repeat of the events of 1914–18 and, rather than looking on the Germans as the harbingers of a New Order, the 'Boches' were regarded as conquerors intent only on plunder.[174] In these circumstances, political attitudes changed markedly. The *secrétaires-généraux* were widely criticised for their apparent willingness to appease the Germans and even attitudes towards the King began to change. His personal courage in remaining with his troops was admired but many regretted that, unlike some other European monarchs, he was not in London to rally support for the struggle against Germany.[175] Looking to the future, most Belgians continued to believe that it would be necessary to carry out profound reforms of their political system but the sufferings of the Occupation fostered a recognition of the value of basic liberties and in consequence support for some form of authoritarian New Order began to evaporate.[176]

The Rexists were well aware of this change in popular attitudes. Though Degrelle and others at first sought to blame it on the evil influence of *ancien régime* politicians, freemasons or Jews, they were soon forced to accept that their initial hopes of rallying a majority of their compatriots to their cause were unrealistic.[177] This realisation was reflected in the tone of Rexist propaganda: the exultant populist tone of the summer of 1940 was replaced by a much harsher emphasis on the need for a determined elite to carry out the revolution. A crude cult of power came to the fore, encouraged by Degrelle who declared in December that 'il ne suffit pas d'avoir raison, il faut avoir la force'.[178] The image presented by the *Formations de Combat* reflected this change well. When it had been created, the militia had presented itself as a symbol of the new mood of national unity which all were welcome to join regardless of their former beliefs. By the end of 1940, the *Formations* had largely shed this conciliatory attitude; instead they portrayed themselves as a martial elite committed to *imposing* their revolution on Belgium.[179] Given these statements, it was scarcely surprising that during the last weeks of 1940 popular anger began to be directed towards the Rexists. This hostility would increase dramatically in the subsequent months but already at this time Degrelle's followers were becoming targets for the abuse and ridicule of their compatriots. In the opinion of many Belgians, they were traitors attempting to profit from the misfortunes of their country and denunciations of the Rexists and, more especially, of their leader featured prominently in the expanding underground press.[180]

In many respects the position of Rex was already clearly defined by the end of 1940. Presented with a choice, Degrelle had opted for the German cause. While the general population was moving in one direction, the Rexists were being pulled by their leader in the opposite direction. The result was a gulf between the majority of Belgians and the Rexist minority which would grow ever wider during the subsequent years of the Occupation. This had not, however, yet become a formal policy of collaboration. His public declarations of support for Germany had been cautious and in their propaganda the Rexists were still anxious to present themselves as a movement for national renewal. Thus, though the choice had been made, it still had to be converted into words, gestures and actions.

Degrelle's choice had not, however, brought him the success which he had anticipated. The history of Rex in 1940 was one of failure and frustration disguised beneath a veneer of arrogant confidence. This failure was threefold. In the first place, Degrelle had proved unable to establish himself as the central political figure within Occupied Belgium. Others such as the King, the Flemish Nationalists or even Henri De Man remained much better placed to benefit from the political situation. Secondly, Degrelle had failed to establish Rex as a mass movement. Though it had expanded during the year, its success had been modest and Rex remained a marginal force. Finally and, in his opinion, most importantly, Degrelle had proved unable to win the support of the German authorities. Shunned by the *Wehrmacht* officials in Brussels, he had failed to open up any alternative means of communication with the leaders of the Third Reich. So, far from emerging as one of the principal leaders of the German-dominated New Europe, Degrelle seemed doomed to remain an isolated figure of no great importance; and it was in a further attempt to break this impasse that at the end of 1940 he decided to make a categorical declaration of support for the Nazi cause. This took place in January 1941 and it was at this point that one adventure ended and another – that of collaboration – truly began.

Chapter Two

January – August 1941

The Choice of Collaboration

COLLABORATION during the Second World War never formed part of the world of modern politics. Its rules and character always remained different, more often resembling a pre-modern society in which patronage and symbolism were of pre-eminent importance. Degrelle, the outsider who had rejected the mundane *moeurs* of inter-war Belgian politics, felt at home in this new world. He was at last freed from the constraints which had dogged his pre-war political career, and his willingness to throw himself wholeheartedly into the spirit of collaboration was his great strength and, ultimately, the reason for his success. Despite all their bluster, his rivals for the favours of the Germans remained tied by their habits and values to the old regime. Degrelle, on the other hand, felt no such constraints and he embraced the new world as wholeheartedly as he had rejected the old. Above all, the *Chef de Rex* understood the importance of the dramatic gesture which would demonstrate to a suspicious and distant German leadership his willingness to adopt their cause. Thus, at some point in mid–December 1940, he decided to abandon all pretence. Rex, he declared to a sceptical José Streel, must suppress its outdated scruples and instead 'cross the Rubicon' by demonstrating its unambivalent solidarity with the Axis cause.[1]

The reasons for Degrelle's decision were several. The influence of certain of his advisers as well as a fear that he had been left behind by those other groups – such as the *VNV* – who had already signalled their willingness to work with the German authorities were undoubtedly important factors. So too was a febrile, desperate lust for power. But, like many of the other decisions which Degrelle had made during his political career, this move was ultimately based less on any rational analysis than on its emotional appeal. The unrewarding pre-war years of political struggle combined with the adulation of his supporters had fostered in the *Chef de Rex* a conviction that he was a Cassandra-like figure who alone possessed an insight into the needs of his country. Collaboration became for Degrelle the fulfillment of this self-image. The role of the statesman forging an alliance with Nazi Germany appealed both to his sense of historical grandeur as well as enabling him to cast himself in the role in which he always felt most comfortable – as the solitary monarch leading his uncomprehending people into a new era.

Degrelle's initial intention was probably to announce his support for Germany at the national Rexist rally scheduled to be held in Liège on 22 December. However, the meeting was postponed until after the New Year and Degrelle – ever reluctant to tolerate any delay – chose to publicise his new stance by means of an article in *Le Pays Réel*.[2] Entitled 'Salut à 1941', it appeared on 1 January, although it had apparently been written several days earlier.[3] Its uncompromising tone and, in particular, the dramatic concluding cry of *'Heil Hitler!'* could leave no reader in any doubt as to Degrelle's pro-German sentiments. Much of it, however, merely restated themes which had already been evident in Degrelle's journalism during the autumn of 1940. He made much of the threat posed to Europe by a decadent English nation, declaring in characteristic style that: 'L'Angleterre est finie, ses ploutocrates vont payer leurs crimes et l'Europe entière, qui connut si longtemps la dictature de l'égoïsme britannique, rugira de bonheur le jour où la jeunesse d'Hitler jettera les derniers ploutocrates dans l'eau du Canal Saint-Georges.'[4] It was his insistence that the war had become a revolution, however, which demonstrated most clearly Degrelle's new-found willingness to declare openly his support for Germany. The conflict, he proclaimed, was no mere military combat but a revolutionary struggle between the old and the new, between the decrepit forces of reaction and those of virile youthful progress: 'ce n'est plus une guerre militaire qui étreint le monde, mais une guerre de religion où des millions de jeunes hommes se sentent solidaires, quel que soit leur pays natal. Qu'ils suivent Hitler ou Mussolini, qu'ils suivent Franco ou Horia Sima, qu'ils suivent Quisling ou Mussert, ou les drapeaux rouges de la Révolution rexiste, tous sont pris par le même idéal politique et social, par la même mystique.'[5] Thus, Degrelle chose to justify his support for Germany in emphatically ideological terms. Collaboration was not for him a mere patriotic necessity but a positive choice determined by the support of Rex for the cause of a New Order revolution. The Rexists were, rather in the manner of the radicals who in various European lands chose to side with the French Jacobins of the 1790s, revolutionaries of the New Europe who rejected conventional boundaries in favour of a broader ideological goal. This article therefore placed Degrelle in the vanguard among the most radical and enthusiastic exponents of collaboration and if, as some have suggested, a distinction should be drawn between 'collaboration de raison' and 'collaboration de sentiment', the Rexist leader was firmly in the latter camp.[6]

As Degrelle had intended, this New Year article had an immediate impact far beyond Rexist ranks and it marked a major turning-point in the history of the movement. Indeed, recognising its importance, the Belgian judicial authorities decided after the war that it was from January 1941 onwards that membership of Rex constituted a crime. All those who had remained in the movement after this clear declaration of support for Hitler were judged to have shared in Degrelle's guilt.[7] Yet, even in this article, there was evidence of some caution on the part of Degrelle. His espousal of collaboration was certainly unambivalent but it was also somewhat limited. As Streel subsequently pointed out, the article had the character of 'un coup de sabre dans l'eau' in that, although it was a dramatic gesture, it had few practical consequences.[8] Degrelle had indeed opted for collaboration but he had done so in a largely symbolic manner. Rather than committing his movement to working with the German authorities, Degrelle had portrayed Rex as working *alongside* Germany to achieve a European revolution. This distinction was in many respects an irrelevance but one consequence was that the Rexists did not suddenly become the agents of the German occupying forces. Indeed, in the subsequent weeks, Degrelle was careful to distinguish between his support for the Nazi cause and his distrust of the *Wehrmacht* administrators of Belgium: 'L'Allemagne militaire ne nous intéresse pas. Nous n'avons pas de solidarité avec l'armée allemande mais avec la révolution National-Socialiste.'[9]

On 5 January, the delayed national Rexist rally finally took place in Liège. It was the first such meeting since the German invasion and it firmly established Rex as a major factor in the political life of Occupied Belgium. The Rexist leaders were anxious that the rally should demonstrate the strength of their movement and its credentials as a serious contender for power. Great care was lavished on its preparation and every effort was made to convince all militants to attend. In the event, according to German observers, an audience of some 5,000 Rexists gathered within the hall.[10] Outside, however, they had to contend with the presence of a vocal group of counter-demonstrators organised by left-wing groups of the Liège region well experienced in disrupting Rexist meetings. Estimates of the size of this hostile crowd varied wildly but, though the Rexists claimed that a small group of trouble-makers had been dispersed without incident, it is clear that in the scuffles between the Rexists and their opponents a number of members of the *Formations de Combat* were injured.[11]

Within the hall Degrelle devoted his two-hour oration to a restatement of the position which he had outlined so dramatically a few days before in *Le Pays Réel*. Once again, he poured scorn on England and portrayed Rex as part of a community of New Order movements fighting under the leadership of Hitler for the liberation of Europe: 'Dans dix ans, l'Europe entière reconnaîtra qu'Hitler l'a sauvée. Nous le voyons dès aujourd'hui et nous avons le courage de dire: *Heil Hitler!*'[12] Degrelle was, however, also careful to present the Rexists as patriotic nationalists. Belgian tricolours and a bust of Léopold III adorned the hall and, with his customary taste for grandiose historical tableaux, the *Chef de Rex* once again reiterated how collaboration with Germany would enable Belgium to recover its position as the cultural and mercantile centre of Europe.

The principal purpose of Degrelle's speech however was to portray Rex as a movement advancing confidently towards power. In his public oration as well as in a private speech he made on the same day to Rexist cadres, he stressed that the movement was no longer constrained by outmoded notions of legality: 'Trop longtemps nous avons eu peur de sortir de la légalité. Depuis le 10 mai [i.e. the German invasion], la légalité ne compte plus, n'existe plus. Le 10 mai la Révolution a commencé, c'est à nous de la faire triompher.'[13] Despite the reverses of the previous months, Degrelle conveyed the impression of believing that power still remained within his grasp. The key to success, he declared, lay in force rather than in numbers. The coming conflict would be won not by an undisciplined flock of supporters but by a determined minority of militants and Degrelle called on the Rexist cadres to follow his leadership with the blind loyalty of dedicated soldiers: 'Ne nous embrassons pas de ce que pense l'opinion politique, des réactions du public. Il n'y a qu'une manière de dire la vérité; la dire crûment. Tant pis pour les mous qui nous quittent. On ne fait pas la révolution avec des mous, mais avec des soldats.'[14]

The combined impact of the Le Pays Réel article and the speech at Liège was enormous. As far as the Belgian public was concerned, Degrelle's extravagant praise of Germany irredeemably discredited the Rexist cause and, henceforth, the popular image of Rex and its leader was one of unscrupulous and abject collaboration.[15] Reactions were scarcely more positive among those sympathetic to the New Order cause. For example, Robert Poulet, writing in Le Nouveau Journal, deplored the fawning tone of Degrelle's speech while Paul De Mont, a former Rexist senator and leader of Rex in Flanders, commented bitterly: 'Il n'y a rien à gagner à une servilité qui ne peut que susciter le mépris . . . on ne négocie pas à genoux.'[16]

The violent tone of Degrelle's speech also gave credence to the alarmist rumours which had been circulating for some weeks of an imminent Rexist coup d'état. In late December the secrétaires-généraux had placed a number of public buildings under the protection of armed gendarmes and, in response to widespread apprehension that the Rexists would use their rally in Liège to launch a putsch, the bourgmestre (mayor) of Brussels ordered on 3 January that the police in the capital be placed on alert.[17] Although the Rexist leadership noisily denied any such ambition,[18] it seems likely that they were largely responsible for these rumours. In private, Degrelle often liked to boast that he stood on the threshold of power and many Rexists, intoxicated by his rhetoric, felt confident that the interim rule of the secrétaires-généraux would soon end. This bluster was not, however, accompanied by any actions. No evidence has survived to suggest that the Rexists ever developed concrete plans for a seizure of power and any such adventure would have been firmly opposed by the Germans. Indeed, the officials of the *Militärverwaltung* explicitly reassured the *secrétaires-généraux* of their support in January and Reeder summoned Degrelle in order to extract from the Rexist leader an assurance that he would not seek to challenge the status quo.[19]

It was not only outside the movement that the declarations of Degrelle inspired apprehension. Though long inured to Degrelle's rapid changes of direction, few Rexist militants had anticipated such a radical espousal of collaboration and the *Chef de Rex*'s outspoken article and subsequent speech at Liège caused widespread astonishment among his followers. Some decided that they could not accept the new orientation of the movement and, according to a former employee, letters of resignation inundated the Rexist headquarters.[20] Many others, equally concerned by Degrelle's declarations, chose to trust in the political judgement of their leader[21] or merely decided to await the consequences of the new policy. Predictably, one such sceptic was José Streel. In his contributions to *Le Pays Réel*, he continued to argue for a more moderate stance, insisting that a policy of collaboration should be based not on ideology but on considerations of national interest: 'On peut aimer ou ne pas aimer les vainqueurs, partager ou ne pas partager, ou ne partager que partiellement leur idéologie: on n'empêchera pas la Belgique de se situer à un carrefour de l'Europe et de se trouver soumise au processus historique d'unification du continent. Les choses étant ce qu'elles sont, au seuil de cette année 1941, l'intérêt de notre pays exige sa collaboration avec les vainqueurs.'[22] For Streel, collaboration remained no more than a passive acceptance of reality. and he reprimanded those who ventured onto the shifting sands of ideological affinity or personal sentiment.

These criticisms were clearly aimed at Degrelle and they bore witness to the clear division which existed within the movement between those Rexists anxious to forge ahead into the intoxicating world of collaboration and those who remained loyal to the cautious policies of 1940. At first, Degrelle appeared unmoved by the unease which his pronouncements had provoked, declaring to the staff of *Le Pays Réel* that there was no alternative but to press forward with the new policy of support for Hitler.[23] Indeed, he had undoubtedly anticipated that his dramatic espousal of the German cause would lead to some defections. Nevertheless the extent of the discontent does seem to have taken him by surprise and he sought to reassure some disaffected supporters by hinting privately that his more radical statements were no more than an attempt to hoodwink the Germans.[24] In public, too, he became more circumspect, avoiding the dramatic tone of his earlier declarations while still seeking to consolidate his pro-German stance. Thus, he apparently agreed to liaise with the more moderate and monarchist New Order newspaper *Le Nouveau Journal* and it was only in his more unguarded moments – notably in an interview with an Italian journalist – that he returned to the tone of his earlier pronouncements.[25] In statements intended for domestic consumption, he was deliberately more cautious. While continuing to insist that the war was a 'guerre de religion' in which Rex stood on the side of the revolutionary forces, he avoided direct references to Hitler and instead stressed the patriotic necessity of collaboration. In a series of public speeches, Degrelle returned again and again to the theme that the Rexists and not the myopic supporters of England were the true patriots. Rex, he declared, was fighting to win a place for Belgium in the New Europe and the ideological affinities between the movement and the Nazis in no way implied an abandonment of national loyalties: 'être camarades de combat ne veut pas dire être des esclaves [ou] des valets, mais des collaborateurs dignes'.[26]

Yet, despite the self-imposed moderation of such comments, there was no mistaking Degrelle's determination to capitalise upon the position he had established in January 1941. He remained optimistic of eventual success and much of his activities during the early months of 1941 were devoted to preparing the movement for the challenges which lay ahead. He continued to stress that the Rexist revolution would be the work of a dedicated elite of activists and accepted that much of the population was hostile to Rex.[27] Nevertheless, Degrelle and his advisers also recognised that the small number of militants at their disposal was not sufficient to assure them of success and during February and March they launched a large-scale recruitment campaign intended to swell the ranks of Rex.

Le Pays Réel was central to this propaganda effort. The circulation of the Rexist newspaper was declining rapidly and after Degrelle's speech in Liège it stood at only 10–15,000 copies.[28] These readers were for the most part committed supporters of Rex and the leadership hoped to recover a wider audience for the newspaper by using it to launch a campaign against those in authority whom they held responsible for the rapid decline in living standards. This first winter was the most difficult experienced by the Belgian people during the German Occupation. In addition to the harshness of the weather, shortages of food and fuel brought real suffering to a large proportion of the population.[29] While most Belgians blamed the rapacious policies of the Germans for their woes, the Rexist press under the direction of Victor Matthys launched a campaign of populist demagogy intended to pin the responsibility on the English blockade of Europe and on the 'maffias politiciennes' who were accused by the Rexist journalists of infiltrating and subverting what Le Pays Réel referred to as 'le Désordre Nouveau'. The message was clear: as long as these men remained in place, there could be no true New Order in Belgium and a massive purge was essential in order to transfer power into the hands of new, disinterested administrators.[30]

The whole thrust of this simplistic propaganda campaign was directed towards the working class. The Rexist leaders exulted in distinguishing between the selfish, anglophile bourgeoisie and the open-minded attitude of the workers whom they declared were turning to Rex. In the early months of 1941 Degrelle addressed a series of public meetings, the majority of which were held in the industrial areas of Wallonia. The reports which appeared in the Rexist press of these meetings highlighted the presence of large numbers of workers in the audience and a major theme of Degrelle's speeches was his commitment to a vast, if rather ill-defined, social revolution.[31]

This Rexist optimism may not for once have been entirely ill-founded. A number of German and Belgian contemporary observers writing in early 1941 also contrasted the patriotic and pro-Allied spirit of the bourgeoisie with the more ambivalent mood of the workers.[32] How well-informed such writers were of the real mood of the working classes clearly remains open to question. Most were, after all, based in Brussels and relied essentially on second-hand accounts. Nevertheless, it would seem that many workers, though they in no sense supported the German cause, also remained alienated from an old political regime which had brought them few real benefits in the previous ten years. The material suffering in the industrial regions of Wallonia during this first winter was especially intense and it is clear that food and employment were the overriding concerns of the workers of these areas. Thus, in contrast to the symbolic patriotic gestures engaged in by students and other predominantly bour-geois groups, worker demonstrations at this time – such as strikes and acts of sabotage – were focussed much more on defending their living standards and on attacking those authorities, principally German but also to some extent Belgian, whom they held responsible for their sufferings. A concerted Nazi propaganda campaign sought to exploit the bitterness and sufferings of the working class. Posters and propaganda tracts promised respect and dignity for the workers in a New Order Europe and incited them to volunteer to work in factories in Germany. Between 1940 and November 1942 some 200,000 Belgian workers chose to do so and, although most probably did so only out of desperation, the Nazi promises may have enjoyed a certain limited appeal among those workers dis-illusioned by the failures of the past.[33]

However, the attempts by Rex to woo disaffected workers brought it only very limited success. Many of the new recruits to the movement at this time do seem to have been drawn from the industrial working class and, especially among the ranks of the *Formations de Combat*, men from working-class and socialist backgrounds formed for the first time a significant element.[34] The volume of these new recruits was not sufficient, though, to transform the overall social character of Rex. Workers re-mained in the minority within the movement and, writing in May 1941, one Rexist worker stressed that its middle-class image remained a serious obstacle to its recruitment efforts in working-class areas.[35] Thus, it is clear that Rex on the whole succeeded in enrolling only on the fringes of working-class communities. Whatever their other grievances, the mass of the workers of the industrial regions of francophone Belgium remained firmly hostile to Degrelle and his movement.

In an effort to lend greater plausibility to their revolutionary credentials, the Rexist leadership devoted considerable energy in the early months of 1941 to efforts to convince former socialist leaders in Wallonia to rally to their cause.[36] But, with the exception of a small group of socialist activists from Charleroi and La Louvière who did join Rex,[37] few militants of the *Parti Ouvrier Belge* (POB) were attracted by this proposed 'union of revolutionaries'. Many had participated in the anti-Rexist campaigns of the 1930s and the German invasion had not inclined them to abandon their anti-fascist convictions. Moreover, the espousal by the POB President, Henri De Man, of ideas of an authoritarian New Order had had little impact on the majority of socialist militants. They had supported enthusiastically his proposed economic plan during the 1930s but, apart from among a small coterie of young journalists and intellectuals, little of De Man's sympathy for wide-ranging political reforms had filtered down into the ranks of the POB.[38]

Yet, though these efforts to win over former socialist activists were largely unsuccessful, the Rexists did briefly win support from one highly unlikely quarter. This took the form of the tentative *rapprochement* between Walter Dauge and the Rexists. Dauge was the son of a miner from the Borinage region near Mons and in the 1930s his revolutionary politics and unaffected proletarian style had come to epitomise the radical political mood of the depressed mining communities of that blighted area. Dauge was a powerful and charismatic orator who had initially been active in radical POB groups such as *Action Socialiste* and he had played a major role in the organisation of strikes in his native region. Yet he cared little for the cautious policies of the POB and had been one of the first and most enthusiastic advocates of a Popular Front of socialists and communists. In the mid-1930s, however, he turned against the Communist Party and, soon afterwards, his radical views also caused him to break away from the POB. Instead, in 1936 he founded his own movement, the *Parti Socialiste Révolutionnaire*, which, although it had little national support, absorbed much of his personal following in the Borinage. Rejecting both the reformist policies of the POB and the dependence of the Communists on the Soviet Union, Dauge remained an uncompromising yet unconventional radical and his internationalist and revolutionary views brought him into alliance in the late 1930s with the small Belgian Trotskyist groups.[39]

Yet this firebrand who had been in the vanguard of the struggle against the fascist threat fell strangely silent after the German invasion of Belgium.

There were persistent rumours that he had met Degrelle and, together with a small group of supporters, Dauge did attend the Rexist rally in Liège in January 1941.[40] This was no idle gesture and, although the erstwhile foe of Rex remained cautious in his links with Degrelle's movement, there seems to be little doubt that he was at this time to some extent sympathetic to Rexist policies.[41] Quite why this should have been so remains unclear and even his friends had difficulty in explaining the marked change in his opinions. The shared antipathy of Rex and Dauge towards the Soviet Union does not appear to have been an important factor and it would seem more probable that Dauge had come to believe that some form of German-sponsored New Order socialism was the only realistic means of bringing about improvements in the material conditions of working people. Having rejected the rival paths of Soviet-directed communism and socialist reformism as well as having witnessed the crumbling of his Trotskyist hopes of a spontaneous working-class uprising, Dauge was by 1940 a rebel devoid of hope and faith who was perhaps peculiarly susceptible to the illusory promises of a New Order.[42]

His infatuation with such ideas was short-lived. Negotiations in 1941 between Dauge and Degrelle concerning a fusion of their two movements never reached a conclusion and it would appear that Dauge drew back from any formal espousal of the Rexist cause.[43] Nor did Dauge's brief flirtation with New Order ideas bring Rex many new recruits. Even the militants of his pre-war party proved reluctant to follow the lead given by their leader and only a handful ever appear to have joined Rex, subsequently serving in the Rexist-sponsored *Légion Wallonie* on the Eastern Front.[44] Although he acted as *échevin* (alderman) and subsequently as *bourgmestre* of his commune during the war, Dauge shunned other political activity and the former revolutionary was rumoured to have turned instead to black market activities.[45] On 30 June 1944, he was assassinated by unknown killers in the Borinage. Amidst the widespread violence of the last months of the Occupation, no grouping claimed responsibility for his murder but it would seem probable that it was the work either of the Communist-directed *Partisans Armés* or, if the somewhat unreliable post-war testimony of a former Rexist killer is to be believed, of a local group of Rexist terrorists.[46]

The failure of Rex to attract widespread working-class support or to win over former socialist activists did not shake Degrelle's public image of boisterous self-confidence. He continued to boast of how he stood on the threshold of power and, despite attempts by figures such as Streel to present a more reassuring and cautious image of the movement proceeding to power by gradual steps, the *Chef de Rex* spoke in terms of an imminent decisive conflict with the manifold opponents of the Rexist revolution.[47] Everything was done to create a mood of expectation amongst Rexist militants. Speeches exhorted them to hold themselves in readiness for 'le jour décisif très prochain' and at rallies the audience sang 'C'est la lutte finale . . .' while the men of the *Formations de Combat* trained for their role as the shock troops and guardians of the revolution.[48]

Such expectations were clearly at odds with the realities of the political situation. Rex could only come to power with the assistance of the German forces and, whatever Degrelle claimed, his outspoken comments in January had not convinced the German authorities either in Belgium or in the Reich to provide Rex with that support. As far as the *Militärverwaltung* was concerned, the January speech was no more than a speculative act by a desperate opportunist. Reeder and his colleagues remained distrustful of Degrelle's impulsive character and unreliable behaviour which they contrasted repeatedly with the sobriety and sincerity of the Flemish Nationalists.[49] Nevertheless, Reeder reluctantly accepted that Degrelle's declarations of support for Germany did make possible some form of limited co-operation with Rex. Thus, from January onwards, the *Wehrmacht* officials in Belgium cautiously increased the modest assistance that they had already provided to Rex. The movement was allowed a free hand to recruit members and organise meetings, its press received financial subsidies and a number of Rexists and their sympathisers began to be appointed by the Germans to positions in the Belgian public administration.[50] There remained, however, clear limits to the amount of support which the *Militärverwaltung* was willing to grant Rex. Von Falkenhausen, the titular head of the *Wehrmacht* regime in Belgium, still refused to receive Degrelle and on the rare occasions when the *Chef de Rex* was able to meet German dignitaries he was forced to try rather desperately to impress his audience.[51]

One obvious means for Degrelle to win the confidence of the Germans was to involve Rex in the military campaigns of the Axis powers and throughout the winter he continued to make a series of somewhat ridiculous proposals for the creation of various Rexist military units, such as an air corps which he claimed would fight against England as well as recovering the Congo from the control of the Pierlot government in London.[52] These ideas were not surprisingly rejected out of hand but in February 1941 a more modest opportunity arose for Degrelle to display his pro-Axis sentiments when the *Wehrmacht* authorities in Belgium decided to enrol local men in their auxiliary transport corps, the *Nationalsozialistisches Kraftfahrer-Korps* (*NSKK*). Not surprisingly, Degrelle promptly volunteered to assist with this task by offering to create a '*Brigade Motorisée Rexiste*'. Announcing this initiative to militants in early March, the Rexist leaders stressed its significance. Rex, they declared, must seize upon this opportunity to impress the German authorities and demonstrate that the Flemish Nationalists (who were also recruiting drivers for the *NSKK*) were not the only group capable of providing volunteers for the German armed forces.[53] Degrelle initially promised to recruit 1,000 drivers but this target was soon substantially reduced and it appears that recruitment proved difficult. Despite an energetic propaganda campaign during March and the favourable material conditions on offer to those who volunteered, few Rexists appeared keen to join the new unit. Eventually, however, it seems that some 300 drivers were enrolled and, contrary to assurances that they would be deployed only in Western Europe, these first Rexists to join the German armed forces subsequently served throughout Europe including the Eastern Front.[54]

The *Brigade Motorisée Rexiste* was a concrete contribution to the Axis war effort but the recruitment of this small number of auxiliaries was clearly unlikely to change German attitudes towards Rex. This remained Degrelle's overriding problem and by March 1941 he was no closer to success than he had been in January. The limited assistance offered by a *Militärverwaltung* evidently still anxious to keep him at arm's length in no way satisfied his considerable ambitions and Degrelle remained convinced that he must deal directly with the leaders of the Reich. But he lacked any obvious means of bringing himself to the attention of Berlin. Only Abetz seemed to offer any hope of success and throughout the winter the *Chef de Rex* continued to visit Paris in the belief that the German ambassador would be able to act as an intermediary between himself and the German leaders. In fact Abetz – whose influence was much less than he liked to suggest – was largely powerless to assist Degrelle and his tentative efforts to help him in January and again in March 1941 were easily rebuffed by the *Wehrmacht* authorities in Brussels.[55]

The problem for the *Chef de Rex* was that he was distrusted by both the conservative and the more radical German leaders. In the opinion of the *Wehrmacht* officials in Belgium, Rex was – as José Streel subsequently observed[56] – 'un élément turbulent et gêneur' whose activities threatened their attempts to work with the Belgian bureaucracy and the Flemish Nationalists, while for the SS and other more radical National Socialists, Rex with its supposedly clerical ideology was a hindrance to their attempts to impose a racial political solution in Belgium. As Heydrich commented dismissively in January 1941, the Nazi regime had no interest in aiding the Rexists as long as they remained loyal to a unified Belgian state which obstructed hopes of a confederation of Flemish and other Germanic peoples.[57] Even Goebbels, who was no ally of the SS and who in the 1930s had had considerable admiration for the Rexist leader's propagandistic skills, was disenchanted with Degrelle. In January he ordered that his declarations should receive only cursory coverage in the German press and in his diary he remarked that Degrelle had proved to be an insubstantial fraud ('ein falscher Fuffziger').[58]

Degrelle was painfully aware of his political impotence. As he subsequently wrote, all of his efforts to attract Nazi support at this time were a dismal failure: 'Tout ce que nous fîmes durant l'hiver 1940–1 pour dégeler l'iceberg allemand échoué sur nos rivages, ne nous conduisit guère plus loin.'[59] This failure inevitably undermined Degrelle's attempts to pose as the future leader of Belgium. While elsewhere in Europe collaborationist figures such as Quisling in Norway and Anton Mussert in the Netherlands were receiving tangible German encouragement and had become figures of some importance, Degrelle began to appear as something of a spent force. Rex no longer inspired the same fear as it had done in January and, in private, there was much talk in pro-German circles of the need to find a more credible standard-bearer for their cause in francophone Belgium.[60]

This failure also had consequences within Rex. As the weeks passed without any tangible evidence of progress, a mood of unease became increasingly evident. Rexists began to lose faith in the optimistic declarations of their leaders and latent tensions within the movement once again surfaced. The organisational structure established in 1940 had been an improvised affair and its ill-defined hierarchy created ample opportunities for rivalry between a number of ambitious individuals. This potential for conflict became a reality with the announcement in February 1941 of a major reorganisation of the movement. In part, these changes were merely an attempt to resolve the problems inherent in the 1940 structure. In line with a number of measures already announced,[61] they sought to establish the hierarchical structures appropriate for a political movement operating on authoritarian principles. Thus, the *Secrétariat-Général* as well as the other central Rexist offices lost much of their former importance and all responsibility for national decisions was concentrated in the hands of a new *Etat-Major du Chef*, to which Degrelle devolved effective responsibility for the administration of the movement. In addition, the powers of the three *Chefs de Région* (of Wallonia, Brussels and Flanders) were extended. They became responsible for all Rexist activities in their areas and were answerable only to Degrelle. On the other hand, the militia, the *Formations de Combat*, was deprived of much of its former autonomy. Within each region it was placed under the effective control of the *Chefs de Région* while at a national level the *Etat-Major de Chef* was empowered to intervene directly in the actions of the *Formations*.[62]

The most important consequence of this reorganisation was the dramatic increase it brought about in the personal power of Fernand Rouleau. The *Lieutenant du Chef de Rex* was widely regarded as having been the author of the changes and not surprisingly he was appointed to head the new *Etat-Major du Chef*. A mere six months after joining the movement, Rouleau had become the undisputed second in command of Rex – a position confirmed by his appointment as Degrelle's deputy during the foreign travels of the *Chef de Rex*.[63] His meteoric rise could hardly fail to annoy both long established Rexist leaders and those who – like Rouleau – had joined Rex in 1940 in the expectation of acquiring substantial power. Indeed, hardly had the new structure been announced, than a dispute arose over the position of Antoine Leclercq. He was a Rexist veteran from Liège who, despite his somewhat volatile character, enjoyed a considerable personal following among the Rexists of his native city.[64] Since 1940 he had been the regional head of Rex in Wallonia but he was downgraded in the reorganisation of February to the rank of *Chef de Province* of Liège. Leclercq at first accepted this new position but he was clearly unhappy at his demotion and during the following weeks he attempted to convince Degrelle to reverse Rouleau's decision.[65] This was, as Leclercq subsequently made clear in a private letter, essentially a personal struggle between himself and Rouleau for the ear of the *Chef de Rex* and in the event it was the *Lieutenant du Chef* who emerged victorious. The demotion was not reversed and during April Leclercq resigned from Rex with the intention of establishing his own pro-German movement.[66] He published a brochure entitled rather optimistically '*Wallons, réveillez-vous!*' and, after receiving the approval of the German authorities, the new party was launched in the summer of 1941 as the *Mouvement National Populaire Wallon* (*MNPW*). This breakaway organisation was not a success. Its attempts to court popularity by posing as an authentically Walloon – rather than a Belgian – movement were unfruitful and few disgruntled Rexists, even in Liège, chose to join Leclercq in his new venture. Devoid of cadres, popular support or coherent leadership, the *MNPW* never became more than a marginal force within the collaborationist world.[67]

The disarray caused by Leclercq's departure may well, however, have been instrumental in provoking the defection from Rex of a second and more substantial group of *liégeois* militants. These were enthusiastic supporters of Nazi ideas who considered Degrelle's espousal of the German cause to have been too cautious and who advocated the dismantling of the unitary Belgian state in favour of the integration of the Walloon race into an expanded Germanic confederation. Their extreme views inevitably attracted the ready support of the more radical Nazi agencies and, with the assistance of the Liège offices of the *SS* police, the *Sipo-SD*, they launched the unambivalently titled *Amis du Grand Reich Allemand* (*AGRA*) on 13 March 1941. These self-proclaimed radicals had little hope of attracting a mass audience but their pan-Germanic ideas were perhaps marginally less fanciful in the eastern city of Liège with its long history of contact with the German world than elsewhere in francophone Belgium and they did win the backing of a number of local Rexists.[68] The *Militärverwaltung* was, however, reluctant to allow *AGRA* to emerge as a direct rival to Rex and at its insistence the new grouping was obliged to limit itself to what the German authorities termed 'kulturpolitischer Betätigung'. This was, moreover, a limitation largely accepted by the first leaders of *AGRA* who preferred to concentrate on cultural propaganda rather than political activity. Only towards the end of 1941 under new leadership did *AGRA* begin to emerge as a more explicitly political challenge to Rex.[69]

The problems encountered by Rex in Liège were not unique. The organisational changes introduced in February provoked dissent through-out the movement and one of the most prominent opponents of the new structure was Rutger Simoens, the *Commandant Général* of the *Formations de Combat*. Although he remained the national head of the militia as well as the commander of its Flemish units, Simoens was deeply unhappy at the way in which the *Formations* had been brought within the political struc-ture of Rex. Rouleau and the regional leaders now possessed substantial powers to intervene in the affairs of the militia and they soon demonstrated this authority by exercising their right to appoint its principal officers.[70] It was apparent that Simoens would not accept this substantial curtailment of his power. He continued to regard the *Formations* as his personal fiefdom and he soon became embroiled in conflicts with the regional leaders of Rex.[71] At the same time, he entered into contact with the leaders of an extremist Flemish collaborationist grouping, the *Algemeen SS Vlaanderen*. It seems that Simoens hoped to regain in this organisation the power which he had lost in Rex and in a letter to the members of the *Formations* in Flanders, as well as in a speech to a rally at Antwerp, he openly encouraged Flemish Rexists to defect to the *Algemeen SS*.[72] Degrelle's public response to this insubordination was to expel Simoens but, in private, he was more conciliatory and for a number of weeks he appears to have sought to persuade the former commander of the *Formations* to return to Rex.[73] These negotiations were, however, unsuccessful and Simoens subsequently went on to have an undistinguished career as a propagandist for a number of Flemish pro-German organisations. Moreover, the de-parture of Simoens proved to be a serious blow to the already weak Rexist organisation in Flanders. Despite attempts by Degrelle to retain their loyalty, many militiamen in Flanders seem to have followed the example of their commander and defected from Rex.[74]

The departures of Leclercq, of the founders of *AGRA* and of Simoens were merely the most prominent examples of dissent within a Rexist movement which by the spring of 1941 appeared to be collapsing under the pressure of its own divisions. Rumours of intrigues and defections were rife, prompting the internal Rexist bulletin to comment with some understatement that: 'Une crise de croissance semble s'être produite dans le Mouvement au cours de ces dernières semaines. Simultanément au Centre et en divers points du Pays, des différends se sont élevés entre quelques Dirigeants et groupes de membres du Mouvement. Quelques cabales ont été montées et il en est résulté un certain malaise . . .'[75] Al-though this article claimed that Degrelle's resolute actions had resolved the problems, the crisis was clearly a serious one. The bubble of optimism which had carried the movement through the first nine months of the Occupation had now burst and, despite the leadership's efforts, Rex would never fully recover the buoyant mood of those early days.

Reeder was, as always, one of the keenest and least sympathetic observers of the difficulties of Rex. In a report written at the end of April, the President of the *Militärverwaltung* contemplated what seemed to him to be an irreversible process of collapse. The responsibility for this situation was, Reeder insisted, essentially Degrelle's. His entire strategy since the German invasion had been 'ein fortgesetztes, nicht immer glückliches Improvisieren' and his impulsive pro-German declarations and rash promises of an imminent acquisition of power had aggravated the problems created by his poor choice of advisers and unskilful management of personal rivalries.[76]

However, just as in January Degrelle had exaggerated the movement's successes, so Reeder was now too hasty in announcing its demise. There remained a great fund of loyalty to the Rexist cause among the long-standing militants of the movement and the problems caused by the internal strife of early 1941, though serious, did not in themselves prejudice its survival. Those leaders who left were replaced and, in general, the local structures of Rex remained intact. In Wallonia the new *Chef de Région* appointed to replace Leclercq was Joseph Pévenasse, an energetic lawyer and Rexist veteran from the Hainaut. He established a powerful regional headquarters in Charleroi and, with the former *Chef de Province* of Namur, Jean Georges, as his deputy, he set about improving the Rexist organisation throughout Wallonia.[77] The provinces were abolished and the *arrondissements* emerged instead as the most important unit in the hierarchy. The powers of the *chefs d'arrondissements* were reinforced and they were assisted by a number of local delegates with responsibility for specific aspects of Rexist activities. In addition, each *arrondissement* was encouraged to establish its own *service de renseignements* and propaganda school. The sections remained the basic level of local organisation but Pévenasse encouraged the grouping of scattered rural sections into districts as well as the division of each section into cells composed of ten members.[78] These changes were not implemented immediately in all areas but their overall impact was undoubtedly to create a much more direct chain of command and for the first time the local structure of Rex took on something of the air of an authoritarian political movement. Even the *Formations de Combat* recovered from the defection of its leader. A new central *Etat-Major* was established for the militia but it had little real influence and, as with the political structure of Rex, it was the regional leaders – notably Albert Constant, the new commander of the *Formations* in Wallonia – who became the real force within the militia.[79]

It was not merely the divisions within the movement which took their toll on Rexist morale. A second and in many ways more significant factor was the fundamental change taking place in popular attitudes towards Degrelle and his followers. Hostility towards Rex had already been evident by the end of 1940 but during the first months of the new year this antipathy became much more marked. Discrimination, sullen hostility and

verbal abuse henceforth formed an unavoidable element of the daily lives
of most Rexists, forcing many to retreat from normal social contact into
the relative security of a ghetto existence. This antipathy towards the
advocates of collaboration marked an important change in the history of
Occupied Belgium. During 1940 divisions between those who hoped for
an English recovery and those who accepted or even welcomed the
apparent German victory had been only one of many divisions within the
population. Traditional conflicts of language, class and political ideology
remained important while the events of May 1940 had fostered new
disputes surrounding the actions of the King and his ministers. In the early
months of 1941, however, these other issues declined in importance and it
was the division between pro-German collaborationists and pro-Allied
patriots which came to dominate Belgian life. Any middle ground rapidly
disappeared and contemporary observers concurred that the population
had in effect become polarised into two very unequal camps.[80]

The emergence of this single overwhelming schism owed much to the
actions of the collaborationist groupings themselves. Without doubt, their
espousal of the Nazi cause had genuinely shocked much of the population.
In Flanders, it had been hoped that the failure of pro-German 'activism'
during the first German Occupation of 1914–18 would prevent a resurgence of such activities; while in francophone Belgium political collaboration was an unexpected – and entirely unwelcome – novelty. In these
circumstances, it was scarcely surprising that most Belgians paid little
attention to the nuances in the positions adopted by the various collaborationist groups. All were 'les embochés', unprincipled opportunists
devoted to serving the cause of the occupying power in every way.

Other less obvious factors also help to explain why hostility towards
collaborators came to play such a dominant role in the life of Occupied
Belgium. In seeking to subsume their differences in support for an Allied
victory and the liberation of their country, the diffuse forces of the
patriotic majority required certain immediate objectives upon which all
could agree. A simple desire to see the expulsion of the Germans was one
such goal;[81] but another was a shared hostility towards all those 'mauvais
Belges' who had chosen to aid the occupiers. The social and ideological
tensions evident in Belgium before 1940 had not disappeared and, if
anything, were exacerbated by the circumstances of the Occupation.
Relations between rich and poor were not improved by the material
sufferings of the war years, the political right became ever more fearful of
a Communist-inspired uprising while the divisions caused by the King's
actions continued to cast a long shadow over the country. Thus, opposition to the collaborationist minority became a necessary rallying-point for
all men of good will and a means for the not entirely united forces of the
patriotic majority to express their sense of common purpose.

The collaborators were also a highly convenient target. Embroiled in a vast global conflict, the unfortunate citizens of Occupied Belgium were the unwilling victims of a situation which lay entirely beyond their control. In reality, nothing they could do would have any influence on the outcome of the military struggle but they inevitably sought some means of giving expression to their anti-German and pro-Allied sentiments. Attacks on German personnel or facilities were one obvious means of doing so but such activities were dangerous and never appealed to more than a minority. The daily – almost casual – persecution of those regarded as traitors was, however, a much easier course of action and one within the capacity of all sections of the population. Every adolescent fired with enthusiasm for the Allied struggle, every housewife bitter at the daily sufferings of the Occupation and every *ancien combattant* anxious to demonstrate his antipathy to 'les Boches' found in hostility towards the collaborators an outlet for his or her sympathies and frustrations.

Rex always bore the brunt of this popular hostility. Although few had any sympathy for the pro-German stance of the Flemish Nationalists, loyalties were on the whole less polarised in Flanders and there was always a feeling – even among some outside Flanders – that their actions had some rationale in the disadvantaged position of the Flemish population within the pre-war Belgian state; but no such considerations clouded popular attitudes towards Degrelle and the Rexists. From early 1941 'cet inverti politique' and his band of mercenaries became the scapegoats for all of the sufferings of the Occupation.[82] Reeder, for example, reporting to Berlin in April 1941, noted a sharp increase in anti-Rexist propaganda and repeated the remarks of a high placed Belgian bureaucrat who commented that the *Chef de Rex* was a worthless charlatan who, had he been German, would have been executed by the Nazis.[83]

The intimidation of Rexist militants gradually extended into almost all aspects of their lives: they received numerous menacing letters, bricks were thrown at their windows and members of Rex were shunned by their relatives or even expelled from the family home.[84] Their appearances in uniform in the street led to scuffles from which they rarely emerged victorious and Rexist meetings were frequently disrupted by counter-demonstrators and hecklers.[85] On occasions, these crowd actions took on a ritualised character reminiscent of older forms of popular protest. For example, at Anhée near Dinant a Rexist was assaulted and a straw effigy of him carried around the village in triumph.[86] Hostility to the agents of Nazism was also a means of expressing optimism in the future. Although organised resistance as yet remained insignificant, many pro-Allied patriots were already compiling black lists of Rexists and other traitors and dire threats were circulating as to the bloody *jacqueries* which would follow any eventual German military defeat.[87]

The Rexists had long been a marginal group in Belgian political life who were used to enduring the incomprehension and ridicule of their compatriots. The emergence of this all-pervading hostility was, however, a novel development. Those who continued to support Rex had to accept that their political choice would have considerable consequences for their public and private lives and, not surprisingly, this was a commitment which not all proved willing to make. Thus, during the spring and early summer of 1941, there appears to have been a further significant reduction in Rexist membership as its less committed supporters withdrew. Though detailed figures are impossible to compile, it would seem that those who left the movement at this time were for the most part drawn from the pre-war membership of Rex. On the whole members of the *petite bourgeoisie*, these were the men and women who had provided the movement with its brief electoral success in 1936 and who had thronged Rexist rallies to hear Degrelle denounce the immorality and corruption of the political elite. They had joined Rex not to participate in some broad movement of European revolution but to protest at the specific failings of the Belgian regime and they felt little instinctive sympathy for the cause of the German invaders.[88]

On the other hand, those militants who remained loyal to Rex were those who accepted Degrelle's assertion that the war had become a revolution and that a Nazi victory was essential both for the achievement of their political goals and the regeneration of Europe. Some were recent converts to Rex but others were long-time supporters of the movement who had come to see their struggle for a Belgian revolution as inseparable from the broader international conflict. These loyalists tended also to be those who were most enthusiastic for a profound and radical transformation of society. Although many were from bourgeois backgrounds, they were not *nostalgiques* in search of some secure Golden Age but radicals intent upon substantial social change. These self-styled revolutionaries of the New Order cause were little concerned by the exodus of their more cautious colleagues. Indeed, many seem to have regarded it as a timely *nettoyage* which would hasten the transformation of Rex into a truly revolutionary movement. Their response to the development of popular hostility was to call on Rexists to take pride in their isolation and they called for the expulsion of those *rexistes honteux* unwilling to give their clear-cut support to the cause.[89]

This belief that there was no place in Rex for the hesitant was shared by their leaders, who recognised that Rex must adopt the characteristics of an authoritarian political movement. Thus, in propaganda and at local meetings an ever greater emphasis was placed on the need for 'un esprit de foi et de discipline sans restriction'. For example, the membership card for 1941 stated starkly: 'Je promets d'obéir sans discuter aux ordres du Chef de Rex, de Servir de toutes mes forces et de verser s'il le faut mon sang pour la Cause de la Révolution Rexiste.'[90] Such dramatic language was still largely rhetorical but, as the gulf of incomprehension and hostility between the Rexists and the patriotic majority widened, so the likelihood of some form of Rexist 'counter-violence' increased. Few Rexists were inclined to accept passively the insults directed at them and a desire to strike back at their many adversaries soon became evident. This was especially so among the members of the *Formations de Combat* who continued with their crude attempts at retribution against those tradesmen – especially those of Jewish origin – whom they accused of black market activities.[91] In addition, in certain localities some Rexists began to resort to more direct forms of retaliation. In one such incident at Herstal near Liège in January, a group of militiamen who had been assaulted by counter-demonstrators at the Liège rally viciously attacked the local democratically-elected mayor causing him injuries from which he eventually died.[92] Other Rexists resorted to more symbolic forms of revenge, such as the newly-appointed head of Rex in Wallonia, Joseph Pévenasse, who struck two fellow lawyers in the *Palais de Justice* of Charleroi who had mocked him for wearing his Rexist uniform during his legal work.[93]

The attitude of the Rexist leaders to such ripostes was ambivalent. Pévenasse's actions were given wide publicity in the Rexist press and were clearly presented as a model for other militants to emulate. The provincial commander of the *Formations* in Namur, for example, wrote to his officers praising Pévenasse's behaviour and advocating that they should carry a riding crop with which to respond in a similar fashion to those who insulted them.[94] On the other hand, there was a general recognition among the Rexist leadership that the wild behaviour of certain elements in the *Formations de Combat* was damaging the reputation of the movement. Strenuous efforts were made in the spring of 1941 to inculcate a mood of discipline and restraint into the militia and instructions were issued reminding militants that the correct response to all provocations was to report the culprits to the police.[95] Constant, the commander of the *Formations* in Wallonia, repeatedly called on his men to shake off their violent and destructive image. The Rexist militia, he declared, should be neither a 'troupe d'aventuriers' nor a 'bande de "gamins"' but a disciplined army able to demonstrate a sense of responsibility and maturity.[96]

If these attempts to impose restraint were to succeed, the leadership sorely needed to be able to reassure their followers that they did indeed stand on the threshold of power. Degrelle and his colleagues did not, however, have any such evidence of progress. The political situation in Belgium remained totally immobile and within a few months the arrogant confidence of the Rexist leaders had given way to a mood of frustration and despair. Degrelle in particular found this enforced inaction intolerable. More than ever convinced that he was the only man who could save Belgium, he was nevertheless forced to stand idly by while the country drifted towards what he considered to be anarchic chaos.[97] It was, as he subsequently admitted, the darkest moment of his political career and, in a mood of some desperation, he wrote directly to Hitler on 10 April expressing his sense of frustration: 'Après six années de lutte très violente, après des mois de cachot et de tourments, je me sens livré à un chômage qui m'est beaucoup plus dur que les luttes du passé et les tourments dans les prisons ... Penser qu'à cette heure incomparable du destin, je suis immobile et stérile, m'est particulièrement amer.'[98] If he could perform no useful role in Belgium during the war, Degrelle pleaded to be allowed to serve as an ordinary soldier in the German armed forces. But this request, like so many of the *Chef de Rex*'s previous appeals, met with no success. His letter probably never reached the German *Führer* and his proposal was rebuffed by the *Wehrmacht* authorities who were advised by Reeder that Degrelle's departure from Belgium would in all probability result in the total collapse of his political movement.[99]

The overwhelming sense of frustration felt by Degrelle was also evident for the first time in the tone of his public declarations. He abandoned his former boisterous optimism and in a number of outspoken articles and speeches admitted that the short-term outlook for Rex was indeed unencouraging.[100] In what became a continual refrain in his declarations during March and April, Degrelle warned that no positive changes could take place in Belgium until after the end of the war. While in January he had portrayed the war as the enactment of the European revolution, the *Chef de Rex* now insisted that they were separate events and that the accomplishment of the Rexist seizure of power must await the resolution of the military conflict. Thus all talk of immediate action disappeared from his rhetoric and Degrelle warned the Rexists that they were at the mercy of forces beyond their control. Nobody could predict whether the war would end within a few months or only after a number of years; and even then it was not certain that a unified Belgium would form part of the New Order Europe. German intentions, he admitted, were clouded in mystery and his unwelcome message for his followers was to master their impatience by concentrating on enhancing the strength of their movement.[101]

As Degrelle knew only too well, however, the real reason for the enforced idleness of Rex was his continued failure to attract German patronage. The Third Reich remained for him an incomprehensible maze and even to casual observers it was clear that the German officials in Brussels chose to treat the Rexist leader with scarcely concealed disdain.[102] Nevertheless, Degrelle had begun to learn something of the harsh world of Nazi politics. In particular, he had realised that success would depend on him proving able to adapt to rapidly changing circumstances. Immutable principles and cautious scruples had no place in the labyrinth of collaboration and the *Chef de Rex*, always a consummate opportunist, began to adapt his stance in order to respond to what he believed to be German wishes.

This attempt to mould a Rexist ideology more palatable to the Nazis took several forms. Aware that his continued commitment to a unified Belgian state was a hindrance in his attempts to woo the more radical Nazi leaders, the *Chef de Rex* increasingly chose to avoid any references to Belgium in his speeches and newspaper articles. The patriotic language still so evident at the Liège rally in January was quietly dropped and instead the Rexist leader began to use much more evasive terms such as 'l'Occident'.[103] Degrelle also seized upon somewhat dubious historical arguments in order to convince a sceptical Nazi audience of the importance of francophone Belgium. Speaking at a Rexist meeting in Liège in April, he declared that the francophone Walloons were not – as was commonly supposed – a disjointed fragment of the French nation but, in fact, a frontier people of Germanic origins with a proud history of resisting integration into the French world. Indeed, Degrelle added somewhat audaciously, the Walloons had always enjoyed closer contacts with Germany than had the Flemish and their claim to a place in the new German-dominated Europe was no more than a return to this long-standing historical tradition.[104]

Degrelle's opportunistic use of this tendentious interpretation of history would in the latter years of the war bring him substantial benefits but in 1941 it had little impact. The Nazi leadership, poised for the attack on the Soviet Union, was in no mood to revise its opinion of a minor political figure who, as Goebbels again remarked in his diary in April, appeared to be on his last legs.[105] Most seriously for Degrelle, the internal problems of Rex caused the *Militärverwaltung* to curtail its hitherto cautious support for the movement. In particular, Reeder and his colleagues decided that, given the uncertainties which surrounded the future of Rex, they could no longer support the nomination of Degrelle's supporters to influential positions in public administration. This decision could not have come at a more inopportune moment for Rex. The popular hardening in attitudes towards the Germans during the winter of 1940–1 had led both the Belgian civil servants and much of the economic elite to retreat from working too closely with the German authorities. Patriotic scruples initially suppressed in 1940 resurfaced and, although Belgian and German officials continued to co-operate on many matters, a new spirit of caution was apparent in Belgian dealings with the *Militärverwaltung*. For Reeder and his colleagues, even this limited obstructionism was a serious threat to their policy of ensuring the effective administration of the country with the minimal deployment of German manpower and they responded in the spring of 1941 by intervening directly in the structures of Belgian internal administration to nominate supporters of New Order ideas who, they felt, would be more willing to implement their commands. The most important of these changes concerned the central government ministries. Despite the dubious legality of such actions, on 1 April the *Militärver-waltung* announced the appointment of a number of new *secrétaires-*

généraux, the influential civil servants who, in the absence of their political superiors, directed each of the Belgian ministries.[106]

The Flemish Nationalists of the *VNV* were inevitably the greatest beneficiaries of these changes. It was their supporters who acquired the most important posts from the German authorities, including the appointment of one of their leaders, Gérard Romsée, to the key post of *secrétaire-général* of the Ministry of the Interior. In contrast, although a francophone magistrate, Gaston Schuind, was nominated as *secrétaire-général* of the Ministry of Justice, no supporter of Rex was appointed to the *collège* of *secrétaires-généraux*. The nomination of Rexists, Reeder reported categorically to Berlin, was impossible both because of the problems within the movement as well as the bitter opposition which any such appointment would provoke from the Belgian bureaucracy.[107] Degrelle was enraged by this exclusion of Rexists from high administrative office and he immediately used the columns of *Le Pays Réel* to disassociate Rex publicly from the policies of the *Militärverwaltung*. Annoyed by such dissent, Reeder decided to call the *Chef de Rex* to order. He summoned Degrelle to what proved to be a stormy meeting at which Reeder apparently imposed a fine on *Le Pays Réel* and threatened to suppress the newspaper in the event of any further dissent. Once again, the President of the *Militärverwaltung* had exposed the weakness of Degrelle's position. His bluster evaporated and, cowed if not truly repentant, the Rexist leader apologised and promised his future support for Reeder's policies.[108]

Though the Rexists sought to present the changes announced on 1 April as a reallocation of administrative tasks of no political importance,[109] they undoubtedly regarded this failure to acquire important governmental posts as a major reverse. The appointment of Romsée to the Ministry of the Interior did, however, give them some modest cause for optimism. Romsée was a dynamic political figure of considerable abilities and his ministry soon emerged as the major focus of New Order and collaborationist influence within Occupied Belgium.[110] Moreover, he was regarded by the Rexists as one of the leaders of the *VNV* most sympathetic to the interests of francophone Belgians and his presence in the Ministry of the Interior aroused hopes among the Rexist leaders that they would at last gain control of the structures of local government in francophone Belgium. By the spring of 1941 little had been achieved in this area. Isolated successes – notably in Charleroi where the Rexist veteran and former parliamentary deputy, Prosper Teughels, had become the mayor – had been more than outweighed by the removal from office of many of those Rexists who had illegally usurped power during the summer of 1940.[111] In March, however, a German decree was issued barring from office all communal officials aged over 60 and, as many of the democratically-elected mayors and aldermen exceeded this age limit, Rex hoped that this decree heralded the entry of their supporters into local

government. In addition, soon after Romsée's appointment, new administrative procedures were announced which increased substantially the
power of the Ministry of the Interior to intervene in the nomination of the
all-important posts of mayors (*bourgmestres*) and aldermen (*échevins*).[112]

Hopes of a rapid and decisive change in the personnel of local government were further encouraged when it was agreed by Degrelle and Romsée
that the appointment of local officials in francophone Belgium would be
the responsibility of a special *cabinet wallon* in the Ministry of the Interior.
As the head of this *cabinet*, Romsée and Degrelle chose a long-standing
somewhat cautious supporter of Rex, Ernest Delvaux, who was assisted by
two deputies, Boulanger and Dessart, both of whom were also Rexists.[113]
Encouraged by these changes, Rouleau established a *Service des Nominations*
headed by Charles Lambinon in the Rexist headquarters which began the
task of identifying those Rexists deemed suitable for recommendation to
the Ministry for posts in local and provincial government.[114] There was
no shortage of enthusiastic applicants but, although a small number of
Rexist *bourgmestres* soon took office in a number of towns including
Verviers,[115] the expected avalanche of new appointments failed to materi-
alise. To the great frustration of Rex, the decree forcing office-holders over
60 years old to retire was implemented very gradually and, in general,
Romsée approached his task in a spirit of prudent caution. The new
secrétaire-général hoped to win popular approval for his reforms and he
therefore preferred, wherever possible, to appoint moderate supporters of
New Order ideas who were untainted by association with Rex. Only in
1942, when all hope of obtaining popular support had disappeared, would
Romsée prove more willing to choose the candidates proffered to him by
Rex.[116]

Frustrated in their ambitions, disappointed by every new development
and harassed by an increasingly hostile population, the Rexists desperately
needed some cause for optimism and they were ready to welcome any
new development which seemed to herald a thaw in the political climate.
Hence, when on 10 May an accord was announced between Rex and the
Flemish nationalist movement, the *VNV*, it was inevitably greeted within
Rex as a harbinger of better times. Degrelle, conscious of the mood of his
followers, encouraged such expectations and, at a press conference held in
the opulent surroundings of his private home, he spoke grandiloquently of
it as a historic agreement which would enable the two movements to
work together to achieve the National Socialist revolution. It was, he
declared, the successor to the ill-fated accord signed by Rex and the *VNV*
in the autumn of 1936 and, like that earlier agreement, this new understanding would ensure the achievement of a unitary but devolved New
Order Belgian state which would respect the distinctive characters of the
two linguistic groups.[117]

Degrelle's desire to present the accord as a major political breakthrough for Rex was not borne out by a detailed examination of its content. The first and most important of its three clauses announced the fusion of the *VNV*, of the pro-German elements of the late Joris Van Severen's *Verdinaso* movement and of the Rexist groups in Flanders (*Rex-Vlaanderen*) into a single New Order party in Flanders. In fact, though nominally a new organisation, this movement would inevitably be dominated by the *VNV* and it was clear that the agreement's principal purpose was to bring about the absorption of the two smaller groupings by the *VNV*. The other two clauses were of much less importance. The second merely stated in general terms that the signatories agreed to recognise Rex as 'le parti unique pour le peuple wallon' while, in the final clause, Rex and the newly-expanded *VNV* undertook to collaborate on 'toutes les questions d'intérêt commun'.[118] This evasive formula amounted to much less than a clear political alliance and, notwithstanding Degrelle's grand declarations, the accord made no reference to a unitary Belgian state.

The limited scope of the agreement reflected its origins in the various negotiations which had long been taking place in Flanders between the several pro-German groupings of the region. As early as the summer of 1940, the *VNV* had proposed the formation of a single party and in October a tentative accord had been concluded between the *Verdinaso* movement and *Rex-Vlaanderen*.[119] These efforts received the firm support of the *Militärverwaltung* which hoped that such a union would reinforce the strength of its ally, the *VNV*, while also ensuring the isolation of those small extremist groups – notably the *Algemeen SS Vlaanderen* – with which the *VNV* had been in conflict during the winter of 1940–1. During the winter, negotiations between the *VNV* and the pro-German elements in *Verdinaso* continued and by April agreement had been reached by the two parties on the formation of a single movement.[120]

The leaders of Rex in Flanders were apparently not party to these talks but they, nevertheless, supported the idea of a union of Flemish New Order groups. Since May 1940, *Rex-Vlaanderen* had operated largely independently of the rest of Rex: it had its own *Etat-Major* and its head, Odiel Daem, was responsible directly to Degrelle.[121] Rexist ideas had only a limited appeal in Flanders and, although it was present throughout the region, *Rex-Vlaanderen* had always remained a relatively small organisation whose support was strongest amongst the professional middle classes of Antwerp, Malines, Gent and certain towns in West Flanders. Its leaders successfully rebuilt the movement after May 1940 but, faced with the opposition of both the *VNV* and the *Militärverwaltung* because of their commitment to a unified Belgium, they frequently found it difficult to operate effectively.[122] Consequently, Daem and his colleagues seem to have decided at an early stage to seek the integration of *Rex-Vlaanderen* into a single New Order party in Flanders. They called repeatedly for such a union[123] and it would seem probable that it was at their initiative that

Rex-Vlaanderen was included in the proposed accord between the *VNV* and *Verdinaso*.

Degrelle had little choice but to accept this *fait accompli*[124] but he hoped to turn it to his advantage by demanding that Rex should receive some form of quid pro quo for the loss of its Flemish organisation. Hence, it was at his insistence that the second and third clauses were added to the agreement and that it was presented to the public as a national accord between Rex and the newly-unified Flemish movement. Although the leaders of the *VNV* apparently accepted these concessions as the price they must pay for the incorporation of *Rex-Vlaanderen*, they regarded them as no more than a sop to the *amour propre* of the *Chef de Rex*. At the press conference held to announce the agreement, the leader of the *VNV*, Staf De Clercq, was careful to portray it as essentially an internal Flemish matter and avoided making any declaration of support for Rex. Moreover, the general tone of his remarks concerning francophone Belgium was far from conciliatory. He stressed the commitment of the *VNV* to the defence of Flemish rights in Wallonia, implying, as he had on several previous occasions, that Wallonia would eventually form part of 'l'espace vital' of Flanders.[125] More immediate difficulties arose over the vexed problem of the status of Brussels. Although largely francophone in composition, the city was surrounded by Flemish-speaking areas and the *VNV* had long been committed to its incorporation into Flanders. The accord avoided any reference to Brussels but the *VNV* leadership made clear that they regarded the city as an integral part of the Flemish community. This was unacceptable to Rex and in the weeks following the accord Degrelle was forced to pose as the defender of the interests of the francophone population warning the *VNV* that he would tolerate no Flemish interference in Brussels and Wallonia.[126]

These disputes revealed the extent to which the accord was an agreement between parties of very unequal strengths. The *VNV* – confident of the support of the *Militärverwaltung* – was in an aggressive and self-assured mood and was not willing to be deflected from its ambitious political goals. Rex, in contrast, was its poor cousin in the collaborationist world. It was in no position to impose its wishes on either the *VNV* or the Germans and Degrelle could only hope that his attempt to reach some form of understanding with the Flemish Nationalists might eventually enable Rex to escape from the impasse in which it appeared trapped.

Critics of Rex in francophone Belgium were not slow to point to the weaknesses of the accord and, even in the German-censored press, reactions to its announcement were largely negative. The editors of the major New Order titles, including Raymond De Becker of *Le Soir* and Paul Colin and Robert Poulet of *Le Nouveau Journal*, stressed that it was an unofficial agreement and they dismissed the claims of Rex to be the 'parti unique wallon' as an absurd presumption. Degrelle, they declared, had merely capitulated to the demands of De Clercq by abandoning his Flemish supporters without obtaining in return any clear guarantees regarding the future of francophone Belgium.[127] In reply, Rexist journalists tried to defend as best they could their accord with the *VNV*, insisting that, whatever its shortcomings, it did at least mark a first step towards the co-operation between the New Order forces of Wallonia and Flanders which would be essential if Belgium was to survive in a German-dominated Europe.[128] The real advantage of the accord in the eyes of most Rexists was, however, its potential political benefits. Although they regretted the loss of *Rex-Vlaanderen* which did indeed soon become totally absorbed within the *VNV*, they sought to use the accord to establish themselves clearly as the sole authorised representatives of the collaborationist cause in francophone Belgium. Internal Rexist circulars boasted of their new quasi-official status and warned militants not to tolerate competition in Wallonia from any other pro-German groups.[129]

Thus, the accord with the *VNV* brought to a head the conflict which had long been looming between Rex and that self-styled 'moderate' wing of francophone collaboration which controlled the New Order press of Brussels. Although Rex was the only pro-German movement of any size in francophone Belgium, this rather heterogeneous milieu of journalists and press barons formed a prominent presence within Occupied Belgium. Through their virtual monopoly of the official media, their statements enjoyed a wide circulation and, as elsewhere in German-occupied Europe, they behaved with the arrogant self-confidence of men who felt that they were the opinion leaders of their country. Some were indeed relatively well-known figures: the writer Robert Poulet had long been prominent among the Maurrassian anti-democrats of the Catholic right, while Paul Colin was a leading art critic and historian who after a youthful flirtation with pacifism had established an influential weekly satirical paper, *Cassandre*, which during the 1930s had ridiculed the *moeurs* of the established Belgian political elite. Their boasts as to their power and influence, however, were in reality little more than vainglorious posturing. Though the New Order titles enjoyed impressive circulation figures (and enriched their proprietors), few of their readers paid much attention to the editorial content of the papers. The newspapers were above all a source of practical information and ponderous articles by lesser figures such as the young Paul De Man (the future guru of American post-structuralism and nephew of the President of the *POB*) passed entirely unnoticed while even the contributions by men such as De Becker and Poulet preached on the whole to the already converted.[130]

These New Order journalists had always held Degrelle in no great esteem and, encouraged by Rex's failure to attract German support, certain among them decided to create their own political grouping which they hoped would supplant Rex as the standard-bearer of the New Order and pro-German cause in francophone Belgium. Raymond De Becker, the editor-in-chief of *Le Soir*, was the leader of these malcontents. He had already made a number of thinly disguised attacks on Degrelle and, after the announcement of the Rex-*VNV* accord, he rapidly won the backing of a number of other figures in the Brussels press – including Robert Poulet of *Le Nouveau Journal* – for his plan to create a broadly-based single party. The basis of support for this movement would, they claimed, come from those many Belgians who were sympathetic to New Order ideals but whom Rex, discredited by its past and by the impulsive behaviour of its leader, had failed to mobilise.[131] Two meetings were held in De Becker's office at *Le Soir* during May 1941 at which agreement was reached on the structure of the new organisation. Baptised the *Parti des Provinces Romanes*, it stated its commitment to the New European Order and called for the construction of a federal Belgian state based on authoritarian and corporativist principles. As well as De Becker and Poulet, the statutes of the new party were signed by a number of prominent New Order figures including Degrelle's erstwhile adviser, Pierre Daye; the pre-war head of *Verdinaso* in Wallonia, Jacques Boseret; Gabriel Figeys of the German-controlled *Radio Bruxelles*; and Henri Bauchau, the founder of the pro-New Order *Service des Volontaires du Travail pour la Wallonie*.[132]

Although the new movement did not intend to commence public activities immediately, there was no doubt that it posed a serious threat to Rex. Unlike the small groups of dissidents who had formed *AGRA* and the *MNPW*, the putative *Parti des Provinces Romanes* enjoyed the support of figures of some national standing and it was not surprising that it should immediately have been strongly attacked by the Rexist leaders. Employing his considerable polemical powers to the full, Degrelle poured scorn on De Becker and his associates in the columns of *Le Pays Réel*. Rex, he thundered, had no intention of being pushed aside by self-important journalists who talked of the need to create a new movement as if a political party could be established as easily as a temperance society: 'On n'improvise pas un parti, ni surtout un chef . . . Rex peut déplaire, mais un fait est certain, c'est qu'il est seul dans son cas.' Forged by many years of struggle, the Rexists were, Degrelle claimed, the indispensable shock troops of the New Order revolution. Certainly, they did not command the support of the majority of Belgians but it was determined minorities and not incoherent popular movements which made revolutions and Degrelle concluded his article with a clear warning to his rivals: '. . . nous prétendons, ayant été la révolution vivante, en rester le moteur. Nous sommes dans la place, nous y resterons.'[133] Intimidated perhaps by this unprecedented outburst, De Becker proposed that he and Degrelle should sign an agreement to refrain from attacks on each other. The *Chef de Rex* was, however, in no mood to make concessions and, apparently ignoring De Becker's overtures, he continued to fulminate against the naïvety of journalists who believed they could convert their readership into a political force.[134]

Degrelle's invective might intimidate but, as he was only too aware, there was little he could do to frustrate the plans of De Becker and his allies. Only the German authorities, it was clear, possessed the power to determine the success or failure of the new movement. The crisis provoked by the *Parti des Provinces Romanes* revealed the change which had taken place in relations between the German authorities and those who supported their goals within Belgium. During the early months of the Occupation, the New Order groups had claimed, not without some plausibility, to represent a significant proportion of Belgian public opinion and had sought to negotiate with the German authorities as equals. By the spring of 1941 this had changed. With the shift in the fortunes of the military conflict and the consequent hardening of attitudes within Belgium towards the German authorities, none of those groups advocating support for the Nazi cause or even an authoritarian reform of the constitution could claim to enjoy mass support. Instead, they were obliged to gravitate – like moths fluttering around a light – towards the German officials who had become their only source of money, influence and, ultimately, power. It was a dependent relationship which dragged them progressively out of the real world of Belgian life into an artificial, closed environment somewhat akin to a medieval court where they competed for the ear of a capricious and wily monarch.

Degrelle had been one of the first to appreciate this reality and, from January 1941 until the final collapse of the Reich, the pursuit of German patronage would be his overriding obsession. The founders of the *Parti des Provinces Romanes* on the other hand clung to the myth that they were a substantial political force in their own right. These pretensions were, however, illusory. By 1941 no army of foot-soldiers stood ready to follow De Becker and his friends into a policy of collaboration which no longer seemed either necessary or desirable. Reeder appreciated the situation to the full. The President of the *Militärverwaltung* rightly judged that the vast majority of francophone Belgians were hostile to the Germans as well as to their supporters. Hence, though he remained convinced that Rex was an outmoded and unreliable organisation which could have no long-term role in German plans for the region, Reeder held out little hope for the emergence of any new pro-German mass movement in francophone Belgium.[135] De Becker was therefore informed by the *Militärverwaltung* in June that his initiative was premature and that approval would not be forthcoming for the *Parti des Provinces Romanes*. A few days later Reeder made his decision public. Writing in the quasi-official German-language newspaper the *Brüsseler Zeitung*, he announced that for the foreseeable future the *Militärverwaltung* would regard Rex and the *VNV* as the only authorised political movements in Belgium. Faced with such explicit

German disapproval, De Becker had little choice but to retreat. In August the meetings of the new party were suspended and they were never resumed.[136]

Not surprisingly, the Rexists greeted the decision of the *Militärverwaltung* with undisguised glee.[137] The movement at last appeared to have received some form of German approval and it was with an air of renewed optimism that a further substantial reorganisation of the internal structure of the movement was carried out during May. The most important change was the abolition of the powerful regions established in February and their replacement by a centralised structure based in Brussels. The *Etat-Major du Chef* remained the focus of political power but it was expanded to include not only the *Lieutenant du Chef*, Fernand Rouleau, but also Degrelle's personal secretary, Félix Francq, and the former head of *Rex-Wallonie*, Joseph Pévenasse. He was appointed to the new post of *Inspecteur Fédéral du Mouvement* and, with the assistance of his deputy, Jean Georges, took charge of the supervision of all local Rexist groups. Rouleau's responsibilities, on the other hand, remained much more general. As Degrelle's trusted adviser, he continued to determine the political strategy of Rex as well as directing the central Rexist offices which were grouped together in a new *Etat-Major du Mouvement*. These consisted of a number of specialised departments, such as the Propaganda Department directed by Victor Matthys, as well as the increasingly important *Service des Nominations*. Finally, the subordination of the *Formations de Combat* to the political leadership of the movement was reinforced. In place of the former regional units, the militia was organised into two *Etendards* based in Brussels and Wallonia which operated under the direction of Rouleau and Pévenasse, who were appointed respectively as *Commandant Fédéral* and *Inspecteur Fédéral* of the *Formations*.[138]

The most durable change introduced in May was the replacement of the network of *arrondissements* by a structure of some 25 *cercles*. These were to remain the principal unit of local Rexist organisation throughout the remainder of the Occupation. They were based on the principal towns of francophone Belgium and varied considerably in size from the very substantial ones in Brussels, Liège and Charleroi whose meetings were frequently attended by several hundred members to the much smaller *cercles* in some provincial towns. Each *cercle* was divided into a number of *groupes* based either on local *quartiers* or, in rural areas, on the constituent towns and villages of the *cercle*. Where possible, these *groupes* were further subdivided into *cellules* and *blocs*. Each *cercle* had an *Etat-Major* composed of its officials as well as of delegates appointed on an *ad hoc* basis to carry out specific tasks but the key figure in each area was invariably the *chef de cercle*. He was the focus of all local Rexist activities and, although they were unpaid volunteers, many *chefs de cercles* dedicated all their time and energies to their Rexist work.[139]

This reorganisation, although substantial, had little impact on the political control of Rex which remained firmly in the hands of Fernand Rouleau. The true nature of the ambitions of the *Lieutenant du Chef* has remained the subject of some controversy. Many Rexists regarded Rouleau as no more than an opportunistic adventurer intent upon personal advancement but it is clear that he did have a number of priorities for the movement. First and foremost, he was determined that Rex should commit itself fully to collaboration. Rexists, he believed, must move beyond mere rhetorical declarations of support for the German cause and should become at every level the loyal adjuncts of the Nazi authorities. To this end, Rouleau fostered close links with German officials and, as one of the few Rexists to speak German fluently, he soon acquired a reputation within Rex as 'l'homme de la Kommandantur'.[140] The *Lieutenant du Chef*'s second priority was the internal transformation of the Rexist movement. He had little sympathy for the rather chaotic traditions inherited from Rex's pre-war political activities and was instead firmly convinced that the movement must adopt the trappings of an authoritarian party. Thus, like other pro-German movements in Occupied Europe, Rex sought rather gauchely to imitate Nazi models. Rituals, uniforms and commands derived from German examples were all introduced and, although the results were rarely impressive, they served to identify Rex still further in the popular mind with the Nazi cause.[141]

Rouleau's ascendancy and the nature of his activities continued to inspire resentment among some long-standing militants. José Streel, for example, subsequently dismissed this period in Rexist history as 'l'aventure Rouleau' when in his opinion the movement had been forced into a policy of uncritical support for Nazi Germany.[142] Several incidents of open dissent arose, most notably in Brussels where a prominent Rexist journalist, Carl Suzanne, and some officers of the *Formations de Combat* circulated a document strongly critical of the *Lieutenant du Chef*. Rouleau, conscious no doubt that he had few friends within the movement, reacted energetically to this relatively minor incident by instigating legal proceedings against his critics, establishing a *tribunal d'honneur* to clear his name and ensuring that Suzanne was expelled from Rex.[143] The real basis of Rouleau's hold over the movement remained his close links with Degrelle. The reasons for Degrelle's support for his ambitious deputy remain difficult to discern. The former *Chef de Rex* denies that he had any special confidence in Rouleau and, at times in the spring of 1941, the two men were reported to have been in conflict with each other.[144] Such disputes do appear however to have been short-lived and on all important matters Degrelle continued to give his backing to his *Lieutenant*. In truth, it seems that the *Chef de Rex*, obsessed with his pursuit of German patronage, had little interest in the affairs of his political movement and found it convenient to devolve responsibility for internal Rexist matters to his deputy.

Moreover, most Rexists proved remarkably willing to accept the leadership of Rouleau. The incidents of dissent in Brussels and elsewhere never seriously threatened his position and it seems that, as popular hostility to the Rexists mounted, many militants came to agree with Rouleau that the only way forward for the movement lay in a closer relationship with the German forces. The consequence was to transform the policy of collaboration from the symbolic level of the declarations of Degrelle into the mundane reality of daily life. Quite apart from the burgeoning relations between local officials of Rex and the German authorities and the participation of Rexist drivers in the German *NSKK*, examples abounded of ordinary militants who volunteered their services to the Germans. Indeed, so common had such advances become that the Rexist leaders were forced to try and restrain their members from making such individual approaches.[145]

This deepening of collaboration was also evident in the ideological positions adopted by Rex. Throughout 1940 Rexist propaganda had remained, despite some innovations, rooted essentially in the concepts and themes of its pre-war past. During 1941 a gradual change took place as Rexist writers became not only ever more fulsome in their praise of the German regime but also adopted Nazi ideas formerly alien to Rex. Most strikingly, the movement became openly committed to 'National Socialism'. During the pre-war years Rexists had often referred to the need for a 'socialisme national' or a 'nouveau socialisme' but 'National Socialisme' with its explicitly German connotations had not formed part of Rexist rhetoric. In 1941, however, it came to predominate in Rexist declarations as both the guiding principle and the declared goal of the movement.[146] This was merely one aspect of what Rexist leaders often admitted in private was a policy of aligning Rex more explicitly with the values and ideology of the Nazi regime. As Joseph Pévenasse declared to a closed meeting of militants in April: 'REX doit être un Mouvement National Socialiste pour entrer dans cette immense confédération européenne [créée] par la main de fer et aussi de justice d'Hitler.'[147] The impact of these changes was also reflected in the political aspirations of the movement. The vague Rexist goal of the pre-war years of a 'révolution des âmes' was discarded in favour of a much harsher vision of a violent revolution which would destroy the structures and personnel of the existing world. Dreams of reconciliation gave way to images of struggle and of incessant conflict and, though some articles in the Rexist press continued to dwell on the mystical essence of their movement, the focus of Rexist interests had turned from the spiritual to the concrete. Rexist ideologists made much of their supposedly socialist inspiration and their propaganda was dominated by bold promises of the material changes which would be brought about by their revolution.[148]

The combined effect of these changes was to deprive Rexism of much of its former distinctiveness and to bring it much closer to the model of German National Socialism. This progressive incorporation of their ideology into a Nazi mould also led the Rexists to redefine their own political role. Initially they had seen themselves as an avant-garde paving the way for a revolution which would be enacted by the whole nation but by 1941 they had abandoned any pretence of popular participation. Condemned to the ghetto existence of collaboration, the Rexists were forced to fall back, like all such extremists at odds with popular opinion, on a Messianic vision of their own role. The people, they declared dismissively, were a 'masse . . . amorphe et veule' and Rexist militants were exhorted to regard themselves as a revolutionary elite. Total dedication and unquestioning obedience were the qualities extolled by a movement which had lost all faith in human nature and which sought to depersonalise even its own supporters. As Matthys, the newly-appointed *Chef de Propagande*, declared: 'Ce que nous cherchons, ce que nous voulons, ce sont des soldats, toujours sur le pied de guerre de la révolution . . . Etre rexiste, c'est militer de toutes ses forces, de tout son temps, de toutes ses possibilités et avec un discipline de soldat pour la révolution.'[149]

Rexist propaganda might threaten a violent revolution against the established forces of Belgian society but this political and economic elite still felt able to look on Degrelle and his followers with more disdain than trepidation. These traditional notables remained apprehensive as to the nature of long-term Nazi plans for the country but they had good reason to be satisfied with their position under the *Militärverwaltung*. Far from destroying their power, the *Wehrmacht* authorities had – as the collaborationist minority never ceased to complain – on the whole reinforced the power of the existing elites. Certainly, many of the pre-war politicians had been marginalised and the German-imposed changes in central and local government had brought into office a number of supporters of New Order ideas, but the system of indirect rule imposed by the German victors sought as far as possible to ensure that Belgian society remained unaltered. Thus, many of the notables of pre-war Belgium continued to play a prominent role in public life during the years of the Occupation. Civil servants, industrialists and Church leaders were all the privileged *interlocuteurs* of the German authorities who, for reasons both practical and, one suspects, emotional, preferred to work with these established leaders of society rather than risking dangerous experiments with untried collaborationist adventurers.

The position of the Catholic Church exemplified this situation. The *Wehrmacht* officials – a number of whom were themselves practising Catholics – placed a high priority on retaining good relations with the Catholic hierarchy and went out of their way to mollify Cardinal Van Roey and his colleagues.[150] For the Rexists, on the other hand, the Church had become a symbol of the social and political order which they were seeking to destroy. They were annoyed by the deferential respect shown by the *Militärverwaltung* towards the Church and *Le Pays Réel* launched frequent attacks on what it alleged was the pro-English sentiments of the ecclesiastical hierarchy. As in 1940, the Rexists were careful to stress that they were not hostile to the Catholic religion. Their target was the Belgian Catholic hierarchy which through its long cohabitation with the democratic political order had, they alleged, become unable to recognise where its true interests lay. Prominent Rexist journalists such as José Streel continued to insist on the advantages which a New Order would bring to the Catholic faith in Belgium and they seized with enthusiasm on instances elsewhere in Europe of support by the Catholic Church for authoritarian regimes.[151]

Conflict at a local level between Rex and the Church authorities had by 1941 become commonplace and in many parishes Rexists became involved in long-running and often bitter disputes with the local *curé*. In turn, many priests did everything within their power to hinder Rexist activities, warning their parishioners of the error of Rexist opinions and refusing to administer communion to those wearing the insignia or uniform of the movement.[152] These local disputes took on a national dimension early in 1941 when the Church hierarchy issued a series of directives which appeared to discriminate against the members of collaborationist movements. In response to the disruptive activities of small groups of Rexist and Flemish Nationalist students in Catholic schools, the pupils of these institutions were forbidden from enrolling in or supporting such organisations. Further, in May, Cardinal Van Roey expressly instructed priests not to allow uniformed militants of pro-German organisations to participate in communion or funeral services.[153] Together with the comments of Van Roey to an audience of Catholic youth leaders in July as well as the refusal of the Church authorities to permit a memorial ceremony for the *Verdinaso* leader, Joris Van Severen, these orders left little doubt as to the sympathies of the Church and they drew a prompt and angry response from much of the pro-German press. Amidst this chorus of denunciation, it was, however, the journalists of *Le Pays Réel* who distinguished themselves by the virulence of their attacks on the Church. Long-standing rancour against the Church's refusal to support Rex in 1936–7 merged with more immediate grievances to produce a torrent of invective against Van Roey and his colleagues for having abandoned, in the eyes of the Rexists, all pretence of political neutrality.[154]

The role of arbiter in this dispute fell inevitably to the officials of the *Militärverwaltung*. They had observed with dismay the deterioration in relations between the Church and the pro-German minority and, to the intense annoyance of the Rexists, they chose once again to pacify the Church rather than to assist their collaborationist supporters. The German authorities apparently suppressed a newspaper article by Degrelle which they judged to be too critical of the ecclesiastical hierarchy and, after negotiations with a representative of the Cardinal, the *Militärverwaltung* agreed that the orders issued by the Church regarding supporters of collaborationist groups could remain in force substantially unaltered.[155] The resolution of this dispute served again to underline the isolation of the Rexists. Having broken with their compatriots, they had received in return little tangible support from those whose cause they had so publicly espoused. Deprived of any means of imposing their will on the Church, Rexist militants could therefore do no more than threaten and intimidate those individual priests who opposed them too ostentatiously.[156]

The anniversary on 28 May 1941 of Léopold III's surrender to the German armies was a melancholy one for the Rexists. The previous year had brought them a long and dispiriting series of reverses offset only by brief and largely illusory moments of optimism, and José Streel must have expressed the feelings of many within the movement when he used the anniversary to lament in *Le Pays Réel* that: 'En Belgique, il y aurait peut-être à faire le bilan de ce qui s'est passé depuis un an. Mais il ne s'est rien passé. Nous avons piétiné sur place, c'est-à-dire reculé . . . on a beaucoup parlé, beaucoup écrit, beaucoup comploté. On tue le temps en attendant que vienne enfin l'heure de l'action.'[157] Events had certainly not worked out as they had hoped. Everywhere they looked within Belgium the new dawn of 1940 had given way to a military and political stalemate which seemed likely to continue for months or even years. The prospects for change were slight and, more than ever, Degrelle and his colleagues longed for a decisive event which would restore the optimism which they had felt in the summer of 1940.

On the morning of 22 June, this wish was suddenly and unexpectedly satisfied. The news of Hitler's attack on the Soviet Union was greeted by pro-German groups throughout Occupied Europe as a glorious event which resolved the last ambiguities surrounding the military conflict. The embarrassing *realpolitik* of the Nazi-Soviet Pact was at an end and the war finally seemed to have taken on the character of a clear-cut struggle between good and evil.[158] The Rexists shared in this elation. For them, the attack on the Soviet Union served both as a belated vindication of the pro-German stance they had adopted in January as well as a real cause for optimism. The new military campaign transformed the war from an Anglo-German struggle for supremacy into a crusade against not only the external Bolshevik threat but also against the internal Communist movements. All Europeans could now identify with these Nazi goals and Degrelle hastened to declare his unconditional support for the German armies advancing in the East. Predicting that Hitler would be in Moscow by Bastille Day, the *Chef de Rex* called on his supporters to shed their remaining hesitations: 'Qu'on finisse avec la peur devant les mots! Nous sommes de toute notre âme avec la jeunesse hitlérienne.'[159] Degrelle's exultant reaction to the attack on the Soviet Union was predictable. Of greater significance was the way in which the new declaration of war also caused more moderate Rexists to abandon their former caution. Almost overnight, men such as José Streel declared their support for the Nazi cause arguing that the war was no longer a mere conflict between nation-states but an apocalyptic struggle between the forces of darkness and light. Henceforth, the only possible victors were Bolshevism or Nazi Germany and as, should the former prevail, Europe would be plunged into 'un état d'anarchie épouvantable, un chaos d'apocalypse', it was imperative for all Belgians to recognise that their future was henceforth inextricably linked to the victory of the German armies in the East.[160]

This argument was not original. Indeed, it rapidly became – and has remained – the standard justification advanced by many of those who opted to support the Nazi cause throughout German-occupied Europe. Its popularity bore witness not merely to the anti-communism current in right-wing circles during the inter-war years but also to contemporary perceptions of the Soviet Union. For most Rexists, raised and educated within the Catholic educational system, the Soviet regime had always appeared as an anti-Christ which threatened the survival of the Catholic faith and even of European civilisation. It was, therefore, in many respects scarcely surprising that they should have greeted the Nazi declaration of war on the Soviet Union with such enthusiasm: but it also soon became evident that many other Belgian Catholics did not share their views. If the Nazi rulers of Belgium hoped that the attack on the Soviet Union would cause the Catholic faithful to rally to the German cause, they were sorely disappointed. There were indeed a few rare instances of young Catholic militants who expressed their support for the Nazi crusade or who even volunteered to fight with the German armies in Russia, but for most Belgians Hitler's new declaration of war merely reinforced their belief that the Nazi regime was engaged on a war of conquest without limit. For these Catholics, the Nazi and Soviet regimes had in effect long since become mirror images of each other and any sympathy they felt for the overthrow of the Soviet regime was greatly outweighed by their more immediate and tangible hostility towards the German invaders of their country.[161] Thus, the declaration of war on the Soviet Union was principally of significance for the manner in which it radicalised those already sympathetic to the Nazi cause to opt decisively for collaboration. For men such as José Streel, the German attack on Russia was the cathartic event which enabled them to shake off their residual hesitations. Already considered by their compatriots to be de facto supporters of Germany, they now passed from a superficially neutral acceptance of the reality of the German Occupation to positive support for the Nazi cause.

For men such as Degrelle and Rouleau, the war in Russia had no such significance. They had long since entered the German camp and they welcomed the new conflict principally as an opportunity to escape from their former isolation. Degrelle has often subsequently described his pleasure on learning of the German attack on Russia. Like Paul on the road to Damascus, he has written, he found himself confronted by a miracle which brought to an end: 'l'année de déboires, de tergiversations et même d'humiliations que nous avions connue d'août 1940 à août 1941'.[162] From the outset Degrelle was determined to exploit the war in Russia to his own ends. The Rexist leader had long believed that direct participation in the German armies offered Rex the best means of attracting the support of the Nazi leaders and it seems that he decided, almost as soon as he learnt of the attack on the Soviet Union, to repeat his request to be allowed to create a volunteer military unit.[163] Moreover, unlike his earlier somewhat eccentric proposals, Degrelle had better reason to believe that on this occasion his suggestion would be favourably received. Foreign volunteers would provide much needed manpower for the new military front as well as assisting Nazi propagandists in their efforts to portray their campaign as a European crusade against Bolshevism. Nor was he acting in isolation. Although the *Chef de Rex* appears to have known little of such initiatives, he was not alone among collaborationist leaders in seeking to participate directly in the war against the Soviet Union. Pro-German leaders throughout Occupied Europe responded to news of the German attack by proposing the creation of similar military units to fight alongside the German armies in Russia.[164]

Predictably, the *Chef de Rex*'s initial response to the news of 22 June was to hurry to Paris where his ally Abetz was already encouraging French collaborationists in their efforts to create a *Légion des Volontaires Français* to fight on the Eastern Front. The German ambassador to France undoubtedly encouraged Degrelle in his parallel efforts but, during the Rexist leader's absence from Brussels, it fell to Rouleau to make the first approach to the *Militärverwaltung*.[165] Not surprisingly, their reaction was discouraging. Quite apart from their political distrust of the Rexists, the professional soldiers of the *Militärverwaltung* were scarcely inclined to look favourably on the enrolment of inexperienced foreign volunteers in the *Wehrmacht*.[166] The Rexists did not, however, allow the matter to drop. On his return to Brussels, Degrelle seconded enthusiastically the efforts of his *Lieutenant* and at length their persistence was rewarded. In early July, the *Militärverwaltung* – acting in all probability on instructions from Berlin – gave permission for the Rexists to create a unit composed exclusively of francophone Belgian volunteers. In exultant mood, Degrelle announced this success to a meeting of the *Formations de Combat* in Brussels on 6 July. Never before, he proclaimed with his usual gusto, had such an opportunity been presented to Belgian youth. They would be able to participate in the most glorious military campaign in history before returning to Belgium as the conquering heroes of the New Europe.[167]

Behind such rhetoric, however, there lay uncertainty and unease. The *Corps Franc 'Wallonie'* – or *Légion 'Wallonie'*, as it soon came to be known – announced in early July differed markedly in some significant respects from the initial proposal made by the Rexists. Most importantly, the unit was limited to francophone Belgians. Degrelle and Rouleau had advocated the creation of a single Belgian unit but this was firmly opposed by the *VNV* and the *Militärverwaltung* who, not without some foundation, saw in it an attempt by Rex to commit the Nazis to some form of unitary Belgian state. During July Degrelle and Rouleau continued to lobby the German authorities to reverse this decision but they had no success and, with the creation of a parallel Flemish Legion by the *VNV*, they were forced to accept that the *Légion Wallonie* would be limited to francophone Belgium in fact as well as in name. This was not the only contentious issue. In their haste to receive German approval for the unit, the Rexist leaders had left unresolved many of the details regarding the structure and operation of the *Légion*. The uniforms to be worn by its members, the oaths of loyalty which would be demanded of them and the exact nature of the *Légion*'s relationship with the German armies were all matters which were studiously avoided when the *Légion*'s creation was announced.[168]

These questions of detail mattered little to Degrelle and Rouleau. For them the overriding consideration was that the new unit should be created as rapidly as possible. The *Chef de Rex* was convinced that the German armies would defeat the Soviet forces within a matter of weeks and he was anxious that the *Légion* should reach Russia in time to participate in the final battles. *Ad hoc* recruitment offices were hurriedly opened and Degrelle undertook a tour of francophone Belgium to whip up popular support.[169] In his speeches, the arguments used by Degrelle to justify the creation of the *Légion* soon took on the air of a familiar litany. Much was made of the peril supposedly posed to Europe by the Soviet Union while a Nazi victory would, Degrelle claimed, inaugurate a New European Order of prosperity and harmony. The Rexist leader was always careful, however, to stress that the principal motivation behind the creation of the new unit was to ensure that Belgium would form part of a unified New Order Europe. The Soviet Union was in this respect no more than a convenient pretext. It was on the battlefields of the East, Degrelle declared, that the future structure of Europe would be decided and, by fighting shoulder to shoulder with the German troops, the Belgian *légionnaires* would win the respect of the Nazi leaders and thereby guarantee their country's place in the New Europe.[170]

In his post-war writings, Degrelle has frequently returned to this argument, stressing how the *Légion* was essentially a means of forcing the attention of the Nazi leaders upon Belgium.[171] Few of his compatriots seem to have shared his views. Most Belgians dismissed the *Légion Wallonie* as the last desperate throw of a discredited adventurer and, although German and Rexist propagandists boasted of the crowds which had besieged the recruiting offices of the *Légion*, the reality was that very few Belgians responded to Degrelle's invitation. No more than a couple of hundred volunteers had been enrolled by mid-July and, even compared with the modest achievements of the other units created at the same time elsewhere in Europe, the initial recruitment for the *Légion Wallonie* was a categorical failure.[172]

Indeed, Degrelle even appears to have had difficulty in winning the support of committed Rexists for his new venture. Degrelle's outspoken declarations of support for Nazi Germany since January 1941 had in no way prepared the Rexists for this direct involvement in a distant military campaign and a strongly-worded circular had to be issued to militants warning them not to fail the movement at this decisive moment.[173] Many Rexists, however, remained unwilling to enrol in what was in effect an auxiliary unit of the German *Wehrmacht*. Degrelle was well aware of this problem and he sought as far as possible to give the *Légion* the air of an autonomous army. Given its exclusively francophone composition, use of the Belgian flag by the *Légion* was impossible but the Rexist leader convinced a reluctant *Militärverwaltung* that the cross of the old Burgundian Empire rather than the explicitly regionalist *Coq Wallon* should be the flag of the *Légion*. Moreover, though the Germans insisted that the volunteers must wear *Wehrmacht* uniforms, Degrelle ensured that they would be emblazoned with a badge in the colours of the Belgian tricolour and that French would be the language of command within the *Légion*.[174] These concessions did, nevertheless, provide only a thin veneer of patriotic credibility and for most Rexists the most important stumbling-block remained the German uniforms to be worn by the *légionnaires*. To wear the uniform of the armies which scarcely more than a year earlier had invaded the country was a step which few – even within Rex – were willing to contemplate and it seems that Degrelle was not above misleading some reluctant recruits into believing that they would in fact wear Belgian army uniforms.[175]

The *Chef de Rex* and his *Lieutenant* were similarly unscrupulous regarding the contentious issue of the King's attitude towards the new unit. Any indication of support on the part of Léopold III would of course have been of enormous propaganda value to Degrelle and he promptly dispatched his customary intermediary Pierre Daye to the palace at Laeken to sound out the King's advisers. Daye was received by Comte Capelle on 15 July but his proposal that the King should make some form of public gesture of approval for the *Légion* was not surprisingly rejected. Capelle's attitude may not, however, have been entirely discouraging. According to Daye, the King's secretary did express some personal sympathy for the courage and ideals of the *légionnaires* – an assertion which Capelle strenuously denied after the war.[176]

In fact, in this matter as in so many others relating to the wartime actions of Léopold III and his entourage, much probably depended on the interpretation one chose to place on certain guarded comments. Since 1940, Léopold had become considerably more wary in his political initiatives and he had little reason to look with favour on Degrelle's activities. Rumours of disparaging remarks made by Degrelle about the King had reached Laeken and his rash adventurism had done much to undermine the more circumspect efforts of the King to reach an understanding with the Nazi leaders. Nevertheless, the suspicion must remain that Capelle may have been less cautious in his comments to Daye than he cared to remember after the war. During his regular conversations with the New Order journalist Robert Poulet, Capelle apparently indicated his sympathy for the idealism of certain légionnaires and there were persistent rumours both within Rex and the Légion that not all of those who had sought the advice of the court as to whether to fight in Russia had been discouraged from doing so.[177] What is however clear beyond any doubt is that Degrelle and Rouleau deliberately set about manufacturing the impression that the King had given his blessing to the creation of the Légion. Rouleau, never one to be constrained by scruples, went a stage further, producing a forged letter purporting to be written by Comte Capelle which expressed the King's support for the Légion. Widely distributed amongst the légionnaires, the existence of this fake soon became known to the King's advisers. They called Rouleau to Laeken but Degrelle's deputy prudently chose to ignore this summons.[178]

Even these unscrupulous tactics brought scant rewards. Although the idea of a crusade against the Bolshevik peril undoubtedly appealed to a certain number of Belgians, only the most idealistic or naïve of these anti-Communists were in practice willing to be associated with a military unit which seemed to be little more than a vehicle for Rexist ambitions. Thus, the Légion failed to attract more than a handful of non-Rexist volunteers and during the last two weeks of the recruitment campaign Degrelle was forced to concentrate instead on enrolling men from within the ranks of his political movement. He boasted – somewhat belatedly – of how the Légion would be composed almost exclusively of Rexists and attempted to bully even journalists from Le Pays Réel into joining the unit.[179] The response within the movement remained, however, less than enthusiastic. Many Rexists were still reluctant to serve in the Légion and, in an attempt to overcome their hesitations, Degrelle chose to take a step which proved to be of the greatest importance both for his own future and that of Rex. At a meeting in Liège on 20 July, the Chef de Rex suddenly announced that he would himself join the Légion as a volunteer.[180]

This dramatic gesture was apparently an impulsive move undertaken, so Degrelle has claimed, without warning either the German authorities or even his family.[181] Nevertheless, it succeeded in transforming the attitudes of many ordinary Rexists towards the new unit. Until Degrelle's dramatic announcement, many Rexists seem to have looked on the *Légion* as a temporary propaganda initiative of little long-term importance. But the example of their leader himself enrolling – despite his total lack of any military training – in the new unit, as well as his refusal to accept any special treatment from the German authorities, convinced many that it was their duty to accompany the *Chef* in his new venture.[182]

Thus, during the last days of the recruitment campaign, several hundred of the most experienced Rexist militants – including a number of *chefs de cercles* – came forward to join the *Légion* with the consequence that on the appointed date of departure of 8 August, 850 volunteers assembled in the Place Royale in Brussels.[183] As the self-proclaimed saviours of Belgium, they formed an unlikely group. Though they did their best to give an appearance of military discipline, there was no disguising the wide disparities in age and experience evident among the recruits. The one fact that united them was that most were Rexists. Many wore Rexist uniforms and it seems that some 730 of their number were members of Rex, most of them drawn from the *Formations de Combat*.[184] The other volunteers were a heterogeneous group. About 30 were members of the small anti-semitic grouping *Défense du Peuple* while others included Tsarist exiles, young Catholic idealists, long-standing anti-communists as well as a number of adventurers who found in the *Légion* an opportunity to escape from material, judicial or domestic difficulties.[185]

These putative national heroes and their supporters gathered first in the Palais des Beaux Arts to hear an emotional speech from Degrelle which, amidst the shifting sands of Rexist opportunism, subsequently came to be treasured by his followers as a rare expression of their central beliefs. What his audience particularly welcomed in this speech was the emphasis which he placed on his Belgian patriotism. Responding directly to the charge of treason which had dogged them since their espousal of collaboration, he claimed for the Rexists the mantle of the true patriots in Occupied Belgium. Unlike those who preferred to cling to outmoded beliefs or to unrealistic dreams, the *légionnaires* – Degrelle declared – were departing to the East as lucid and realistic nationalists determined to win a place for their country in the New Europe.[186] As the rapturous reception which his speech received indicated, this was a theme which many Rexists welcomed. Despite the undoubted ideological evolution which had taken place within the movement during the previous winter, most Rexists still preferred to see themselves not as the soldiers of some National Socialist revolution but as patriots serving their nation in a time of trial. Indeed, one of the most striking features of the creation of the *Légion* was that it was accompanied within Rex by a return to a more moderate and patriotic basis for their actions. For the first time since the summer of 1940, the Rexists felt confident that they could justify their actions in patriotic terms and, after the frustrations of the previous winter, there seems to have been a general feeling of relief that they had succeeded in returning to the right course.

These patriotic arguments did, however, rest on the flimsiest of bases. Nothing could hide the total dependence of the *Légion* on the German authorities and the nationalist veneer Degrelle sought to give to the unit was at every turn contradicted by the circumstances of its creation. Thus, when the *Chef de Rex* boasted on 8 August of the patriotism of the new soldiers, he did so standing beneath a huge photograph of the German *Führer* and, in reality, the entire cost of the recruitment campaign had been met from German funds. Even the military band which played the Belgian national anthem during the march past of the *légionnaires* belonged to the *Wehrmacht*.[187]

If the immediate impact of the formation of the *Légion* was to give to Rex a more moderate air, its more durable effect was to deepen still further the gulf between the Rexists and their compatriots. Military collaboration, more perhaps than any other form of pro-German activity, was seen by the population as an act of free will. To don the uniform of the conqueror was an unambivalent act and one with a long lineage in European history. Thus, despite their protestations of their patriotic intent, the creation of the *Légion* was regarded by the majority of Belgians as a monstrous crime for which there could be no excuse. This attitude of popular incomprehension was clearly evident during the march by the *légionnaires* through the streets of Brussels to the Gare du Nord. Although a large crowd of curious onlookers had gathered to witness the bizarre spectacle, they showed little sympathy for the new soldiers and local police officers apparently turned their backs on the volunteers.[188]

For the Rexists, on the other hand, the departure of the *légionnaires* was a moment charged with emotion. After the enforced idleness of the winter, they at last had the opportunity to act and the commemoration of the emotional events of 8 August subsequently became a major ritual in the Rexist calendar.[189] Few of those Rexists who gathered in the fine rain to watch their *légionnaires* depart could have imagined the future which lay in store for the untried soldiers. Degrelle had spoken with his usual bravura of his willingness to die for his beliefs but he had privately reassured his fellow volunteers that they would be no more than *soldats de propagande* serving behind the front lines before participating in the victory parades in a liberated Moscow.[190] In fact, the war in the East proved to be anything other than a brief if exotic *Blitzkrieg*. The *Légion* was never to return from the front for more than brief periods of recuperation and, within a few months, many of its members were to die in obscure battles on the killing fields of the Ukraine. Far from acting as a springboard for the acquisition of power, the *Légion* became – like some monstrous cuckoo – the *raison d'être* of Rex, continually depriving the movement of its energy, manpower and resources; while, for the *légionnaires*, the optimistic new dawn of August 1941 proved to be merely the prelude to a long nightmare from which only death or the end of the war in 1945 would give some form of release.

Chapter Three

August 1941 – Spring 1942

Rex without Degrelle

WITH THE departure of its leader at the head of the *Légion*, the survival of Rex as an effective force within Occupied Belgium seemed to hang in the balance. Despite the euphoria engendered by the formation of the *Légion*, the political situation within the country remained as unpromising as ever. Moreover, by depriving Rex of many of its most experienced and capable militants, the *Légion Wallonie* had created serious difficulties of organisation which those Rexists who remained behind would have to address. All observers were agreed that those who had joined the *Légion* in August were primarily those faithful veterans who had served the Rexist cause through all of the vicissitudes in its fortunes and who had always constituted the core of its organisation. Thus, as Rexist propagandists were always quick to point out, the new soldiers were far from being the young rootless adventurers often attracted by visions of distant campaigns. On the contrary, they were established men, often of quite mature years, who had abandoned both their jobs and their responsibilities to their families in order to answer Degrelle's call to arms.[1] Many had directed Rexist *cercles* or units of the *Formations de Combat* which were now abruptly deprived of their leaders. Degrelle, desperate to acquire the largest possible number of recruits for his new venture, paid little attention to this decimation of the local structure of Rex. The *Légion* already threatened to eclipse all of his other priorities and it was only a few days before his departure that he recognised that a small group of experienced figures must remain behind to staff the central *Etat-Major* of the movement.[2]

Degrelle does not appear to have considered the selection of these interim leaders to have been of great importance. He confidently believed that the *légionnaires* would return to Belgium before the onset of winter and the chances of any change in the political situation within the country during the intervening months appeared remote. His selection of these leaders was complicated by a further resurgence in the personal rivalries among the Rexist leaders. In particular, the creation of the *Légion Wallonie* had once again brought to a head the long-standing tensions surrounding the power exercised within Rex by Fernand Rouleau. Already established as the *de facto* deputy of Degrelle, the *Lieutenant du Chef* had further reinforced his authority by taking charge of the organisation of the new military unit.[3] Rouleau considered himself to be the interim head of the *Légion* and it seems probable that he initially intended – perhaps with the connivance of certain German officials – to use the *Légion* as his own power base which would gradually absorb the remnants of the civilian Rexist organisation. The *Chef de Rex*'s sudden decision to serve in the *Légion* disrupted these plans. Though Degrelle would be only an ordinary soldier in the unit, he would clearly be the dominant political force. Rouleau therefore apparently changed his mind, suggesting instead to the *Chef de Rex* that he should remain in Belgium as the interim leader of Rex during Degrelle's absence.[4]

Degrelle, however, refused this request. He insisted that Rouleau remain a member of the *Légion* and both he and Rouleau left with the other recruits on 8 August. Behind the scenes a struggle for control both of the *Légion* and possibly of Rex had now begun and relations between the two men continued to deteriorate rapidly after their arrival at the training camp for the *Légion* in eastern Germany. The details of what actually occurred remain enveloped in the mists of complicated intrigues but it is clear that Degrelle had come to regard his deputy with the deepest mistrust. Rouleau, as the ordnance officer of the *Légion*, enjoyed close relations with the German officers and made frequent visits to Berlin. These contacts, as well as his apparent attempts to build a personal following among the *légionnaires*, inevitably aroused suspicions as to his intentions and rumours soon began to circulate that the German authorities would force Degrelle to return to Belgium leaving Rouleau as the undisputed head of the *Légion*.[5] Whether there was any substance to these stories remains unclear but Degrelle seized upon them to act decisively against his deputy. In a furious rage, he accused Rouleau of orchestrating a plot against him and within a few hours the *Lieutenant du Chef*, whether at the instigation of the Germans or because he genuinely feared for his life, disappeared from the ranks of the *Légion*.[6]

Thus, Rouleau's involvement with Rex ended – as it had begun – in an atmosphere of some mystery. He was never to return either to Rex or to the *Légion* and both his real motivation and the means by which he emerged so rapidly as the *adjoint* of Degrelle must remain matters for conjecture. Perhaps – despite Degrelle's denials – it was indeed true that he was financing Rexist activities or that he was an agent of some part of the Nazi hierarchy. Yet, whatever the truth, his involvement in Rex personified a certain opportunistic style of collaboration which in Belgium as elsewhere in German-occupied Europe was most evident during these early years of the war. Like innumerable other adventurers who offered their services to the Nazi authorities, traded in scarce commodities, or climbed aboard the German propaganda machine, Rouleau was a man of no fixed convictions who saw in the Occupation merely an opportunity for personal advancement. As the fortunes of battle changed, many of these 'non-political' collaborators retreated from public view, preferring either to foster links with the Resistance and the Allies or taking refuge in more discreet pro-German activities. This was the course followed by Rouleau who after his departure from Rex disappeared into the murky – and, one suspects, for him congenial – world of the Nazi police. For some months, he was occasionally glimpsed in Brussels in the company of German officials but he soon moved to Paris where he was variously reported to be an agent of the SS police, the *Sicherheitsdienst* (SD), and a recruiter for the Charlemagne division of the *Waffen-SS*. He later worked for the SD in Tunisia and at the end of the war was serving with an SS cavalry division in Hungary. From there, he succeeded in fleeing – apparently with a considerable fortune – first to Switzerland and then, a few months later, to Spain where he was employed from 1946 as a chemical engineer. He lived in La Coruna and Madrid and during a minor court case in 1951 was described as a former soldier in the Nationalist armies. Protected from Belgian justice by his connections with the Francoist police and seemingly untroubled by Spain's transition to democracy, he died in exile in 1984 aged 81.[7]

Rouleau's hurried departure from Rex marked the end of Degrelle's policy of entrusting the administration of the movement to those new men who had joined Rex in the summer of 1940. Though he remained in so many other respects an impulsive adventurer, his experiences with figures such as Rouleau and Simoens had made the *Chef de Rex* cautious in his choice of assistants and all of the principal leaders of the movement after the summer of 1941 were men who had served Rex throughout its turbulent history. A hierarchy of seniority had been re-established and power in effect returned to the informal coterie of journalists and in-tellectuals who had gathered around Degrelle at Louvain in the mid-1930s. It was one of this group, Victor Matthys, who on the eve of his departure to Germany Degrelle chose to direct Rex during his absence. Appointed by Degrelle as *Chef ad interim* 'jusqu'à mon retour à la fin de la guerre',[8] Matthys was in some respects a surprising choice. Only 27 years old in 1941, he was, even by the standards of the youthful Rexist movement, exceptionally young and had few obvious qualifications for the tasks which would confront him. A journalist by profession, Matthys was the principal editor of *Le Pays Réel* but his only experience of administration within the Rexist headquarters was as the head of the propaganda depart-ment created in May 1941. Matthys' principal qualification for his new post was, however, clearly his unwavering personal loyalty to Degrelle. Matthys had been one of the *Chef de Rex*'s closest associates for almost ten years and, on appointing him, Degrelle described the new *Chef de Rex ad interim* as 'mon plus vieux et plus fidèle collaborateur'.[9] Matthys' back-ground was very different from those of most of the aspiring journalists and intellectuals who formed the first nucleus of Rexists. In contrast to the sons of the respectable provincial Catholic bourgeoisie who dominated the movement in its early years, Matthys was illegitimate and had been raised by his mother in modest circumstances. He had few formal educational qualifications and when he first met Degrelle he was working as a lowly employee in the offices of the *Association Catholique de la Jeunesse Belge* in Louvain. Matthys did, however, share both Degrelle's irreverent humour and his enthusiasm for a Catholic spiritual renewal in Belgium and he rapidly became one of the *Chef de Rex*'s inner circle of advisers, specialising in the direction of the Rexist press.[10]

Matthys was far from evidently suited to be the leader of a New Order political movement. His physical appearance was unimpressive and his poor health had even caused him to be exempted from military service.[11] Moreover he was an inexperienced and somewhat awkward public speaker who possessed none of the oratorical gifts of Degrelle. However in private Matthys was a skilful administrator and, although his interim leadership of Rex was to last far longer than either he or Degrelle had anticipated, he proved to be an effective guardian of the movement. His personal commitment to Rex was beyond question. It had long been the focus of his life and he never seems to have doubted that Rex did indeed offer the only hope for the salvation of the country. Similarly, he was a whole-hearted supporter of collaboration with Nazi Germany. Although during his tenure of the affairs of Rex he would often be at pains to hold the movement at a certain distance from the German authorities, he was an uncritical admirer of the Nazi regime and in the early months of 1941 he had already used his position as *Chef de Propagande* to encourage Rexist imitation of the structures and ideology of Nazism. Matthys' commitment to these political goals was to some extent contradicted by his personal irreverence. Like many of those who had joined Rex during its early days at Louvain, the new *Chef de Rex ad interim* never succeeded in shaking off entirely that irreverent *esprit farceur* which had characterised the student origins of the movement. Even as Rex plunged deeper into collaboration, Matthys retained the mark of those early years, mocking the pomposity of those in authority be they the pre-war political elite or even the German authorities. José Streel, who knew Matthys well, stressed this division within Matthys between his sincere commitment to the goals of Rex and an attitude of student irresponsibility which refused to engage fully with the dark events in which he was implicated. When after the war he was apprehended and subsequently prosecuted for his wartime crimes, Matthys was one of the few leading Rexists who mounted an impressive and reasoned explanation of his collaborationist career, taking upon himself responsibility for many of the most incriminating Rexist actions. Yet, almost to the last, he retained that irreverent aspect to his character which led him to comment to Streel on one occasion during the Occupation: 'On ne sait pas comment tout ça finira, mais on se sera tout de même bien amusé.'[12]

Conscious no doubt of Matthys' inexperience, Degrelle took care to surround the new leader with more experienced advisers. Joseph Pévenasse as *Inspecteur Fédéral du Mouvement* assumed responsibility for Rexist local organisation and the *Formations de Combat*, while the veteran militant Maurice Vandevelde retained control of the finances of the movement. In addition, José Streel was appointed by Degrelle as *Conseiller Politique* of Rex. This was a new post and its responsibilities were initially vague but in practice the leader-writer of *Le Pays Réel* soon emerged as the principal adviser of Matthys.[13] Degrelle's intention was that these new leaders should merely act as the custodians of the Rexist organisation during what he expected to be his brief absence. His instructions to Matthys were to deal with 'l'expédition des affaires courantes du mouvement' and he discouraged the *Chef de Rex ad interim* from seeking to launch any new initiatives.[14] This was not merely a matter of practicalities. It also reflected Degrelle's deep disenchantment with the political situation in Occupied Belgium. He had become convinced that further progress was impossible and his departure for Russia was in effect an admission that he had abandoned the struggle for power within the country in favour of winning the support of the Germans from outside. Thus, his political strategy had taken on the simple form which it would retain until the final collapse of the Reich in the flames of Berlin: namely the pursuit of Nazi patronage through military success. Only with the return of the battle-hardened *légionnaires* did he believe that political progress would again become possible in Belgium and, as his speech on 8 August clearly demonstrated, he was already contemplating the rewards which would await the victorious Rexist soldiers: 'un jour nous reviendrons. Ayant tout donné, nous pourrons alors tout prendre'.[15]

The Rexists who stayed behind in Belgium did not, however, share fully their leader's attitude and many – including Matthys – were reluctant to abandon the political struggle entirely during the absence of the *légionnaires*. Thus, while not explicitly contradicting Degrelle's guide-lines, the new *Chef de Rex ad interim* promptly asserted that there should be no diminution in Rexist activity and, in a forceful message which was read out to all of the *cercles* on 7 September, he put forward his own strategy for the future development of Rex, declaring unambivalently: 'Je vous promets que vous serez commandés, je me promets que je me ferai obéir.'[16] Nor did Matthys limit himself to words. Conscious that his most obvious potential rival was Joseph Pévenasse, he used the occasion of a joint meeting of the Brussels *cercles* in September to receive a public oath of loyalty from the *Inspecteur Fédéral*. This was a dramatic gesture more akin perhaps to the feudal world than to a modern political movement but it proved effective and, after the incessant conflicts of the previous year, Matthys' determination to assert his personal authority appears to have been widely appreciated within Rex.[17]

Inevitably, the most important priority for Matthys and his colleagues was to overcome the organisational problems caused by the departure of the *légionnaires* and in his September message he called on all militants to dedicate themselves totally to this task: 'A l'égal des absents, nous devons nous considérer tous comme des soldats mobilisés qui ne peuvent connaître aucun repos avant la victoire, qui ne peuvent connaître d'autre occupation que le combat, d'autre objectif que la conquête.'[18] Rex, Matthys declared, must turn its back on its former civilian character and, in what would become a familiar refrain over the subsequent years, he insisted that the only hope for the future lay in emulating the authoritarian structures of other New Order movements. No longer would any 'esprit de clan' or sterile democratic discussion be allowed to disrupt the movement. Membership of Rex, Matthys and his colleagues insisted, was a total and irrevocable commitment and there could be no place in the movement for those unwilling to accept its rules.[19]

The whole thrust of Matthys' policies was directed towards ensuring that Rex became a self-contained, inward-looking movement. Despite his announcement in September of a recruitment drive supposedly intended to double the membership of Rex, few efforts were in practice made to enrol new members and the energies of militants were instead directed towards matters of internal organisation.[20] Matthys repeatedly warned his followers that they must expect to remain isolated from the majority of their compatriots and all dreams of leading a vast popular crusade had been abandoned in favour of making their movement a secure bastion within a hostile world.

These efforts were given greater impetus by the ever more pronounced antipathy of the population towards the Rexists. Those around them seized every opportunity to demonstrate their hostility to the Rexists and all that they represented. Shops, cafés and other businesses owned by militants of the movement were often deserted by much of their former non-Rexist clientele while other shopkeepers refused to serve the supporters of Rex.[21] One indication of the extent of such discrimination was that some Rexists began to experience material difficulties and a new organisation, *Solidarité Rexiste*, had to be established during 1941 with the aim of helping those in need of assistance. The departure of the *légionnaires* exacerbated these difficulties by depriving many Rexist families of their bread-winner and another organisation, *Solidarité Légionnaire*, had to be created to care for the relatives of the absent soldiers.[22]

Discrimination was supplemented by violence. Scuffles between Rexists and their opponents had long been commonplace but there was a sudden escalation in this violence in September 1941 when the Rexist *chef de cercle* in Tournai, Paul Gérard, was murdered at his home and a second Rexist militant, Jean Oedekerke, was killed by a parcel bomb sent to the Brussels offices of the *Formations de Combat*. These were the first Rexists to be assassinated and this sudden and apparently well-organised outbreak of violence inevitably had considerable repercussions both within and beyond the ranks of the movement. Political assassination was a relative novelty within Belgium and, though few mourned the victims of these attacks, many Belgians feared what they might herald.[23] In fact, they proved – at least in the short-term – to be isolated instances. The Brussels parcel bomb was apparently the work of Communist militants while the murder of Gérard was the work of a small group of local patriots who were soon arrested by the Nazi police.[24] The reaction within Rex to these attacks was one of anger and dismay. Long inured to blacklists and death threats, the Rexists were nevertheless entirely unprepared for this violence which their new leaders tried to blame variously on Communist assassins, agents of the government-in-exile in London and common criminals.[25] In an attempt to restore morale, the funerals and memorial services for the two victims were transformed into demonstrations of Rexist strength and, in his orations, Matthys promised the mourners that Rex had now reached the final stage in its quest for power, declaring: 'nous devons accepter nos morts, comme les conséquences naturelles de notre combat et comme les conditions de notre victoire'.[26] *Tableaux d'honneur* glorifying the Rexist martyrs were inaugurated in many *cercles* but the leadership also prudently acquired a small number of weapons and armed members of the *Formations de Combat* were present at the memorial service for Gérard. Although the German authorities accepted the need to distribute both arms permits and some hand-guns to vulnerable Rexist leaders, they still remained opposed to any general arming of the Rexists and discouraged all public display of this weaponry.[27]

The main priority for Rex remained the internal reorganisation of the movement and by the end of the year much had been achieved in this respect. The disruption caused by the departure of local and national leaders with the *Légion* had been overcome, the *cercles* were once again operating effectively and Matthys and his colleagues had established themselves as the unquestioned leaders of the movement. Consequently, as 1941 drew to a close, a cautious mood of optimism was evident within the movement. Despite the hostility of their compatriots and the murders of Gérard and Oedekerke, the Nazi attack on the Soviet Union was still regarded as the key event which had revealed the true sense of the international conflict and had opened the way to political progress. A consensus in favour of collaboration had at last emerged within the movement and even that most cautious of Rexists, José Streel, in an article entitled 'Degrelle avait raison' published in December 1941 praised Degrelle's initial pro-German declarations in January as an act of remarkable historical prescience.[28] This new mood of confidence was most clearly evident at a rally held at Liège in December 1941. This was the first occasion on which Matthys had addressed a mass meeting of Rexist militants and he used the occasion to present a confident and determined picture of the future of the movement. Dispensing with the lyrical extravagances and vague promises so typical of Degrelle's speeches, the interim leader of Rex recalled the many disappointments which the movement had experienced during the previous year but then went on to present the establishment of the *Légion* as the decisive event which had resolved all of these difficulties. Although its effects were yet to make themselves felt, the *Légion* – Matthys insisted – would be the vehicle which would win German favour and bring Rex to power and, with the German advances in the East apparently heralding a definitive military victory for the Axis powers, Matthys concluded his speech with an enthusiastic paeon of praise to Hitler, the man destined to be the leader of the New Europe.[29]

All Rexist hopes were, thus, focussed on the new tactic of military collaboration and in the autumn of 1941 the movement recruited a second military unit, the *Gardes Wallonnes*, which like the *Légion Wallonie* was to form part of the *Wehrmacht*. Its intended tasks were much less ambitious than those of the *Légion*. The *Gardes Wallonnes* were not to be front-line troops and would operate only within the jurisdiction of the *Militärverwaltung* (i.e. Belgium and the Nord and Pas de Calais in France) where they would guard places of strategic importance such as airfields, bridges and railway lines.[30] The initiative to create this auxiliary corps had come from the German administrators of Belgium who, as always, were anxious to reduce to a minimum the number of German soldiers deployed in the Occupied territories. As early as the spring of 1941, the *Wehrmacht Kommandostab* in Brussels had approached the leaders of Rex and of the *VNV* to suggest that they should recruit local military units to take over certain tasks from the German forces. Both Degrelle and the *VNV* responded favourably, hoping no doubt that, though the duties of the new soldiers would be mundane, the existence of these troops would strengthen their political position.[31] Thus, during May and June the plans for the new units were finalised and the *VNV* began to recruit volunteers for the new *Vlaamse Wacht*. Rex, on the other hand, was slower in launching its new corps and it was only on 6 July that Degrelle announced simultaneously the creation of the *Légion Wallonie* and of the *Gardes Wallonnes*. In doing so, the *Chef de Rex* did all he could to glorify the modest responsibilities of this auxiliary corps, the name of which had been chosen to recall the Walloon soldiers who in the seventeenth and eighteenth centuries had fought in the Habsburg armies. This 'armée de l'intérieur', he claimed with little justification, confirmed Rex's status as the only legal political movement in francophone Belgium and its soldiers would form the nucleus of a future New Order Belgian army.[32]

Yet, despite Degrelle's extravagant claims, the new unit was slow in

coming into existence. The simultaneous creation of the *Légion Wallonie*
and *Gardes Wallonnes* was a task beyond the modest capacities of Rex
and in mid-July the *Militärverwaltung* decided to suspend recruitment for
the *Gardes Wallonnes*, directing potential volunteers instead towards the
Légion.[33] Hence, it was only in September that the Rexist leaders turned
their attention once again to the *Gardes Wallonnes*. A new recruitment
campaign was launched aimed primarily at members of the *Formations
de Combat* but, unlike the very public recruitment drive for the *Légion
Wallonie*, little publicity was given to the new unit's creation. The reasons
for this discretion were primarily political. While the *Légion* had been
conceived as a propaganda initiative intended to impress both the Belgian
population and the German authorities, the *Gardes* were – at least in Rexist
eyes – an armed force operating within Belgium which might prove to be
of decisive importance in any eventual struggle for political power. The
Rexists were therefore eager to ensure that the *Gardes* were overwhelmingly
composed of reliable supporters of Rex and those non-Rexists who did
join were required also to join the *Formations de Combat*.[34]

Despite the depletion of the *Formations* by the creation of the *Légion*, a
significant number of Rexist militiamen were prevailed upon to join the
Gardes Wallonnes and the first battalion which assembled on 17 November
was composed of several hundred Rexists.[35] The relative success of this
recruitment drive undoubtedly owed much to the well-paid and secure
employment which service in the *Gardes* appeared to offer. It also provided
further evidence of the support which existed within Rex for the new
policy of military collaboration. Not all of the new recruits were mere
opportunists and some of those who entered the *Gardes Wallonnes* at this
time clearly did so in the belief that their participation, however modest,
in the ranks of the *Wehrmacht* would hasten the victory of the Rexist cause.

Therefore the political significance of the creation of this auxiliary corps
was considerably greater than the modest assistance it provided to the
German armies would suggest. As José Streel admitted, the guard duties
allocated to the new unit could be accomplished equally well by simple
mercenaries[36] and few of the arguments advanced to justify the creation of
the *Légion Wallonie* could be applied to the *Gardes Wallonnes*. Far from
participating in the crusade to save Europe from Bolshevism, the soldiers
in the new unit would be assisting the Germans directly by protecting
their installations in Belgium against potential attacks by Belgian patriots.
Thus, much more so than the *Légion*, the creation of the *Gardes Wallonnes*
demonstrated the willingness both of ordinary Rexist militants and of their
leaders to associate themselves directly with the German cause. Convinced
that they had at last discovered a means of winning Nazi support, they
were eager to exploit every opportunity to participate in the German
military campaigns, whatever the cost might be for Rex.

In the case of the *Gardes Wallonnes*, this cost was far from insignificant.

The creation of the new unit once again weakened the organisational structure of Rex and, while it was expected that the *légionnaires* would soon return from the war in the East, the men of the *Gardes Wallonnes* were lost to the movement until the conclusion of all hostilities. The greatest cost paid by Rex for the creation of both the *Gardes Wallonnes* and the *Légion Wallonie* was the virtual decimation of the *Formations de Combat*. Total membership of the Rexist militia had fallen to no more than 1,000 by the end of 1941.[37] From Wallonia alone, 900 men had left the *Formations* for service in the two military units while many others were reported to have withdrawn because of popular hostility or in order to work in Germany. In Charleroi, for example, membership of the militia had fallen from 700 to 210 and in many smaller towns – including Mons and Namur – only small groups of the old, the very young and the infirm remained by late 1941.[38] The leaders of Rex did their best to rectify this position. A thorough reorganisation of the militia's internal structure was carried out in January 1942 and a series of inspections and training exercises organised.[39] Matthys was, however, well aware that these efforts had had only a marginal impact and he frankly admitted after the war that the *Légion Wallonie* and *Gardes Wallonnes* had robbed the *Formations* of 'leurs éléments les plus dynamiques et les plus vigoureux'. The same point was made somewhat more colourfully by a local Rexist official in Brussels when he observed in November 1941 that the militia had become little more than an 'armée Mexicaine'.[40]

The same optimism which led so many ordinary Rexist militants to join the German armies was also at the root of the unexpected decision of José Streel to assume responsibility for the political affairs of Rex. Streel was a journalist and intellectual with no experience of administrative tasks and, despite being named as *conseiller politique* in August 1941,[41] it seemed at first unlikely that he would seek to exert much influence over Rex. In the event it was this diffident man, rather than the experienced Pévenasse, who proved the more willing to assist Matthys in the leadership of Rex during the absence of Degrelle. Some weeks after the departure of the *légionnaires*, Streel suggested to Matthys that a *Service Politique* be established within the national headquarters of Rex with responsibility for the political direction of the movement. Streel proposed himself as the head of the new department and, as he remarked after the war, his new-found enthusiasm for political activity was in part the consequence of 'la sorte de ferveur qui gagnait nos milieux' at the time of the creation of the *Légion*.[42] Possessing few of the attributes necessary for a military career, he had had no wish to participate in the adventures of the *Légion* but instead hoped to assist its cause by preparing the way for the acquisition of power within Belgium. Streel recognised that any successful seizure of power by the inexperienced Rexists would require careful preparation and he intended that the *Service Politique* should pave the way by developing the necessary policies as well as by infiltrating trusted supporters of Rex into positions of influence throughout central and local government.[43]

There was also a second, unstated purpose for Streel's proposal. By the autumn of 1941, his commitment to the cause of collaboration with Nazi Germany was beyond question. He remained convinced however that this policy of collaboration should always be limited to certain specific domains and he feared that the appointment of the inexperienced and impressionable Matthys might lead to a return to what he regarded as the indiscriminate and unprincipled 'adventurism' of the Rouleau era. Thus, Streel hoped to capitalise upon the more moderate orientation of the movement evident in Degrelle's speech on 8 August 1941 and, by establishing the *Service Politique*, to create a bastion for his own more moderate and nationalist views within the leadership of Rex.[44]

José Streel had always stood at an opposite pole within Rex to men such as Rouleau. A Rexist veteran rather than a new entrant, cautious rather than impulsive, a man of conviction rather than an opportunist, Streel was the most original thinker in Rex and, in deciding to pass from the realm of journalism to that of political activity, he was attempting to put into action his long held belief in the need for a profound political and spiritual revolution. His very personal vision of the crisis of modern society had changed little during more than ten years as a journalist and writer and, even during the German Occupation, he remained strongly influenced by the formative experiences of his youth. Born in 1911, Streel – like Matthys – was illegitimate and had been raised by his mother in modest circumstances in the industrial town of Jemeppe-sur-Meuse near Liège. He was a diligent and talented pupil and, unusually for somebody of his modest origins, Streel won a scholarship to attend the University of Liège where he received a doctorate for his work analysing the ideas of Henri Bergson and Charles Péguy. The writings of both men clearly exercised a considerable influence over the young Streel, as did those of other Catholic writers such as Jacques Maritain, Léon Bloy, and, inevitably, Charles Maurras, whose works he had discovered at the age of 14 and who would remain an important influence on Streel throughout his adult life.[45] During his university days, Streel contributed to a number of Catholic publications but in 1932 he came to the attention of a wider audience through his essay entitled 'Les jeunes gens et la politique'. In this polemical work, Streel posed as the spokesman of a new post-Maurrassian generation of young Catholics alienated from the established Catholic Party and the spiritual pieties of the *Association Catholique de la Jeunesse Belge*. Echoing the stance adopted at the same time by many younger Catholic intellectuals elsewhere in Europe, Streel declared that the need was to create an engaged and heroic Catholic faith which would challenge the established liberal order and offer an alternative to the materialism of fascism and communism.[46]

Streel had first met Degrelle in 1930 and, like so many others, he fell under the spell of the young publisher. He soon became a regular contributor to Rexist publications and was subsequently appointed as editor of the weekly '*Rex*' and later of the daily newspaper *Le Pays Réel*.[47] The clarity and consistency of his writings distinguished Streel from most of his colleagues in the Rexist press and he was one of the very few Rexist journalists whose opinions attracted an audience beyond the confines of the movement. Yet Streel always kept himself apart from the political activities of Rex preferring to trust to the talents and judgement of Degrelle. In character, he was very different from the turbulent and extrovert *Chef de Rex*. Shy, hesitant and reserved in conversation, Streel always retained the air of a young provincial somewhat ill at ease in Brussels. He was seen only rarely at the numerous literary and political events of the era and preferred the company of a few intellectual friends and of his young family.[48]

The revisionists who in recent years have sought to rehabilitate certain pro-Nazi intellectuals have often argued that their heroes strayed almost accidentally into collaboration through a mistaken assumption that Germany had achieved a definitive military victory in 1940. Had he lived, Streel would have had no sympathy for such arguments. He came to regard his espousal of collaboration as the culmination of his intellectual reflections and, though his personal loyalty to Degrelle and to the Rexist movement undoubtedly played its part in determining his wartime stance, it was his interpretation of modern European history which lay at the heart of his justification of collaboration. In common with Bainville, Maurras and many other Catholic writers of the early twentieth century, Streel insisted that since the eighteenth century, Europe had fallen victim to a seductive liberal ideology which had fostered the horrors of unrestrained economic growth and had divided the peoples of Europe from their Christian heritage. Liberalism was, however, a specious creed. Devoted to abstract principles, it ignored the deeper irrational realities which alone could ensure the survival of a civilisation. Hence, it had produced no lasting achievements and had culminated in the early years of the twentieth century in a profound spiritual crisis which manifested itself in the scepticism and nihilism of the intellectual elite and in the disguised barbarism of modern popular culture.[49]

Europe, Streel believed, was threatened with ruin but fortunately a broad intellectual and political reaction had taken place against the easy pleasures of liberal individualism. This revolution offered the possibility of salvation because it worshipped no abstract creed and based itself on what Streel referred to insistently as the 'realities' of the modern age: 'La révolution qui s'accomplit sous nos yeux marque un retour aux réalités empiriques, aux exigences de la vie, à la primauté de l'organique sur l'idéologique.'[50] This 'révolution du vingtième siècle' was the cause to which Streel pledged his personal allegiance. Although he remained a practising Catholic during the German Occupation, he had abandoned his youthful hopes of some form of Catholic spiritual reconquest of society. Instead, it was this secular vision of a wide-ranging regeneration and rejuvenation of Europe which had become the focus of his hopes. This reorientation in Streel's ideology was also reflected in his attitude to Italian Fascism and German Nazism. In his writings in the early and mid-1930s, he had defined his vision of a specifically Catholic revolution against the supposedly materialist and pagan values of these totalitarian creeds. However, in common with many of those who remained loyal to Rex during its drift towards the extreme-right of the political spectrum in the immediate pre-war years, he gradually tempered his hostility to the Italian and German regimes. The demise of hopes of a 'third way' between fascism and liberalism had led Streel in effect to accept that fascism – and even Nazism – did indeed form part of the same broad anti-liberal revolution. All were united by a common spirit which, in characteristically Bergsonian terms, Streel portrayed as a 'mystique créatrice' challenging the sterility of liberal rationalism.[51]

The Second World War became for Streel the decisive encounter between the old liberal order and the forces of regeneration. Although he was optimistic that events such as Mussolini's March on Rome in 1922 would in retrospect be seen as having had the same historical significance as the storming of the Bastille in 1789, he recognised that the success of the 'révolution du vingtième siècle' was not assured. Even the most remorseless historical force could be destroyed by human ignorance or folly and it remained possible that Europe would fail to seize the historical opportunity with which it was presented. All would depend, therefore, on the outcome of the war and in his wartime journalism Streel continually portrayed Europe as standing at a crucial moment in its history, when it could either progress towards a new High Middle Ages or collapse into the barbarism of the Dark Ages.[52]

If European culture did survive, Streel foresaw a new golden age in which the natural, fragile order of civilisation would be restored. He frequently employed organic metaphors describing this new world as one in which communities, purged of the alien, cosmopolitan influences of the liberal era, would regain their unity. There was an indisputably nostalgic air to this vision and, like many influenced by the ideas of Maurras, Streel never freed himself entirely from the spell of a harmonious pre-industrial world. Yet he vehemently denied that he sought to reverse the course of history. The new order, he declared, would not retreat from the complexities of industrial society but would overcome them. Above all, Streel fervently believed that the restructuring of society would end the moral and material alienation of the industrial working class from the social order. In the new world, their labour would be valued in human rather than economic terms and a spirit of common service for the community would replace exploitation by plutocratic capitalism.[53]

This utopian vision had little in common with the oppressive conformity and bureaucratic structures commonly associated with fascist states. There was to be no formal state ideology but instead a new value structure in which selfish individualism was superseded by what Streel considered to be the values of the old Christian civilisation of Europe such as fraternity, loyalty and faith.[54] Nor would there be an intrusive state apparatus. A strong state, a single party and an undisputed leader were, Streel admitted, all essential for the accomplishment of the revolution but he envisaged that these would subsequently wither away as institutions of local self-government such as corporations took their place. These would ultimately form the basis of a devolved society in which the mechanisms of external constraint would be unnecessary and the specious liberal contract between governor and governed would be replaced by a united popular community.[55]

This ideology with its strange amalgam of naïve Catholic idealism and crude historical determinism won few converts in the stark circumstances of the German Occupation. The attention of both the readers of Le Pays Réel and their patriotic opponents was absorbed by other more pressing concerns and they took little interest in such intellectual speculations. The importance of Streel's ideas lies in the light which they shed on the complex intellectual heritage which on occasions lay behind an individual's espousal of collaboration. Throughout much of Europe, the previous twenty years had been a period of unprecedented fluidity when the widespread conviction that the liberal political and economic system was exhausted had given rise to a plethora of projects and movements which often transcended the traditional categories of the political spectrum. Established labels such as left and right, or socialist, liberal and conservative came to seem somewhat outmoded and, though most such initiatives proved transitory and insubstantial, these 'non-conformist' ventures of the 1930s often provided the bridge by which certain intellectuals subsequently entered the world of collaboration.[56] In Streel's case his initial enthusiasm in the early 1930s to define a new form of Catholic politics which challenged the values and institutions of a secular liberal world set him on an intellectual course which culminated in his espousal of collaboration with a Nazi regime which in its principles and actions stood in categorical opposition to the Catholic religion.

The key to this progression from Catholic idealism to pro-Nazi collaboration lay in Streel's anxiety to see all contemporary developments as the enactment of a broad historical conflict between the forces of decline and regeneration. Collaboration with Germany became for him nothing less than a necessity imposed by history in order to prevent the collapse of the West in an anarchy of dissolution. In the early months of the Occupation, Streel, as we have seen, was reluctant to endorse collaboration fully and his writings at that time went no further than to argue that the military defeat of May 1940 gave Belgium no choice but to work with Germany. However, as we have seen, with the German invasion of Russia, Streel abandoned this measured tone and henceforth he had no hesitation in portraying the war as an apocalyptic struggle against the materialistic, barbarian enemies of western civilisation.[57]

This rigid analysis of the nature of the conflict proved to be an intellectual prison from which Streel was never to escape. During the latter years of the war he recognised that the ascendancy of extremist elements within the Reich gave little hope that a German victory would in fact herald an authentic European revolution. Hence, in January 1943 he withdrew from all political activity and his writings during the remaining years of the war displayed an increasing belief that the real solution to the crisis of modern Europe was moral rather than political in nature.[58] Streel remained convinced to the last that an Allied victory would only hasten the demise of European civilisation. Thus, even from his post-war prison cell he observed with little optimism the reconstruction of Europe, writing sombrely in 1945: 'les Barbares sont aux portes et leurs émissaires sont déjà dans la Cité. L'Occident est menacé de sombrer dans le byzantinisme politique et la dissolution morale'.[59]

Yet, although, perhaps more than any other Rexist of importance, Streel was convinced of the intellectual and political rectitude of collaboration, this conviction always went hand in hand with a belief that it was a policy which must be followed with the greatest caution. The spectacle of an unprincipled collaboration based on an abandonment of all patriotic loyalties was one which continually haunted Streel. He felt a profound loyalty to his country which went much deeper than any repetition of conventional formulae and his wartime journalism was dominated by an insistence that collaboration must always be reconciled with an overriding commitment to the interests of Belgium. This led him into conflict with those Rexists anxious to work directly with the German authorities and he frequently exhorted the Rexists to avoid all servility in their dealings with the German forces and to guard against the danger of 'dénationalisation'. Collaboration, he rather optimistically insisted, must always be practised in a dignified spirit of partnership, declaring: 'La collaboration est une chose. L'aplatissement en est une autre qui confine à la trahison.'[60]

Streel was especially anxious that the advocates of collaboration should not be drawn into a derivative imitation of German ideology. In each country the New Order revolution must take its own distinctive form and he regarded those extremists who mouthed Germanic phraseology and advocated the introduction of Nazi policies in Belgium as infantile opportunists lacking in both scruples and realism: 'Les idées nouvelles sont comme des explosifs qu'il est dangereux de laisser aux mains des enfants. Quand on ne sait comment les manier, il en résulte des catastrophes.'[61]

For Streel, as for many other Belgian collaborationists, Germany always remained a distant land of which he knew little. He derived no pleasure from his few contacts with German officials and throughout the war retained an instinctive antipathy to Nazi ideas. They were, in his opinion, the product of an alien culture dominated by a very distinct national psychology and, though the spirit of the Nazi revolution was to be admired, its wholesale application in Belgium would be an unwelcome and doomed enterprise.[62]

This vision of an almost abstract collaboration which would avoid contamination by Nazism demonstrated clearly the political impact which Streel hoped his *Service Politique* would have on the direction of Rex. He saw the new office as the means whereby Rex would pursue a policy of collaboration by working alongside the German authorities in a spirit of common purpose. Above all, Streel hoped to use his new position to ensure that Rex should remain loyal to its own past. Though he accepted the need for some minor alterations in Rexist ideology in order to adapt to new realities, the basic tenets of its pre-war Rexist beliefs were, he believed, still valid. Moreover, it was only by keeping faith with these ideas that the Rexists would ensure their political success. Collaboration, he continually reminded the readers of *Le Pays Réel*, must be based on the firm ground of realism and avoid the temptations of servile imitation. In a typically trenchant comment in November 1941, he declared: 'l'orthod-oxie rexiste ne se mesure nullement à l'enthousiasme qu'on éprouve pour l'uniforme feldgrau'.[63]

Streel's views were not to the liking of many within the movement and his relations with Degrelle were not always easy. The *Chef de Rex* shared little of Streel's instinctive caution and apparently referred to him with some frustration on one occasion as a 'petit pion de province dont les scrupules l'empêcheront d'aller loin'.[64] Nevertheless, Matthys recognised the value of Streel's proposal and gave his approval for the creation of the *Service Politique* which came into operation during the autumn of 1941.[65] It was intended that the department should be responsible for all of the political activities of Rex and, with the handful of staff at his disposal, Streel created specialised sub-sections responsible for the various areas of public life.[66] Its further expansion was, however, hampered by the perpetual Rexist problem of finance. In the latter years of the war Rex would benefit from substantial grants from its German sponsors, but at this time its resources remained very limited. The salaries of those employed by the movement were low and, despite continual appeals, the modest income provided by a declining membership seems never to have been sufficient even to cover the basic needs of Rex.[67] Financial insolvency often threatened and that the movement survived at all during the early years of the war seems to have owed much to somewhat imaginative methods of accounting coupled with German hand-outs and, one must suspect, periodic injections of funds from Degrelle's not inconsiderable personal wealth. The *Service Politique* maintained itself only through those donations which Streel was able to collect from businessmen sympathetic to Rex or anxious to curry favour with the movement and all attempts to give it a sounder financial basis – including an approach to the influential industrial magnate, the Baron de Launoit, who had helped to finance the Rexist press in 1936 – proved unsuccessful.[68]

Despite these difficulties, the *Service Politique* soon established itself as the foremost department of the *Etat-Major* and, though Streel combined his direction of the department with his journalistic activities, his new position firmly established him as the most influential adviser of the *Chef de Rex ad interim*.[69] This duumvirate of Matthys and Streel was further reinforced at the end of 1941 by the appointment of Marcel Dupont to the new post of *Chef des Cadres Territoriaux*. A *représentant de commerce* by profession, Dupont was a faithful Rexist veteran of few political ambitions who took charge both of the secretariat and finances of the *Etat-Major* as well as supervising the operation of local Rexist groups.[70] As such, he took over much of the work formerly accomplished by Pévenasse whose *Inspectorat Fédéral du Mouvement* rapidly lost much of its importance. Thus, though Pévenasse remained a prominent figure at Rexist rallies, he lacked a clear power base within the movement and by the end of 1941 he seems to have retained little influence over the formulation of policy.[71]

The reasons for this shift in power remain unclear. Pévenasse did not appear to resist his demotion and he subsequently left to join the *Légion Wallonie*. Hence, it is possible that he was reluctant to remain in Belgium at a time when events on the Eastern front seemed to be of pre-eminent importance. It is, however, also likely that Matthys and Streel deliberately sought to reduce the power of their more experienced colleague. Pévenasse was a senior figure with substantial personal support within Rex whom Matthys may well have regarded as a potential threat to his leadership. Moreover, he was an impulsive emotional man who typified the combative and extremist image of Rex which Streel was anxious to change. Whatever the explanation Pévenasse's withdrawal was of considerable importance for the future direction of Rex. He was to remain absent from Belgium until 1943 and his departure, by confirming Matthys and Streel as the effective leaders of the movement, opened the way to the introduction of the more moderate policies favoured by Streel.[72]

These personnel changes took place, moreover, at a time when the relations between Rex and the *Militärverwaltung* were at last beginning to be placed on a firmer footing. This change owed little if anything to the strenuous efforts of Degrelle and the Rexists to convince the Germans of their importance. Instead, it was largely a by-product of the increasing hostility faced by the German administrators of Occupied Belgium and their consequent need to seek out new, more dependable agents to implement their policies. The Germans, as we have seen, had arrived in Belgium with few political ambitions regarding the francophone population. Faithful to the instructions they had received from Hitler, the *Wehrmacht* administrators initially regarded Wallonia largely as a future *terre de colonisation* for the Flemish nation where the German armies should do no more than maintain public order and promote industrial output. Therefore they paid little attention to political matters, preferring to develop a working relationship with the established leaders of society.[73] During the latter months of 1941, this policy did, however, gradually change. In part, the impulse for this change came from within the Third Reich. Certain Nazi leaders such as Himmler and Heydrich were coming to regard the Walloons as a 'lost' Germanic people and, encouraged perhaps by an awareness of this change in attitude, Reeder and his colleagues began to take a belated interest in the political potential of the francophone Belgians. Cultural policies were inaugurated intended to raise the francophone Belgians out of their 'politisch-kulturellen Apathie' and to foster an awareness of their Germanic heritage. To this end, Reeder encouraged a programme of pro-German cultural activities and gave financial assistance to those small groups such as the *Communauté Culturelle Wallonne* of Pierre Hubermont and *AGRA* willing to act as the standard-bearers for the new ideas.[74]

Rex had no place in this cultural process. In the opinion of the *Militär-verwaltungschef*, Degrelle's movement was wedded irredeemably to a 'Belgicist' and francophone outlook and he hoped that the pro-German cultural groups would eventually supersede Rex as the basis of collaborationist activity in the region. Nevertheless, Reeder also recognised that his grand design for a cultural reorientation of Wallonia could only be a very long-term goal. For the immediate future, he was faced with more pressing problems which – as he reported to Berlin in December 1941 – gave him little option but to work with the Rexists. Despite their many faults, they remained the only substantial pro-German grouping and to abandon them after they had sent their elite to fight on the Eastern front would be politically unacceptable. Thus the other pro-German groups were instructed to confine their activities to the cultural domain and for the first time the *Militärverwaltung* began, in the last months of 1941, to provide significant political assistance to Degrelle's supporters.[75]

This support for Rex was, in part, a reflection of the failure of rival groups such as the *MNPW* and *AGRA* to establish themselves as credible alternatives to Rex but it also illustrated the limited nature of the options open to the German administrators by the end of 1941. Their overriding short-term concern was always to control Belgium with the minimal deployment of German manpower and, while they had initially been able to rely on the acquiescence of much of the Belgian bureaucracy, the subsequent polarisation of political loyalties had imposed serious strains on this cohabitation. The structure of the Belgian civil service headed by the committee of *secrétaires-généraux* remained in place and continued to work with the German authorities on many matters of a mundane nature. But the realisation – first evident in the spring of 1941 – among these civil servants that the German military victory was far from assured caused a discernible hardening in their attitudes towards Reeder and his colleagues. On the German side the need to mobilise all resources for a total war against not only Great Britain but also now the Soviet Union and, from December 1941, the United States, made it imperative that they find agents willing to act as the executants within Belgium of policies designed explicitly to aid the Nazi war effort. The ineluctable consequence of these developments was to oblige the *Militärverwaltung* to turn to the collab- orationists of the *VNV* and of Rex. Contacts multiplied between the Rexist *cercles* and the German authorities and, for the first time, the Germans began to contemplate integrating substantial numbers of Rexists into local government to act as the executants of their decrees.[76]

This *de facto* alliance between the *Militärverwaltung* and the Rexists would become progressively closer as the war continued. Reeder never abandoned his aim of making the Walloon people more aware of their Germanic roots[77] but the circumstances of the later war years offered little hope for an effective cultural policy and the imperative need for reliable allies always took precedence. Faced on every side by passive obstruction or active resistance, the *Wehrmacht* officials in Brussels discovered to their evident distaste that they needed the Rexists just as much as Degrelle's supporters were dependant on the protection and support offered by the Germans. His increased contact with the Rexists did little, however, to cause the President of the *Militärverwaltung* to revise his low opinion of Rex and, more especially, of Degrelle whom he continued to regard as an untrustworthy adventurer.[78] However Reeder's often outspoken criticisms of the Rexist leader disguised his position of weakness. In reality, the Rexists had become the indispensable agents of the German authorities in Wallonia.

This enforced partnership was also not without consequences for Rex. It brought the movement out of its isolated position and, rather than remain- ing disruptive outsiders critical of the status quo, the Rexists became – like the supporters of the *VNV* in Flanders – to some extent an element of the established order of German-occupied Belgium. Within Rex, this new quasi-official status discouraged the extremist revolutionary mentality which had been evident during the first year of the Occupation and contributed to the ascendancy of Streel's more moderate views. On the other hand, by drawing the movement ever more directly into the admin- istration of Occupied Belgium, it reinforced the pro-German stance of Rex. Collaboration ceased to be a matter of symbolic gestures and boisterous declarations but became the principal daily activity and, eventually, the all- absorbing *raison d'être* of the movement.

In February 1942, the patient efforts of Matthys and Streel to rebuild the

Rexist organisation were suddenly interrupted by the arrival from Russia of a *légionnaire*, Jean Vermeire, bearing new orders from Degrelle. The fierce hardships of the Russian winter as well as skirmishes with enemy forces had severely depleted the *Légion* to the point that it was threatened with disbandment. For Degrelle this would have been an intolerable humiliation and he ordered his supporters to recruit several hundred new volunteers immediately.[79] These instructions caused astonishment among the Rexist leaders. Contact between Belgium and the Eastern Front had not been easy and, though the Rexist leadership had known something of the problems encountered by their comrades in Russia, they had regarded the creation of the *Légion* as a once and for all effort.[80] Nevertheless, there could be no question of ignoring Degrelle's orders and a recruitment campaign was immediately launched with the initial aim of enrolling 300 new soldiers by the end of February. The Rexists were under no illusion that even this modest target would be easy to achieve and Pévenasse wrote to militants of the need for 'un authentique miracle de Rex'. Their task was made all the more difficult by Degrelle's insistence that only 'rexistes sûrs' should be recruited. Ever since the *Légion*'s creation, the *Chef de Rex* had been embroiled in a series of acrimonious disputes with non-Rexist *légionnaires* who resented his attempts to subordinate the unit to his personal control and he clearly hoped to use the opportunity presented by this further recruitment effort to consolidate his hold over the *Légion*.[81]

Vermeire, Pévenasse, Matthys and other leaders toured the Rexist *cercles* throughout Brussels and Wallonia in search of potential recruits. It was not an easy task. Recruitment for the *Légion* as well as for the *Gardes Wallonnes* had already absorbed most of those militants who were attracted by a military career and those who had remained behind were, on the whole, unwilling to forsake their families and jobs to participate in such adventures. Moreover, while in August 1941 it had appeared that the *Légion* would be participating in a harmless *promenade militaire*, those who joined this second contingent were all too aware that they would be drawn into a violent war against a determined enemy. As one Rexist wife wrote unambivalently to her husband: 'On veut vous envoyer mourir au front russe; je ne veux pas que tu parte . . . Tu dois quitter ce mouvement et ne pas aller à la *Légion Wallonie*.'[82] In response, the Rexist leader tried to reassure the hesitant with promises that the Nazi armies were poised for victory in the East and that the new recruits would be joining the *Légion* only for the final triumphant advance before returning to form the political elite of the new Belgium. The time had come, declared Pévenasse in a circular to all militants, for those 'enfants gâtés' of Rex to prove that they too were willing to risk their lives for the cause and, in an evident attempt to set an example, a number of *chefs de cercles* as well as Brahy, the commander of the *Formations de Combat*, and Pévenasse himself were among the first to enrol in the new contingent.[83]

All these efforts were, however, largely in vain and the Rexist leadership was obliged to resort to what in effect amounted to a policy of conscription. Addressing a major rally in Brussels on 22 February, Matthys ordered all but a few of the local and national Rexist leaders to join the *Légion*. The survival of the military unit, he declared, was of paramount importance for the future both of Belgium and of Rex and the disruption that the departure of these experienced men would inevitably cause to the movement within the country was a price which the Rexists must accept: 'Il importe peu que certains secteurs soient actuellement laissés en friche si à l'heure décisive nous avons ces hommes qui forceront le destin.'[84]

This order was unambivalent and on the appointed date of 10 March some 450 volunteers assembled on the Grand Place in Brussels, before marching past the Rexist headquarters in the avenue du Midi.[85] Unlike the first contingent of volunteers, the departure of these new *légionnaires* was an emphatically Rexist event and it seems that the vast majority were indeed members of the movement. The superficially impressive total had, however, been achieved only by transferring a number of men from the *Gardes Wallonnes* and, despite the presence of Pévenasse and other senior Rexist officials, the most prominent group in the new unit were 150 or so teenage boys from the *Jeunesses Rexistes*. Some of these short-trousered soldiers were as young as 15 or 16 years old and they formed a distinct unit under the command of their leader John Hagemans, the *Prévôt* of the *Jeunesses Rexistes*.[86]

Although it remains unclear whether Degrelle or the Rexist leaders in Belgium were responsible for the decision to enrol these adolescents, the recruitment campaign had from an early stage paid much attention to attracting their support. Special meetings of the *Jeunesses Rexistes* had taken place and the decisions of Hagemans and of several of his assistants to volunteer were given wide publicity.[87] Strenuous efforts were made to reassure the recruits and more especially their parents that they would come to no harm and Hagemans and other Rexist leaders reportedly promised that the young soldiers would only make propaganda tours of Germany, the Balkans and liberated areas of Russia before returning to Belgium for the new school year in the autumn.[88] On their arrival in Russia, however, all such assurances were rapidly forgotten and Degrelle insisted that the members of the *Jeunesses Rexistes* must join the other *légionnaires* at the front. Hagemans was apparently outraged by this deception but his protests to the *Chef de Rex* were to no avail and many of these adolescent soldiers – as well as Hagemans himself – subsequently perished in the fierce battles in the Caucasus region during the summer and autumn of 1942.[89]

The consequences of this further recruitment campaign were predictable. The *Jeunesses Rexistes* were decimated by the departure of their leaders and, though Hagemans' successors attempted to remedy the situation, the youth groups never recovered from these losses.[90] The impact on the adult organisation was also substantial. Rex had once again been deprived of many of its most experienced militants and the impact of these departures was compounded by the decision of Matthys to censure those local Rexist officials who had defied his orders to join the *Légion*. The *Chef de Rex ad interim* was clearly anxious to stamp out any such disobedience and, a few days after the departure of the new contingent of volunteers, he dismissed a number of officials who had failed to respond to his orders.[91]

Thus, the recruitment campaign's success had been achieved only at the price of further weakening the structure of the movement and, ultimately, of sending a large number of Rexist youths to their deaths in Central Asia. By any standard it was a Pyrrhic victory, but few in the Rexist leadership seem to have subsequently felt any remorse on learning of these deaths. Collaboration was a harsh world in which there was little place for the weaknesses of human emotions and the Rexist leaders remained convinced that any sacrifice was worthwhile in order to obtain the all-important political support of the Nazi leadership. Their eyes fixed unswervingly on this illusory final goal, the Rexists were doomed to advance ever further into an abyss which would bring only death, popular odium and, ultimately, disaster for their cause.

Chapter Four

Spring – Autumn 1942

Between Moderation and Extremism

IN POPULAR memory, collaboration is recalled principally as the unscrupulous pursuit and abuse of power. The image of the collaborator as an arrogant, ambitious figure profiting from the presence of the German armies to exert arbitrary, dictatorial control over his compatriots while at the same time servilely executing every German order – however base it might be – is one which recurs throughout Occupied Europe. It is, nevertheless, an image markedly at variance with the position of the Rexists during much of the German Occupation of Belgium. Rex, tied umbilically to the ever more grandiose ambitions of Degrelle, was indeed engaged in the pursuit of power at almost any cost and during the final years of German rule it would eventually come close to attaining its goal. But for much of the Occupation, the Rexists remained a marginal group obliged to content themselves with the semblances of power. Certainly, their ever closer relationship with the *Militärverwaltung* did bring them some tangible rewards, and the Rexists leapt hungrily upon even the slightest symbols of success and authority, but such posturing was often little more than nervous play-acting. Though they happily used the Rexists to perform certain essential tasks, the Germans continued to withhold approval of their political ambitions and without this support the Rexists always lacked much of that arrogant confidence commonly associated with pro-German collaborators. Instead, they remained a frustrated group unable to enact their cherished revolution and trapped in a position which, as the war progressed, came to seem less and less promising.

This nervous, defensive mood was particularly evident in 1942 during Degrelle's long absence on the Eastern front. With the departure of Pévenasse to join the *Légion*, a period of transition within Rex had drawn to a close. Matthys and Streel were securely established as the leaders of the movement and they appeared well placed to relaunch Rex as a political force within Occupied Belgium. Both the network of *cercles* introduced in mid-1941 and the changes which had taken place in the central headquarters enabled the leadership to exercise more effective control over the wide range of Rexist activities. Rex remained a somewhat chaotic confederation where – as Streel subsequently observed – a superficially imposing hierarchy often disguised 'la plus aimable pagaille'.[1] A considerable improvement had nevertheless taken place. Structures of command existed and were respected, while the appointment of loyal, unambitious men such as Dupont and Constant to posts such as *Chef des Cadres Territoriaux* and Commander of the *Formations de Combat* ensured that the movement was no longer threatened by a resurgence of the bitter personal rivalries so evident during the previous year.

Yet, despite these advantages, much of the energies of Matthys and Streel during 1942 were to be devoted not to new initiatives but to the defence of existing positions. This reflected the general sense of insecurity which gradually enveloped the movement as the German Occupation entered its third year. The early months of 1942 formed in this respect a crucial watershed. In late 1941, as we have seen, Rexist morale was probably higher than at any time during the previous year but, as during the following months it became evident that the war on the Eastern front and the creation of the *Légion Wallonie* had done little – at least in the short term – to resolve the political stalemate within Occupied Belgium, so the mood of the Rexists changed to one of pessimism and frustration. Doomed apparently to remain an isolated, marginal group, the Rexists no longer felt entirely confident that, in a much more uncertain world, they were indeed the men of the future.

This decline in Rexist morale was all the more striking because it was in marked contrast to the ebullient, aggressive mood of the *VNV* which continued to attract new recruits and whose leaders remained convinced that they were poised to become the undisputed masters of the country.[2] The Rexists remained in almost every respect the poor cousins of the Flemish Nationalists within the collaborationist world. Not only did they lack the *VNV*'s access to German political support but they had still received no clear signal from the Nazi authorities that Belgium would indeed survive as a political unit within any future German-dominated Europe. For all of the opportunist changes enacted in Rexist ideology by Degrelle, the Rexists remained firmly committed to some form of binational Flemish-Walloon state and they increasingly feared that the favouritism shown to the Flemish by the *Militärverwaltung*, combined with the continued absence of German support for the creation of a collaborationist government in Belgium, indicated a secret Nazi plan to dismember the country. In fact, such fears were exaggerated. Leading Nazis – including Hitler himself – did indeed regard Belgium as an artificial diplomatic creation and intended that any future German-imposed political settlement in the country would reflect the aspiration of the Flemish for some form of national autonomy. Such vague principles fell far short of a clear commitment to abolish a unitary Belgian state however and no consensus existed within the highest reaches of the Reich or even in Hitler's mind as to Belgium's future status.[3] The Rexists, though, had little insight into the confused improvisation which characterised Nazi decision-making and – in common with many other francophone Belgians – they feared that Wallonia would either be absorbed into the German Reich or, at best, be forced to act as the colony of a Greater Flanders. For the Rexists neither option was attractive and, despite the constraints imposed by German censorship, Streel and other Rexists used their press to hint at the difficulties which this ominous silence created for those seeking to work with the German authorities.[4]

Uncertainties over the outcome of the war added to Rexist unease. The spring of 1942 was perhaps the last moment when an outright German victory seemed a realistic – if distinctly unlikely – possibility and the Rexist press greeted with enthusiasm the renewed German offensive in the East.[5] But the reverses subsequently suffered by the Axis forces rapidly undermined this optimism. *Le Pays Réel* was obliged to admit that Germany had lost the military initiative and, as the *Wehrmacht* commenced defensive preparations on the French and Belgian coasts, the Rexist leaders attempted to discount the widespread rumours of an imminent Allied invasion. Uncomfortable Napoleonic analogies had already begun to surface in the minds of many militants and by the summer of 1942, whatever their public efforts to present a brave face, the Rexist leaders were privately beginning to contemplate the possibility of some form of German military collapse.[6]

Rexist justifications of collaboration had to be revised to adapt to these new realities. It was no longer possible to portray the German victory as an assured fact and the Rexists, like many other supporters of the Nazi cause throughout Europe, increasingly sought refuge from the uncomfortable realities of the military situation by adopting a crude historical determinism. If the latest German communiqués could not be used to justify their support for the Nazi cause, a broader historical process had to be invoked instead. Thus, José Streel, for example, sought to distract his readers' attention from the events on the various military fronts by reassuring them that an 'accidental' Allied victory would be no more successful in arresting the New Order revolution than had been Wellington's victory at Waterloo in preventing the liberal revolution of the nineteenth century. The victory of the New Order cause was ordained by history: 'C'est la vie qui exige que cette révolution se fasse . . . Une éventuelle – très éventuelle – victoire des Anglo-Saxonnes ne pourrait contrarier le cours des choses. Dans la meilleure hypothèse, elle aurait pour seul résultat de modifier le personnel, l'étiquette et le style de la révolution du XXe siècle. Cela est, dès à présent, certain.'[7] Even Streel seems at times to have found such arguments unconvincing and he was forced instead to compare collaboration to a wager. There could not, he admitted, be any guarantee of victory. All would depend not only on the course of the military struggle but also on the attitude adopted by the Nazis towards Belgium in the event of a German victory and, like Pascal pondering the existence of God, the Rexists could only hope that their stance would be justified by subsequent events.[8]

In this uncertain atmosphere Rex no longer possessed a strategy for the immediate acquisition of power. Rumours of a Rexist *coup d'état* continued to circulate intermittently in Brussels but Matthys clearly lacked the authority to launch a direct challenge to the status quo and he and his colleagues discounted hopes of an imminent political breakthrough. Instead, the *Légion Wallonie* became the focus of Rexist hopes. Degrelle's promise of his triumphal return at the head of the *légionnaires* was the dream which fortified many ordinary militants during these difficult times and the leadership remained confident that the *Légion* would eventually achieve the double feat of winning German support for their cause as well as acting as the decisive political force within Belgium.[9]

Hopes of the return of the conquering heroes were, however, repeatedly dashed. Throughout 1942 the *Légion* had little respite from the bloody conflicts of the Eastern front where it was frequently to the fore in German offensives. Unlike many of the other units of foreign volunteers who fought in Russia, the Walloon *légionnaires* soon distinguished themselves as courageous and effective soldiers but it was a reputation achieved only at considerable cost. In February, almost 200 *légionnaires* were killed or wounded in one battle in the Ukraine while the losses incurred from the ravages of disease and enemy action during the *Légion*'s subsequent role in the summer offensive in southern Russia were such that, despite the reinforcements sent from Belgium, the effective strength of the *Légion* was no more than 200 men by October. Degrelle was to the fore in these military campaigns. To the considerable surprise of both his colleagues and the German officers, the Rexist leader proved to be no mere *soldat de propagande*. He was often in the thick of the action and in recognition of his achievements was awarded the Iron Cross and promoted to the rank of lieutenant. His involvement in battle did not, however, cause Degrelle to lose sight of his political ambitions. Through a series of manoeuvres during 1942, he consolidated his personal ascendancy over the *Légion* which by the end of the year had become an emphatically Rexist – or even Degrellian – unit. Similarly, his absence from Belgium did not lead Degrelle to abandon his pursuit of German favour and he sedulously exploited his growing military reputation to forge friendships with those German officers whom he encountered in Russia.[10]

Though they greeted the *Légion*'s triumphs with enthusiasm, the Rexists in Belgium were painfully aware of the cost of this military adventure. News of the first substantial losses reached Brussels in late March and throughout 1942 obituary notices for *légionnaires* featured prominently in the columns of *Le Pays Réel*.[11] Many of those who died were the relatives or friends of militants and the difficulties of communication with the front meant that there was often a long and agonising wait before they received news of their loved ones.[12] Grief and mourning became all too familiar rituals in the Rexist world and the activities of the *cercles* were inevitably overshadowed by concern for the *légionnaires*. Expressions of solidarity with the volunteers in Russia took myriad forms. Memorial services were held in honour of the dead and visits organised to those wounded soldiers hospitalised in Brussels. Collections of money, of warm clothing and even of items such as skis took place regularly while numerous parties were held for the families of the *légionnaires*.[13]

There was, however, in reality little that could be done to help their distant soldiers, and the leaders of Rex tried instead to focus the attention of their followers on the need to restore the internal structure of the movement. A new generation of officials had to be found to replace those who had departed to the East and, despite the *Etat-Major*'s best efforts, there was a continual shortage of candidates for responsible positions at both a central and local level. In these circumstances, external activity was necessarily limited and once again a proposed recruitment campaign was postponed indefinitely.[14] This concern with organisational matters never caused Streel to lose sight of his central ambition of establishing Rex as a bastion of moderate collaborationist opinion. Distinctions between 'moderate' and 'extremist' definitions of collaboration are easily exaggerated. Subtle nuances of opinion within the pro-German minority paled into insignificance when compared with the chasm which separated collaborators from the patriotic majority. Moreover, the very concept of a moderate 'patriotic' collaboration has often been exploited by certain former collaborationists and those who share their views in an attempt to lend credibility to their wartime actions.[15] Nevertheless, there was a clear distinction between Streel's undoubtedly sincere belief that collaboration should be pursued within certain limits and those other Rexists – including Degrelle – who had long since abandoned any pretence at restraint. Although Streel sought at his trial to exaggerate his moderating influence, it was no mere illusion summoned up to impress his post-war judges.[16] Under his control, a modest change did indeed take place in the direction of Rex. He halted the increasing radicalism which had been so evident during 1941 and the opportunism of men such as Rouleau and Degrelle gave way to a more coherent – and limited – definition of collaboration. This change did not go unnoticed beyond the ranks of Rex. Though it failed to tame popular hostility towards the movement, it did lay the basis for a gradual *rapprochement* between Rexism and those more cautious pro-German figures such as the editor of *Le Soir*, Raymond De Becker, who had formerly dismissed Rex as the epitome of unprincipled collaboration but who now began to praise its 'orientation fermement nationale'.[17]

The success of Streel's strategy depended in large measure on the continued absence of Degrelle. Rumours of a visit by the *Chef de Rex* to

Belgium came to nothing and, as Degrelle has freely admitted, his isolated position on the Eastern front gave him little opportunity to exert any control over Rexist actions.[18] During most of 1942 he was fully absorbed by his military – and political – activities within the *Légion* and he left the front only once in June to make a brief visit to Berlin, as well apparently as Rome and Bucharest.[19] In the capital of the Reich Degrelle held discussions with a number of Nazi officials including representatives of the Ministries of Foreign Affairs and Propaganda as well as a delegation of his Belgian allies including Matthys, Alfred Lisein, the *Chef des Cadres Politiques* of Rex, and Paul Colin, who directed the New Order newspapers *Le Nouveau Journal* and *Cassandre*. At his meeting with these Belgian emissaries, Degrelle was in an ebullient mood, talking at length of his exploits at the front and boasting that he would soon be more powerful than Mussert, the Dutch pro-Nazi leader. Far from providing the Rexists with clear political directions, however, Degrelle proved to be interested only in efforts to advance his own interests and those of the *Légion*. Even when he did refer to the hoped-for revolution in Belgium, it was significantly the *Légion* rather than Rex which he envisaged playing the leading role, declaring: 'La *Légion* . . . est l'école du Mouvement, l'école précieuse, l'école indispensable pour tous ceux qui voudront affronter les responsabilités de la Révolution.'[20]

Degrelle's visit to Berlin was the first occasion on which he had been able to meet such a wide variety of German officials and it was an indication that his political reputation within the Third Reich was finally beginning to rise. One somewhat indirect consequence of this visit was that Degrelle was allowed to recruit for the *Légion* among the thousands of francophone Belgian prisoners of war who had remained imprisoned in camps in Germany since May 1940. The Rexists had always claimed that a substantial number of these men were sympathetic to their cause and, during his visit to the German capital, Degrelle made the release of these supporters a major theme of his discussions. The *Reichspressechef*, Dr Dietrich, was one of those to learn of Degrelle's request and he raised the issue at dinner with Hitler on 27 June with the result that the *Führer* issued a verbal order that Degrelle be allowed to select prisoners to be liberated. The *Wehrmacht* authorities responsible for the POWs were, however, opposed to any mass releases and it was only in September that they reluctantly agreed that up to 300 prisoners could be liberated provided that they joined the *Légion*.[21] Degrelle was more than happy to agree to this condition and he penned an effusive letter to be distributed in the camps in which lyrical descriptions of the spirit of *cameraderie* and of adventure within the *Légion* were mixed in with details of the material benefits available to volunteers. A recruiting team headed by Joseph Pévenasse toured Germany during the autumn of 1942, often using lists drawn up by Rexist *cercles* in Belgium of POWs believed to be sympathetic to the cause.

Despite these efforts and the promise that all volunteers would be accorded several weeks leave in Belgium prior to joining the *Légion*, the campaign was on the whole a failure. The POWs proved no more susceptible to Degrelle's blandishments than their compatriots in Belgium and, according to the German authorities, only 140 had by the end of 1942 exchanged imprisonment for service in the *Légion*. A good number of these appear to have been opportunists who used the *Légion* solely as a means to escape from detention and, although a few further prisoners were subsequently enrolled, the POW camps never became the significant source of additional manpower that Degrelle had hoped.[22]

With Degrelle's mind distracted by these other concerns, responsibility for the direction of Rex lay firmly in the hands of Matthys and Streel. But, while Streel's intentions were well defined, those of Matthys were far less clear. The *Chef de Rex ad interim* was in no sense a nominal figure-head and, though he allowed considerable freedom of action to Streel, he always retained overall control of the movement. Moreover, Matthys was not firmly committed to Streel's policy of moderation. His instincts were more radical and the violent rhetoric of Matthys' speeches often formed a marked contrast to the more cautious formulations of Streel.[23] Streel could not therefore take the support of his superior for granted and he had to counter the influence on Matthys of a number of more radical advisers. Typical of these was Léon Van Huffel. This somewhat pedantic young historian and journalist was one of a small number of Belgian intellectuals attracted by the claims advanced by a number of German academics that the Walloons were in fact a Germanic race. He had worked originally for De Becker's *Le Soir* until his radical pro-German opinions had caused his dismissal and, although he never joined Rex, Van Huffel subsequently became the Berlin correspondent of *Le Pays Réel*. He had long been in contact with SS officials in Brussels and he profited from his presence in the German capital to develop close links with senior figures in the expanding SS empire. As an exponent of extreme pro-German views, Van Huffel had no sympathy either for Belgian nationalism or for Degrelle's dream of a resuscitated Burgundian empire, proposing instead that Wallonia should be integrated into a pan-Germanic empire. During 1942 Van Huffel travelled regularly to Brussels seeking to convince the Rexist leaders that their continued loyalty to a united Belgium was leading the movement into an impasse. Nobody in Berlin, he insisted with some exaggeration, considered the survival of a Belgian state to be a serious possibility and the Rexists should seek instead the patronage of the ever more powerful SS.[24]

Though Van Huffel's arguments undoubtedly appealed to Matthys, his efforts did not meet with immediate success. The counsels of caution emanating from Streel proved more persuasive and Rexist actions throughout 1942 remained rooted in the principles laid down by the *Chef du*

Service Politique. Nevertheless, Van Huffel's views were significant for the light which they shed on the uncertainty which still surrounded Rexist tactics. Though the movement's choice of collaboration had been emphatic and was to all intents and purposes irreversible, there remained much to be resolved as to the form which that collaboration should take. Streel and Van Huffel in this respect reflected different trends and an increasing division opened up within the movement during 1942 between those whose espousal of collaboration was still couched in the language of patriotism and those who wished to cast all caution to the wind in pursuit of Nazi favour.

One symptom of this underlying tension was the confused ideological positions which the movement adopted as it oscillated between themes traditional to the Rexist struggle and innovations drawn from the new language of German National Socialism. There was of course nothing new in Rexist journalists seeking to imitate the themes of Nazi propaganda. Already in 1941 an evolution in Rexist ideology towards a German model had been clearly evident. During 1942 however this process gathered pace and became to some extent a struggle for the soul of the movement between the rival attractions of tradition and innovation. This ideological conflict could not be divorced from other more pressing considerations. In the increasingly exposed position which many Rexist militants found themselves in by 1942, matters of ideological nuance must have seemed almost absurdly irrelevant. The evolution of the war, the isolated position of the Rexists within Belgium and their consequent dependence on German protection were all forces which worked to push the movement remorselessly towards an extremism born out of a combination of fear and desperate ambition.

In 1942, however, the movement remained poised rather awkwardly between its past beliefs and the necessities of the present and future. This was most clearly evident in the confusion which surrounded the loyalties of the movement. Men such as Streel continued to portray Rex as a royalist and patriotic movement and, when paying tribute to the heroism of the *légionnaires*, he was at pains to stress that they were fighting above all for their country.[25] Such declarations were in part a response to the unceasing cries of treason levelled at the Rexists by their compatriots, and other Rexist journalists and militants echoed Streel in seizing on every opportunity to demonstrate their patriotic credentials.[26] By 1942 other loyalties were also competing for a place in Rexist hearts. The funeral notices in *Le Pays Réel*, for example, declared that the fallen *légionnaires* had given their lives for Belgium, Europe and the National Socialist revolution, while at Rexist meetings the portraits of Léopold III now shared their place of honour with photographs of Degrelle and of Hitler, 'le Chef et le Guide du Continent'.[27] Thus, though many militants still paid lip-service to the language of patriotism, one senses that the true focus of their loyalties was shifting remorselessly from the Belgian tri-colour and the royal prisoner in the château of Laeken to the *Führer* and swastika of the Third Reich.

Similar tensions surrounded the importation of Nazi racial ideas into Rexist propaganda. Rexists had long been concerned about the need to defend the health of the community through what they termed 'social medicine'[28] but the jargon of pseudo-scientific racism had never played a prominent role in the movement. Yet, despite protests from Streel, a racialist hue gradually began to colour Rexist propaganda. Much of this was rather superficial and there was no real attempt to adopt in their entirety the biological theories of the Nazis. Nonetheless they were happy to draw on its language and stereotypes presenting, for example, the Anglo-Americans and their Soviet allies not only as ideological enemies but also as degenerate racial groups. Racism became to some extent a new fashion within the movement and one of the most influential Rexist journalists, Jean Denis, wrote a long series of articles on the subject for *Le Pays Réel* in which he ingeniously tried to demonstrate that Nazi-style racial ideas were in no sense incompatible with long-held Rexist beliefs.[29]

Inevitably, this racism was accompanied by a heightened anti-semitism. Ever since 1940 the alleged dangers posed by the Jews had been a promi-nent feature of Rexist propaganda as well as a frequent subject for dis-cussion at local Rexist meetings. Employing themes drawn from the standard repertoire of European – and more especially francophone – anti-semitism, the image the Rexists presented of the Jews was a familiar one of a dark force intent upon exploiting every opportunity to advance their own interests. The Jews were in effect parasites whose unlimited ambitions and corrupting influence on public morals could only be countered by Draconian measures which would destroy their power and wealth.[30] Un-pleasant though it was, this rhetoric was also entirely unoriginal. Anti-Jewish sentiments of this kind had been common currency in much of the francophone world since at least the Dreyfus era and their exploitation by the Rexists reflected in part the popularity which a journalistic anti-semitism had enjoyed during the inter-war years among those Belgians attracted by French right-wing political ideas.[31]

Gradually, however, such prejudices gave way to a more integral and radical anti-semitism. Biological science replaced social and economic grievances as the basis for their attacks and, rather than merely calling for a special statute for the Jewish community, Rex advocated the physical ex-pulsion from Europe of this malignant racial group.[32] The reasons for this change were in part crudely opportunistic. Popular anti-semitism had always been a weak force in Belgium. The small size of the Jewish com-munity and its largely assimilated character made it difficult to portray it as a significant threat to the country and only in Antwerp had Jewish in-fluence in the diamond industry given rise to local anti-semitic campaigns.

But, as elsewhere in western Europe, the influx of Jews seeking refuge from persecution in Poland and Germany during the inter-war years had given rise to new resentments. The German propaganda agencies in Occupied Belgium did their best to exploit such feelings and showings of anti-semitic films and exhibitions were organised throughout the country.[33] These attracted a significant audience and, though most Belgians clearly looked on Nazi anti-semitic campaigns as no more than another German peculiarity, the Rexist leaders seem to have hoped that anti-Jewish propaganda might be one means of winning support among an otherwise hostile population.

This Rexist espousal of racial anti-semitism was more than an opportunistic gesture: it also reflected their more general infatuation with Nazi ideas, as well as the personal enthusiasms of Matthys who was well known amongst the Rexist leadership for his strongly anti-semitic opinions. In an uncompromising article in Le Pays Réel in December 1941, the Chef de Rex ad interim criticised those who discriminated between assimilated and non-assimilated Jews. All Jews, he declared, were identical and the only possible solution was the root-and-branch destruction of their power.[34] Once again these radical opinions were, however, opposed by José Streel. The day before Matthys' outspoken article, he had published an article insisting that the measures already initiated by the German authorities were sufficient to neutralise harmful Jewish activities and he opposed calls for additional legislation as well as denouncing manifestations of what he termed 'vulgar' anti-Jewish rabble-rousing. For Streel the Jewish 'problem' was always more cultural than political. Though he shared in the anti-semitic assumptions current throughout the movement, he regarded the power of the Jews as a symptom of the more general ascendancy of liberal ideas. Hence, he saw little value in repressive legislation and, during the latter war years, he protected individual Jews from the German police while continuing to advocate the elimination of Jewish influences from European civilisation.[35]

Such tensions between those anxious to emulate Nazi models and the defenders of a 'traditional' Rexism also surfaced in differences over the role that socialism should play in the movement's ideology. Since its foundation, Rex had adopted the rhetoric and ideals of 'social Catholicism' with a vigour which was rare in Belgian Catholic life. They had long denounced the material and, more especially, the spiritual sufferings of the industrial working class and called for the workers to be accorded an honoured place in society.[36] There were, however, clear limits to such expressions of sympathy. In its early years, the movement was overwhelmingly middle class in composition and few Rexists had direct experience of the needs of the workers. Moreover, the Socialist Party and the trade union movement were continually denounced by the Rexists for their materialist ideology and their exclusive identification with the workers at the expense of the wider community. During the war years, however, Rex shed much of its anti-socialism. Even since early 1941, Rexist propaganda had concentrated on attracting the support of the working class and under the leadership of Matthys the movement made much of its commitment to a radical socialist revolution as well as attacking the selfish – and pro-English – industrialist elite.[37] Attacks on the wealthy few won the support of all Rexists but divisions soon appeared within the movement when Matthys, seconded on occasions by Degrelle, adopted a class war rhetoric which seemed to imply an exclusive identification with the interests of the workers against those of the bourgeoisie.[38] Understandably, many Rexists were unhappy at this condemnation of the middle-class world which had spawned the movement and to which many of its militants still belonged. Streel and Jean Denis, for example, both responded to Matthys' attacks on the middle class by insisting that it was not the bourgeoisie which should be attacked but, rather, 'l'esprit bourgeois' with its egotistical and unheroic mentality.[39]

Given such divisions, it was not surprising that efforts by Rexist propagandists to articulate the basis of their supposedly socialist beliefs were singularly unsuccessful. Despite their ceaselessly reiterated claims – again drawn from Nazi examples – to represent an 'authentic' socialist tradition cleansed of the influences of Marxism and Liberalism, their socialism never amounted to more than an amalgam of empty slogans coupled with vague promises that Rexist socialism would respect 'the personality of man' while ensuring the ascendancy of community interests over those of individuals.[40] Even these vacuous gestures were sufficient to worry those, like Streel, who were reluctant to see any change in central Rexist beliefs. Though the *Chef du Service Politique* was willing to praise socialism as a means of achieving the twin goals of national integration and of social solidarity, he insisted that this was entirely different from the left-wing ideologies of the pre-war era. Socialism, he declared, should be regarded more as a method of social organisation than as a political creed and he remained committed to the vision of a devolved corporatist structure of society which had long formed the basis of Catholic social doctrine. Streel envisaged no radical redistribution of wealth and, in marked contrast to Matthys' calls for a violent workers revolution, he repeatedly used his column in *Le Pays Réel* to defend the interests of the lower middle class by advocating special legislation to protect small businessmen against the threat posed by large enterprises.[41]

Confusion was, thus, a major feature of Rexist wartime ideology. An incoherent *mélange* of loyalties competed for the support of Rexist militants who were uncertain whether they were patriots serving the King and the national interest, Catholic idealists pursuing a vision of an ideal Christian city, or the avant-garde of a violent Nazi revolution. Such confusion was not wholly new but nor was it ultimately of any great significance. While Rexist rhetoric of the 1930s had reflected the real feelings and aspirations of certain sections of the population, the Rexist ideology of the war years lacked not only clarity but also plausibility and relevance. Rexist insistence that a New Order of justice would emerge from collaboration with those German forces who were responsible for such widespread oppression and suffering could appeal only to those blinded to reality by great naïvety, unscrupulous ambition or obstinate loyalty to an outdated pre-war ideal.

It was not, therefore, merely the issue of collaboration which divided the Rexists from the vast majority of their compatriots. The whole thrust of their ideology was also profoundly at variance with the mood of the population. In Belgium, as in France and elsewhere in Europe, the experience of German occupation provoked a major shift in political attitudes in favour of a renewed faith in the values of free expression and of participatory government. The former watchwords of 'authority', 'order' and 'hierarchy' which had been used so indiscriminately in the 1930s fell rapidly from favour and, with the exception of those conservatives fearful of a Communist *coup d'état*, the general aspiration – as expressed in the substantial underground press and in reports on public opinion reaching the London government – was for reforms which would increase rather than circumscribe popular participation. Criticisms of the failings of the pre-war regime (and its personnel) were still voiced frequently but it was now the organisations of the Resistance and not foreign authoritarian regimes which many Belgians wished to see as the inspiration for a new political system.[42] Rex was at odds with this new popular mood. Rather like a fish stranded by the retreat of the tide, its ideologists could find no resonance in a population who regarded the ideas of the Rexists as no more than the irrelevant legacy of an obsolete intellectual fashion.

Rexist ideological disputes during the war years were, therefore, little more than quarrels in a vacuum; and it was this same separation from the aspirations and concerns of their compatriots which helped to fuel the internecine disputes which in Belgium – as elsewhere in German-occupied Europe – were a prominent feature of relations between different movements within the collaborationist community. The combination of isolation and of unrestrained ambition was a powerful cocktail which created an atmosphere of rivalry and mutual distrust among the various supporters of the Nazi cause. With the departure of many of its more turbulent spirits, Rex had attained a certain internal peace but throughout 1942 conflict intensified between the movement and those other pro-German groups intent upon usurping its position as the standard-bearer of collaboration in francophone Belgium.

The attitude adopted by Rex during these squabbles also provided further evidence of the tensions within the movement between its different tendencies. Though the Rexist leaders had energetically opposed the efforts of De Becker and his fellow journalists to create the *Parti des Provinces Romanes* in 1941, they had initially been remarkably tolerant of those groupings which had emerged on the extremist margins of the collaborationist world. Organisations such as the *Communauté Culturelle Wallonne* (*CCW*), the *Amis du Grand Reich Allemand* (*AGRA*) and the *Mouvement National Populaire Wallon* (*MNPW*) were no more than fringe groupings of idealists and opportunists, whose grandiose titles were in inverse relationship to their minimal importance. They posed little direct threat to Rex and, as long as they did not challenge their political supremacy, the Rexist leaders were on the whole content to work with them. So, for example, Rexist militants participated in the branches of the *CCW* and there was some contact between the two organisations on cultural and social matters.[43] Good relations also developed between the Rexists and the Antwerp-based anti-semitic league *Défense du Peuple* led by a lawyer, René Lambrichts, which was gradually extending its operations to francophone Belgium. Members of *Défense du Peuple* served in the *Légion Wallonie* and at a local level Rexist groups participated in the activities of the league and sent delegates to its meetings. Matthys encouraged this *rapprochement*. As we have seen, he shared fully their anti-Jewish prejudices and not only was his article in *Le Pays Réel* in December 1941 intended as a rejoinder to Streel's more moderate opinions but at a meeting with representatives of *Défense du Peuple* he apparently reassured them of Rexist support for their militantly anti-semitic ideas. A few days later he used the occasion of a public rally in Liège to declare that Rex and the anti-semitic league were allies fighting for a common cause.[44]

The ascendancy of Streel brought to an end this tolerant attitude and instituted in its place a policy of clear-cut opposition to the smaller pro-German groups.[45] This was first evident in Liège where a committee composed of representatives of all the collaborationist groupings had been established under the patronage of the local German *Propaganda Staffel*. This committee was intended to bring to an end the local rivalries between the Liège *cercle* of Rex and the two dissident groupings, the *MNPW* and *AGRA*, which had broken away from Rex in the early months of 1941. It initially operated quite effectively and – with the encouragement of the local German authorities – Antoine Leclercq, the former head of *Rex-Wallonie* who now directed the tiny *MNPW*, proposed in February 1942 that Rex, *AGRA* and the *MNPW* should sign an accord of mutual co-operation. The Rexist leadership in Liège at first appeared sympathetic to this proposal, but the reaction of the national Rexist leaders was unambiguous. Streel had no sympathy either for *AGRA* and the *MNPW*'s naïve enthusiasm for Nazi Germany or their commitment to the supposedly Germanic origins of the francophone Walloons and he rejected Leclercq's proposal out of hand. Rex was, the national leadership insisted, the only authorised political movement in francophone Belgium and the members of *AGRA* and the *MNPW* should abandon their activities and apply instead to join the Liège *cercle* of Rex.[46]

A few weeks after the collapse of these negotiations in Liège, Streel and his colleagues launched a major national initiative intended to assert the hegemony of Rex within the collaborationist community. With a vitriol which was remarkable in a press operating under German censorship, the *Chef du Service Politique* led a furious verbal assault on the extremist rivals of Rex, whom he dismissed as: 'l'inévitable écume de toutes les révolutions. Cette faune va depuis la franche canaille jusqu'à l'imbécile béat, en passant par toutes les variétés d'aventuriers plus ou moins frottés de basse police'.[47] This tone was sustained throughout the spring and summer of 1942, as a torrent of more or less justified accusations were heaped on the leaders of *AGRA* and the *MNPW*. With one eye no doubt on hoping to influence the German authorities, the Rexist press proclaimed that the leaders of these organisations represented nobody but themselves and, whilst some might be simple-minded enthusiasts or 'demi-intellectuels', most of these latter-day Jacobins were no more than base opportunists whose extremist rhetoric masked a murky past in Masonic or pro-French organisations. Having belatedly rallied to the German cause, these 'kleptomanes' and 'derviches hurleurs' were now seeking to acquire a spurious credibility by posing as the advocates of total collaboration and of National Socialism.[48]

A circular sent to Rexist cadres by Matthys and Streel on 1 June set out clearly their new attitude. In line with Streel's strategy of charting a more moderate course for the movement, it stated that all Rexists should resign from those groups such as *Défense du Peuple* whose radical views were at variance with those of Rex. Ideological scruples were, however, clearly allied to more political calculations. Though neither *AGRA* nor the *MNPW* was more than a fraction of the size of Rex, Streel and Matthys feared, not without some justification, that both movements might eventually seek to supplant Rex. All offers of co-operation from these groupings, the circular made clear, must therefore be rejected: 'Tous contacts, tout rapprochement, toute "coordination" seront *brutalement* refusés.'[49] The impact of this new policy soon became apparent. Relations with *Défense du Peuple* deteriorated rapidly and, even if not all Rexists immediately followed the instructions of their leaders, few members of Rex appear to have remained active in the anti-semitic league which began instead to develop closer links with *AGRA* and the *MNPW*.[50] Even relations with Pierre Hubermont's cultural organisation, the *Communauté Culturelle Wallonne* (*CCW*), which devoted itself to the less controversial – if rather vain – task of stimulating among the Walloon people an awareness of their Germanic heritage, were adversely effected. The June circular deplored what Streel and Matthys claimed were this grouping's political ambitions and an order appears to have been issued to Rexist militants to resign from the *CCW*. The Rexist leaders were especially annoyed by the attempts of the *CCW* to nominate its supporters for posts in local and central government. Rex regarded such positions as its own monopoly and, in a letter to Romsée at the Ministry of the Interior, Streel described the candidates proposed by the *CCW* as pro-Walloon extremists whose appointment would prejudice the integrity of the Belgian state.[51]

It was, however, for *AGRA* that Rex reserved its greatest hostility. Early in 1942 control of this grouping had passed to two new unscrupulous leaders, Scaillet and Gérits, who – apart from using *AGRA* as a vehicle for their self-enrichment – reorganised the movement in order to give it a more explicitly political role.[52] Under their aggressive leadership, *AGRA* posed as a movement of extremist revolutionaries whose publications combined a slavish imitation of Nazi propaganda with a crude populist socialism. It rejected the concept of a united Belgian state and, plundering the racial theories of National Socialism, claimed that the Walloons were a lost Nordic race who should return to the German Reich. Popular support for *AGRA* was non-existent and, although small branches of the movement were established in the principal towns of Wallonia, it was only in Liège that it was able to operate with any success. Contemporary estimates of its membership in 1942 varied between 1,200 and 2,500 but the quality of this membership was open to question. The unsophisticated demagogy of its leaders and the substantial material benefits offered to members attracted recruits who were described by one New Order observer as 'un véritable mercenariat'.[53]

Despite its all too evident flaws, there was little doubt that *AGRA* constituted the most serious challenge to Rex since De Becker's abortive efforts in May 1941. Like similar movements which appeared elsewhere in German-occupied Europe during the latter years of the war, its opportunist leaders clearly hoped that by adopting an extremist stance they would attract the patronage of those radical Nazi groupings – such as the *SS* – which were gaining power within the Reich. Such a tactic was indeed successful in Flanders where the formerly insignificant *DeVlag* movement led by Jef van de Wiele rapidly emerged with *SS* support during 1942 and 1943 as a serious rival to the more moderate *VNV*.[54] Rex, which was distrusted in *SS* circles because of its Catholic origins and hesitant attitude towards Nazi ideas, was clearly vulnerable to a similar challenge and from the spring of 1942 onwards the Rexist leadership made strenuous efforts to prevent *AGRA* from emerging as a fully-fledged political movement. Militants were forbidden from joining the rival movement and Rex systematically opposed all candidates nominated by *AGRA* for posts in local government as well as seeking to convince the *Militärverwaltung* to end its modest financial support for the movement.[55]

Scaillet and Gérits were not, however, easily intimidated and, while protesting that they had not sought conflict with Rex, they continued to boast that they alone were pure National Socialist revolutionaries.[56] This self-confidence was not entirely unfounded: *AGRA* did not collapse under the Rexist onslaught. It retained the support of elements within the German administration and also benefited from the influential assistance of its allies in the radical pro-German press of Charleroi where the two daily papers – *La Gazette de Charleroi* and *Le Journal de Charleroi* – both lent their support to the movement.[57] Hence, although *AGRA* never acquired anywhere near the importance of *DeVlag* in Flanders, it remained a vocal irritant to the Rexists and it was only in 1943, after in effect stealing many of *AGRA*'s ideological clothes, that Rex proved better able to act against its extremist rival.[58]

Countering the actions of other pro-German groups was only one facet of Streel's strategy for establishing Rex as the major bastion of a 'moderate', patriotic collaboration with Germany. The central element of his policy was the appointment of Rexist militants and their supporters to positions in central and local government. As well as strengthening the movement's position in advance of the hoped-for Rexist revolution, Streel hoped that the entry of the movement into public administration would help to foster a more moderate spirit within Rex by bringing its militants into contact with the complexities of government.[59] Since early in 1941 the *Militärverwaltung* and its appointee and close ally, the Flemish Nationalist *secrétaire-général* of the Ministry of the Interior Gérard Romsée, had begun a process of transforming the character of Belgian central and local government by dismissing a number of key office-holders and replacing them with Flemish Nationalists and other New Order figures. This revolution from within was initially stimulated by the reluctance of many officials to enact German orders but it soon developed into an attempt to remould the structures of Belgian administration along authoritarian lines. Romsée was the key figure in this policy. As a British report observed, he was the closest equivalent in wartime Belgium to Quisling in Norway[60] and he used to the full his powers as the administrative head of the Ministry of the Interior to enact wide-ranging changes in the personnel and spirit of government. Romsée was particularly concerned to make changes in local administration where most of the democratically-elected mayors and aldermen remained in office. Many of these pre-war figures were arbitrarily dismissed and replaced by more malleable nominees and the process of change was gradually extended to many other areas of the public sector such as education and public works which, though of less immediate political significance, also formed part of Romsée's overall plan for a New Order administrative revolution.

Despite the scale of these changes, Rex had been slow to benefit. Neither Romsée nor the German authorities had been eager to provoke anger by appointing Rexists to prominent public positions and only a handful of Degrelle's supporters were chosen for posts in central and local government during 1941.[61] Streel was determined to reverse this policy and as early as September 1941 he published an outspoken article in *Le Pays Réel* attacking Romsée's cautious attitude.[62] In addition, he made the entry of Rex into public administration the principal priority of his new *Service Politique*. Every effort was made to encourage militants to apply for posts in all areas of public administration and close links were fostered between the *Service Politique* and Romsée's advisers in the Ministry of the Interior. Regular weekly meetings took place between Rexist officials and representatives of the *cabinet wallon* of the Ministry of the Interior and they worked together to identify those Rexists suitable for nomination to governmental posts.[63]

Streel's efforts soon began to bear fruit. In the final weeks of 1941 a number of Rexists were appointed to posts in local government and officials of the movement began to speak optimistically of their chances for future success.[64] This change formed part of the more general *rapprochement* between Rex and the *Militärverwaltung* during the winter of 1941–2. In the appointment of officials, as in many other fields, the Germans were forced to accept that, with the polarisation of the population into pro- and anti-German camps, only the supporters of Rex could be relied upon to act as faithful executants of their policies.[65] Thus, in early 1942 the pace of the replacement of local mayors and aldermen appears to have quickened substantially and supporters of Rex featured prominently amongst the new appointees. The exact extent of this change is difficult to quantify but that it took place is clearly evident from Rexist documents. Early in 1942 Streel was still deploring the absence of Rexists from positions of importance but the tone changed during the subsequent months as articles in *Le Pays Réel* boasted of the achievements of Rexist-directed communes. In August 1942 the *chef de cercle* of Mons was able to state that almost all communes with a population of over 5,000 in the Borinage region had a Rexist mayor and, though this level of success may have been exceptional, the long lists of local government officials attending Rexist functions bore witness to the scope of the changes which had taken place. By October 1942, the national rally held in Brussels was reported to have been attended by almost 300 Rexist mayors and aldermen.[66]

As well as changing the personnel of government, Romsée and the *Militärverwaltung* also introduced structural reforms intended to create a more efficient and hierarchical system of administration. The most important of these was the creation of a series of *grandes agglomérations* to administer the principal cities of Belgium. These replaced the former chaotic network of autonomous urban communes with a new single administration responsible for an entire conurbation. The advantages of such a rationalisation had long been accepted but the arbitrary manner of its introduction was widely resented and, whatever administrative improvements they might bring, the new authorities were widely perceived as collaborationist institutions established to serve German aims.[67] During 1942 four such *grandes agglomérations* were established in francophone Belgium to administer La Louvière, Charleroi, Liège and Brussels and control of these powerful new authorities inevitably became a major focus of collaborationist rivalries.

As the only substantial pro-German movement, the Rexists felt they had a right to control the new councils. There was, however, no shortage of other candidates both from within and even beyond the collaborationist community and the special commissariat created by the Ministry of the Interior to oversee the establishment of the *grandes agglomérations* was not at first disposed to capitulate to Rexist demands.[68] Nevertheless, the movement did win control of the conurbations of La Louvière and Charleroi. In both cases Rexist mayors were appointed and supporters of Rex enjoyed a clear majority within the council chambers.[69] These cities were, however, in the province of Hainaut where Rex had few collaborationist rivals. In Liège, the situation was very different and the establishment of the new council of *Grand Liège* was preceded by bitter rivalries between the candidates of several different pro-German organisations. When it was eventually established in November, the new council sought to achieve a balance between these groups. Three Rexist aldermen were appointed along with six non-Rexist ones and a mayor and one other alderman who were only loosely affiliated to Rex. Events, however, worked to the Rexists' advantage. Within a few weeks the new mayor and three non-Rexist aldermen resigned after receiving threats from Resistance groups and their replacement by a Rexist mayor and two additional pro-Rexist aldermen ensured that Rex did after all win control of the new council.[70] Only in Brussels were Rexist ambitions frustrated. They had hoped that a pre-war Rexist senator, Léon Brunet, would be appointed as the mayor of the capital but both the *Militärverwaltung* and the *VNV* were firmly opposed to the appointment of a francophone mayor of what they intended should eventually become a predominantly Flemish city. Thus, a Flemish *bourgmestre* was nominated and, although Brunet became the *premier échevin*, only two other Rexist aldermen were appointed to serve on the council.[71]

Rexist advances within local government were accompanied by a similar expansion in its influence within the five provinces of francophone Belgium. Apart from in the Hainaut where a supporter of Rex, Leroy, had been allowed to usurp the position of provincial governor in the summer of 1940, the Germans had initially preferred to leave the francophone provincial administrations in the hands of non-political figures.[72] But, as with other areas of government, the increasing reluctance of these officials to comply with German orders eventually obliged Reeder to intervene. In March 1942 the governors of Namur and Liège were replaced by two

New Order nominees. Though the new governor of Namur, the Prince de Croy, was not a member of Rex and had before the war been a supporter of Joris Van Severen's small New Order movement, *Verdinaso*, his candidature received Rexist support while the appointee in Liège, Georges Petit, was a former Rexist parliamentary candidate.[73] Moreover, in 1943, Rex achieved partial recompense for its disappointment over control of *Grand Bruxelles* with the nomination of one of its supporters, Gillès de Pélichy, as governor of the province of Brabant which included the capital in its territory.[74] Finally, in the spring of 1944, another supporter of Rex, Dewez, was appointed as governor of the rural province of Luxembourg.[75]

Yet, as in a number of other areas of government, not all of these Rexist appointees proved to be reliable agents of the movement. Once in office, both De Croy and Petit sought to distance themselves from Rex[76] while Leroy, the governor of the Hainaut, proved to be something of a fair-weather friend to the movement. He was soon on bad terms with the local Rexist leaders and during the latter war years he sought to protect his own future by cultivating links with a Resistance intelligence network.[77] The effects of such opportunism were, however, to some extent offset by the appointment of Rexists to the delegations of *députés permanents* who worked alongside the governors within each provincial administration. By 1944 Rex controlled the delegations in the provinces of the Hainaut, Liège and the Luxembourg[78] and, in a number of cases, these *députés* became a major force within the provincial administration. This was particularly so in the Hainaut and Namur where Joseph Pévenasse and Jean Georges respectively both used their authority ruthlessly as *députés permanents* to further Rexist goals. Moreover, Rex also gradually colonised the *arrondissements* into which each province was subdivided. These were administered by *commissaires* whose powers had traditionally been largely nominal but, as part of its drive for greater efficiency in local government, Romsée's Ministry of the Interior increased their responsibilities while at the same time choosing new appointees favourable to New Order ideas. By 1944 seven of these *commissaires* were described by the German authorities as supporters of Rex.[79]

Rexist infiltration of central government never developed to the same extent as in provincial and local administration. Though a number of militants did acquire posts as civil servants within the central ministries,[80] by 1942 no supporter of Rex had been appointed to the all-important *collège* of *secrétaires-généraux* which continued to act as a surrogate internal government of Belgium. In August 1942 partial recompense was made with the appointment by the German authorities of Edouard De Meyer as *secrétaire-général* of the Ministry of Public Works. De Meyer was nominally of pro-Rexist sympathies but he proved to be a technocrat and engineer who concerned himself largely with the affairs of his own ministry and made little impact on the overall character of the *collège*.[81] This absence of a Rexist figure of significance was all the more galling because of the success of the *VNV* in obtaining the appointment of a number of its leaders such as Romsée and Leemans to key positions in the *collège* of *secrétaires-généraux*. At this most important level of administration, the Rexists seemed doomed to remain impotent outsiders and, in their frustration, they vented their anger on the staff of Romsée's Interior Ministry. The pro-Rexist head of its *cabinet wallon*, Ernest Delvaux, was accused by the Rexist leaders of having allowed the Flemish Nationalists a virtual monopoly over certain areas of government and in March 1942 Matthys and Streel unsuccessfully approached Romsée to suggest that Delvaux be replaced by Alfred Lisein, the *Chef des Cadres Politiques* of Rex.[82]

The real reason for the virtual exclusion of Rexists from central government did not lie with the Ministry of the Interior but with the *Militär-verwaltung*. Though Reeder recognised the necessity of working with the Rexists at a local level in Wallonia, he remained reluctant to appoint their supporters to positions of national authority. Despite the undoubted cooling which had taken place in relations between the German authorities and the civil servants who still constituted the majority of members of the *collège* of *secrétaires-généraux* a cautious *modus vivendi* still existed. Points of tension did inevitably arise – notably concerning the introduction of labour conscription legislation – but on the whole both sides preferred the status quo to any revolutionary changes. For the Belgian civil servants (as well as for the industrialists, judiciary and other elements of the Belgian pre-war elites with whom the *secrétaires-généraux* worked closely), the system of indirect rule operated by the *Militärverwaltung* offered a modicum of independence as well as protection from the excesses which they feared if the *Wehrmacht* administrators were to be replaced by a civilian regime dominated by the SS and staffed by Belgian collaborationists. On the other hand, as Reeder was at pains to explain to his superiors in Berlin, the *secrétaires-généraux* provided effective and economical administration of Belgium, while ensuring through the appointment of members of the *VNV* to certain key posts that the immediate economic and political needs of Germany could be met.[83] In these circumstances, Reeder had little incentive to appoint to high office Rexists who for the most part also lacked the relevant qualifications. No member of Rex could, for example, rival the accomplishments of Romsée who had attended the universities of Louvain, Berlin and Paris and had been a *VNV* parliamentary deputy since 1929.[84] Throughout its history, Rex had remained a movement of journalists, intellectuals and the provincial middle classes who, though well suited for political polemic or local administration, had little aptitude for the more demanding responsibilities of national government.

The most attractive prizes were therefore always to remain beyond the grasp of the Rexists and they were obliged to turn their attention instead to the less glamorous areas of the public sector. Militants were incited by their leaders to emulate the hated Jews by seizing every opportunity, however modest, to infiltrate governmental institutions[85] and this process of colonisation soon became a goal in itself divorced from any political benefits which it might bring the movement. No public office was too obscure to escape the attention of Streel and his colleagues who frequently expended inordinate efforts on ensuring the appointment of a supporter to a post of meagre significance. Thus, for example, the Rexist leadership seized with enthusiasm on the opportunities which arose to nominate their supporters to posts in the various New Order-inspired public institutions which were established during the Occupation. Certain of these, such as the *Office National du Travail*, were influential organisations but others such as the *Commissariat à l'Education Physique* and the various pseudo-corporatist guilds created to represent different trades and professions were phantom bodies with no real power.[86]

This obsession with the control and infiltration of public organisations also extended far beyond the formal institutions of government. Education was, for example, one area where the Rexists were especially anxious to extend their influence. Political involvement in educational appointments in Belgium had long been commonplace and, rather like the Vichy government in France, the Rexists regarded the schools as having been corrupted by the ills of the pre-war order. Therefore the movement was keen to ensure the promotion of teachers who supported its vision of a new more physical and practical educational system purged of the evils of individualism and effete intellectualism. Lists of suitable candidates were drawn up and the *Service Politique* worked closely with the *Commission Consultative de l'Enseignement* which Romsée had established to vet appointments to vacant teaching posts. Once again, however, Rexist ambitions were to go largely unfulfilled. Despite its New Order composition, the commission proved reluctant to accept quiescently all Rexist nominations and supporters of the movement only ever remained a small and beleaguered minority within the teaching profession. Efforts to influence the appointment of school inspectors and administrators or to introduce educational reforms proved ineffectual and it was left to individual Rexist teachers to do what they could to influence their very unwilling pupils.[87]

Of more immediate value to Rex was the appointment of its supporters to posts in the judiciary and the police. The judicial system was considered by the Rexists to be one of the key bastions of the democratic *ancien régime* but the magistrate chosen by the German authorities to act as *secrétaire-général* of the Ministry of Justice, Gaston Schuind, proved to be a cautious apolitical figure who was disinclined to favour Rexist appointments to the judiciary.[88] In the police, however, the situation was more encouraging. An increasing number of communal police forces were now under the control of Rexist mayors and aldermen who not surprisingly had proved anxious to reinforce their somewhat precarious authority by appointing like-minded Rexists to posts within the police. Thus, the *Service Politique* encouraged militants to sit the police entrance examinations as well as ensuring the appointment of pro-Rexist former army officers to the new police training-schools.[89]

It was, however, the national paramilitary police, the *Gendarmerie*, which most interested the Rexist leaders. Since mid-1941, the *Militärverwaltung* and the Ministry of the Interior had begun to expand and reform this force with the hope of making it an instrument of their policies as well as a means of ensuring public order within Belgium. A pro-German Flemish officer, Colonel Van Coppenolle, was appointed in October 1941 to enact these changes and at the same time Rex was given permission to recruit 200 of its supporters to serve as officers in the *Gendarmerie*.[90] A number of Rexists did indeed subsequently enter the *Gendarmerie* training-school at Vottem-lez-Liège, but they were too few to make much impact. In the autumn of 1942, however, Rex made infiltration of the *Gendarmerie* a major priority. The *Service Politique* attempted to gather information on the political views of all of the officers in the force and the Rexist *cercles* were instructed to exert pressure on militants to choose service in the *Gendarmerie* in preference to any other public sector career.[91] These efforts were not without success and a new wave of Rexists entered the *Gendarmerie*, though not on the scale hoped for by Van Coppenolle and the Rexist leaders. By 1943 about 1,500 new recruits had been enrolled in the force throughout Belgium and, according to Reeder, most of these were members of collaborationist groupings, including Rex. These new *gendarmes* were, however, too few to transform the overall character of the *Gendarmerie* which remained a bastion of anti-German views, many of whose members were also active in the Resistance. The supporters of Rex in the force were an isolated group and, though the *cercles* were encouraged to maintain close contact with them, their presence within the *Gendarmerie* proved to be of little real benefit to Rex.[92]

Yet, though the rewards were rarely commensurate with the effort expended, the appointment of Rexists to posts in the manifold branches of the public sector remained a major focus of the movement's activities for much of the remainder of the Occupation. As Matthys subsequently admitted, the laborious task of seeking out suitable candidates for posts absorbed the energies of many Rexist officials and to some extent filled the vacuum left by the collapse of their hopes of an imminent revolution.[93] This was a process which had various consequences for the character of the movement. Above all, it contributed to a 'professionalisation' of Rex. In the past its militants had been drawn from a wide variety of social backgrounds but, as the infiltration of state institutions gathered pace, so the movement came to be predominantly one of public sector bureaucrats. This was not a change unique to Rex. Throughout German-occupied

Europe the supporters of collaboration gradually became a professional caste, absorbed into a variety of military and civilian bureaucracies. Thus, the old-style Rexist militant who combined his enthusiastic participation in the life of Rex with a professional life separate from the movement disappeared to be replaced by full-time officials whose positions in public administration – or the German forces – enabled them to devote themselves entirely to the Rexist cause.

Exercising effective political control over those militants appointed to public offices became a major concern of the Rexist leaders. Some of those who acquired a post with the assistance of Rex soon chose to forget their debt to the movement and, in an effort to counter such behaviour, all Rexists nominated to positions in government were required to swear an oath of allegiance to Rex as well as contributing a fixed proportion of their income to the movement.[94] In addition, a special organisation – the *Cadre Politique* – was created in order to provide Rexist office-holders with a clear status within the movement. Directed at first by Joseph Pévenasse and, after his departure to Russia, by Alfred Lisein, this organisation spawned local *cadres politiques* which operated within many of the Rexist *cercles* and which sought to inculcate loyalty among office-holders as well as providing a forum for them to exchange practical information.[95]

Not surprisingly, their large-scale entry into public administration did little to enhance the reputation of the Rexists in the eyes of an already hostile population. In many towns and villages throughout francophone Belgium, local communities found that their elected mayors and aldermen had been summarily dismissed by a decree of the Ministry of the Interior and replaced by Rexist nominees. This transfer of power inevitably provoked a major change in attitudes towards the Rexists. Long shunned and ridiculed by the majority of the population, they now stood at the centre of public life. Rexist militants and their sympathisers were in charge of the *Hôtel de Ville* and their pronouncements concerning food rationing, public order and a host of other matters of local concern were to have a direct impact on the well-being of many communities.

For most Belgians, the spectacle of Rexist nominees replacing democratically-elected officials confirmed their belief that Degrelle and his followers were little more than unscrupulous opportunists intent upon profiting from the German presence to advance their own careers. Rexist propagandists, on the other hand, were understandably at pains to present a rather different analysis of their entry into public administration. Unlike the corrupt placemen of the democratic *ancien régime*, the Rexist nominees were, they insisted, motivated by a genuine desire to serve the interests of the entire community: 'Pour nous une fonction publique n'est pas une "place" honorifique ou rénumératrice qui doit flatter la vanité ou satisfaire les appétits d'un agent électoral: c'est un poste de combat pour le bien de la communauté.'[96] Reports in *Le Pays Réel* publicised instances of flagrant corruption which the new appointees claimed to have uncovered and boasted of how in Rexist-controlled communes 'la politicaille du village' had been replaced by a new era of efficient 'depoliticised' administration. Rexist *bourgmestres* and *échevins*, the Rexist press claimed, were energetic technocrats whose experience in business and industry had equipped them to introduce new principles of order and discipline into the archaic structures of government.[97]

The reality rarely accorded with this ideal. Some Rexist office-holders were indeed well-intentioned men who sought to serve the interests of the community, caused little harm and proved willing to help those of their fellow citizens in trouble with the German authorities. A very few even seem to have achieved a certain measure of popularity and received only minimal prison sentences after the liberation.[98] Such rare examples were however greatly outweighed by instances of Rexist *bourgmestres* and *échevins* who servilely accomplished German commands or who exploited their positions of authority to their own frequently illicit ends. Despite the promises of a new honesty in local government, several Rexist appointees were dismissed from office during the war for corruption, while the post-war trials of others – such as Louis Froment, the *échevin* in charge of food provisioning for Liège – revealed a life of debauchery based upon the misappropriation of public funds.[99] As the Occupation entered its final dark years, many drew closer to the German authorities and some Rexist office-holders became free-lance agents of the Nazi police and even participated in the arrest of their fellow citizens.[100] The overwhelming impression was less one of unredeemed evil than of pompous incompetence. Many Rexist authorities spent money extravagantly on grandiose projects of public works and, having at last acceded to power, the Rexist appointees rejoiced in the trappings of authority by attending official functions in their Rexist uniforms or by raising the flag of the movement over the town hall.[101]

As infiltration of the manifold branches of administration was largely the responsibility of José Streel, it was inevitable that it should also have reflected his wish to chart a more moderate course for Rex. He tried to ensure that less extreme Rexists were appointed to the more important positions of authority, preferring even on occasions to support the candidatures of non-Rexists rather than of extremist members of his own movement.[102] The impact of his moderating influence was, however, always very limited. Because of the small number of militants at his disposal, Streel was never able to exclude from public office all those Rexists with whose views he did not agree and in practice it was more often Romsée's Ministry of the Interior which vetoed applications by the more extreme supporters of Rex. In addition, once appointed to positions in local government, even the most moderate of Rexists frequently resorted to desperate measures in a vain attempt to reinforce their authority. For Streel, acting at a national level, distinctions between 'patriotic' and extremist collaboration seemed valid but in the polarised situation which prevailed in much of francophone Belgium by 1942, such considerations were irrelevant. Surrounded by a hostile and increasingly violent population, Rexist officials had little choice but to seek assistance from any quarter, even if that meant working with the German police or exacting crude reprisals on a populace which made no secret of the fate it hoped would befall Rexist appointees.[103]

Streel's failure to influence to any significant extent the selection and policies of Rexists in public administration well illustrated the broader problems which confronted his entire policy of moderation. Any attempt to restrain Rex from adopting a categorically pro-Nazi stance ran counter to the logic of the stark division between a small collaborationist minority and the patriotic majority of the population. Streel hoped to straddle this divide in the illusory hope that Rex could occupy a middle ground which had in fact long since disappeared. Thus, throughout 1942, the movement was confronted by a number of issues which presented Streel and his colleagues with a stark choice between pro-German collaboration and anti-German patriotism.

One such issue concerned the always difficult relations between the pro-German minority and the Belgian Catholic Church. After the disputes of 1941, the Catholic hierarchy and the leaders of Rex and the *VNV* were once again brought into conflict in the early months of 1942 by the contentious problem of funerals for members of collaborationist movements. The Church authorities had already ordered in 1941 that uniformed members of such groups should not be allowed to participate in religious services but this issue was given a new immediacy by the deaths of those members of Rex and the *VNV* serving with the German armies on the Eastern front. It was clear that the funerals and memorial services for these men would inevitably take on a political character and in February 1942 an acrimonious exchange took place between the Church and the *VNV* concerning the arrangements for the funeral of Tollenaere, the head of the *VNV* militia who had died while serving in the Flemish legion in Russia.[104]

The first incident of this kind to involve Rex occurred early in April when a priest refused to officiate at the funeral of a Walloon *légionnaire* at Châtelet and a German military chaplain had to be called upon to direct the service.[105] A conference of bishops on 10 April apparently resolved to take a firm stance against the collaborationist groups over this issue and within a few days similar problems arose at other funerals of members of the *Légion Wallonie* at Châtelineau, Braine l'Alleud, Frameries and Fleurus. In each case, the local *curé* refused to permit delegations of uniformed militants to attend the services or to allow flags or non-liturgical music to be used for what they deemed to be political ends.[106] The response of the

Rexist leaders was one of predictable outrage. Articles in Le Pays Réel denounced the inveterate politicking of the Catholic hierarchy and accused the Church of hypocrisy in imposing Draconian conditions on Rexist services while allowing funerals for members of Resistance groups to be turned into patriotic demonstrations.[107] It is not difficult to see why the stance of the Church provoked such anger. The Rexists believed that the légionnaires had given their lives for their country and yet they were to be permitted only semi-secret funerals more appropriate for common criminals than for putative national heroes. It was, moreover, an issue of especial sensitivity for those Rexists who still regarded themselves as sincere Catholics. They had looked with sorrow on the estrangement of Rex from the Church and had long hoped that some form of reconciliation would prove possible. Streel was once again the spokesman of such traditional Rexist views, using the columns of Le Pays Réel to argue consistently for an alliance between the Church and the advocates of New Order ideas. Clearly alarmed by the anticlerical tone of much col-laborationist journalism, he called for the Catholic faith to be accorded a privileged position in a New Order Belgium and continued to stress the many points of convergence which he claimed existed between the ideas advanced by the advocates of a New Order and the teachings of the papacy contained in encyclicals such as Quadragesimo Anno.[108]

This hope of some form of reconciliation with the Church was one which also seems to have held some appeal for Degrelle who apparently sent a letter to Cardinal Van Roey from Russia early in 1942.[109] Van Roey and his fellow bishops had little interest in effecting a reconciliation with the advocates of collaboration however and the subsequent evolution of the dispute over funerals for légionnaires soon destroyed all hope of any compromise. On 24 April, Matthys wrote to Van Roey proposing that Brussels cathedral be used for a memorial ceremony for all of the Rexist dead and asking for clarification of the conditions under which priests were authorised to officiate at funerals. The Cardinal's response was uncompromising: the cathedral could not be used for such a service and no priest would participate in any funeral which had the character of a politi-cal event. In response, a further torrent of articles by Rexist journalists – including Streel – attacked the Belgian Catholic hierarchy, often in crudely anticlerical terms, as the agents of Anglo-Saxon liberalism and atheistic communism.[110] Once again, it fell to the Militärverwaltung to act as the arbiter in this conflict. As during earlier disputes between the Church and collaborationist movements, the German administrators of Belgium pre-ferred to placate the bishops rather than support their political protégés. Peace and order remained the overriding priorities for Reeder and his colleagues and it seems likely that they prevailed upon the Rexists to abandon their conflict with the Church. In an abrupt reversal of their former stance, the Rexist Etat-Major advised its followers on 28 April that funerals for *légionnaires* would in future be conducted by a chaplain of the *Wehrmacht* and that the memorial service planned for Brussels cathedral would take place under German auspices in a military barracks in Brussels.[111]

The Catholic Church had good reason to be satisfied with the outcome of this conflict. In a series of speeches and pastoral letters during the spring and summer of 1942, the bishops reiterated their uncompromising position towards funerals of collaborationists[112] while being able to absolve themselves of all responsibility for events at those services conducted by German chaplains. The Rexists, on the other hand, had suffered a further humiliating reverse and the verbal fury which they continued to vent at Cardinal Van Roey and his colleagues spoke eloquently of their underlying weakness.[113] Trapped between the mutual interest of the Church and of the *Militärverwaltung* to preserve their *modus vivendi*, the Rexists lacked any means of achieving their aims. Thus, almost all subsequent Rexist funerals were conducted by German military chaplains.[114] Only rarely could one of the small band of pro-Rexist priests be prevailed upon to brave the wrath of his superiors by officiating at Rexist funerals and on other occasions it was only the threat of physical violence which obliged highly reluctant priests to conduct Rexist funeral services.[115] It was therefore scarcely surprising that Catholic priests should have remained a favourite target for Rexist hostility. During the Occupation priests were almost unique in having a relative freedom to express their opinions from the pulpit and many used this privilege to express their patriotic sentiments, as well as to condemn the actions of those 'mauvais Belges' who had opted to side with the Nazis. In turn, many Rexists came to regard the clergy almost as a pro-English fifth column within Belgium. Their political intrigues were frequently the subject of discussion at local Rexist meetings, militants were encouraged to compile reports on priests who delivered anti-German sermons and in the last years of the Occupation the clergy not surprisingly often bore the brunt of Rexist violence.[116] At a national and local level an atmosphere of unambivalent hostility had been firmly established between the Church and Rex and, speaking at a rally in Charleroi in August 1942, Matthys must have voiced the views of many Rexists when he declared: 'Il y a un temps pour tout . . . Lorsque la possibilité nous en sera donnée, nous agirons et les ennemis de la révolution paieront! Nous ne voulons pas confondre la religion avec le clergé politicien. Mais le respect que nous témoignons à la Religion ne nous empêcherons pas d'appliquer, au moment venu les mesures nécessaires.'[117]

The use of German military chaplains to bury their dead demonstrated unequivocally the extent to which the Rexists had become social pariahs within their own land. Shunned by the institutions of Belgian society and the focus of almost unanimous popular antipathy, the Rexist community increasingly took on the appearance of a beleaguered camp and this profound isolation was further underlined by the decision of Matthys in the spring of

1. Léon Degrelle presents the Rexist flag to the *Formations de Combat*, August 1941.

2. Léopold III in the grounds of the palace of Laeken during the Occupation.

3. Eggert Reeder, head of the *Wehrmacht Militärverwaltung* in Belgium.

4. Group of Rexist volunteers at the ceremony for the departure of the *Légion Wallonie* to Germany on 8 August 1941.

5. Volunteers for the *Légion Wallonie* in Brussels on 8 August 1941.

6. Rexist militiamen of the *Formations de Combat*, 8 August 1941.

Women and children at the *Gare du Nord* in Brussels prior to the departure of the *Légion Wallonie*, 8 August 1941.

9. Victor Matthys, *Chef ad interim* of Rex, presents a Burgundian flag to the *Jeunesses Rexistes*, March 1942.

8 (facing page). Member of the *Jeunesse rexiste féminine*.

10. Members of the *Etat-Major* of Rex at the ceremony for the departure of further volunteers for the *Légion Wallonie* in Brussels, 10 March 1942.

11. Members of the *Légion Wallonie* in *Wehrmacht* uniforms at the memorial service held on 21 May 1942 for *légionnaires* who had died on the Eastern Front.

12. General view of the memorial service, 21 May 1942.

13. Matthys and other members of the *Etat-Major* at the funeral of the Rexist *bourgmestre* of Charleroi, Prosper Teughels, assassinated by the Resistance in November 1942.

14. Members of the Rexist youth leaving for a camp in Germany.

15 (above left). Gérard Romsée (in civilian suit), *secrétaire-général* of the Ministry of the Interior, at a ceremony for the *VNV* militia.

16 (above right). Paul Colin, director of the collaborationist newspapers *Le Nouveau Journal* and *Cassandre* assassinated by the Resistance in April 1943.

17. Degrelle with his wife and children.

8. Degrelle and Matthys at a rally in the *Palais des Beaux Arts* in Brussels, 2 May 1943.

9. Choir of the *Jeunesse Légionnaire*.

21. *SS* representative in Belgium, Richard Jungclaus, at a reception for war correspondents.

20 (facing page). Degrelle, standing in front of a bust of Hitler, addresses an anti-Bolshevik meeting in Brussels on 27 June 1943.

22. Jean Vermeire, representative of the *Chef de Rex* in Berlin.

23. Degrelle and *SS* General Gille being presented to Hitler and Himmler, February 1944.

24. Degrelle (right), Himmler (centre) and *SS* General Gille (left), February 1944.

25. Ceremony for the *Légion Wallonie* in front of Charleroi Town Hall, 1 April 1944.

26. Degrelle among Walloon workers in Germany, June 1944.

27. Families of members of the *Légion Wallonie* at the Children's Home for the *Waffen-SS* in Bouillon.

28. Degrelle at the funeral of his brother Edouard in Brussels, July 1944.

29. Ceremony held in Brussels in August 1944 to commemorate the anniversary of the departure of the *Légion Wallonie* to the Eastern Front.

30. The liberation of Brussels, September 1944.

31. Collaborators under arrest after the liberation, September 1944.

32. Group of female collaborators with shaven heads in Charleroi in September 1944.

1942 to order a 'mobilisation' of Rexist militants. In a letter sent to all Rexists on 5 May, the *Chef de Rex ad interim* called on them to join an elite group of militants who would be mobilised by Rex in the event of an emergency. In order to prepare them for this task, those Rexists who came forward were required to attend a two-week military training course at Contich near Antwerp under the direction of officers of the *Wehrmacht* and *Gardes Wallonnes*.[118] In part, these measures were intended to rebuild some form of Rexist militia after the virtual collapse of the *Formations de Combat* but its principal purpose was clearly defensive. Surrounded by a hostile population and confronted by an uncertain military situation, Matthys and his colleagues hoped that the creation of an elite corps of militants who had undergone military training would enable Rex to defend itself against the dangers posed by a Resistance uprising or a landing by Allied troops.[119]

The response to Matthys' appeal was not discouraging and an initial training camp reserved for members of the *Formations de Combat* was held at the end of May. Under the supervision of their leader, Albert Constant, 233 Rexist militiamen underwent a course of basic military and police training.[120] It had initially been stated that those Rexists who had attended the camp would form a reserve for the *Gardes Wallonnes* under the control of the movement[121] but, while the members of the *Formations* were at Contich, it was suddenly announced that they would instead form part of the German-controlled *Hilfsfeldgendarmerie*. This part-time auxiliary police force had originally been composed solely of German civilians resident in Belgium but early in 1942 the *Militärverwaltung* decided that in view of the decline in public order it should be expanded to include 'zuverlässigen Flamen und Wallonen'.[122] The Rexist training programme at Contich presented the German authorities with a convenient opportunity to enrol the first Belgian members of this new police force and the Rexist leaders appear to have had little choice but to accept the German order. Its announcement to the members of the *Formations de Combat* at Contich did, nevertheless, arouse considerable opposition. A number of the Rexist militiamen had already been unhappy at the harsh conditions in the camp and many – including Constant – were angry that they had apparently been duped into effectively becoming auxiliaries of the German police.[123]

Despite this opposition, the Rexist leadership pressed ahead with the mobilisation programme. A special unit, the *Service M*, was established in the Rexist *Etat-Major* to oversee its development and circulars instructed local Rexist officials to make it their principal priority.[124] Already the training courses at Contich were being seen as only the first step towards a more general militarisation of Rex and in the summer of 1942 the *Service M* asked the *cercles* to provide details of arms and petrol dumps, of potential safe houses and of members willing to participate in unspecified 'sacrifice missions'.[125]

It was, however, the camps at Contich which remained the keystone of the mobilisation programme. Apparently unconcerned that those militants who underwent the training courses would in effect serve as agents of the German police, the Rexist *Etat-Major* organised three further camps at Contich during the autumn of 1942.[126] The evident reluctance of many militants to attend these courses now that they were linked to service in the German police did cause difficulties. Matthys was forced to write twice to all those who had responded to his initial appeal insisting that they must honour their promise.[127] Nonetheless, a significant number failed to attend the camps and many of those who did do so subsequently refused to join the *Hilfsfeldgendarmerie*.[128] There were no doubt several reasons for this reluctance but it would seem to suggest that, despite the movement's whole-hearted espousal of collaboration, a substantial proportion of Rexists were unwilling to become quite so intimately associated with the Nazi cause. Though they were willing to serve in the German forces when – as in the case of the *Légion Wallonie* or *Gardes Wallonnes* – it seemed to be directly related to Rexist political goals, service in the German police was a further step which some at least remained reluctant to take.

No further camps were organised after 1942 but efforts continued to convince Rexists to enter the *Hilfsfeldgendarmerie*. According to Matthys, 85 to 90 per cent of those trained at Contich did subsequently agree to join the German police reserve and German and Rexist reports indicate that as many as several hundred Rexists were serving as part-time German police auxiliaries.[129] In many cases – as Matthys was at pains to stress – their responsibilities were purely nominal[130] but in certain localities the enthusiasm of the Rexists or of their German commanders led to them playing a more active role. In Namur and Dinant, for example, regular bimonthly exercises of the *Hilfsfeldgendarmerie* were held and after the liberation a number of Rexists were prosecuted for their role in *Hilfsfeldgendarmerie* operations directed against Resistance groups or men evading German labour conscription measures.[131]

The participation of Rexists in the *Hilfsfeldgendarmerie* left unresolved the problem of how the movement could recreate a militia capable of protecting its militants and accomplishing an eventual seizure of power. Unlike the *VNV*, which in 1942 was able to deploy thousands of uniformed men on the streets of Brussels in a demonstration of its strength,[132] Rex possessed no substantial paramilitary organisation and this issue would remain a central preoccupation of the Rexist leaders throughout the remainder of 1942. Several possibilities were considered but in practice the only option remained some form of renovation of the *Formations de Combat*. In February Albert Constant had been appointed to head the *Etat-Major* of the *Formations* and he laboured with considerable determination to instil greater discipline and organisation into the depleted ranks of the militia.[133] A flood of memoranda and training schedules emanated from the Rexist headquarters, encouraged by Victor Matthys who in his speeches and circulars exhorted all able-bodied Rexists to enrol in the *Formations*.[134] Their efforts did, however, achieve little. Recruitment for the *Légion Wallonie* and *Gardes Wallonnes* had already absorbed many young Rexist men and few of the older more experienced militants seemed willing to join an organisation which was regarded, even within Rex, with some derision. Thus, despite Matthys' hopes that the militia would be able to present an imposing front at the national rally in Brussels planned for October, few new recruits were attracted and the *Formations de Combat* continued to consist of little more than small isolated groups of men.[135]

These efforts at reform were, moreover, undermined by differences between Constant and Matthys as to the purpose which such a militia should serve. Constant still regarded the *Formations de Combat* as a surrogate national army acting to preserve public order and serving as a 'rassemblement national' for all men of goodwill. Matthys, on the other hand, saw little value in creating a patriotic 'garde civique' and instead wished to establish an aggressive and explicitly political militia modelled on the examples of the Nazi *SA* and *SS*.[136] These differences gradually caused Constant to lose the confidence of Matthys and in January 1943 he offered his resignation.[137] It was promptly accepted by Matthys but, by depriving the militia of its most effective organiser, Constant's departure merely made even more intractable the problem of re-establishing an effective Rexist paramilitary force.

This task was made all the more urgent by the intensification of attacks on Rexist militants by the burgeoning Resistance groups. After the first isolated attacks in September 1941, armed assaults on supporters of Rex recommenced in the spring of 1942 and from then on the regular reports sent by Reeder to his superiors in Berlin catalogued an accelerating spiral of attacks on Rexist militants and buildings.[138] Much of this violence was Communist-inspired. Freed by the attack on the Soviet Union from the difficult position of superficial neutrality imposed on them during the winter of 1940–1, the Belgian Communist Party (*PCB*) had entered wholeheartedly into the Resistance, bringing to it a new determination and energy. In contrast to the more conventional military outlook of other patriotic organisations such as the *Armée Secrète* who preferred to act as the adjuncts of the Allies, the *PCB* sought to wage a pitiless guerrilla warfare against the German occupiers and their Belgian agents. Their underground newspaper, *Le Drapeau Rouge*, called as early as March 1942 for an all-out struggle 'jusqu'à le dernier nazi ait été chassé du pays et le dernier traître châtié' and small groups of partisans, in which former volunteers in the Spanish Civil War were often prominent, began to operate in Brussels and the industrial centres of Wallonia in the spring of 1942.[139]

In response, the Rexist leaders tried as best they could to protect their supporters. In February 1942, an agreement was reached with the German authorities under which a limited number of Rexists were issued with permits to carry arms but the acquisition of such weapons was still difficult and most Rexist *dirigeants* remained unarmed in the face of increasingly audacious attacks.[140] Local Rexist groups also sought to improve their security: elaborate precautions were adopted at meetings and bodyguards were appointed to guard vulnerable figures.[141] But most Rexists regarded these *ad hoc* measures as ineffectual and some began to advocate more drastic measures. As early as June 1942 militants in La Louvière were apparently considering gathering together their supporters in a protected camp[142] while others throughout Belgium began to demand that Rex instigate reprisal attacks against the Resistance activists and their supposed patrons. Opinion was still clearly divided within the movement as to the legitimacy of such actions. While in July 1942, the *chef de cercle* of Braine l'Alleud was still counselling his members to show self-restraint in the face of such attacks, in November of the same year a meeting of the *cercle* of Philippeville discussed the creation of Rexist counter-terrorist squads which it was intended would take the law into their own hands.[143]

The national leaders shared in the exasperation felt by many of their supporters. There was no official policy of authorising reprisal actions but Matthys, in particular, believed that the Rexists had no choice but to respond in kind to Resistance attacks. When in June the Rexist *bourgmestre* of Ransart and former *chef de cercle* of Charleroi Jean Demaret was shot dead in his office by a Resistance militant disguised as a *gendarme*, Matthys' immediate reaction was to order Albert Constant to organise the assassination of a local magistrate. The head of the *Formations* did subsequently visit Charleroi but, despite the enthusiasm shown by certain local Rexists, the matter was allowed to drop.[144] Nevertheless the threat made by Matthys in his address at the funeral of Demaret was emphatic. Rex, he declared, had been too passive in its reaction to such murders and the time had now come to act: 'Je déclare donc que chaque fois qu'un Rexiste tombera, un de nos ennemis sera abattu.'[145] Such threats were to be repeated frequently by Matthys during the subsequent months. When in July and August, in two separate incidents, Rexists serving in the German transport corps, the *NSKK*, and the *Légion Wallonie* shot dead civilians who they claimed had insulted them, the *Chef de Rex ad interim* singled out their actions for praise, declaring in an *Ordre du Jour* issued to the *Jeunesses Rexistes* and *Formations de Combat* that they marked 'une étape dans l'histoire du Mouvement'.[146] A few weeks later in a speech at Tournai and a strongly worded article in *Le Pays Réel*, Matthys reiterated his support for decisive action. The Rexists, he declared, had been deprived of the protection of the police and judicial authorities and, though they accepted the deaths of their comrades as the cost of the achievement of their revolutionary goals, they were justified in resorting to the primitive morality of revenge: 'Des soldats savent combattre mais aussi abattre . . . Certains de nos camarades ont déjà montré l'exemple. Ne pleurons pas, ne gémissons pas, préparons-nous au combat, passons aux actes!'[147]

The bloody language of Matthys was not, however, matched by equivalent actions. Rex possessed neither the means nor as yet the clear will to respond in kind to the Resistance violence. In Spa on 20 September members of the *Formations de Combat*, acting apparently on orders received from Matthys' office, did sack the home of the local *bourgmestre* whom they suspected of complicity in a wave of attacks on local Rexists.[148] However the orders from the Rexist headquarters specified that the mayor himself should not be harmed and, despite his threatening public statements, even Matthys seemed reluctant to authorise violent attacks. Torn between the desire for revenge and the hope that the German or even the Belgian authorities might prove able to act against the perpetrators of such violence, the Rexist leadership gradually became more circumspect. They took no steps towards initiating a policy of reprisal killings and Matthys himself became more cautious in his public declarations preferring not to give encouragement to those militants who talked wildly of engaging their fellow citizens in open combat.[149]

There was little discernible public sympathy for those Rexists who fell victim to the Resistance assaults. Some Belgians did regard such attacks as premature or counter-productive but most seem to have applauded the assassinations.[150] Unlike the anonymous representatives of the Occupying forces, the followers of Degrelle were clearly identifiable targets and the murder of a local Rexist frequently seemed to do more than any distant Allied military victory to raise popular morale. The emerging alliance of Great Britain, the Soviet Union and the United States had convinced many Belgians that the defeat of the German Reich was inevitable and their minds turned to dreams of the bloody purge which would accompany the final liberation. The innumerable and often ephemeral underground publications now circulating within the country did much to excite popular anger with lurid and frequently exaggerated descriptions of collaborationist activities. More than ever, the Rexists became scapegoats for the frustrations of the population and such was the violence of the threats levelled at 'cette vermine immonde' who had betrayed the country that it prompted two bourgeois observers to remark apprehensively in 1942: 'On craint que la guerre finie, il se produise dans notre pays de terribles remous. L'esprit de vengeance est poussé au paroxysme et, à entendre ce qui se colporte, les représailles s'exerceront sans aucune pitié.'[151]

Popular antipathy towards the Rexists continued to escalate remorselessly in all areas of public and private life. Their rallies were shunned, their funerals heckled and their marches disrupted. Some lost their jobs or, like the Uccle hairdresser who wrote in desperation to *Le Pays Réel* in 1942, struggled to make ends meet after their businesses were boycotted by their non-Rexist clientele.[152] At school the children of Rexists were insulted by their class-mates and their teachers; their post was intercepted and doctors were accused of neglecting the Rexist sick in their care.[153] As the numerous requests for pen-friends from *légionnaires* and *Gardes Wallonnes* published in *Le Pays Réel* indicated, friends and families often abandoned those who volunteered for the German armies while even in the Stalags in Germany, where many francophone Belgian soldiers still languished, Rexists were insulted or attacked by their comrades.[154]

In these circumstances, many Rexists felt they had little choice but to withdraw from the outside world. The vision of a moderate, principled collaboration presented by Streel may have accorded with the wishes of many militants but most recognised that it was no longer a viable possibility. Some chose to abandon Rex and, in contrast to the *VNV* which was still expanding, the overall trend in Rexist membership in 1942 appears to have been downwards.[155] Most remained loyal however and many of these responded to the hostility of their compatriots by retreating ever further into the limited protection offered by the German authorities. Though the difficulties encountered by the mobilisation programme had demonstrated the reluctance of many to become too closely associated with the German police, at a more superficial level the Rexists gave an impression of unconditional support for the Nazi cause by applauding frenetically at any mention of Hitler or by giving their children incongruous Germanic names.[156]

Above all, the Rexists gradually adopted the attitudes of a group who stood outside the rest of the community. In common with supporters of the Nazi cause elsewhere in Occupied Europe, their alienation from their compatriots and dependence on German favour propelled the Rexists towards seeing themselves as foreigners within their own land. They claimed exemption from the requisitioning and rationing imposed on their fellow citizens and, as early as December 1941, many were apparently even questioning whether they had to pay taxes to the Belgian authorities.[157] This attitude was encouraged by propaganda which portrayed the Rexists as a revolutionary elite struggling to impose their will on an alien population. Crude elitism of this kind was a prominent feature of collaborationist rhetoric throughout German-occupied Europe but it rarely reached such extremes as in Rexist speeches and publications. Any sense of popular support was banished and instead the Rexists were incited to regard themselves as 'légionnaires du front de l'intérieur' who on the decisive day of action would, 'baïonnette au canon', impose their revolution on an uncomprehending nation.[158] The slogans, iconography and even the songs of Rex reflected the harshness of their rhetoric. Though the sardonic cartoons of 'Jam' in *Le Pays Réel* still recalled the student iconoclasm of the early years of Rex, much more typical of the new spirit of the movement was the song 'Fer, Sang et Feu' distributed to militants in 1942:

Gardons toujours nos glaives
Brillants pour le combat
Préparons-nous sans trêve
Car le sang coulera.

Craignons la peur traîtresse
Et non pas la douleur.
Ni pitié, ni faiblesse,
Durcissons notre coeur.

Fer, sang et feu,
Combat pour l'idéal.[159]

Chapter Five

Autumn 1942–January 1943

The Decisive Turning Point

THROUGHOUT German-occupied Europe, the final months of 1942 formed a decisive watershed when the ambivalences of the preceding three years were crushed by the remorseless march of the global military conflict. On the battlefields, the reverses suffered by Rommel in North Africa were followed by the siege and eventual surrender in January 1943 of the German armies at Stalingrad. The impact of these first major German defeats was reinforced by the Allied resolve – proclaimed at the Casablanca conference of January 1943 – to pursue the military struggle until the unconditional surrender of Nazi Germany. Expectations of a prolonged stalemate or of some form of compromise peace largely evaporated and were replaced by a recognition that the war had become a trial of military strength between two clearly-defined coalitions. This awareness that the conflict had entered upon its decisive phase was deepened by important changes in Nazi policy. The invasion of the unoccupied southern zone of Vichy France, the imposition on much of Occupied Europe of labour conscription measures which led to the deportation of large numbers of workers to Germany as well as the increasingly apocalyptic tone adopted by Nazi propaganda were all developments which swept away the superficial veneer of European co-operation within the German empire. Exploitation and repression were now the clearly established determinants of Nazi policy towards its subject peoples and – within Germany as beyond – it was clear that only whole-hearted obedience and commitment would satisfy Hitler and his acolytes.

In Belgium, as elsewhere, the overall impact of these changes was to create a simpler, harsher world in which black and white superseded the manifold shades of grey so evident during the preceding years. For many people, of course, life continued much as before, but even for those who shunned any direct involvement in the conflict the events of war intruded ever more directly into the banalities of daily existence. The developing battle of wits between the German police and their Resistance adversaries, the defensive preparations by the German forces for an Allied landing on the coast, the nightly sound of Allied bombers passing overhead and, above all, the deportation of large numbers of men to work in the factories of the Reich served to bring the conflict into the lives of many ordinary people. Most Belgians had, of course, little doubt as to where their sympathies lay in this global war. They remained in the overwhelming majority firm in their support for the Allied cause: but, while in the early years of the Occupation this support had been a predominantly sentimental matter, it subsequently became a much more intense matter. Both the development of internal resistance to the German forces and the prospect that Belgium might once again become the front line of battle required many more ordinary men and women to decide whether they wished to carry their support for the Allied cause from the realm of symbolic gestures to concrete actions replete with potentially serious consequences.

The war not only intruded into private lives but also became the determining factor in all political choices. The relatively conciliatory stance adopted by the *Wehrmacht* officers of the *Militärverwaltung* ensured that the cautious 'cohabitation' continued between the German authorities and the *secrétaires-généraux*, the Catholic Church and the industrialists; but in what remained of the political sphere only one elemental division prevailed. Collaboration and Resistance were the twin poles around which all political activity gathered and not only was a position outside of these two camps all but impossible but within each camp it was those who were most whole-hearted in their commitment who increasingly gained the upper hand. This was especially so among the advocates of collaboration, for whom the pressure of external events was reinforced by the clash of personal ambitions and by the often desperate pursuit of Nazi patronage. Belgium was far from being unique in this respect. Elsewhere in Occupied Europe, notably in Norway and France, there was a similar hardening in the positions adopted by the collaborationist minorities in response to the pressure of circumstances and the demands of the German authorities. Men such as Quisling and Laval, formerly so anxious to present themselves as intermediaries between their countries and the victorious Germans were now obliged to adopt a new rhetoric of choice and of overt identification with the ideology and goals of the Nazi regime.[1]

These months were of especial significance for the Rexist movement, still awkwardly poised between the unconditional enthusiasms of Degrelle and the more circumspect policies of its interim leadership. If any period can be said to have been decisive in the wartime history of Rex, it was undeniably the hectic months between September 1942 and January 1943. Its starting-point was the decision by Streel in September to redouble his efforts to establish Rex as a bastion of moderation within the collaborationist camp. His principal initiative was the creation in September 1942 of a *Conseil Politique* of Rex. Acting with the support of Matthys, the *Chef du Service Politique* intended that this consultative body should be composed principally of those non-Rexist francophone advocates of collaboration, notably in public administration and the German-censored press, who had formerly remained aloof from Rex. Its initial purpose was merely to improve co-operation between Rex and these more moderate elements but, as Streel explained after the war, he hoped that it would be the first stage towards the creation of a more broadly-based anti-democratic and collaborationist movement: 'Je voulais passer du cadre étriqué du rexisme à quelque chose de nouveau qui aurait reçu une nouvelle appellation et fait appel à un nouveau personnel. Dans ce but je m'efforçai par des contacts personnels de grouper autour du mouvement des sympathies prêtes à s'affirmer dans le cadre d'une formation plus vaste.'[2] The first meeting of the *Conseil Politique* held on 25 September was attended by representatives of the Brussels collaborationist press including Paul Colin and Pierre Daye from *Le Nouveau Journal* and Raymond De Becker and Pierre De Ligne of *Le Soir*, as well as Letesson of the Liège newspaper *La Légia*. Also present were Paul Garain of the New Order trade union, the *Union des Travailleurs Manuels et Intellectuels (UTMI)*, Ernest Delvaux of the Ministry of the Interior and Edouard De Meyer, the pro-Rexist *secrétaire-général* of the Ministry of Public Works, as well as representatives of the *Ordre des Médecins, Commission de la Bourse*, and of New Order local authorities.[3] On the other hand, no representative from the more radical pro-Nazi newspapers or from extremist groups such as *AGRA*, the *MNPW* or *Défense du Peuple* was invited to join the new organisation.

The initial success of the *Conseil Politique* owed much to broader military and political events. Men such as Colin, De Becker and Poulet were by the autumn of 1942 prophets without a cause. Not only had the evolution of the war undermined their principal justification of collaboration as a patriotic necessity but the polarisation of the country into two unequal camps of pro-Allied patriots and emphatically pro-German collaborationists had destroyed the centre ground of moderate, 'realistic' opinion which they had claimed to represent. Moreover, their hope that a New Order Belgium might take its place among the states of an Axis-dominated Europe had all but disappeared. The political eclipse of the King, still languishing in the palace of Laeken, was ample proof of the lack of interest manifested by the Nazi leadership in a Belgium remodelled along authoritarian lines. Instead, it was the *SS* and its pan-Germanic ideology which increasingly set the tone of German policy-making, raising the spectre of a dismemberment of the Belgian state or even its incorporation into an expanded Reich.[4]

Thus these New Order figures were faced with a stark choice between advancing further into the world of collaboration or withdrawing entirely from the political stage. Some chose the latter path. Henri De Man, former President of the *Parti Ouvrier Belge* and royal adviser, who had been such an influential figure in the months after the military defeat, rediscovered his distaste for the world of political intrigue, choosing not only to abandon public life but to withdraw to an isolated chalet in the French Alps to muse on the failure of his dreams.[5] Others, however, opted to persevere with collaboration and, for them, Streel's initiative offered a welcome opportunity to escape from their marginal position. From the spring of 1942, there had been indications that men such as De Becker, Poulet and Colin were willing to swallow their pride and ally themselves with Rex. Streel encouraged this process. He met Robert Poulet to discuss the possible content of a common political programme and in *Le Pays Réel* he was careful to praise the proposals advanced by De Becker for the structure of a future Belgian state.[6] Therefore, when the *Conseil Politique* was proposed, these journalists reacted enthusiastically. Robert Poulet, while not actually joining the *Conseil*, published a series of articles in *Le Nouveau Journal* calling for the urgent creation of a *parti unique* of all pro-German forces in which he accepted that Rex would play the leading role. De Becker's reaction was even more favourable. Under the headline 'En marche vers l'unité', the editor of *Le Soir* praised the declarations of the Rexist leaders which, he claimed, demonstrated that all francophone collaborationists in Belgium now spoke 'un véritable langage commun, issu d'une réelle communauté d'idéal'.[7]

In parallel with the establishment of the *Conseil*, Streel encouraged a *rapprochement* between Rex and the Flemish nationalist movement, the *VNV*. Since the accord of May 1941, relations between the two groups had deteriorated rapidly. The *VNV* had violated almost immediately the spirit if not the wording of the agreement by seeking to extend its activities to Wallonia. Many Flemish Nationalists had long regarded francophone Belgium and even northern France as part of the *espace vital* of the Flemish nation and in the summer of 1941 the *VNV* appointed a leader for 'Wallonie en Zuid-Vlaanderen' and launched a monthly journal entitled *Ons Vaderland* aimed at those many francophone Belgians who were of Flemish extraction. A number of local *VNV* groups were subsequently set up, notably in the Hainaut, and though these efforts met with little success they were sufficient to arouse the ire of the Rexists.[8] In August 1941 Streel denounced the 'foyers de trouble' which the *VNV* was seeking to establish in southern Belgium and Rexist militants were warned to be vigilant for any evidence of *VNV* activity. Squabbles over the future status of Brussels and the power enjoyed by the *VNV* in central government added to tensions between the two movements and by January 1942 the Rexists seemed anxious to end the May accord which they dismissed as no more than a temporary arrangement based on 'considérations d'opportunité'.[9]

Yet by the following summer this hostility had all but disappeared. Streel praised the moderate stance adopted by the *VNV* regarding the future status of Brussels and in October Matthys spoke optimistically of the improved relations between Rex and the Flemish nationalist movement.[10] The reasons for this *rapprochement* are not difficult to identify. Surrounded by an increasingly hostile environment the two movements had every reason to work together and in October 1942 the sudden death of the leader of the *VNV*, Staf De Clercq, led to the appointment as his successor of a much more conciliatory figure, Hendrik Elias, who renounced De Clercq's imperialist and anti-Belgian rhetoric in favour of seeking to work within the institutions of the Belgian state.[11] This evolution within the *VNV* was greatly aided by the development of *DeVlag* (the *Duits-Vlaamse Arbeidsgemeenschap*), a radical grouping led by Jef Van de Wiele which rejected the traditional goal of an independent Flemish homeland in favour of the incorporation of Flanders into the German Reich. Initially a purely cultural organisation, *DeVlag* received the energetic support of the *SS* and it was at their instigation that Van de Wiele decided in October 1942 to establish *DeVlag* as a mass political movement.[12] In response to this direct challenge, the leaders of the *VNV* began to look to the New Order groups in francophone Belgium to form a common front against the threats posed by annexation and the activities of Nazi-sponsored radicals. Streel met Elias on several occasions during the autumn of 1942 and, though their meetings had few immediate consequences, they apparently revealed a considerable convergence of views.[13]

These political initiatives by Streel were reinforced by his use of the columns of *Le Pays Réel* to attack the advocates of total collaboration. Frequently using events in France as a means of making thinly disguised comments on the Belgian political situation, he declared that extremism was for some people an illness or a profession which must be countered by the creation of a bloc of moderate and principled collaborationists: 'Il s'agit aujourd'hui de distinguer ceux qui veulent une collaboration effective dans la loyauté et la dignité, de ceux qui sont prêts à livrer notre peuple aux plus dangereuses aventures.'[14] The centre-piece of any new movement must, Streel insisted, be a clear commitment to a bilingual federal Belgian state. Only by presenting such a common front could the Belgian collaborationists ensure for their country its rightful historical role as the crossroads of Europe. The bleak alternative was that the country would be dismembered by Flemish and Walloon extremists and that it would sink into the protectorate status of a Croatia, Montenegro or 'sous-Slovaquie'.[15]

Not for the first time, however, Streel's apocalyptic attitude was not entirely shared by Matthys. Though he supported the initiatives of the *Chef du Service Politique*, Matthys saw his principal priority during these months as the regeneration of Rex after the difficulties of the spring and summer. To this end, he decided to organise a national rally in Brussels on 25 October, the first such event since the dramatic meeting at Liège in January 1941. The venue for this show of strength was in itself significant. The Rexist leaders were anxious to counter the impression that Brussels was a Flemish city and they chose to hold the meeting in the vast Palais des Sports, the scene of many of Degrelle's most dramatic pre-war meetings.[16]

In deference to the sensibilities of the Flemish Nationalists and their allies in the German administration, the rally was officially described as a meeting of the three Brussels *cercles* of Rex. In reality it was attended by several thousand militants who had travelled to the capital from all areas of francophone Belgium.[17] The Rexist leaders may initially have hoped that Degrelle would be present to address his followers but his return from the East was once again postponed and he sent only a brief message of support to the assembled Rexists.[18] Instead the centre-piece of the rally was a major speech by Matthys. He predictably devoted much of his speech to seeking to reassure his audience that, whatever the vagaries of the military campaigns, the triumph of their cause was ineluctable. Though he admitted the possibility of an Allied victory, he declared that not even this catastrophe could prevent the formidable social revolution which was maturing and of which the Rexists were the pioneers. Matthys was, however, forced to admit that the immediate political outlook was bleak. No change to the frustrating stalemate within Belgium was in view and the *Chef de Rex ad interim* could only reiterate to his audience the need to prepare for an eventual, unspecified, day of action: 'Plus que jamais le mot d'ordre est Révolution d'abord. Votre objectif doit être: formation, organisation, conquête.'[19]

His emphasis on a social revolution as well as his verbal attacks on the selfish bourgeoisie, the Jews and 'le clergé politicien' reflected Matthys' own radical impulses. Nonetheless the speech was no mere diatribe and the emphasis he placed on more long-standing Rexist ideas such as the importance of the family demonstrated Matthys' anxiety to fuse both the traditional and the novel elements in Rexist ideology. This same balance was also evident in the important section of his speech which he devoted to the future political structure of Belgium. Degrelle had long been keen to emphasise the close historical links between francophone Belgium and Germany but in this speech Matthys went much further in presenting the Walloons as a Germanic people. Adopting the racial theories advanced by various German academics and popularised by innumerable Nazi publications, the *Chef de Rex ad interim* declared that by blood, history and *moeurs*, Wallonia did indeed belong to 'l'espace germanique'. But he went on to stress that the Germanic character of the Walloons in no way prejudiced Belgian unity. On the contrary, he argued, it demonstrated the indissoluble racial bond which united the Walloons and the similarly Germanic Flemish nation and which formed the basis of the Belgian state: 'Nous sommes fermement attaché à ce minimum qu'est l'unité étatique des deux communautés qui forment la Belgique d'aujourd'hui. Ces provinces sont unies par une communauté de destin, indiscutable et séculaire . . . Notre fidélité jalouse à notre propre Patrie est la garantie la plus certaine de la fidélité que nous saurons témoigner au monde germanique.'[20]

Matthys' skilful use of Nazi ideas to rebuff those who sought a division of Belgium into two distinct ethnic communities meant that his acceptance of the Germanic character of the Walloons amounted to little more than a symbolic change. While demonstrating the willingness of Rex to adopt the rhetoric of Nazism, he had avoided making any real change in Rexist policies and, as Reeder succinctly observed, Matthys' comments signified 'allerdings noch keine Abkehr von dem Gedanken des belgischen Einheits-staates'.[21] Streel too recognised the real significance of the *Chef de Rex ad interim*'s declarations. Though he had formerly been noisy in his con-demnation of those who claimed that the Walloons were a Germanic people, he declared his cautious support for the new policy provided it was used to reinforce the cause of a united Belgium.[22]

Despite the absence of Degrelle, the rally in Brussels undoubtedly had a beneficial impact on Rexist morale. It was attended by an array of col-laborationist and German delegates as well as by representatives of the numerous communal authorities under Rexist control and, if nothing else, it proved to a hostile population and a sceptical German audience that Rex was still a significant political force. Its impact was, however, to be only very transitory. Already before the rally took place, two new crises had arisen which in the subsequent weeks would absorb the attention of the Rexist leaders. Moreover, both of these issues – the introduction of labour conscription and an unprecedented wave of attacks on the supporters of Rex – once again demonstrated that the cautious position articulated by Matthys in his speech was no longer viable. The only real choice was between withdrawal or total collaboration.

On 6 October, the *Militärverwaltung* suddenly announced legislation making all men aged between 18 and 50 years and all women aged between 21 and 35 liable for labour service in the German Reich. During the preceding months, other more limited forms of labour conscription within Belgium had been announced but the introduction of such sweeping measures came as an unwelcome shock to the population. It inevitably recalled memories of the mass deportations which took place during the first German Occupation of 1914–18 and the immediate popular response was one of anger and despair.[23] For once, the Rexist leaders shared in the mood of their compatriots. They had learned of the decrees in September and were quick to realise that such arbitrary measures would destroy whatever slender hope remained of winning popular support for their cause. The newly created *Conseil Politique* was hastily convened on 25 September and it agreed that: 'Il faut s'efforcer d'éviter cette réquisition qui évoquerait les déportations de l'autre guerre et serait d'un effet psy-chologique déplorable et pourrait interrompre toute politique de collabor-ation.'[24] The Rexists and their allies sought to convince the German authorities to adopt an alternative programme devised by Hendrickx, the pro-New Order director of the *Office National du Travail*, for the mobil-isation of the labour force within Belgium. These efforts were entirely in vain. The German administrators in Brussels were well aware that the deportations would have a catastrophic impact on popular morale and had opposed their introduction. But their arguments had had little impact in Berlin where the forced mobilisation of foreign labour to work in German factories was regarded as essential for the Nazi war effort.[25]

Thus, after a series of fruitless negotiations, the Rexists were forced to abandon all hope of reversing or modifying the German decrees. But *Le Pays Réel* continued to treat the matter very cautiously and, according to a post-war account by Matthys, the Rexist leadership even contemplated suspending the entire policy of collaboration.[26] If this was indeed so, it would seem unlikely that it ever received serious consideration. At the very least such a major change in policy would have required the approval of Degrelle and he remained isolated with the *Légion* in the distant Caucasus region of Central Asia. Thus, the Rexist leadership was obliged to support, however reluctantly, the labour conscription legislation. In a strongly worded circular distributed to the *cercles* on 21 October, the Rexist leaders swallowed their misgivings declaring that 'en Nationaux-Socialistes, nous collaborons à fond pour la réussite de cette ordonnance'. A few weeks later this choice was made public. Writing in *Le Pays Réel*, Victor Meulenyzer explained that, though Rex did not watch with 'gaieté de coeur' the deportation of Belgian workers to Germany, labour conscription was essential in order to ensure the victory of the National Socialist cause.[27]

Nor was this support purely symbolic. In its circular of 21 October, the Rexist *Etat-Major* ordered its supporters to collect information on 'tous les éléments associaux, trafiquants, "swings" et fils de famille, sans occupation régulière' who would benefit from a period of labour in Germany.[28] These lists were clearly intended for the German authorities and in practice the definition of antisocial elements was soon extended to include all those believed to be opposed to Rex. Moreover, though the Rexists claimed that the denunciation of such 'social parasites' was the most effective means of protecting the honest members of the working class from deportation, their real motive was more self-interested. Some Rexist officials frankly admitted that they hoped that as recompense for helping the German authorities their own supporters would be exempted from the labour conscription measures.[29] Certain officers in the *Formations de Combat* apparently refused to participate in this work but other militants had no such scruples and within a few months a number of lists had been forwarded to the German authorities. In Brussels members of Rex were even reported to have visited small businesses to assess whether they should be closed down and their owners deported to work in Germany.[30] Such zeal soon brought its intended reward. From the outset, the *Militärverwaltung* had agreed that prominent Rexists would not be deported and, after further negotiations, the Rexist *Etat-Major* was finally able to announce in March 1943 that the German authorities had accepted that all militants who submitted justified requests would be exempted. Close relations soon developed between the Rexist *cercles* and the German *Werbestellen* responsible for the enactment of the labour conscription measures and, in practice, few if any Rexists were obliged to join their compatriots in the factories of the Reich.[31]

The mass deportation of Belgian men to Germany was a major turning-point in the history of the Occupation. Though the legislation was principally applied only to certain age groups of young men, it served as the catalyst which more than any other single factor mobilised popular hatred against the Occupying forces and their Belgian allies. The remorseless decline in living standards, the activities of the Nazi police and the numerous constraints imposed on daily life by German decrees and regulations had all played their part in alienating the Belgian people from the Occupying forces but it was the labour conscription legislation which for the first time brought the mass of ordinary citizens into direct conflict with the German authorities. Conditions in the German factories were frequently harsh and, rather than report for this unpleasant and ill-paid work, thousands of young men chose to go into hiding. Thrust into a clandestine existence, these *réfractaires* provided a steady stream of volunteers for the burgeoning Resistance organisations.[32]

For their part, the Rexists had once again chosen, after some weeks of hesitation, to support the German authorities against their own compatriots. Ultimately unwilling or unable to countenance abandoning collaboration, they were obliged to support a policy which could only prejudice the Rexist cause. Moreover, by choosing to assist the German authorities in return for effective exemption from the labour conscription measures, the Rexist leaders had reinforced their status as a separate caste who seemed willing to put their interests and those of the Occupying power above those of their country.[33]

A similar combination of self-interest and loyalty to the German cause also determined the Rexist response to the escalation in Resistance attacks on Rexist militants which occurred during the last months of 1942. Assaults on Flemish Nationalists and other collaborationist figures were also stepped up but the Rexists remained the principal target of the Resistance. For example, of 19 pro-German figures murdered between August and November 1942, 12 were members of Rexist organisations.[34] No supporter of Rex was too lowly to be immune from such attacks, but it was the murders of a number of prominent local leaders which had the greatest impact. On 11 November, Charles Hénault, a medical doctor and the long-time *chef de cercle* of Verviers, was shot dead by the *Partisans Armés* while a few days later on the 19th the *bourgmestre* of *Grand Charleroi* and former parliamentary deputy, Prosper Teughels, was killed outside his home. Finally, on 16 December, the *Abbé* Kaumont of Lasnes-Chapelle St

Lambert, one of the few remaining Rexist priests and a confidant of some of the leaders of the movement, fell victim to the Resistance assassins.[35]

Many militants were reported to be 'affolés' by this wave of attacks and they began to take on the air of hunted men, avoiding travelling alone and barricading themselves in their houses at night.[36] Some became reluctant to accept public offices and in Liège, as already mentioned, the newly-appointed mayor and some of his colleagues resigned, the mayor un-heroically seeking sanctuary in a sanatorium.[37] Fearing that such examples might provoke a wave of resignations, Streel and Matthys responded by sending a letter to all Rexist office-holders on 27 November in which they detailed the efforts they had been making to guarantee the security of their supporters. It was symptomatic of the fear gripping the movement at this time that the letter conceded that if matters did not improve it might prove necessary to withdraw all Rexists from positions in public adminis-tration. However the two Rexist leaders were adamant that the time had not yet come for such a drastic step and the letter concluded with exhor-tations to their militants to remain at the 'poste de combat' which they had assumed.[38]

But how was their security to be improved? Streel's initial preference was for the Belgian judicial and police authorities to act more decis-ively in identifying the perpetrators of the attacks. To this end, he and Matthys had some months earlier visited Schuind, the secrétaire-général of the Ministry of Justice, to ask for greater efforts in this field. Yet, though Schuind apparently reassured them that he regarded those re-sponsible for such attacks as criminals and that every effort would be made to apprehend them, this interview had little effect. No arrests were made and, as Matthys and Streel admitted in their November letter to office-holders, the Belgian police and judiciary manifestly lacked both the means and the will to act against the Resistance groups.[39] Instead, Streel proposed that special units be established within the polices communales of Rexist-controlled local authorities to specialise in the investigation of these mur-ders. This proposal offered little hope of immediate results however and Matthys chose instead to adopt a more radical course. In two virtually hysterical letters written to the German authorities in November, he called for stern reprisals to be taken against the civilian population. Substantial fines, he demanded, must be imposed on the localities where such attacks took place, all former Belgian army officers and prisoners of war must be arrested and ten known Communists should be executed in response to every murder of a supporter of collaboration.[40]

Matthys repeated these Draconian demands in subsequent meetings with German officials.[41] For some months previously, the Militärverwaltung had been imposing fines on communes where Resistance violence took place and, in response to pressure from Matthys, a special fund was established into which these fines were paid and from which all collaborationists could claim in proportion to the loss or injury which they had suffered. In addition, the Germans accepted that the system of arms permits should be extended so that all those Rexists appointed to public offices would be allowed to carry weapons.[42]

These limited measures were, however, insufficient to appease the *Chef de Rex ad interim* who, according to Reeder, also demanded that the Rexists be allowed to resort to measures of 'Selbsthilfe' in response to the Resistance attacks. Already in his letter to the German military commander of Brussels on 14 November Matthys had threatened that, if effective action was not taken by the German authorities, Rex would be forced to take the law into its own hands. The *Militärverwaltung* was firmly opposed to any such 'counter-terrorism' by the advocates of collaboration and no evidence exists to suggest that the Rexist leadership were at this time in fact planning attacks on suspected Resistance militants.[43] Matthys' threat was therefore probably little more than an attempt to force the German authorities to take more drastic steps. Prominent among these was Matthys' repeated insistence that the Germans should execute Belgian hostages in reprisal for attacks on collaborationists. The German authorities had frequently arrested local dignitaries and suspected Communist sympathisers in response to Resistance actions but, though they had ordered the execution of a number of these political hostages in the Nord and Pas-de-Calais of France, Reeder and Von Falkenhausen had long resisted calls both from Berlin and from Belgian collaborationists to extend this policy to Belgium, arguing that such executions would be ineffective and counter-productive. Finally, however, they gave way and eight hostages were executed at Charleroi on 27 November 1942. These were the first of many such executions: between November 1942 and July 1944, 240 political prisoners (drawn from among those hostages against whom clear evidence of Resistance involvement was said to exist) were executed in reprisal for Resistance actions.[44]

The role played by Matthys in provoking this change in German policy was in all probability relatively unimportant. The executions in Charleroi were publicly stated to be in response to the murders of the Rexist *bourgmestre*, Teughels, and of other collaborationists and in his report to his superiors in Berlin Reeder admitted that the executions were principally intended to calm the members of Rex and other pro-German groups. This was a theme which Reeder enlarged upon at his post-war trial during which he presented the execution of hostages as largely the product of pressure from Degrelle and the Rexists. Reeder's account should not, however, be accepted at face value. The officials of the *Militärverwaltung* undoubtedly did believe that executions were ineffective in countering Resistance activities but their decision to proceed with them was the product of a complex matrix of pressures brought to bear by a number

of collaborationist groups within Belgium as well as by repeated interventions by their military and political superiors in Berlin. In these circumstances, to isolate the demands of Matthys and of other Rexists as the
decisive factor would be misleading. At most, their appeals can only have
served to reinforce what was an already inevitable concession to other
more influential pressures.[45]

Nevertheless, Matthys' unambivalent espousal of such extreme measures
demonstrated once again the difficulty of seeking to contain collaboration
within certain limits and served to exacerbate the tensions within the
Rexist leadership between its more moderate and extreme elements. These
tensions became more acute during the autumn of 1942 as a modest
improvement in the finances of the movement enabled a number of new
figures to join the staff of the Rexist headquarters. These men came to the
Rexist *Etat-Major* from the local *cercles* and the *Légion* and, on the whole,
they allied themselves with those in the Rexist leadership who had long
been anxious to kick over the traces of Streelian moderation.[46] Prominent
among these long-standing radicals within the Rexist headquarters was
Charles Lambinon. This former commercial traveller had never formed
part of the inner group of Rexist leaders and had few obvious qualifications
beyond a talent for office administration.[47] But during 1941 and 1942
he gradually developed a position of considerable autonomy within the
Rexist *Etat-Major* establishing the grandly titled *Bureau d'information, de
renseignements et de documentation (BIRD)*, the official responsibilities of
which were to collect information on members of Rex as well as their
opponents. Lambinon had a taste for this police work and the introduction
of labour conscription provided him with ample opportunity to display his
talents. He enthusiastically took charge of collecting the lists of those
'antisocial elements' deemed suitable for deportation to Germany as well
as asking the Rexist *cercles* for details of Communist militants and former
career soldiers of the Belgian army. Such information was in all probability
passed on to the various German police authorities with whom he was said
to be in contact and Lambinon was clearly eager that *BIRD* should become a Rexist police force. Streel was firmly opposed to any such change
and rejected Lambinon's request that *BIRD* be allowed to take charge of
the pursuit of those responsible for attacks on Rexist militants. Streel's
attempts to limit the scope of *BIRD*'s activities were, however, largely
ineffectual. Lambinon was convinced that Rex must take the offensive
against the Resistance groups and in the final months of 1942 he was already engaged in surveillance operations of figures, including the *procureur
du Roi* in Charleroi, whom he suspected of involvement in Resistance
activities.[48]

Lambinon was an ambitious figure anxious to exploit whatever opportunities collaboration offered for self-advancement but by late 1942
his belief in the need for more extreme measures was shared by many

other Rexists. Resistance terrorism, the absence of any significant political breakthrough and the unfavourable evolution of the war all appear to have contributed to a general mood of frustration within Rex. Morale was lower than at any time since the spring of 1941 and, more than ever, it seemed to many that the only hope lay in the return of the *Légion*. As one Rexist wrote desperately to his *légionnaire* brother in late November: 'A quand le retour de nos chers légionnaires? Il s'avère de plus en plus nécessaire; tu auras appris . . . l'assassinat de Teughels. C'est épouvantable et si cela continue nous serons bientôt réduits à une poignée. Vite vos mitrailleuses pour faire de la bonne besogne!'[49]

Thus, it was with understandable euphoria that the Rexists learnt at the end of November that Degrelle was at last to return to Belgium on leave accompanied by approximately 160 *légionnaires*.[50] Matthys and Streel hastened to Germany to meet the returning heroes who were spending one week at the training camp of the *Légion* at Meseritz. They found Degrelle remarkably unchanged by the long months at the front line. He had learnt not a word of German and, far from having adopted the discipline of a soldier, he had retained his impulsive, ebullient and somewhat anarchic character. He privately reassured the Rexist leaders that his experiences in the German armies had in no way changed his political attitudes and, in an emotional speech delivered at Meseritz, once again proclaimed that the *légionnaires* were Belgian patriots fighting for the salvation of their country.[51]

Streel was greatly reassured by these first meetings with Degrelle but his optimism was to prove to be short-lived. A few days later Degrelle and the Rexist leaders travelled to Berlin where they met the correspondent of *Le Pays Réel*, Léon Van Huffel, who remained an enthusiastic exponent of radical Germanic ideas. Released from the privations of the front, Degrelle was initially disinclined to pay attention to the journalist's long monologues on the Germanic origins of the Walloons. He was more anxious to enjoy the social pleasures of the German capital and, to the despair of Van Huffel, declined a meeting with SS officials in favour of paying a visit to the wife of a German general. Nevertheless, Van Huffel persisted and the next day Degrelle did agree to visit the offices of the SS where for the first time he met leading members of Himmler's entourage including apparently Gottlob Berger, the head of the SS headquarters, the *SS-Hauptamt*.[52]

This meeting on 19 December proved to be a revelation for Degrelle. During their wide-ranging discussions on the future of Belgium and of the *Légion Wallonie* and the Rexist movement both sides were anxious to impress each other. Despite their doubts as to his political reliability, the SS saw two principal attractions in forging closer links with Degrelle. Firstly, it would provide them with a further ally in their struggle against the *Wehrmacht* officers of the *Militärverwaltung* and, secondly, the entry of the *Légion Wallonie* into the *Waffen-SS* would assist their aim of transforming the military wing of the *SS* into the political army of the New Europe. As for Degrelle, the appeal of an alliance with the *SS* requires little explanation. It would at last provide him with access to the inner decision-making counsels of the Reich and, with his adroit sense of political opportunity, he abandoned his pro-Belgian declarations of a few days previously, assuring the *SS* officials that he was fully committed to restoring the Walloons to their rightful role as a Germanic people within the Reich.[53]

As Streel afterwards recalled, the effect on the *Chef de Rex* of this meeting with the *SS* was immediate and profound: 'Degrelle en revint littéralement transformé. C'est comme si un monde nouveau venait de se révéler à lui. On avait réussi à le persuader que l'avenir était à la *SS* et que seuls ceux qui auraient son appui pourraient jouer un rôle.'[54] His newfound enthusiasm was not, however, entirely unpremeditated. As a consummate political tactician, Degrelle had long been aware of the increasing power of the *SS* and, through a study of his correspondence and actions, it is possible to trace the *Chef de Rex*'s growing interest in the *SS* during the months preceding the meeting in Berlin.[55] As early as September 1941 he had made efforts to contact the *SS* and, though he does not appear to have met any *SS* representatives during his brief visit to Berlin in June 1942, he probably did encounter Van Huffel. Moreover, after Degrelle's return to the front line, the *Légion Wallonie* was placed for a number of weeks under the command of Steiner, the head of the *SS* Viking Division. The *Chef de Rex* was by all accounts greatly impressed by the superior spirit and material conditions of the *Waffen-SS* troops and, after a meeting with Degrelle, Steiner wrote to the *SS* headquarters in September 1942 advocating the transfer of the *Légion Wallonie* to the *Waffen-SS*.[56]

But, despite these contacts, Degrelle's closest links within the Nazi bureaucracy prior to December 1942 were still with non-*SS* figures such as the diplomat Otto Abetz, to whom he had addressed a further long missive in September.[57] Moreover, though he must have been aware of *SS* antipathy to a united Belgium, Degrelle continued to present himself as a Belgian nationalist. Indeed, in his dealings with German officials during 1942 he seemed to go out of his way to stress the patriotic purpose of the *Légion* declaring for example in an interview with the *Deutsche Allgemeine Zeitung* that: 'Ce n'est pas comme Wallons que nous sommes partis au Front de l'est, mais la Légion "Wallonie" est la légion des volontaires belges d'expression française. Pour nous, nous sommes des nationalistes qui combattent pour une Belgique nouvelle dans une Europe rénovée.'[58] These apparently contradictory gestures would seem to indicate that, as he has admitted, it was only in Berlin in December that Degrelle finally decided to ally himself with the *SS*. Berger, he has recalled, seemed to him to be a man of elephantine stupidity wedded to an absurd racial vision of world history but it was obvious that he and his *SS* colleagues were the coming men of the Third Reich. The generals and diplomats of the *ancien régime* were destined to disappear and, if he was to play any role in the New Europe, it was clear that he must win the support of Himmler and his assistants.[59]

In his many post-war justifications of his activities, the *Chef de Rex* has often dwelt on the patriotic motive behind his new policy. Listening to Berger, he claimed to have become aware of the threat of dismemberment which hung over Belgium and resolved to avert this danger by winning the *SS* over to his nationalist opinions.[60] In reality Degrelle's change of direction owed less to any concern for the national interest than to his own overweening ambition. During his meetings in Berlin, the *SS* officials had dwelt on the failings of the *VNV* which, attached to a narrow provincial outlook and dependant on the support of the *Militärverwaltung*, would have no place in an *SS*-designed New Europe.[61] The comparison with Rex must have been more than evident to Degrelle, especially as the *SS* was already providing financial assistance to extremist Walloon groups and had begun to recruit for the *Waffen-SS* in the region. Thus, as he remarked frankly to Romsée, his alliance with the *SS* was above all an accommodation to the changed power structure within Germany: 'La politique de l'Anschluss se fera dans notre pays avec ou contre moi; je préfère qu'elle se fasse avec moi.'[62] Having made his choice, the *Chef de Rex* was unshakeable in his new resolve. He had smelt the seductive whiff of power and on his return to Belgium in mid-December Degrelle threw himself into political intrigue with a renewed enthusiasm which flagrantly contradicted his assurances to Reeder that he intended only to rest during his stay in the country.[63]

Streel was understandably appalled by Degrelle's abrupt change of direction. An alliance with the *SS* was the antithesis of everything for which he had striven and both in Berlin and after their return to Brussels he made strenuous efforts – in person and via the columns of *Le Pays Réel* – to make Degrelle change his mind.[64] These efforts were to no avail. Never one to listen to the rational arguments of others, Degrelle was intoxicated by the prospect of an alliance with the *SS* and refused to heed either the warnings of Streel or those of Elias, the head of the *VNV*, whom Streel had arranged for Degrelle to meet in the hope that his experience of the ways of the *SS* might make the *Chef de Rex* reconsider his new policy. Degrelle dismissed the Flemish nationalist movement as 'foutu' and instead concentrated his attention on winning the support of Jef Van de Wiele, the malleable head of the pro-*SS* Flemish group *DeVlag*, and of *SS-Brigadeführer* Richard Jungclaus who since April 1942 had been Himmler's representative in Belgium.[65]

At public functions in the weeks after his return to Belgium, Degrelle made no secret of his determination to 'marcher à fond'. Addressing

Belgian volunteers in the German transport corps he praised the comradeship of Germanic peoples within the *NSKK*, while at a reception given in
his honour by the New Order *Association des Journalistes Belges* he spoke
grandiloquently of the glorious future which awaited Brussels as one of
the major cities of a new German Empire.[66] But, with his characteristic
taste for the dramatic gesture, Degrelle chose to make the first full statement of his 'neue Marschrichtung'[67] at a large Rexist rally held in the
Palais des Sports in Brussels on 17 January 1943. The style of this meeting
was a careful imitation of Nazi party rallies and, in front of the assembled
Rexist militants as well as numerous German and foreign dignitaries,
Degrelle delivered a major speech which impressed even such a sceptical
observer as Reeder by the power of its oratory.[68] Its climax was a vivid
portrayal of the supposedly Germanic heritage of Wallonia. Charlemagne,
the bishops of Liège and the Burgundian monarchs were all conscripted by
the Rexist leader to buttress his singular interpretation of history in which
he presented the Walloons as a Germanic frontier people struggling over
the centuries against the alien influences of French culture. The war, he
continued, had provided Wallonia with the opportunity to return to these
Germanic roots: 'Il faut qu'on sache que, fils de la race germanique . . .
nous avons repris conscience de notre qualité de Germains, que dans la
communauté germanique nous nous sentons chez nous.'[69] Matthys had, of
course, already made similar remarks in his October speech but on this
occasion Degrelle made no attempt to use the Germanic origins of the
Walloons to justify the continued unity of Belgium. Instead, he fully accepted that the future of the francophone Belgians lay *within* an expanded
Germanic Empire. The political significance of these remarks was clear.
The idea of a federation encompassing all of the German racial groups of
Europe was in effect the programme of the *SS* and the entire speech was
clearly intended by Degrelle to prove his support for the aims of Himmler
and his associates.

In other respects, however, Degrelle's speech was much more evasive.
He provided no details of the form which the new relationship between
Wallonia and Germany should take, merely declaring that: 'Notre petite
Patrie, c'est l'Occident; mais notre grande Patrie c'est la Communauté
Germanique au sein de laquelle nos camarades sont morts.'[70] Moreover,
though he dismissed the centralised Belgian state created in 1830 as a
deformation of history, Degrelle was careful not to reject completely some
form of Walloon-Flemish partnership and he once again praised the era of
the Burgundian empire as one of harmony and joint endeavour between
the two peoples. Such evasive phraseology served a deliberate purpose.
Though anxious to convince the *SS* of his willingness to participate in
their Germanic Empire, Degrelle's political ambitions remained considerably wider than the narrow frontiers of Wallonia. Thus, he did not wish to
be seen as an advocate of the simple annexation of Wallonia by Germany

and throughout the remaining years of the war he would always leave open the possibility of some form of unified Walloon-Flemish entity within the expanded Reich.[71]

These subtleties were, however, much less important than the way in which Degrelle's speech fundamentally altered the terms upon which collaboration was based. Until January 1943, it had been presented by the Rexists as a *contract* between Belgium and Germany. The justifications of that contract were several: the German military victory in Western Europe, the need for a political revolution within Belgium and, from June 1941, the crusade against the Bolshevik peril. All of these justifications defined collaboration in restrictive, exclusive terms. However close the relationship might be, it remained a pact between two separate entities whose distinctiveness was not prejudiced by their mutual endeavours to achieve certain goals. On 17 January Degrelle abandoned this contractual vision of collaboration and instead presented Wallonia and Germany as a single entity. The consequence of this fusion of the interests of Germany and Wallonia was to destroy all notion of a limit to collaboration. Walloon co-operation with the Reich ceased to be motivated by self-interest but became self-fulfilment, the expression of Wallonia's racial and historic destiny. Nazi policies were, by definition, also those of Wallonia and the Walloon people owed an unconditional loyalty to the leaders of the Third Reich.[72]

Degrelle's speech on 17 January marked what might be termed the highest stage of collaboration. What had begun two years earlier as a part-opportunistic, part-principled policy of co-operation with the Occupying forces had become an open-ended commitment to support the Nazi regime in every way. Not content to identify with the German cause, Degrelle now advocated even the physical absorption of the Belgian lands and people into a Germanic empire. Above all, however, the speech completed Degrelle's transformation into a power-seeker on the stage of the German Reich. All scruples were forgotten in what had become an unrestrained pursuit of the Nazi patronage which he now believed was the only way that he could hope to acquire power. Thus, as Degrelle has freely admitted, the ideological content of his speech was much less important than its political significance. He attached no great value to the alleged Germanic character of the Walloons and claimed that he would have happily declared that they were Hindu in origin if it would have appeased the Nazi leaders: '. . . Moi cette germanité des Wallons ne m'impressionait pas outre mesure, mais les Allemands étaient baba devant cette découverte.'[73] Thus, in his post-war accounts of his actions, he has presented the speech as an instance of Degrellian sleight of hand outwitting the ponderous Germans. By convincing the Nazi leaders that he was a convert to their pseudo-scientific racial doctrines, Degrelle has argued that he intended to ensure the survival of some form of Belgian state within the Nazi empire.[74]

This may indeed have remained his final goal but, in reality, such patriotic justifications had long since become no more than a convenient pretext for his pursuit of power. Drawn like a moth towards the fading lights of Berlin, Degrelle was from January 1943 of peripheral importance in his native land. He had become an essentially German figure, of significance only in the internecine conflicts which would dominate the last years of Hitler's regime. The corollary of this process was a weakening of the bonds between Degrelle and his political movement. Though he remained the undisputed leader of Rex, Degrelle no longer took much interest in developments within Belgium and observed with only a distracted eye the fortunes of the movement. Therefore the speech which superficially marked Degrelle's return amongst his followers in fact signalled the point of separation between Rex and its leader. In the final years of the war Degrelle and Rex were increasingly to operate in different political arenas and, instead of the leader of a Belgian political movement, Degrelle became a solitary adventurer seeking crumbs of prestige and power amidst the ruins of the besieged Reich.

Chapter Six

January – Autumn 1943

The Pursuit of Total Collaboration

DEGRELLE'S speech was a rock thrown into the small pool of Belgian collaboration. Most Belgians dismissed the latest declarations of the *Chef de Rex* as the ravings of an opportunist who had long since lost any hold on reality.[1] Among his fellow collaborationists, however, Degrelle's dramatic espousal of the ideas of the *SS* aroused intense and widely divergent reactions. Men such as Raymond De Becker and Robert Poulet regarded the speech as a negation of their commitment to a united Belgian state and, after seeking in vain some form of reassurance from the *Chef de Rex*, De Becker and his colleague Pierre De Ligne resigned from the *Conseil Politique* of Rex, which rapidly ceased to be an institution of any significance.[2] After lengthy negotiations with the *Militärverwaltung*, De Becker was allowed to publish a series of articles in *Le Soir* strongly critical of Degrelle's new course. But Robert Poulet was prevented by the German censors from voicing his similar criticisms and he resigned as editor of *Le Nouveau Journal*, commenting that he considered the *Chef de Rex* to be 'de plus en plus fou'.[3] Not all of their colleagues in the pro-German press did, however, share their views. Paul Colin, the director of *Le Nouveau Journal* and *Cassandre*, was well aware of the historical absurdities of Degrelle's speech but he too was attracted by the idea of an alliance with the *SS* and, declaring that all political initiatives contained a necessary element of risk, he not only praised the *Chef de Rex*'s change of direction but became one of his closest political allies.[4]

Such flexibility held no appeal for José Streel. The rally at the Palais des Sports had amply fulfilled his worst expectations and he promptly withdrew from both *Le Pays Réel* and the *Service Politique* of the Rexist *Etat-Major*, insisting that Degrelle had betrayed both Rex and his country by proclaiming 'sa confiance illimitée et inconditionnelle dans [un] chef d'état étranger dont il se proclame le soldat politique'.[5] Fearful of the consequences of the departure of such a prominent figure, Matthys and the administrators of *Le Pays Réel* sought to reach a compromise whereby Streel would have remained within the movement in a less public capacity. This idea seems initially to have had some appeal for Streel but the negotiations soon proved fruitless, not least because of an intemperate intervention by Degrelle, and Streel severed all links with Rex accepting instead an offer from De Becker to become a regular columnist for *Le Soir*.[6]

In letters to Rexist friends, Streel bitterly denounced 'les enthousiasmes chimériques, les ambitions maladroites et les erreurs politiques' of Degrelle.[7] But with the passage of time he came to look on his departure from Rex as a liberation. Released from his political responsibilities, he felt better able to express his personal views and his contributions to *Le Soir* during 1943 and 1944 were devoted largely to historical and moral subjects.[8] Yet, although Streel played no part in collaborationist politics, he never abandoned his belief in the need to work with Germany. The Bolshevik menace remained the dominant factor which, as he wrote privately to Reeder in February 1943, made an Axis military victory ever more essential.[9] Nonetheless he had few illusions as to the political consequences of such a victory. He recognised that the ascendancy of extremist forces both in the Third Reich and within Belgium had effectively destroyed all hope of a New Order Belgium emerging from the war and, during the last years of the Occupation, he was to be little more than an eloquent relic of an obsolete cause.

Streel was not the only Rexist leader dismayed by Degrelle's abrupt change of course. Paul Lisein, the *Chef des Cadres Politiques*, and Albert Constant, the head of the *Formations de Combat*, resigned from Rex in the weeks after the rally while other senior figures, such as Victor Meulenyser, made clear to Degrelle their personal opposition to his new stance.[10] Their concern was shared by many ordinary militants. For several weeks Degrelle's speech was apparently the principal subject of discussion in the local *cercles* and many Rexists were clearly alarmed by the tone and content of Degrelle's pronouncements.[11] José Streel was held in high esteem by many within the movement and a number of militants followed his example by resigning from Rex. As an internal report was subsequently obliged to admit: 'Nous avons vu s'en aller quelques camarades – fort peu nombreux d'ailleurs – qui n'avaient pas assez de muscle, qui n'avaient pas surtout assez de confiance en eux-mêmes, pour entreprendre l'audacieuse aventure à laquelle le Chef nous conviait tous.'[12]

Degrelle did not initially appear concerned by these resignations. As in January 1941, he had doubtless foreseen that his speech would prompt some defections and he made no attempt to placate Streel or the other discontented Rexist leaders. He insinuated that Streel's departure had been motivated by the greater financial rewards on offer at *Le Soir* and he tried in vain to use his influence with the German authorities to prevent Streel from joining De Becker's newspaper.[13] Nor was Degrelle interested in a reconciliation with his opponents outside the movement. At a dinner arranged by Paul Colin for the principal journalists of the francophone collaborationist press, he presented his new opinions in such a provocative manner that his critics, including Robert Poulet, had little choice but to walk out.[14] To those who remained loyal to him, Degrelle was more reassuring. In private he was happy to admit that his conversion to a Germanic Wallonia was not to be taken entirely seriously. Such ideas were, he insisted, of interest only to Nazi racial theorists and the real purpose of his speech was to lure the SS and their allies into entrusting him with substantial political power.[15]

These private remarks were complemented by a series of articles in Le Pays Réel in which Rexist journalists attempted to minimise the significance of Degrelle's declarations. Matthys was to the fore in this campaign, reassuring militants that, although the speech had contained certain new 'précisions', its novelty should not be exaggerated. The espousal of the cause of a Germanic empire was, he argued, no more than a recognition that traditional nation-states were outmoded and that new and more flexible principles of sovereignty offered the best hope for the future of their country. Nor, he insisted, should the Rexists fear that they would become subservient Germanophile collaborators. On the contrary, Degrelle's new course would ensure that the Walloons would become free and equal citizens of a Germanic empire in which the most influential posts of responsibility would be open to them. Only Léon Van Huffel refused to adopt this reassuring tone. The Berlin correspondent of Le Pays Réel to some extent replaced Streel as the official ideologue of Rex and, far from seeking to minimise the significance of Degrelle's speech, he wrote articles which displayed a full-blooded commitment to the SS rhetoric of race, soil and 'popular community'.[16]

The private and public efforts of Degrelle and his colleagues ensured that there was no mass exodus from Rex. The departures which did take place were on a relatively small scale and it is clear that many militants did not grasp the full significance of Degrelle's change of direction. Nor was it easy, both materially and emotionally, for many militants to bring themselves to break with Rex. The gulf which now divided the Rexists from the patriotic majority was so great that few could hope that by withdrawing from Rex they would be rehabilitated in the eyes of their compatriots. The movement had, moreover, in many cases come to dominate their lives. Some owed their jobs either directly or indirectly to Rex while many others, especially those who had been active in the movement since its beginnings, had an enormous emotional investment in the cause. To leave Rex at this stage, simply because of the rhetorical flourishes of Degrelle, would have seemed to be a betrayal of their many friends and relations within the movement or serving with the Légion Wallonie on the Eastern Front. Thus, rather than contemplate such a rupture, many must have preferred to trust to the political genius of their leader whose abrupt changes of direction had in the past been vindicated by subsequent events.[17]

These nervous militants must also have received reassurance from a further speech which Degrelle gave to Rexist cadres on 4 April in which he idealised the Burgundian empire of the early modern era as a golden age of Walloon and Flemish common endeavour. This Burgundian theme became a central feature of Degrelle's rhetoric in 1943 and was soon picked up by a number of other Rexist leaders, prompting the SS police representatives in Brussels to deplore the emergence of a marked 'burgundisch-belgizistischen Tendenz' in Rexist ideology.[18] Nothing characterised better the air of unreality which permeated collaborationist rhetoric in the latter years of the war than this nostalgia for a distant historical age, and it further contributed to the public perception of Degrelle as an opportunist desperate to exploit any theme which might cloak his megalomania with a spurious credibility. For Degrelle – and to a lesser extent also for Rex – this idealisation of the Burgundian dukes who in the fifteenth century briefly succeeded in uniting a heterogenous collection of territories in a middle kingdom between France and the Holy Roman Empire served several practical purposes. Most obviously, it provided Degrelle with a historical tradition which he could exploit to invest his actions with some superficial glamour. In his recruitment campaigns for the *Légion Wallonie*, the Rexist leader drew repeatedly upon the imagery of the Burgundian empire. The *légionnaires* were, he declared, the spiritual descendants of the knights of the Burgundian empire fighting against myriad adversaries for the survival of their country. For impressionable adolescents raised on the rather more staid glories of the Belgian state, it was a theme which may have had a certain superficial appeal and it perhaps helps to explain why so many of the recruits for the *Légion* in 1943 and 1944 were young men with few political views.[19]

More importantly, however, Degrelle's Burgundian rhetoric served as a surrogate Belgian nationalism. The collaborationists of the later war years were obliged to conform to the ideological themes laid down by their political masters. But, rather in the manner of the Stalinist leaders of post-war Eastern Europe, they occasionally resorted to a coded rhetoric which permitted them to express ideas which did not meet with official approval. Thus Degrelle's glorification of the dukes of Burgundy was in part an indirect means of gesturing to his supporters that, whatever his public servility to Nazi racial ideas, he remained loyal to some form of Walloon-Flemish confederation. In addition, it also formed part of the repertoire of weapons employed by Degrelle in his campaign to win the maximum possible political authority from the leaders of the Third Reich. He had not made his spectacular leap of January 1943 in order to become the ruler of an undistinguished Walloon *Gau* within an expanded Reich. The limited horizons of Walloon regionalism were always constricting to his immense personal ambition and, with his incorrigible taste for grand historical tableaux, Degrelle undoubtedly did see himself as the future leader of a Low Countries state operating within a loose confederation of

Germanic peoples.[20] His Burgundian rhetoric was the public symbol of this goal and it provided the *Chef de Rex* with an almost infinitely flexible geographical formula as he sought to win from the Nazi leaders a political role wider than the frontiers of Wallonia.

It was the pursuit of this ambition which was to draw Degrelle continually away from Belgium to Germany during the latter years of the war; and at the end of January he returned to Berlin accompanied by Matthys and Paul Colin. During the two weeks that Degrelle spent in the German capital, he was extraordinarily active. He met representatives of the *Wehrmacht*, of the *SS-Hauptamt* and *Reichsicherhauptamt*, of the *Reichsjugendführung* and of the Ministries of Propaganda and of Foreign Affairs as well as addressing an audience of approximately 2,000 Belgian workers and *légionnaires* assembled on the Reichssportsfeld in Berlin.[21] His speech on this occasion contained little of consequence but the overall effect of the visit was to confirm his growing reputation within the Nazi world. The most tangible manifestation of this success was the verbal order issued by Hitler on 31 January that: 'wir mit allen Mitteln Degrelle unterstützen müssten, da er für uns der einzig wirklich brauchbare Belgier sei'.[22] Like many such orders of the *Führer*, this command issued almost casually to the German Foreign Ministry had few practical consequences. It did not signal any change in the established Nazi policy of avoiding any definitive decision regarding the future of Belgium and it brought Degrelle no immediate rewards. At the very least, however, it did indicate that his espousal of the *SS* cause had at last provided Degrelle with access to the highest levels of decision-making within the Reich. There is little doubt that Hitler shared the *SS* conviction that Belgium and much of northern France must eventually form part of a Germanic empire and in May 1942 the *Führer* had consulted the work of the German ethnologist Petri which claimed to demonstrate the Germanic origins of the Walloons.[23] Although Hitler was not willing to contemplate any short-term change in policy towards Belgium, the *Führer*'s long-term plans were evolving in ways favourable to Degrelle. Political success might still be a long way off but the *Chef de Rex* was no longer the obscure outsider who in the first winter of the Occupation had struggled so unsuccessfully to attract the attention of the Nazi leaders.

From Berlin, Degrelle returned to Brussels where he did his best to encourage expectations that he would soon be accorded substantial power. He was soon restless to leave Belgium again, however, travelling this time to France where he spent three weeks during February in Paris and on the Riviera coast. Degrelle used this opportunity to renew his friendship with Abetz who once again showed himself eager to assist the ambitions of his Belgian protégé. As Degrelle must by now have been aware, the German ambassador in Paris possessed little real influence and a rumour that thanks to Abetz the *Chef de Rex* would soon be accorded a meeting with Hitler was no more than another of Degrelle's many flights of fancy.[24]

The central political purpose behind these various discussions with German officials in Berlin, Brussels and Paris was to build a broad coalition of support for his cause amongst the leaders of the Reich. Unlike, for example, Jef Van de Wiele, the leader of *DeVlag* in Flanders, Degrelle had no intention of becoming a pawn of the *SS* and he continued to seek the support of any other element of the Nazi hierarchy which might help him to fulfil his ambitions. He appears to have had few scruples in such discussions, adapting his tone to suit each meeting and often advocating ideas regarding the future of Belgium which differed significantly from the Germanic racial ideas he had presented to the *SS*.[25] These meetings also enabled Degrelle to make a number of specific requests to the Nazi authorities. Foremost among these was his wish to bring about the transfer of the *Légion* from the *Wehrmacht* to the *Waffen-SS* but he also had other more fanciful ambitions for the development of the *Légion*, including its expansion into a regiment and the creation of a second similar unit which would fight alongside the Axis forces in North Africa.[26] In addition, he put forward a variety of other proposals, including the recruitment of a *Bataillon Féminin* which would serve in the German Red Cross, the creation of a new organisation – the *Honneur Légionnaire* – to take charge of the moral and material welfare of the families of *légionnaires* and the fusion of the *Jeunesses Rexistes* and the other pro-German Walloon youth groups into a new single movement – the *Jeunesse Légionnaire* – to be led by former soldiers of the *Légion*.[27] The collaborationist press remained as always an area of Degrellian ambition. He had long hoped to expand his power beyond the confines of the discredited *Le Pays Réel* and he proposed that he and Paul Colin be allowed to take control of the mass-circulation *Le Soir* which was not only highly profitable but also remained, under the direction of De Becker, the principal opponent of his pro-*SS* stance.[28]

These various demands met with a mixed response. Some, such as the creation of the Red Cross units, the *Honneur Légionnaire* and the *Jeunesse Légionnaire*, were approved without difficulty but others were dismissed by the German authorities as merely unrealistic or politically unwise. Even in *SS* circles, many doubts understandably remained as to Degrelle's reliability, not least because of what was perceived to be his Catholic political inspiration.[29] There still remained clear limits to the degree of support which the Nazis were willing to accord to Degrelle and no immediate decision was taken to transfer the *Légion* to the *Waffen-SS* while his proposal to seize control of *Le Soir* was once again rebuffed.

The nature of the proposals made by Degrelle at this time also demonstrated how far his policies had become distinct from those of the Rexists. During his discussions with German officials in January and February 1943, he made few references to Rex, hinting to the representatives of the *SS-Hauptamt* that he intended eventually to dissolve the movement and replace it with a new political organisation based on the *Légion*.[30] How serious a project this was remains unclear. It may have been designed principally to appease the *SS* authorities who, Matthys claimed in his post-war memoirs, unsuccessfully pressed Degrelle to break with his former political colleagues.[31] Even if this was so, it would seem that by 1943 Degrelle envisaged little long-term future for Rex. In part, this was simply because of his devotion to the *Légion*. It had come to dominate both his private calculations and his public statements and he clearly preferred to pose as the political head of the *Légion* rather than as the *Chef de Rex*.[32] The *Légion* was, moreover, by 1943 largely independent of Rex. It had developed its own bureaucracy, possessed a network of recruiting offices in Belgium and Germany and, with the creation of the *Jeunesse Légionnaire*, had acquired its own youth movement.

Degrelle's detachment from Rex seems also, however, to have been based on a recognition that there was no longer an obvious role within collaboration for a civilian political movement. Partly because of the intensity of the popular antipathy which they faced and partly because of their own infatuation with military structures, pro-Nazi groups throughout Europe in the final years of the war moved away from conventional political structures to movements – such as the *Milice* in France – which were in effect political armies. Often modelled on the example of the *SS*, these units seemed to represent the only viable future and Degrelle as always was keen not to be left behind. Indeed, as early as 5 January 1943 at a meeting with Jungclaus, the *SS* representative in Belgium, he had requested permission to establish what he termed an *Allgemeine Wallonische SS*.[33] This would not, it seems, have formed part of the *SS* military hierarchy but would have been a political militia modelled probably on the example of a similar organisation, the *Algemene SS-Vlaanderen*, which had operated since 1940 in Flanders. Degrelle's proposal was in the event rejected by Berger and Himmler who, still doubtful of Degrelle's political credentials, decided that the time was not ripe to create such a corps.[34] Nevertheless it served as an indication of the way in which Degrelle was searching for an alternative long-term basis for his political activities in Belgium.

In the meantime, Degrelle took little interest in Rex. He was content to allow the trusted – and unthreatening – Matthys to remain as the interim leader and during his visits to Belgium played little role in Rexist affairs, prompting Reeder to lament that: 'Degrelle nutzt seine Anwesenheit im Lande weniger zur Reorganisation und Verstärkung seiner Partei aus, als vielmehr zu politisch taktischen Verhandlungen und Besprechungen.'[35] Degrelle has himself subsequently boasted of his disengagement from Rex, claiming that he never set foot in the movement's headquarters after August 1941.[36] This was a considerable exaggeration but on the rare occasions that he did intervene actively in the direction of Rex, he seems to have been concerned principally to subordinate the movement to the *Légion*. Therefore, for example, he declared that all future Rexist leaders should serve a *stage* in the *Légion* and, according to Reeder, he encouraged the promotion of former *légionnaires* to positions of authority within Rex.[37] On the whole, however, he simply ignored the existence of Rex. Félix Francq, who directed the *Cabinet du Chef de Rex*, remained his direct representative within the Rexist hierarchy but Francq seems to have concerned himself only with the management of the financial interests of the Degrelle family and played no part in the decision making of the movement.[38] Degrelle's status came to amount to little more than that of a *deus ex machina* whose infrequent interventions in Rexist affairs were principally intended to serve his own interests or those of the *Légion*.

The corollary was that the Rexists came to enjoy little influence over the policies of the man who remained their leader. During the latter war years, Degrelle surrounded himself with an informal network of advisers and personal confidants of whom the principal figures were not Rexist officials but men whose loyalty was to Degrelle as an individual. Foremost among these until his assassination was Paul Colin, the director of *Le Nouveau Journal* and of *Cassandre*. The two men made unlikely allies. In contrast to the ebullient Degrelle, Colin was a self-regarding intellectual whose espousal of collaboration seems to have owed much to his scorn for a Belgian political establishment which he felt had never adequately recognised his talents. His wartime press activities brought him considerable wealth and influence and he was an omnipresent figure in the claustrophobic village life of the Brussels collaborationist community. He was appointed as the President of the pro-German *Association des journalistes belges* and seemed to possess an insatiable appetite for intrigue and polemic which created around him what one observer described as 'un tourbillon de passions et de haines'.[39] The alliance between him and Degrelle was one based on shared ambition. Colin had never been a member of Rex and he was privately scornful of the personal qualities of Degrelle and the Rexists. But he was also quick to recognise that Degrelle's achievements in the *Légion* had placed him in a pre-eminent position among Belgian francophone collaborationists and during 1942 he had sought to effect a *rapprochement* with the Rexist leader. Similarly, though he had no interest in the racial ideology of the *SS*, the power enjoyed by Himmler's men lured him towards them. As he remarked bluntly to Streel: 'Nous avons cru que les militaires ici présente [i.e. in Brussels] représentaient la politique officielle allemande. Nous avons ainsi négligé tout un vaste secteur et perdu de vue la puissance croissante des SS et de leur idéologie. Nous n'avons pas mise sur la bonne carte.'[40] Such sentiments could easily have been expressed by Degrelle and the close links between the two men were symbolised by the somewhat ludicrous nomination of the physically unimpressive Colin as an honorary corporal in the *Légion Wallonie*. Colin's goal was still, however, personal power. He assured journalist colleagues that Degrelle was a mere 'pantin' who could be easily manipulated and he evidently saw himself playing a major role in any future regime established under the aegis of Degrelle.[41]

Colin's death in April 1943 at the hands of young patriotic assassins forced Degrelle to rely instead upon a number of *légionnaires*. None of these could pretend to the importance of Colin but they provided Degrelle with the circle of intimates and reliable adjuncts upon whom he had always relied. The two most influential were Joseph Pévenasse and Jean Vermeire. Since leaving Belgium in early 1942, Pévenasse, the former head of *Rex-Wallonie* and *Inspecteur Fédéral du Mouvement*, seems to have become increasingly critical of what he regarded as the hesitant policies of the Rexist leadership. During 1942 he helped Degrelle to consolidate his political control of the *Légion* and was chosen by him to convey his message to the Rexist rally in the Palais des Sports in October. Subsequently Degrelle gave him responsibility for recruitment for the *Légion* amongst Walloon workers and prisoners-of-war in Germany and also entrusted him with the efforts to seize control of the *Service des Volontaires du Travail pour la Wallonie*.[42] Unlike Pévenasse, Jean Vermeire had never been a figure of importance in Rex. Only 21 years old at the time of the German invasion, he had been a reporter on *Le Pays Réel* before becoming the war correspondent for the Rexist newspaper with the *Légion*. Despite or perhaps because of his youth, Vermeire soon attracted the attention of Degrelle and in the summer of 1943 was chosen by him as his 'ambassador' in Berlin where he worked to reinforce the alliance between Degrelle and the leaders of the SS. Significantly, Vermeire never became a member of Rex and, as he subsequently admitted, his appeal for Degrelle was partly as an outsider untainted by close association with a Rexist movement from which Degrelle was anxious to distance himself.[43]

While Degrelle pursued his personal political trajectory, the principal consequence for Rex of Degrelle's dramatic speech on 17 January was that it resolved the tension evident during the previous year between those anxious to press forward with total collaboration and those who still wished to keep the movement at a certain distance from the German authorities. After January 1943, this problem no longer existed. Degrelle had charted a course of unlimited collaboration with Nazi Germany and Rex duly followed its master's lead. It was Matthys who presided over the consequent reorientation of the movement. Despite his support for Streel's policies during 1942, he seems to have had no qualms about accepting the new stance of Degrelle and he responded to the resignations of Streel and other moderates by reorganising the Rexist headquarters to create a more hierarchical structure based on a series of departments.[44]

The most important of these was the *Département Politique* which continued on a somewhat expanded scale the work of the former *Service Politique*.[45] To replace Streel as head of the department, Matthys chose

Léon Brunet, a pre-war Rexist senator who in 1942 had been appointed as *premier échevin* of *Grand Bruxelles*. Brunet was a prosperous *notaire* who formed part of the small social elite of Brussels collaborators. Like Paul Colin, he was frequently to be seen at the receptions and dinners held at the German embassy as well as hosting his own parties for German officials and their Belgian allies at his Rhode Saint Genèse villa.[46] He had little interest in the details of Rexist administration and had been chosen by Matthys principally as a figure-head whose presence would reassure militants worried by Streel's abrupt departure. The effective responsibility for directing the work of the new department fell to its new deputy head, Louis Collard. He came from a very different world to that of Brunet. Born in Liège in 1915, his background was typical of many young members of the Belgian lower middle class who had drifted without any clear purpose in the difficult economic circumstances of the 1930s. Educated at a Catholic *collège*, he was an early supporter of Rex and in 1936 joined the staff of the movement, playing a leading role in the organisation of the Rexist electoral triumph in the Luxembourg province. A chaotic, impulsive worker, Collard devoted all of his energies to the Rexist cause and subsequently took charge of the organisation of many of Degrelle's major public rallies. However, as the fortunes of Rex began to wane, so Collard drifted away from the movement. After a period of military service, he worked briefly in the *Sarma* department store before being recalled to the army. He was released from POW camp in October 1940 but showed no sign of wishing to return to Rex and, after unsuccessfully attempting to obtain a post in the *Commissariat aux Prix et aux Salaires*, he returned to Liège where his only 'collaborationist' activity was to try to sell some building materials to the Germans.[47] When in September 1942, a pro-Rexist industrialist, Van Reck, agreed to fund the salary of an additional employee in Streel's *Service Politique*, Collard, however, was chosen for this post. He once again threw himself into his responsibilities with great energy, with the result that only a few months after rejoining Rex Collard was selected by Matthys for what proved to be a position of considerable importance within the Rexist hierarchy.[48]

The other major change introduced by Matthys was to establish Charles Lambinon's *BIRD* as a separate department, entitled the *Département de Sécurité et d'Information (DSI)*. Its formal responsibilities included the collation of information on the enemies of Rex as well as vetting Rexist and other pro-German candidates for public posts, but the new department was also made responsible for ensuring greater protection for Rexist militants against Resistance attacks. This open-ended brief gave Lambinon the freedom he had long been demanding to establish a Rexist police force. As Matthys rather laconically observed, Lambinon possessed 'le goût de cette besogne' and the new department became little more than a free-lance collaborationist police unit working alongside the German police.[49]

The other changes in the administrative organisation of Rex were of less importance but all demonstrated a commitment to bring about a more hierarchical structure for the movement. A *Département de Discipline Intérieure* was created which, under the direction of Georges Jacobs the first commander of the *Légion Wallonie*, was intended to ensure 'une cohésion parfaite entre tous les membres du Mouvement et une discipline très stricte vis-à-vis de la Hiérarchie'. In a similar vein, the Rexist journalist Jean Denis was appointed to head a *Département Culturel*, one of the principal tasks of which was to bring greater discipline into the somewhat chaotic ranks of the *Mouvement des Femmes Rexistes* (*MFR*) and the grouping for young women *Foi dans la Vie*.[50] A *Département de Contrôle et de Coordination* took charge of the allocation of arms permits to militants as well as distributing compensation to the victims of Resistance violence while the *Chef des Cadres Territoriaux*, Marcel Dupont, remained responsible for the appointment of local Rexist officials, the collation of local reports and other routine administrative tasks.[51]

The major challenge facing the reorganised movement was the by now familiar one of Resistance terrorism. After a brief lull at the beginning of the New Year, there was a recrudescence of such attacks during the early months of 1943 culminating in the audacious murder of Paul Colin as he was leaving his office in Brussels.[52] But it was once again the rank-and-file members of Rex who bore the brunt of the Resistance violence. By April 1943, Rexist sources estimated that 50 of their supporters had been killed during the Occupation, and among the latest victims of these 'attentats de quartier' were a militant in the *Mouvement des Femmes Rexistes* and a wheelchair-bound veteran of the Great War.[53]

The effect of these killings on Rexist morale was substantial. Those militants appointed to positions in local government were regarded as especially vulnerable to attack and both the Ministry of the Interior and the German authorities complained that it was becoming increasingly difficult to find volunteers for certain prominent public posts in Wallonia.[54] Moreover, the atmosphere of fear engendered by the Resistance had a major impact on local Rexist activities. From Liège, Charleroi and Verviers, German police officials reported that many members had withdrawn from Rex to await better times. Meetings were said to be sparsely attended and exhortations from local *chefs de cercles* to remain faithful to the cause went unheeded.[55] These problems were not unique to Rex. The other small pro-German groups in Wallonia were similarly effected while popular hostility towards Flemish collaborationist groups also increased. Nonetheless antipathy to collaborators in Flanders never reached the same intensity as in francophone Belgium. There were fewer assassinations, public meetings were still possible and *DeVlag* still reported some success with its recruitment efforts.[56] Such traditional political activities were by 1943 all but impossible in Wallonia. Especially in the industrial areas, public hostility was so intense and the threat from Resistance groups so omnipresent that Rex was gradually forced to abandon acting in the public sphere. It ceased in effect to be a political movement and, despite the positions of public authority occupied by many Rexists as mayors or civil servants, collaboration became essentially a private activity carried on either under the armed protection of the German forces or in barricaded secrecy.

The Rexist *Etat-Major*, absorbed by its own reorganisation, was slow to respond to what Matthys subsequently described as 'cet état de guerre civile et de terreur'.[57] At the general meeting of Rexist cadres held on 4 April not even a rousing speech from Degrelle and the all too familiar appeals to militants to regard themselves as the 'soldats du front intérieur' seem to have done much to overcome the evident torpor.[58] A cult of the fallen martyrs of the Rexist revolution continued to be encouraged. Obituaries of the dead crowded the pages of *Le Pays Réel* and a roll-call of those militants who had given their lives for the 'idéal révolutionnaire' became a regular and emotional ritual at meetings.[59] But for practical action against the Resistance, the Rexist leaders still looked primarily to the German authorities. They remained convinced that the *Militärver-waltung* possessed the capacity to restore public order but that it was holding back from taking decisive action because of fear of alienating the *secrétaires-généraux* and other elements of the Belgian elite. The Rexists therefore joined with Flemish collaborationist leaders in lobbying the German authorities to cast off all hesitations. These efforts culminated in a meeting on 15 April at which Reeder sought to reassure the leaders of all of the pro-German movements of the progress being made in countering the Resistance attacks. A delegation of five Rexists, including Matthys and Louis Collard, attended this meeting at which they proposed a number of additional measures including the use of sympathetic Belgian *Sûreté* officers to investigate the clandestine Communist organisation. The most important Rexist proposal was that a special '*Schutzgarde*' be created to protect vulnerable public office-holders in Wallonia. This idea was firmly rejected by Reeder and it is unclear whether Matthys intended that these bodyguards would have operated within the communal police forces or as a militia under Rexist or German control. Nevertheless, Matthys' proposal was one to which the Rexist leaders would return later in 1943 as their faith in the capacity of the German police and military gradually waned and they attempted to define their own independent response to the Resistance violence.[60]

Reeder, anxious to display his own moderation, alleged after the war that the Rexist leaders also sought permission at this meeting to launch their own 'counter-terrorist' reprisal attacks against the Resistance and its supposed bourgeois patrons. The contemporary German report of the meeting made no reference, however, to any request and it would seem unlikely that any such formal proposal was in fact made.[61] Reprisal killings were certainly contemplated by the Rexists. When José Streel made a rare visit to the offices of *Le Pays Réel* shortly after the murder of Colin, he claimed to have overheard Matthys and others discussing the possibility of murdering the wives of two ministers in the London government, Paul-Henri Spaak and Camille Gutt. Streel acted promptly to warn Madame Spaak of this danger and after the war remained convinced that he had saved the lives of the two women.[62] Despite many similar threats, no attacks were authorised by the Rexist leadership during 1943. Even those crimes widely believed at the time to have been carried out by Rex were the responsibility of others. For example, a series of violent attacks during January 1943 on prominent Brussels figures with known patriotic and pro-English sympathies were generally assumed to have been the work of the Rexists but were in fact carried out by a Flemish terrorist group closely linked to *DeVlag*.[63] For all of the violence of their rhetoric, the Rexist policy was one of discouraging such 'unofficial' actions and, as the creation of the *DSI* demonstrated, they hoped instead to assist the German police in uncovering the perpetrators of the attacks on their supporters.

Matthys, in particular, seems to have become convinced that little purpose would be served by isolated acts of revenge. Unlike in 1942 when he had praised the unilateral actions taken by certain Rexists and had threatened that Rex might take the law into its own hands, he now sought to reassure his supporters by stressing the high success rate achieved by the German police in identifying the Resistance terrorists.[64] These calls for restraint were reinforced by dire promises of the violence that would be unleashed against their enemies after the Rexist seizure of power. Violence today was excluded by promises of an eventual blood-bath at some date in the future. Speaking, for example, at Colin's funeral in April, Degrelle described in lurid terms the merciless war which the *légionnaires* would wage on the Resistance groups and their patrons when they returned from the East at the end of the war: 'Nos armées n'hésiteront pas plus ici qu'elles s'hésitèrent là-bas [i.e. in the East], dans les plus horribles mêlées. On a voulu le sang. On l'aura. Ce sont des soldats qui le jurent.'[65] Promises of action in the distant future were not sufficient to satisfy all within the beleaguered Rexist community and it is clear that only firm opposition from the German authorities prevented some Rexists from taking matters into their own hands. For example, speaking at the funeral of another victim of a Resistance attack in April, Ruelle, the new *Chef de l'Etat-Major* of the *Formations de Combat*, must have expressed the thoughts of many Rexists when he declared rhetorically to the body of the fallen Rexist: 'Tu sais que seule la discipline qui nous est imposée nous interdit de venger ton sang dans le sang. Mais un jour viendra qui tout paiera.'[66]

Whether that day of vengeance would ever come must have seemed doubtful to those many militants who reacted with despair to the deteriorating military and security situation; but among the national leadership, there was a remarkable air of resilience and even of optimism during the early months of 1943. For those who had chosen to rally to the new policies of Degrelle, it seemed that his alliance with the SS offered a real prospect of power. Rex was at last in tune with the broader shift towards radicalism which was taking place within the Third Reich during the war years. Conservative forces such as the Foreign Ministry and the *Wehrmacht* which had proved most resistant to the overtures of Degrelle lost ground and the political beneficiaries were the SS and their allies. This internal radicalisation of the Third Reich accelerated as the military situation became more desperate, with the consequence that a curious inverse relationship gradually developed between the broader military fortunes of the German armies and the specific political fortunes of Degrelle and the Rexists. While the reverses suffered on the battlefields raised the possibility for the first time of a total defeat of the Nazis and their allies, the political repercussions of this impending collapse within the Third Reich worked to the advantage of Degrelle and his supporters. This created what might be described as a schizophrenic tension within Rex between those militants – generally those of the rank and file most exposed to the external dangers – who were intensely conscious of the developing catastrophe and those other Rexists – often within the national leadership – who through ideological self-delusion or simple myopia focussed solely on their political success within the crumbling Nazi fortress.

This division was clearly evident during the spring of 1943 as, despite the intensification of the Resistance onslaught on Rex, the leadership launched a series of political initiatives intended to capitalise on the opportunities opened up by Degrelle's new course. Central to Rexist ambitions after January 1943 was the alliance with the SS. As an internal Rexist report frankly admitted, the principal goal of the leadership during 1943 was to 'aligner le Mouvement aux forces de l'Ordre de la SS, qui sont les seules forces révolutionnaires authentiques de l'Europe'.[67] Thus, while in 1942 they had shunned contact with the representatives of the SS, the Rexist leaders now courted Himmler's chief agent in Belgium, Richard Jungclaus, anticipating – not without reason – that he would be the true arbiter of political power in the country when the *Militärverwaltung* had finally been replaced.[68]

An essential element of this strategy was to refashion the structure and ideology of Rex in imitation of the SS. This aping of the SS took many forms but it was not surprisingly the self-conscious elitism of the SS to which the Rexist leadership responded most readily. The beleaguered Rexists had long since come to regard themselves as a heroic minority struggling to impose their revolution on an uncomprehending populace and the SS rapidly became the ideal revolutionary elite which they sought to emulate. The effects were on the whole more superficial than profound.

Rex remained to the last an obstinately chaotic and amateurish movement and in comparison with the *VNV* the training and discipline of Rexist militants was always rudimentary.[69] Nevertheless, some progress was made. Uniforms had long been commonplace but these were now supplemented by the introduction of a formal ritual for use at national and local meetings and by oaths demanding unwavering loyalty to Degrelle, the movement and the Walloon race.[70] The language of Rex was also changed in other ways. Hitler, the *Führer* of all the Germanic peoples, was saluted at the end of meetings while in correspondence conventional formulae were gradually abandoned in favour of more revolutionary phraseology such as '*Camarade*', '*Au Chef*' and, increasingly, '*Sieg Heil!*'[71] The unstated intention of many of these measures was clearly to innoculate the Rexists against the impact of a hostile world. A cult of secrecy was encouraged which went far beyond the needs of security and internal directives made much of the need for local groups to cut themselves off from alien external influences. All births, marriages and deaths were to be marked by the movement and, like the members of an enthusiastic religious sect, militants were encouraged to have no private life separate from Rex. Even the most modest position of responsibility was declared to be 'une mission sacrée' and those who failed to show sufficient zeal were denounced as 'rexistes d'opérette'.[72]

While Rex sought to flatter the SS by imitation, Degrelle pressed forward with his more direct efforts to win their support. As we have seen, it was never part of his intention to become Himmler's vassal but in the spring of 1943 he did take significant steps towards reinforcing his links with the SS. Part of the explanation for Degrelle's behaviour at this time may have lain in the complicated circumstances of his private life. During his absence at the front, his relations with his French-born wife had gone into a marked decline. While Degrelle was widely rumoured to have acquired a number of mistresses in Berlin, Paris and Brussels,[73] his 'lebenslustigen' wife found solace in a relationship with an Austrian *Luftwaffe* officer, *Sonderführer* Hellmuth Pessl, who had first visited her home on the pretext that he was preparing an article on Degrelle. For a time, they were to be seen together in Brussels restaurants and Madame Degrelle apparently presented Pessl with a number of lavish presents. In March 1943 while in southern France with her husband, she decided to end the relationship with Pessl and told Degrelle what had occurred. His first reaction was to seek a divorce but, conscious of the possible political consequences, he soon changed his mind and, instead, decided with typical impetuosity to challenge the *Luftwaffe* officer to a duel. This somewhat unlikely possibility was averted by the German authorities who insisted that it would violate an order issued by the *Führer* outlawing all duels for the duration of the war. In the meantime, Pessl, who seems to have behaved throughout rather in the manner of a figure from a romantic operetta, showed no intention of abandoning the relationship. He wrote numerous letters to Madame Degrelle, arranged to meet her when she made a visit to Paris and proposed that they should elope together. She, however, remained resolved to end the affair pleading unsuccessfully with Pessl to return the letters which she had written to him.

Denied the opportunity of more elementary forms of redress, Degrelle sought to institute legal procedures against the *Luftwaffe* officer. The *Luftwaffe* was opposed to the prosecution of Pessl and Degrelle visited Jungclaus to enlist the support of the SS in the pursuit of the case. Matters did, however, rapidly reach their own conclusion. While Madame Degrelle – still full of remorse – talked of committing suicide, the hapless Pessl – overwrought with emotion – also declared his intention of taking his own life and wrote a number of dramatic letters to Degrelle, Hitler and others. Then, late in the evening of 12 April, Degrelle telephoned the German police to inform them that Pessl had indeed committed suicide. Arriving at the scene, they found the *Luftwaffe* officer's body lying close to Degrelle's house. Their investigation, however, soon raised doubts as to the true circumstances of Pessl's death. He had died of bullet wounds to the head and heart yet he did not possess a gun, no cartridges were found near the body and shortly after the alleged suicide another man had been seen running away from the scene. The German police not surprisingly concluded that in all probability Pessl had been killed – possibly at his own request – by one of Degrelle's *légionnaire* bodyguards. They passed on these findings to their superiors but at a meeting in Brussels between Reeder and representatives of the SS police it was decided, on political grounds as well as because moral right was judged to be on Degrelle's side, that no further action would be taken. This decision was communicated to the *Luftwaffe* as well as to Kaltenbrunner, Berger and Himmler of the SS who all apparently agreed that the matter should be left unresolved.[74]

What impact, if any, this affair had on Degrelle's political activities remains unclear. News of the incident was successfully suppressed and there is no evidence that the SS leaders used it to bring pressure to bear on Degrelle. But it had once again displayed his reliance on the SS to whom – as Jungclaus remarked in his report on the incident to Berger – 'er sich politisch unterstellt fühlt'.[75] Therefore it is perhaps not so surprising that at a meeting with Himmler only a few weeks later Degrelle should have made further concessions to the ideas and ambitions of the SS. This meeting between Degrelle and Himmler occurred during the night of 23–24 May on the personal train of the *Reichsführer-SS* at Rastenburg in East Prussia.[76] It was the first opportunity that Degrelle had had to meet the head of the SS and, not surprisingly, highly extravagant descriptions of their discussions have featured prominently in Degrelle's post-war accounts of his actions. In fact, the meeting served both a specific and a more general purpose. The first was to ratify the transfer of the *Légion Wallonie* from the *Wehrmacht* to the *Waffen-SS*. This marked the fulfilment of one of Degrelle's principal goals. He had long been convinced that only membership of the *Waffen-SS* could enable the *Légion* to develop as an elite military unit while at the same time serving as an effective vehicle for the promotion of his own political aims. Therefore, under the terms of the agreement signed by the two men, the *Légion* became part of the *Waffen-SS* on 1 June 1943, taking the title soon afterwards of the *SS-Sturmbrigade Wallonien*.[77]

In broader political terms the meeting marked the completion of the political realignment which Degrelle had commenced in December 1942. As in his first encounters with the representatives of the SS in Berlin, he seems to have been somewhat dazzled by the opportunities presented by an alliance with Himmler and the meeting was dominated by Degrelle's efforts to convince the *Reichsführer-SS* of his political sincerity. Himmler too was willing to make some limited concessions. He readily agreed that the *Légion* would retain a number of special privileges within the *Waffen-SS* including its own Belgian commanders and Catholic chaplain and also conceded that French should remain the language of command. These gestures were not devoid of a certain symbolic importance but they did not have the wider political implications which Degrelle has subsequently claimed and seem to have been principally intended to facilitate the acceptance by the *légionnaires* of their transfer into the *Waffen-SS*.[78]

On political as opposed to military matters, it was Degrelle and not Himmler who made concessions. In a document which he composed during these negotiations and presented to Himmler, Degrelle accepted that the sole aim of political activity in Wallonia should be the preparation of the return of the Walloon race to the Reich. Moreover, in contradiction to many of his public statements on the subject, he agreed that the continued association of Wallonia and Flanders was only a temporary necessity imposed by the economic interdependence of the two communities and by the persistence of 'eine belgische Empfindlichkeit' in the minds of the population. An energetic cultural, political and social policy, he optimistically assured Himmler, would gradually resolve these obstacles and he anticipated that within one or two generations the Walloon people would come to accept their full integration into the Reich.[79]

This charter for the annexation of Wallonia by the Reich revealed the desperate search for power which lay at the heart of Degrelle's manoeuvring. There is no doubt that he still hoped to achieve a unified Belgium or even, in his moments of self-delusion, a larger 'occidental' or Burgundian state; but these aims were always secondary to his pursuit of personal power. In his post-war publications, Degrelle has been careful to disguise this fact, claiming, for example, that he convinced the *Reichsführer-SS* at this meeting to accept his plans for a Greater Belgium.[80]

In fact, the inverse was the case. Confronted by the firm convictions of Himmler, Degrelle was forced to abandon his pretence as the defender of Flemish-Walloon unity. For all his bluster it was a sacrifice which he was more than ready to make and, although he would continue to hope for a modification in Nazi policy, this underlying willingness to defer to the aims and ideology of the SS would remain at the heart of his political strategy for the remainder of the war.

The meeting with Himmler also marked a further stage in Degrelle's disengagement from his own political movement. Little mention was made of Rex during the discussions and Himmler clearly regarded Degrelle primarily as the political head of the *Légion Wallonie*. As for Degrelle, the transfer of the *légionnaires* to the *Waffen-SS* clearly enhanced his conviction that it was the *Légion* and not Rex which would bring about the National Socialist revolution in Wallonia. This was evident in a speech which he gave to new *légionnaires* in June 1943, soon after the meeting with Himmler. After the standard ritualistic references to the genius of Adolf Hitler, Degrelle pronounced that: 'Soldats du Fuehrer vous serez aussi les soldats politiques de l'après-guerre qui viendront planter ici [i.e. in Wallonia] le drapeau de la révolution victorieuse. Pour nous, la SS Brigade Wallonie est le moyen qui fera triompher l'idée nationale-socialiste'.[81]

Significantly, the Rexists were also obliged to recognise this change in the balance of power between Rex and the *Légion*. Matthys and his colleagues had long accepted that the armed force of the *Légion* offered the only real hope of establishing their rule in Belgium[82] but, in his statement heralding the news of the transfer of the *Légion*, Matthys acknowledged for the first time that as soldiers of the SS the *légionnaires* would also form the political elite of that revolution. The former division between Rex as the political movement and the *Légion* as a purely military unit was clearly no longer valid and the *Chef de Rex ad interim* tacitly recognised that the task of Rex was to assist the *Légion*, declaring: 'nous voyons dans une légion puissante le moyen le plus certain et peut-être le seul de donner à la Révolution nationale-socialiste dans nos provinces l'assise populaire et la force qui lui sont également nécessaires'.[83]

Yet, though in effect it signified a further stage in the subordination of their movement to the *Légion*, the Rexist leadership welcomed the news of the transfer to the *Waffen-SS*. In his statement, Matthys declared that it was an event 'd'une importance capitale' which demonstrated that the Germanic origins of the Walloons had been recognised by the highest authorities of the Reich.[84] A major reason for this enthusiasm was that the Rexist leaders, in common with many others in Belgium, believed that Degrelle had won from Himmler the promise of substantial political power. They knew few details of the discussions with Himmler but the very fact that both he and Jef Van de Wiele of *DeVlag* had both been accorded interviews with the *Reichsführer-SS* seemed to suggest that they were the chosen protégés of the Nazis. For a number of weeks rumours circulated in Brussels of an imminent *coup d'état* by Degrelle acting in conjunction with *De Vlag* and, though these were no more substantial than previous such rumours, they demonstrated the dominant position that he had now acquired within the collaborationist camp in Belgium.[85]

The political ascendancy of Degrelle and his allies was aided by the reverses suffered by many of the other contenders for power within the pro-German community. The *VNV* did remain a substantial force but it was now being seriously challenged by *De Vlag*, while in francophone Belgium any more moderate alternative to the Germanophile enthusiasms of Degrelle had finally collapsed. Streel's *Conseil Politique* had briefly offered men such as Robert Poulet and Raymond De Becker a means of recovering some of their former influence. But Degrelle's speech in January had, as we have seen, destroyed this *rapprochement* and instead Rex and Degrelle did all within their power during 1943 to silence their remaining critics within the collaborationist press. After Paul Colin's death, they prevented Robert Poulet from returning to *Le Nouveau Journal* and eventually succeeded in tranforming the paper into a mouthpiece for their extreme views.[86] In the case of *Le Soir*, they were, however, less successful. Despite repeated efforts by both Degrelle and the Rexists, the combined opposition of the *Militärverwaltung* and of influential elements of the Belgian elite ensured that control of the most important francophone newspaper always eluded their grasp.[87]

This modest victory for the opponents of Degrelle was of little real significance. The underlying problem faced by those who still advocated a moderate collaboration based on a New Order Belgian state under the leadership of Léopold III was that such ideas no longer possessed any relevance. The progress of the war combined with the ascendancy of extremist elements within both Belgium and the Third Reich left no room for anything other than total collaboration. Léopold III, isolated in his château in Laeken, seems to have believed that an agreement with Hitler remained possible but he refused to contemplate any contact with Degrelle[88] and, in reality, nobody of importance within the Third Reich still imagined that the Belgian King would find a place within a Nazi-dominated Europe. As events in Italy and Rumania demonstrated, monarchs were part of the debris of the political *ancien régime* which must be swept away if Nazism was to create a racially and socially pure Europe. Instead, their new allies were men such as Doriot or Darnand in France or more implausibly Mussolini, newly installed in the puppet Republic of Salo, who could mimic the revolutionary rhetoric of an ever more millenarian Nazism. Degrelle was admirably suited to play this role in Belgium but the King and his allies were no more than an irrelevance. This was finally acknowledged by Raymond De Becker who as editor of *Le Soir* was by the summer of 1943 the sole prominent exponent of a limited 'patriotic' collaboration. In an outspoken speech to the editorial staff of *Le Soir* on 3 September 1943, he denounced the Nazi authorities for having destroyed all hope of building a dignified partnership between Belgium and Germany in favour of fostering groups of mercenaries slavishly devoted to their cause. As he had no doubt intended, this swan-song reached the ears of the Germans and De Becker was promptly dismissed from his editorial post.[89]

Thus, in the last years of the war, the only serious challenge to Degrelle and Rex came from those small sects which had emerged on the radical fringes of collaboration. A number of these, including Leclercq's *MNPW*, had all but disappeared. Two did, however, remain of some importance. These were the *Communauté Culturelle Wallonne* (*CCW*) led by Pierre Hubermont and the *Amis du Grand Reich Allemand* (*AGRA*) still directed from Liège by Gérits and Scaillet. Degrelle's speech in January had brought the ideology of Rex much closer to both the Germanophile Walloon nationalism of the *CCW* and the radical National Socialism of *AGRA* and Reeder optimistically declared that the basis now existed for joint action by the pro-German movements of Wallonia.[90] Relations between Rex and the other two movements did show some modest signs of improvement. The Rexist press ceased its attacks on these fringe groups and Degrelle and Hubermont met in January 1943 to discuss collaboration between Rex and the *CCW*. In private Degrelle and the Rexists were still scornful of the supporters of *AGRA* but the *AGRA* weekly, *Notre Combat*, gave a cautious welcome to Degrelle's speech and for the first time the leaders of *AGRA* appear to have expressed some interest in working with Rex.[91]

Reeder's hopes of a new dawn in relations between the collaborationist groups were to prove short-lived. In the spring the youth wing of *AGRA* was forcibly absorbed into Degrelle's new *Jeunesse Légionnaire* while in Namur approximately 200 *AGRA* members defected to Rex prompted by rumours of Communist infiltration of *AGRA* as well as by the immoral and criminal activities of the local *AGRA* leadership.[92] The principal point of conflict between the two movements did, however, concern recruitment by *AGRA* for the *Waffen-SS*. This had commenced in 1942 and by the following year it seems that perhaps some 200 Walloons were serving in *Waffen-SS* units.[93] The challenge that even this small-scale recruitment posed to Rex was twofold. Not only did it threaten the status of the *Légion Wallonie* as the only front line Walloon military unit but it also demonstrated the reluctance of elements within the SS to commit themselves fully to support for Degrelle and his allies. Rex did their best to undermine the *AGRA* recruitment campaign but they were powerless to crush it completely and, according to Matthys, it was this potential threat which was a major motivation behind Degrelle's decision to seek the transfer of the *Légion* to the *Waffen-SS*.[94]

The entry of the *Légion Wallonie* into the *Waffen-SS* in June 1943 provided Degrelle and the Rexists with the opportunity to act decisively

against these fringe groups. They chose to consider this event as sig-
nifying Nazi recognition of Rex as the sole authorised political grouping in
Wallonia and promptly set about seeking the forced amalgamation into
Rex of all other pro-German groupings.[95] Their new policy was first
evident at the *journées d'études* organised by the *CCW* at Dinant from 25 to
27 June 1943. Representatives of all Walloon collaborationist groupings
attended this conference which was intended to demonstrate the unity of
purpose of the various pro-German groups. In fact it was dominated by
the aggressive behaviour of the substantial delegation of uniformed Rexists
headed by Louis Collard of the *Département Politique* who – together with
representatives of the recently established pro-*SS Cercle Wallon* – were
intent upon discrediting Hubermont's *CCW*.[96]

AGRA was also exposed to the hostility of Rex. The agreement between
Degrelle and Himmler not only resulted in the integration of the *AGRA
Waffen-SS* volunteers into the *Légion*[97] but also deprived *AGRA* of the
support of its principal German patron. Rex exploited this weakness by
fostering divisions within *AGRA* between those who rejected any contact
with Rex and those more willing to work with the rival movement.[98]
Gérits, who had taken over from Scaillet as the formal leader of *AGRA*,
was one of those who had come to see an agreement with Rex as the only
way forward and in July 1943 he accepted a Rexist proposal that the
members of the German transport corps, the *NSKK*, who had been
recruited by *AGRA* should be integrated with those *NSKK* volunteers
enrolled by Rex.[99] The fusion of the two groups took place at a ceremony
attended by both Degrelle and Gérits and, although in his speech Gérits
was keen to stress that the new *NSKK* unit was not the prelude to a total
fusion of the two movements,[100] the Rexists persisted in their efforts to
undermine *AGRA*'s independent existence. By the autumn of 1943 Rex
had all but succeeded in this aim. A number of leading *AGRA* members
were lured into joining or rejoining Rex and the local groups of the
movement gradually evaporated.[101] Only a few loyalists remained and,
although it still had some supporters among the journalists of the extremist collaborationist press of Charleroi, *AGRA* largely ceased its activities during the last year of the Occupation.[102]

With the virtual demise of *AGRA*, it was the newly established *Cercle
Wallon* (*CW*) which emerged during 1943 as the most formidable opponent of Rexist political ambitions. This organisation had developed
from the groups of the same name which had been set up by the German
authorities in the Reich during 1942 to care for the increasing numbers of
Walloon workers. In the autumn of 1942 the *Militärverwaltung* had approved their expansion into Wallonia to look after the families of those
working in Germany[103] and it was at this stage that the *Cercle Wallon* began
to take on a more explicitly political character. The driving-force behind

its development appears to have been a German official, Dr Sommer, who from 1941 was the representative in Belgium of an unidentified branch of the *SS*, possibly the *Rasse- und Siedlungshauptamt (RuSHA)*. A somewhat mysterious figure dressed always in civilian clothes, Sommer claimed to be an ethnologist but he held the rank of a captain in the *SS* and his offices were in the headquarters of the *SS* police, the *Sipo-SD*, in the Avenue Louise.[104]

In order to establish the *Cercle Wallon* in Belgium, Sommer turned to the small number of francophone intellectuals and journalists who expounded pan-Germanic and annexationist ideas. He chose as its *secrétaire-général* Fernand-Marie Collard. Not to be confused with Louis Collard of Rex's *Département Politique*, he was a young journalist who – after working for both Henri de Man's *Le Travail* and *Le Soir* – had been appointed as the editor of *L'Effort Wallon*, a weekly newspaper published in Berlin for Walloon workers in Germany.[105] Collard exploited this position to establish himself as a supporter of extremist pro-*SS* opinions. He used *L'Effort Wallon* to make outspoken criticisms of the conservatism of the collaborationists in Belgium and in 1942 De Becker, Colin, Matthys and Streel apparently sought unsuccessfully to oust him from his editorial post.[106] Collard emerged unabashed from this conflict and, returning to Belgium in 1943 to take charge of the *Cercle Wallon*, he gathered around him a loosely united group of intellectuals and unscrupulous *condottieri* who exalted in proclaiming the Germanic character of the Walloon race. Léon Van Huffel, despite his links with Rex, became a member of the *Cercle* but its most important activists were Roger De Moor, a pre-war member of the *Jeunesses Socialistes*, who became its assistant secretary and Camille Ernalsteen, an engineer born in Belgium but who had spent most of his life in Germany. Apparently an agent of both the *Abwehr* and the *Sipo-SD*, Ernalsteen was first active at *Le Soir* where he tried to undermine the position of De Becker but by 1942 he had become the trusted aide of the secretive Dr Sommer.[107]

The men of the *Cercle Wallon* in no sense formed a political movement and could claim no popular following within Belgium. Nonetheless they were in tune with the extremist atmosphere of the times and, with Degrelle and Rex still not firmly established as the allies of the *SS*, they attracted significant Nazi patronage. Apart from the support of Sommer, the *Cercle* also received assistance from the *Militärverwaltung*, the *Dienststelle Jungclaus* and from the Brussels office of Rosenberg, the Reich Minister for the Occupied Eastern Territories which was responsible for the sequestration of Jewish property in Belgium.[108] This enabled it to organise holidays for Walloon children in Germany and to launch a journal, *Le Bulletin de l'Ouest*; but its most important initiative was to establish a series of *Maisons Wallonnes* in the principal Walloon towns. Directed by Paul

Garain, these were intended to act as centres of cultural and social activities based on National Socialist principles but they also enabled the *Cercle Wallon* to establish a limited network of local groups.[109]

It was not, however, so much these activities as the success of the *Cercle* in attracting German patronage which threatened Rex. By 1943 collaboration amounted to little more than the pursuit of Nazi sponsorship and the *Cercle Wallon* was a direct challenge to the efforts of Rex to emerge as the only authorised spokesman of pro-German opinion within francophone Belgium. In response, a bitter rivalry soon developed between the two groups for SS support both within Belgium and in Berlin.[110] At the domestic level, the Rexists opposed any expansion in the scale of the *Cercle's* activities and they succeeded, after lengthy manoeuvring, in convincing the *Dienstelle Jungclaus* and the representative in Belgium of the *Hauptamt für Volkswohlfahrt* that the new Nazi-style public-health organisation being established in Wallonia, *Bien-Etre du Peuple*, should be directed by Rex rather than by the *Cercle Wallon*.[111] Rex won a further victory when in May 1943 Collard left Belgium to attend the *Waffen-SS* officer training school at Bad Tölz in Bavaria. Collard was regarded by some in the SS as a future leader of Wallonia in preference to Degrelle and his training at Bad Tölz was undoubtedly intended to equip him for his future political responsibilities.[112] During his absence, however, the *Cercle Wallon* lost much of its former dynamism. Responsibility for the organisation was officially shared between De Moor and Garain but in reality Garain sought to separate the *Maisons Wallonnes* from the *Cercle*. He had apparently decided to ally himself with Rex and in mid-1943 he briefly held the rank of a *chef de service* within the Rexist *Département Politique*. Strongly encouraged by the Rexist leadership, Garain brought the *Maisons* within the Rexist sphere of influence, expelling those staff who opposed Rex and appointing new figures sympathetic to the movement.[113] In addition to fostering these divisions within the *Cercle Wallon*, the Rexists steadily deprived it of much of its German support within Belgium. By the summer of 1943, the SS representative in Brussels, Jungclaus, had decided to give his backing to Rex and, with his assistance, they were finally able to bring about the departure of Dr Sommer from Belgium by the end of 1943.[114]

Though the *Cercle* soon ceased to pose a serious threat to Rex within Belgium, its supporters remained influential in Berlin. At the initiative of the *SS-Hauptamt*, a *Deutschwallonische Arbeitsgemeinschaft* (*DeWag*) had been established in April 1943.[115] This body was presumably intended to serve much the same purpose as *DeVlag* in Flanders and its creation indicated the distrust still felt by some elements within the SS towards Degrelle. Collard and his allies were the founder members of *DeWag* and Ernalsteen moved from Brussels to Berlin to take charge of the new organisation under the supervision of the inevitable Dr Sommer. Although officially limited to the care and welfare of Walloon workers in Germany, *DeWag* soon sought to expand its activities into Belgium. It was, however, never able to establish more than a minimal presence in the country, largely, it seems, because of opposition from the *Militärverwaltung* which feared the prospect of further internecine strife within the collaborationist camp.[116]

DeWag, nevertheless, remained an influential pressure group within the Reich where its supporters used their control of *L'Effort Wallon* to ridicule the pretensions of Degrelle, describing him in June 1943 as an 'Unter-Hitler' and 'Pfennig-Mussolini'.[117] Such activities soon attracted the ire of Degrelle. He had no intention of allowing his labours to be prejudiced by a small group of journalists and he succeeded in instigating a *coup* within *L'Effort Wallon* whereby power was transferred to a pro-Rexist editor-in-chief.[118] This was just the beginning of a concerted campaign by Degrelle to undermine the power of *DeWag* in Berlin. After the transfer of the *Légion* to the *Waffen-SS*, a *Wallonische Verbindungsstelle* was established in the *SS-Hauptamt* staffed by *légionnaires* who were able to act as the advocates of his cause. In addition, he appointed one of his closest aides, Jean Vermeire, as his personal representative in Berlin with the clear intention not only of winning SS support but also of wresting control of *DeWag* from the hands of his opponents. This was eventually achieved. By January 1944, Vermeire was being described as the *délégué général* of *DeWag* and, although Collard, Ernalsteen and their allies would remain active in Germany during 1944, they possessed neither the resources nor the Nazi patronage necessary to mount a serious challenge to Degrelle.[119]

Therefore, by 1944 Degrelle and Rex had finally succeeded in their goal of emerging as the sole significant advocates of collaboration within francophone Belgium. By that time, this was of course no more than a Pyrrhic victory but, given the disadvantages under which Rex and its leader had laboured, it was nevertheless a considerable feat. They had prospered in the jungle of collaborationist intrigue where so many others, apparently better placed than they, had failed. First in the aftermath of the Belgian military defeat they had succeeded in outmanoeuvring those figures, including Léopold III and Henri De Man, who had believed themselves destined to act as the architects of a *rapprochement* between Belgium and the apparently victorious German Reich. Subsequently, Rex and Degrelle had neutralised and eventually defeated De Becker and his colleagues from the pro-German press of Brussels, before finally successfully repulsing the efforts of the radicals of *AGRA* and the *Cercle Wallon* to win the ear of the all-important SS. This success was not, of course, entirely the work of Rex. To a large degree it was the product of the all too evident failings of their opponents, coupled with the repercussions of the broader military conflict. Perhaps most importantly, however, Rex and Degrelle also benefited from the inability of the leaders of the Third Reich to implement an agreed policy towards Belgium. The subsequent political impasse frustrated the efforts of those such as Léopold III who had hoped to reach an agreement with Germany and at the same time it provided Rex and Degrelle with the opportunity necessary to advance their own credentials as the principal francophone standard-bearers of collaboration. Nevertheless, such factors should not be allowed to mask the undoubted part that Rex and Degrelle played in bringing about the downfall of their various rivals. Unlike the *VNV* in Flanders, they manoeuvred with considerable skill in ruthlessly suffocating or marginalising all potential challengers to their position until by 1944 they stood alone as the representatives of the pro-German cause in Wallonia.

To the general public, the manoeuvrings of these rival collaborationist groups were of no real significance. The underground press seized enthusiastically upon any evidence of dissensions among the supporters of the German cause as evidence of the corrupt opportunism which they believed lay at the heart of all collaboration; but for most Belgians the fluctuating fortunes of different collaborationists held little interest. It was instead the actions of the German authorities and their allies at a local level which had the greatest impact upon the pattern of their lives. By 1943 supporters of Rex were present at all levels of central, provincial and local government and this process of infiltration remained a dominant concern of the Rexist leadership during the latter years of the war. The reorientation of the movement initiated by Degrelle in January 1943 had if anything only served to heighten still further their obsessive concern with controlling even the most obscure backwaters of the public sector and, as the officials of the German *Sipo-SD* remarked, this work so absorbed the energies of Rexist officials that other more important tasks were frequently neglected.[120]

Responsibility for the infiltration of Rexists into government lay with the *Département Politique*. This still operated on the principles established by Streel but, under the direction of Louis Collard, it became a much more regimented and efficient organisation which by the autumn of 1943 was in the process of establishing a vast *fichier* containing details of the entire personnel of local government.[121] The basis of Rexist infiltration remained, as before, the close relationship between the *Département Politique* and the staff of the *Cabinet Wallon* of Romsée's Ministry of the Interior. The head of the *Cabinet*, Delvaux, and his two deputies, Boulanger and Dessart, worked closely with Rex to identify militants suitable for appointment to the considerable range of posts that were under the control of the Ministry. Louis Collard visited the Ministry at least once a week and Matthys and Delvaux also met regularly to discuss the choice of Rexists for more senior positions.[122] Although some Rexists continued to criticise what they regarded as the excessive caution of the *Cabinet Wallon*,[123] relations between the Rexist leaders and the Ministry of the Interior were considerably more amicable than had formerly been the case. There was no longer much competition between Rexists and other candidates for the available posts and, far from Rex forcing the hand of the Ministry, it was more often the *Cabinet* which was anxious to make use of Rex to find candidates for the many vacant positions. Rex, it is clear, also avoided conflict with the Ministry by not proposing for important posts those of its supporters regarded as particularly extreme and when Romsée's *Cabinet* objected to Rexist office-holders explicitly assisting the German authorities over specific issues the Rexist *Etat-Major*, according to Collard, deferred to the wishes of the Ministry.[124]

Some indication of the extent of Rexist infiltration of public adminis-tration can be gleaned from statistics compiled by the German authorities. In a report to his superiors in March 1944, Reeder stated that 174 *échevins* and 206 *bourgmestres* were members of Rex while within central govern-ment one *secrétaire-général* (De Meyer), three *directeurs-généraux*, four *di-recteurs*, two *commissaires-généraux* and ten other unspecified important officials were members of the movement.[125] These figures omit many Rexists serving in other areas of the public sector but they do demonstrate that the weight of Rexist infiltration remained focussed on local govern-ment. Within the central administration, it was the supporters of the *VNV* who still held the most important posts and Rex now recognised that the root cause of this imbalance lay not with the Ministry of the Interior but with the 'Flamenpolitik' of the *Militärverwaltung*. The Rexists complained vociferously to the German authorities about this discrimination and their complaints were also taken up by Degrelle in a letter to Himmler in October 1943. But these protests achieved little. Reeder continued to deny that there was any deliberate policy of excluding Rexists from central administration and he pointed – not without reason – to the difficulties which the movement had experienced in finding candidates of sufficient calibre to fill high governmental posts.[126]

Rexist infiltration of local government did not mean that every com-mune passed under Rexist control. There were approximately 1,520 com-munes in francophone Belgium[127] and a Rexist report of late 1943 admitted that only approximately one in eight of these was in their hands. Com-munes did, however, vary greatly in size and Rexist influence was con-centrated on those – notably the three *grandes agglomérations* – which contained the largest population. Thus, according to the same report, 70 per cent of the population of francophone Belgium was resident in communes directed by Rexist nominees and Matthys claimed that by the summer of 1944 this figure had risen to 85 per cent.[128] As in previous years, the task of this corps of *bourgmestres* and *échevins* was stated to be the destruction of the corrupt *ancien régime* of self-interest and its replace-ment by an impartial and depoliticised administration. Rexist propaganda boasted of the efficiency of their administrations and called for increased salary levels which would reflect the new professional attitude of office-holders.[129] These claims to impartiality were, however, little more than a sham. The Rexist appointees were also intended to act as the soldiers of the National Socialist revolution and commands issued to them by the Rexist leadership – such as that issued in May 1944 ordering Rexists in local government to draw up lists of Belgians who were evading labour conscription – ensured that in effect they served only the interests of Rex and the German Reich.[130] The *Département Politique*, moreover, did all it could to tie its appointees to the movement. All Rexist applicants for governmental posts were required to sign an open-dated letter of resignation before assuming their functions and the *cadre politique* structure within each *cercle* was reinforced. A special periodical, *Informations administratives et politiques*, was distributed to Rexist officials and meetings of *députés permanents*, *commissaires d'arrondissement* and *bourgmestres* were held to make these militants more aware of their revolutionary duty.[131]

The number of Rexist *bourgmestres* and *échevins* remained relatively constant from mid-1943 onwards and the attention of the Rexist leaders turned instead towards taking control of subsidiary posts within the machinery of local administration. Amidst the impending military catastrophe, they nevertheless found time to launch attempts at seizing control of those organisations such as the *Société Nationale des Chemins de Fer Vicinaux* and the bank *Crédit Communal* which were composed of representatives of local authorities.[132] More importantly, Rexist *bourgmestres* and *échevins* used their authority to ensure the appointment of their sympathisers to posts within local administration. Thus, during the latter years of the Occupation, a significant influx of Rexists took place into the bureaucracy of local government where they found employment as *secrétaires communaux*, *receveurs communaux* or even as air-raid wardens.[133] It was in the substantial bureaucracies of the *grandes agglomérations* of Charleroi, La Louvière and Liège that the opportunities for such favouritism were greatest. In 1943 and 1944, Rex reinforced its hold over the council chambers of these cities[134] and a considerable number of Rexists were appointed as *chefs de districts* or as the directors of agencies such as the *commissions d'assistance publique* and the burgeoning *services de ravitaillement*.[135]

Above all, the Rexists remained anxious to infiltrate their supporters into the communal police forces. Control of the police was regarded as essential if they were to transform the towns and cities of francophone Belgium into reliable Rexist fiefdoms and it was once again in the *grandes agglomérations* that the greatest changes were made. Each of these cities attempted – largely in vain – to recruit substantial numbers of additional policemen as well as enrolling members of collaborationist groups into a temporary *police supplémentaire*.[136] In addition, the Rexist councils did all they could to promote those few officers sympathetic to their views. In La Louvière, for example, a supporter of Rex, Lecocq, was appointed as the *commissaire de police*[137] while in Liège the Rexist rulers of the city displayed especial zeal in attempting to mould the communal police into a tool of their designs. They promoted pro-German police officers, encouraged the recruitment of Rexists as well as *AGRA* militants and former *légionnaires* into the police force and made financial bonuses available to those officers who distinguished themselves in anti-Resistance activities.[138] Yet, despite all of these efforts, the results – both in Liège and elsewhere – were limited. The position of the Rexists was too weak and the opposition of the majority of police officers was too implacable for more than small groups of pro-Rexist police to emerge and their ambition of an effective collaborationist police force remained unfulfilled.

Rexist hopes of controlling the *Gendarmerie Nationale* proved similarly illusory. As we have seen, the infiltration of supporters of the movement into this national police force had been a major priority in 1942 and this remained the case during the last years of the Occupation. Efforts were made to concentrate *gendarmes* of New Order views in special anti-terrorist units and Rex enjoyed considerable influence in the *Gendarmerie* training schools enabling it, for instance, to vet all applicants seeking to enter the officer school at Tervuren.[139] But these measures failed to transform the character of the *Gendarmerie* and a Rexist report in the autumn of 1943 admitted that their efforts had been an all but total failure. Despite the enrolment of 'plusieurs centaines' of sympathetic recruits, almost all units of the *Gendarmerie*, it reported, remained centres of pro-English sentiment and those *gendarmes* sympathetic to Rex felt isolated and demoralised.[140]

Their failure to take control of the local police and the *Gendarmerie* illustrated well the problems encountered by Rex in its efforts to infiltrate the institutions of government. Although with the connivance of the German authorities and of Romsée's Ministry of the Interior, they were able to ensure the appointment of their supporters to posts in many areas of public administration, the fierce opposition which these new appointees faced seriously circumscribed their power. Faced at every turn by obstruction and sabotage, many Rexist office-holders achieved little and the energy consumed on their appointment often greatly outweighed the contribution which they subsequently made to the Rexist cause.

This imbalance between the efforts expended and the meagre rewards which such infiltration often brought was most clearly evident in the case of the various new public institutions which were established in wartime Belgium. These were emphatically New Order creations and, although the scale of their activities was limited, they attracted the attention of the Rexists as harbingers of what they hoped would be much more wide-ranging changes in the structure of government. Two of these, *Action Familiale* and *Bien-Etre du Peuple*, were essentially social welfare organis-ations. *Action Familiale* was supposed to assume responsibility for all areas of family policy but, despite some financial assistance from the *Militärver-waltung*, it never had more than a nominal existence.[141] On the other hand,

Bien-Etre du Peuple did have a limited impact. Funded exclusively by the German authorities, it established branches in the major centres of population which, from December 1943, provided pre- and post-natal care, child care facilities and food and other assistance for the elderly and needy. It boasted of its commitment to New Order concepts of social welfare and firmly opposed what it declared to be the bourgeois notions of charity represented by its much larger rivals such as the Catholic-sponsored *Secours d'Hiver*. The predominantly female staff of *Bien-Etre du Peuple* were trained in Germany and, although Rex tried to disguise its role in the organisation, all of its leading personnel were in fact Rexists who had been selected for this work by the leadership of the movement.[142]

The institution of this kind in which the Rexist leadership invested by far the greatest effort was, however, the *Service des Volontaires du Travail pour la Wallonie (SVTW)*. This was not a Rexist creation. The *Volontaires du Travail* had been established in the immediate aftermath of the defeat by a group of Catholic royalists anxious to participate in the reconstruction of their country and in late 1940 it had been divided into two largely autonomous Flemish and Walloon organisations which operated under the indirect supervision of the *secrétaires-généraux*. The francophone *Service* subsequently established a number of work-camps for young people and by July 1941 1,342 volunteers had passed through its camps. The ideology of the *Volontaires du Travail* with its emphasis on loyalty to the dynasty and the virtues of work in the service of the nation was clearly authoritarian in nature but, like the *Chantiers de la Jeunesse* established at the same time in Vichy France, it was above all a product of the distinctive atmosphere created by the military defeat and was not necessarily pro-German or collaborationist in character.[143]

The complicated history of Rexist involvement with the *Volontaires* can only be summarised briefly here. At first, they welcomed its creation. A number of militants participated in its work and an unknown but apparently significant number of *Volontaires* joined the *Légion Wallonie* in 1941. Indeed, one of its leading officials, Lucien Lippert, was to become the military commander of the *Légion* from June 1942 until his death in February 1944.[144] However, as the Rexist commitment to the Nazi cause hardened, so they became critical of the *attentiste* and even pro-English attitudes which they discerned within the *Volontaires du Travail* and by the autumn of 1942 they were contemplating seizing control of the organisation.[145] A major impulse behind this change in attitude was the intense speculation that the German authorities might introduce a system of obligatory labour *within* Belgium. This would have complemented the conscription of Belgian labour for work in Germany and was supported by both the SS and *Reichsarbeitsführer* Hierl. Their intention was to use the *Volontaires du Travail* as the basis for the scheme and not only the Rexists but also Romsée's Ministry of the Interior and the *Communauté Culturelle*

Wallonne became anxious to gain control of an organisation which seemed destined to play a major role in Belgian life.[146]

During a visit to Berlin, Matthys discussed the future of the *SVTW* with officials of Hierl's *Reichsarbeitsdienst* (*RAD*) and Rex was subsequently invited to designate Rexists who could form the core of an explicitly pro-German *SVTW*. Fifty male and female militants including Joseph Pévenasse and a number of *légionnaires* were chosen and in March 1943 they left for Germany where they received training from the *RAD*.[147] By May they were ready to return to Belgium and both the German authorities and the Rexist press began to exert pressure on the *SVTW* to accept these Rexists into their ranks. In mid-June, the German authorities forcibly dismissed the leaders of the *SVTW* imposing in their place the Rexists and *légionnaires* trained in Germany. A Rexist nominee, Dollard, was named as the new head of the *Volontaires* but the real power lay in the hands of his assistant, Lieutenant Closset, and of Pévenasse who was appointed as adviser to Dollard.[148]

The new leaders encountered fierce opposition from the rank and file of the *SVTW* and two of the work-camps were razed by *Volontaires* opposed to this forcible take-over of their organisation.[149] Pévenasse was at the heart of the often violent efforts of the new leaders to exert their authority and, possibly acting on orders from Degrelle, he seems to have been intent upon transforming the *SVTW* into an antechamber for the *Légion Wallonie*. This went beyond the original intentions of Matthys and Collard who seem to have attempted to restrain Pévenasse's activities. Their influence over their former colleague was, however, limited and Pévenasse and his allies persisted in their efforts to crush all opposition within the *SVTW*.[150] These violent disputes forced Romsée to intervene. The *secrétaire-général* of the Ministry of the Interior had initially supported the integration of the *légionnaires* but, in mid-July, he dismissed Dollard and Pévenasse and nominated a more moderate leadership headed by De Decker.[151] By now the authorities in Berlin appeared to have lost interest in an obligatory labour scheme within Belgium and Romsée's actions received the support of the *Militärverwaltung* which predictably preferred to support its trusted ally rather than the turbulent and pro-*SS légionnaires*. Somewhat more surprisingly, Romsée also received cautious support from Louis Collard who apparently assured the *secrétaire-général* that Rex would allow the stabilisation of the *SVTW* under its new leadership.[152]

Hopes of a truce in the struggle for control of the *SVTW* did, however, prove to be short-lived. Despite Collard's promises, the *Département Politique* of Rex soon began to foment disruption amongst the *Volontaires*. Collard attempted to bully and bribe De Decker into reinstating Rexists within the organisation and, when rebuffed, he succeeded, with the support of the *Dienstelle Jungclaus* and possibly of the *Militärverwaltung*, in placing a number of Rexists in the officer training camp of the *SVTW*.[153]

Romsée opposed these activities and appointed a new figure, Van Craen, as the head of the *Volontaires*. However Van Craen allied himself with Rex and appointed a number of Rexists to influential positions, obliging Romsée to intervene once again, this time in order to dismiss Van Craen.[154]

Decimated by these rivalries, the *SVTW* had been reduced by the end of 1943 to a small group of recruits and the *secrétaires-généraux* finally decided to liquidate the remnants of the organisation.[155] Rex refused to allow the demise of a body in which it had invested so much effort and in April 1944 created its own organisation with an almost identical title.[156] This was almost entirely Rexist in composition and, although its President, Closset, was officially received by *Reichsarbeitsführer* Hierl, it was shunned by the vast majority of the former personnel of the *SVTW*. It only ever operated on a small scale and formed in effect an adjunct of the Rexist movement: young employees of the Rexist *Etat-Major* were required to undergo a period of training in the *SVTW* and its camps were guarded by armed members of the Rexist protection group, the *Formations B*.[157]

The tortuous history of Rexist efforts to infiltrate the *Volontaires du Travail* served once again to demonstrate their impotence. Though they eventually won control of the *SVTW*, they did so only at the cost of destroying whatever importance the organisation had formerly possessed. The Rexists, however, never appeared to question the value of infiltrating all available positions of authority, continuing even as the Allied armies rolled towards Belgium in the summer of 1944 to plot the capture of minor posts which had hitherto evaded their grasp.[158] The rationale for this obsessive concern with the process of infiltration remained that the acquisition of posts of public authority was a means of preparing for their long-heralded seizure of political power. In reality the real reasons why it always remained such a dominant concern were rooted in the nature of the German Occupation and, more especially, in the character of Rex itself. During the latter war years, the overriding concern of the officials of the *Militärverwaltung* remained to ensure that control of Belgium was accomplished with the minimal deployment of German manpower and resources. This obliged the German authorities to continue to work as far as was possible with the *secrétaires-généraux* and other elements of the elite, but the extent to which these figures were willing to respond to the dictates of a visibly waning German power was by now limited. In response, Reeder and his colleagues were forced more than ever to rely on Rex and its Flemish equivalents who came in effect to form a parallel 'unofficial' administration working alongside the official Belgian bureaucracy.[159]

It was not merely Nazi needs which forced the Rexists to assume posts of public responsibility. Much of the impetus also came from within Rex. In part this was a consequence of the structure of the movement's *Etat-Major*. In 1943 and 1944, the *Département Politique* under the leadership of

Louis Collard came to dominate the national headquarters and was in effect able to impose its priorities on the movement. Foremost amongst these was the policy of infiltration, of which Collard always remained both the most enthusiastic exponent and the principal architect. This impetus from above was, however, also reinforced by pressure from below. The rank and file of the movement's evident enthusiasm for acquiring all positions of authority was such that on more than one occasion Matthys felt obliged to warn his followers that Rex was not merely a vehicle for the gratification of personal aspirations. As early as September 1941, for example, he warned that: 'REX est un mouvement idéaliste: nous n'existons pas pour procurer des places ou des postes à des amis . . . L'activité de nos Cercles et de nos Groupes ne peut, sous aucun prétexte, être entièrement consacrée à ce secteur important mais *limité*.'[160] Clearly, crude personal ambition often lay at the heart of this quest for public positions. Political parties in Belgium have a long tradition of providing posts in the public sector for their supporters and many Rexists evidently saw no reason why their movement should break with this custom. Many applied for posts for which they were singularly under-qualified and there were prominent instances of Rexists who exploited their new-found positions of authority for corrupt or dissolute ends.[161] Despite such cases greed was not the only spur. The long roll-calls of Rexist office-holders murdered by the Resistance indicated that nomination to such a post was unlikely to appeal to the simple adventurer and collaboration offered many less hazardous opportunities for personal enrichment. Moreover, most Rexist appointees showed remarkable dedication in the face of adversity. Despite the dangers to which they were exposed, no substantial wave of resignations by Rexist office-holders ever occurred, even in the final desperate months of the Occupation.[162]

Therefore, for many Rexists ambition formed part of a broader complex of emotions and motivations. For some the acquisition of public office was perceived as no more than a deserved recompense. Support for the German cause did, after all, expose Rexists and their families to considerable opprobrium or even danger and there was a feeling in Rexist ranks that a post in local administration was the due reward for such hardships. But in many cases the most important motivation behind the Rexist scramble for positions of authority was a craving for status combined with a perverse sense of personal idealism. Rexist propaganda continually stressed that its militants were an enlightened minority forced to lead their uncomprehending compatriots towards the New Order, and this rhetoric undoubtedly fostered in many Rexists a state of mind in which they saw it as their duty to shoulder the hazardous responsibilities of public office.[163] This was reinforced by an often almost desperate desire to appear as the leaders of a local population who despised and shunned them. Few Rexists had ever exercised any official functions and appointment as *bourgmestre, échevin* or even to a more modest post provided these militants with the opportunity they had longed for to act out their dreams. Ambition in such cases was secondary to a real – if profoundly misguided – sense of civic responsibility and in the *Monsieur Homais* world of many modest Rexists their acquisition of a position of local responsibility served, above all, to prove to their community that they were indeed idealists determined to serve the common good.

Whether naïvely well-intentioned or merely intent upon personal advancement, almost all Rexist office-holders did encounter implacable opposition from their fellow citizens who quite rightly saw their appointment as primarily intended to serve the interests of the German authorities. Mutual incomprehension often degenerated into violence and the last years of the Occupation abounded with examples of local confrontations between Rexist office-holders and their opponents. Arguments in streets or cafés often led to exchanges of insults, scuffles or even to shots being fired. In a typical incident, the *bourgmestre* of Philippeville, Gabriel Claes, was drinking in a café with a fellow Rexist in September 1943 when he became embroiled in a dispute with the son of the proprietor. Fuelled not a little by drink, tempers soon became frayed and the row culminated in Claes firing his revolver at his opponent. Fortunately, he missed his target and, aided by the other customers, his intended victim escaped unscathed.[164] Such incidents could, however, take a more serious form when the Rexists chose to appeal for help to the German police and many of the incidents of Rexists denouncing their compatriots to the German authorities undoubtedly arose from quarrels of this kind.[165]

Conflict was particularly intense between Rexist officials and those who could more rightly claim to be leaders of the community. Pre-war political figures, local teachers and, above all, priests frequently became embroiled in acrimonious disputes with the Rexists. The privileged position enjoyed by the Catholic Church within Occupied Belgium ensured that religious services remained the principal opportunity to voice patriotic opinions with relative impunity and Rexists had long been vigilant in their surveillance of such ceremonies. Incidents of Rexists disrupting services or denouncing priests to the German authorities were commonplace[166] and received encouragement from the example of Degrelle's own behaviour. During a visit to his home town of Bouillon in July 1943 he deliberately sought confrontation with the local priest by attending mass dressed in his new *SS* military uniform. In accordance with the orders of the bishops, the priest refused to administer the sacraments to Degrelle, whereupon the Rexist leader and his bodyguards dragged the priest out of his church and imprisoned him in the cellar of the Degrelle family home. The German authorities eventually intervened to ensure the release of the unfortunate priest but the Belgian Church authorities reacted by excommunicating Degrelle, a sanction which he was subsequently able to have lifted by the chaplain of the *Légion Wallonie* and the German military chaplaincy.[167]

Such local confrontations, whether spontaneous or – as in this case – clearly premeditated, were less sinister than the activities of Lambinon's *Département de Sécurité et d'Information (DSI)*. This gradually emerged during 1943 as a collaborationist police force assisting the German authorities directly in their often murky war against the Resistance. Although Lambinon's appointment as the head of the *DSI* in January 1943 had been the culmination of persistent pressure on his part, he was initially slow to seize upon the opportunities offered by his new position. For a number of months the *DSI* had a nominal existence and it was only in the summer of 1943 that Lambinon established its first unit, the *Brigade Z* in Brussels, and set about making the department what one Rexist subsequently described as 'un état dans un état' in Rex.[168]

Some of the staff of the *DSI* were Rexist militants but most were recruited by Lambinon in the *demi-monde* of adventurers and drifters which existed on the margins of the collaborationist world. An *agent touristique*, a hairdresser, a driver, a former waiter and even an announcer from a greyhound race-track were all chosen by him as agents for the new organisation.[169] Dubious personal morality and lack of any evident commitment to the Rexist cause were no obstacle to membership of the department. As the head of the *Brigade Z*, Lambinon appointed a former inspector in the *Police Judiciaire* from Liège, Jules Funken, who, after being dismissed from the Belgian police, had joined the *Légion Wallonie* before finding in the *DSI* a congenial opportunity to avoid the rigours of the Eastern Front.[170]

Lambinon's choice of assistants hastened the transformation of the *DSI* into a free-lance police unit operating largely independently of Rex. He fostered links with a number of the German police organisations working in Belgium, and the *DSI* and its *Brigade Z* began to assist these German agencies on an *ad hoc* basis. Such collaboration was, however, hampered by the deep distrust with which many Nazi police officials – notably in the *Sipo* in Brussels – regarded Lambinon's organisation. They strongly criticised its amateurism and corruption and, for this reason, the German authorities withheld the right to carry out arrests of suspects from both the *DSI* and the *Brigade Z*.[171]

This distrust was well justified. A number of the agents of the *DSI* were no more than unscrupulous mercenaries and Lambinon himself apparently enjoyed a luxurious style of life which was out of all proportion to his official income.[172] Many of the operations of his department took place on or close to the frontier between anti-Resistance actions and simple banditry. The *Brigade Z*, for example, chose to specialise in the pursuit of prosperous Jews, an activity which provided its members with ample opportunities for extortion.[173] In August 1943 one such incident led to the arrest of members of the brigade by the German *Feldgendarmerie* and, a few weeks later, the involvement of the *DSI* in corrupt foreign exchange dealings led the German police to arrest Lambinon and his principal assistants. Thanks to the efforts of his friends within the German police as well as of the Rexist leadership and their allies in the *Dienstelle Jungclaus*, Lambinon and his associates soon regained their freedom but the incident did little to enhance German perceptions of the new police unit.[174] Corruption also went hand in hand with a taste for violence. Lambinon's agents were ineffectual policemen who compensated for their lack of expertise by habitually resorting to the physical intimidation of those unfortunate enough to fall into their hands and violent assaults and rudimentary torture soon became commonplace in the cells of the *DSI* building in the Place Rouppe in Brussels.[175]

This combination of inefficiency and corruption seriously hindered the *DSI*'s development. It employed no more than a handful of agents during 1943[176] and, unlike the *Algemene SS-Vlaanderen* in Flanders, failed to establish itself as a recognised adjunct of the German police authorities. The efforts of Lambinon to extend his activities from Brussels to Wallonia were similarly slow to bear fruit. A *DSI* unit was created in Liège under the direction of Funken in the summer of 1943 but it rapidly became embroiled in a campaign of terrorism and banditry and was rapidly dissolved.[177] Instead, Lambinon turned his attention to the local Rexist police units which already existed in La Louvière and Charleroi. These were in some respects comparable to the *DSI* but in origin they owed nothing to Lambinon's department. In La Louvière, the Rexist police was the creation of a local Rexist leader, Edgard Duquesne, who worked closely with the pro-German communal police and the Rexist city council. In Charleroi, the Rexist police unit was responsible directly to the authorities of *Grand Charleroi* and the effective head of the brigade, Henri Merlot, was both an *échevin* of the city and the local *chef de cercle* of Rex.[178] The principal purpose of the *Bande Duquesne* and the *Police Merlot*, as they were respectively known, was to counter the activities of the Resistance and both worked closely with the German police. Their methods were violent including, in the case of the La Louvière brigade, the use of torture and members of both units were also implicated in cases of petty theft.[179] While the development of the Charleroi brigade was always hindered by poor recruitment and weak leadership, Duquesne's unit in La Louvière was relatively efficient and was regarded by Lambinon as the ideal which he sought to emulate in his own activities.[180]

Duquesne came to an agreement with Lambinon in the summer of 1943 whereby his unit was attached to the *DSI* as its *Brigade A* and he was appointed as the Inspector of the *DSI* for the provinces of the Hainaut and Namur. Similarly, the *Police Merlot* of Charleroi became the *Brigade E* of the *DSI* and Lambinon demonstrated his authority over the brigade by summoning its members to participate in his operations in Brussels and by expelling those of its agents who opposed him.[181] Lambinon's control over both of these units during 1943 should not, however, be exaggerated.

Their principal loyalty remained to the Rexist leaders of their home towns and effective integration into the *DSI* only began in December 1943 when their members participated in a training school organised by Lambinon at Genval. A few days later, the first joint operation involving all brigades of the *DSI* took place when, together with *Wehrmacht* forces, they carried out a military-style campaign against the Resistance in the hills around the town of Huy.[182]

Even so, the *DSI* units in La Louvière and Charleroi always remained intimately connected to the local Rexist hierarchy. Members of the brigades were also officials of the *cercles*, and local militants acted as informers. This was particularly so in La Louvière where an *échevin* served as the brigade's secretary and the *chef de cercle*, Oscar Cus, even participated in the interrogation of suspects.[183] The situation in Brussels was very different. There, the *DSI* and the *Brigade Z* formed a separate shadowy world which had few links either with local Rexist groups or with the *Etat-Major*.[184] Militants knew little of *DSI* activities and Lambinon kept himself apart from the Rexist leadership. He visited the headquarters of the movement only infrequently and was apparently referred to by other Rexist officials – presumably not without some irony – as 'notre Himmler'.[185] As the head of the *DSI*, Lambinon sent regular reports on his activities to Matthys but the *Chef de Rex ad interim* exercised little effective control over the department. Rumours of Matthys' supposed participation in the *DSI*'s police operations and black market intrigues remained unproven and, by his own admission, he took little interest in Lambinon's activities. On rare occasions, the reports he received do seem to have prompted Matthys to make somewhat half-hearted attempts to constrain the scale or nature of the *DSI*'s actions and he claimed after the war to have repeatedly insisted that the department should not assist German efforts to apprehend those Belgians seeking to evade labour conscription. Not surprisingly, these orders were blatantly disregarded by Lambinon who continued to look on the *DSI* as his personal fiefdom.[186]

Lambinon's autonomy from the Rexist leadership was, however, an exception to the trend within the movement towards a more hierarchical and centralised structure. The architect of this process was the young *Chef-adjoint* of the *Département Politique*, Louis Collard. Collard's rise within Rex during 1943 was meteoric. Less than a year after returning to the movement in the autumn of 1942, he had asserted his control over all important areas of Rexist activity and had established himself as the most influential adviser of Matthys. Léon Brunet, the *Chef du Département Politique*, was no more than a nominal figure-head who visited the Rexist offices only infrequently and it was Collard who took charge both of the internal direction of the *département* as well as its relations with external bodies, including most importantly all dealings with the German authorities.[187] During his post-war interrogations, Collard was not surprisingly at pains to present himself as a loyal official who had done no more than act on the orders of his superiors. In reality Collard was the man who more than any other determined the policies of Rex during the last year of the Occupation and who established himself indisputably – alongside Degrelle and Matthys – as the third man of Rex.[188]

Collard's dramatic rise from obscurity to become the *de facto* head of the Rexist bureaucracy was ascribed by many to his personal ambition. For example, Henry Marcovitz, an employee of the German *Sicherheitsdienst* (*SD*) who in his post-war prison cell wrote detailed reports on Rex for the Belgian judicial authorities, described Collard as a consummate intriguer who skilfully manipulated the personal rivalries which flourished in the hothouse atmosphere of the Rexist *Etat-Major*. Marcovitz laid particular stress on the close relationship between Collard and Matthys. According to his somewhat colourful description, Collard cynically exploited the natural laziness and other vices of his superior in order to reinforce his own authority over the movement.[189] There was clearly some truth in Marcovitz's account. He was not alone in noting Collard's influence over Matthys, and Matthys himself had no hesitation after the war in describing the *Chef-adjoint* of the *Département Politique* as 'le plus intime et le plus influent' of his aides.[190] As two men of the same generation and from similarly modest backgrounds, they soon became close friends and Collard was frequently to be seen at Matthys' side on public and private occasions. The *Chef de Rex ad interim* was, however, no mere tool of Collard. Possibly worn down by eighteen months as the effective leader of the movement, Matthys was clearly more than content to devolve much of the administration of Rex to his energetic subordinate but he continued to exercise considerable influence over the political direction of the movement.

Nor should Collard's ascendancy be attributed solely to his undoubted ambition. He was also a man of considerable bureaucratic talents. Matthys praised Collard's dynamism and 'formidable force de travail' and his appreciation was shared by other well-informed observers. Degrelle, for example, writing from the front line in August 1944, remarked of Collard that he had been 'épaté par son travail et par ses étonnantes qualités'.[191] Indeed, as one of his erstwhile colleagues noted after the war, there was something manic about Collard's prodigious energies. He appeared to devote himself entirely to his work refusing to delegate even the most trivial matters of detail and had little social life outside of the offices of the *Etat-Major*.[192]

Collard was in effect one of the very few specialists in the world of collaboration. Most allies of the Nazi cause turned their hand to such diverse activities as journalism, public speaking or even military leadership. Collard, as his defence counsel was keen to point out at his trial, seems never to have made a public speech and published no newspaper articles.[193] The ascendancy of this unremarkable figure, who amidst the myriad uniforms of Rex was dressed always in a civilian suit, symbolised a new form of collaboration which came to the fore in the last years of the war. By then, Rex was irredeemably isolated from the vast majority of the population and had little need of journalists, politicians or still less of orators. It had become an administrative and military machine and, as an internal report – written probably by Collard – in December 1943 remarked, the organisation had ceased to be a primarily political move-ment.[194] Thus, like the Third Reich which in its dying days fell under the control of *apparatchiks* such as Bormann, Himmler, Kaltenbrunner and Speer, Rex required men who could adapt to this new world. Collard, with his administrative talents, amply filled this need and he typified a white-collar style of leader who became increasingly influential within Rex in the latter war years and who existed, occasionally somewhat uneasily, alongside military figures drawn from the *Légion*.

This bureaucratisation of Rex was most evident in the expansion in the size and responsibilities of the *Département Politique*. Under Collard's di-rection, it came to overshadow completely the other departments of the *Etat-Major*, whose duties were reduced to matters of routine adminis-tration. Its personnel multiplied tenfold to a full-time staff of sixty and each of the ten areas of responsibility originally identified by Streel became an office in its own right.[195] The men who staffed the *département* were, almost without exception, very similar to Collard. His four principal assistants were Jean Colman, Albert Regnard, Michel Saussez and Carlos Jacques. With the exception of Jacques, they were young men under 30 years old and all had joined the *Etat-Major* in late 1942 or early 1943. The backgrounds of Colman and Regnard were almost identical. Both were *petit bourgeois employés* who had left with Degrelle for the Eastern front in August 1941 and who had joined the *Département Politique* on being demobilised from the *Légion*.[196] Michel Saussez, on the other hand, was from a working-class family of the Borinage. His father was a miner but, with financial assistance from a local benefactor, Saussez had been able to attend the University of Louvain where he soon rallied to the Rexist cause. He subsequently returned to his native area as a schoolteacher and worked actively for the Rexist *cercle* of Mons in a number of administrative posts before joining the *Département Politique* in November 1942.[197] In contrast, Carlos Jacques was a prosperous Brussels industrialist and a veteran of the 1914–18 conflict who had been active in *ancien combattant* associations. But he too was primarily a bureaucrat and, although a member of Rex since 1935, he joined the *Département Politique* only in May 1943.[198] Together with Louis Collard, these four men constituted a new generation of Rexist leaders. They were in no sense politicians and shunned public attention. Instead, they were anonymous *apparatchiks* well suited to direct a move-ment which had come to regard even its compatriots as an enemy.

The problems faced by Rex in the summer of 1943 demonstrated the need for strong leadership. The steady retreat of German forces on the Eastern front and the sudden collapse of Mussolini's regime in Italy in July were unwelcome developments which inevitably had a considerable impact on the morale of the Rexist rank and file. The propagandists of the movement did their best to present these events in the most encouraging light, assuring their readers that the Italian defection had clarified the true sense of the war as a struggle between the Nazi revolution and its enemies while stressing the resources which Germany was holding in reserve for the decisive battle.[199] On the whole, nonetheless, they preferred to distract their readers from the depressing catalogue of military reverses by pointing to the broader significance of the conflict. Fascism and National Socialism were expressions of the will of history and could not, Le Pays Réel rather nervously insisted, be 'des explosions sans lendemain'. This recourse to a crude determinism was taken up by Matthys. Speaking at a Rexist rally in September 1943 under a banner proclaiming 'Fidélité', he declared that the Nazi cause was sacred and that not even the presence of Stalin's Cossacks camped in the Grand Place of Brussels would be able to prevent its remorseless historical triumph.[200]

In private, the Rexist leaders were rather less sanguine. Degrelle had warned them of the exhaustion of German forces in Russia and they no longer hoped for a Nazi victory. However they still felt able to joke about the postponement of the long-awaited Allied liberation and the leadership remained optimistic that an outright German defeat might be averted.[201] Indeed for a few brief weeks in the summer of 1943 it seemed that events might be moving in their favour. Military developments during the previous year had created an atmosphere in which it had seemed that the war would continue ineluctably until the Allies achieved a complete victory. The failure of the Allies to invade northern Europe in 1943 and the consequent strains in relations between the Soviet Union and the western powers as well as the unexpected resilience demonstrated by the German armies in Italy appeared to indicate that a decisive Allied victory might not be a realistic possibility. The consequence was to create speculation – at least in pro-German circles – that some form of compromise peace might after all prove possible.[202] The relative stalemate also gave rise to more dramatic scenarios. Within the Axis camp, some began to dream of a reversal of alliances in which Britain and the United States would join with Germany in confronting the Bolshevik threat or even that Nazi Germany and Soviet Russia would revive the Ribbentrop-Molotov pact, enabling the entire German military might to be deployed against the western Allies. Indeed, during the summer of 1943, there were some tentative signs of a rapprochement between Germany and the Soviet Union. Both regimes softened the tone of their propaganda attacks and in Stockholm tentative contact between emissaries of the two countries seems to have been established.[203]

The Rexist leaders of course knew nothing of these shadowy events but they sensed the possibility of some change in the current balance of forces. Significantly, it was the idea of a 'revolutionary' union of Nazism and Soviet communism which most appealed to them. In private conversations, they strongly advocated such an alliance and, demonstrating how far they had come since the anti-Bolshevik crusade of 1941, Degrelle declared publicly that, if forced to choose between capitalism and communism, he would ally himself with the latter.[204] Not surprisingly, such heresies seem to have worried some militants but Degrelle's views received strong support from Matthys who had long stressed the socialist element in Rexist ideology. The bourgeoisie were, he insisted, the principal enemy of Rex and he boasted of the affinity of temperament which he claimed existed between Rexists and Communists.[205]

The alluring possibilities of the summer were, however, soon dissipated. Contacts between Germany and the Soviet Union were broken off and at the vast tank battle at Kursk the Red Army gained a decisive military advantage.[206] Thus, the war returned to its former remorseless course, while within the country the Resistance redoubled its campaign of terror against the agents of the Nazi cause. By November Reeder reported that approximately sixty Rexists had been murdered so far that year and, writing in *Le Pays Réel* in September, Matthys declared that the Rexists were obliged to operate in an 'atmosphère de guerre civile larvée' in which the normal protection afforded by the rule of law no longer applied.[207] This was a comment with which many of his compatriots would have agreed. The Belgian government in London issued a series of decrees in December 1942 modifying the law to facilitate the post-war prosecution of collaborators.[208] These were in part intended to discourage Resistance attacks on collaborators by reassuring the population that effective action would be taken after the liberation against those who had served the Nazi cause. Although news of the decrees broadcast by the BBC was widely welcomed,[209] it seems to have done little to prevent more immediate action. Indeed, by appearing in some sense to give official approval to such attacks, the decrees may have served to fuel further violence. It was, as before, the more radical Resistance groups – notably the Communist-led *Partisans Armés* – which took the lead in waging war on the collaborationist minority and their actions received strong encouragement from much of the underground press. In a typical statement, the paper *La Belgique Nouvelle* declared in 1943: 'Entre les Patriotes et les Sbires d'un flamingantisme malsain et du rexisme, une lutte à mort est ouverte; elle durera aussi longtemps que l'Allemagne occupera notre pays ... Le terrorisme est l'arme des opprimés. Dans le passé, des régimes autrement puissants que les leurs ont été secoués, freinés dans leur despotisme et se sont même écroulés sous ses coups. Il faut que chaque rexiste ou mauvais flamingant ... se rende bien compte qu'il n'échappera pas au châtiment;

qu'il n'est plus en sécurité nulle part; que la mort le guette nuit et jour, que le passant qu'il coudoie ou qui l'approche, que l'inconnu ou le mendiant qui vient sonner chez lui, que l'ami même qu'il reçoit à sa table, peut être celui-là même envoyé pour l'exécuter.'[210]

Such language appears to have enjoyed ready approval from the majority of the population who sympathised with the Resistance attacks and participated enthusiastically in the intimidation of the pro-German minority. Even in comparison with much of the rest of German-occupied Europe where the population was similarly polarised into two unequal camps, the depth of bitterness towards the collaborationist minority in Belgium – and more especially in Wallonia – was exceptional. As Reeder remarked, the division between the Rexists and their pro-Allied compatriots was by now total and communication across the divide became virtually impossible.[211] The Rexist press claimed that children as young as eight years old had been assaulted and even the posters advertising the *Légion Wallonie* had to be guarded night and day against attack. Attacks on homes of Rexists were commonplace and in the Borinage members of the movement received rope nooses through the post. Elsewhere, near Ciney the cows of a militant were daubed with swastikas while in Charleroi unwary Rexists were reported to have been attacked in the streets at night and stripped of their clothes.[212]

Not surprisingly, many Rexists became intensely suspicious of all those outside of the movement with whom they came into contact. Jean Colman of the *Département Politique* was one of many militants who feared that even his neighbours were plotting his demise, prompting him to write in panic to the German police to request protection.[213] The Rexists were, however, all too aware that the German authorities could offer them only an imperfect security and pressure mounted inexorably for the movement to take its own revenge on its enemies. Vague promises of bloody retribution at an unspecified future date were no longer sufficient to satisfy many exasperated local militants and, as Matthys subsequently admitted, a desire for immediate reprisals had become 'le courant général' within the movement.[214]

In the summer of 1943 this frustration took concrete form when a number of radical elements took matters into their own hands. The perpetrators of this improvised violence were frequently demobilised *légionnaires* or members of the *Légion* employed in the substantial network of recruitment, propaganda and welfare offices of the *Ersatzkommando* of the *Légion* which now existed within Belgium. In Brussels, for example, a group of *légionnaires* formed a vigilante squad which pillaged the offices of patriotic organisations and assaulted members of a cinema audience in Anderlecht who had ridiculed a newsreel film of Degrelle.[215] Not all of this violence was political. In July 1943 a *légionnaire* on leave in Namur shot dead a man in a street brawl while a few weeks later two members of the

Ersatzkommando murdered a Brussels café-owner. They claimed that the victim was a member of the Resistance but it soon emerged that the two *légionnaires* had been in dispute with him over an unpaid drinks bill and they were prosecuted under *SS* law.[216]

It was in Liège that Rexist violence took its most organised form. This first became evident in July 1943 at the funeral of a pro-German policeman who had been assassinated by the Resistance. The priest was unwilling to proceed with the service in the presence of uniformed *légionnaires* but he was forced to change his mind after being threatened by a number of armed Rexists. The funeral over, the Rexists locked the *curé* in his cellar and pillaged his home.[217] Soon after this incident, an organised gang of Rexists committed to terrorism emerged in the city. The central figure of this group was Jean Pirmolin. He was a long-standing Rexist who, after service in the *Légion Wallonie*, had returned to Liège as the local representative of *Honneur Légionnaire*, the welfare organisation for the families of *légionnaires*. A violent man who boasted of his role in atrocities in Russia, Pirmolin soon became a prominent figure at Rexist events in his home town and gathered around him a number of like-minded militants.[218]

Pirmolin's group also became part of the *DSI*. Lambinon's assistant, Funken, was a frequent visitor to Liège during the summer of 1943 and at a meeting on 21 August he encouraged Pirmolin to organise assassinations of local dignitaries known for their patriotic views.[219] Lists of suitable victims were drawn up and in the course of the following days Pirmolin and his associates murdered two leading figures in the Liberal party in Liège as well as a police inspector against whom Pirmolin held a personal grudge. Soon afterwards, the same men carried out a number of armed robberies – including one of a casino at Noville outside Liège – sharing the booty between themselves and the Rexist movement.[220] The Belgian police acted swiftly to discover the authors of these crimes. Within a few weeks they had arrested some of Pirmolin's accomplices and, although he and one of his assistants initially evaded capture by enrolling in the German *Sicherheitsdienst* (*SD*), he too was arrested in March 1944. This success was, however, short-lived as the local German military commander intervened to transfer all of the group into the hands of the German military judicial authorities and they were released without charges a few months later.[221]

The extent to which the Rexist hierarchy were involved in the actions of Pirmolin's band remains unclear. Some local Rexist figures, such as Gaston Chavanne, a *député permanent* of the province of Liège, were certainly directly implicated[222] but it appears that Dargent, the *bourgmestre* of *Grand Liège*, and Bomans, the *chef de cercle*, may have done no more than express approval for Pirmolin's actions after they had taken place.[223] When Pirmolin and his accomplices were interrogated by an *SS* judge in 1944, they also claimed that they had acted on orders from the national leadership of Rex.[224] The judge unsuccessfully sought permission to interrogate Matthys but it seems unlikely that, with the exception of Lambinon, anybody within the Rexist *Etat-Major* was aware of Pirmolin's plans. Both during his post-war interrogations and in an article in *Le Pays Réel* in September 1943, Matthys denied that the Rexist leadership had played any part in the murders and he apparently opposed the efforts by Rexists in Liège to protect Pirmolin and his associates from the Belgian judicial authorities.[225]

Nevertheless, even if they were not directly implicated in the murders at Liège, the events there did indicate that the Rexist leaders were unable or even unwilling to prevent violent-minded radicals from initiating their own actions. In his article denying any responsibility for the killings at Liège, Matthys avoided condemning the murderers and, raising the possibility of other similar actions, the interim *Chef de Rex* commented: 'Il ne faudrait pas compter sur nous pour désavouer ces garçons. Ils agiraient à l'encontre des instructions et des ordres qu'ils ont reçus, mais pas plus que le Mouvement lui-même, ils ne porteraient la responsabilité réelle des actes meurtriers qu'éventuellement, et à notre plus vif regret d'ailleurs, ils commettraient.' The true responsibility, he declared, for such murders lay with those who organised and permitted the Resistance attacks on supporters of Rex. It was they – and in particular the elite of pre-war Belgium – who had created the atmosphere of terror in which the Rexists were forced to respond in kind.[226] Matthys' attitude to Rexist violence was fundamentally ambivalent: while remaining unwilling to direct or authorise violent actions, he had apparently come to accept their inevitability. This was a significant shift in his position. As we have seen, after initially praising Rexist violence in the summer of 1942, he had sought – no doubt under pressure from Reeder – to prevent such individual initiatives by pointing to German police successes and by promising a bloody *règlement de comptes* after the Rexist acquisition of power. But by the autumn of 1943, he had lost faith in the capacity of the German authorities to offer effective protection and, emboldened by the alliance with the SS, he no longer felt obliged to defer to the counsels of caution emanating from the *Militärverwaltung*. This combination of a Rexist movement both more desperate to protect itself against an omnipresent danger and more confident in its radical allies opened the way for the violent actions of 1944.

The threat posed by the Resistance also reinforced the decline in Rexist membership which had already taken place after Degrelle's speech in January. Although it is impossible to quantify, German and other observers were convinced of the reality of this decline and examples of individuals who withdrew from Rex in 1943 are easy to identify.[227] The Rexists did admit to defections by those whom they described as bourgeois members of weak resolve but boasted that this purification of their ranks had been more than compensated for by new recruits from what they termed the 'milieux populaires'.[228] While Rex did have some very modest success in attracting working-class support during the latter years of the war, this claim was highly implausible. New members were a rare phenomenon at Rexist meetings and one to be boasted of in local reports. Indeed, most *cercles* paid little attention to recruitment and concentrated instead on the more realistic task of enrolling the wives and other close relatives of existing members.[229]

There seems little doubt that Rexist membership was in decline and the effects of this decline were most evident at a local level. During the summer of 1943 a virtual collapse in Rexist membership was reported from certain localities, particularly the more isolated rural areas of southern Belgium. In Chimay, for example, Albert Constant deplored the 'funeste épidémie de découragements, de reculements et d'opportunisme' which he had witnessed among his fellow Rexists and in many villages a Resistance attack on one militant was often sufficient to prompt many others to abandon the movement.[230] These withdrawals were reflected in the local organisation of Rex. In the rural province of Luxembourg, which in 1936 had given Rex its most dramatic electoral successes, membership of the *cercle* of Neufchâteau had fallen to 13 by late 1943 and its remaining members were reallocated to the *cercle* of Virton, while elsewhere in the same province declining numbers forced the fusion of the *cercles* of Marche and of Bastogne.[231] Similar problems were reported from other provinces. In the Hainaut, the *cercle* of Soignies was closed and its membership attached to La Louvière and in the province of Liège the *cercles* of Huy and of Waremme were apparently combined into a single unit. Finally, in what was claimed to be a measure to improve co-ordination, the three *cercles* in the capital were replaced by a single *Région de Bruxelles*.[232] Thus, the total number of *cercles* fell from 23 to 17 during 1943, while those which did survive often had difficulty in retaining the support of their members. In Liège, for example, reports deplored absenteeism by local officials and a substantial number of militants refused to renew their financial contributions. Elsewhere, warnings were issued to militants to remain loyal or to risk punishment by 'les Durs et Purs' of Rex. Such threats were, however, ineffectual and the activity of many *cercles* was reported by the German *Sipo-SD* to be limited to internal administration and recruitment for military units.[233]

Reeder, that most unsympathetic observer of Rex, stressed repeatedly in his reports of the latter war years that the Rexists formed an insignificant proportion of the francophone population, estimating in August 1943 their total membership to be only approximately 8,000.[234] This figure, which seems to have been derived from an internal German police report of May 1943,[235] provides the most reliable assessment of the strength of the movement during the latter years of the Occupation. It should, however, be treated with some caution. No membership lists have survived to corroborate this estimate and no indication was provided by Reeder as to whether it took into account the membership of Rexist-affiliated organisations and of military and para-military units. It would seem that the figure of 8,000 was intended as an assessment of the number of militants who were under the direct control of the Rexist *Etat-Major*. As such, it probably included not only the membership of the *cercles* but also those

Table

Membership of Rexist and 'Degrellian' Organisations in 1943 and 1944[236]

Organisation	Membership
Local *cercles* of Rex	Approximately 8,000
Formations de Combat	600–850 men in 1943
Mouvement des Femmes Rexistes	300–400 women in 1943 and 1944
Foi dans la Vie	Approximately 200 young women in 1943 and 1944
Walloon units of German Red Cross	100 women in 1943 and 1944
Légion Wallonie	1,850 men in November 1943[a]
Gardes Wallonnes	1,500 men in 1943 and 1944
NSKK (German Transport Corps)	1,600 men in 1943
Jeunesse Légionnaire	2,000 children and adolescents in 1943[b]
Volontaires du Travail (*SVTW*)	200 men and women in 1943 and 1944
Formations B	300–500 men in 1944 only

Notes

a Approximately 2,500 men served in the *Légion Wallonie* at some time during 1943 and 1944.

b Of these, only the *cadre*, numbering some 300 young men and women in 1943 and 1944 can be regarded as in any sense fully politicised.

men serving in the *Formations de Combat* or in military units who remained in contact with their *cercles*. It was not an estimate of all those enrolled in pro-Rexist or Degrellian organisations and some indication of the membership of these other bodies is provided in the Table.

The figures given in this table should not be regarded as cumulative. Some are no more than rough estimates and, as the information is drawn from several unrelated sources and refers to calculations made at different times, it undoubtedly includes a certain amount of double counting. Nor should all those enrolled in these organisations be regarded as committed supporters of Rex, of Degrelle, or even of the German cause. The *NSKK* transport corps, for example, contained a number of members of *AGRA* while many of those serving in both the *Gardes Wallonnes* and the *NSKK* were regarded by their German commanders as no more than opportunist mercenaries.[237] Thus, although the figures provided in the table would suggest a possible total figure of 15,000, a more realistic assessment of the number of committed supporters of Rex or of Degrelle in 1943 and 1944 would seem to be approximately 12,000.

It should be emphasised that this figure does not include all those popularly regarded as forming part of the Rexist community. It takes into account only those who were members of Rex or of affiliated organisations and excludes those who, though sympathetic to the cause, did not participate actively in the movement. The most important group of these Rexist sympathisers were the families of Rexist militants and of other 'Degrellian' organisations. These wives, children, parents and even brothers and sisters did not always share the political views of their relative but in the polarised circumstances of Occupied Belgium many did come to embrace the Rexist cause and they formed a penumbra of sympathisers which it is impossible to quantify. Despite these caveats, it is clear that Reeder was justified in claiming that the Rexists formed only a very small minority of the population. The figure of 12,000 amounted to only approximately 0.31 per cent of the population of Brussels and Wallonia and, even employing the most generous definition, the Rexist community could not have exceeded 1 per cent or at most 1.25 per cent of the population.[238]

These figures demonstrate the extent to which the Rexists had by the latter years of the war almost become a political irrelevance. A marked decline had occurred in Rexist support during the war and the number of committed Rexist militants in the last year of the Occupation was no more than half the number estimated for the winter of 1940–1.[239] Above all, these figures paled into insignificance in comparison with the numbers who supported and, indeed, became actively involved in the patriotic activities of the Resistance. Collaboration was no more than a marginal phenomenon and, as liberation remorselessly approached, so the day of its final political extinction became ever more imminent.

Chapter Seven

Autumn 1943–
September 1944

Impotent Success and Final Failure

IN MANY respects, the last year of the Occupation was no more than a parenthesis between the political upheavals of the early war years and those which would follow the liberation of September 1944. Despite their disappointment at the slow pace of the Allied advance, almost all Belgians recognised that an eventual German withdrawal was now all but inevitable and their attention turned instead to the political struggles which lay ahead. Much remained uncertain about the future structure of Belgium. The government in London had done a great deal towards redeeming its reputation after the defeat of May 1940 but few in the Resistance – least of all the expanding Communist Party – were content to allow it to return in the baggage-train of the Allied armies and re-establish the old political order. A strong if ill-defined desire for wide-ranging social and political change was in the air and the underground press abounded with plans which would sweep away the entrenched divisions of class, language and religion in favour of a new, more democratic society. Casting a long shadow over all such speculations was the unresolved problem of the King. Until his deportation to Germany in June 1944, Léopold III remained confined to his palace at Laeken outside Brussels and refused all entreaties by intermediaries to recognise the government in London. Despite the failure of his own attempts to reach an understanding with the Nazi regime, he remained convinced that he alone represented political legitimacy and that he would form his own government after the German withdrawal.

Alongside these manifold uncertainties, collaboration seemed to be no more than a bankrupt irrelevance. No longer able to find its justification in the realities of the military situation or the promises offered by the Occupying power, it was composed solely of uncritical enthusiasts for the Nazi cause who were doomed to political – or even physical – extinction after an Allied liberation. They were men living on borrowed time confined to an unreal existence on the margins of Belgian life.

This was, of course, especially true of the Rexists. For them the last year of the Occupation was a time of unprecedented fluctuations in their fortunes. The remorseless advance of the Soviet armies in the East and the preparations by the Allies for a landing in northern Europe as well as the hostility of their compatriots served as constant reminders of the sword of Damocles which hung over their heads. But the inverse relationship already evident earlier in 1943 between the broader fortunes of the Nazi cause and the specific fortunes of Degrelle and the Rexists became ever more marked during this final phase of the Occupation. As the Third Reich entered ever more clearly into its death throes, so the cause of Degrelle and his allies within the crumbling Nazi empire blossomed. Degrelle's speech in January 1943 and his subsequent meeting with Himmler in May had already laid the basis for this remarkable political success but the military feats of the *Légion Wallonie* during the winter of 1943–4, combined with Degrelle's indefatigable talent for self-publicity, provided it with substantial further impetus. By the spring of 1944, the *Chef de Rex* had become the unlikely but undisputed hero of New Order Europe, fêted in Berlin, Brussels and Paris while, in an unprecedented gesture, the German authorities permitted the *Légion* to parade in full battle order through the streets of the Belgian capital. In a dramatic reversal of fortune and against all the odds, Rex and its young leader had come to personify the spirit of the Nazi New Europe and, while the other pro-German movements in Belgium disintegrated in an atmosphere of self-doubt and failure, the Rexists retained during the spring and summer of 1944 a confidence and resolve which belied the desperate realities of their situation.

These important developments notwithstanding, much else changed little within Rex during the last year of the Occupation. The overriding concern of the militants remained their personal security and much of the energies of the Rexist leadership were devoted to ensuring effective protection for their supporters against ever more audacious Resistance attacks. Moreover, the political strategy of the movement remained unchanged. Long before the autumn of 1943, Rex had already opted for collaboration 'cent pour cent' with the Nazi authorities and its policies during 1944 were merely the consequence of this fundamental choice. As Matthys declared succinctly at a rally on 12 September 1943, the objective of Rex was: 'la collaboration la plus complète, et la plus efficace possible au combat de l'Allemagne contre tous les ennemis de l'Europe et de la Révolution, sous le commandement suprême du Fuehrer'.[1] This simple goal dominated every facet of the movement's life. Rexist rhetoric, uniforms and titles were all modelled closely on Nazi examples while at a local level the movement's followers gradually ceased to have any existence independent of the Nazi authorities. Instead, they became the adjuncts and auxiliaries of the Germans, seconding every aspect of the increasingly harsh Occupation regime.

The pursuit of total collaboration drew the Rexists remorselessly into a 'looking-glass world' of their own making. An air of unreality pervaded all facets of Rexist propaganda during the final year of the Occupation: military defeats were transformed into victories, the crude imperialism of the Nazis became the basis of a New European Order and even the material sufferings imposed on the Belgian people by the Occupying forces were heralded as the prelude to a new authentic socialism. How far the Rexists themselves believed in their inherently absurd assertions is of course open to question. Trapped in an indefensible position, it was hardly surprising that they should have resorted to ever less plausible arguments. Yet something about their espousal of this perverse vision went beyond a desperate attempt at self-justification. In that strange vacuum in which collaboration operated during the final years of the war, the capacity for self-delusion was enormous. Deprived of social contact with those beyond the ranks of the pro-German minority, even the most lucid spirits took refuge in a vision of the world which could make no sense to those who did not share their utter isolation. Thus, although there certainly were cynical spirits who recognised the absurdities of their position, there were also many others within Rex for whom their emotional commitment to the cause was so overwhelming that it enabled them to voice its rhetoric with sincerity.

This was perhaps especially so in the case of the leaders of the movement. As Matthys observed after the war, collaboration had become 'une confrérie initiatique', in which the principal figures led an existence 'en dehors de la vie réelle'.[2] Although aware of the decline in Nazi fortunes, these leaders maintained throughout the last year of the Occupation a spirit of ceaseless activity which almost until the last minute failed to grasp the imminence of the German retreat. This myopia was reinforced by Degrelle's unexpected political success. Having laboured so long to attract the attention of the Nazi leaders, it was perhaps predictable that the Rexist leaders would react with euphoria to any signs of Nazi favour. The consequence was to destroy much of the private realism which had hidden behind the bombast of Rexist public rhetoric during the early years of the war. The trappings of success heaped on Degrelle by the leaders of the Reich acted as a stimulant which drove the Rexists forward and, far from capitulating to a mood of defeatist despondency, the new generation of leaders who now controlled the destiny of Rex presided over what amounted to a modest renaissance in Rexist activity during the final months of the Occupation.

These new leaders acted largely without the assistance of Degrelle for, although he was present in Belgium for much of 1943, he continued to distance himself from the affairs of the movement. This was to some extent due to his health. In the summer, Degrelle was seriously ill with diptheria which at one stage it was feared might prove fatal; but, although he subsequently made a full recovery and appeared at several Rexist rallies, his speeches on these occasions were little more than vacuous calls for optimism coupled with dire warnings as to the consequences of an Allied or Communist victory.[3] Degrelle, it was clear, no longer had any great interest in Rex and he devoted his energies instead to a number of personal projects. One of these was to launch a mass circulation newspaper in Brussels modelled on the highly successful format of *Paris-Soir* in France. In part, this new title was intended to supplant *Le Soir* which continued to evade his political control and which had retained its dominant position within the German-censored Brussels press. His overriding motive, however, appears to have been crudely commercial. Degrelle was well aware of the large profits to be made in the press world and, regardless of any political considerations, he was determined to seize upon this business opportunity. After prolonged negotiations with the German authorities, the new newspaper – entitled *L'Avenir* – appeared on 29 July 1943 and, although it was fully owned by Degrelle's company, *La Presse de Rex*, and its editor was the Rexist journalist Victor Meulenyser, every effort was made to disguise its origins. *L'Avenir* fostered a highly sensationalist style avoiding all political comment to the extent that its many critics within the collaborationist press described it as pro-English in tone. Yet in those dark times the paper obviously responded to a popular desire for escapism and, in stark contrast to *Le Pays Réel*, it was an immediate financial success. Its initial circulation was 70,000 growing to 100,000 by 1944 and *L'Avenir* made a profit of as much as 600,000 BF a month for the already ample coffers of Degrelle.[4]

Nor was *L'Avenir* the only such venture by the *Chef de Rex*. Ever since his early days as a publisher, he had always had a keen eye for commercial opportunities and during 1943 he purchased a large Jewish-owned perfume company, *Les Parfumeries de Bruxelles*, from its German sequestrators; even borrowing money from Rexist funds for the purpose. Once again, this proved to be a lucrative move which, whatever its dubious morality, paid handsome financial dividends for Degrelle.[5] Coupled with the wealth of his wife's family, these activities enabled Degrelle to live in an opulent style. His house in the Forêt de Soignes was furnished with valuable antiques and he was also negotiating to purchase a tract of land near Cannes in the south of France.[6]

These commercial actions never took precedence over Degrelle's political ambitions. Throughout late 1943 and 1944, these remained focussed on the twin goals of the further expansion of the *Légion Wallonie* and the consolidation of his personal prestige within the Third Reich. During most of 1943, the *Légion* was resting at its training camp in Germany. Many of its original members had been demobilised and the major priority was the recruitment and training of new soldiers. In contrast to his neglect of Rex, Degrelle took a prominent role in these efforts, appearing frequently at propaganda events in Belgium which drew a limited but steady stream of new recruits.[7] By the autumn of 1943, the *Légion* could boast almost 2,000 men but the moulding of these disparate elements into an effective military unit posed many problems. There was a continual shortage of officers which was only partly overcome by the secondment of many of its more experienced soldiers to officer training schools such as the *SS* school at Bad Tölz.[8] Disputes between the *Légion*'s commanders and its German liaison officer exacerbated these difficulties, as did the long-standing personal and political rivalries within the unit. Degrelle had considerably strengthened his hold over the *Légion* since August 1941. Many of those soldiers most opposed to him had died in battle or been demobilised and those who had replaced them were on the whole young men with few political convictions. In addition, Degrelle had found in Lucien Lippert a military commander for the *Légion* who, though not a member of Rex, could be relied upon to support his plans. Nevertheless, there remained some dissident elements, including the chaplain *Abbé* Fierens, who had only reluctantly accepted the transfer to the *Waffen-SS* and who still hoped to recover the *Légion* from its subordination to Degrelle's personal interests.[9]

As regards his wider political ambitions, Degrelle's pursuit of Nazi patronage had by the end of 1943 come to concentrate almost exclusively on consolidating his relationship with the *SS*. They had become the major political force within the Third Reich and, although figures within the *Führer*'s entourage such as Bormann still acted as a brake on Himmler's personal ambitions, the *SS* would clearly dominate the construction of any future Nazi-dominated Europe. Degrelle, ever the alert courtier, recognised this shift in power and he met Himmler's assistant, Gottlob Berger, on two separate occasions in Berlin in October and November 1943. For the *SS*, Degrelle's principal value was as part of their plan to replace the *Wehrmacht* Military Administration in Brussels by a civilian Nazi administration in which they would have a pre-eminent role and, not for the first time, Degrelle proved happy to act as an accomplice in their designs. At their instigation, he wrote to Hitler denouncing the anti-National Socialist policies of *Militärverwaltungschef* Reeder and advocating the appointment of a *Höherer SS- und Polizeiführer* who could reverse the decline in public order within Belgium.[10]

There is no evidence that Hitler ever received this missive but, unfortunately for Degrelle, a copy did reach Reeder. The President of the *Militärverwaltung* had shortly before been the recipient of a fulsome letter of praise (as well as a large bouquet of flowers) from Degrelle and was therefore all the more annoyed, if not entirely surprised, by this further evidence of the *Chef de Rex*'s duplicity. Reeder seized upon the opportunity to launch a further withering attack on Degrelle. In a letter to Fieldmarshal Keitel, the supreme commander of the *Wehrmacht*, he detailed with evident pleasure Degrelle's actions and castigated in outspoken terms the 'geistigen Beweglichkeit und Phantasie' which made the Rexist leader entirely unworthy of German favour.[11] Reeder's hostility was not the obstacle it had been earlier in the war and, aided by the SS, Degrelle had good reason to hope that he would eventually win real power in Belgium. Nevertheless Reeder and his allies in Berlin remained powerful enough to block any immediate progress and Degrelle was once again forced to abandon the field of political intrigue for that of battle. On 2 November he left Brussels for the *Légion*'s training camp and shortly afterwards he and his soldiers returned to the front line of the desperate military struggle against the Soviet armies.[12]

Degrelle was to remain away from Belgium for more than three months and in his absence the Rexist leaders sought to restore as best they could the rather battered morale of their followers. After the reverses in Italy and Russia, an experienced Rexist journalist, Julien Carlier, had been appointed in September to the new post of *Chef de Propagande Active* and during the autumn he and a group of associates toured Belgium addressing the *cercles* of the movement.[13] With titles such as 'Raisons d'espérer malgré tout', these speeches were clearly intended to rally the demoralised, and their tone was no doubt similar to the articles which Carlier also con- tributed at the same time to *Le Pays Réel*. Aggressive, millenarian and utterly devoid of any subtlety, these challenged those with any doubts to depart: 'Que les cowards s'en aillent. Nous ne sommes pas de ces rats qui fuient le navire quand il menace de sombrer.' A few days later, Carlier returned to the attack: 'On accepte le combat avec toutes ses difficultés et ses risques. Ou l'on déserte . . . Pas de flottement dans nos rangs? Personne ne bouge? En avant donc. Serrons les dents. La route est belle.'[14]

Such words might rally some waverers, but they could do nothing to resolve the most serious cause of unease amongst Rexist militants which remained the threat to their personal security. The leaders of the move- ment were well aware of the seriousness of this problem but they also recognised that there was no easy solution. In a lengthy report drawn up in the autumn of 1943 and intended probably for the SS, the Rexist leadership detailed in sombre terms the 'état d'anarchie' which reigned in Belgium. Neither the ineffectual gestures by the *secrétaires-généraux* nor the cautious efforts to transform the Belgian police undertaken by the *Militärverwaltung* had done anything to reverse the escalation in violence and the only solution, they claimed, lay in a wholesale transfer of power to committed Belgian National Socialists.[15]

No such political initiative was, however, likely in the near future and in the meantime the Rexists could do no more than devise more effective means of protection. One such plan considered by Matthys and Collard during 1943 was the creation of a special *police supplémentaire* to protect Rexist *bourgmestres* and *échevins*. It was intended that these bodyguards would be recruited by sympathetic New Order communes and discussions to this end were held both with local authorities as well as with the

Ministry of the Interior.[16] A series of administrative obstacles did eventually force the Rexist leaders to abandon this project and they turned instead to Jungclaus, the representative of the SS in Belgium, proposing to him the creation of a corps of full-time Rexist bodyguards who would operate under the protection of the SS. Jungclaus, who was anxious both to consolidate his links with Rex and to increase the forces in Belgium under his command, was sympathetic to this suggestion. During the autumn of 1943, negotiations proceeded between his deputy for Walloon affairs, Moskopff, and Louis Collard which culminated in an agreement announced on 20 November to establish the new unit, officially entitled the *Etendard de Protection Paul Colin* in memory of the assassinated collaborationist journalist but more commonly referred to as the *Formations B*. It was to be composed initially of approximately 300 men who would serve as armed bodyguards for those Rexist militants, especially local *bourgmestres* and *échevins*, who were deemed to be especially vulnerable to Resistance attack. The *Formations B* would operate under Rexist commanders but Jungclaus retained ultimate responsibility for the unit and it was his office which provided the necessary finance and arms as well as a pass placing the bodyguards under the protection of SS justice.[17]

Already on the defensive against attempts by the SS to circumscribe its authority, the *Militärverwaltung* could do little but approve the creation of this new unit.[18] Reeder was, however, able to extract one important concession from the Rexists. On 1 November the *Wehrmacht* authorities had established a new auxiliary police unit, the *Zivilfahndungsdienst*, which was intended to assist the German *Feldgendarmerie* in the pursuit of the many young Belgian men who had refused to enrol for labour service in Germany. Thus, in return for approval for the *Formations B*, the *Militärverwaltung* apparently insisted that the Rexists should also recruit volunteers for this new police force. Rex agreed to this condition and the new body was also announced to Rexist militants as the *Formations A* on 20 November.[19] The neutral title was clearly intended to disguise any close association with the German police but in reality the *Formations A* operated under the direct command of the German authorities and formed part of the *Zivilfahndungsdienst*. Few Rexists appear to have been attracted to join the new unit. Perhaps because of the reluctance of many militants to assist the Germans in the enforcement of labour conscription or because of what the Rexist leaders subsequently claimed was a deliberate policy of sabotage on their part, the *Formations A* never had more than a nominal existence and, although there were instances of Rexists who threw themselves enthusiastically into the pursuit of those evading the labour conscription legislation, the majority of the agents of the *Zivilfahndungsdienst* had no connection with Rex.[20]

Recruitment for the *Formations B*, on the other hand, was much more successful. The initial target of 300 volunteers was soon achieved and in

January 1944 training began at a barracks in Namur.[21] The recruitment campaign had been directed principally at the remaining members of the *Formations de Combat* as well as at young Rexists who, in return for service in the *Formations B*, were promised exemption from the labour conscription legislation. A number of experienced Rexists also enrolled but the majority of the new bodyguards appear to have had no prior association with Rex. Some had served in auxiliary units of the *Wehrmacht* such as the *NSKK* but most were young unemployed men attracted by the pay, extra rations and protection from deportation to the factories of the Reich which the *Formations B* offered.[22]

The establishment of the *Formations B* was only one of many ways in which the Rexist movement worked closely with the representatives of the SS in Belgium during the last year of the Occupation. While continuing to collaborate with the *Militärverwaltung* on many practical matters, it was increasingly to the *Dienstelle Jungclaus* that the Rexists turned for political assistance. This was, of course, partly the work of Degrelle. During his visits to Belgium, he met Jungclaus frequently and relations between the two men appear to have been warm.[23] But much of the credit for the close relationship between Rex and the SS in Belgium was due to the efforts of Matthys and Collard in gradually winning the confidence of Jungclaus and detaching him from the pro-Flemish and anti-Rexist prejudices still prevalent in SS circles. One early indication of their success had been the departure from Belgium of Dr Sommer, the erstwhile patron of the *Cercle Wallon*, and both Jungclaus and his deputy for Walloon affairs, SS-*Hauptsturmführer* Moskopff, had by 1944 become close allies of the Rexist leaders offering them what Marcovitz of the *Sipo-SD* described as their 'appui total et inconditionnel'.[24]

The benefits for Rex of this support were manifold. In addition to paying for the *Formations B*, the SS provided a considerable financial subsidy for the Rexist coffers of between 500,000 BF and 1,000,000 BF per month during 1944.[25] Consequently, the movement was for the first time during the Occupation assured of adequate funding and this new-found prosperity was reflected in a steady increase in the salaries paid to employees of the Rexist *Etat-Major*. The most important assistance provided by the *Dienstelle Jungclaus* was, however, political. Rex had at last acquired a firm ally among the manifold agencies of the Third Reich and on several occasions in 1944 Moskopff proved willing to defend Rexist interests, even travelling to Berlin to rebuff allegations made by those who remained distrustful of Degrelle and his political movement.[26]

Much of the optimism evident amongst the Rexist leaders during the last year of the Occupation was the consequence of this close relationship with the representatives of the SS. In fact, unknown to the Rexists, a decision had already been taken in principle at a meeting in Berlin on 3 January 1944 initiated by Hitler and attended by representatives of the

Reich Chancellery and the *Wehrmacht* to replace the Military Administration in Belgium with a Civil Administration in which the *SS* would inevitably be the dominant force.[27] The Rexists knew nothing of these high-level developments but they seem to have sensed that some sort of change was in the air and in a forthright article published in *Le Pays Réel* on 1 January 1944 Matthys gave voice to their newly confident mood, declaring: 'nous ne connaissons d'aucune manière l'inquiétude de demain. Nous ne connaissons que la certitude de la victoire.' The *SS*, he declared, was the guide and inspiration of the Rexists: 'la *SS* est . . . un esprit, une révolution, le symbole de l'unité grand-germanique naissante et de la fidélité sans condition au Fuehrer'.[28] Never before had the Rexist leadership been so explicit in linking their cause to that of the *SS*, and the *Chef de Rex ad interim* was similarly forthright in the distinction he drew between the communist and capitalist enemies of National Socialism. The Rexists, he insisted, were revolutionaries of the New Europe and, echoing the comments which he had already made during 1943, he identified the English and the Americans as the principal adversaries of Rex: 'Le fait que nos Légionnaires sont engagés sur le front de l'Est n'a aucune signification politique. Au contraire, leurs préférences personnelles . . . les orienteraient d'une manière certaine vers d'autres fronts et pour eux, comme pour nous, l'Anglo-Saxon n'est pas moins l'ennemi que le Russe soviétique. Et même, pour la plupart d'entre nous, l'instinct révolutionnaire aidant, l'Anglo-Saxon est-il davantage l'ennemi!'[29]

This mood of arrogant confidence was also evident in the major reorganisation of the Rexist headquarters announced by Matthys on 3 January 1944. The series of departments introduced in early 1943 had proved to be too unwieldy and these further changes were principally intended to create a more hierarchical structure. The most important innovation was the establishment of a *Secrétariat de l'Etat-Major* headed by Louis Collard. While retaining his responsibilities as *Chef-adjoint du Département Politique*, this new post enabled Collard to exercise more direct control over the other central offices of Rex and his secretariat assumed responsibility for all personnel matters as well as monopolising contact with the German authorities.[30] Collard's trusted subordinates also benefited from this reorganisation. Michel Saussez was named as his assistant in the new *Secrétariat de l'Etat-Major* while Jean Colman took over much of the day-to-day direction of the *Département Politique*. With the exception of Lambinon's *DSI*, all areas of the *Etat-Major* were now explicitly subordinated to Collard's control and, as Matthys withdrew into a more presidential role, it was Collard who in effect directed the central headquarters of Rex.[31]

Other less important reforms also announced in January reinforced the trend towards a more centralised structure. The veteran *Chef des Cadres Territoriaux*, Marcel Dupont, was obliged to retire and responsibility for supervision of the local *cercles* passed to Julien Keutgen, the former *chef de cercle* of Verviers.[32] Financial affairs were concentrated in a new *Département des Finances* which operated under the control of Degrelle's personal secretary Félix Francq while responsibility for the women's organisations passed to a new *Inspection Générale des Organisations Féminines* which operated under the direction of the Rexist *Etat-Major*.[33]

These organisational reforms were accompanied by further attempts to improve the protection of Rexist militants. Despite the creation of the *Formations B*, many Rexists remained unconvinced that sufficient had been done to counter the many dangers which they faced. While bodyguards might discourage the opportunistic, almost casual assassinations which had proliferated during 1943, they would do nothing to deter the more professional Resistance groups and there appears to have been widespread agreement within Rex on the need to give a higher priority to the paramilitary structures of the movement. Thus, among the reforms announced by Matthys on 3 January was the creation of an *Inspectorat de la Milice*. The responsibilities of this new office within the *Etat-Major* were twofold. In the first place, it assumed command of the *Formations de Combat* with the intention of re-establishing an effective Rexist militia. Secondly, the Inspectorate was intended to provide a single unified command within Belgium for all of the military and paramilitary forces of Rex. The *VNV* had already established a similar command structure in the autumn of 1943 and the Rexist leaders clearly hoped that the new office would for the first time bring those auxiliary German units such as the *Gardes Wallonnes* and the Walloon *NSKK* under Rexist operational control.[34]

Joseph Pévenasse was named as the new *Inspecteur de la Milice*. The former *Chef de Rex-Wallonie* and *Inspecteur Fédéral du Mouvement* was in many respects the obvious choice for this post. Throughout his long career in Rex, he had taken a strong interest in its various paramilitary groups and his appointment was welcomed by men such as the former head of the *Formations de Combat* Albert Constant as an indication that the leadership had finally recognised the importance of the militia.[35] Yet, given the apparently strained relations between the combative Charleroi lawyer and Matthys and Collard, his nomination to this key post was nevertheless a surprising one. Pévenasse's service in the *Légion Wallonie* and the *Volontaires du Travail* had consolidated his reputation as a radical opposed to what he regarded as the excessive caution of Matthys and Collard. It would therefore seem unlikely that he was the preferred choice of the Rexist leaders, and Matthys did indeed imply after the war that Pévenasse's appointment had been insisted upon by Jungclaus of the SS.[36] Whatever the truth of this assertion, the divisions between Pévenasse and his new colleagues should not be exaggerated. The renovation of the paramilitary structures of Rex was a goal upon which all of the leadership could agree and during January Collard and Pévenasse collaborated closely on drawing up the priorities for the new Inspectorate.[37]

The establishment of the *Formations B*, the close alliance with the *Dienstelle Jungclaus* and the reorganisation of the Rexist headquarters were all developments which led the Rexist leaders to regard the future with greater optimism than had been the case during the previous year. A difficult corner appeared to have been turned and, taking their cue from Matthys' New Year article, the propagandists of *Le Pays Réel* adopted a noisy, confident tone which on occasions recalled the optimism felt by the Rexists during the first months of the German Occupation. Like other collaborationist organs, the Rexist daily was obliged to echo the tortuous and frequently ludicrous interpretations of the course of the military struggle presented by the Nazi propaganda apparatus.[38] While the German propagandists on the whole preferred to minimise or even deny Allied successes, however, the Rexists showed a greater willingness to accept the gravity of the military situation. Despite Nazi claims that an Allied landing in northern Europe was an impossibility, *Le Pays Réel* carried a number of articles accepting the likelihood of such an invasion and at a private meeting of militants in January 1944 Pévenasse warned them to expect an invasion during the coming months. The prospect that the military front line might reach Belgium did not appear to worry unduly many in the Rexist leadership. Indeed, at least in public, they welcomed such an eventuality as the catalyst which would bring about the decisive conflict between the forces of reaction and those of National Socialism.[39] How far such statements disguised a more private desperation is ultimately impossible to gauge. The precautions for escape taken by a number of Rexists in 1944 indicate that not all within the movement viewed the advance of the Allies in quite so sanguine a manner. But for many within the Rexist elite the opportunity to engage their enemies in open conflict – regardless of the eventual outcome – does seem to have held a genuine appeal. The deaths of Rexists on the Eastern front and at the hands of the Resistance within Belgium had long accustomed them to the prospect of violent conflict and some clearly found the prospect of martyrdom preferable to the humiliation of defeat. An almost millenarian attitude seems to have taken hold of sections of the movement in which they envisaged Rex rising Phoenix-like from the ashes of a Nazi military defeat. In one such article in *Le Pays Réel* in February 1944, a Rexist journalist declared dramatically: 'Même si quelques-uns d'entre nous doivent se balancer aux réverbères du boulevard Anspach [in Brussels], les Rexistes ne manquent pas d'enfants qui pourront reprendre leur combat dans cinq, dix ou vingt ans et assurer le triomphe de leur cause.'[40]

This belief that National Socialism was a remorseless historical force destined to overcome all opposition dominated Rexist propaganda during 1944. Belgian nationalism no longer formed part of the Rexist creed and the ideologists of the movement concentrated instead on presenting the Rexists as the soldiers of a pan-European National Socialist Revolution.

This 'Europeanist' rhetoric was a major feature of Rexist public pronouncements during 1944. Like collaborationists elsewhere in Europe during the last desperate years of the war, the Rexists were anxious to present the military conflict as a struggle to defend Europe against its enemies. Rexist propaganda made much of the 'unEuropean' (and multi-racial) character of the Soviet and Anglo-American armies while the soldiers of the Third Reich and its remaining allies were portrayed as the guardians of European civilisation. This higher loyalty to a European cause had an evident appeal for a Rexist movement which could no longer defend its actions in purely Belgian terms and, comparing themselves self-consciously to the foreign volunteers who had aided the armies of revolutionary France in the 1790s, the Rexists declared themselves somewhat implausibly to be the soldiers of a future united National Socialist Europe.[41]

In other respects, Rexist propaganda of 1944 made uninspiring reading. The times were hardly conducive to prolonged reflections and Rexist journalists contented themselves with a monotonous hymn of praise to Nazism as the 'synthèse de toutes les vérités, de toutes les certitudes'.[42] Turgid glorifications of the achievements of the National Socialist regime in Germany alternated with crude attacks on their adversaries. Predictably, it was the soldiers of Himmler who were singled out for especial praise. The SS had become the model which Rex yearned to emulate and Le Pays Réel abounded with articles calling for a comparable 'élite nouvelle, forte et saine' which could raise Belgium out of 'les boues de la décadence'.[43] Violence and a cult of the virility of youth had replaced the former concern with a spiritual 'révolution des âmes' and, though some Rexist veterans such as Serge Doring occasionally warned of the need to base any revolution on continuity with the past, the Rexist press was largely the stronghold of extremists who advocated a nihilistic revolution of destruction.[44]

On the rare occasions when the Rexist propagandists of the latter war years paused to consider the new regime that they wished to achieve, they offered what they claimed was a socialist order of labour corporations, youth leagues and social welfare organisations. This obsession with the socialist credentials of the movement often amounted to little more than a crude attempt to pose as the true revolutionaries opposed to the allegedly reactionary aims of their patriotic opponents. Thus, in a major speech on May Day 1944, Matthys declared that Rex was 'le grand mouvement des travailleurs socialistes au service de la Révolution et de notre Peuple'[45] and Rexist propagandists frequently stressed the substantial material benefits which they claimed that their National Socialist revolution would bring to the working people of Belgium. Behind the slogans, however, there was little substance. Despite efforts to claim that theirs was 'notre vieux socialisme populaire enfin retrouvé' which, unlike Marxism, was based on national traditions and on the primacy of the community, Rexist socialism offered merely a plethora of bureaucratic institutions derived from Nazi models. '*Rex = Ordre = Socialisme*' was the slogan most frequently employed by the propagandists of the movement during 1944 and it well conveyed the concern with state regimentation which formed the basis of their supposedly socialist rhetoric.[46]

This dour, Nazi-inspired vision won Rex few converts. Those many Belgians in search of radical social changes had no reason to support the agents of a conquering power which by crushing working-class organisations while working with employers' groups had exacerbated social inequalities. Instead, the Rexist pretensions at adopting a socialist rhetoric merely provided further evidence of the bankruptcy of a movement which had lost both its intellectual rationale and its social basis. Such questions of ideology were, however, very remote from the concerns of most Rexists. Their choice of collaboration had long since ceased to be a matter of intellectual commitment and most no doubt paid little attention to the arguments advanced by their propagandists. Other issues had a greater claim on their attention, of which the most important was the threat posed to their security by the Resistance. This remained the overriding concern of most Rexist militants who, whatever comfort they might draw from the political successes of the movement, were all too aware of the activities of well-organised Resistance units determined to eradicate the traitors who had espoused the German cause.

In these circumstances, the security precautions adopted by the Rexists became ever more elaborate. Those who possessed weapons carried them at all times while one Rexist *bourgmestre* near Namur was reported to have installed a special lock on the door of his office to ensure that it could only be opened from the inside.[47] Everything was done to ensure secrecy and even anonymity. Publications such as *Le Pays Réel* and *National Socialisme* were distributed by private couriers so as not to expose their recipients to attack and some militants even used false names for their gas and electricity bills.[48] All Rexist meetings were accompanied by intensive security measures and in Brussels some militants were issued with special cards specifying that, should they fall victim to a Resistance attack, they were to be hospitalised in the German-controlled Hôpital Brugmann. Even in illness, the Rexists were segregated from their compatriots.[49]

Yet, despite all these measures, the number of attacks on Rexists and their families increased remorselessly. Reeder reported more than 50 attacks on Rexists or their property during December 1943 and January 1944. Some militants had by now been attacked several times and the *Jeunesse Légionnaire* was obliged to establish a home for Rexist children whose fathers had been killed in Russia or on the 'front de l'intérieur'.[50] The majority of these actions were the work of the *Partisans Armés* (*PA*) which was the most active of the Resistance armed units in much of Wallonia. Opinions varied among Resistance and patriotic organisations as to the priority which should be given to attacks on collaborators. The army officer dominated *Armée Secrète* sought to establish itself along the lines of a conventional army and, with some local exceptions, preferred to conserve its forces for the day when it could assist an Allied liberation of Belgium. The pro-Communist *PA*, on the other hand, formed part of a broad coalition of largely left-wing groups, the *Front de l'Indépendance*, and saw its role as a guerrilla force engaged in clandestine warfare against the German forces and their allies. The Partisans carried out numerous attacks on German personnel and installations but they reserved a particular enthusiasm for the suppression of collaborators. Special assassination squads were created to 'semer la terreur dans les rangs des traîtres embrigadés par l'ennemi'[51] and at the close of 1943 a national campaign was launched against those collaborators who had been appointed by the German authorities to posts in local government. The underground newspaper *Front* published in January 1944 an unambivalent warning addressed to all such men to resign or face the consequences: 'Nous vous donnons un mois. Un mois pendant lequel il vous sera loisible de méditer, de prendre une décision. Après ces trente jours, le bras vengeur des patriotes s'abattra sur vous, à l'heure où vous y penserez le moins.'[52]

This threat did not go unheeded. In the Borinage, 15 Rexist *bourgmestres* were reported to have resigned but many others remained in place and were among those who were shot or who had their homes dynamited during a wave of *PA* attacks on collaborationist office-holders in February.[53] Despite these efforts to target particular collaborationist groups, the war that the Partisans waged against the pro-German minority was ruthless and essentially indiscriminate. With limited information at their disposal and continually in fear of denunciation, local commanders had little means of discriminating between potential victims and many clearly regarded all followers of Degrelle as legitimate targets. Proof of Rexist membership was often sufficient for a *PA* attack to be authorised[54] and, inevitably, a good number of their victims appear to have been obscure Rexist militants of little political importance. Well protected by bodyguards, the Rexist elite remained on the whole beyond their reach.

The large number of attacks remained the central preoccupation of the Rexist leadership. More advice was issued to militants on the best means of protecting themselves against attack and a further modest distribution of pistols took place.[55] Access to sufficient numbers of arms did, however, remain difficult. The *Militärverwaltung* was adamant in its opposition to a general arming of the Rexist membership and throughout 1944 it remained the Resistance, supplied by Allied air drops and raids on German depots, rather than the collaborationist groups who found it easier to acquire weapons. The Rexist leaders also made further visits to the Belgian Ministry of Justice and to the *Militärverwaltung* to demand more effective action against the Resistance. The replies they received, however, gave them little reassurance. Although the *Wehrmacht* administration continued to execute Belgian hostages in retaliation for attacks on collaborators, Reeder refused to consider any new measures, merely advising the Rexists to trust in his policy of reinforcing the Belgian police.[56] On the other hand, De Foy, the new *secrétaire-général* of the Ministry of Justice, and not a man regarded as sympathetic to Rex, appears to have been more frank. He admitted the impotence of the police to act against the Resistance and expressed his understanding at Rexist exasperation remarking, according to several Rexist sources, that 'le sang appelle le sang'.[57]

Comments such as this encouraged the Rexists to see themselves as a beleaguered group who could rely only upon themselves for their protection. As Matthys recalled after the war: 'Nous nous sommes considérés comme une communauté d'hommes sur qui pesait une menace perpétuelle mais qui ne jouissait plus de la protection des organes sociaux habituels. Réduits à un état primitif de légitime défense, cette communauté devait trouver en elle-même sa protection et défendre le droit de ses membres à la vie.'[58] Though this argument was clearly intended to provide a retrospective justification for Rexist crimes, it is evident that Matthys and his colleagues did see themselves as obliged to resort to measures of self-defence. Indeed, building on the policy of tacit support for Rexist 'counter-terrorism' already evident at the time of the murders in Liège in September 1943, Matthys explicitly threatened in his New Year message of 1 January 1944 that Rex would henceforth revenge the deaths of its supporters.[59]

In the violent atmosphere of the times, this warning went unnoticed. For the Resistance forces, already engaged in a bitter war with the German police, the comments of Matthys were an irrelevance and, as the attacks on their militants continued, Rex moved from threats to concrete, bloody acts. On 30 January the Rexist *chef de cercle* of Namur, Gignot, and his wife were murdered in their home by a Resistance unit.[60] In response, Charles Lambinon, the head of the *DSI*, travelled to Namur where, accompanied by three soldiers from the training school of the *Légion Wallonie*, he drove to the home of François Bovesse. He was the pre-war Governor of the province of Namur and a popular Liberal politician who, as Minister of Justice at the time of the Rexist electoral triumph of 1936, had come to symbolise for many Rexists the hated democratic regime. Already in 1940 the Rexist press had attacked him for shirking his responsibilities as Governor during the German invasion and a Rexist crowd demonstrated outside his house.[61] On this occasion, however, the danger was more mortal. Early on the morning of 1 February, the four Rexists called at the politician's home claiming to be members of the Gestapo and, when he asked to see proof of their identity, they opened fire killing him almost instantly.[62]

The perpetrators of this attack fled but few had any doubt as to their identity and a few days later Matthys all but admitted responsibility for the murder. Although the attack had been planned and executed by Lambinon without seeking the approval of the Rexist leadership, Matthys chose to approve it as responding to the 'nécessités du moment'.[63] Speaking at the funeral of Gignot, he praised those who had enacted such 'prompte et bonne justice' for the murder of the *chef de cercle*.[64] The significance of this speech was substantial. Through their willingness to work with the German authorities, the Rexists had of course already been implicated in the deaths and suffering of many of their compatriots but Rex had never hitherto acknowledged responsibility for a political murder. On this occasion, however, all pretence at innocence was rejected and, as Matthys acknowledged after the war, the murder of Bovesse in effect inaugurated the Rexist 'counter-terrorist' campaign which would develop during the summer of 1944. Moreover, the attack on Bovesse set a model which would be imitated in subsequent Rexist crimes. The movement lacked both the means and the intelligence necessary to identify those Resistance units responsible for the attacks on their supporters. Instead, they resorted to reprisal actions against those dignitaries – such as Bovesse – whom the Rexists claimed were in effect the patrons of the Resistance groups.[65]

The murder of Bovesse, thus, marked a major turning-point but it did not lead immediately to an abandonment of all restraint on the part of the Rexist leadership. For almost six months there would be no further officially sanctioned reprisal actions and Rex would continue to lag behind those Flemish collaborationist groups such as *DeVlag* which continued to carry out numerous reprisal attacks, including the murders on 28 February 1944 of Alexandre Galopin, the Governor of the *Société Générale de Belgique* and architect of the policy of limited economic co-operation with the German authorities.[66] Any residual reluctance on the part of the Rexist leadership to involve themselves directly in political murders was rendered increasingly redundant by the unrestrained enthusiasm for such actions among many of their followers. In Liège, Namur, Mons and no doubt other localities, groups of Rexists came together during the first months of 1944 to organise their own forms of 'counter-terrorism'. Near Mons, for example, five opponents of Rex were killed early in 1944 by a group of unidentified New Order terrorists who, it seems, may have included Michel Saussez and Jean Colman of the *Département Politique* of Rex.[67] There is no evidence that the Rexist leadership approved these local initiatives but nor is there any evidence that they tried to prevent them. The desperate circumstances of 1944 were not conducive to tight central control over all local actions and, having admitted in the case of Bovesse the general principle of reprisal actions, the Rexist leaders could hardly object when certain of their supporters followed their example. Indeed, Matthys gave further encouragement to such radicals when he announced in February 1944 the creation of an *Insigne du Sang* to be awarded to those

Rexists who distinguished themselves in direct combat with the enemies of the Revolution.[68]

This tacit support for violence was also evident in the tolerant attitude adopted by the Rexist leadership towards the actions of Lambinon's *Département de Sécurité et d'Information* (*DSI*) which in the last year of the Occupation continued to operate on the more disreputable fringes of the German police apparatus. As in 1943, Lambinon remained a law unto himself, keeping his department apart from the central Rexist headquarters and maintaining only perfunctory relations with the leadership of the movement. Yet, despite their exclusion from the detail of *DSI* operations, the Rexist leaders made no efforts to curtail the department's activities and Matthys and Collard lent intermittent but effective support to Lambinon's long-term ambition of transforming his ragged and corrupt group of agents into the *Sûreté* of the future National Socialist Belgian state.[69]

During the first months of 1944, the *DSI* gradually expanded the scale of its activities. Its central organisation was improved, new agents and administrators were recruited and Lambinon at last obtained sufficient weapons for all *DSI* agents to be armed for the first time.[70] Obstacles to further expansion did, nevertheless, remain. A *DSI* brigade was reconstituted in Liège and a new unit created during 1944 in Mons. But in both cases difficulties in finding a competent leader seriously hampered their development and, although plans existed to create further units at Namur, Braine l'Alleud and Tournai, these appear never to have come to fruition.[71] Of the four existing brigades in La Louvière, Charleroi, Huy and Brussels, it was the *Brigade A* in La Louvière which remained the most effective. Composed of as many as 18 agents, it worked closely with both the German police and the Rexist communal administration and remained the model which the other units sought to emulate. Co-ordination between the brigades was, however, still limited. The provincial units of the *DSI* worked closely with the Rexist *cercles* and, despite Lambinon's persistent efforts to assert his supremacy, they were frequently reluctant to accept directives from the *DSI* headquarters.[72]

Relations between the *DSI* and the German authorities also remained poor. In April 1944, all of the brigades – consisting at that time of approximately 30 agents, including Lambinon and his assistants – participated in a large-scale operation carried out by the German authorities against the Resistance in the hills near Chimay south of Namur.[73] But, in general, the *Sipo-SD* continued to regard the *DSI* with great distrust, refusing to allow its Brussels brigade, the *Brigade Z*, to arrest suspects. Lambinon made repeated efforts to have this limitation on its activities withdrawn but the German police proved obdurate. They had little faith in either the competence or the honesty of the head of the *DSI* and they only relented when in the spring of 1944 Lambinon, acting with the support of Matthys and Collard, presented an ambitious plan for the development of the *DSI* including an expansion in its size and financial resources as well as training for its staff in Germany.[74]

This project was discussed at a meeting on 2 May between Matthys, Collard, Lambinon and the principal officers in Belgium of the *Sipo-SD*.[75] Many of these German officials, including Canaris, the head of the *Sipo-SD* in Belgium, remained opposed to any collaboration with the *DSI* but they were apparently prevailed upon by their superiors in the Reich to suppress their scruples and the meeting resulted in a cautious expansion in the role of the *DSI*. Financial support for the department was increased substantially and, although the proposed expansion in its staff and training programme were postponed until a future date, the *Brigade Z* was at last accorded the right to carry out arrests. The conditions imposed were, however, restrictive: not only must the *DSI* work exclusively for the *Sipo-SD* and hand over all detainees within 48 hours of their arrest but Lambinon was required to submit a weekly report on his activities to Jungclaus and Canaris.[76]

Nevertheless, this agreement provided Lambinon with the freedom he required to expand the scope of the activities of the *Brigade Z* during the last four months of the Occupation. Acting under the direct control of Lambinon and his assistant Vervloet, the brigade – now composed of some 15 agents – operated throughout the Brussels area distinguishing itself by its crude and violent methods.[77] A *légionnaire* transferred briefly to the brigade was astonished by the daily violence which he witnessed and one such incident in July, when the *Sipo-SD* were summoned to the offices of the brigade in the Place Rouppe to collect a strangled corpse, almost led to the demise of the hard-won agreement with the German police. Informed of this as well as of other excesses, Canaris ordered that the *Brigade Z* should no longer be allowed to carry out interrogations but, in the chaotic circumstances of the summer of 1944, Lambinon proved able to circumvent this order with impunity.[78]

The activities of the *DSI* during the last months of the Occupation undoubtedly constituted one of the darkest chapters in the history of Rex. Yet, despite the agreement in May with the *Sipo-SD*, Lambinon's department never succeeded in establishing itself as an important element of the German police structure within Belgium. With the partial exception of its La Louvière brigade, the staff of the *DSI* carried out little police work of any consequence and it always remained a more or less tolerated free-lance group to whom the German authorities occasionally allotted certain tasks. This was, however, of little comfort to those unfortunate enough to fall into its hands. How many there were of these victims is impossible to establish with any certainty. The La Louvière brigade alone was apparently responsible for some 600 arrests while the contemporary reports of the *DSI* claimed that its brigades carried out 324 arrests in the first four months of 1944, a figure which had risen to 492 by the end of June.[79]

These statistics were no doubt no more than rough approximations but it would seem plausible to estimate the total number of those arrested by the *DSI* during 1943 and 1944 as being in the region of 1,500.

The Rexist leaders recognised that Lambinon's *DSI* provided only a highly indirect method of countering the challenge posed by the Resistance. Any more effective response had to be based on the internal transformation of Rex into a more military-style organisation and during the early months of 1944 a number of such plans were under consideration. The principal driving-force behind these changes was the *Inspecteur de la Milice*, Joseph Pévenasse, who from his appointment in January 1944 had thrown himself energetically into his new responsibilities, commissioning reports and policy documents, writing articles for the Rexist press and explaining his ideas at local meetings.[80] In addition, he supervised the training and operation of the *Formations B*. The first members of the new unit completed their training on 5 February and were deployed as bodyguards for prominent militants. It was intended that eventually every Rexist office-holder should be guarded by a member of the *Formations B* and Pévenasse decreed that the corps should be doubled in size from the initial 300 to 600 members. In addition, as it expanded, some of its men were also used to protect convoys of munitions as well as the camps of the *Volontaires du Travail*.[81] It was monotonous work and there were predictable instances of undiscipline and corruption among the often ill-qualified recruits. Some became involved in banditry and purges had to be carried out of the more untrustworthy bodyguards. Yet, despite these problems, the unit continued to expand and by June 1944 some 460 members of the *Formations B* were in service providing much needed protection for militants throughout francophone Belgium.[82]

The second strand to Pévenasse's activities were his efforts to strengthen links between Rex and the *Gardes Wallonnes* and the Walloon units of the German transport corps, the *NSKK*. When they had been established in 1941, the intention had been that, although both of these units would operate under German military command, they would remain closely tied to Rex. Their original Rexist membership had, however, soon been swamped by recruits unconnected with the movement and, although Rex had successfully countered efforts by *AGRA* to seize control of them, contact between the movement and the two units amounted by 1944 to little more than the symbolic presence of delegations from the *Gardes Wallonnes* and *NSKK* at Rexist functions.

Pévenasse's efforts to bring them back into the Rexist fold were, however, hampered by the internal problems which by the end of 1943 had brought both units to the brink of dissolution. In the case of the *Gardes Wallonnes*, morale appears always to have been very low. Scattered for the most part throughout the province of Hainaut as well as the Nord and Pas de Calais of France, its members guarded installations of military importance such as bridges, railway lines, canals, factories and even work-camps for Russian prisoners of war.[83] These dreary, menial tasks did little to foster any sense of political commitment and, as a Rexist report early in 1944 observed, the *Gardes* – far from forming the nucleus of a future New Order Belgian army – had sunk into 'une situation stagnante, particulière-ment débilitante, tant morale que physique'.[84] Incompetent officers, intense rivalry between different units and widespread corruption and violence had all become prominent features of the *Gardes* and made them the object of ridicule even among members of other pro-German organisations. The *Wehrmacht* authorities were forced to disband certain units regarded as beyond redemption and an intelligence report drawn up for the Belgian authorities in London in October 1943 estimated that no more than 50 per cent of the *Gardes* could be regarded as loyal to the German cause.[85] The situation in the Walloon *NSKK* was much the same. While many of its Walloon *sous-officiers* were incompetent or corrupt, the officers were for the most part ill-educated Germans who took no interest in the welfare of their soldiers. By February 1944 the moral and material condition of the corps was described as 'bedauerlich' and most of its best soldiers were reported to be making desperate attempts to leave.[86]

The principal cause of the difficulties of both units lay in the very poor quality of their recruits. There certainly were examples, even during the latter years of the war, of long-standing Rexists who joined the *Gardes* and *NSKK*[87] but they formed only a small minority among units composed for the most part of drifters and unfortunates drawn from the least dis-tinguished sectors of society. This was an impression amply confirmed by the post-war trials of members of the *Gardes* and Walloon *NSKK* which presented a melancholy spectacle of men who had enrolled in an attempt to escape from chronic poverty or in order to save themselves from deportation to Germany.[88] Some were diagnosed as mentally subnormal, while others, aged as young as 16, were 'jeunes voyous' already well known to the courts. A criminal record seemed, as one post-war judge observed, to be a positive recommendation for membership of the *Gardes Wallonnes* and cases abounded of petty criminals who had hastily joined up in order to escape the attentions of the Belgian police.[89]

In part, the recruitment pattern of both the *NSKK* and *Gardes Wallonnes* (as well as the *Formations B* and, to a lesser degree, the *Légion Wallonie*) demonstrated the failure of Rex to appeal to more established sections of the Belgian population. But it also reflected the profound social crisis which afflicted the urban, industrial centres of Belgium during the latter years of the war. With unemployment soaring, food rations scarce and black market prices prohibitively high, there were unprecedented levels of destitution. This suffering was most intense among traditionally vulnerable groups: the elderly, unskilled workers and, above all, the young. Many young Belgian men were presented with an unenviable choice between working in Germany or an uncertain (and materially difficult) clandestine existence in Belgium and it was scarcely surprising that in these circumstances some should have found the pay and other benefits offered by collaborationist military units alluring. Thus, as in many other areas of Occupied Europe, the auxiliary units of the German forces in Belgium became a point of refuge for those who saw few other options for survival. Needless to say, few of these recruits made good soldiers. Some rapidly deserted while others stayed behind only to engage in thefts, pillaging and black market activities. Protected by their uniforms from the Belgian police, the *Gardes* could often act with impunity and there were numerous instances of assaults by *Gardes* on civilians with whom they came into conflict.[90]

Pévenasse tried in various ways to effect improvements in these units. New command structures were introduced and, where possible, incompetent officers were moved to less important posts.[91] In addition, the *Inspecteur de la Milice* encouraged the deployment of the *Gardes Wallonnes* in a more active military role and special squads of *Gardes* were established in Mons and Namur which worked alongside the Gestapo and the *Feldgendarmerie* in the pursuit of Resistance militants.[92] The results of these reforms were, however, modest. No real improvement in the overall quality of the units was achieved and, despite the *Wehrmacht* authorities forcing all *Gardes Wallonnes* in June to swear an oath of loyalty to Hitler, desertions continued to take place.[93] Rexist efforts to reassert some form of direct control over the two military formations proved similarly ineffectual. Pévenasse did successfully oppose a proposal by the *Wehrmacht* to create a civilian reserve for the *Gardes Wallonnes* which would have acted as a further drain on the limited manpower at the disposal of the Rexists. But, although Reeder reported in April that Pévenasse had created a single command structure for all its military and paramilitary units, its importance was very limited and effective control of both the *Gardes Wallonnes* and *NSKK* always remained in the hands of their German commanders.[94]

For Pévenasse, these efforts to renovate the *Gardes Wallonnes* and *NSKK* were only the prelude to a more general militarisation of the Rexist movement. He believed that the time for civilian organisation had passed, declaring bluntly in a speech: 'Plus de civils, rien que des soldats de la Révolution.'[95] This was a slogan in tune with the desperate circumstances of the time and mirrored other proposals advanced by Rexists for a root-and-branch reorganisation of their movement. For example, Louis Abrassart, a Rexist veteran from Binche, wrote a report in February 1944 arguing that Rex should emulate the underground Communist party by organising its militants into a network of secret armed cells.[96] Pévenasse was convinced that only one model was appropriate for the movement: that of the *SS*. His consistent goal during 1944 was to integrate all supporters of Rex, apart from the *légionnaires*, into an *SS* militia which he hoped would contain as many as 10,000 militants. As early as January 1944, he had proposed to Collard that Rex should imitate the *Allgemeine SS* which had operated in Flanders since 1940[97] and, although Collard's response was unenthusiastic, Pévenasse pressed ahead with his plan. Speaking in March 1944, he once again stressed that only an elite force modelled on the *SS* could meet the challenge of an Allied invasion: 'un débarquement soulèverait un volcan. En face des communistes déchaînés, ce n'est pas l'esprit "garde-civique" qui triomphera, il n'y a que l'esprit de la *SS – légion de l'intérieur* – qui soit capable de mobiliser nos camarades qui se dresseront *un contre cent* parce qu'ils attendent depuis des années cette heure-là.'[98]

This categorical support for an *SS*-style organisation distinguished Pévenasse from his colleagues in the Rexist *Etat-Major*. Although his opinions attracted some support from the Rexist rank and file, none of the other leaders of the movement seem to have shared his views. They distrusted the personal ambitions of the *Inspecteur de la Milice* and no doubt recognised that the creation of an *SS*-style militia would in effect mark the final demise of any autonomous Rexist movement. They preferred instead to investigate other, less radical, alternatives for the reorganisation of Rex. One such possibility was to emulate the *Milice* directed by Joseph Darnand in Vichy France. During the early months of 1944 the activities of the newly-appointed *Secrétaire Général au Maintien de l'Ordre* in the Vichy government attracted much interest and admiration in collaborationist circles in Belgium. Having long criticised the vacillation and impotence of the pro-German groups in France, the Belgian press now hailed Darnand as the saviour who would impose the necessary revolutionary unity.[99] Moreover, the *Milice* had the advantage that, rather than subsuming the political direction of the movement within an *SS* structure, it maintained the traditional distinction between the political leadership and a subordinate militia. The Rexist leadership collected documentation relating to Darnand's activities and in February 1944 a delegation headed by Albert Regnard of the *Département Politique* visited France to study the operation of the *Milice* at first hand. Carrying a letter of introduction to Darnand from Matthys in which the *Chef de Rex ad interim* expressed his 'voeux ardents pour le succès de vos entreprises d'épuration', the delegation visited Darnand's offices in Paris and, after witnessing the operations of the *Milice* against the Maquis of the Haute Savoie, returned to Belgium full of praise for the achievements of the French organisation.[100]

The wide range of activities initiated by Rex during the early months of 1944 contributed to the impression of a movement which had recovered its self-confidence and sense of purpose. Yet, behind their proud boasts of imminent success, there remained a hidden nervousness. Throughout January and February, all Rexists were preoccupied by the fate of Degrelle and the *légionnaires*. When the *Légion* had returned to the front in

November, it had been larger, better equipped and better armed than ever before. Its training programme was, however, far from complete and in the opinion of its German liaison officer it was capable only of participating in defensive manoeuvres. But Degrelle had other ideas. His political ambitions depended on building the reputation of the *Légion* as an elite military unit and, within a few weeks, it became embroiled – largely, it seems, at Degrelle's instigation – in a bloody counter-attack against the Red Army. This soon turned into a fiasco and, by the end of January, the *Légion* was one of the units encircled by Soviet forces at Tcherkassy in the Ukraine.[101] For the Rexists, it was a time of great anxiety. Each day the military communiques became more sombre while the Belgian radio from London gloated enthusiastically over the apparent demise of Degrelle and his men. However, suddenly in mid-February, news arrived which transformed Rexist spirits: contrary to all expectations, the *Légion* had managed to extricate itself from the Soviet encirclement and rejoin the German lines. The cost had, though, been enormous. The *Légion* had been forced to abandon all of its equipment and, of its almost 2,000 members, fewer than half had survived. Approximately 1,100 men, including the *Légion*'s military commander, Lucien Lippert, had died on the field of battle.[102]

Among the fortunate survivors was Léon Degrelle who was flown immediately to Berlin where he was fêted by a German propaganda machine desperate for war heroes. Late in the evening of 20 February, the *Chef de Rex* was received by Hitler who presented him with the *Ritterkreuz*.[103] It was the first time since 1936 that Degrelle had met the *Führer* and, although nothing of substance was discussed at their one hour meeting, it reinforced his image as a hero of the New Order Europe. The Rexists reacted with predictable euphoria to the news from Berlin and, when Degrelle returned to Belgium on 22 February, a large delegation – including Matthys and, significantly, Jungclaus – travelled to the frontier to greet him. A rally was hastily organised in honour of the conquering hero at the Palais des Sports on 27 February. The large hall was full to capacity and, amidst genuine if well-disciplined acclamations, Degrelle made a speech which, though it contained no more than vacuous expressions of undying fidelity to the Nazi cause, was delivered with his customary skill and verve. He was the man of the moment and the rally was followed by a lavish reception hosted by Gillès de Pélichy, the pro-Rexist provincial Governor of Brabant.[104]

Not since 1936 had Degrelle tasted such success and he had no intention of allowing the least opportunity for self-publicity to go to waste. The speech in Brussels was followed by visits to Charleroi and Liège where he was received by the Rexist administrations of these cities.[105] But Belgium had become too small a stage for the *Chef de Rex* and he soon travelled on to Paris where he addressed a rally at the Palais de Chaillot on 5 March. Dressed in his *SS* uniform with his military decorations prominently displayed, the war hero made a rousing speech in which he posed as the symbol of the New Europe fighting to save its civilisation from the ravages of Asiatic and American barbarians. The audience of several thousand French collaborationists included De Brinon, Doriot, Déat and Darnand and, after the rally, Degrelle met these French leaders at a reception hosted at the German embassy by his long-standing ally, Abetz. Accompanied by a number of Rexist leaders including Matthys, Collard, and the *Chef de la Propagande Active*, Julien Carlier, as well as by Moskopff of the *Dienstelle Jungclaus*, Degrelle made the most of his visit to the French capital. In the following days he was the guest of honour at a series of social events and the somewhat unlikely military hero clearly made a substantial impression on the French collaborationist community.[106]

Encouraged by his reception in Berlin, Brussels and Paris, Degrelle hoped that his military feats would provide him with the springboard to power in Wallonia, Belgium, or even some fanciful reconstituted Burgundian state. Not for the first time his optimism was misplaced. His links with the SS combined with his new-found military prestige did indeed leave him strongly placed to emerge as the eventual ruler of some form of puppet regime in Wallonia in the increasingly implausible circumstances of a German victory. In the meantime Degrelle remained for the Nazi elite little more than a convenient propaganda tool whom they could use to provide some threadbare plausibility for their European crusade against Asiatic Bolshevism and Anglo-American plutocracy. Even Degrelle's supposed allies within the Nazi elite proved reluctant to advance his cause. This was especially true of the all-important SS. Degrelle met Himmler on 20 February at the time of his audience with Hitler but the two men do not appear to have discussed political issues and the *Reichsführer-SS* made no effort during the subsequent months to assist the ambitions of the Rexist leader. On the contrary, at the decisive meeting between Himmler and Hitler held on 12 July 1944 to arrange the replacement of the *Wehrmacht* authorities in Belgium by a German civilian administration, the head of the SS did not propose any role for Degrelle within the new regime and referred in dismissive terms to the Rexist leader's political unreliability compared with the Flemish collaborationists. These private comments to Hitler display the hypocrisy which lay behind Himmler's support for Degrelle. Though many within the SS hierarchy were by 1944 no doubt genuinely convinced of the Rexist leader's merits, at the highest levels Himmler and his entourage regarded him essentially as a convenient mechanism for undermining Reeder's authority in Brussels and winning new recruits for the armies of the *Waffen-SS*. As a future political leader of importance, he still lacked plausibility.[107]

Both Degrelle and his supporters were blind to these obstacles. In the strange spring of 1944, everything seemed possible and a mood of euphoria overwhelmed all but the most disabused of Rexists. To the intense annoyance of Reeder, the Flemish Nationalists and the *collège* of *secrétaires-généraux*, Degrelle's return to Belgium from France in mid-March soon gave rise to wild rumours which, as always, were fanned enthusiastically by the Rexists. Degrelle was said to be about to be appointed as the 'Darnand belge' and the Rexists began asking civil servants whether they would work for a new government headed by Degrelle.[108] The *Chef de Rex* did his best to turn these dreams into reality, hosting a lavish reception for the German and collaborationist elite at his home in the Drève de Lorraine at which cognac, champagne and expensive wines all flowed in abundance. At this and other such events, he boasted of his intentions when he was appointed *Staatsführer* of Belgium, even daring to insult Canaris, the head of the *Sipo-SD* in Belgium, whom he accused of organising surveillance of his activities.[109]

The contrast could not have been more striking with the situation during the first years of the Occupation. Then it had been the Flemish Nationalists of the *VNV* who had seemed poised for success while the Rexists had been the impotent outsiders: but by 1944 these positions were reversed. Many Flemish leaders had come to regard the policy of collaboration with the Germans as an error and, as Degrelle and his supporters exulted in the prospect of power, the Flemish nationalist movement disintegrated amidst internal divisions and mutual recriminations.[110]

One event above all others symbolised the reversal in political fortunes. This was the march by the *Légion Wallonie* through the streets of Charleroi and Brussels on 1 April. The survivors of Tcherkassy had returned to Belgium at the end of March and rumours soon began to circulate of a parade in Brussels by the *légionnaires*. Fears of provoking an Allied bombing raid on the Belgian capital caused it to be repeatedly postponed. Finally, however, German approval was obtained and the *légionnaires* assembled on the morning of 1 April on the Grand Place of Charleroi where, in the presence of Sepp Dietrich of the *Leibstandarte Adolf Hitler*, military decorations were awarded to the veterans.[111] The *Légion* then travelled on to Brussels and in bright afternoon sunshine paraded through the boulevards of the capital. To add to the effect, the column of *légionnaires* was motorised for the occasion, with *matériel* borrowed from Sepp Dietrich's troops, and Degrelle, smiling broadly, rode triumphantly on a tank at the head of his troops accompanied by his young children. A substantial number of dignitaries had assembled on the steps of the Bourse in the centre of Brussels to greet the returning heroes, including the Rexist leadership, German officers and the five provincial governors of Wallonia as well as representatives of French and Flemish collaborationist groups. The *secrétaires-généraux* had, however, declined an invitation to attend, as had Gottlob Berger of the *SS* headquarters who was concerned that his presence at this Degrellian event might alienate the Flemish Nationalists.[112]

Despite being given only a few hours notice, a large crowd gathered in

Brussels to watch the march. Some were merely curious onlookers but the vast majority consisted of Rexists and the friends and families of the *légionnaires*. For them, this was in many respects their finest hour. After the repeated disappointments of the previous years, they could at last enjoy the appearance if not the reality of success. As a wife of a *légionnaire* was reported to have declared: 'Cela nous venge de bien de choses'.[113]

A march by a collaborationist military unit in full battle order through a capital city appears to have been a unique event without parallel elsewhere in German-occupied Europe[114] and it confirmed Degrelle's status as a leading figure in the Nazi propaganda pantheon. But it brought him no closer to real political power and, as the initial euphoria receded, so Degrelle came to recognise the need to redouble his efforts to woo the Nazi elite. This he did with characteristic energy, seeking by a combination of charm, bluster and intrigue to consolidate his political position. The pursuit of Nazi favour drew Degrelle remorselessly to the Reich. Like others among the diminishing band of pro-Nazi collaborators in Occupied Europe, the Rexist leader recognised that it was in the offices, restaurants and corridors of Berlin that the real key to power lay. He therefore spent little time in Belgium and his brief visits to his native land were devoted more than ever to relaxation rather than to political activity. The consequence was to loosen still further his ties to Rex. The movement had become little more than a relic of his political past and he continued to comment privately to German officials that his long-term aim was to dissolve Rex in order to base his support exclusively on the *Légion*.[115]

Two of Degrelle's initiatives during these months did, nonetheless, have consequences for Rex. These were his attempts to resuscitate a Rexist presence in Flanders and to build a coalition of support among the French collaborationists in Paris. Both policies formed part of Degrelle's grandiose ambition of emerging, after a German military victory, as the ruler of a political unit larger than Wallonia. In meetings with Nazi leaders and journalists, he reiterated his support for the integration of the Walloons into a Germanic confederation. These apparently unambivalent statements were invariably accompanied by the qualification that this Germanic empire could only come about slowly and should take the form of a loose confederation.[116] In this way Degrelle hoped to leave open the possibility that some form of Walloon–Flemish association could be retained, or even that Wallonia might become the focal point of a larger union of 'the Germans of the West' incorporating not only the Low Countries but also the territories of eastern France which had once formed the Burgundian empire.

In Flanders, Degrelle still remained nominally tied by the terms of the May 1941 agreement between Rex and the Flemish nationalist movement, the *Vlaams Nationaal Verbond* (*VNV*). Since Degrelle's rejection in December 1942 of the *rapprochement* between the two movements advocated by José Streel, this had become a dead letter. While Degrelle had plunged ever more deeply into a policy of total collaboration, the *VNV* under the cautious leadership of Elias had sought to distance itself from the German authorities and had become embroiled in an intense conflict within Flanders with the pro-*SS Duits-Vlaamse Arbeidsgemeenschap* (*DeVlag*) led by Jef Van de Wiele. Not surprisingly, Degrelle recognised Van de Wiele to be a kindred spirit in his struggle to undermine the authority of the *Militärverwaltung*. He met the leader of *DeVlag* on a number of occasions during 1943 and, although he seems rightly to have regarded Van de Wiele as a man of little political talent, the two leaders appear to have agreed on the framework for a joint Flemish-Walloon administration in Belgium after a German military victory.[117] This agreement was of little real significance but it reflected their confidence that, as protégés of the *SS*, they would soon be invested with substantial political power. Moreover, Van de Wiele gave public expression to this alliance when in June 1943 the two men attended a major anti-Bolshevik rally in Brussels at which Van de Wiele declared (in French): 'Nous sommes d'accord, Degrelle et moi, pour conduire notre peuple [*sic*] vers son glorieux avenir. Cet avenir se situe dans le Reich germanique.'[118]

This personal alliance between Degrelle and Van de Wiele did, however, prove to be short-lived. Although the leader of *DeVlag* continued to attend Rexist ceremonies during 1944,[119] he had by then come to share the alarm long felt by his rivals in the *VNV* that the rise in Degrelle's political fortunes could prejudice German support for the cause of an independent Flanders. Like many other collaborationist leaders in wartime Europe, the leaders of *DeVlag* and the *VNV* had an exaggerated belief in the coherence of Nazi decision-making and they therefore misinterpreted the German propaganda machine's opportunistic exploitation of Degrelle as signalling Nazi support for the Rexist leader's extravagant political ambitions. Fearful that the Nazi regime was on the verge of concluding a political agreement with Degrelle, they bombarded German officials in Belgium during the spring of 1944 with alarmist descriptions of the adventurism and disguised Belgian nationalism which they detected behind the Rexist leader's pro-Nazi gestures.[120]

Thus, when Degrelle sought in 1944 to build support for his cause in Flanders, he was forced to turn instead to the former members of *Rex-Vlaanderen*. They had been absorbed into the *VNV* under the terms of the May 1941 accord but few of these Rexists had found the Flemish nationalist movement to be a congenial home. Some had served in the *VNV* militia or in the Flemish Legion recruited by the *VNV* to fight on the Eastern Front but many others had followed the example of their former leader Odiel Daem who, after initially participating in the expanded *VNV*, had soon abandoned his political career.[121] Already in April 1943 Degrelle had addressed a private meeting of former leaders of *Rex-Vlaanderen* in an

Antwerp hotel at which, while reiterating that the Rex-*VNV* accord remained in force, he had encouraged them to preserve their distinctive identity. By the spring of 1944 Degrelle was less cautious. Encouraged by the Rexist leaders, he believed that his new political profile would enable him to recreate his old political organisation in Flanders. Efforts were made to involve former members of *Rex-Vlaanderen* in the celebrations marking the triumphant return of the *Légion* and in April it was announced that two of Degrelle's most enthusiastic supporters from France, Jean Azéma and Jean Hérold-Paquis, would address public meetings in Gent and Antwerp.[122]

This disguised revival of Rexist activity in Flanders was, however, cut short by the opposition of the *Militärverwaltung*. Reeder was well aware that his days as German administrator of Belgium were numbered. Threatened on the one hand by an Allied invasion and, on the other, by Hitler's decision in January 1944 to approve the creation of a *Zivilverwaltung*, his power nevertheless remained intact, as did his determination to thwart Degrelle's political ambitions. Thus, he issued an order that all pro-Degrelle meetings in Flanders should be banned and seized the opportunity caused by Degrelle's disruptive activities to deliver to his superiors in Berlin his most crushing assessment to date of the political talents of the Rexist leader: 'Es zeigte sich immer wieder, dass Degrelle, sowie es auf politische Fragen ankommt, sprunghaft, leicht beeinflussbar, politisch oft ungeschickt und charakterlich manchmal unzuverlässig ist . . . Durch sein Temperament und gewisse Charaktereigenschaften bedingt, zeigen sich bei Degrelle oft politische Phantastereien und Uberschätzungen, die nichts mehr mit gesunden Optimismus oder gar realpolitischen Erwägungen zu tun haben.'[123]

Compared with the obstacles which still frustrated Degrelle in Belgium in 1944, France must have appeared to the Rexist leader to be a land of relative opportunity. One of the more bizarre features of the last year of the Occupation was the considerable effort expended by Degrelle and his allies on forging links with collaborationists in Paris and Vichy. His rally in the Palais de Chaillot in Paris had fostered illusions of grandeur in the *Chef de Rex* who began to dream of leading a grand alliance of French-speaking National Socialists. Indeed, if his post-war reminiscences are to be believed, he even hoped that he would emerge as the leader of a vast West European state which, along with Germany and the Slavonic lands, would be one of the three geopolitical units of a Nazi-controlled Europe.[124]

There was of course nothing new in contact between the Rexists and sympathetic figures on the French extreme right. As early as 1936, Robert Brasillach had published a pamphlet eulogising the youthful, virile Degrelle while French right-wing organs such as *Je Suis Partout* had given much coverage to the pre-war Rexist movement.[125] These contacts appear, however, to have come to an end in 1940. The hesitant and divided Vichy regime did not enjoy a good reputation among Belgian collaborationists and it was common in Rexist circles to bemoan the failure of the defeated French nation to adapt to the new European order. Degrelle was of course always a frequent visitor to France but it was only in 1943 that figures from the Parisian collaborationist community began to visit Brussels. At the same time, Matthys and Louis Collard obtained passports to travel to France and a number of Rexist delegations made the journey to Paris, including the one which observed the operation of Darnand's *Milice*.[126]

The central figure in these burgeoning contacts appears to have been Julien Carlier, the head of Rexist propaganda. He visited France on several occasions and it may well have been through him that two French collaborationists, Jean Hérold-Paquis and Jean Azéma of *Radio-Paris*, became associated with Rex. In 1944 both men were outspoken supporters of Degrelle who toured Belgium addressing audiences on the close comradeship between Walloon and French National Socialists.[127] It was Azéma, a young man of the same generation as many of the Rexist leaders, who was loudest in his praise for Degrelle. As well as becoming the Paris correspondent of *Le Pays Réel*, he used his frequent contributions to the French press to advance the Rexist leader's cause as the potential leader of French collaborationists alienated by the failures of Vichy.[128] The Burgundian Cross, he forecast, would soon become 'le symbole unique des Nationaux-Socialistes d'expression française' while Degrelle, he proclaimed after the march by the *Légion* in Brussels, was the man on horseback whom Paris-based collaborationists had long been seeking to rescue them from their sterile internecine intrigues. A few weeks later Azéma enrolled in the *Légion Wallonie*, declaring that its soldiers possessed the spirit of idealism and fraternity which was so absent amongst French National Socialists.[129]

Although both men professed an allegiance to Jacques Doriot's *PPF*, neither Hérold-Paquis nor Azéma were figures of the first rank and their infatuation with Degrelle was not shared by the principal French collaborationist leaders. They respected Degrelle's military achievements but found it difficult to take his political ambitions seriously and viewed with some condescension his pretensions to leadership of all francophone National Socialists.[130] The political situation within the French collaborationist community was, moreover, far from favourable to the Rexist leader. Degrelle's hopes of success lay in winning the support of those radical Paris-based collaborationists who had long distrusted the hesitant stance of the Vichy regime. The Nazi-imposed reorganisation of the Vichy government in January 1944 had, however, brought a number of the Paris radicals such as Marcel Déat into the Laval government and had reinforced the powers of those in Vichy – such as Joseph Darnand and Philippe Henriot – who were the most enthusiastic advocates of total collaboration. Some Parisian collaborationists still dreamt of building a French National

Socialist regime independent of Vichy but the new, more radical character of the Vichy government had removed any hope of German sponsorship for this cause and left Degrelle with only the support of embittered individuals such as Azéma.

At Vichy, the cause of Degrelle had few advocates. The Rexist leader has subsequently boasted of his wartime links with Joseph Darnand but, although the head of the *Milice* made a brief visit to Brussels in April 1944,[131] there is no evidence of the two men having had any political discussions until after the Allied liberation of France and Belgium. In November 1944 Degrelle addressed the remnants of the French collaborationist leadership in exile at the castle of Sigmaringen in Germany. After a warm introduction by Darnand, he delivered a characteristically bombastic speech to an audience which included Déat, De Brinon and Otto Abetz in which he assured the demoralised and still divided French exiles that the victory of the German armies was ineluctable. He subsequently visited French troops at the *SS* Training School at Neweklau but his grandiose plan to combine the French Charlemagne *SS* division with the *Légion Wallonie* to form an 'Occident' army corps came to nothing.[132]

The failure of these attempts to extend his influence beyond francophone Belgium was a disappointment to Degrelle but it did not undermine his confidence. Degrelle's ambitions during the war were a remarkable combination of extravagant fantasies and hard-headed realism and he never lost sight of his essential goal of winning the support of the leaders of the Reich. The transformation of the *Légion Wallonie* into an elite military unit was central to this ambition. In part, his concern for the *Légion* was the consequence of his own somewhat unexpected taste for the military life. The impulsive, chaotic and *bon vivant* Rexist leader made an implausible soldier but, unlike many other European collaborationists who did no more than make propaganda tours of the front line, he participated actively in the battles of the *Légion Wallonie* and shared in the physical hardships. In a volume of thoughts supposedly composed in Russia and published in 1944 under the title of *Feldpost*, he idealised the life of the front line soldier which, he declared, was the only one to be 'vraiment droite, désintéressée, sans bravure et sans marchandage'.[133] Degrelle's new self-image as a simple 'soldat du front' masked, however, his political calculations. He rightly recognised that the *Légion* was the most effective means of winning the confidence of the Nazi leaders and also provided him with a military force capable of imposing and sustaining his rule in Wallonia. As he declared in a speech in Berlin in June 1944: 'Seuls des fusils, des canons, des tanks seront assez forts pour mater les ploutocrates . . . La révolution socialiste ne se fera pas facilement après la guerre . . . Il faut que nous soyons une armée. Il faut que nous soyons des milliers à rentrer au pays.'[134]

Thus, it is impossible to exaggerate the extent to which Degrelle's thoughts in the last year of the Occupation were dominated by the *Légion*. Its organisational autonomy from Rex was by now almost complete. During 1943 and 1944 an *Ersatzkommando für Wallonien der Waffen-SS*, headed by Moskopff of the *Dienstelle Jungclaus* and staffed by a substantial bureaucracy of demobilised and seconded *légionnaires*, took charge of the administration of the *Légion* within Belgium. Its manifold responsibilities incorporated much which had formerly been accomplished on a voluntary basis by the Rexists. Recruitment for the *Légion* was carried out by a network of permanent recruitment offices directed by the *Ersatzkommando* and a special service of the *Ersatzkommando*, the *Honneur Légionnaire* later renamed the *Entraide Nationale-Socialiste pour les Waffen-SS*, took over the distribution of food rations and other benefits to the families of *légionnaires*.[135]

The *Ersatzkommando* was responsible not to the Rexist leaders but to Degrelle and the German authorities. Inevitably, strong personal links often existed between the Rexists and the men of the *Ersatzkommando* but the two organisations operated largely independently of each other and, as Louis Collard commented after the war, most members of the Rexist leadership visited the *Ersatzkommando* offices only in order to send letters to Degrelle.[136] Rex and the *Légion* had become in effect parallel Degrellian hierarchies within Belgium and, although Degrelle never carried through his stated intention of dissolving Rex, the *Ersatzkommando* provided him with an alternative basis for his future political activities within the country.

This division between Rex and the *Légion Wallonie* was reinforced by their very different social composition. By the end of 1943 possibly as many as 90 per cent of the *légionnaires* were new recruits and only a small proportion of these had any prior connection with Rex. For example, of the 120 men enrolled in January 1944, only 23 were members of the movement: 101 described themselves as workers, craftsmen or as unemployed and it is clear that the majority of the *légionnaires* of the latter war years were young working-class men whose motivation for joining the *Légion* was more material than ideological. As early as the summer of 1943 the *Légion*'s chaplain estimated that only some 25 per cent of its soldiers could be described as idealists, while the others were mercenaries or adventurers.[137] Many of these were adolescents who, like their colleagues in the *NSKK* or *Gardes Wallonnes*, found in the *Légion* a refuge from labour conscription or the material difficulties of wartime Belgium. But the status of the *Légion Wallonie* as a front line military unit also drew to it a number of men from the fringes of society who joined the *Légion Wallonie* rather as they might formerly have joined the French Foreign Legion. A few indeed were veterans of the French unit while others had been in Spain during the Civil War.[138] Volunteer military units of this kind have always attracted men temperamentally unsuited to more conventional lives and the Belgian army unit formed in 1950 to fight with the United Nations forces in Korea contained a similar element of adventurers 'en quête d'un nouveau départ'.[139] The *Légion*, however, also acted as an asylum for those in search of an escape from more pressing difficulties. Post-war trials of *légionnaires* revealed a number of cases of men who had enrolled in order to escape the clutches of Belgian justice. Hardened criminals, the chronically impoverished and the mentally subnormal were all present in the *Légion* of the latter years, even if many soon deserted in order to escape the perils of the front line. Desperate to enrol as many recruits as possible, the *Légion* rarely if ever rejected anybody and during 1944 some were recruited directly from German and Belgian prisons.[140] Thus, though the *Légion* never declined to the level of auxiliary German units such as the *Gardes Wallonnes*, it did come to contain a strong element of those whom one young veteran of 1941 described as: 'des gars bizarres que l'on préférerait ne pas rencontrer le soir au coin d'un bois'.[141]

During the spring of 1944, Degrelle devoted much of his energies to a propaganda campaign intended to attract new recruits for his military unit. The heavy losses sustained during the escape from the Soviet armies at Tcherkassy had reduced the *Légion* to a virtual rump, making it imperative to enrol a substantial number of new soldiers as rapidly as possible. Degrelle's ambitions, however, went beyond merely restoring the *Légion* to its former size. Immediately after his return from Tcherkassy, he seems to have conceived the idea of expanding the unit from a brigade to a division and this soon became his overriding obsession as he toured Belgium and Germany during the coming months seeking out the several thousand additional recruits who would be required.[142] Not surprisingly, he recognised that the limited numbers of men being enrolled by the offices of the *Ersatzkommando* would not meet his needs and he hoped to recruit more substantial contingents from auxiliary units such as the *Gardes Wallonnes*[143] as well as from the large number of Belgian men unwillingly conscripted for labour service in Germany.

One of Degrelle's obstinate beliefs during the latter years of the war was that those Belgian men working in factories in Germany were more eager than their compatriots in Belgium to serve in the *Légion Wallonie*. As with his earlier efforts to convince Belgian prisoners of war in Germany to join the *Légion*, there is little evidence that this was in fact so but Degrelle nevertheless undertook during the early summer of 1944 a substantial tour of Germany speaking to audiences of Belgian workers. With his customary wild optimism, he hoped that this recruitment drive would yield as many as 10,000 new soldiers and he was concerned that the Nazi authorities might not permit the 'liberation' of so many Belgian workers. He therefore conceived the plan of mollifying the Germans by providing them with the names and addresses of an equivalent number of Belgian men who had evaded the labour conscription measures and who could be deported to Germany to replace those who joined the *Légion*. Whether Degrelle ever received the approval of the German authorities for this bizarre project remains unclear[144] but it is unlikely that they ever took it very seriously. Not only was it highly implausible that many Belgian workers would renounce their admittedly disagreeable work in German factories to fight on the Eastern front but the lists of replacement Belgian workers would in themselves be of little value. The real difficulty that faced the German authorities was not to identify additional workers but the enforcement of the existing labour conscription measures. Many thousands of Belgian men had chosen to avoid deportation to Germany by going into hiding and it was unlikely that these new recruits would prove any more amenable to a summons to work in the Reich.

These practical difficulties were of little concern to Degrelle and he persevered with the project, instructing the Rexist leadership to collect names of Belgian men who could be deported to Germany. Orders were issued to the local *cercles* and a lieutenant from the *Légion* was seconded to the Rexist headquarters to oversee the compilation of the lists. Degrelle's plan did, however, meet with opposition from an unexpected quarter. His hitherto faithful deputy, Victor Matthys, refused to carry out the order. Possibly the task of identifying additional Belgian men for deportation to Germany aroused the scruples of the *Chef ad interim* of Rex or he may simply have resented the way in which Rexist resources were once again to be put at the disposal of the *Légion*. Whatever the reality, Degrelle acted swiftly to circumvent Matthys' opposition. The more pliant Louis Collard was summoned to meet Degrelle at his home and was given detailed instructions for the compilation of the lists.[145] These were then conveyed to the Rexist *cercles* in an urgent order issued by Collard on 13 May in which he made it clear that this task was imposed on the Rexists by an 'ordre exprès et formel du Chef le Sturmbannführer et Commandeur Léon Degrelle'. Degrelle's original intention may have been to collect as many as 40,000 names but in Collard's circular this was reduced to the still substantial total of 10,000. Only one week was allowed for the preparation of the lists which, he added, should include all those deemed suitable for work in Germany but who 'jusqu'à ce jour, ont échappé indûment à la réquisition'.[146]

The real significance of this affair was the extra test it imposed on the commitment of ordinary Rexists. Despite the complete identification of the movement with the Nazi cause, most Rexists had never formerly been called upon to assist the German authorities so directly in their work. Many had, of course, already had contact with the German police and some had even denounced individuals whom they believed to be engaged in 'terrorist' Resistance activities. These were, however, individual initiatives while Degrelle's order now obliged his followers to participate in the identification of 'innocent' compatriots for deportation to the Reich. A number of *cercles*, notably in Brussels, immediately set about this task but others dragged their feet. Almost a month later, many had still not provided any lists and a stern circular had to be issued reminding them of the importance of the information. The reasons for this tardiness can only be guessed at. In some cases, it may have reflected an unwillingness to assist the German authorities in what was essentially a police matter but others may simply have recognised the futility of the task. Whatever the case, their hesitations seem gradually to have been overcome and, after repeated requests, it appears that almost all *cercles* did eventually provide lists of some sort.[147]

The sense of urgency had soon evaporated. Degrelle's tour of Germany during June and July did attract some new recruits from among Belgian workers but in nothing like the numbers which he had anticipated.[148] The expansion of the *Légion* into a division was postponed and the issue of replacing the volunteers by additional workers from Belgium never arose. Nevertheless, the staff of the Rexist *Etat-Major* proceeded diligently with their work and by the liberation they had collected the names of 6,000 to 7,000 men.[149] Because of the Allied advance, this information was never communicated to the German authorities but the very existence of the lists bore witness to the willingness of many – if not all – Rexists to participate in activities directly harmful to their compatriots. Not even assisting in the potential mass deportations of ordinary Belgian citizens was, it seemed, too great a step for a movement which had divorced itself from the national community.

For most Rexists, Degrelle's insistence that they assemble these lists of names must have been no more than a minor distraction from their more pressing concerns. Foremost among these was the imminent prospect of an Allied invasion of northern Europe, probably on or very close to the Belgian coast. This invasion had already been widely anticipated during the previous summer and there were very few Rexists who denied that it would in all probability occur at some point during the summer of 1944. In preparation for this eventuality, the Rexist leaders devised elaborate security plans. They believed that the invasion would be accompanied by an uprising of Communist-led Resistance forces and they designated a series of fortified buildings in which the families of militants could be assembled. Isolated regions such as the Luxembourg were to be evacuated of all Rexists while every able-bodied militant would be mobilised to help maintain public order.[150] A special department, the *Service K*, was established in the *Etat-Major* to draw up lists of Rexists requiring protection as well as to assemble those resources – such as food, vehicles, petrol and armaments – which would be essential for the continued operation of the movement. Finally, in an attempt to raise morale, Matthys undertook a tour of Belgium in May and early June in order to inspect the security precautions.[151]

These measures did not go unnoticed by the underground press which mocked the desperation and panic they believed was widespread in Rexist ranks.[152] At least among the leadership, however, the mood seems to have been more one of grim resolution. Most had been anticipating an Allied invasion for almost two years and, as it drew closer, they steeled themselves for the trials ahead. Despite the practical difficulties, a number of rallies and smaller meetings continued to take place and directives from the *Etat-Major* optimistically encouraged local groups to seek out new recruits for the Rexist cause.[153] During the spring of 1944 the Allies carried out bombing raids on a number of Belgian cities in an attempt to damage the railway network prior to their invasion. These caused almost 10,000 civilian deaths and the Rexist propagandists sought somewhat forlornly to capitalise on the discernible if transient decline in the pro-English sentiments of the population which resulted from the raids. The Rexist press relentlessly condemned the 'barbarism' of the Allies and, under headlines such as 'Les yeux s'ouvrent', praised the new mood of realism which they claimed to discern in the population.[154]

The best indication of the attitude of the Rexist leaders at this time was a 'Note Générale' written by Louis Collard which was distributed on 13 May, the same day that he announced Degrelle's orders for the compilation of the lists of potential deportees. This substantial document intended for the local officials of the movement denied that the Rexists had any reason to fear the future. The security precautions were, Collard insisted, 'une preuve de réalisme et l'expression de notre volonté de combattre et de vaincre' while the German forces assisted by the Rexists would crush ruthlessly any attempt by the Resistance forces to foment an uprising within Belgium. Above all, Collard insisted that the political prospects of the movement were better than ever before. The reorganisation of the militia, the establishment of the *Formations B*, the expansion in the *DSI* and Degrelle's political successes were all decisive developments which, Collard concluded, indicated that Rex would soon achieve substantial power.[155]

Thus, when the invasion did finally take place on 6 June in Normandy, rather than further east as anticipated, the initial reaction of many Rexists was not one of despair. In common with other members of the pro-German minority, they seemed relieved that the long period of waiting was at an end and were confident that the German armies would achieve a decisive victory over their Anglo-American enemies. To the amazement of more realistic German observers, both Rexists and Flemish collaborators appeared convinced that the initial reverses suffered by the *Wehrmacht* were no more than a ruse designed to lure more of the Allied forces onto the continent. Nothing, it seemed, could shake their faith in the German armies and, even once the invaders had secured their beach-heads in

Normandy, many still believed that the V1 missiles first deployed in June 1944 would reverse the course of the conflict.[156]

As Matthys remarked at his trial, this confidence could only appear in retrospect to have been based on blind stupidity[157] but it was the logical conclusion of the process of self-delusion which had been developing over the previous years. Their strange existence within the collaborationist vacuum combined with their sense of exaltation at Degrelle's apparent political success rendered the Rexist leaders largely impervious to the omens of disaster. How far this optimism was shared by their followers is, however, difficult to assess. Even at this late stage, a few attempted to disguise their past through timely displays of pro-English sentiments while others sought to curry favour by supplying money or information to Resistance groups.[158] The number of such defections was relatively small, however, and at no point in the summer of 1944 was there a general collapse in Rexist confidence comparable to that which appears to have occurred after the fall of Mussolini in 1943. German reports testified to the confidence displayed by local Rexist officials and the total membership of the movement appears to have remained largely static. The time for rats to leave a sinking ship had long since passed and those resignations which did occur were offset by the enrolment of the wives and children of militants as well as of other supporters of the German cause anxious to acquire the protection accorded to members of Rex.[159]

Most Rexists saw no alternative in the desperate situation created by the Allied invasion other than to draw still closer to the German authorities. José Streel's ambition of a Rexist movement which espoused collaboration while remaining apart from the Germans had long since been rendered obsolete and the dividing line between Rexist and German organisations had all but disappeared. Groups such as the *Formations B* and the *DSI* were little more than offshoots of the German forces while the financial assistance provided by Jungclaus' office destroyed the last vestiges of the movement's financial autonomy. As Rex became integrated into the Nazi military and administrative apparatus, so the Rexists themselves became in many ways more German than Belgian in character. This was the final and most extreme stage of collaboration. They wore the uniforms of the conqueror and employed both his titles and language. They enjoyed the rations reserved for German citizens and many bought their food in shops reserved for German personnel. The Rexist police travelled in the Mercedes cars of the Occupying forces while in daily life members of Rex mimicked German habits and customs. In private as in public, they sought the company of Germans inviting them to their homes and even, in a few cases, marrying German women. Germany, one Rexist remarked, had become his second home but, in truth, it was for many their first and only home.[160]

It would therefore be ridiculous to define the pro-German stance of the Rexists during 1944 in terms of certain specific actions. Collaboration had become the dominant, all-determining fact of their lives and, though some still attempted to distance themselves from extreme actions such as the compilation of the lists of Belgian workers demanded by Degrelle or the activities of Lambinon and his colleagues, all were aware that it was no longer possible to maintain an existence independent of the German forces. Collaboration had to be embraced in its grim entirety or not at all. The corollary of this integration into the German world was the ever more complete exclusion of the Rexists from the lives of their compatriots. While earlier in the war militants had often protested at being ostracised by non-Rexists, they now positively sought the security offered by isolation. Innumerable circulars warned members of the need for internal discipline and, in a further step towards complete segregation, the *Jeunesse Légionnaire* planned to establish its own schools for the children of supporters of the Nazi cause. All unnecessary contact with those beyond the ranks of Rex was avoided and Louis Collard warned in March 1944 that to communicate any details of Rexist activities to those outside the movement, amounted to 'trahison pure et simple'.[161] Despite such threats, there were leaks of information, notably through the actions of individuals who joined Rex in order to provide intelligence to the Resistance, the *Gendarmerie* or the Allied intelligence services. No such spies ever appear to have operated in the Rexist headquarters but they did have some success at a local level where one was the *chef de cabinet* of the *bourgmestre* of Liège while another even succeeded in becoming the German-appointed mayor of the town of Philippeville.[162]

The principal challenge to Rex came not from internal subversion but from direct attacks. The security measures taken by the Rexists as well as the successes of the German police did bring about a brief dip in the number of attacks during the spring of 1944[163] but the Allied invasion led to a prompt and dramatic escalation in Resistance activity. According to statistics compiled by the Belgian police, there were 94 attacks on pro-German individuals during May which resulted in 74 deaths. In June, this rose to 151 attacks and 110 deaths and in July there were 286 attacks resulting in 217 deaths.[164] These were national figures and only a proportion of the victims were Rexists but Degrelle's followers remained a favourite target of the Resistance and their supporters featured prominently amongst the dead.

The atmosphere during these final months of the Occupation was described by many observers as akin to a civil war. For example, the Brussels lawyer and future Minister of Justice, Paul Struye, in a confidential report written for the government in London in the summer of 1944 remarked anxiously: 'Des haines fratricides déchirent le pays, elles déchaînent des instincts de cruauté qu'on croyait éteints dans notre peuple.'[165] Written in the heat of the moment, such descriptions tended to exaggerate the reality. The situation in Belgium never became a civil war, if only because the imbalance in numbers between the collaborationist minority and the pro-Allied majority was so great. Nor, unlike large areas of southern and eastern Europe, did Belgium ever degenerate into a quasi-anarchic situation in which authority had evaporated. There was indeed a substantial increase in lawlessness and criminality but the legal and police structures remained in place and continued to act as a restraint upon individual actions. The exception to this atmosphere of relative normality was the conflict between the Resistance and the collaborationist minority. Both operated outside of the normal patterns of daily life and, just as the Belgian police possessed neither the means nor ultimately the will to control Resistance actions, so the German forces were increasingly unwilling to act as a restraint upon the Rexists and other collaborationists. The consequence was to create the opportunity for the two groups to pursue largely with impunity a conflict which rapidly developed its own momentum of terrorism and counter-terrorism.

The initiative in this struggle always lay with the Resistance which possessed the advantages of numbers, surprise and anonymity. The struggle they waged against the collaborationist minority was pitiless. Rather like the political and sectarian killings in Northern Ireland, their gunmen would strike suddenly at close range before disappearing into the crowd as rapidly as they had emerged. There seemed to be no hiding-place for the Rexists. In July the *Partisans Armés* boasted that their units had launched 'une terrible besogne d'épuration' and the attacks rapidly spread to regions such as the Brabant Wallon which had hitherto been relatively quiet. Assaults occurred on Rexists at all times of the day and night – in their homes, in their offices, in the streets or on crowded buses and trains. Significantly, *Le Pays Réel* no longer gave detailed accounts of each attack but limited itself to a stark roll-call of those martyrs who had fallen for the National Socialist cause.[166]

Once again, it was not the well-guarded national leaders who fell victim to these attacks. Apart from Jean Danly who died in August in a random Allied air attack on his car,[167] no member of the Rexist headquarters was killed during the Occupation. Instead, it was their supporters in the towns and villages of Wallonia who bore the brunt of the violence. Public office-holders, notably *bourgmestres*, remained a favourite target but, with the deployment of the *Formations B*, these officials were now better protected and the Resistance turned their attention to other more vulnerable sections of the movement. Members of the *Légion Wallonie* on leave and adolescents of the *Jeunesse Légionnaire* as well as rank-and-file militants were frequent victims of Resistance attacks.[168] However it was the increasing number of attacks on the parents, wives and even occasionally the children of Rexists and *légionnaires* which attracted the most attention.[169] There were several examples of families virtually wiped out by such attacks and it is clear that, as far as groups such as the *Partisans Armés* were concerned, all those associated with Rex were legitimate targets. As Matthys remarked: 'Si nous étions aveuglés par nos illusions, la Résistance était éclairée par ses certitudes.'[170]

It is impossible to establish with any certainty the total number of Rexists killed during the Occupation. The circumstances of the times did not lend themselves to accurate record keeping and the spectacular figures advanced since the war by Degrelle and other former Rexists are undoubtedly grossly exaggerated. Victor Matthys proposed the more plausible total of approximately 700 Rexist dead and, although this too may have been an exaggeration, the true figure undoubtedly amounted to several hundred.[171]

The Resistance attacks made the Rexists fugitives within their own country. Some sent their families away to distant havens[172] while others abandoned their homes. Those who lived in the countryside or in small towns felt especially vulnerable to attack and during 1944 there was a steady exodus of Rexists from rural areas towards the greater security offered by larger towns. Some fled as far as Brussels believing, perhaps with some justification, that only the anonymity of city life would enable them to escape the attentions of the Resistance.[173] Belgium had become an alien land for the Rexists and in the last weeks of the Occupation one group of militants even began to produce an underground newspaper entitled *L'Action Directe: journal clandestin d'Ordre Nouveau*. Its crudely typed format closely resembled the style of newspaper produced by patriotic groups but the irony was that it was now the Rexists who were entering this clandestine world while their adversaries prepared for the liberation and a return to legality.[174]

The Rexist leaders and their German allies continued to seek some means of countering the Resistance attacks. Extra staff were recruited for the *Formations B* and, on the rare instances when they were able to mobilise sufficient forces, the German authorities launched large-scale offensives against Resistance groups active in a particular area.[175] However such actions on the whole achieved little and many Rexists resorted to cruder forms of guaranteeing their security. Foremost amongst these was the mania for compiling lists of local patriotic dignitaries who were to be arrested – or even shot – by the German forces in the event of an attack on a Rexist. Already as early as 1942 some such lists appear to have been drawn up by Rexists anxious to guarantee their security or flaunt their power within the local community, but it was in the last year of the Occupation that their number increased spectacularly with numerous examples of militants supplying the German authorities with the names of potential hostages.[176] Some openly boasted of the existence of these lists in the hope of deterring Resistance attacks. Others were more pessimistic, merely drawing some consolation from the knowledge that their deaths would not pass unavenged. As one prominent Rexist in Bastogne was reported to have remarked: 'Si on me fait disparaître, j'ai cette fiche de consolation qu'une dizaine de personnes seront arrêtés.'[177] During the summer of 1944 this proved all too often to be the case as prominent local citizens were arrested by the Germans in response to attacks on Rexists or merely as a precautionary measure. Many of these hostages were simply imprisoned but others were shot or deported to camps in Germany. Local Rexists encouraged the Germans in this work and on occasions carried out their own arrests. In Mons, for example, the brigade of the *DSI* accompanied by officials of the *cercle* arrested a dozen hostages in July who were transferred to a Brussels prison.[178]

The taking of hostages is a traditional response by a beleaguered community and has many parallels in the histories of other occupied territories both past and present. It remains unclear, however, whether the drawing up of lists of potential hostages was a spontaneous reaction on the part of local militants or was organised by the national leadership. The opponents of Rex had no doubt that a general instruction had been issued by the Rexist *Etat-Major* to local groups to draw up lists of hostages and it was alleged after the war that the *Département Politique* had also provided the names of potential hostages to the *Militärverwaltung*. No evidence has survived of such lists and, not surprisingly, the Rexist leaders denied after the war that they had ever encouraged their members to supply the German authorities with the names of hostages.[179] These issues of responsibility are, however, ultimately of less importance than the mentality which the compilation of these lists revealed. The Rexists had become a community at war with their compatriots. Like conquerors in a foreign land or colonialists anxious to subdue a restive population, they resorted to crude forms of intimidation which they knew would inevitably result in deaths and suffering.

The same overriding logic of revenge also lay behind the decision of the Rexist leadership to return to the policy of 'counter-terrorism' initiated in February with the murder of Bovesse. The incident which provoked this bloody response was the murder by a unit of the *Armée Secrète* of the brother of the *Chef de Rex*, Edouard Degrelle, on 8 July. He was a pharmacist in Degrelle's native town of Bouillon in the Ardennes who, although he had made no secret of his support for his brother's views, had never played more than a very modest role in Rex. For his assassins – who included three gendarmes – it was sufficient that he was a known sympathiser of the German cause and they must have been aware that his murder would inevitably lead to reprisals.[180] Immediately after the assassination, the German authorities arrested 46 local men but this did not satisfy the Rexists and late in the evening of 9 July Jean Danly, the head of the *Service d'action sociale* in the Rexist *Etat-Major*, Paul Flament of the *DSI* and Matthys' chauffeur Pierre Manfroid arrived in Bouillon determined to exact vengeance. They intended to murder several local figures but, in the event, they could find only one, Henri Charles, who like Degrelle's brother was a pharmacist. He was shot by Danly on the steps of his home and the three assassins fled the town pursued by a German police patrol which, after a dramatic car chase, succeeded in apprehending the men.[181]

Under interrogation, the three Rexists readily admitted that the attack had been masterminded by Charles Lambinon who, they claimed, had acted on the orders of Matthys. This was apparently confirmed in a report sent by the Rexist *Etat-Major* to the *Dienstelle Jungclaus* which intervened to ensure their release.[182] Danly was killed a few weeks later and the other participants in the murder disappeared after the war, making it impossible to establish with certainty the extent of Matthys' involvement. After the war he disclaimed all responsibility for the crime insisting that the killers had acted on their own initiative;[183] but the participation of his chauffeur as well as the testimony of those involved strongly suggests that the *Chef de Rex ad interim* did in fact give his approval to what he must have known would be an act of bloody revenge.

Matthys may well have been influenced by the knowledge that Degrelle would wish to see the death of his brother avenged. Indeed, when the *Chef de Rex* returned in haste from Germany on 10 July, he immediately demanded additional measures, declaring that 'un malheur appelle un autre malheur'. He insisted that the German police arrest three further hostages in Bouillon and in an angry telegram to Himmler he called for Draconian measures to be taken against the entire Belgian population including the immediate execution of 100 hostages. In a reply sent to Jungclaus, the *Reichsführer-SS* ignored these demands but ordered Jungclaus to initiate a 'radikalen Gegenterror' against those responsible for Resistance attacks. Such promises were not, however, sufficient to appease Degrelle and, in response to his continued pressure for vengeance, the three additional hostages were killed in cold blood by the German police near Bouillon on 21 July.[184]

The murders at Bouillon formed part of a wave of Rexist reprisal actions during the final months of the Occupation. Already in a number of localities militants had launched their own bloody campaigns against their enemies. At Ottignies in the Brabant Wallon, unidentified Rexists burst into the church and seized a priest well known for his pro-Allied views. He was bundled into their car and, shortly afterwards, his corpse was found in a nearby wood. Elsewhere, a *comité de représailles* was created by Rexists and their allies in Namur while in Mons another group, the *Bande Chéron*, was responsible for at least eight murders during July and August.[185] This chaotic and indiscriminate violence owed nothing to central planning and was the antithesis of Matthys' intention of limited 'counter-terrorism' directed against prominent patriotic dignitaries. The leadership were, as Matthys subsequently admitted, aware of these local initiatives[186] but, even had they wished to do so, there was little that they could have done to restrain their followers. Many Rexists had decided that the time had come to settle outstanding scores and, once initiated, this orgy of violence was impossible to contain.

The Rexists who carried out these murders were often men from the fringes of the movement who had joined Rex or one of its paramilitary units during the war years. In Charleroi, for example, many of the worst crimes were the work of the *Formations B*, three of the most sinister of whose members were termed by their colleagues, the 'Pieds Nickelés'. Two of this trio died before the end of the war but the third, Honoré Navez, who had only joined Rex in 1943, did survive to stand trial and achieved the melancholy distinction of being condemned to death ten times. It was criminal figures such as Navez who gave to some Rexist groups of the latter war years the character of 'un gang américain'.[187] But not all of the murders committed by Rexists during 1944 were the work of such men. The *Bande Chéron* in Mons, for example, included an electrical engineer and a schoolteacher among its number while Louis Bertrand, the head of the *Formations B* in Charleroi and the inspiration behind many of its violent actions, was a small-time greengrocer who had first joined Rex in 1936. He worked closely with another long-standing Rexist business-man, Henri Merlot, who directed the Charleroi brigade of Lambinon's *DSI*.[188] Not all Rexist veterans did, of course, share their views and even at this late stage several militants withdrew from the movement rather than be involved in these atrocities.[189] Nevertheless, the prominent role played by experienced militants in this terrorism highlighted the radicalisation which had occurred within the ranks of Rex. The Allied advance, the 'psychose de terreur' fostered by the Resistance attacks and the millenarian rhetoric of the Rexist leaders came together to create an apocalyptic atmosphere in which the Rexists, seeing their own dreams crumble to dust, struck out blindly against the victors of tomorrow.[190]

This rapid escalation in violence soon spread to the Rexist headquarters. Lambinon and his associates in the *DSI* and the leaders of the *Jeunesse Légionnaire* as well as certain employees of the *Département Politique* and the *Ersatzkommando* formed a loose coalition of radicals who encouraged and even participated in the wave of local terrorism.[191] In the summer of 1944 these elements distributed a number of tracts within the Rexist offices in Brussels including a stencilled manifesto circulated to all members of the *Etat-Major* in June which demanded reprisals against those members of the bourgeoisie deemed to be the 'moral accomplices' of the Resistance. In language which perhaps unconsciously revealed the experiences of a number of Rexists in the Belgian Congo, these radicals claimed that large-scale counter-terrorism was now unavoidable: 'les membres des mouve-ments d'Ordre Nouveau vivent perpétuellement dans une sorte de jongle et dans la jongle on applique les lois de la jongle, on tue pour n'être pas tué, on "liquide" les indigènes simplement suspects, on répond à la terreur par une super-terreur. C'est l'A.B.C. du métier de colon, et cela doit devenir le principe premier de notre action de défricheurs de la brousse politicienne . . . nous souhaitons personnellement qu'on frappe fort, qu'on frappe dur, qu'on frappe impitoyablement.'[192] A few weeks later, the underground Rexist paper, *L'Action Directe*, returned to the same theme encouraging its readers to jettison all outmoded scruples: 'Nous DEVONS pour protéger la vie des nôtres nous montrer de féroces justiciers, nous DEVONS faire de notre coeur une pierre . . . nous DEVONS fermer les yeux avec une joie sadique, nous DEVONS pour vivre, tuer, tuer encore non pas comme des soldats mais comme des fauves.'[193]

The unofficial leader of these radicals was, not surprisingly, Joseph Pévenasse. His dissatisfaction with the leadership of Matthys and Collard had intensified during 1944 and, although the three men had worked together in seeking to renovate the Rexist militias, an undercurrent of tension appears to have always been present. Finally, in the early summer Matthys and Collard decided to act against the *Inspecteur de la Milice*. Pévenasse was abruptly stripped of his responsibilities and departed from the Rexist headquarters.[194]

Much regarding the exact circumstances of this crisis remains unclear. Pévenasse disappeared in Germany in 1945 and events can only be reconstructed from the testimony provided by Matthys and Collard to their post-war interrogators. It is evident, however, that it was the culmination of the long-standing differences between Pévenasse and his superiors. In part, this was a personal struggle between Collard and the *Inspecteur de la Milice* for control of the Rexist headquarters. Collard had, as we have seen, long sought to concentrate power within the *Etat-Major* in his own hands and he appears to have consistently attempted to undermine Pévenasse's autonomy by, for example, in April transferring the former administrator of the *Formations B*, Pierre Pauly, from Pévenasse's *Inspectorat* to his own secretariat.[195] The immediate cause of Pévenasse's downfall was, however, secret discussions which he had been holding with the SS representative in Belgium, Richard Jungclaus. At these meetings, the *Inspecteur de la Milice* apparently proposed the transfer of the *Formations B* into an *Allgemeine SS* operating under SS control. This was an idea in line with his long-standing ambition of incorporating Rex into an SS-style military organisation and it was no doubt welcomed by Jungclaus who was eager to resolve the manpower shortage which hindered his implementation of the energetic police measures demanded by Himmler.[196] But, unfortunately for Pévenasse, Matthys learnt of these discussions, apparently from Moskopff, Jungclaus' deputy for Walloon affairs and a close ally of the Rexist leaders. Matthys was, it seems, incensed. He had long opposed the creation of an *Allgemeine SS* and he apparently told Pévenasse that he would prefer to dissolve the *Formations B* rather than allow them to pass out of Rexist control.[197] In addition, he must also have suspected, probably not without reason, that this proposal was merely the prelude to more far-reaching changes which would have seen him ousted from power within Rex in order to make way for Pévenasse and his fellow radicals.

Thus, encouraged no doubt by Collard, Matthys moved decisively against Pévenasse. The *Chef de Rex ad interim* announced that he was assuming personal control of all policy towards the Rexist militias and a furious Pévenasse departed from the Rexist headquarters, according to an eye-witness, 'en claquant la porte'.[198] He was never to return, spending much of the last weeks of the Occupation in his native Charleroi where he encouraged local militants in their terrorist campaigns. Although Pévenasse was not formally dismissed as *Inspecteur de la Milice*, his responsibilities were assumed by Louis Collard who in addition to his other titles was appointed to the new post of *Chef d'Etat-Major de la Milice* and in effect took command of the *Formations B*.[199] Pévenasse's sudden departure ended any prospect of a transfer of power within the Rexist leadership. Radicals within the movement remained dissatisfied with Matthys and Collard but no obvious candidate now existed to replace them and they could only hope that Degrelle might intervene to impose external figures drawn from the *Jeunesse Légionnaire* or the *Légion Wallonie*.[200]

The prospect of any such intervention was, however, remote. When on 10 July he had returned to Belgium on receiving the news of his brother's death, Degrelle had announced to Himmler that it was his duty at this crucial time to remain with his men in Belgium.[201] If this had proved to be the case, the history of Rex during the last weeks of the Occupation might have been rather different; but Degrelle's resolve lasted scarcely more than a week. A few days after his return he may have made a brief visit to Paris and on 22 or 23 July he impulsively left Brussels again to rejoin the *Légion* which had been deployed on the Estonian front.[202] Degrelle was not to return before the liberation and, apart from a brief excursion into the Ardennes during the von Runstedt offensive in December 1944, he has never since set foot on Belgian soil. But even before his departure his political career within his native land had already ended and during these final weeks of the Occupation Degrelle appeared remarkably unconcerned as to the fate of his followers in Belgium. On 13 August he wrote a long, optimistic letter to Matthys from the front line in which he described his military adventures, reassuring his deputy that a reversal in German military fortunes remained possible. However, having rediscovered his taste for the military life, Degrelle was clearly in no hurry to return to the less heroic atmosphere of Belgium. He informed Matthys that he intended to remain at the front for the foreseeable future and, apart from requesting that his wife and family were cared for, he had no instructions to pass on to the Rexist leaders.[203]

Thus, Matthys and Collard were left to respond as best they could to the rapidly evolving political and military situation. This responsibility fell essentially on Louis Collard. Matthys had by now largely withdrawn from the cares of daily administration and during July and August 1944 it was Collard who ruled supreme over the Rexist headquarters. He was a skilled but domineering administrator who cajoled and threatened the other staff as he continued to mould the Rexist bureaucracy into a tool of his wishes. But, as his powers increased, so his unpredictable and aggressive nature became more evident. His impulsive marriage in June to a young official in the Rexist women's organisation had little impact on his total dedication to his work and, apart from brief visits to the *SS* offices in Berlin, he was rarely absent from the *Etat-Major*.[204] In addition, the influence of an artificial stimulant which he had been taking for a number of months caused Collard's behaviour to become increasingly erratic. As a medical expert reported at his trial, the drug provoked 'un état permanent d'excitation psychique et motrice' which increased yet further his capacity for work but also led to sudden outbursts of irrational anger.[205]

The subordination of the movement to the whims of a young, despotic figure who himself took refuge in a frenetic commitment to administration conveys well the void in which Rex operated during these last months of the Occupation. Though the efforts of Collard ensured that there was no slackening in the activities of the Rexist headquarters until the very eve of the liberation, the world of the Rexist leaders became ever more marked by their isolation from the external world. This was certainly not true of all of the leadership. Protected by the anonymity of life in a large city, inconspicuous members of the *Etat-Major* continued to lead remarkably normal lives. Charles Raty, the administrator of the Rexist press and Degrelle's brother-in-law, for example lived throughout the Occupation in the Brussels suburb of Uccle where his neighbours portrayed him as a quiet, unassuming man who never discussed politics and appeared interested only in his stamp collection.[206] But such normal patterns of life had long become impossible for the principal leaders who lived in securely guarded flats (often sequestrated from their Jewish owners) and only ever mixed with fellow Rexists.[207] This isolation seems to have encouraged an air of decadence and corruption in which traditional constraints on behaviour seemed irrelevant. Provincial Rexists who visited the *Etat-Major* were alienated by the general atmosphere of immorality and irresponsibility which they sensed among a leadership who, conscious of the fragility of their existence, seemed determined to savour to the full the last drops of power which the faltering Nazi hold on Belgium offered them.[208] The possibility of any reversal of policy had long since become inconceivable. Instead, rather like men trapped in a cave with a diminishing supply of oxygen who are aware of their predicament but are powerless to alter it, they pursued their policies with a blind determination which, as Matthys subsequently wrote, could only be explained as a product of: 'l'extraordinaire existence en vase clos que nous avons menée, de cet isolement spirituel . . . dans lequel nous avons été confinés. Pendant ces années, je n'ai connu, et je n'ai vu que des hommes qui pensaient, qui jugeaient et qui sentaient comme moi.'[209]

Rexist actions during the last weeks of the Occupation were a strange combination of lucidity and blindness. Aware for the first time of the imminence of their defeat, they nevertheless persisted in actions which not only confirmed but reinforced the errors of the previous years. Collaboration, they now recognised, was a bankrupt tactic but it was one with which they refused to break and which led them on to commit crimes which condemned beyond redemption not only them but also their cause.

The new-found realism of the Rexist leaders was evident in their response to both the external military situation and developments within Belgium. Everything, as they were only too aware, would depend on the outcome of the battles taking place in France and, as the Rexists observed these events, it gradually dawned on them that the German armies were indeed doomed to defeat. The distant conflicts on the Eastern front had always had an unreal character about which it had been easy for the Rexists to be relatively sanguine. But the battles in France opened their eyes and, as their faith in German military resilience evaporated, so the tone of their propaganda changed markedly. The Rexist press finally admitted that the military situation was desperate[210] and, once the Allied forces had broken out of their bridgehead in Normandy, it was obvious even to the leaders of Rex that their advance had gained a momentum which was unlikely to be contained before the Rhine. Thus, even if – as some apparently hoped – the Germans did regroup in order to delay the Allies at the Somme,[211] the Rexists were forced to accept that a Nazi retreat from Belgium had become an all too imminent probability. The year 1944 was proving to be a repeat of 1918 and they could only hope that the new weapons being developed would at some stage reverse the imbalance of forces and enable the German armies to return.

The internal situation was similarly discouraging. Compared with much of German-occupied Europe, Belgium had always enjoyed a relatively high standard of living but during these last months many of the normal features of life were severely disrupted. Food supplies became uncertain, while Allied bombing and shortages of fuel and vehicles brought the usual means of communication virtually to a standstill. Daily life was difficult but it was not impossible and the majority of the population, buoyed up by the advance of the Allied armies, bore these hardships with fortitude. The Rexists, however, had no such cause for optimism. During the exceptionally hot days of the summer of 1944, the intensity of the conflict between the Rexists and their opponents increased remorselessly. Armed bands of Resistance fighters, bandits, or of men who fell somewhere between the two categories, roamed the country engaging the Germans and their collaborationist allies in gun battles.[212]

To these factors was added the unexpected shock of the attempted assassination of Hitler on 20 July. In public, the Rexists heralded the *Führer*'s escape as providential but, even if they hoped that the consequent purge would strengthen the hand of radicals sympathetic to Rex, they were forced to accept that even the survival of the Nazi cause within Germany was no longer assured.[213] Closer to home, the fortunes of the Rexists were also effected by Hitler's decision, taken on 12 July, finally to replace the *Wehrmacht* administration in Brussels by a *Zivilverwaltung* headed by a *Reichskommissar*. This change was no surprise. In January the *Führer* had already decided in principle to end von Falkenhausen and Reeder's remarkably long custodianship of German affairs in Belgium and it finally brought the administration of the country in line with the civilian SS-dominated regimes which governed most of German-occupied Europe.[214] This was the transformation for which Degrelle and the Rexists had so long striven and the arrival in Brussels on 18 July of Grohé, the former *Gauleiter* of Cologne, as the new *Reichskommissar* inevitably gave rise to much speculation in collaborationist circles. Shortly before his final departure to the front line, Degrelle hastened to meet the new ruler of Belgium hopeful that Grohé would sweep away the *secrétaires-généraux* in favour of a radical pro-Nazi government. In a letter to the *Reichskommissar*, he stated this aim with customary frankness, declaring: 'Nous avons déjà les communes et les provinces, faisons un coup d'état et emparons-nous du restant.'[215] Hopes of a marked change in Nazi policy in Belgium were, however, to be bitterly disappointed. As Matthys noted in a circular sent to local Rexist officials only two days after Grohé's arrival, the new German administrators lacked both the means and the will to implement radical changes.[216] Jungclaus was indeed finally named as *Höherer SS- und Polizeiführer* with wide police powers but it was already too late for the aggressive counter-terrorist measures so long demanded both by the Rexists and by Himmler to have any impact on the Resistance forces. Most importantly, Grohé proved to be a man of moderate instincts. He retained the *secrétaires-généraux* and in a remarkable move appointed Reeder, the symbol of German caution, as his deputy. Even in apparent defeat, the former *Militärverwaltungschef* was, it seemed, destined to return to frustrate Rexist ambitions.[217]

Thus during the few weeks of its existence the *Zivilverwaltung* enacted few new policies of any consequence and the Rexists were once again deprived of the prize of national political power. Instead, they were obliged to respond to a Resistance which launched itself with unprecedented energy upon the German forces and, more especially, their collaborationist allies. All but certain that the German Occupation was now about to end, the Rexist leaders might have been expected to have concentrated on protecting their depleted ranks of supporters but in fact this awareness of their impending doom drove them forward into one final paroxysm of violence. In August they announced that the hour for 'revolutionary action' had arrived and during the last three weeks of the Occupation Matthys and Collard presided over an unprecedented wave of attacks on their opponents.

This criminal violence was, as the Rexist leaders admitted at the time, partly intended to appease the 'sentiment profond et finalement incoercible' of many of their followers.[218] Pressure for radical measures had continued to build during the weeks following the assassination of Edouard Degrelle. Early in August, for example, a delegation of Rexist officials from Mons had visited Brussels to discuss security in their area with Matthys, possibly receiving from him approval for the murder which occurred soon after-wards of a local patriotic judge.[219] But it was in Charleroi that Rexist terrorism took its most dramatic form. Nowhere in Belgium had the Resistance attacks on supporters of Rex been as intensive as in Charleroi and its environs. The industrial centre of the Hainaut with its small, working-class communities and its strong Socialist tradition provided an ideal environment for the operation of Resistance groups. According to a source close to the *Partisans Armés*, their units assassinated 137 traitors in the Charleroi area from the end of May to 12 July 1944 and the underground newspaper *Front* boasted that eight pro-German figures had been killed by the Partisans in the same region during the week of 16 to 24 July alone.[220] These statistics were probably inflated but it is clear that assassinations of collaborators were taking place at a rate of almost one a day in the Charleroi area during the summer of 1944. In response, Rexist terrorism gathered momentum remorselessly during the last two months of the Occupation. The Belgian police catalogued no fewer than 21 separate acts of violence committed by Rexists between 23 July and 17 August while a survey of the post-war trials of Charleroi Rexists reveals approxi-mately 20 major instances of Rexist violence in the area during July and August 1944 which resulted in the deaths of more than 40 Resistance figures, local dignitaries and innocent bystanders.[221]

The trials after the liberation of those responsible for this violence demonstrated the extent to which Rexist terrorism in the Charleroi region had become an institutionalised phenomenon. Funerals of murdered Rexists were, for example, frequently the occasion for premeditated mob violence during which the houses of patriots were pillaged and set on fire.[222] In addition, well-organised hit-squads of Rexist terrorists operated within the *Formations B* in Charleroi under the direction of its local com-mander Léon Bertrand. He in turn received his orders from more senior figures, including Joseph Pévenasse who helped Bertrand and his col-leagues to identify potential targets and to arrange the practical details of operations.[223]

The local terrorist campaigns in Charleroi and elsewhere also received assistance from some staff of the Rexist *Etat-Major*. In one such case an *ad hoc* coalition of radicals from the Rexist headquarters murdered seven local dignitaries at Wavre and Huy on Sunday 6 August. The original idea for these killings had come from local militants anxious to avenge the deaths of their comrades but it was taken up enthusiastically by a group of national figures, including predictably Charles Lambinon and *légionnaires* from the *Ersatzkommando*. With Jungclaus' approval, they travelled from Brussels to carry out the assassinations accompanied by a number of other figures who had volunteered their services, including Paul Mezzetta of the *Jeunesse Légionnaire* and Albert Regnard from the *Département Politique*.[224]

It was incidents such as this which undoubtedly influenced the decision of Matthys and Collard to abandon all restraint. The new policy was announced by the *Chef de Rex ad interim* at a national rally held in Brussels on 13 August. For the last time, the Rexists gathered in the Palais des Beaux Arts for what was stated to be the most important event in the history of Rex since Degrelle's dramatic espousal of the ideas of the SS on 17 January 1943. Despite the difficulties of travelling to Brussels, approximately 2,000 militants as well as Jungclaus and other German dignitaries were present to hear Matthys announce that 'nous sommes arrivés à l'heure de l'action révolutionnaire'.[225] The political struggle, he proclaimed, had reached its final phase: 'ce qui exclut formellement pour le proche avenir, les demi-teintes et les demi-convictions. Notre idée politique doit s'affirmer à nouveau, dans toute son intransigeante pureté, dans toute sa rigueur et en dehors de tout esprit de compromis.'[226] The Rexists, he declared, had demonstrated 'une patience excessive' in allowing their supporters to be picked off like rabbits by the Resistance. But this chapter in their history was closed and it was now they who would seize the offensive in attacking their enemies. As an article published in *Le Pays Réel* the following day was careful to stress, this did not mean that the Rexists had become mere 'buveurs de sang' and in a faint echo of Matthys' calls earlier in the year for a limited, 'scientific' counter-terrorism the Rexist daily promised that their avenging violence would be concentrated on those prominent personalities whom, it obstinately continued to insist, were the inspiration behind the Resistance actions.[227] This was, however, no more than a gesture. The real message of Matthys' speech was that all violence was legitimate and, amidst what *Le Pays Réel* claimed was frenetic applause from the assembled militants, the Rexist leader concluded his speech with the unambivalent declaration that: 'Maintenant, c'est à nous d'attaquer tout ce qui entrave notre route, c'est à nous de nous affirmer les plus forts, c'est à nous de nous faire redouter par tous les moyens.'[228]

The Belgian population did not have to wait long to discover the consequences of these threats. Only four days later, on the morning of 17

August, the Rexist *bourgmestre* of *Grand Charleroi*, Oswald Englebin, was killed together with his wife and son in a Resistance attack on his heavily protected car at Courcelles on the outskirts of Charleroi. Englebin, who had had a reputation as something of a moderate figure, had taken over as mayor after his predecessor, Teughels, had himself fallen victim to a Resistance attack and the assassination of a figure of such importance so soon after Matthys' speech could not but lead with grim inevitability to bloody Rexist reprisals. Indeed, soon after the attack Pévenasse and the *échevins* of *Grand Charleroi* as well as a group of the *Formations B* arrived in Courcelles and, after attempting without success to apprehend the attackers, began arresting local figures as well as setting fire to houses and public buildings.[229]

What gave these events their unique character in the grim catalogue of Rexist atrocities was the immediate decision of Victor Matthys that the Rexist leadership should take charge of the reprisal actions. Matthys learnt of Englebin's death early in the afternoon of 17 August and he presided soon after at a meeting – attended by Collard, Lambinon, Louis Jacobs of the *Ersatzkommando*, Léon Bertrand from Charleroi and Moskopff of Jungclaus' staff – at which it was agreed that the reprisals would be carried out by members of the Brussels *Etat-Major* acting in conjunction with local Charleroi militants.[230] Moskopff, for his part, assured the Rexist leaders of Jungclaus' support. The head of the *SS* in Belgium no doubt saw in the proposed reprisals an opportunity to implement Himmler's oft-repeated demand for violent counter-terrorist measures and, exploiting the new powers granted to him as *HSSPF* of Belgium, he ensured that the Rexists were allowed a free hand by ordering that all German police be withdrawn from Charleroi until the following day.[231] During the afternoon and evening feverish preparations went ahead for this unprecedented operation. At a meeting of the staff of the Rexist headquarters, volunteers were enrolled and these were supplemented by additional forces summoned by Collard from the *Volontaires du Travail* as well as from the Brussels staff of the *Formations B*. These men were then divided into teams and, where necessary, were issued with more powerful weapons.[232]

By midnight the preparations had been completed and the Rexists drove in a convoy of 13 vehicles to the offices of the *Formations B* in Charleroi. They were met there by Pévenasse, who throughout the day had directed Rexist activities in the town with evident enthusiasm. The approximately 25 Rexists from Brussels were combined with more than 100 local militants and Matthys, Collard and Pévenasse hastily agreed upon a list of 100 local dignitaries who were to be arrested.[233] During the night teams of Rexists – including Matthys and the other leaders – toured Charleroi seeking out their victims and setting fire to a number of houses. But, despite Matthys' order that in the absence of the intended targets their wives should be arrested instead, they met with only limited success. All too aware of the likely consequences of Englebin's death, many local figures had gone into hiding and only some 20 detainees were brought to the offices of the *Formations B*. There, they were partially stripped and deprived of their valuables before being taken to Courcelles where the house nearest to the scene of Englebin's murder had been requisitioned as a makeshift prison.[234] Matthys and Collard arrived soon afterwards and gave the command that the hostages should be killed. A number of the Rexists from Brussels were apparently reluctant to carry out this order but, after pressure from Lambinon and possibly Matthys, sufficient volunteers were found and the 19 victims, including several women and a priest, were shot one after the other at close range. Their corpses were then dumped unceremoniously at the place where Englebin had been assassinated. By dawn the mission was accomplished and the Rexist staff returned to Brussels where they were offered a drink and congratulated by Matthys on their act of revolutionary vengeance.[235]

Together with those murdered in other reprisals committed in the Charleroi area in the aftermath of Englebin's death, the total number of those killed on 17–18 August amounted to 27, making the 'tuerie de Courcelles' by far the most horrific of all Rexist atrocities. Those who died were ordinary citizens chosen almost at random not because of their links with the Resistance but, as Matthys subsequently explained to his post-war interrogators, because they were deemed to have contributed to 'le climat moral' in which attacks on Rexists had come to be regarded as legitimate.[236] It was, however, the direct involvement of the Rexist leadership which gave this atrocity its unique character. The Charleroi Rexists would have been all too capable of carrying out their own reprisals but, seized by a 'folie sanguinaire',[237] Matthys and his colleagues directed and gloried in a terrorist act which in its scale and ruthlessness was almost without precedent in Belgium. Nothing could have demonstrated more starkly the failure of the Rexist cause. From a fringe political organisation, it had descended to the level of a band of criminal outlaws who could excel only in the black arts of violence.

Although somewhat overshadowed by the horror of Courcelles, Rexist activities continued almost unabated during the final weeks of the Occupation. By now it was clear that the arrival of the Allies was imminent and all militants were incited to consider themselves soldiers in the front line 'où il faut savoir mourir, et savoir tuer'. Under the vigilant supervision of Louis Collard, the Rexist headquarters appears to have operated much as normal and in many localities there was similarly a remarkable air of normality which belied the rapid approach of the Allied armies. In Brussels local groups continued to hold meetings while in Charleroi plans were going ahead for the official inauguration of a memorial to Englebin.[238]

But it was once again terrorist operations which dominated these weeks. Many of these were directed by Louis Collard who, since his appointment as *Chef d'Etat-Major de la Milice*, exerted direct control over such matters. Originally a supporter of Matthys' efforts to restrain Rexist terrorism, Collard's attitude changed markedly during the summer of 1944. He began to work closely with Lambinon's *DSI*[239] and he played a prominent role in the planning and execution of the major operation carried out by the Germans and their allies from 26 to 28 August against Resistance units active near Ciney in the hills south of Namur. Few German troops could be spared for the operation and at the end of July Collard visited the Gestapo offices in the nearby town of Dinant to arrange the participation of Rexist forces.[240] Subsequently, as many as 600 Rexists took part in this military-style campaign under the command of the former head of the *Légion*, Pierre Pauly, including contingents from the *Légion Wallonie* training camp, the *Gardes Wallonnes*, the *DSI* and about 100 members of the Brussels *Formations de Combat* as well as a considerable number of rank-and-file militants. Despite the numbers involved, the operation achieved little. The Resistance groups evaded their pursuers who resorted instead to widespread intimidation, pillaging and violence against the local population.[241]

Unable to engage the Resistance groups in direct combat, the Rexists vented their frustration on those dignitaries who they still claimed acted as the patrons of the Resistance. This insistence that the Resistance groups were no more than a conspiracy orchestrated by the reactionary bourgeoisie had become in effect the alibi for an indiscriminate campaign of violence against a social and political elite who, with the advance of the Allies, stood poised to return to power. Rex, with its crude rhetoric of social revolution, found it convenient to use this elite as scapegoats for their own failures and, during the last days of August, as many as 20,000 copies of an anonymous tract signed 'La Brigade Rouge' were distributed from the Rexist *Etat-Major* to the homes of figures of the Belgian bourgeoisie. Its tone was at first quite measured, detailing the attacks perpetrated on Rexists and their families, but the threat directed at the recipients in its final paragraphs was emphatic: 'Lorsqu'il s'agit de tuer ou d'être tué, plus aucune discussion n'est possible: on tue.'[242]

Thus, during these last days of the Occupation, the Rexists struck out at any vulnerable local and national dignitaries. Typical of such attacks was the murder of *bâtonnier* Braffort, a prominent figure in the Brussels legal world, who was killed in response to an attempt on the life of George Dubois, Degrelle's lawyer and a well-known Rexist sympathiser. As soon as Collard learnt of this attack, he ordered Lambinon's *DSI* to arrest a number of leading legal figures. An informer in the Rexist police was able to warn nearly all of the intended victims but Braffort was arrested by the *DSI* on 22 August and at a meeting at Collard's home that evening it was decided – despite a plea by Dubois from his hospital bed that no more blood be spilt – that he should be murdered. Collard's assistants in the *Département Politique*, Colman, Regnard and Saussez, went to the headquarters of the *DSI* where, with the assistance of Lambinon's men, they beat Braffort unconscious and drove him to a wood outside Brussels before murdering him in cold blood.[243]

At his trial, Matthys claimed that he was unaware of many of these crimes and it does seem that, after organising the reprisals at Courcelles, the *Chef de Rex ad interim* played little further part in Rexist activities. Soon after returning from Charleroi, Matthys took the strange decision to leave Brussels to spend a holiday at a Rexist hotel in Dinant and he returned to the Belgian capital only on the eve of the German evacuation.[244] Quite why he should have chosen to leave Brussels at this critical moment remains unclear. Perhaps not even the imminent arrival of the Allied armies could lead him to break with the ritual of an August holiday but it may also have reflected the feelings of despair and even of remorse which seem to have overcome him in the aftermath of the Courcelles killings. Whatever the explanation, however, Matthys' departure provided a fitting conclusion to the evolution which had taken place in power within Rex during the latter years of the Occupation. Matthys had abandoned all but a semblance of authority and it was Louis Collard who ruled supreme over the movement.

Collard had little time in which to enjoy his power. Suddenly, at the end of August the Germans began to retreat from Belgium, evacuating their forces from nearly all of the country within a few days. This precipitate withdrawal took the Rexists largely by surprise. Despite the evidence of the previous months, they had not expected the Germans to retreat so abruptly, believing instead that their withdrawal would be preceded by prolonged battles within Belgium itself. Thus, when the German troops began to flood east, the Rexists, along with other collaborators, were presented with a stark choice between accompanying them or remaining behind to face the revenge of the Resistance and the military justice promised by the government-in-exile. In many cases, Rexists had only a few hours in which to make this choice and it was not surprising that, amidst the atmosphere of general panic, only a few, generally those of a more moderate ilk, chose to remain in Belgium.[245] Most opted instead for exile. Some hoped to continue the Rexist struggle from the Reich but most were simply anxious to escape the retribution of their compatriots and, although a few perhaps cherished the hope of returning to Belgium once popular passions had subsided, others undoubtedly hoped to begin a new life in a distant land.[246]

The evacuation was chaotic and undignified. The Rexist leaders had access to cars or were able to hitch a lift from the German forces[247] but most militants had no such means at their disposal. Hastily arranged trains from the Gare du Nord in Brussels were the salvation of many but others, especially those from rural areas, were forced to requisition lorries or even horses in order to make their escape.[248] All fled towards the East, occasionally pausing for a few days in eastern Belgium before finally crossing the German frontier. In total, between 5,000 and 10,000 Rexists appear to have joined this exodus to the Reich where most were lodged in a number of villages and small towns near Hannover.[249] Not all proved able to escape: many were overtaken by the rapid pace of the Allied advance or were taken prisoner by the Resistance. A few chose to make a last stand firing wildly at the Allied troops while others attempted, less heroically, to escape detection by taking to the hills or by participating in the patriotic celebrations.[250] A few even managed to enrol in Resistance groups but the pursuit of those suspected of collaboration was remorseless and nearly all Rexists, along inevitably with a number of innocent citizens, were eventually rounded up and interned in prisons or detention camps. Some were roughly treated[251] but in general the *épuration* in Belgium was more orderly than in much of Europe. Most Resistance groups proved content to hand their prisoners over to the legal authorities and those instances of violence which did occur – such as the Rexist pharmacist in Péruwelz who was reportedly dragged into the Grand Place of the town and lynched from a convenient lamp post – were largely the product of spontaneous mob action.[252]

These unfortunates were, however, for the most part only the small fry of the movement. The Rexist leaders had fled and the manner of their departure was entirely appropriate to their status in Occupied Belgium. They left not as the exponents of a defeated political cause but as the humiliated, detested servants of a departing conqueror. And, like the remnants of any defeated army, they pillaged as they went. On the eve of departure, Lambinon's men in the *DSI* – probably acting with the approval of Collard or Matthys – carried out a number of robberies of Brussels jewellers, the booty of which was shared out equally between the robbers and the Rexist treasury. The ostensible purpose seems to have been to bolster the funds of the movement but, in reality, political motives had given way to mere plunder and their example was imitated by many other Rexists who profited from their last hours on Belgian soil to pillage at random, arriving in Germany laden down with the spoils of their crimes.[253]

Conclusion

DURING the spring and summer of 1946 a strange spectacle unfolded at the
Concordia theatre in Charleroi. Its usual repertoire of light comedies and
variety shows was abandoned and the 2,000 seat theatre became instead
the improvised court-room for a trial which in effect marked the conclusion of the Rexist adventure. Under the system of military justice
established by the Belgian government to investigate those accused of
collaboration, it was the *Conseil de Guerre* of Charleroi which was responsible for judging those Rexists implicated in the horrific murders carried
out at Courcelles during the final, desperate days of the German Occupation. There were 97 defendants who, with the prominent exception
of Degrelle, included almost the entire Rexist leadership. Not all were
present in person. Some of those who had played a major part in the
events of 18 August, such as Charles Lambinon and Joseph Pévenasse,
had evaded capture and were tried in their absence. But many others,
including the former *Chef ad interim* of Rex Victor Matthys and his deputy
Louis Collard, had been apprehended and were brought to court to
respond to the forbidding array of charges levelled at them.

Only a few years before, the Concordia theatre had been the venue for
major Rexist rallies but it now became the setting for a trial which
symbolised the moral and political bankruptcy of the Rexist cause. Wearing
large numbers round their necks to identify them, the defendants sat in the
front rows of the theatre while the hastily adapted stage was occupied by
the judges and lawyers. The murders at Courcelles remained a vivid
memory for many in Charleroi and when the trial began in May a large
crowd gathered early in the morning to hurl abuse at the defendants as
they arrived. But hopes of rapid, dramatic judgements soon gave way to
legal arguments and lengthy presentations of evidence and it was soon
only the journalists and a small number of housewives who continued to
attend the proceedings regularly. The spectacle was not an edifying one.
Some of the defendants, such as Matthys, achieved a modest dignity,
accepting their responsibility for the killings and seeking to make sense of
the tortuous series of events which had led to them. But others – including
Collard – took refuge in implausible bouts of amnesia or sought to elicit

the sympathy of the court through elaborate protestations of remorse. All but a very few had the air of defeated men, unable to take pride in their past actions or to see any hope for the future. In August the trial finally ended and death sentences were passed on all of the principal defendants. An appeal to the *Cour Militaire* followed and Matthys, Collard and a number of the other Rexist leaders also faced a second trial in Brussels in 1947 for their role in the crimes of Lambinon's *Département de Sécurité et d'Information*. It was, however, in the *Gendarmerie* barracks in Charleroi that Matthys, Collard and 25 other Rexists were finally executed in November 1947 for their role in the killings at Courcelles. There were no dramatic last statements. All were shot in the back in less than half an hour and their bodies buried immediately afterwards in the town cemetery.[1]

The trial in the Concordia theatre was merely one of the most dramatic of thousands of similar trials which took place of members of Rex and its affiliated organisations after the liberation. With due respect for the appropriate legal procedures and in the circumstances remarkable thoroughness, the military justice authorities proceeded with what amounted to the last rites for Rex. Amidst the volume of cases and the emotions provoked by the war, there were inevitably some miscarriages of justice. Those prosecuted in the immediate aftermath of the liberation were, on the whole, treated more harshly than those whose trials were delayed until after the final defeat of Germany. In addition, the sentences passed on defendants reflected some discrimination between different categories of collaborationist actions. It was usually the more blatant or public acts which received the sternest sentences. Thus, for example, those who had worn German military uniforms or who had contributed to the German-controlled press were generally given harsher sentences than those whose services to the economic or political interests of Germany had been more discreet but also perhaps more significant.[2] The total number of prosecutions of Rexists remains unknown but more general figures of those accused of collaboration were compiled. There were 57,052 individuals prosecuted between 1944 and 1949 for various collaborationist offences, of whom 53,005 were found guilty. Of these, 21,709 were judged by courts in Brussels or Wallonia. Among the various categories of convictions in francophone Belgium, 12,597 were found guilty of acts of 'military' collaboration and 7,258 of 'political' collaboration. Overall, 89 per cent of those convicted nationally were men and 11 per cent were women; 54 per cent were aged between 16 and 30 and 41 per cent were unmarried.[3]

Prosecution of the Rexists was aided by the evident clarity of their crimes. The continued existence – however fortuitous – of the Pierlot government in London ensured that, unlike many of those accused of collaboration in France who could assert with some plausibility that they had merely been serving the legally-constituted Vichy government, the Rexists were able to claim no higher authority for their actions. They had indeed been rebels and to have remained a member of Rex after Degrelle's initial unambivalent statement of support for Germany in January 1941 was regarded by the post-war authorities as sufficient grounds for prosecution.[4] The Rexist defendants responded to the charges in various ways. Some shunned any defence and appeared in court dressed proudly in their Rexist uniforms. Others boasted of their timely actions during the last months of the Occupation on behalf of Resistance or intelligence organisations. Some challenged the legality of the decrees issued by the London government which provided the basis for much of the post-war prosecution of collaborators; while a few sought, with varying degrees of success, to convince the court of their mental irresponsibility.[5] Most Rexists however could do little more than attempt to refute certain particularly incriminating accusations while pleading that their actions had been motivated by a misplaced desire to serve the best interests of their country. Many expressed regret for their wartime actions and, though a good number of these statements were no more than attempts to curry favour with their judges, there does appear to have been a widespread recognition among former Rexist militants that the policy of collaboration had indeed been a mistake.[6] Some claimed that they had been the dupes of the Germans while others presented themselves as victims of the intoxicating rhetoric of Degrelle. In a characteristic expression of regret, the former *chef de cercle* of La Louvière, Oscar Cus, declared: 'J'ai servi une cause que je croyais juste. Maintenant, je comprends que le national-socialisme a commis des horreurs et que Rex a failli à sa tâche.'[7]

This defence that the Rexists had been, in the words of Matthys, the victims of 'la folle sincérité de nos illusions'[8] had little influence on their judges. 'La trahison n'est pas un idéal' remarked one lawyer at the post-war trials and very few Rexists proved able to convince the courts that they had indeed acted in good faith.[9] Many received long periods of imprisonment and some, generally those who had been directly implicated in the deaths of their compatriots, were sentenced to death.[10] Most of these death sentences were, however, subsequently commuted to life imprisonment and in the later 1940s the Ministry of Justice initiated a policy of gradually releasing almost all of those found guilty of wartime crimes. Some were taken to the French frontier and expelled from the country but many others were simply released within Belgium and a special body was set up to facilitate the 'reintegration' of the former collaborators into society. The reasons for this change in policy were essentially pragmatic. Popular passions had subsided and, with the re-establishment of the democratic parliamentary regime and Belgium's integration into a structure of Cold War alliances, little purpose appeared to be served by maintaining large numbers of former collaborators in detention. This process was facilitated by the mood of the detainees. The passage of time had fostered among many former Rexists a bitterness at their treatment by the post-war authorities but, with the exception of a small core of unrepentant 'nostalgiques', few wished to resume any involvement in politics. They recognised that the Rexist adventure was at an end and most sought simply to forget the past either by emigrating or by resuming as far as possible the pattern of their former lives.[11]

The exhaustion of the Rexist cause revealed during the post-war trials had already been evident during the months that many Rexist refugees spent in Germany after the liberation of Belgium. The thousands of Rexists, *légionnaires* and camp followers who had fled from the Allied advance in September 1944 joined the vast numbers of displaced persons trapped within the diminishing frontiers of the Third Reich. Some found employment in German factories while many young men were enrolled – often unwillingly – in the ranks of the *Légion Wallonie* which continued to fight against the Soviet armies in Eastern Europe. Most of the refugees were, however, housed in a number of villages near Hannover where a Rexist *Etat-Major* was re-established under the direction of Louis Collard and Jean Colman. Matthys played little role in Rexist affairs and instead spent much of his time in Berlin where he assisted Degrelle's efforts to win Nazi support for his increasingly unreal political ambitions.[12]

Morale amongst the Rexist exiles was always low. Beset by material hardships and by rumours of the treatment of former collaborators in liberated Belgium, they found it difficult to believe the assurances of Degrelle that Germany would snatch victory from the jaws of defeat. Instead, this winter of exile was for many militants a period of 'disin-toxification' from the illusions which had sustained them during the years of the German Occupation.[13] With the German retreat from Belgium, Rex had lost its sole remaining rationale and in the enforced idleness of exile there were many who began to criticise the rash opportunism of Degrelle which had led the movement to identify so completely with the Nazi cause. Only among the leaders did some residues of optimism remain. Degrelle, for whom the constraints of external reality had long since lost any force, persevered in his quest for Nazi favour and when the German armies launched their surprise counter-offensive in the Belgian Ardennes in December 1944 he hastened to join the advancing German forces, declaring that he wanted to be the first Belgian to enter 'liberated' Brussels. Although the *Chef de Rex* spent Christmas in a requisitioned château in the Ardennes and was joined soon after by Matthys and Collard at the head of a self-styled *Comité de Libération Wallon*, the German offensive rapidly ground to a halt in the heavily wooded Ardennes.[14] Hopes of a triumphant return to power collapsed and the Allied counter-attack soon forced the Rexist leaders to return to Germany where they observed as demoralised spectators the final disintegration of the Reich. Although the *Légion* par-ticipated in the bloody last ditch battles against the Soviet armies advancing on Berlin, further political activity seemed pointless and at a meeting of

Degrelle, Matthys and Collard at Beckerode on 30 March, the Rexist movement was officially dissolved.[15]

All thoughts had now turned to escape and, as the Allied armies advanced through western Germany in the spring of 1945, a number of leading Rexists including Joseph Pévenasse and Charles Lambinon melted away into the ruins never to be seen again.[16] Some, including José Streel, chose to return to Belgium hoping that they would escape detection amidst the large numbers of conscripted workers and former prisoners of war flooding back from the defeated Reich. Most, including Streel, were apprehended almost immediately but a few Rexists did succeed in leading a secret life for some months in Belgium before eventually being arrested.[17] Others fled further afield. A very few eventually reached Spain or South America, but both Matthys and Collard travelled south through Germany in the hope of finding sanctuary in Switzerland. In common with many other such refugees, they were, however, refused entry at the Swiss frontier and were forced to retreat instead into the Austrian Alps where there were vague hopes that the Nazi armies would make a final stand. Soon this area too came under Allied control and Matthys was arrested on 31 July in a remote Alpine cottage after attempting to make contact with his wife. Collard was more successful at evading capture but he too was finally apprehended by the Belgian *Sûreté* in Innsbruck in February 1946.[18]

Characteristically, Degrelle was more fortunate. He left the remaining units of the *Légion* outside Berlin at the end of April and fled north through Denmark and Norway – both of which remained under German control – to Oslo where he commandeered a light aeroplane. With five colleagues, he flew over much of liberated Europe before crash-landing the aeroplane on a beach at San Sebastian in northern Spain.[19] The *Chef de Rex* was at first anything but a welcome guest. Already embarrassed by the presence of the Vichy regime's Prime Minister Pierre Laval, the Francoist regime wished to expel Degrelle but both the British and the Americans refused to accept responsibility for him and efforts to bring the fugitive to justice soon became bogged down in bilateral negotiations between the Spanish and Belgian governments. In return for handing over the *Chef de Rex*, Franco hoped to receive some form of diplomatic recognition from the Belgian government but, although the Spanish authorities subsequently softened their stance, the Belgian Foreign Minister, Paul-Henri Spaak, refused to allow the fate of Degrelle to become the subject of what he termed a 'marchandage diplomatique'. In August 1946 Degrelle suddenly disappeared from the hospital where he had been convalescing from injuries sustained during the crash-landing and the Spanish government subsequently denied any knowledge of his whereabouts. In fact, the Rexist leader was being protected by influential Spanish friends and he remained in hiding for some ten years before gradually reappearing in public in the late 1950s. The Belgian authorities continued to seek his extradition for war crimes but, once he had managed to obtain Spanish nationality, such hopes became unrealistic and in 1983 the government finally announced that, if the *Chef de Rex* did ever return to Belgium, he would be expelled at the frontier as an 'étranger indésirable'.[20]

During his long exile, Degrelle has remained frozen in the attitudes he adopted during the war years. He has prospered financially and at one stage ran a construction firm which was involved in building bases for the US air force in Spain. His wife was imprisoned in Belgium for some years but she chose not to join her husband in Spain after her release and he subsequently remarried a niece of Joseph Darnand, the former head of the French collaborationist *Milice*.[21] As the last surviving pro-Nazi leader of importance, Degrelle has acquired something of a mythic status among European neo-fascist groups. This is a role which the former *Chef de Rex* has sedulously fostered. In a long series of books and interviews, he has constructed a substantial mythology surrounding his wartime actions, telling elaborate tales of his supposed intimacy with the Nazi leaders and presenting himself as the heir to the European National Socialist tradition.[22] The inaccuracies of Degrelle's historical accounts are not difficult to establish, but his more political statements have on occasions brought him to wider attention. In 1986 his oft-repeated assertion that the Holocaust was no more than a Jewish-inspired fabrication led to him being sued unsuccessfully by a Jewish woman whose family had died during the war and Degrelle has also long maintained close links with elements in the French *Front National*. His writings are occasionally to be found on sale at *Front National* rallies and he is not surprisingly a friend and admirer of the *Front*'s leader Jean-Marie Le Pen whose bombastic demagoguery bears more than a passing resemblance to Degrelle's own former political style.[23]

Exile has not, however, restored the *Chef de Rex*'s fortunes in his native land. His outspoken comments and occasional appearances on Belgian television enjoy a certain *succès de scandale* but, with the exception of small groups of nostalgic admirers, few in Belgium regard him as anything more than a bizarre relic of a bygone era. Nor is it merely Degrelle who has remained an isolated figure. Although the often tortuous history of post-war Belgium has produced a wide variety of movements of political protest, the extreme right has remained, at least until recent years, a political force of marginal importance.

The development of the Cold War and, more especially, the intense political controversy provoked by the wartime actions of Léopold III encouraged the emergence of a patriotic, authoritarian right in the immediate post-liberation years. Shortly before their withdrawal in 1944, the German authorities had transferred the King from his palace in Laeken to the Reich and in his absence his brother, Prince Charles, assumed the throne as regent at the liberation. Léopold's efforts to reach some form of agreement with Germany in 1940, combined with his obstinate refusal in the latter war years to accept the legitimacy of the government-in-exile in London, aroused strong emotions in Belgium after the liberation and, when the King was finally released from German custody in 1945, negotiations between him and the government on the terms for his return to the throne failed to reach an agreement. Léopold went into exile in Switzerland but he never abandoned his intention of recovering a throne from which he believed he had been deposed by the machinations of the politicians and he received strong support not only from the Catholic ecclesiastical hierarchy and many Catholic politicians but also from a number of right-wing leagues. Strongly anti-communist and royalist in character, these groups were in effect the heirs to the ex-combattant leagues of the inter-war years. Although often accused by their adversaries of being a refuge for former collaborationists, they were largely composed of members of non-communist resistance groups such as the *Armée Secrète* and the *Mouvement National Royaliste* for whom the fate of Léopold had become a symbol of the antipathy they felt towards the post-war parliamentary regime.[24] In March 1950 a national referendum produced a narrow majority in favour of the King and in July Léopold finally returned to the royal palace in Brussels. His presence did, however, spark off widespread protests in Brussels as well as in the industrial regions of Wallonia. The King initially refused to bow to these pressures and for a number of days a major constitutional crisis or even some form of civil war appeared imminent. Finally, however, on 1 August Léopold was prevailed upon to accept a compromise solution whereby he agreed to abdicate in favour of his son, Baudouin.[25]

Léopold's reluctant withdrawal consigned the authoritarian right to the political wilderness and none of the extremist movements which emerged during the 1950s and 1960s succeeded in attracting a mass audience. Nevertheless, especially in certain of the lower-middle-class *quartiers* of Brussels such as Ixelles, St Josse and St Gilles, an anti-parliamentary right-wing culture survived. Based on a Poujadist rhetoric of economic grievances, this *commerçant* right focussed much of its anger on the Catholic Party, now renamed the *Parti Social Chrétien* (*PSC*), which it accused of having abandoned the defence of middle-class interests in favour of a quasi-Socialist Christian Democracy. With the support of some intellectuals as well as of certain figures on the traditionalist wing of the *PSC*, these protest groups articulated an ideology of economic and political reform, combined with anti-communism and Belgian nationalism, which on occasions was strongly reminiscent of pre-war Rexism. Indeed, a former member of the *Légion Wallonie*, Jean-Robert Debbaudt, briefly re-established a Rexist movement which won a modest 2,764 votes in Brussels in the elections of 1974.[26]

It was, however, only in the 1980s that the extreme right began to regain wider support. The impetus came originally from Flanders where the long-standing extreme-right undercurrent in Flemish nationalism gave rise to a mass political movement, the *Vlaams Blok*, which won almost 11 per cent of the popular vote in Flanders in the 1991 elections. In Brussels and Wallonia the advance of the extreme right has been less spectacular but nevertheless important. The transient success enjoyed in the early 1980s by the *Union Démocratique pour le Respect du Travail (UDRT)* has given way to a *Front National* modelled on the example of the French movement. This has absorbed many of the militants of other extreme-right franco-phone groups and, although hindered by its lack of the charismatic leadership and mass membership enjoyed by Le Pen's movement in France, it won significant levels of support in Brussels and certain areas of Wallonia in the 1991 elections.[27]

The increase in electoral support for extreme-right groups in the 1980s has, however, been based essentially on the construction of a new ideo-logical platform which bears little resemblance to the ideas represented by Rex. In Belgium, as in much of Europe, the extreme right of the 1980s has been much more than 'old wine in new bottles'. The composition of the wine has also changed. There remain certain points of convergence, such as a hostility to a parasitic political elite combined with a prominent commitment to the defence of the family. But the essential inspiration and character of the right of the 1980s reflect the enormous changes which have taken place in Belgian society since the 1930s. Far from being nostalgic, it seeks to appeal directly to current discontents. Thus, while Rex was Catholic and provincial in origin, the right of the 1980s articulates the concerns of a predominantly urbanised, secular population. It makes little appeal to traditional Belgian nationalism and, in contrast to the anti-capitalist emphasis of much Rexist propaganda, espouses a neo-liberal ideology of market forces. Above all, the electoral appeal of the 1980s right has been based around a virulent antipathy to non-European im-migrant groups and the economic and social danger which they are alleged to represent. Though this rhetoric draws in its most extreme forms on the racist ideas of the Third Reich, and also to some extent mirrors hostility in inter-war Belgium to Jewish immigration from Eastern Europe, the emphasis on the threat to employment and, above all, to law and order supposedly presented by the Turkish and North African immigrant groups reflects present-day concerns and had no significant parallel in the Belgian right of the 1930s.[28]

This absence of any significant Rexist legacy in the post-war history of Belgium underlines the categorical failure of the movement. This went much deeper than the mere fact of the German defeat. Collaboration had destroyed Rex and, if by some bizarre circumstance Nazi Germany had emerged victorious from the war, Rex would none the less have remained a failure. The destructive effect of collaboration on Rex was threefold. First and foremost, it destroyed its political and ideological coherence. As José Streel repeatedly warned the Rexists in his wartime journalism, by tying themselves so closely to the cause of a self-serving and oppressive conqueror they ceased to be a movement with roots in Belgian political life but became an imitative branch of German National Socialism. Secondly, collaboration destroyed what little credibility the Rexists possessed in the eyes of their compatriots. Although there was widespread popular support in 1940 for some form of accommodation with Germany, Degrelle and the Rexists never succeeded in establishing themselves as the legitimate representatives of this opinion. Instead, discredited by the opportunism of their leader and by the indecent haste with which they sought to capitalise upon the defeat, they were regarded as unscrupulous *condottieri* intent upon seeking personal advantage rather than the salvation of their nation. Finally, collaboration destroyed the Rexists themselves. The leaders of the Third Reich had not sought collaboration in German-occupied Europe and, when it did emerge, they had no policy other than to exploit the collaborationist forces for their own ends. This was rooted in the nature of National Socialism. It was in essence a nihilist journey of destruction and, as the more perceptive among the wartime collaborationists had long noted,[29] the various – often conflicting – representatives of the Nazi regime in Brussels shared an inability to conceive of Belgium as anything other than a resource to be exploited. Through a combination of greed, opportunism and ideological conviction, the Rexists allowed themselves to be sucked into this maelstrom which destroyed not only their political credibility but also in many cases their lives.

Only in one perverse respect could Rex be judged to have been a success. This was in its dealings with the Nazi authorities. In 1940 everything seemed likely to militate against the emergence of the Rexists as a major force in Occupied Belgium and yet they had established themselves by 1944 as the favoured protégés of the Nazis in francophone Belgium. This success was in many respects more apparent than real. Degrelle's wild statements that he had been designated as the ruler of a pro-Nazi Burgundian empire or even as Hitler's heir apparent remain no more than figments of his ever fertile imagination[30] and even in 1944 Hitler, Himmler and the other Nazi leaders were still deeply suspicious of the character and ambitions of the Rexist leader. Yet such qualifications should not be allowed to disguise the unlikely achievement of the Rexists in winning the support – however grudging – of the Nazi elite. In 1940 the Flemish Nationalists of the *VNV*, the Socialist leader Henri De Man and, above all, Léopold III appeared far better placed to become the chosen partners of the German forces. Yet, by the latter war years, the demoralised *VNV* leaders were seeking to escape the German embrace, De Man had fled to lonely exile in the French Alps and Léopold III had withdrawn into sullen reflection in the palace of Laeken. Instead, it was the Rexists – along with the extremists of *DeVlag* in Flanders – who had become the indispensable partners of the Nazi rulers of Belgium.

This achievement was a product both of the strengths and the weaknesses of Rex and, more especially, those of its leader. The political skills of Degrelle, though ill-suited to the normal processes of pre-war Belgian politics, equipped him admirably for the very different world of collaboration. His substantial personal charm, ruthless opportunism and taste for complex intrigues gave him advantages which none of his rivals possessed. Degrelle was from the outset a whole-hearted collaborationist who never lost sight of the basic truth that the collaborators were no more than courtiers seeking the favour of the Nazi elite. Unconstrained by considerations of personal dignity or ideological consistency, he manoeuvred ceaselessly within the labyrinth of the Third Reich until finally – aided by the military feats of the *Légion Wallonie* – he achieved at least a partial reward.

This success was, however, ultimately also a product of Degrelle's failings as a political leader. The *Chef de Rex*'s messianic sense of his own destiny enabled him to throw himself into collaboration with an enthusiasm which his more circumspect rivals – constrained by patriotic scruples or merely by an awareness of external realities – could never equal. It was this capacity to close his eyes to developments both in Belgium and on the various military fronts which enabled him to press forward with the policy of collaboration when both the course of the military conflict and the oppressive policies of the German authorities in Belgium caused others to hesitate or withdraw. Whatever his post-war statements, there is no evidence that Degrelle ever seriously contemplated departing from the collaborationist path he had chosen. He had become addicted to the pursuit of power within the Nazi empire and neither the outcome of battles nor the sufferings of his compatriots could lead him to break with that course. Thus, Degrelle's success was in large part a product of his capacity to share in the process of self-deception which enveloped much of the Nazi elite during the later years of the war. At a time when many of the initial exponents of collaboration began to think of their fate after a Nazi defeat, the *Chef de Rex* lived for the present, trusting to his own skills to extricate himself and his followers from any ensuing difficulties. Rather like the sailor who remains behind when all his colleagues have abandoned a sinking ship, he did indeed win a semblance of power but it was an entirely Pyrrhic victory brought about in large measure through the withdrawal of his rivals. In short, Degrelle and Rex were only able to succeed once Nazi Germany had already lost the war.

The final reflection on the failure of the Rexists must, however, be the limited importance of the phenomenon of collaboration. As was stressed at the outset of this study, collaboration was in no sense a historical accident. Its emergence during the Occupation was the product neither of some strange mental aberration nor even of the exceptional circumstances of the war years. On the contrary, it was a revelation of the divisions which already existed within pre-war Belgian society.[31] Nevertheless, both in popular memory and in historical studies, the extent and importance of collaboration has often been exaggerated. As the large number of films, fictionalised accounts and newspaper and magazine articles devoted to the subject bear ample witness, the actions of those who supported the Nazi cause retain a capacity to attract popular interest which is rivalled by few other historical events. In Belgium, as elsewhere in former German-occupied Europe, this popular obsession with collaboration reflects both the still vivid memories of the war years as well as the more general fascination with the failures and weaknesses of the human character. Its inevitable consequence has, however, been to inflate collaboration beyond its true proportions. Rather as in France where post-war attempts to minimise the significance of collaboration have given way since the 1960s to a tendency to present the French as having been 'a nation of collaborators', so in Belgium fascination with the actions of the Rexists and the Flemish collaborationist groups – as well as figures such as Léopold III and Henri De Man – has threatened to obscure the reality that only a small minority opted for the German cause.[32]

Nor is it merely the extent of collaboration which it is all too easy to exaggerate, it is also its significance. As has been stressed repeatedly during this study, collaboration – and, to a lesser extent, resistance – were only ever the actions of a few. Though there was no doubt that in 1940 a majority of the nation leaned towards some form of accommodation with Nazi Germany just as in the latter war years an even more emphatic majority supported the Allied cause, only small minorities chose to throw themselves actively into either camp. The lives of most Belgians were less clear-cut and less heroic. Only *in extremis*, confronted by material desperation or the pressure of family or friends, did many individuals find themselves thrust into making – frequently almost against their will – the dramatic choices symbolised by collaboration or resistance. The majority, whatever their personal sympathies, formed part of neither camp and it is in their actions, with all the daily ambivalences and moments of human weakness and modest heroism, that the real experience of the German Occupation of Belgium resides.[33]

It was also in this grey world between collaboration and resistance that the major forces of Belgian social and political life were to be found. It was no accident that both the resistance and collaborationist groups declared themselves to be in their very different ways 'revolutionaries' for both were, in many respects, revolts by powerless groups on the margins of the Belgian social and political order.[34] This was true not only of the Rexists, but also of the Flemish Nationalists of the *VNV* whose espousal of collaboration reflected the failure of the Belgian inter-war political system to respond effectively to the new aspirations felt by many Flemish people. Similarly, within the Communist-led resistance groups the predominance of young working-class men who had felt most directly the effects of the economic depression of the 1930s indicated how resistance was often as much a rejection of the pre-war order as of the German presence. This was also the case with much of the non-Communist resistance. Especially in the latter war years, groups such as the *Armée Secrète* were able to count on the support of men from within the heart of the Belgian social and political elite. But the initial core of their support – and throughout the war much of their leadership – came from outside of these elites. They were on the whole members of the lower middle class, frequently from an *ancien combattant* or army-officer background, who had provided Rex with much of its electoral support in the mid-1930s but whose intransigent patriotism led them to refuse to accept the military defeat of 1940. These 'résistants de la première heure' were not, however, merely opposed to the traditional German enemy. Their choice of resistance also reflected their opposition to the supposed internal threat from Communism and, above all, to what they regarded as the corrupt and ineffectual political regime. This antipathy to the parliamentary regime, combined with sympathy for schemes of authoritarian constitutional reform or even a royal dictatorship, underlay their actions throughout the Occupation and it was far from surprising that these groups should have provided many of the most enthusiastic supporters of Léopold III in his post-war attempts to return to the throne.

In contrast, the powerful forces of Belgian politics and society – the political leaders, the major industrialists, the Catholic Church, the legal and administrative elites and even the trade union bureaucracies – shunned both collaboration and resistance. Their actions during the difficult war years were in effect a prolonged exercise in the 'politics of accommodation'. In the aftermath of the defeat of 1940, the military situation led them to espouse a cautious *rapprochement* with the German conqueror but, once the course of the war changed, they sought instead to distance themselves from the German authorities – often instigating somewhat symbolic disputes with the *Militärverwaltung* – and to establish discreet but close links with the formerly isolated government-in-exile in London. It was the Catholic Church under the leadership of Cardinal Van Roey which provided the clearest case of such 'accommodation' but its actions were, to a large extent, mirrored by those of the *secrétaires-généraux* of the governmental ministries, the legal authorities in the Palais de Justice and the financial and industrial elite which formed the 'comité Galopin'.[35] The motivation behind their actions was not merely self-interested. They certainly sought to protect their personal power but, in doing so, they also believed that they were acting in the best interests of the nation. Their overriding priority was to ensure the continuity of the social and political structures and the extremes of collaboration and resistance formed no part of this policy. Instead, in common with elites in many other German-occupied countries, these leaders of Belgian society preferred to place the sober preservation of the social and political status quo before the illusory appeals of gesture and sentiment.

The principal challenge to these elites came not from the German or Allied authorities but from the Belgian population. Certainly, at different stages in the war, they feared both a Nazi-imposed collaborationist *coup* and an Allied-sponsored resistance government. But in the event neither Reeder and his *Wehrmacht* colleagues nor their British successors in Brussels after the liberation of September 1944 proved to be interested in favouring those from the collaborationist or the resistance camps who had risked their lives for their respective military causes. Instead they chose to work with and, in effect, to reinforce the power of the established social and political elites who provided the combination of social order and industrial production which favoured the fulfilment of their military goals.

It was, therefore, only by a revolution from within the population that major change could have been enacted. In 1940 it appeared briefly that this might be the case. The manner of the German victory threw discredit upon almost the entire pre-war elite and seemed to open up a bewildering vista of new political possibilities. In the event, however, neither the collaborationist nor the resistance groups proved able to rally a broad coalition of support capable of bringing about major social and political change. In the case of the Rexists, and of the collaborationists more generally, this failure was almost immediate. After the autumn of 1940, their pretensions to represent the opinions of the population were to sound increasingly hollow. For the Resistance, however, their failure was for a long time more disguised. As elsewhere in Occupied Europe, the suf-ferings of the latter war years created a widespread hope, and indeed the expectation, that the eventual defeat of Nazi Germany would be accompanied by large-scale social and political change. But the structures for bringing about this transformation were absent. The resistance groups possessed neither the armed strength nor ultimately the will to mount a major challenge to the status quo. For some months during the winter of 1944–5 an uneasy coexistence of the old and the new prevailed, with the returning ministers from London sharing power with new political figures drawn from the ranks of the Resistance. But, after the Allied military authorities succeeded in enforcing the disarmament of the resistance groups in the autumn of 1944, the initiative passed to the established political forces and the social and political continuity which they represented. Rewarded with medals, glorified in speeches and immortalised in statues, the resistance movements nevertheless ceased to play an important political role and it was largely the institutions and policies of the pre-war years which prevailed.[36]

Viewed in this broader context, the Rexists appear inevitably as little more than a slight historical footnote. Collaboration in Belgium, as in much of German-occupied Europe, was a historical phenomenon the origins of which proved to be more important than its consequences: it was significant not for what it achieved (or even failed to achieve) but for how its existence revealed the social, ideological and political tensions at work within inter-war Belgium. Collaboration was the expression of these tensions and revealed the failure of the country to find a satisfactory political structure to replace the nineteenth-century hegemony of the francophone bourgeoisie. Combined with the economic difficulties of the inter-war years, this failure encouraged the development of dissident groups such as the Rexists and the *VNV* whose radical opposition to the pre-war order led them in 1940 to reject conventional patriotic norms in favour of working with the German forces. Collaboration did, however, rapidly prove to be a political cul-de-sac. Shunned by the majority of their compatriots and unrewarded by the Nazi rulers, the collaborationists became a besieged minority whose desperation was reflected in their increasingly extreme rhetoric. As the war turned to the advantage of the Allies, even the apparent military logic of their pro-German stance evaporated and collaboration became an adventure devoid of any purpose. Though Rexist propagandists might proclaim that they were the agents of a 'National Socialist revolution', self-advancement or, more frequently, self-preservation had taken the place of any political programme. Long before the German retreat of September 1944, the movement had become a political irrelevance and the subsequent trials of Rexist militants served merely as the public expression of its demise. Collaboration had become a disaster which not only destroyed the lives of many followers of Rex, but also consigned their movement to a political oblivion from which there was to be no escape.

Notes

Introduction

1 See M. Conway 'Building the Christian City: Catholics and Politics in Inter-War Francophone Belgium', *Past and Present* No. 128 (Aug. 1990), pp. 117–51.

2 For an excellent modern synthesis of the course of Belgian history, see E. Witte and J. Craeybeckx *La Belgique politique de 1830 à nos jours* (Brussels, 1987).

3 See J. Stengers 'Belgium' in H. Rogger and E. Weber (eds.) *The European Right: A Historical Profile* (London, 1965), pp. 133–56.

4 E. Witte and J. Craeybeckx *Op. cit.*, p. 157; M. Claeys-Van Haegendoren 'L'Eglise et l'Etat au XXe siècle', *Courrier hebdomadaire du CRISP* No. 542–3 (1971); E. Gerard *De Katholieke Partij in crisis* (Leuven, 1985).

5 L. Schepens 'Fascists and Nationalists in Belgium 1919–40' in S.V. Larsen, B. Hagtvet and J.P. Myklebust *Who were the Fascists* (Bergen, 1980), pp. 501–16; F. Balace 'Fascisme et catholicisme politique dans la Belgique francophone de l'entre-deux-guerres', *Handelingen van het XXXIIe Vlaams filologencongres* (Leuven, 1979), pp. 146–64.

6 E. Gerard 'La responsabilité du monde catholique dans la naissance et l'essor du rexisme', *La Revue Nouvelle* Jan. 1987, pp. 67–77; G. Hoyois *Aux origines de l'Action Catholique: 'Monseigneur Picard* (Brussels, 1960).

7 E. Defoort 'Le courant réactionnaire dans le catholicisme francophone belge 1918–1926', *Revue belge d'histoire contemporaine* VIII (1977), pp. 81–149.

8 M. Conway 'Building the Christian City...', *Past and Present* No. 128 (Aug. 1990), pp. 127–40. See also R. De Becker *Le livre des vivants et des morts* (Brussels, 1942).

9 J.-M. Etienne 'Les origines du rexisme', *Res Publica* IX (1967), pp. 87–110; P. Vandromme *Le loup au cou de chien* (Brussels, 1978), pp. 13–53; G. Hoyois 'Monseigneur Picard et Léon Degrelle', *Revue générale belge* XCV (Nov. 1959), pp. 83–94.

10 J.M. Mayeur *Histoire du Christianisme des origines à nos jours XII Guerres mondiales et totalitarismes 1914–1958* (Paris, 1990), p. 191.

11 J.-M. Etienne *Le mouvement rexiste jusqu'en 1940* (Paris, 1968), pp. 14–29.

12 F. Balace 'Fascisme et catholicisme politique...', *Handelingen van het XXXIIe Vlaams filologencongres*, p. 162; E. Gerard 'La responsabilité du monde catholique...', *La Revue Nouvelle* Jan. 1987, pp. 70–1.

13 J.-M. Etienne *Le mouvement rexiste*, pp. 64–6; *Le Pays Réel* (henceforth *Le PR*) 26 Feb. 1941, pp. 1 and 3, 'Echec aux politiciens...'; Interview between Carl Peeters and José Gotovitch 24 Mar. 1972, *Centre de recherches et d'études historiques de la seconde guerre mondiale* (henceforth *C2GM*); J. Gérard-Libois 'Rex 1936–1940', *Courrier hebdomadaire du CRISP* No. 1226 (1989), p. 13.

14 E.g. *Annales parlementaires de Belgique* Sénat 2 July and 24 Nov. 1936, Speeches of X. De Grunne and E. Delvaux.

15 L. Degrelle *Les Taudis* (Louvain, 1929); *Annales parlementaires de Belgique* Chambre des Représentants 25 June and 29 Oct. 1936, Speeches of C. Leruitte; J.-M. Etienne *Le mouvement rexiste*, pp. 92–5.

16 R. De Smet, R. Evalenko and W. Fraeys *Atlas des élections belges* (Brussels, 1958), pp. 59–60; R. Verlaine *Sans haine et sans gloire* (Liège, [1944]), pp. 103–4; *Le Soir* 10 Apr. 1941, p. 1, 'Les équivoques du 11 avril'; *Le PR* 4 Aug. 1942, p. 1, 'Trente-deux mois...'

17 J.-M. Etienne *Op. cit.*, pp. 119–22; *Le PR* 22 Oct. 1942, p. 1, '25 octobre'; J.-C. Ricquier 'Auguste De Schryver: souvenirs politiques et autres', *Revue Générale* May 1982, pp. 20–1.

18 J. Gérard-Libois and J. Gotovitch *L'an 40* (Brussels, 1971), p. 34; J. De Launay *Histoires secrètes de la Belgique* (Paris, 1975), pp. 197–200; E. Krier 'Le rexisme et l'Allemagne', *Cahiers d'histoire de la seconde guerre mondiale* (henceforth *Cahiers*) V (1978), pp. 173–220; *Die Tagebücher von Joseph Goebbels. Sämtliche Fragmente Teil I 1924–1941* (Munich, 1987) II, pp. 699 and 722 and III, pp. 105, 265 and 401; R. De Becker 'La collaboration en Belgique', *Courrier hebdomadaire du CRISP* No. 497–8 (1970), pp. 9–10.

19 J.-M. Etienne *Le mouvement rexiste*, pp. 99–102; *Le PR* 11 May 1941, p. 3, 'De l'accord REX-*VNV* de 1936 . . .'; P. Vandromme *Le loup au cou de chien*, pp. 105–16; A. Crahay *Une vie au XXe siècle* (Brussels, 1988), p. 75.

20 E. Gerard 'La responsabilité du monde catholique . . .', *La Revue Nouvelle* Jan. 1987, pp. 73–4; M.-H. Jaspar *Souvenirs sans retouche* (Paris, 1968), pp. 204–15.

21 C.-H. Höjer *Le régime parlementaire belge de 1918 à 1940* (Uppsala, 1946), pp. 236–58; *Le Soir* 18 Oct. 1936, p. 2, 'Le gouvernement Van Zeeland contre la dictature'.

22 J.-M. Etienne *Le mouvement rexiste*, pp. 133–40; A. Dantoing *La 'collaboration' du Cardinal* (Brussels, 1991), pp. 208–11; *Le PR* 11 Apr. 1943, p. 1, 'Des vaincus du 11 avril 1937 . . .'

23 A. Dantoing *Op. cit.*, pp. 212–13; E. Gerard 'La responsabilité du monde catholique . . .', *La Revue Nouvelle* Jan. 1987, pp. 75–6.

24 J.-M. Etienne *Op. cit.*, pp. 141–62; J.-M. Frérotte *Léon Degrelle, le dernier fasciste* (Brussels, 1987), pp. 143–5; *Le PR* 19 Mar. 1942, pp. 1 and 4, 'Chapelles politiques'.

25 J. Willequet *La Belgique sous la botte: résistances et collaborations 1940–1945* (Paris, 1986), pp. 29–34; J.-C. Ricquier 'Les souvenirs politiques d'Etienne de la Vallée Poussin', *Revue Générale* Mar. 1981, pp. 21–2; *Annales parlementaires de Belgique* Chambre des Représentants, 17 and 18 May and 6 Dec. 1938, Speeches of P-H Spaak; R. De Becker *Le livre des vivants et des morts*, pp. 178–92, 207–10 and 213–16.

26 Secrétariat du Roi *Livre Blanc 1936–1946* (No place, 1946) I, pp. 14–19; J. Willequet *Op. cit.*, pp. 23–4 and 34–6.

27 See J. Touchard 'L'esprit des années 1930' republished in P. Andreu (ed.) *Révoltes de l'esprit: les revues des années 1930* (No place, 1991), pp. 195–262; Z. Sternhell *Ni droite ni gauche: l'idéologie fasciste en France* (Paris, 1983); M. Smith 'Neither Resistance nor Collaboration: Historians and the problem of the Nederlandse Unie', *History* LXXII (1987), pp. 255–7; G. Hirschfeld 'Collaboration and Attentisme in the Netherlands', *Journal of Contemporary History* XVI (1981), pp. 473–5.

28 F. Van Langenhove *La Belgique en quête de sécurité 1920–1940* (Brussels, 1969).

29 J. Vanwelkenhuyzen *Les avertissements qui venaient de Berlin* (Gembloux, 1982); J. Gérard-Libois and J. Gotovitch *L'an 40*, pp. 23–81.

30 E.g. *Le PR* 22 July 1939, p. 1, 'La guerre des nerfs continue . . .', 6 Sept. 1939, p. 1, 'Un pathétique discours de Léon Degrelle' and 11 Sept. 1939, p. 1, 'Veut-on la guerre en Belgique?'

31 See, for example, the comments of a prominent Rexist in José Streel (henceforth JS) Notice pour mon défenseur: [première suite], *C2GM*, Fonds José Streel.

32 E. Krier 'Le rexisme et l'Allemagne', *Cahiers* V (1978), pp. 196 and 219; Collection of letters in *C2GM*, C 11/22; L. Degrelle *La Cohue de 1940* (Lausanne, 1949), pp. 85–6; J.-M. Etienne *Le mouvement rexiste*, pp. 163–7.

33 See P. Ory *Les collaborateurs 1940–1945* (Paris, 1976), pp. 11–35.

34 The concept of 'pillarisation' was originally developed to describe modern Dutch society: A. Lijphart *The Politics of Accommodation: Pluralism and Democracy in the Netherlands* (Berkeley, 1968).

35 R. Brasillach *Notre Avant-Guerre* (Paris, 1968), pp. 207–12; P. Vandromme *Le loup au cou de chien*, pp. 82–3; M.-H. Jaspar *Souvenirs sans retouche*, pp. 188–9; Albert Constant *Pro Justicia* (henceforth *Pro Just.*), 2 Oct. 1945, Auditorat Général près la Cour Militaire (henceforth *Aud. Gén.*), Doss. Albert Constant, Instruction (henceforth Inst.), Doct. 86–7.

36 P. Vandromme *Le loup au cou de chien*, pp. 13–25; R. De Becker 'La collaboration . . .', *Courrier hebdomadaire du CRISP* No. 497–8 (1970), pp. 32 and 59.

Chapter One

1 J. Vanwelkenhuyzen 'Regards nouveaux sur mai 1940' in *Actes du Colloque d'histoire militaire belge 1830–1980* (Brussels, 1981), pp. 261–78; J.-L. Charles *Les forces armées belges au cours de la deuxième guerre mondiale 1940–1945* (Brussels, 1970), pp. 22–61.

2 J. Gérard-Libois and J. Gotovitch *L'an 40*, pp. 346–51; H. Bernard *La Résistance 1940–1945* (Brussels, 1969), p. 25.

3 J. Stengers *Léopold III et le gouvernement: les deux politiques belges de 1940* (Paris-Gembloux, 1980).

4 J. Vanwelkenhuyzen and J. Dumont *1940: le grand exode* (Paris-Gembloux, 1983); J. Gérard-Libois and J. Gotovitch *L'an 40*, p. 168.

5 P. Delandsheere and A. Ooms *La Belgique sous les Nazis* (Brussels, No date) I, p. 91; J. Wynants *Verviers 1940* (No place, 1981), pp. 123–46.

6 P. Struye *L'évolution du sentiment public en Belgique sous l'occupation allemande* (Brussels, 1945), pp. 18–20; H. Bernard *La Résistance*, p. 24.

7 P. Struye *Op. cit.*, p. 20; J.-C. Ricquier 'Le Vicomte Eyskens: souvenirs et commentaires', *Revue Générale* (Aug.–Sept. 1983), p. 12.

8 M. Smith 'Neither Resistance nor Collaboration', *History* LXXII (1987), pp. 251–78.

9 J. Gérard-Libois and J. Gotovitch *L'an 40*, pp. 129–30. The predominantly German-speaking territories of Eupen, Malmédy and St Vith which had been annexed by Belgium from Germany after the First World War were re-integrated into the Reich. In 1944 they returned once again to Belgium.

10 A. De Jonghe *Hitler en het politieke lot van België (1940–1944)* (Antwerp-Utrecht, 1972) I, pp. 186–98.

11 J. Gérard-Libois and J. Gotovitch *L'an 40*, pp. 185–99; M. Van den Wijngaert 'La politique du moindre mal: la politique du Comité des Secrétaires-Généraux en Belgique sous l'occupation allemande, 1940–1944', *Revue du Nord* Special Number (1987), pp. 63–72.

12 See note 10.

13 A. De Jonghe *Hitler en het politieke lot van België* I, pp. 259–312.

14 J. Gérard-Libois and J. Gotovitch *L'an 40*, pp. 298–305; A. De Jonghe 'La lutte Himmler-Reeder pour la nomination d'un *HSSPF* à Bruxelles', *Cahiers* IV (1976), pp. 14–32.

15 J.-M. Etienne *Le mouvement rexiste*, p. 163; *Le PR* 1 Apr. 1942, p. 4, 'Chronique du Mouvement' and 9 June 1942, p. 2, 'Les légionnaires et les prisonniers'; Victor Matthys (henceforth VM) to Reeder, date unknown, copy in Simar to *Chefs de Groupes* 21 Nov. 1942, *C2GM*, C 11/321.8.

16 J. Gérard-Libois and J. Gotovitch *L'an 40*, pp. 105–22.

17 Journal de V. Matthys p. 1, *C2GM*; *Le PR* 30 Nov. 1940, Magazine, pp. 1 and 3, 'Israël en Pyrenées' and 20 Nov. 1942, p. 1, 'Notre camarade Jean Teughels...'; *Le Soir* 5 Nov. 1947, p. 5, 'Conseil de Guerre de Bruxelles'.

18 Mémoire de V. Matthys pp. 5–6, *C2GM*; J.-M. Etienne *Le mouvement rexiste*, p. 165.

19 L. Degrelle *La Cohue*, pp. 89–99.

20 J. Gérard-Libois and J. Gotovitch *L'an 40*, p. 114; *Le PR* 1 Sept. 1940, p. 1, 'Un martyr rexiste'.

21 J. Gérard-Libois and J. Gotovitch *L'an 40*, pp. 114–15; P.J. Teughels to *Conseil Général* 2 July 1940, *C2GM*, C 11/115; W. Dannau *Ainsi parla Léon Degrelle* (Strombeek-Bever, 1973) VI, pp. 225–36; J.-M. Charlier *Léon Degrelle: persiste et signe* (Paris, 1985), pp. 217–21.

22 Circular from *Conseil Général* 8 June 1940, *C2GM*, C 11/113; *Die Tagebücher von Joseph Goebbels* IV, p. 193.

23 Circular to members of *Conseil Général* 24 May 1940, Vandevelde to R. Ledoux 15 June 1940 and Vandevelde to C. Damman 14 July 1940, *C2GM*, C 11/106, C 11/105 and C 11/189.

24 J.-L. Hondros *Occupation and Resistance: The Greek Agony* (New York, 1983), p. 26; P. Hayes *Quisling* (Newton Abbot, 1971), pp. 210–45.

25 Avis of *Directoire* of Rex-Liége 15 June 1940 and Vandevelde to *Le Soir* 16 July 1940, *C2GM*, C 11/110 and C 11/113; *Le Soir* 7 June 1946, p. 3, 'Les Conseils de Guerre'.

26 Resolution of *Conseil Général* 26 June 1940, *C2GM*, C 11/108.

27 *Conseil Général* to Léopold III 7 June 1940, *C2GM*, C 11/109.

28 Circular and Resolution of *Conseil Général* 8 June and 2 July 1940, *C2GM*, C 11/108 and C 11/113; Interview between Carl Peeters and José Gotovitch 24 Mar. 1972, p. 56, *C2GM*.

29 A. Zégels to Léon Degrelle (henceforth LD) 4 June 1940 and Rex-Auderghem to *Conseil Général* 6 July 1940, *C2GM*, C 11/327 and C 11/110; L. Degrelle *La Cohue*, p. 265.

30 Note from *Directoire* of Rex-Liége to *Conseil Général* 18 June 1940 and F. Van Overstraeten to *Conseil Général* 26 July 1940, *C2GM*, C 11/321.9 and C 11/112.

31 Declarations of Rex-Liége 12 and 15 June 1940, *C2GM*, C 11/110.

32 P. Janssens 'Les Dinasos wallons 1936–41' (Université de Liège Mémoire de licence, 1982), pp. 215–17; Légion Nationale Feuille d'ordre No. 2 21 Aug. 1940, *C2GM*, C 8/5.

33 J. Gérard-Libois and J. Gotovitch *L'an 40*, pp. 218–30.

34 C. Damman to Vandevelde 24 July 1940, *C2GM*, C 11/189.

35 Vandevelde to *Chefs de Région* 12 July 1940, *C2GM*, C 11/262.

36 Note from *Directoire* of Rex-Liége to *Conseil Général* 18 June 1940 and Vandevelde to C. Damman 14 July 1940, *C2GM*, C 11/321.9 and C 11/189.

37 Vandevelde to *Conseil Général* 12 July 1940, *C2GM*, C 11/114; Journal de V. Matthys pp. 1–2, *C2GM*.

38 Madame J. Beval to Vandevelde 4 July 1940, *C2GM*, C 11/112. Re the press, see J. Gérard-Libois and J. Gotovitch *L'an 40*, pp. 307–20; E. De Bens *De Belgische dagbladpers onder Duitse censuur* (Antwerp-Utrecht, 1973), pp. 139–60.

39 L. Degrelle *La Cohue*, pp. 112–13 and 247; J. Denis 'Mémoire justificatif d'un condamné à mort', p. 25, *Aud. Gén.*, Doss. Jean Denis, Information (henceforth Info.), Doct. 53; Vandevelde to Madame J. Beval 6 July 1940, *C2GM*, C 11/112; *Le Soir* 7 June 1946, p. 3, 'Les Conseils de Guerre'; *Tätigkeitsbericht* (henceforth *TB*) 8, 3 Sept. 1940, p. 528.

40 L. Degrelle *La Cohue.*, pp. 98–103; 'Les mémoires de Pierre Daye', *Dossier du mois* No. 12 (Brussels, 1963), pp. 14–15.

41 'Les mémoires de Pierre Daye', *Dossier du mois* No. 12, pp. 14–16; W. Dannau *Ainsi parla Léon Degrelle* VI, p. 274; J. Stengers *Léopold III et le gouvernement*, pp. 88–90.

42 C. Raty to Vandevelde 26 July 1940, *C2GM*, C 11/113; 'Les mémoires de Pierre Daye', *Dossier du mois* No. 12, p. 16; P. Delandsheere and A. Ooms *La Belgique sous les Nazis* I, pp. 241–2.

43 E. Jäckel *Frankreich in Hitlers Europa* (Stuttgart, 1966), pp. 66–70; P. Ory *Les collaborateurs*, pp. 12–20 and 37–8.

44 L. Degrelle *Hitler pour mille ans* (Paris, 1969), p. 102; J.-M. Charlier *Léon Degrelle*, p. 239; E. Krier 'Le rexisme et l'Allemagne', *Cahiers* V (1978), p. 184.

45 J. Gérard-Libois and J. Gotovitch *L'an 40*, pp. 43–7; B. de Jouvenal *Un voyageur dans le siècle* (Paris, 1979), p. 379.

46 See R. Paxton *Vichy France: Old Guard and New Order 1940–1944* (London, 1972), pp. 63–8.

47 *L'Eventail* 30 May 1980, p. 7, 'Léon Degrelle, le procès qui n'a jamais eu lieu'; 'Les mémoires de Pierre Daye', *Dossier du mois* No. 12, p. 16.

48 R. Devleeschouwer 'L'opinion politique et les revendications territoriales belges à la fin de la première guerre mondiale 1918–1919' in *Mélanges offerts à G. Jacquemyns* (Brussels, 1968), pp. 207–38; P. Janssens 'Les Dinasos wallons'.

49 E.g. L. Degrelle *La Cohue*, pp. 109–20.

50 Mémoire de V. Matthys pp. 9–14, *C2GM*.

51 E. Brasseur to Vandevelde 3 Aug. 1940 and Vandevelde to E. Brasseur 4 Aug. 1940, *C2GM*, C 11/112.

52 J.-M. Charlier *Léon Degrelle*, p. 236.

53 Notes of meeting on 7 Aug. 1940, *C2GM*, Papiers Pierre Daye; *Le Soir* 16 Aug. 1940, p. 2, 'L'entrevue Laval-Degrelle à Paris'; F. Kupferman *Laval* (Paris, 1987), p. 255.

54 According to certain sources, Pierre Daye and Edouard and Lucienne Didier (whose salon had been a meeting-place in pre-war Brussels for those who inclined towards

sympathy for Germany) were also present: *Le Soir* 30 Nov. 1946, p. 4, 'Conseil de Guerre de Bruxelles'; 'Les mémoires de Pierre Daye', *Dossier du mois* No. 12, p. 18; B. de Jouvenal *Un voyageur dans le siècle*, p. 394. Re the Didiers, see J. Gérard-Libois and J. Gotovitch *L'an 40*, pp. 43–7.

55 L. Degrelle *La Cohue*, pp. 388–9.

56 M. Brelaz *Henri De Man, une autre idée du socialisme* (Geneva, 1985); P. Dodge *Beyond Marxism: The Faith and Works of Hendrik De Man* (The Hague, 1966); J. Willequet *La Belgique sous la botte*, pp. 95–101.

57 W. Wagner *Belgien in der deutschen Politik während des Zweiten Weltkrieges* (Boppard, 1974), pp. 201–2; *L'Eventail* 30 May 1980, p. 7, 'Léon Degrelle'.

58 'Les mémoires de Pierre Daye', *Dossier du mois* No. 12, p. 18; L. Degrelle *La Cohue*, pp. 277, 390 and 392–3; M.-H. Jaspar *Souvenirs sans retouche*, p. 240.

59 L. Degrelle *La Cohue*, p. 394.

60 M. Brelaz *Léopold III et Henri De Man* (Geneva, 1988), pp. 207–20.

61 De Man remarked to de Jouvenal in Paris in August that any long-term collaboration between himself and Degrelle would be impossible, but added (in a reference to the Germans) 'il le faudra bien à présent, puisqu'*ils* le veulent': B. de Jouvenal *Un voyageur dans le siècle*, p. 395.

62 A. Dantoing 'L'épiscopat belge en 1939–1940: De la neutralité à la présence' (Université Catholique de Louvain-la-Neuve Docteur en philosophie et lettres, 1990), p. 615.

63 *Recueil de documents établi par le Secrétariat du Roi concernant la période 1936–1949* (No place, 1949), pp. 82–4.

64 L. Degrelle *La Cohue*, pp. 153–4 and 383–4.

65 *Ibid.*, pp. 142–8 and 158–9; Mémoire de V. Matthys p. 25, *C2GM*.

66 J. Gérard-Libois and J. Gotovitch *L'an 40*, pp. 207–10; L. Degrelle *La Cohue*, pp. 159–70.

67 L. Degrelle *La Cohue*, pp. 404–5.

68 Notes of meeting on 1 Aug. 1940, *C2GM*, Papiers Pierre Daye; 'Les mémoires de Pierre Daye', *Dossier du mois* No. 12, pp. 16–17; Comte Capelle *Au Service du Roi* (Brussels, 1949) II, p. 77.

69 Capelle to Daye 2 Aug. 1940, *C2GM*, Papiers Pierre Daye.

70 Capelle to Daye 16 Aug. 1940, *C2GM*, Papiers Pierre Daye; L. Degrelle *La Cohue*, pp. 120 and 269–70.

71 L. Degrelle *Lettres à mon Cardinal* (Brussels, 1975), pp. 33–4.

72 Notes of meeting on 21 Aug. 1940, *C2GM*, Papiers Pierre Daye; 'Les mémoires de Pierre Daye', *Dossier du mois* No. 12, p. 19; L. Degrelle *La Cohue*, pp. 271–9; *Recueil de documents établi par le Secrétariat du Roi*, pp. 81–3; Comte Capelle *Au Service du Roi* II, pp. 78–9.

73 J. Gérard-Libois and J. Gotovitch *L'an 40*, p. 211.

74 See pp. 9–14.

75 A. Dantoing *La 'collaboration' du Cardinal*, pp. 111–322. I am indebted to Alain Dantoing for sharing with me his unparalleled knowledge of the Church during the Occupation.

76 A. Dantoing *Op. cit.*, pp. 213–23; Chanoine Leclef *Le Cardinal Van Roey et l'occupation allemande en Belgique* (Brussels, 1945), pp. 82–3 and 85; L. Degrelle *La Cohue*, pp. 213–18.

77 A. Dantoing *Op. cit.*, pp. 223–8.

78 *Le Soir* 16 Aug. 1940, p. 2, 'L'entrevue Laval-Degrelle à Paris'; *Recueil de documents établi par le Secrétariat du Roi*, p. 83.

79 W. Wagner *Belgien in der deutschen Politik*, p. 200; L. Degrelle *La Cohue*, pp. 396–9; General Van Overstraeten *Sous le joug: Léopold III prisonnier* (Brussels, 1986), p. 44.

80 *Le PR* 29 Oct. 1942, p. 1, 'En marche vers l'unité'; J. Denis 'Mémoire justificatif...' p. 102, *Aud. Gén.*, Doss. Jean Denis, Info., Doct. 53; General Van Overstraeten *Sous le joug*, p. 76.

81 Vandevelde to E. Brasseur 4 Aug. 1940, *C2GM*, C 11/112; W. Wagner *Belgien in der deutschen Politik*, p. 201; *Le Soir* 5 June 1946, p. 2, 'Les Conseils de Guerre'; L. Degrelle *La Cohue*, pp. 249–51; Interview between Carl Peeters and José Gotovitch 24 Mar. 1972, pp. 44–5, *C2GM*. *Le Soir* had already reappeared under the control of pro-

German editors without the permission of the paper's owners. This 'unofficial' *Le Soir* continued to be published throughout the Occupation.

82 L. Degrelle *La Cohue*, pp. 247–8; Journal de V. Matthys p. 2, *C2GM*.

83 *Le PR* 18 Sept. 1940, p. 8, 'Dans le Mouvement' and 2 Oct. 1940, p. 2, 'Dans le Mouvement Rexiste'.

84 Vandevelde to LD 10 Sept. 1940 and to Doring 12 Sept. 1940, *C2GM*, C 11/190 and C 11/116; *Le PR* 5 Feb. 1941, p. 2, 'Dans le Mouvement'.

85 *Le PR* 21 Sept. 1940, p. 2, 'Dans le Mouvement Rexiste'.

86 Extrait du Bulletin des Dirigeants 25 Jan. 1941, *C2GM*, C 11/92; Interview with Léon Degrelle 14 July 1988; Interview with Paul Jamin 11 Dec. 1987.

87 See note 85; E. Brasseur to Vandevelde 3 Aug. 1940, *C2GM*, C 11/112.

88 Albert Constant *Pro Just.*, 18 Apr. 1946, *Aud. Gén.*, Doss. Albert Constant, Inst., Doct. 219–20; Unofficial list of Rexist leaders and Peeters to Damman 13 Aug. 1940, *C2GM*, C 11/88 and C 11/112; *Le PR* 11 Oct. 1940, p. 8, 'Rex Flandre au service de la communauté populaire'.

89 See note 85.

90 Anonymous letter 17 Apr. 1987, Private Papers of the Author.

91 Interview between Carl Peeters and José Gotovitch 24 Mar. 1972, p. 37, *C2GM*; JS Notice pour mon défenseur: deuxième suite, *C2GM*, Fonds José Streel; Interview with Léon Degrelle 14 July 1988.

92 *TB* 15, 7 Apr. 1941, p. 1466; Anonymous letter 17 Apr. 1987, Private Papers of the Author.

93 Telegram from *Chargé d'affaires* at Madrid 10 Feb. 1951, Archives of the Ministry of Foreign Affairs Brussels, Doct. 11179. I am grateful to José Gotovitch for kindly making a copy of this telegram available to me.

94 Ch. d'Ydewalle *Degrelle ou la triple imposture* (Brussels, 1968), p. 195; Sylvain Jadoul *Pro Just.*, 28 Aug. 1945, *Aud. Gén.*, Doss. Pierre Pauly, *Cour Militaire*, Doct. 10; Interview between Carl Peeters and José Gotovitch 24 Mar. 1972, p. 37, *C2GM*; E. De Bruyne *Les Wallons meurent à l'est: La Légion Wallonie et Léon Degrelle sur le Front russe 1941–1945* (Brussels, 1991), p. 30.

95 Sylvain Jadoul *Pro Just.*, 28 Aug. 1945, *Aud. Gén.*, Doss. Pierre Pauly, *Cour Militaire*, Doct. 10; Anonymous letter 17 Apr. 1987, Private Papers of the Author.

96 E.g. Daye to LD 10 Sept. 1940, *C2GM*, Papiers Pierre Daye.

97 Rouleau to Vandevelde 23 Aug. 1940, *C2GM*, C 11/190; *Le PR* 18 Sept. 1940, p. 8, 'Dans le Mouvement'.

98 Interview with Léon Degrelle 14 July 1988.

99 *Le PR* 4 Oct. 1940, p. 1, 'Ouvriers et agriculteurs'; Bulletins du mouvement rexiste Nos. 1–3, 20 Sept., 25 Oct., and 30 Nov. 1940, *C2GM*, C 11/162–4.

100 Bulletin du mouvement rexiste No. 1, 20 Sept. 1940, *C2GM*, C 11/162; Vandevelde to Vanderveken 29 May 1940, *C2GM*, C 11/107; *Le PR* 11 Oct. 1940, p. 8, 'Cadre du mouvement rexiste en Flandre'.

101 Région de Bruxelles Bulletin du 20 décembre 1940 and Rex-Wallonie Liste des titulaires de cartes de dirigeants 20 Feb. 1941, *C2GM*, C 11/91 and C 11/321.2.

102 Bulletin du mouvement rexiste No. 1, 20 Sept. 1940, *C2GM*, C 11/162.

103 B. Peeters *Le monde d'Hergé* ([Tournai], 1983), p. 16.

104 *Le PR* 25–6 Aug. 1940, p. 1, 'Belgique', 30 Aug. 1940, p. 1, 'De Londres à Anvers' and 31 Aug. 1940, p. 1, 'Sabotage et patriotisme'; Bulletin du mouvement rexiste No. 2, 25 Oct. 1940, *C2GM*, C 11/163.

105 *Le PR* 25–6 Aug. 1940, pp. 1 and 3, 'L'Europe va naître' and 3 Sept. 1940, p. 1, 'Un an de guerre'.

106 *Le PR* 4 Sept. 1940, p. 1, Le devoir de présence' and 8 Sept. 1940, p. 1, 'Le martyre n'est pas une solution'.

107 *Le PR* 15 Sept. 1940, p. 1, 'Intérêt de la Patrie . . .', 1 Oct. 1940, p. 1, 'La vie des peuples' and 27 Oct. 1940, p. 1, 'Devoirs présents des Belges'.

108 *Le PR* 25–6 Aug. 1940, p. 1, 'Pourquoi notre retard?'

109 *Le PR* 25–6 Aug. 1940, p. 1, 'Belgique' and 22 Sept. 1940, pp. 1 and 2, 'Un déblaiement préalable'.

110 *Le PR* 28 Aug. 1940, p. 1, 'Les Traîtres de Limoges', 6 Sept. 1940, pp. 1–2, 'La paix

sociale . . .' and 18 Sept. 1940, p. 1, 'Aucun pardon . . .'
111 *Le PR* 28 Aug. 1940, p. 1, 'Les Traîtres de Limoges'.
112 *Le PR* 25–6 Aug. 1940, p. 6, 'La conception individualiste . . .', 4 Sept. 1940, p. 5, 'L'intérêt des Wallons' and 13 Sept. 1940, pp. 1–2, 'Le problème du corporatisme'.
113 E.g. *Le PR* 6 Sept. 1940, pp. 1–2, 'La paix sociale . . .'
114 *Le PR* 8 Sept. 1940, p. 1, 'Le martyre n'est pas une solution'.
115 Note from *Directoire* of Rex-Liége to *Conseil Général* 18 June 1940 and Rex-Ixelles to *Conseil Général* 14 July 1940, *C2GM*, C 11/321.9 and 323.22; *Cassandre* 22 Nov. 1942, p. 1, 'Echos et Indiscrétions'.
116 J. Legrain to Rex 7 July 1940, *C2GM*, C 11/115; F. Spruyt to [*Etat-Major* of Rex] 24 Dec. 1943, *Aud. Gén.*, Doss. Marcel Dupont, Info., Doct. 69. See pp. 66–8.
117 *Gazette de Liége* 27 June 1945, p. 1, 'Au Conseil de Guerre'; *Le PR* 13 Nov. 1940, p. 1, 'Léon Degrelle . . .'; Rex-Wallonie Extraits de l'Ordre de Service 5 Feb. 1941, *C2GM*, C 11/321.1.
118 *Le PR* 1 Nov. 1940, 21 Nov. 1940 and 4 Jan. 1941, p. 2, 'Dans le Mouvement'.
119 Louis Richard *Pro Just.*, 12 July 1945, *Aud. Gén.*, Doss. Albert Constant, Documentation Générale, Doct. 1–5; *Le PR* 2 Oct. 1940, p. 2, 'Dans le Mouvement Rexiste'.
120 VM *Pro Just.*, 3 Oct. 1945, *Aud. Gén.*, Doss. VM, Info., Doct. 206; *Le PR* 7 Jan. 1941, p. 3, 'Le rassemblement de Liége'; Documentation Jans 366.
121 See p. 62.
122 J. Gérard-Libois and J. Gotovitch *L'an 40*, p. 298.
123 *Ibid.*, p. 301; *Jahresbericht der Militärverwaltung* June 1941, Section A, p. 43.
124 E. De Bens *De Belgische dagbladpers*, pp. 149–51; *Le Soir* 7 June 1946, p. 3, 'Les Conseils de Guerre'; L. Degrelle *La Cohue*, p. 248.
125 M. Smith 'Neither Resistance nor Collaboration', *History* LXXII (1987), p. 258; Y. Jelinek 'Storm-troopers in Slovakia: the Rodobrana and the Hlinka Guard', *Journal of Contemporary History* VI (1971), p. 104; J.-P. Azéma *De Munich à la Libération* (Paris, 1979), pp. 101–7.
126 A. De Jonghe 'La lutte Himmler-Reeder . . .', *Cahiers* V (1978), p. 45; *Die Tagebücher von Joseph Goebbels* IV, pp. 325 and 454–5.
127 Rouleau to Vandevelde 14 Oct. 1940, *C2GM*, C 11/132; *Le PR* 16 Oct. 1940, p. 2, 'Dans le Mouvement Rexiste'.
128 *Akten zur Deutschen Auswärtigen Politik 1918–1945* Serie D Band XI.I (Bonn, 1964), pp. 289–90.
129 *Ibid.*, pp. 288–93; W. Wagner *Belgien in der deutschen Politik*, pp. 202–5.
130 A. De Jonghe 'La lutte Hitler-Reeder . . .', *Cahiers* V (1978), p. 45; Report by Reeder for *Auditeur Général* Wilmart 2 May 1949, *C2GM*, Procès von Falkenhausen, Doct. 351.
131 See previous note; L. Degrelle *La Cohue*, p. 409.
132 Louis Collard (henceforth LC) to [Burtomboy] 30 Nov. 1940, *Aud. Gén.*, Doss. LC, Inst., Doct. 137.19; J.-M. Charlier *Léon Degrelle*, pp. 246–7; A. De Jonghe 'La lutte Himmler-Reeder . . .', *Cahiers* V (1978), p. 45.
133 E.g. *Jahresbericht der Militärverwaltung* June 1941, Section A, p. 7.
134 Reeder to *OKH* 26 Jan. 1943, *C2GM*, Procès von Falkenhausen, Doct. 117; L. Degrelle *La Cohue*, pp. 113–14.
135 P. Hayes *Quisling*, pp. 264–6; R. Paxton *Vichy France*, pp. 69–74.
136 L. Degrelle *Hitler pour mille ans*, p. 103; Interview with Léon Degrelle 14 July 1988.
137 See p. 26; *Le PR* 29 Sept. 1940, p. 1, 'Le cloaque politicien' and 16 Oct. 1940, p. 1, 'La Révolution doit être totale'.
138 M. Steinberg *L'étoile et le fusil: la question juive 1940–1942* (Brussels, 1983), pp. 134–5.
139 *Le PR* 22 Sept. 1940, p. 1, 'Belges d'abord ou Anglais?', 10 Nov. 1940, p. 1, Jam cartoon and 28 Nov. 1940, p. 3, 'Les atrocités britanniques . . .'
140 J.-P. Brunet *Jacques Doriot* (No place, 1986), pp. 312 and 324.
141 *TB* 11, 1 Dec. 1940, p. 890; P. Delandsheere and A. Ooms *La Belgique sous les Nazis* I, pp. 145–6.
142 *Le PR* 29 Sept. 1940, p. 1, 'Le cloaque politicien', 4 Dec. 1940, p. 5, 'Au pilori', 7 Dec. 1940 Magazine, p. 1, Jam cartoon and 20 Dec. 1940, p. 1, 'Politiciens et Froussards'.

143 M. Steinberg *L'étoile et le fusil*, p. 16; *Le PR* 7 Nov. 1940, p. 1, 'Prélude au grand nettoyage'.
144 *Le PR* 17 Nov. 1940, p. 1, 'Les Maffias' and 19 Nov. 1940, p. 1, 'La Dictature maçonnique'.
145 *Le PR* 30 Nov. 1940 Magazine, pp. 1 and 3, 'Israël en Pyrénées', 17 Dec. 1940, p. 5, 'Les avocats juifs . . .' and 19 Dec. 1940, p. 1, 'Les Juifs tabou'; M. Steinberg *L'étoile et le fusil*, pp. 133–45.
146 Bulletin du mouvement rexiste No. 3, 30 Nov. 1940, *C2GM*, C 11/164; *Le diocèse de Tournai sous l'occupation allemande* (Tournai-Paris, 1946), pp. 83–4.
147 Chanoine Leclef *Le Cardinal Van Roey et l'occupation allemande*, pp. 84–5 and 257–9.
148 *Le PR* 8 Dec. 1940, p. 1, 'Sermons politiciens'; A. Dantoing *La 'collaboration' du Cardinal*, pp. 223–5; C. Chevalier 'La presse francophone et l'église catholique en Belgique sous l'occupation allemande (1940–1944)' (Université Catholique de Louvain-la-Neuve Mémoire de licence, 1986), pp. 174–6 and 184–5.
149 *Le PR* 23 Nov. 1940, p. 1, 'Une agitation inopportune' and 22 Dec. 1940, p. 1, 'Ne pas confondre'.
150 *Le PR* 31 Dec. 1940, 'Léon Degrelle a parlé . . .'
151 P. Delandsheere and A. Ooms *La Belgique sous les Nazis* I, pp. 206–7; *Vers l'Avenir* 9 May 1946, p. 4, 'Célestin Renard'. See also pp. 91–3.
152 Interview between Carl Peeters and José Gotovitch 24 Mar. 1972, p. 38, *C2GM*; *Le PR* 19 Sept. 1940, p. 1, 'Un limogeard corrigé'.
153 *Le PR* 4 Oct. 1940, p. 1, 'Le Franc-Maçon Thelismar . . .' and 'Ici: Limogeard', 5 Oct. 1940, p. 2, 'D'un jour à l'autre', p. 8, 'La séance tumultueuse . . .' and 'Rex mène l'action . . .' and 8 Oct. 1940, p. 1, 'Le nettoyage'; A. Delattre *Mes Souvenirs* (Cuesmes, 1957), p. 225.
154 *Le PR* 6 Oct. 1940, p. 1, 'Nos souhaits de nouvel-an aux juifs', 8 Oct. 1940, p. 1, 'Le nettoyage' and 10 Oct. 1941, p. 4, 'Un an de combat . . .'; M. Steinberg *L'étoile et le fusil*, pp. 105–7.
155 *Le PR* 6 Oct. 1940, p. 1, 'Ça doit finir'.
156 JS Notice pour mon défenseur: quatrième suite, *C2GM*, Fonds José Streel.
157 *Le PR* 13 Oct. 1940, p. 1, 'L'union des partis'.
158 *Ibid*; R. Poulet 'Un plaidoyer non prononcé', p. 22 (Private Collection); P. Janssens 'Les Dinasos wallons', p. 229; *Le PR* 25 Oct. 1940, p. 1, 'Le Parti Unique' and 9 Nov. 1940, p. 1, 'L'Ordre nouveau de Madame la Générale'.
159 *Le PR* 25–6 Aug. 1940, p. 1, 'Pourquoi notre retard?' and 27 Aug. 1940, p. 1, 'Une guerre qui est une révolution'.
160 *Le PR* 13 Nov. 1940, p. 2, 'Dans le Mouvement', 5 Dec. 1940, p. 8, 'Léon Degrelle parle aux mineurs de Frameries', 10 Dec. 1940, p. 2, 'Devant une foule enthousiaste . . .' and 31 Dec. 1940, p. 1, 'Léon Degrelle a parlé . . .'
161 *Le PR* 27 Oct. 1940, p. 1, 'Devoirs présents des Belges' and 9 Nov. 1940, p. 1, 'L'Ordre nouveau . . .'
162 E.g. *Le PR* 22 Dec. 1940 Magazine, p. 1, 'Il y a soixante-quinze ans . . .'
163 Albert Constant *Pro Just.*, 2 Oct. 1945, *Aud. Gén.*, Doss. Albert Constant, Inst., Doct. 86–7; Interview between Carl Peeters and José Gotovitch 24 Mar. 1972, p. 45, *C2GM*.
164 R. Paxton *Vichy France*, pp. 66–7 and 70–1; LD to *Formations de Combat* (henceforth *FC*) of Brussels 6 July 1941, *C2GM*, C 11/275.
165 Vandevelde to LD 4 Oct. and Vandevelde to Rouleau 19 Oct. 1940, *C2GM*, C 11/190 and C 11/133; Daye to Paternostre and Paternostre to Daye 10 and 11 Sept. 1940, *C2GM*, Papiers Pierre Daye.
166 E.g. *Le PR* 2 Oct. 1940, p. 1, 'La tradition dans la Révolution', 3 Oct. 1940, p. 1, 'Il ne suffit pas de courir . . .' and 28 Nov. 1940, p. 1, 'Au seuil de l'ordre nouveau'. See also M. Conway 'Du catholicisme à la collaboration: le cas de José Streel' in *Belgique en 1940: une société en crise, un pays en guerre* (Brussels, 1993), pp. 305–26.
167 Bulletin du mouvement rexiste No. 4, 20 Dec. 1940, *C2GM*, C 11/165.
168 *Le PR* 22 Dec. 1940 Magazine, p. 8 and 10 Jan. 1941, p. 2, 'Dans le Mouvement'.
169 P. Delandsheere and A. Ooms *La Belgique sous les Nazis* I, p. 153.

170 *TB* 10, 1 Nov. 1940, pp. 701–2; *TB* 11, 1 Dec. 1940, p. 858; *TB* 12, 3 Jan. 1941, p. 1011.

171 P. Delandsheere and A. Ooms *Op. cit.* I, p. 152; *TB* 12, 3 Jan. 1941, p. 1015; P. Struye *L'évolution du sentiment public*, pp. 24–5; J. Gotovitch 'Photographie de la presse clandestine de 1940', *Cahiers* II (1972), pp. 141–2.

172 J. Gérard-Libois and J. Gotovitch *L'an 40*, pp. 356–76.

173 *Ibid.*, pp. 354–5.

174 P. Delandsheere and A. Ooms *Op. cit.* I, p. 208; J. Gotovitch 'Photographie de la presse clandestine', *Cahiers* II (1972), pp. 138–9 and 144.

175 P. Struye Complete manuscript version of *L'évolution du sentiment public* Report One pp. 9–10 and 12, *C2GM*, W 3; J. Gotovitch *Op. cit.*, pp. 140–1 and 145.

176 P. Struye *L'évolution du sentiment public*, pp. 29–31.

177 *Le PR* 1 Nov. 1940, p. 1, 'Le crime posthume', 19 Nov. 1940, p. 1, 'La Dictature maçonnique' and 31 Dec. 1940, p. 1, 'L'année terrible'.

178 *Le PR* 3 Dec. 1940, p. 2, 'Deux mille cinq cents rexistes . . .' and 31 Dec. 1940, p. 1, 'Léon Degrelle a parlé . . .'

179 Albert Constant *Pro Just.*, 1 Feb. 1946, *Aud. Gén.*, Doss. Albert Constant, Inst., Doct. 160; *Le PR* 11 Oct. 1940, p. 8, 'La Formation de Combat . . .' and 28 Jan. 1941, p. 2, 'Prestation de serment chez les *FC* Bruxellois'.

180 *Le PR* 20 Dec. 1940, p. 5, 'Sermons politiciens'; J. Gotovitch 'Photographie de la presse clandestine', *Cahiers* II (1972), pp. 148–50.

Chapter Two

1 JS *Pro Just.*, 24 May 1945, *Aud. Gén.*, Doss. JS, Info.; J.-M. Charlier *Léon Degrelle*, pp. 252 and 257.

2 Bulletins du mouvement rexiste Nos. 3 and 4, 30 Nov. and 20 Dec. 1940, *C2GM*, C 11/164 and C 11/165.

3 Interview between Jean Vermeire and José Gotovitch 25 Mar. 1971, p. 57, *C2GM*.

4 *Le PR* 1 Jan. 1941, p. 1, 'Salut à 1941'.

5 *Ibid.*

6 See P.M. Dioudonnat *Je suis partout: les Maurrassiens devant la tentation fasciste* (Paris, 1973), p. 358.

7 E.g. *Journal des Tribunaux* 6 May 1945, p. 322, 'Conseil de Guerre de Liège'.

8 JS Analyse de l'acte d'accusation: première suite p. 11, *C2GM*, Fonds José Streel.

9 *Le PR* 18 Feb. 1941, p. 3, 'Les messages de Rex'; L. Degrelle *La Cohue*, p. 455.

10 *TB* 13, 2 Feb. 1941, p. 1149. Other estimates of the attendance varied between 6,000 and 12,000: P. Delandsheere and A. Ooms *La Belgique sous les Nazis* I, p. 239; *Le PR* 8 Jan. 1941, p. 3, 'Le rassemblement rexiste et la presse'.

11 J. Gérard-Libois and J. Gotovitch *L'an 40*, pp. 383–5; *Le PR* 7 Jan. 1941, p. 3, 'Le rassemblement de Liége'; 'Faits et anecdotes . . .' 18 June 1941, *C2GM*, PD 40; *La Meuse* 2 July 1946, p. 2, 'Au Conseil de Guerre'.

12 *Le PR* 7 Jan. 1941, p. 3, 'Le rassemblement de Liége'; *La Légia* 6 Jan. 1941, pp. 1 and 3, 'Un rassemblement rexiste'.

13 *Le PR* 7 Jan. 1941, p. 3, 'Le rassemblement de Liége'.

14 *Ibid*; *Le PR* 7 Jan. 1941, p. 1, 'A Liége devant 10,000 militants . . .'

15 P. Delandsheere and A. Ooms *La Belgique sous les Nazis* I, p. 236; Ch. d'Ydewalle *Degrelle ou la triple imposture*, p. 183.

16 P. De Mont to Daye 4 Jan. [1941], *C2GM*, Papiers Pierre Daye; *Le Nouveau Journal* 3 Jan. 1941, p. 1, 'L'Occupant et nous'.

17 General Van Overstraeten *Sous le joug*, pp. 113 and 117; P. Delandsheere and A. Ooms *La Belgique sous les Nazis* I, pp. 238–9.

18 *Le PR* 7 Jan. 1941, p. 1, 'A Liége devant 10,000 militants . . .' and 15 Jan. 1941, p. 1, 'Manoeuvres et provocations'.

19 *TB* 13, 2 Feb. 1941, p. 1150.

20 General Van Overstraeten *Sous le joug*, pp. 117 and 119; Interview between Jean Vermeire and José Gotovitch 25 Mar. 1971, p. 58, *C2GM*; *La Meuse* 12 Dec. 1945, p. 1, 'Joseph Mignolet...'; R. Vincent to Daye 31 Jan. 1941, *C2GM*, Papiers Pierre Daye; Interview with Madame R. Meunier 8 Feb. 1988.

21 For example, one militant from Bastogne who remained loyal to the movement after January 1941 commented 'Oui, j'évoluais insensiblement par la force des choses; je considérais les paroles du Chef comme l'Evangile. Que voulez-vous, on était fanatisé!', *L'Avenir du Luxembourg* 10 May 1946, p. 1, 'Au Conseil de Guerre d'Arlon'.

22 *Le PR* 5 Jan. 1941, p. 1, 'Collaborer'. See also *Le Soir* 30 Jan. 1941, pp. 1–2, 'Les trois mobiles...'

23 Interview between Jean Vermeire and José Gotovitch 25 Mar. 1971, pp. 59 and 63, *C2GM*.

24 Albert Constant *Pro Just.*, 2 Oct. 1945, *Aud. Gén.*, Doss. Albert Constant, Inst., Doct. 86–7.

25 R. Poulet 'Histoire du Nouveau Journal', pp. 28–9 (Private Collection); *Le Soir* 4 June 1947, p. 5, 'Conseil de Guerre de Bruxelles'; Radio Vatican 14 Feb. 1941 cited in BBC Daily Digest of Foreign Broadcasts 14 Feb. 1941, *C2GM*, Fonds INBEL/732.

26 *Le PR* 30 Jan. 1941, p. 2, 'Dans le Mouvement', 4 Feb. 1941, p. 1, 'Occupants et hitlériens' and p. 3, 'Le Chef de Rex...' and 4 Mar. 1941, p. 3, 'Les messages de Rex'.

27 *Le PR* 11 Feb. 1941, p. 3, 'Les messages de Rex'.

28 *Le Soir* 14 June 1946, p. 2, 'Les Conseils de Guerre'; J. De Launay *Histoires secrètes de la Belgique*, p. 219.

29 R. Gobyn 'La vie quotidienne pendant la seconde guerre mondiale: une combinaison étrange d'individualisme et de solidarité' in *1940–1945 La vie quotidienne en Belgique* (Brussels, 1984), pp. 54–62.

30 *Le PR* 18 Jan. 1941, p. 1, 'Sous le signe du désordre nouveau', 18 Feb. 1941, p. 1, 'Il faut en finir', 19 Feb. 1941, p. 1, 'Pourquoi vous aurez faim', 25 Feb. 1941, p. 3, 'Les messages de Rex', 27 Feb. 1941, p. 3, 'Billet de Verviers', 1 Mar. 1941, p. 1, 'Et la Belgique?', 4 Mar. 1941, p. 3, 'Nominations partisanes à Soignies' and 19 Mar. 1941, p. 1, 'La Révolution doit être faite...'; JS *Pro Just.*, 24 May 1945, *Aud. Gén.*, Doss. JS, Info.

31 *Le PR* 11 Feb., 25 Feb. and 4 Mar. 1941, p. 3, 'Les messages de Rex' and 12 Mar. 1941, p. 1, 'Le meeting de Frameries'; *TB* 14, 2 Mar. 1941, p. 1311. Degrelle held twelve meetings during the first three months of 1941, addressing audiences as large as 1,000 people.

32 *TB* 12, 3 Jan. 1941, pp. 1021–2; J. Del Marmol to J. Rens 17 Apr. 1941, *C2GM*, PM 14; P. Struye *L'évolution du sentiment public*, pp. 36–8.

33 F. Selleslagh 'L'emploi' and L. Schepens 'La mentalité de la population' in *1940–1945 La vie quotidienne en Belgique*, pp. 157 and 220.

34 Bulletin du mouvement rexiste No. 5, 25 Jan. 1941, *C2GM*, C 11/166; *Le PR* 31 Dec. 1940, p. 1, 'Léon Degrelle a parlé...' and 23 Jan. 1941, p. 2, 'Rex accueille...'; Pévenasse circular to militants 17 Feb. 1942, *Aud. Gén.*, Doss. Albert Constant, Documentation Générale, Doct. 90bis.

35 Bulletin des dirigeants 20 May 1941, *C2GM*, C 11/99.

36 Journal de V. Matthys p. 4, *C2GM*.

37 These included Marcel Parfondry and Henri Horlin of the *POB* and Charles Nisolle of the *Parti Socialiste Révolutionnaire*. They held discussions with local Rexist militants, as well as with Degrelle, as a result of which they decided to join Rex: Charles Nisolle *Pro Just.*, 18–25 June 1945, *Aud. Gén.*, Doss. Charles Lambinon, Inst., Doct. 47–56; *Le PR* 4 Feb. 1941, p. 3, 'Le Chef de Rex fait acclamer...' and 7 Dec. 1941, p. 1, 'Les nouveaux députés permanents...'; L. Degrelle *La Cohue*, p. 185; C. Legein 'Le Parti Socialiste Révolutionnaire (Le Mouvement Trotskyiste en Belgique de 1936 à 1939)' (Université Catholique de Louvain Mémoire de licence, 1982), pp. 363–4.

38 See J. Gotovitch 'Du Collectivisme au Plan de Travail' in *1885–1985: Du Parti Ouvrier Belge au Parti Socialiste* (Brussels, 1985), pp. 123–43.

39 R. Lefebvre 'Dauge et le Daugisme' (Université Libre de Bruxelles Mémoire de licence, 1979).

40 *Ibid.*, p. 80; *Le PR* 9 Jan. 1941, p. 3, 'La réunion rexiste de Liége'.

41 Charles Nisolle *Pro Just.*, 18–25 June 1945, *Aud. Gén.*, Doss. Charles Lambinon, Inst., Doct. 47–56; *Le Soir* 1 May 1941, p. 1, 'Fécondité du mouvement ouvrier . . .'; L. Degrelle *La Cohue*, pp. 203–7.

42 G. Figeys Carnets 3 Mar. 1946, pp. 89–90, *C2GM*, JP 093.

43 *Ibid*; *Le PR* 5 July 1944, p. 2, 'Walter Dauge a été abattu'. A Rexist document of May 1941 described Dauge as the *Chef* of the Rexist trade union (the *Ordre du Travail Nationale-Socialiste*) but he was never active in this organisation: *EM du Chef de Rex* 12 May 1941, *C2GM*, C 11/98.

44 The Rexist press frequently referred to the presence of former Daugistes in the *Légion Wallonie*: *Le PR* 30 July 1941, p. 1, 'La croisade contre le bolchevisme' and 28 Sept. 1941, p. 3, 'Entre camarades'. See also G. Figeys Carnets 3 Mar. 1946, pp. 89–93, *C2GM*, JP 093.

45 R. Lefebvre 'Dauge et le Daugisme', pp. 80–3; *Le PR* 14 Feb. 1942, p. 3, 'W. Dauge affirme qu'il est innocent'; C. Legein 'Le Parti Socialiste Révolutionnaire', p. 326.

46 Marcel Destrain *Pro Just.*, 31 July 1945, *Aud. Gén.*, Doss. LC, Inst., Doct. 91–9. See also G. Figeys Carnets 3 Mar. 1946, pp. 90–1, *C2GM*, JP 093; R. Lefebvre 'Dauge et le Daugisme', pp. 82–3.

47 *Le PR* 23 Feb. 1941, p. 1, 'Magistrature couchée', 19 Mar. 1941, p. 1, 'Il y a un an . . .' and 30 Mar. 1941, p. 1, 'Le présent et Rex'.

48 *Le PR* 28 Jan. 1941, p. 2, 'Prestation de serment . . .', 4 Feb. 1941, p. 3, 'Le Chef de Rex fait acclamer . . .' and 11 Feb. 1941, p. 3, 'Les messages de Rex'.

49 *TB* 13, 2 Feb. 1941, p. 1150.

50 *Ibid*; *TB* 14, 2 Mar. 1941, p. 1311; *TB* 16, 9 May 1941, pp. 1647–8.

51 General von Falkenhausen *Mémoires d'outre-guerre* (Brussels, 1974), p. 300; Souvenirs de H. Forsteneichner p. 1, *C2GM*, PF 3.

52 P. Delandsheere and A. Ooms *La Belgique sous les Nazis* I, p. 274; Radio Vatican 14 Feb. 1941 cited in BBC Daily Digest of Foreign Broadcasts 14 Feb. 1941, *C2GM*, Fonds INBEL/732.

53 Bulletin du mouvement rexiste No. 6, 1 Mar. 1941, *C2GM*, C 11/167; *Chef de Rex-Wallonie* to Rexist militants 2 Mar. 1941, *Aud. Gén.*, Doss. Joseph Pévenasse, Doct. 914.

54 *TB* 14, 2 Mar. 1941, p. 1312; *Chef de Rex-Wallonie* to *Chef de la Province de Namur* 5 Mar. 1941, *Chef de Rex-Wallonie* to *Cdt. Régional FC de la Wallonie* 24 Mar. 1941 and Constant to Cdt. Jacobs 24 Apr. 1941, *Aud. Gén.*, Doss. Joseph Pévenasse, Docts. 914 and 913 and Doss. Albert Constant, Inst., Doct. 12; *Le PR* 13 and 27 Mar. 1941, p. 2, 'Dans le Mouvement'. See also pp. 240–2.

55 E.g. *Le PR* 19 Jan. 1941, p. 1, 'Un artisan de l'Europe nouvelle'; A. De Jonghe 'La lutte Himmler-Reeder . . .', *Cahiers* V (1978), pp. 46–7.

56 JS Au sujet de l'article 115 [pp. 4–6], *C2GM*, Fonds José Streel.

57 A. De Jonghe 'La lutte Himmler-Reeder . . .', *Cahiers* IV (1976), p. 41 and V (1978), p. 46.

58 *Die Tagebücher von Joseph Goebbels* IV, pp. 454–5 and 512; W. Boelcke *Kriegspropaganda 1939–1941* (Stuttgart, 1966), p. 597.

59 L. Degrelle *Hitler pour mille ans*, p. 104; L. Degrelle *La Cohue*, pp. 459–61.

60 General Van Overstraeten *Sous le joug*, pp. 122–3.

61 E.g. Bulletin du mouvement rexiste No. 5, 25 Jan. 1941, *C2GM*, C 11/166.

62 Bulletin du mouvement rexiste No. 6, 1 Mar. 1941, *C2GM*, C 11/167; *Le PR* 1 Mar. 1941, p. 2, 'Dans le Mouvement'.

63 Bulletin du mouvement rexiste No. 6, 1 Mar. 1941, *C2GM*, C 11/167; *TB* 15, 7 Apr. 1941, p. 1466.

64 *La Meuse* 4 Dec. 1946, p. 2, 'Au Conseil de Guerre'; *TB* 16, 9 May 1941, p. 1647.

65 See p. 43. See also note 62 and *Le PR* 26 Mar. 1941, p. 2, 'Dans le Mouvement'.

66 *TB* 16, 9 May 1941, p. 1647; 'Propositions confidentielles du Chef du *MNPW* à Monsieur le Capitaine Dalldorff . . .' 26 May 1942, *C2GM*, C 13/7; L. Degrelle *La Cohue*, pp. 508–9.

67 Dalldorff to *OFK* 589 30 May 1941 and to Propaganda Abteilung Belgien 9 July 1941 and 6 Oct. 1941 and 'Rapport à Monsieur Dalldorff . . .', *C2GM*, C 13/4, C 13/5.2

and C 13/5.1; Documentation Jans 313; *La Légia* 13 Oct. 1941, p. 2, 'Une réunion du Mouvement National Populaire Wallon'; *La Meuse* 2 Nov. 1945, p. 2, 'Au Conseil de Guerre' and 24 Feb. 1947, p. 2, 'Cour Militaire'. See pp. 136–7.

68 Documentation Jans 1 and 73; Report of Propaganda Abteilung Liège 27 Aug. 1941, *C2GM*, C 5/23.

69 *TB* 18, 21 Dec. 1941, p. 2120; Gaillard to *Kreiskommandantur* (*KK*) of Namur 22 Apr. 1943, *C2GM*, C 5/27. See also pp. 138–9.

70 Bulletin du mouvement rexiste No. 6, 1 Mar. 1941, *C2GM*, C 11/167; *Le PR* 1 Mar. 1941, p. 2, 'Dans le Mouvement'; Constant to *Chef de Rex-Wallonie* 17 May 1941, *Aud. Gén.*, Doss. Albert Constant, Inst., Doct. 35.

71 Albert Constant *Pro Just.*, 18 Apr. 1946, *Aud. Gén.*, Doss. Albert Constant, Inst., Doct. 219–20.

72 LD to Officials of *FC* (Flanders), *C2GM*, C 11/269; Louis Richard *Pro Just.*, 12 July 1945, *Aud. Gén.*, Doss. Albert Constant, Documentation Générale, Doct. 1–5.

73 LD to Officials of *FC* (Flanders) 16 Apr. 1941, *C2GM*, C 11/269; *Le PR* 19 Apr. 1941, p. 2, 'De Bewegung in Vlaanderen'; *TB* 16, 9 May 1941, pp. 1646–7.

74 *Le PR* 22 Apr. 1941, p. 3, 'Préparons-nous pour l'après-guerre!' and 24 Apr. 1941, p. 2, 'Dans le Mouvement'; *Le Soir* 14 Feb. 1947, p. 5, 'Conseil de Guerre de Bruxelles'.

75 Bulletin du mouvement rexiste No. 6, 1 Mar. 1941, *C2GM*, C 11/167; *Le PR* 27 Mar. 1941, p. 2, 'Dans le Mouvement'; L. Degrelle *La Cohue*, p. 461.

76 *TB* 16, 9 May 1941, pp. 1648–9.

77 Bulletin du mouvement rexiste No. 6, 1 Mar. 1941 and Rex-Wallonie Bulletin des dirigeants 15 Apr. 1941, *C2GM*, C 11/167 and C 11/321.3; *Le PR* 26 Mar. 1941, p. 2, 'Dans le Mouvement'; Speech by Pévenasse [12 Apr. 1941], *Aud. Gén.*, Doss. Joseph Pévenasse.

78 See note 77; Untitled article by Pévenasse, *C2GM*, C 11/321.5; Documentation Jans 126; *Le PR* 8 Apr. 1941, p. 2, 'Dans le Mouvement'.

79 Historique de l'organisation des *FC* and Constant to *FC* units [Apr. 1941], *C2GM*, C 11/263 and C 11/264.

80 P. Struye *L'évolution du sentiment public*, pp. 34–6; Anonymous report 'La situation à la fin de septembre 1941', *C2GM*, W 3/37.

81 J. Willequet *La Belgique sous la botte*, pp. 104–9.

82 *Le PR* 15 Jan. 1941, p. 1, 'Manoeuvres et provocations'; R. Verlaine *Sans haine et sans gloire*, pp. 175 and 181.

83 *TB* 15, 7 Apr. 1941, p. 1465.

84 *Vers l'Avenir* 13 Feb. 1946, p. 3, 'Conseil de Guerre de Namur'; *L'Avenir du Luxembourg* 10 May 1946, p. 1, 'Au Conseil de Guerre d'Arlon'; Charles Nisolle *Pro Just.*, 18–25 June 1945, *Aud. Gén.*, Doss. Charles Lambinon, Inst., Doct. 47–56; Raymond Camby *Pro Just.*, 17 July 1945, *Aud. Gén.*, Doss. VM, Info., Doct. 22–36.

85 *TB* 15, 7 Apr. 1941, pp. 1465–6; *Le PR* 4 Mar. 1941, p. 3, 'Les messages de Rex'; *Vers l'Avenir* 16–17 Mar. 1946, p. 2, 'Léon Degrelle à Namur'; P. Delandsheere and A. Ooms *La Belgique sous les Nazis* I, pp. 401–2.

86 *Le PR* 13 May 1941, p. 2, 'Des antirexistes arrêtés à Anhée'.

87 'Faits et anecdotes . . . exposés par le Capitaine BEM Monjoie' 18 June 1941 and J. Del Marmol to J. Rens 5 July 1941, *C2GM*, PD 40 and PM 14; P. Struye *L'évolution du sentiment public*, p. 68.

88 Interview between Jean Vermeire and José Gotovitch 25 Mar. 1971, pp. 59–63, *C2GM*; R. Verlaine *Sans haine et sans gloire*, p. 175.

89 Backx to LD 3 Nov. 1941, *C2GM*, C 11/279.

90 Membership card 1941, *C2GM*, C 11/323.15. See also Bulletin du mouvement rexiste No. 5, 25 Jan. 1941, *C2GM*, C 11/166; Documentation Jans 83.

91 *Le PR* 29 Jan. 1941, p. 1, 'Les *FC* anversois . . .', 14 Mar. 1941, p. 3, 'Devant la carence des autorités . . .', 18 Mar. 1941, p. 2, 'La police de St Gilles . . .' and 27 Mar. 1941, p. 2, 'Dans le Mouvement'.

92 *La Meuse* 1 July 1946, p. 2, 'Les agresseurs du bourgmestre Duchatto . . .' and 2 July 1946, p. 2, 'Au Conseil de Guerre'.

93 *Le PR* 27 Feb. 1941, p. 6, 'Une bonne leçon . . . et un exemple', 1 Mar. 1941, p. 2, 'Les bienfaits de la crevache' and 17 May 1941, p. 3, 'Le Conseil de Discipline . . .'

94 Dreumont to *Cdts. de Groupe* 6 Mar. 1941, *Aud. Gén.*, Doss. Joseph Pévenasse, Doct. 916.
95 *Le PR* 30 Mar. 1941, p. 1, 'Pas de meetings aujourd'hui'; Bulletin des dirigeants 20 May 1941, *C2GM*, C 11/99.
96 Constant to *Inspecteur Provincial* of Brabant Wallon 30 Mar. 1941, *Aud. Gén.*, Doss. Albert Constant, Inst., Doct. 33; Le Gorlois to *FC* officers of Wallonia 16 Apr. 1941, *C2GM*, C 11/281.
97 L. Degrelle *La Cohue*, pp. 481 and 508; Journal de V. Matthys pp. 4–5, *C2GM*.
98 LD to Hitler 10 Apr. 1941 cited in A. De Jonghe 'La lutte Himmler-Reeder . . .', *Cahiers* V (1978), p. 168.
99 *Ibid* V (1978), pp. 168–70; *TB* 16, 9 May 1941, p. 1649; L. Degrelle *La Cohue*, p. 515.
100 *Le PR* 13 Apr. 1941, p. 1, 'Pâques de grisaille' and 20 Apr. 1941, p. 1, 'La guerre et l'avenir'.
101 *Ibid*; L. Degrelle *Discours prononcé à Liége le 27 avril 1941* (Liège, No date); *Le PR* 23 Mar. 1941, p. 1, 'Parti unique?', 30 Mar. 1941, p. 1, 'Le présent et Rex', 22 Apr. 1941, p. 3, 'Préparons-nous pour l'après-guerre!' and 6 May 1941, p. 3, 'Le Chef de Rex exalte . . .'
102 J. Del Marmol to J. Rens 17 Apr. 1941, *C2GM*, PM 14.
103 E.g. *Le PR* 7 May 1941, p. 1, 'Nationalisme et l'Occident' and 11 May 1941, p. 1, 'La déclaration du Chef de Rex'.
104 L. Degrelle *Discours prononcé à Liége*, pp. 9–11.
105 *Die Tagebücher von Joseph Goebbels* IV, p. 613.
106 *TB* 15, 7 Apr. 1941, p. 1443. See also E. Verhoeyen 'Les grands industriels belges entre collaboration et résistance: le moindre mal', *Cahiers* X (1986), pp. 88–99.
107 *TB* 15, 7 Apr. 1941, pp. 1449–51 and 1466–7; *TB* 16, 9 May 1941, p. 1648; *Le Soir* 2 Apr. 1941, p. 2, 'Nos nouveaux Secrétaires Généraux'.
108 *Le PR* 30 Mar. 1941, p. 1, 'Le présent et Rex'; *TB* 15, 7 Apr. 1941, pp. 1467–8; Journal de V. Matthys p. 5, *C2GM*; L. Degrelle *La Cohue*, pp. 464–5.
109 *Le PR* 6 Apr. 1941, p. 1, 'Objectifs immédiats'.
110 *Le Soir* 2 Apr. 1941, p. 1, 'Les nouveaux Secrétaires Généraux'; J. Willequet *La Belgique sous la botte*, p. 164.
111 *Le PR* 3 Apr. 1941, p. 1, 'L'arrivée de M. Romsée . . .' See also *Le PR* 28 Feb. 1941, p. 4, 'Billet du Centre' and 11 Apr. 1941, p. 1, 'Notre camarade . . .'
112 *Le PR* 9 Mar. 1941, p. 1, 'Un fameux nettoyage . . .'; *TB* 16, 9 May 1941, p. 1657; *Moniteur Belge* 30 May 1941, pp. 3808–9.
113 VM *Pro Just.*, 14 and 21 May 1947, *Aud. Gén.*, Doss. LC, Enquête Complémentaire, Farde C, Docts. 19 and 20–6; *Le Soir* 13 May 1947, p. 4, 'Les Conseils de Guerre' and 28 and 29 May 1947, p. 5, 'Les Conseils de Guerre de Bruxelles'.
114 JS *Pro Just.*, 24 May 1945, *Aud. Gén.*, Doss. JS, Info; *Le PR* 17 Apr. 1941, p. 2, 'Dans le Mouvement'; *Inspecteur Fédéral* to *Chefs de Cercles* 11 June, 24 July, 13 and 25 Aug. 1941, *C2GM*, C 11/169, 172, 173 and 174.
115 *Le PR* 11 May 1941, p. 8, and 13 May 1941, p. 3, 'Notre camarade . . .'
116 *Cercle de Mons Cadre Politique* Meeting of 21 Feb. 1942, *C2GM*, C 11/321.10; Letter to P. Herlemont 30 June 1941, *C2GM*, W 3/20; J. Wynants 'Verviers, l'autorité communale en 1940–1941', *Cahiers* II (1972), pp. 163–4 and 167. See also pp. 139–48.
117 *Le PR* 11 May 1941, p. 1, 'La déclaration du Chef de Rex'. Re the 1936 accord, see J.-M. Etienne *Le mouvement rexiste*, pp. 99–102.
118 *Le PR* 11 May 1941, pp. 1 and 4, 'La réunion d'hier matin . . .'
119 A. De Jonghe 'La lutte Himmler-Reeder . . .', *Cahiers* IV (1976), pp. 17–19; *Le PR* 23 Oct. 1940, p. 1, 'Un accord . . .'; P. Janssens 'Les Dinasos wallons', p. 228.
120 *TB* 13, 2 Feb. 1941, pp. 1147–9; *TB* 14, 2 Mar. 1941, p. 1308; *TB* 16, 9 May 1941, pp. 1642–4; A. De Jonghe *Op. cit.*, pp. 20–52; P. Janssens *Op. cit.*, pp. 235–6.
121 *Le PR* 1 Jan., 30 Jan. and 5 Feb. 1941, p. 2, 'Dans le Mouvement'.
122 *Le PR* 11 Oct. 1940, p. 8, 'Cadre du mouvement rexiste en Flandre', 4 Jan. and 23 Feb. 1941, p. 2, 'Dans le Mouvement'; Journal de V. Matthys p. 4, *C2GM*; L. Degrelle *La Cohue*, pp. 475–6.
123 *Le PR* 2 Oct. 1940, p. 2, 'Dans le mouvement rexiste', 11 Oct. 1940, p. 8, 'Rex Flandre . . .' and 8 May 1941, p. 2, 'De Bewegung in Vlaanderen'.

124 See *Le PR* 14 May 1941, p. 2, 'Dans le Mouvement'.
125 *Le PR* 11 May 1941, pp. 3–4, 'La communication du leider du *VNV*'. See also General Van Overstraeten *Sous le joug*, pp. 120–4 and 128; *Le PR* 4 Jan. 1941, p. 1, 'Pour un compromis des Belges' and 1 Apr. 1941, p. 1, 'A propos d'espace vital'.
126 *Le PR* 16 May 1941, p. 1, 'Positions de Rex et du *VNV* . . .' and p. 3, 'Les précisions de Rex et du *VNV* . . .'
127 *Le Soir* 13 May 1941, p. 1, 'En marge de l'accord Rex-*VNV*'; *Le Nouveau Journal* 12 May 1941, p. 1, 'Les principes et les méthodes'; *Cassandre* 11 May 1941, p. 1, 'Fusions et "partis uniques" '; *Le Journal de Charleroi* 13 May 1941, p. 1, 'Evénement historique?'
128 *Le PR* 16 May 1941, p. 1, 'A propos de Bruxelles'; *Le Soir* 15 May 1941, p. 1, 'Le Peuple et l'Etat'.
129 Bulletin des dirigeants 20 May 1941 and Constant to *Cdts. d'unités FC*, *C2GM*, C 11/99 and C 11/321.4.
130 *Biographie Nationale* XXXV (1969), pp. 140–5; J. Willequet *La Belgique sous la botte*, pp. 81–91; E. De Bens 'La presse au temps de l'occupation de la Belgique (1940–44)', *Revue d'histoire de la deuxième guerre mondiale* XX (1970), pp. 27–8; J. Stengers 'Paul De Man, a collaborator?' in L. Herman, K. Humbeeck and G. Lernout (eds.) *(Dis)continuities: Essays on Paul De Man* (Amsterdam, 1989), pp. 43–50.
131 *Le Soir* 22–3 Mar. 1941, pp. 1–2, 'Les tâches du jour' and 13 May 1941, p. 1, 'En marge de l'accord Rex-*VNV*'; *Le Nouveau Journal* 12 May 1941, p. 1, 'Les principes et les méthodes'.
132 'Pour un Parti Unique des Provinces Romanes' 19 May 1941, Untitled note (Doct. 313) and De Becker and Daye to founders of Party 5 Aug. 1941, *C2GM*, Papiers Pierre Daye; Documentation Jans 137.
133 *Le PR* 18 May 1941, p. 1, 'Rex ou quoi?'
134 De Becker to Daye 19 May 1941, *C2GM*, Papiers Pierre Daye; *Le PR* 20 May 1941, p. 3, 'Léon Degrelle parle à Namur . . .', 22 May 1941, p. 1, 'Le temps de la critique . . .' and 10 June 1941, p. 3, 'Bruxelles a vécu . . .'
135 *Jahresbericht der Militärverwaltung* June 1941, Section A, pp. 44–5.
136 Documentation Jans 137; *Le Soir* 30 June 1941, p. 1, 'Un important article du Président Reeder'; De Becker and Daye to founders of Party 5 Aug. 1941 and Daye to Herlemont 16 Aug. 1941, *C2GM*, Papiers Pierre Daye.
137 *Le PR* 4 July 1941, p. 1, 'Une leçon et un avertissement'.
138 Rex Statut du Mouvement [1941], Bulletin des dirigeants 20 May 1941 and Historique de l'organisation des *FC*, *C2GM*, C 11/86, C 11/99 and C 11/263; Albert Constant *Pro Just.*, 18 Apr.1946, *Aud. Gén.*, Doss. Albert Constant, Inst., Doct. 219–20.
139 See previous note; *Le PR* 27 June and 18 Sept. 1941, p. 3 and 19 Oct. 1941, p. 2, 'Chronique du Mouvement'; Documentation Jans 193.
140 Interview between Jean Vermeire and José Gotovitch 25 Mar. 1971, pp. 70–4, *C2GM*.
141 See notes 140 and 142. For a similar example of emulation of Nazi models, see Y. Jelinek *The Parish Republic: Hlinka's Slovak People's Party 1939–1945* (New York-London, 1976), pp. 44–6.
142 JS *Pro Just.*, 24 May 1945, *Aud. Gén.*, Doss. JS, Info.
143 Rouleau to Vandevelde 16 May 1941, *C2GM*, C 11/133; Région de Bruxelles Ordres hebdomadaires des *FC* 17 May 1941, *Aud. Gén.*, Doss. Jean Colman, Inst., Doct. 69; *Le PR* 4 May 1941, p. 2, 'Dans le Mouvement'.
144 Interview with Léon Degrelle 14 July 1988; *TB* 16, 9 May 1941, p. 1646; Louis Richard *Pro Just.*, 12 July 1945, *Aud. Gén.*, Doss. Albert Constant, Documentation Générale, Doct. 1–5.
145 E.g. *L'Avenir du Luxembourg* 28 Feb. 1946, p. 1, 'Au Conseil de Guerre' and 5 June 1946, p. 1, 'Le Gestapiste de Bourcy . . .'; *Le PR* 2 May 1941, p. 2, 'Dans le Mouvement'.
146 *Le PR* 8 July 1941, p. 1, 'Pourquoi "Nationaux-Socialistes"?'; Bulletin des dirigeants 15 Dec. 1941, 'De la démocratie au national socialisme', *C2GM*, C 11/184.
147 Speech by Pévenasse [12 Apr. 1941], *Aud. Gén.*, Doss. Joseph Pévenasse.
148 *Le PR* 1 May 1941, p. 1, 'Peuple de chez nous!', 24 June 1941, p. 3, 'Au Camp des FC de Mons' and 28 June 1941, p. 1, 'Il y a la manière . . .'
149 *Le PR* 4 June 1941, p. 3, 'Nos camps de Pentecôte', 6 June 1941, p. 1, 'Tous les

rexistes . . .', 10 June 1941, p. 3, 'Bruxelles a vécu . . .', 15 June 1941, p. 3, 'Chronique du Mouvement' and 26 June 1941, p. 1, 'L'Indiscipline Nationale'.

150 A. Dantoing 'Le hiérarchie catholique et la Belgique sous l'occupation allemande', *Revue du Nord* LX (1978), pp. 315–17.

151 E.g. *Le PR* 6 Mar. 1941, p. 1, 'La Bibliothèque de Louvain' and 8 Mar. 1941, p. 1, 'Les beautés de l'enseignement "religieux"' and 27 Mar. 1941, p. 2, 'Dans le Mouvement'.

152 *Le PR* 13 Feb. 1941, p. 3, 'Un incident scandaleux à Warsage' and 18 Feb. 1941, p. 3, 'Les messages de Rex'.

153 Chanoine Leclef *Le Cardinal Van Roey et l'occupation allemande*, pp. 93–4 and 181–2; *Le diocèse de Tournai sous l'occupation allemande*, p. 117.

154 Chanoine Leclef *Op. cit.*, pp. 93 and 261–75; C. Chevalier 'La presse francophone et l'église catholique', pp. 161 and 190–3; *Le PR* 18 May 1941, p. 1, 'Les prières interdites', 6 June 1941, p. 1, 'Pour la paix des consciences' and 2 Aug. 1941, p. 1, 'Une offensive qui se précise'.

155 Chanoine Leclef *Op. cit.*, pp. 97–8 and 182–6.

156 *Le PR* 22 July 1941, p. 1, 'Des incidents pénibles'; *Vers l'Avenir* 9 July 1946, p. 2, 'Conseil de Guerre de Namur'. See also pp. 148–50.

157 *Le PR* 28 May 1941, p. 1, 'Le 28 mai'. See also *Le PR* 10 June 1941, pp. 1 and 3, 'Bruxelles a vécu . . .' and 22 June 1941, p. 1, 'L'impuissance anglaise'.

158 E.g. J.-P. Brunet *Jacques Doriot*, pp. 359–60.

159 *Le PR* 24 June 1941, p. 3, 'Au Camp des FC de Mons' and 20 July 1941, p. 1, 'Pour la croisade contre Moscou'.

160 *Le PR* 25 June 1941, p. 1, 'Il faut choisir entre l'Ordre et le Bolchevisme' and 27 June 1941, p. 1, 'Croisades et Guerres'.

161 *TB* 17, 22 Sept. 1941, p. 1814; P. Struye *L'évolution du sentiment public*, p. 82.

162 L. Degrelle *La Cohue*, p. 526; P. Dastier 'Degrelle parle', *Dossier du mois* No. 6/7 (Brussels, 1963), p. 10.

163 *Le PR* 30 June 1941, p. 1, 'L'heure des Wallons'; J. Mabire *Légion Wallonie: au Front de l'Est 1941–1944* (Paris, 1987), p. 9.

164 E.g. R. Salas Larrazabal 'La Division "Azul"', *Guerres mondiales et conflits contemporains* XL (1990), p. 48; J.-L. Hondros *Occupation and Resistance*, p. 72.

165 O.A. Davey 'The Origins of the *Légion des Volontaires Français contre le Bolchevisme*', *Journal of Contemporary History* VI No. 4 (1971), pp. 29–45; INBEL 1 Dec. 1941 No. 1, *C2GM*, Fonds INBEL/1087; Henry Marcovitz *Pro Just.*, 7 Mar. 1946, *C2GM*, PF 3; J.-M. Charlier *Léon Degrelle*, pp. 267–8.

166 Interview between Carl Peeters and José Gotovitch 24 Mar. 1972, p. 47, *C2GM*.

167 LD to FC of Brussels 6 July 1941, *C2GM*, C 11/275. Degrelle also announced at the same time the establishment of a second military unit (the *Gardes Wallonnes*) which would assist the German armies within Belgium. Its creation was, however, subsequently postponed until the autumn: see pp. 109–11.

168 E. De Bruyne 'Un aspect de la collaboration militaire dans la Belgique francophone 1941–1945', *C2GM*, JP 732; *Le PR* 8 July 1941, p. 1, 'Un corps franc "Wallonie" . . .' and 'Aux armes!'

169 Interview between Jean Vermeire and José Gotovitch 25 Mar. 1971, p. 70, *C2GM*; *L'Avenir du Luxembourg* 31 May 1947, p. 1, 'Au Conseil de Guerre d'Arlon'; *Le PR* 9 July 1941, p. 1, 'Gardes Wallonnes et Corps Franc' and 13 July 1941, p. 2, 'Chronique du Mouvement'.

170 *Le PR* 13 July 1941, p. 1, 'Pourquoi participer à la lutte contre le Bolchevisme?' and 20 July 1941, p. 1, 'Pour la croisade contre Moscou'; Sylvain Jadoul *Pro Just.*, 28 Aug. 1945, *Aud. Gén.*, Doss. Pierre Pauly, *Cour Militaire*, Doct. 10.

171 L. Degrelle *Hitler pour mille ans*, p. 111; L. Degrelle *La Cohue*, pp. 517–18.

172 *Le PR* 15 July 1941, p. 1, 'La croisade contre Moscou' and 4 Jan. 1942, p. 2, 'Les grandes heures . . .'; Radio Zeesen 28 Aug. 1941 cited in *C2GM*, Fonds INBEL/732; Comte Capelle *Au Service du Roi* II, p. 127; R. Salas Larrazabal 'La Division "Azul"', *Guerres mondiales et conflits contemporains* XL (1990), pp. 49–50.

173 *Inspecteur Fédéral* to *Chefs de Cercles* 14 July 1941, *C2GM*, C 11/171.

174 L. Degrelle *La Cohue*, p. 519; VM *Pro Just.*, 12 Sept. 1945, *Aud. Gén.*, Doss. VM, Info., Doct. 48–51.

175 André Renotte *Pro Just.*, 13 July 1946, *Aud. Gén.*, Doss. Albert Constant, Documentation Générale, Doct. 111–16; Henry Marcovitz *Pro Just.*, 7 Mar. 1946, *C2GM*, PF 3. Degrelle strenuously denies that he gave any such assurance: Interview with Léon Degrelle 14 July 1988.

176 'Les mémoires de Pierre Daye', *Dossier du mois* No. 12, pp. 21–2; Comte Capelle *Au Service du Roi* II, p. 127; *Recueil de documents établi par le Secrétariat du Roi*, pp. 365–7; *La Meuse* 5 Sept. 1945, p. 1, 'Conseil de Guerre'.

177 Comte Capelle *Op. cit.* II, pp. 106 and 209; R. Poulet 'Mémoire confidentiel à S.A.R. le Régent' [Jan. 1946], p. 3 (Private Collection); Mémoire de V. Matthys pp. 20–2, *C2GM*.

178 P. Pauly *Pro Just.*, 4 July 1945 and Louis Richard *Pro Just.*, 12 July 1945, *Aud. Gén.*, Doss. Pierre Pauly, Info., Doct. 18 and Doss. Albert Constant, Documentation Générale, Doct. 1–5; Interview between Carl Peeters and José Gotovitch 24 Mar. 1972, p. 56, *C2GM*. Matthys subsequently admitted to Capelle that the letter had indeed been forged: Comte Capelle *Au Service du Roi* II, pp. 209–10.

179 *Le PR* 1 Aug. 1941, pp. 1 and 3, 'La Légion "Wallonie" . . .'; R. Poulet 'Prison Diary' 12 July 1946, p. 6 (Private Collection); J. Denis 'Mémoire justificatif d'un condamné à mort' p. 52, *Aud. Gén.*, Doss. Jean Denis, Info., Doct. 53.

180 *Le PR* 22 July 1941, p. 1, 'Le Chef de Rex s'engage . . .' and p. 3, 'Devant trois mille Rexistes liégeois'.

181 L. Degrelle *Hitler pour mille ans*, pp. 108–9; P. Dastier 'Degrelle parle', *Dossier du mois* No. 6/7, p. 10. See also E. De Bruyne *Les Wallons meurent à l'est*, p. 32.

182 L. Degrelle *La Cohue*, pp. 525–6.

183 *Le PR* 10 Aug. 1943, p. 4, 'Une émouvante cérémonie d'hommage . . .'; JS Au sujet de l'article 115 [p. 10], *C2GM*, Fonds José Streel; Légion Belge 'Wallonie' Historique, p. 3, *C2GM*, W 4. Later in August and in September, small groups of additional volunteers joined the *Légion* bringing its total strength to approximately 1,000 men.

184 *Le PR* 9 Aug. 1941, p. 1, 'La Légion est partie' and 2 Sept. 1941, p. 3, 'Les nominations de bourgmestres'; Report by Reeder 23 Aug. 1941, *C2GM*, Procès von Falkenhausen, Doct. 118.

185 *L'Ami du Peuple* 11 Oct. 1941, p. 2, 'Une conférence de Me Lambrichts . . .' and 18 Oct. 1941, p. 2, 'Légion Wallonie'; *Le PR* 11 Jan. 1942, p. 1, 'Capitaine Dupré . . .', 1 May 1942, p. 7, 'Une émouvante cérémonie . . .' and 3 Jan. 1943, p. 1, 'Nos héros . . .'; André Renotte *Pro Just.*, 13 July 1946, *Aud. Gén.*, Doss. Albert Constant, Documentation Générale, Doct. 111–16; Mathieu to A. De Bruyne 4 Nov. 1985, *C2GM*, JP 722; E. De Bruyne 'Un aspect de la collaboration militaire dans la Belgique francophone 1941–1945', *C2GM*, JP 732; L. Degrelle *La Cohue*, pp. 522–3.

186 *Le PR* 9 Aug. 1941, pp. 1 and 6, 'La Légion est partie' and 'Le message du Chef'.

187 VM *Pro Just.*, 12 Sept. 1945, *Aud. Gén.*, Doss. VM, Info., Doct. 48–51; *Le PR* 9 Aug. 1941, p. 6, 'La Légion est partie'; L. Degrelle *La Cohue*, p. 519.

188 P. Struye *L'évolution du sentiment public*, p. 83; *Le PR* 9 Aug. 1941, pp. 1 and 6, 'La Légion est partie'; INBEL 30 Nov. 1941 No. 2, *C2GM*, Fonds INBEL/981; *Cassandre* 10 Aug. 1941, p. 1, 'Echos et Indiscrétions'.

189 *Le PR* 10 Aug. 1941, p. 1, 'Les devoirs de la Légion qui reste' and 10 Aug. 1943, pp. 1 and 4, 'Une émouvante cérémonie . . .'; Interview between Carl Peeters and José Gotovitch 24 Mar. 1972, p. 48, *C2GM*.

190 *Le PR* 1 Aug. 1941, pp. 1 and 3, 'La Légion "Wallonie" . . .'; Sylvain Jadoul *Pro Just.*, 28 Aug. 1945, *Aud. Gén.*, Doss. Pierre Pauly, *Cour Militaire*, Doct. 10.

Chapter Three

1 *TB* 18, 21 Dec. 1941, pp. 2063–4; *TB* 23, 15 Apr. 1943, p. 2940; JS Au sujet de l'article 115 [p. 8], *C2GM*, Fonds José Streel.

2 *Le PR* 7 Aug. 1941, p. 3, 'Chronique du Mouvement'.

3 *Le PR* 31 July 1941, p. 1, 'La croisade contre le bolchevisme'; Ch. d'Ydewalle *Degrelle ou la triple imposture*, p. 195.

4 Henry Marcovitz *Pro Just.*, 7 Mar. 1946, *C2GM*, PF 3; Sylvain Jadoul *Pro Just.*, 28 Aug. 1945 and Gilbert Delrue *Pro Just.*, 8 Sept. 1945, *Aud. Gén.*, Doss. Pierre Pauly,

Cour Militaire, Docts. 10 and 13; JS *Pro Just.*, 24 May 1945, *Aud. Gén.*, Doss. JS, Info.

5 Interview between Jean Vermeire and José Gotovitch 25 Mar. 1971, pp. 72–3, *C2GM*; Henry Marcovitz *Pro Just.*, 7 Mar. 1946, *C2GM*, PF 3; E. De Bruyne *Les wallons meurent à l'est*, pp. 34–5.

6 See note 5; Anonymous letter 17 Apr. 1987, Private Papers of the Author; *La Belgique Indépendante* 7 Jan. 1943, cited in *C2GM*, Fonds INBEL/980. According to Carl Suzanne, one of those who had opposed Rouleau earlier in the year, he received a postcard from Degrelle after the August crisis, which declared: 'Mon cher Suzanne, tu avais raison. Il [i.e. Rouleau] a failli m'avoir. Il est chassé de la Légion': Interview between Carl Peeters and José Gotovitch 24 Mar. 1972, p. 48, *C2GM*. Degrelle now insists that he only acted against Rouleau at the insistence of the Belgian officers of the *Légion*: Interview with Léon Degrelle 14 July 1988.

7 Interview between Carl Peeters and José Gotovitch 24 Mar. 1972, pp. 48–9, *C2GM*; INBEL 14 June 1942 No. 2, *C2GM*, Fonds INBEL/1087; Anonymous letter 17 Apr. 1987, Private Papers of the Author; Telegram from *Chargé d'affaires* at Madrid 10 Feb. 1951, Archives of the Ministry of Foreign Affairs Brussels, Doct. 11179; Interview with Léon Degrelle 14 July 1988.

8 Orders of *Chef de Rex* 7 Aug. 1941, *C2GM*, C 11/100.

9 *Ibid.*

10 VM *Pro Just.*, 12 Sept. 1945, *Aud. Gén.*, Doss. VM, Info., Doct. 48–51; Interview with Léon Degrelle 14 July 1988; R. De Becker *Le livre des vivants et des morts*, p. 70; J.-M. Etienne *Le mouvement rexiste*, p. 72.

11 VM *Pro Just.*, 12 Sept. 1945, *Aud. Gén.*, Doss. VM, Info., Doct. 48–51; *La Meuse* 5 Mar. 1947, pp. 1 and 3, 'Des Tueurs rexistes . . .'

12 Les cahiers verts de José Streel p. 154, *C2GM*, Fonds José Streel; L. Degrelle *Lettres à mon Cardinal*, p. 134; Interview with Paul Jamin 11 Dec. 1987; R. De Becker 'La collaboration . . .', *Courrier hebdomadaire du CRISP* No. 497–8 (1970), pp. 31 and 59.

13 Orders of *Chef de Rex* 7 Aug. 1941, *C2GM*, C 11/100.

14 Journal de V. Matthys p. 6, *C2GM*.

15 *Le PR* 9 Aug. 1941, p. 6, 'Le message du Chef'.

16 Message du *Chef de Rex ad interim* 7 Sept. 1941, *C2GM*, C 11/134; *Le PR* 4 Sept. 1941, p. 1, 'Journée Légionnaire' and 12 Sept. 1941, p. 2, 'Chronique du Mouvement'.

17 *Le PR* 16 Sept. 1941, p. 1, 'Le Chef de Rex ad interim . . .'. The *chef de cercle* of Brussels-West wrote to Degrelle: '. . . vous avez eu la main heureuse en choisissant le Chef Matthijs. C'est le meilleur révolutionnaire que nous ayons à Rex. Il a su parfaitement s'imposer': Backx to LD 3 Nov. 1941, *C2GM*, C 11/279.

18 Message du *Chef de Rex ad interim* 7 Sept. 1941, *C2GM*, C 11/134; *Le PR* 10 Aug. 1941, p. 1, 'Les devoirs de la Légion qui reste' and 7 Sept. 1941, pp. 1 and 8, 'Aux côtés de la Légion'.

19 Message du *Chef de Rex ad interim* 7 Sept. 1941, *C2GM*, C 11/134; *Le PR* 17 Sept. 1941, p. 1, 'Le premier devoir . . .'; '*EM* du mouvement rexiste' [Feb. 1942], *C2GM*, Fonds INBEL/963.

20 Message du *Chef de Rex ad interim* 7 Sept. 1941, *C2GM*, C 11/134; *Le PR* 2 Sept. 1941, p. 3, 'Les nominations de bourgmestres', 14 Sept. 1941, p. 1, 'Nous allons doubler nos effectifs' and 21 Sept. 1941, p. 1, 'Mesures de protection . . .'

21 *TB* 18, 21 Dec. 1941, p. 2063; *Le PR* 25–6 and 28 Dec. 1941, p. 2, 'Solidarité Légionnaire'.

22 Bulletin des dirigeants 20 May 1941 and *Vouloir* [1941] No. 1, *C2GM*, C 11/99 and 323.17; *Le PR* 2 Aug. 1941, p. 3 and 21 Nov. 1941, p. 1, 'Solidarité Légionnaire'.

23 *Le PR* 19 Sept. 1941, p. 1, 'A toutes les Formations du Mouvement' and 3 Oct. 1941, p. 1, 'Jean Oedekerke est tombé . . .'; Plaidoyer prononcé par Victor Matthys devant le Conseil de Guerre de Charleroi p. 2, *C2GM*, JP 258; P. Struye *L'évolution du sentiment public*, p. 74.

24 See J. Gotovitch *Du rouge au tricolore: les communistes belges de 1939 à 1944* (Brussels, 1992), pp. 154–5 and E. Verhoeyen 'Un groupe de résistants du Nord-Hainaut: la Phalange Blanche', *Cahiers* XII (1989), pp. 163–205. Verhoeyen's excellent study dismisses as highly improbable the claims of the Tournai group to have acted on the orders of a British intelligence organisation.

25 De Zutter to Constant 2 Oct. 1941 and Leclercq to Constant 12 Oct. 1941, *Aud. Gén.*, Doss. Albert Constant, Correspondence of *légionnaires*, Docts. 2 and 3; *Le PR* 20 Sept. 1941, p. 1, 'La victoire seule venge les morts', 21 Sept. 1941, p. 1, 'Mesures de protection...', 7 Oct. 1941, p. 2, 'Les légionnaires jurent de venger...', 22 Oct. 1941, p. 1, 'Les criminels et leurs victimes' and 15 Nov. 1941, p. 1, 'Les "héros" de Tournai'.

26 *Le PR* 21 Sept. 1941, p. 1, 'Une foule recueillie a exalté...' and 9 Oct. 1941, pp. 1 and 3, 'Réponse à la mort'; 'Ordres pour les funérailles du Cde Jean Oedekerke' and 'Le discours de Victor Matthys', *C2GM*, C 11/290.

27 *Le PR* 24 Sept. 1941, p. 1, 'L'hommage de Rex...' and 26 Nov. 1941, p. 2, 'Chronique du Mouvement'; Albert Constant *Pro Just.*, 4 July 1946 and Marc Feyaerts *Pro Just.*, 8 Oct. 1944 and 7 Aug. 1946, *Aud. Gén.*, Doss. Albert Constant, Inst., Docts. 237, 305–9 and 313; Reusch to VM 15 Oct. 1941 and *OFK* Brussel to *EM* of Rex 7 Oct. 1941, *C2GM*, C 11/154 and 220.

28 *Le PR* 14 Dec. 1941, p. 1, 'Degrelle avait raison'.

29 *Le PR* 23 Dec. 1941, p. 3, 'Deux mille militants liégeois...'. See also *Le PR* 18 Oct. 1941, p. 1, 'Notre caution' and *Vouloir* Dec. 1941, *C2GM*, C 11/323.17.

30 'La Garde Wallonne', 'Conditions d'engagement dans les Gardes Wallonnes' and 'Garde Wallonne: Détachement de Namur', *C2GM*, C 11/274bis/1, 2 and 7.

31 L. Van Daele 'De Vlaamse Wacht Juni 1941–September 1944' (Rijksuniversiteit Gent Mémoire de licence, 1986), pp. 31–41; JS Au sujet de l'article 115 [pp. 15–16], *C2GM*, Fonds José Streel.

32 LD to *FC* of Brussels 6 July 1941, *C2GM*, C 11/275; *Le PR* 5 July 1941, p. 2, 'Chronique du Mouvement' and 1 Apr. 1942, p. 3, 'Nos gardes wallonnes'; JS Analyse de l'acte d'accusation: première suite p. 7, *C2GM*, Fonds José Streel.

33 IIe Etendard *FC* Ordre spécial No. 5 11 July 1941, *Aud. Gén.*, Doss. Albert Constant, Inst., Doct. 26; Georges to *Chefs de Cercles* 12 July 1941, *C2GM*, C 11/170; *Le PR* 19 July 1941, p. 5 and 22 July 1941, p. 2, 'Chronique du Mouvement'.

34 IIe Etendard *FC* Ordres hebdomadaires 13 and 27 Sept. 1941 and Ordre spécial 2 Oct. 1941, *Aud. Gén.*, Doss. Albert Constant, Inst., Doct. 28–30 and Documentation Générale, Farde H, Docts. 8 and 11; *Le PR* 24 Oct. 1941, p. 1, 'Gardes Wallonnes'.

35 The total number of Rexist volunteers is not known but *Etendard II* of the *Formations de Combat* provided at least 300 volunteers: Constant to *Etat-Major Fédéral* (henceforth *EMF*) of *FC* 1 and 5 Nov. 1941 and IIe Etendard *FC* Ordres hebdomadaires 31 Oct. 1941, *Aud. Gén.*, Doss. Albert Constant, Inst., Doct. 241 and Documentation Générale, Farde H, Docts. 27 and 29.

36 *Le PR* 25 Jan. 1942, p. 1, 'Les Gardes Wallonnes'.

37 Historique de l'organisation des *FC* and Organisation des moyens de transports 1 May 1942, C 11/263.

38 Albert Constant *Pro Just.*, 26 Jan. 1946 and Constant to *EMF* of *FC* 27 Sept. 1941, *Aud. Gén.*, Doss. Albert Constant, Inst., Doct. 152–3 and Documentation Générale, Farde H, Doct. 9.

39 IIe Etendard *FC* Ordre spécial 11 Oct. 1941, Ordres hebdomadaires 25 Oct. 1941 and *EMF* of *FC* Ordres hebdomadaires 1 Jan. 1942, *Aud. Gén.*, Doss. Albert Constant, Documentation Générale, Farde D, Docts. 9 and 14–15 and Farde A, Doct. 4–7; Historique de l'organisation des *FC*, *C2GM*, C 11/263; *Le PR* 24 Oct. and 8 Nov. 1941, p. 3, 'Chronique du Mouvement'.

40 VM *Pro Just.*, 25 Nov. 1946, *Aud. Gén.*, Doss. LC, Inst., Doct. 210–11; Backx to LD 3 Nov. 1941, *C2GM*, C 11/279.

41 See p. 106.

42 JS *Pro Just.*, 24 May 1945, *Aud. Gén.*, Doss. JS, Info. An undated document in the archives of the *C2GM* is most probably the report submitted by Streel proposing the creation of the *Service Politique*: 'Note pour le *Chef de Rex ad interim*...', *C2GM*, C 11/223.

43 JS *Pro Just.*, 24 May 1945 and JS 'Note écrite à annexer au procès-verbal de mon audition du 24 mai 1945' 27 May 1945, *Aud. Gén.*, Doss. JS, Info; R. Poulet 'Prison Diary' 12 July 1946 (Private Collection).

44 JS *Pro Just.*, 24 May 1945, *Aud. Gén.*, Doss. JS, Info.

45 Questionnaire addressed by Alain Dantoing to Madame Hepp, widow of Streel, pp. 2–3, JS to Cardinal Van Roey 2 Dec. 1945 and JS Mémoire I Famille, Enfance, Jeunesse, *C2GM*, PS 16 and Fonds José Streel. Despite his subsequent criticisms of Maurras, Streel described himself in January 1946 as an 'ancien maurrassien': *Le Soir* 23 Apr. 1942, p. 1, 'L'unité dans la diversité'; *Le PR* 26 Apr. 1942, p. 1, 'L'Etat corporatif et l'ordre de demain'; JS Letter of 19 Jan. 1946, *C2GM*, Fonds José Streel.

46 J. Streel *Les jeunes gens et la politique* (Louvain, 1932). The early political career of Streel is analysed in greater detail in M. Conway 'Du catholicisme à la collaboration: le cas de José Streel' in *Belgique en 1940: une société en crise, un pays en guerre*, pp. 305–26.

47 JS to Cardinal Van Roey 2 Dec. 1945, *C2GM*, PS 16; J.-M. Etienne *Le mouvement rexiste*, pp. 69 and 72.

48 JS to [*Le Soir*] 8 Feb. [1943], *Aud. Gén.*, Doss. JS [Supplementary File 6, Doct. 10]; G. Figeys Carnets 21 Feb. 1946, pp. 49–50, *C2GM*, JP 093; R. Poulet 'Prison Diary' 8–11 July 1946 (Private Collection); J. Willequet *La Belgique sous la botte*, pp. 189–92. Degrelle has often praised Streel in the most extravagant terms, describing him for example as the Robert Brasillach of Belgium: L. Degrelle *Lettres à mon Cardinal*, p. 174.

49 JS to Dominique 6 Jan. 1946, *C2GM*, Fonds José Streel; J. Streel *La Révolution du vingtième siècle* (Brussels, 1942), pp. 42–59 and 122–6. Streel felt a deep alienation from the modern era describing it as 'le règne des passions élémentaires et des conformismes tyranniques': Speech prepared by José Streel for his trial [1945], p. 3, *C2GM*, Fonds José Streel.

50 JS Chronique des Instituteurs 12 Apr. 1942, *Aud. Gén.*, Doss. JS, Chroniques radiophoniques; *Le Soir* 26 Mar. 1942, p. 1, 'L'essentiel et l'accessoire'.

51 J. Streel *La Révolution du vingtième siècle*, pp. 21 and 60–4; *Le Soir* 19 June 1941, p. 1, 'L'Idéalisme, symptôme de décadence', 5 Mar. 1942, p. 1, 'Le frisson sacré' and 9 July 1942, p. 1, 'Le triomphe de l'avenir'.

52 *Le Soir* 20 Mar. 1941, p. 1, 'Révolution et Radicalisme' and 30 July 1942, p. 1, 'La fin du Renanisme'; *Le PR* 30 Oct. 1941, p. 1, 'Le siècle du fascisme'; J. Streel *La Révolution du vingtième siècle*, p. 73.

53 Les cahiers verts de José Streel pp. 246 and 254–60, *C2GM*, Fonds José Streel; *Le Soir* 3 Apr. 1941, p. 1, 'La lutte des classes . . .'; JS Chronique des Instituteurs 26 Oct. 1941, *Aud. Gén.*, Doss. JS, Chroniques radiophoniques.

54 *Le Soir* 9 July 1942, p. 1, 'Le triomphe de l'avenir' and 30 July 1942, p. 1, 'La fin du Renanisme'; J. Streel *La Révolution du vingtième siècle*, pp. 137–8.

55 J. Streel *La Révolution du vingtième siècle*, pp. 105–17 and 210–11; *Le Soir* 27 Feb. 1941, p. 1, 'Le Chef'; *Le PR* 17 Jan. 1941, p. 1, 'Il ne s'agit pas . . .' and 14 Mar. 1941, pp. 1–2, 'La nouvelle organisation . . .'

56 See for example J.-L. Loubet del Bayle *Les non-conformistes des années 30* (Paris, 1969); P. Burrin *La dérive fasciste: Doriot, Déat, Bergery 1933–1945* (Paris, 1986).

57 *Le PR* 14 Dec. 1941, p. 1, 'Degrelle avait raison' and 6 May 1942, p. 1, 'La guerre et l'ordre nouveau'; JS Analyse de l'acte d'accusation: première suite pp. 9–11, *C2GM*, Fonds José Streel.

58 JS Mémoire: Après mon départ de Rex, *C2GM*, Fonds José Streel.

59 Speech prepared by José Streel for his trial [1945], p. 3 and Les cahiers verts de José Streel pp. 31–5 and 105, *C2GM*, Fonds José Streel.

60 *Le PR* 24 Oct. 1941, p. 1, 'L'originalité de Rex' and 31 Jan. 1942, p. 1, 'Mettons à profit . . .'; *Le Soir* 30 Jan. 1941, pp. 1–2, 'Les trois mobiles . . .'

61 *Le PR* 1 Apr. 1941, p. 1, 'A propos d'espace vital', 8 Nov. 1941, p. 1, 'Nos sentiments et nos intérêts' and 11 Dec. 1941, p. 1, 'Les petits pays . . .'

62 R. De Becker 'La collaboration . . .', *Courrier hebdomadaire du CRISP* No. 497–8 (1970), p. 10; JS Notice pour mon défenseur [première suite], *C2GM*, Fonds José Streel; *Le PR* 4 Sept. 1941, p. 1, 'Les étapes du corporatisme' and 15 Oct. 1941, p. 1, 'La neutralité est dépassé'.

63 *Le PR* 26 Nov. 1941, p. 1, 'La collaboration et son esprit' and 24 Oct. 1941, p. 1, 'L'originalité de Rex'.

64 *La Meuse* 7 Aug. 1945, p. 1, 'La détention perpetuelle à José Streel'.

65 The exact date of the establishment of the *Service Politique* remains unclear. Streel stated that he became the *Chef du Service Politique* in October 1941 but some documents suggest that it existed as early as September: JS Observations sur l'acte d'accusation p. 1, *C2GM*, Fonds José Streel; Thysen to Renauld 8 Sept. 1941, *C2GM*, C 11/226.

66 JS Notice pour mon défenseur (cinquième suite), *C2GM*, Fonds José Streel; LC *Pro Just.*, 27 Nov. 1946, *Aud. Gén.*, Doss. VM, Info., Doct. 154–5.

67 Dietvorst to VM 16 Oct. 1941, *C2GM*, C 11/154.

68 JS 'Note écrite . . .' 27 May 1945, *Aud. Gén.*, Doss. JS, Info.; LC *Pro Just.*, 12 May 1947 and VM *Pro Just.*, 14 and 20 May 1947, *Aud. Gén.*, Doss. LC, Enquête Complémentaire, Farde C, Doct. 19.

69 JS Au sujet de l'article 115 [pp. 16–17], *C2GM*, Fonds José Streel.

70 Once again, the exact date of the appointment is not known but it had taken place by December 1941: *Inspecteur Fédéral* to *Chefs de Cercles* 24 Dec. 1941, *C2GM*, C 11/182; LC *Pro Just.*, 21 Mar. 1946, *Aud. Gén.*, Doss. Marcel Dupont, Info., Section 5; *Le PR* 21 Feb. 1942, p. 3, 'Chronique du Mouvement'.

71 *Le PR* 23 Dec. 1941, p. 3, 'Deux mille militants liégeois . . .' After Pévenasse's departure to the *Légion*, Jean Georges replaced him as *Inspecteur Fédéral* but he seems to have paid little attention to this task: *Le PR* 25 Mar. 1942, p. 2, 'Chronique du Mouvement'.

72 Significantly, when Pévenasse did return, he opposed what he regarded as the undue hesitancy and moderation of the Rexist leaders in Belgium: see p. 231.

73 A. De Jonghe 'La lutte Himmler-Reeder . . .', *Cahiers* IV (1976), pp. 10–14 and V (1978), pp. 45–51; TB 18, 21 Dec. 1941, p. 2020.

74 *TB* 17, 22 Sept. 1941, p. 1863; *TB* 18, 21 Dec. 1941, pp. 2021 and 2064.

75 *TB* 18, 21 Dec. 1941, pp. 2061–4.

76 See pp. 139–48.

77 E.g. *TB* 22, 31 Dec. 1942, p. 2758.

78 See, for example, Reeder to *OKH* 26 Jan. 1943, *C2GM*, Procès von Falkenhausen, Doct. 117; Reeder to Keitel 19 Nov. 1943, *C2GM*, C 11/124bis, Doct. 11.

79 *Le PR* 11 Feb. 1942, p. 3, 'L'appel du Chef de Rex'; J. Mabire *Légion Wallonie*, pp. 28–9. The number of able *légionnaires* had fallen to only 350 by February 1942; Légion Belge 'Wallonie' Historique p. 7, *C2GM*, W 4; Pierre Pauly *Pro Just.*, 20 June 1945, *Aud. Gén.*, Doss, Pierre Pauly, Info., Doct. 18.

80 JS Au sujet de l'article 115 [p. 10], *C2GM*, Fonds José Streel. Some demobilised *légionnaires* had already returned to Belgium and reported on their experiences in Russia: e.g. *Le PR* 13 Jan. 1942, p. 3, 'Deux légionnaires exaltent . . .'

81 *Le PR* 11 Feb. 1942, p. 1, 'La Légion vous attend!'; Pévenasse circular 17 Feb. 1942, *Aud. Gén.*, Doss. Albert Constant, Documentation Générale, Doct. 90bis; JS Au sujet de l'article 115 [pp. 10–11], *C2GM*, Fonds José Streel.

82 *L'Avenir du Luxembourg* 6 Nov. 1946, pp. 1–2, 'Au Conseil de Guerre'.

83 Pévenasse circular 17 Feb. 1942, *Aud. Gén.*, Doss. Albert Constant, Documentation Générale, Doct. 90bis; *Le PR* 11 Feb. 1942, p. 1, 'La Légion vous attend!', 17 Feb. 1942, p. 3, 'Les rexistes de Charleroi, Mons, Tournai et La Louvière . . .' and 18 Feb. 1942, p. 1, 'La magnifique réponse du Hainaut . . .'

84 *Le PR* 24 Feb. 1942, pp. 1, 3 and 4, 'Notre Légion de l'Est . . .' and 'Le discours du Chef ad interim'; P. Delandsheere and A. Ooms *La Belgique sous les Nazis* II, pp. 85–6.

85 *Le PR* 11 Mar. 1942, p. 1, 'Pour la Patrie et pour l'Europe'. On the morning of the parade, the Rexist offices were damaged by a bomb attack and another small bomb exploded during the parade injuring some Rexist bystanders: P. Delandsheere and A. Ooms *La Belgique sous les Nazis* II, pp. 106–7; Police Report of 10 Mar. 1942, *Aud. Gén.*, Doss. VM, Info., Doct. 118; *Le PR* 17 Mar. 1942, p. 3, 'Chronique du Mouvement'. Re the number of volunteers, see: Légion Belge 'Wallonie' Historique p. 20, *C2GM*, W 4; Sylvain Jadoul *Pro Just.*, 25 Aug. 1945, *Aud. Gén.*, Doss. VM, Info., Doct. 64–70. *Le Pays Réel* reported that the contingent was divided into six platoons, each composed of 75 men: *Le PR* 11 Mar. 1942, p. 1, 'Pour la Patrie et pour l'Europe'. Reeder stated, perhaps inaccurately, that only 380 volunteers had been recruited: *TB*

20, 15 June 1942, p. 2346.

86 Pierre Houpline *Pro Just.*, 4 Mar. 1947, *Aud. Gén.*, Doss. Joseph Pévenasse, *Cour Militaire*, Doct. 1b; Légion Belge 'Wallonie' Historique p. 20, *C2GM*, W 4; *Le PR* 28 Apr. 1942, p. 1, 'Dans Bruxelles ensoleillée...' and 12 Feb. 1943, p. 1, 'Nos héros...'; Sylvain Jadoul *Pro Just.*, 28 Aug. 1945, *Aud. Gén.*, Doss. Pierre Pauly, *Cour Militaire*, Doct. 10; J.-M. Charlier *Léon Degrelle*, pp. 277–8. Apparently, more *Gardes Wallonnes* had wished to depart but were retained in the country on the orders of the German authorities. In the summer, however, a further 190 *Gardes* were permitted to join the *Légion*: *Le PR* 6 Mar. 1942, p. 1, 'Six cents légionnaires se sont inscrits...', 23 July 1942, p. 1, 'Nouveau départ de volontaires...' and 26 Aug. 1942, p. 4, 'Un nouveau contingent...'

87 *Le PR* 13 Feb. 1942, p. 1, 'Pour le service du Chef...', 19 Feb. 1942, p. 3, 'La J.N.S. de Liége...' and 26 Feb. 1942, p. 3, 'Notre groupe de combat...'

88 Sylvain Jadoul *Pro Just.*, 25 Aug. 1945, *Aud. Gén.*, Doss. VM, Info., Doct. 64–70; Gilbert Delrue *Pro Just.*, 8 Sept. 1945, *Aud. Gén.*, Doss. Pierre Pauly, *Cour Militaire*, Doct. 13; *L'Avenir du Luxembourg* 6 July 1946, pp. 1–2, 'Les joyeux compères...'

89 It was rumoured that Hagemans, overcome with remorse at these deaths, deliberately sought his own death: Henry Marcovitz *Pro Just.*, 7 Mar. 1946, *C2GM*, PF 3; Sylvain Jadoul *Pro Just.*, 28 Aug. 1945, *Aud. Gén.*, Doss. Pierre Pauly, *Cour Militaire*, Doct. 10.

90 Documentation Jans 303; *Le PR* 19 Aug. 1942, p. 1, 'Nos jeunesses'. Hagemans returned briefly to Belgium in April in an attempt to solve the problems of the Rexist youth organisation: *Le PR* 18 Apr. 1942, p. 1, 'Le prévôt de la J.R. ...'

91 *Le PR* 19 Mar. 1942, p. 3, 'Chronique du Mouvement'.

Chapter Four

1 JS Au sujet de l'article 115 [p. 17], *C2GM*, Fonds José Streel.

2 P. Struye *L'évolution du sentiment public*, pp. 76–7 and 103–5.

3 W. Wagner *Belgien in der deutschen Politik*, pp. 293–6.

4 E.g. *Le Soir* 19 Mar. 1942, pp. 1 and 3, 'Les difficultés de l'avenir'; *Le PR* 25 July 1942, p. 1, 'Notre pari'.

5 *Le PR* 21 Mar. 1942, p. 1, 'Voilà le printemps...'

6 *Le PR* 24 Apr. 1942, p. 8, 'Harceler n'est pas débarquer', 21 July 1942, p. 1, 'Le problème du second front' and 25 Aug. 1942, p. 3, 'Une magnifique réunion...'; JS Chronique des Instituteurs, Radio Bruxelles 25 Oct. 1942, *Aud. Gén.*, Doss. JS (Supplementary File No. 5).

7 *Le Soir* 23 Oct. 1942, p. 1, 'Il y a modérés et modérés'.

8 *Le PR* 25 July 1942, p. 1, 'Notre pari' and 30 Aug. 1942, p. 3, 'Le pari de la collaboration'.

9 Bulletin des dirigeants No. 4, 15 Dec. 1941, *C2GM*, C 11/184; *Le PR* 5 Mar. 1942, p. 1, 'La situation présente' and 10 May 1942, p. 1, 'Le 10 mai'; *TB* 20, 15 June 1942, p. 2343; Extract from report of *Sipo-SD* 15 June 1942, German Records Microfilmed at Alexandria (henceforth GRMA) T 501 173 125.

10 Légion Belge 'Wallonie' Historique pp. 12–31, *C2GM*, W 4; *Le PR* 2 Apr. 1942, p. 1, 'Combats glorieux et sanglants...', 19 Apr. 1942, p. 1, 'La Croix de Fer au Chef de Rex', 11 Oct. 1942, p. 1, 'Onze Croix de Fer...' and 10 Aug. 1943, p. 4, 'Une émouvante cérémonie...'; *TB* 21, 15 Sept. 1942, p. 2555; E. De Bruyne *Les Wallons meurent à l'est*, pp. 50–65.

11 *Le PR* 20 Mar. 1942, p. 1, 'La glorieuse offensive...' and 14 Apr. 1942, p. 2, 'Nécrologie'; JS Au sujet de l'article 115 [p. 11], *C2GM*, Fonds José Streel.

12 *Le PR* 24 Mar. and 8 Oct. 1942, p. 2, 'Chronique de la Solidarité Légionnaire'.

13 E.g. *Le PR* 10 Jan. and 12 Dec. 1942, p. 1, 'Un léger sacrifice...', 10 Mar. 1942, p. 3, 'Chronique du Mouvement', 15 Sept. 1942, p. 1, 'Le Cercle de Tournai...', 4 Oct. 1942, p. 2, 'Service Légionnaire' and 29 Nov. 1942, p. 1, 'La Légion Wallonie...'

14 *Le PR* 14 Mar. 1942, p. 1, 'Avec la Légion' and 7 Apr. 1942, p. 1, 'Les occasions de servir'; *EMF* of *FC Ordres hebdomadaires* 19 Sept. 1942, *Aud. Gén.*, Doss. Albert

Constant, Documentation Générale, Farde C, Doct. 4–5; *TB* 20, 15 June 1942, p. 2343; G. Figeys Mémoire [1944], *C2GM*, JP 093; P. De Ligne 'Résumé des rapports mensuels de nos correspondants en province: juillet 1942' 18 Aug. 1942, *C2GM*, Fonds INBEL/964.

15 This has been particularly so in the case of Robert Poulet whose wartime actions as editor of *Le Nouveau Journal* have often been presented (not least by himself) as a patriotic duty imposed by the necessities of the time. See A. Dantoing 'Du fascisme occidental à la politique de présence: Robert Poulet' in *Belgique en 1940: une société en crise, un pays en guerre*, pp. 337–43.

16 JS *Pro Just.*, 24 May 1945 and 'Note écrite . . .' 27 May 1945, *Aud. Gén.*, Doss. JS, Info.

17 De Ligne to VM 25 Jan. 1943, *C2GM*, Papiers Pierre Daye, See pp. 160–1.

18 A. De Jonghe 'La lutte Himmler–Reeder . . .', *Cahiers* V (1978), pp. 52–3; Interview with Léon Degrelle 14 July 1988.

19 *En Avant* Aug. 1942, p. 1, 'Camarades ouvriers'; *L'Effort Wallon* 28 June 1942, p. 1, 'Degrelle à Berlin'. No surviving official documentation confirms that Degrelle visited Rome and Bucharest but these visits are referred to in *Le Pays Réel* as well as in private correspondence: Informations reçues de Belgique 9 Dec. 1942, *C2GM*, Fonds INBEL/964; *Le PR* 25 July 1942, pp. 1–2, 'Reprenant son commandement au Front de l'Est . . .' and 13 Sept. 1943, p. 1, 'Le Chef de Rex exhorte ses militants'.

20 Journal de V. Matthys p. 7, *C2GM*; Reeder to *OKH* 26 Jan. 1943, *C2GM*, Procès von Falkenhausen, Doct. 117; *Le PR* 30 June 1942, p. 1, 'Rencontre avec le Chef' and 1 July 1942, p. 1, 'A Berlin avec Léon Degrelle . . .'; *En Avant* Aug. 1942, p. 1, 'Camarades ouvriers'; *La Meuse* 5 Sept. 1945, p. 1, 'Conseil de Guerre'.

21 *Le PR* 30 June 1942, p. 1, 'Rencontre avec le Chef'; H. Trevor-Roper (ed.) *Hitler's Table Talk* (London, 1953), pp. 536–7; *TB* 21, 15 Sept. 1942, p. 2555; A. De Jonghe 'La lutte Himmler–Reeder . . .', *Cahiers* V (1978), pp. 53–5.

22 Degrelle to POWs in INBEL No. 0754 16 Apr. 1943, *C2GM*, Fonds INBEL/965; Gendarmerie Nationale Momignies *Pro Just.*, 6 June 1945, René Vandenplas *Pro Just.*, 28 Sept. 1945 and Jules Sandron *Pro Just.*, 19 Oct. 1945, *Aud. Gén.*, Doss. Albert Constant, Inst., Doct. 192–5 and Doss. Joseph Pévenasse, Docts. 1011 and 1014; *TB* 22, 31 Dec. 1942, p. 2746.

23 E.g., see pp. 133–4.

24 *Le Soir* 8 and 16 June 1946, p. 2, 'Les Conseils de Guerre'; *L'Effort Wallon* 28 June 1942, p. 3, 'L'idée de la nation dans l'histoire de Belgique'; JS *Pro Just.*, 24 May 1945, *Aud. Gén.*, Doss. JS, Info.; JS Mémoire: A partir de ma rupture avec Rex, *C2GM*, Fonds José Streel.

25 *Le PR* 31 May 1942, p. 1, 'Les prisonniers et les Légionnaires' and 21 July 1942, p. 1, 'La collaboration dans la camaraderie'. Streel was similarly dismissive of those who sought to construct a Walloon consciousness as an alternative to the unitary Belgian state, declaring: 'Il n'existe pas de nationalité wallonne, ni de conscience nationale wallonne, ni de communauté populaire wallonne . . . La Wallonie n'est qu'une expression géographique, sans aucun contenu populaire positif.' *Le PR* 14 June 1941, pp. 1 and 6, 'Politiciens et Aventuriers' and 23 Aug. 1942, p. 1, 'L'impasse à éviter'.

26 *Le PR* 19 Apr. 1942, p. 3, 'Les "Anciens Belges" étaient-ils des "barbares"?', 11 July 1942, p. 1, ' "Nous, wallons . . ." ', 30 July 1942, p. 2, 'La défense de la musique belge . . .' and p. 4, 'Le Cercle de Tournai . . .' and 4 Oct. 1942, p. 4, 'Les Belges au service . . .'

27 *Le PR* 23 Dec. 1941, pp. 3 and 6, 'Deux mille militants liégeois . . .', 3 Apr. 1942, pp. 1 and 3, 'La prestation de serment de la Brigade Motorisée . . .', 26 May 1942, p. 2, 'Une soirée recréative chez les Gardes Wallonnes' and 4 Oct. 1942, p. 2, 'Chronique du Mouvement'. Robert Poulet wrote to Streel to protest at this watering down of Rex's patriotic loyalties: Poulet to JS 27 May 1942, *C2GM*, Fonds José Streel.

28 *Le PR* 27 Feb. 1941, pp. 1 and 3, 'Le Racisme, la Race et la Médecine Sociale'.

29 *Le PR* 28 Sept. 1941 Magazine, 'Un représentant de la civilisation . . . bolcheviste', 5 Oct. 1941, pp. 1 and 3, 'Les funérailles de Jean Oedekerke', 7 Nov. 1941, p. 2, 'Racisme biologique et spirituel', 9 Jan. 1942, p. 2, 'Mystique raciale', 16 Jan. 1942, p. 2, 'La race: essence de l'Etat' and 11 Apr. 1942, p. 1, 'Nos combats'. See also Jean

Denis 'Mémoire justificatif d'un condamné à mort' pp. 187–8, *Aud. Gén.*, Doss. Jean Denis, Info., Doct. 53.

30 See pp. 51–2; *Le PR* 8 Apr. 1942, p. 1, 'Le danger juif', 5 June 1942, p. 1, 'Secouons le joug d'Israël' and 4 July 1941, p. 3, 'Chronique du Mouvement'. The highly influential Rexist cartoonist 'Jam' frequently presented stereotypically Jewish figures in his cartoons: e.g. *Le PR* 24 June 1941.

31 See, for example, the comments of Léo Moulin in *Pourquoi Pas?* 23 Nov. 1983, p. 93, 'Le cas Robert Poulet...'

32 *Le PR* 23 June 1942, p. 1, 'Les étoiles jaunes' and 23 July 1942, p. 1, 'De quoi vivent-ils ces juifs?'

33 M. Steinberg *L'étoile et le fusil*, pp. 169–71.

34 LD to his family 31 Oct. 1941, *Aud. Gén.*, Doss. VM, Pièces à Conviction, Doct. 31–3; *Le PR* 6 Dec. 1941, p. 1, 'Les juifs seront matés' and 27 Oct. 1942, p. 2, 'Une grande manifestation...' See also M. Steinberg *L'étoile et le fusil*, pp. 34–5 and 149–50.

35 *Le PR* 5 Dec. 1941, p. 1, 'Anti-sémitisme d'état', 1 Aug. 1942, pp. 1 and 6, 'Les forces hostiles au nouvel ordre' and 7 Aug. 1942, p. 1, 'Sabotage judiciaire'; *Le Soir* 9 July 1942, p. 1, 'Le triomphe de l'avenir'; Conseil de Guerre de Bruxelles Procès-verbal de l'audience publique 6 Aug. 1945, *Aud. Gén.*, Doss. JS, Jugement et Appel; JS to [Humblet] 31 Oct. 1945, *C2GM*, Fonds José Streel.

36 E.g. L. Degrelle *Les Taudis*.

37 *Le PR* 15 Oct. 1941, p. 2, 'Le scandale du CCI' and 18 Apr. 1942, p. 1, 'Démagogie capitaliste'.

38 *En Avant* Aug. 1942, p. 1, 'Camarades ouvriers'; *Le PR* 27 Oct. 1942, p. 2, 'Une grande manifestation...'

39 *Le PR* 17 July 1942, p. 1, 'L'esprit bourgeois et le bétail électoral'.

40 *Le PR* 22 July 1942, p. 2, 'Qu'est-ce que le socialisme?' and 31 July 1942, p. 2, 'Socialisme'; *En Avant* Aug. 1942, p. 2, 'Victor Matthys... a parlé à Charleroi'.

41 J. Streel *La Révolution du vingtième siècle*, pp. 149–91; *Le PR* 5 Nov. 1941, p. 1, 'Le chômage du petit commerce', 10 Dec. 1941, p. 1, 'Le statut de la propriété immobilière', 9 Jan. 1942, p. 1, 'Et les classes moyennes?', 30 Oct. 1942, pp. 1 and 4, 'Notre socialisme', 8 Nov. 1942, p. 1, 'L'ordre nouveau sera socialiste' and 27 Nov. 1942, pp. 1 and 4, 'Socialisme ancien et nouveau'; JS Chronique des Instituteurs 10 May 1942, *Aud. Gén.*, Doss. JS, Chroniques radiophoniques.

42 *Le Peuple* [Summer 1941] pp. 1–3, 'Editorial'; J. Del Marmol to J. Rens 1 Jan. 1942, *C2GM*, PM 14; P. Struye *L'évolution du sentiment public*, pp. 63–4, 94–8 and 123–5. Re France, see F. Bédarida 'Vichy et la crise de la conscience française', in J.-P. Azéma and F. Bédarida (eds.) *Vichy et les Français* (Paris, 1992), pp. 89–92.

43 The head of the *CCW*, Pierre Hubermont, volunteered in February 1942 to join the *Légion Wallonie* but subsequently changed his mind: P. Hubermont 'Mémorandum remis à Me. Thomard', *C2GM*, W 3/71; R. De Hoe to Hubermont 24 July 1942, *C2GM*, W 3/73; *Le PR* 24 Feb. 1942, p. 4, 'Le discours du Chef ad interim' and 6 Mar. 1942, p. 3, 'Chronique du Mouvement'; VM *Pro Just.*, 14 Mar. 1946, *Aud. Gén.*, Doss. VM, Info., Doct. 210–13.

44 *L'Ami du Peuple* 11 Oct. 1941, p. 2, 'Une conférence de Me. Lambrichts à Liége', 18 Oct. 1941, p. 2, 'Légion Wallonie', 8 Nov. 1941, p. 2, 'Notre meeting anti-juif...', 22 Nov. 1941, p. 4, 'A Soignies...' and 20 Dec. 1941, p. 1, 'Tout est bien... qui finit bien'; *Le PR* 6 Dec. 1941, p. 1, 'Les juifs seront matés' and 23 Dec. 1941, p. 3, 'Deux mille militants liégeois...'; M. Steinberg *L'étoile et le fusil*, p. 150.

45 *Le PR* 31 Jan. 1942, p. 1, 'Mettons à profit...'; JS *Pro Just.*, 24 May 1945, *Aud. Gén.*, Doss. JS, Info.

46 Procès-Verbal Comité de Coordination 5 Feb. 1942, Leclercq to Dalldorff 4 Apr. 1942, Text of Leclercq's proposed accord, Lodewick to Leclercq (undated) and 'Propositions confidentielles du Chef du *MNPW* à Monsieur le Capitaine Dalldorff...' 26 May 1942, *C2GM*, C 13/7.

47 *Le PR* 22 Aug. 1942, p. 1, 'Effectifs réduits'; *TB* 20, 15 June 1942, p. 2343.

48 *Le PR* 17 June 1942, p. 1, 'L'excès de zèle...', 18 June 1942, p. 1, 'Partout les mêmes intrigants et sots, gonflés de vanité: les convulsionnaires', 28 June 1942, p. 1, 'Convertis et kleptomanes' and 9 Aug. 1942, p. 1, 'Unité sacré et indivisible'.

49 VM to *Cadres Territoriaux* 1 June 1942, *C2GM*, C 11/146.

50 *L'Ami du Peuple* 27 June 1942, p. 2, 'L'activité de la ligue' and 4 July 1942, p. 2, 'Notre meeting à la Brasserie Flamande'. Paul Jamin attended a meeting of *Défense du Peuple* at this time and well recalls Lambrichts' fury at the new stance of Rex: Interview with Paul Jamin 11 Dec. 1987.

51 See note 49; *TB* 20, 15 June 1942, p. 2343; A. Van Hal to *CCW* 9 July 1942, R. De Hoe to Hubermont 24 July 1942, Streel to Romsée 9 Oct. 1942 and Hubermont to Romsée 27 Oct. 1942, *C2GM*, W 3/73 and C 4/3 and 353.

52 *TB* 20, 15 June 1942, p. 2343; Gaillard to *KK* of Namur 22 Apr. 1943, *C2GM*, C 5/27.

53 *Notre Combat* 1 Oct. 1942, p. 8, 'Ce que pense l'AGRA'; Report on *AGRA*, Doct. PP14 B 11 Oct. 1942, *C2GM*, C 5/29; *TB* 21, 15 Sept. 1942, p. 2554; P. De Ligne 'Résumé des rapports mensuels de nos correspondants en province' 18 Aug. 1942, *C2GM*, Fonds INBEL/964.

54 See p. 162.

55 *TB* 20, 15 June 1942, p. 2343; JS to Romsée 9 Oct. 1942, *C2GM*, C 4/353; VM *Pro Just.*, 14 Mar. 1946, *Aud. Gén.*, Doss. VM, Info., Doct. 210–13; Journal de V. Matthys p. 9, *C2GM*.

56 *La Gazette de Charleroi* 25–6 July 1942, 'Qu'est-ce que l'AGRA?' cited in *C2GM*, C 5/32; *Notre Combat* 1 Oct. 1942, pp. 1 and 5, 'Devons-nous accepter comme membres . . . ?'

57 *Le Journal de Charleroi* 28 July 1942, p. 1, 'Un mouvement digne de sympathie' and *Mons-Tournai* 24 Aug. 1942, 'Première manifestation de l'AGRA à Bruxelles' cited in *C2GM*, C 5/32. The conflict between *AGRA* and Rex was always most intense in Liège where, presumably in an attempt to subvert their rival, the members of the Rexist *cercle* apparently applied *en bloc* to enter *AGRA* during the summer of 1942. This application was refused by the *AGRA* leadership. See note 56 and Gaillard to *KK* of Namur 22 Apr. 1943, *C2GM*, C 5/27.

58 See pp. 195–6.

59 JS Notice pour mon défenseur: cinquième suite, *C2GM*, Fonds José Streel.

60 Naval Intelligence Division *Belgium* (No place, 1944).

61 Lambinon to *Chef adjoint* of Dinant 16 Sept. 1941, *Aud. Gén.*, Doss. Charles Lambinon, Inst., Doct. 70; *National Socialisme* 15 May 1943, p. 4, 'Rapport du Chef des Cadres Territoriaux'.

62 *Le PR* 2 Sept. 1941, pp. 1 and 3, 'Les nominations de bourgmestres'.

63 Pévenasse to *Chefs de Cercles* 20 Nov. 1941, *C2GM*, C 11/181; JS 'Note écrite . . .' 27 May 1945, *Aud. Gén.*, Doss. JS, Info.; VM *Pro Just.*, 21 May 1947, *Aud. Gén.*, Doss. LC, Enquête Complémentaire, Farde C, Doct. 20–6; *Le Soir* 13 May 1947, p. 4, 'Les Conseils de Guerre'.

64 *Le PR* 8 Nov. 1941, p. 2, 'Hommes d'Ordre Nouveau . . .'; *National Socialisme* 15 Apr. 1944, p. 8, 'Antoine Dupont . . .'; *Chef du Service des Nominations* to *Chefs de Cercles* of Namur, etc. 12 Nov. 1941, *Aud. Gén.*, Doss. Charles Lambinon, Inst., Doct. 18.

65 P. Delandsheere and A. Ooms *La Belgique sous les Nazis* I, p. 507. See pp. 118–20.

66 *Le PR* 1 Jan. 1942, p. 1, 'L'année qui vient', 5 Feb. 1942, p. 3, 'Les premiers résultats . . .', 5 Mar. 1942, p. 1, 'La situation présente', 22 May 1942, pp. 1 and 3, 'Une grande journée . . .', 25 Aug. 1942, p. 2, 'Chronique du Mouvement' and 27 Oct. 1942, p. 1, 'Une grande manifestation . . .'

67 W. Ganshof van der Meersch *Réflexions sur la répression des crimes contre la sûreté extérieure de l'état belge* (Brussels, 1946), pp. 25–7.

68 JS to Louis Abrassart 16 Oct. 1942, *C2GM*, C 11/231; JS *Pro Just.*, 4 Oct. 1945, *Aud. Gén.*, Doss. JS, Cour Militaire, Doct. 12.

69 In *Grand La Louvière*, a pro-Rexist *bourgmestre* (Gorain) presided over a *collège* of six *échevins* which contained three Rexists (Fourmois, Duhainaut and Hubert); *Moniteur Belge* 22 Aug. 1942, p. 5162; *Le Journal de Charleroi* 13 Sept. 1946, p. 4, 'Enfin, la Bande Duquesne va payer', 21 Feb. 1947, p. 5. 'Les échevins de l'ex-Grand La Louvière' and 5 Mar. 1947, p. 3, 'Conseil de Guerre de Charleroi'. The *collège* of *Grand Charleroi* was composed of ten nominees, of whom six were Rexists; the *bourgmestre*, Teughels, and five *échevins*, Denis, Desclin, Englebin, Grevesse and Sarlet. Two other

échevins, Dujacquier and Ligot, appear to have had pro-Rexist sympathies: *Le PR* 1
Sept. 1942, p. 2, 'Le nouveau collège échevinal . . .'; *Le Journal de Charleroi* 30 June and
1 July 1945, p. 1, 'Les échevins du "Gross Charleroi" . . .' and 10 and 24 July 1945, p.
1, 'Conseil de Guerre de Charleroi'; *Informations administratives et politiques* Sept. 1943,
pp. 9–12, 'Le service social communal'.

70 See note 51; *La Légia* 7–8 Nov. 1942, p. 3, 'Le nouveau Collège . . .' and 23 Nov.
1942, p. 2, 'Le bourgmestre de Liége . . .'; *Le PR* 8 Nov. 1942, p. 2 and 20 Jan,
1943, p. 3, 'Les nouveaux échevins . . .' and 7 Mar. 1943, p. 1, 'Notre camarade
Dargent . . .'; *Journal des Tribunaux* 23 Sept. 1945, pp. 466–9, 'Conseil de Guerre de
Liège'. The Rexist majority was composed of Dargent and of four *échevins*, Bomans,
Fréson, Froment and Tavier. In addition another *échevin*, Boutier, was reported to
have subsequently joined Rex.

71 *TB* 22, 31 Dec. 1942, p. 2754; *Le PR* 27 Sept. 1942, p. 1, 'Le Grand-Bruxelles . . .';
VM and LC *Pro Just.*, 20 and 24 May 1947, *Aud. Gén.*, Doss. LC, Enquête Complémentaire, Farde C, Docts. 19 and 20–6; *Le Soir* 5 Mar. 1946, pp. 1–2, 'Conseil de
Guerre de Bruxelles' and 10 Mar. 1946, p. 3, 'Les Conseils de Guerre'. Only one
échevin, Bottemmanne, was a member of Rex but his colleague, Gillès de Pélichy, was
a friend of Degrelle and a reliable supporter of the movement.

72 J. Gérard-Libois and J. Gotovitch *L'an 40*, p. 195.

73 *TB* 20, 15 June 1942, p. 2360; P. Delandsheere and A. Ooms *La Belgique sous les Nazis*
II, pp. 154–5; *Le Journal de Charleroi* 29 Oct. 1945, p. 1, 'Jean Hancotte et le Prince de
Croy . . .'; *La Meuse* 7 Feb. 1945, p. 1, 'Conseil de Guerre de Liège'; JS *Pro Just.*, 24
May 1945, *Aud. Gén.*, Doss. JS, Info.

74 *TB* 25, 15 Nov. 1943, pp. 3435–6; VM *Pro Just.*, 20 Sept. 1945, *Aud. Gén.*, Doss.
VM, Info., Doct. 55–8.

75 *TB* 27, 10 Apr. 1944, p. 3861; *L'Avenir du Luxembourg* 21 Feb. 1946, p. 1, 'Au Conseil
de Guerre'.

76 See for example *Vers l'Avenir* 9–10 Mar. 1946, p. 3, 'Au Conseil de Guerre de
Namur'; *Sambre et Meuse* 5 Sept. 1946, p. 2, 'Conseil de Guerre de Namur'.

77 The *cadre politique* of the *cercle* of Mons described Leroy in 1942 as a 'rexiste-ersatz en
demi-teintes' while another Rexist said of him in 1944 'il mérite une balle dans la tête':
Cercle de Mons, Cadre Politique, Meetings of 22 and 29 May 1942, *C2GM*, C 11/321.10;
Le Courrier de l'Escaut 14 July 1946, p. 1, 'Conseil de Guerre de Tournai (A)'; *Vers
l'Avenir* 11 and 20 and 21 Apr. 1946, p. 2, 'Conseil de Guerre de Namur'.

78 *TB* 21, 15 Sept. 1942, pp. 2566–7. In the Hainaut, three pro-Rexist *députés* were
appointed in 1941 to be joined later in the Occupation by two more. In Liège – as in
the Luxembourg – three Rexists served as *députés permanents* while in Namur at least
two Rexist *députés* were appointed. In the Brabant, one *député* was Rexist.

79 *Informations administratives et politiques* Sept. 1943, p. 32, 'Activité des Cadres Politiques'; *TB* 26, 1 Mar. 1944, p. 3635.

80 The exact number of Rexists appointed to posts in the central governmental bureaucracy is not known, though German reports provide some details: see p. 201. Certain
of the Rexist *fonctionnaires* also attended rallies of the movement; *Le PR* 18 Jan. 1943,
p. 1, 'La cérémonie' and 4 May 1943, p. 1, 'Le Chef de Rex glorifie le travail'.

81 *Le PR* 15 Aug. 1942, p. 1, 'M. De Meyer est nommé . . .'; Mémorandum aux
autorités allemandes [Autumn 1943], *C2GM*, C 11/324.

82 VM *Pro Just.*, 14 and 21 May 1947, *Aud. Gén.*, Doss. LC, Enquête Complémentaire,
Farde C, Docts. 19 and 20–6; *Le Soir* 28 and 30 May 1947, p. 5, 'Conseil de Guerre de
Bruxelles'.

83 E.g. *TB* 18, 21 Dec. 1941, pp. 2000–3; *TB* 21, 15 Sept. 1942, p. 2517.

84 *Le Soir* 2 Apr. 1941, p. 2, 'Nos nouveaux Secrétaires-Généraux'.

85 Simar to *Chefs de Groupes* 21 Nov. 1942, *C2GM*, C 11/321.8.

86 JS to *Chefs de Cercles* 29 Oct. 1942 and Communication de l'Office National du
Travail, *C2GM*, C 11/225 and C 11/318.2; *La Meuse* 11 Sept. 1946, p. 2, 'L'Office du
Travail . . .' and 12 Sept. 1946, p. 2, 'Au Conseil de Guerre'; *Le Journal de Charleroi*
17–18 May 1947, p. 3, 'Le procès de l'Office du Travail'; *Le PR* 25 June 1943, p. 1,
'Le Commissaire aux Sports . . .'

87 *Inspecteur Fédéral* to *Chefs de Cercles* 11 June 1941, Simar to *Chefs de Groupes* 18 July 1942, JS and Dupont to *Chefs de Cercles* 29 July 1942 and JS to Abrassart 16 Oct. 1942, *C2GM*, C 11/169, 321.8, 226 and 231; *Le PR* 4 Sept. 1941, p. 3, 'Plus de nominations politiciennes . . .'; *Le Soir* 1 Apr. 1947, p. 4, 'Conseil de Guerre de Bruxelles'; *La Meuse* 6 July 1945, p. 1, 'A la deuxième chambre . . .' See also the collection of letters in *C2GM*, PL 1/332.

88 *Le PR* 19 Apr. 1942, p. 1, 'La conspiration des robins'; Simar to *Chefs de Groupes* 21 Nov. 1942, *C2GM*, C 11/321.8; Mémorandum aux autorités allemandes [Autumn 1943], *C2GM*, C 11/324.

89 *Inspecteur Fédéral* to *Chefs de Cercles* 24 July and 15 Sept. 1941 and JS to *Chefs de Cercles* 9 Oct. 1942, *C2GM*, C 11/172, 178 and 228.

90 R. Van Doorslaer 'La police belge et le maintien de l'ordre en Belgique occupée', *Revue du Nord* Numéro Spécial (1987), pp. 75–8; *Inspecteur Fédéral* to *Chefs de Cercles* 1 Oct. 1941, *C2GM*, C 11/180.

91 JS and Dupont to *Chefs de Cercles* 26 June 1942, JS to *Chefs de Cercles* 9 Oct. 1942 and JS to *Cadre Politique* 20 Oct. 1942, *C2GM*, C 11/228; JS to *Cadre Politique* 2 Dec. 1942 and JS to *Chefs de Cercles* etc., 17 Dec. 1942, *Aud. Gén.*, Doss. JS (Supplementary File 7, Docts. h and k); *Le Soir* 28 Mar. 1947, p. 5, 'Le procès Romsée'.

92 See previous note; R. Van Doorslaer *Op. cit.*, p. 77; *TB* 23, 15 Apr. 1943, p. 2962; JS and Dupont to *Chefs de Cercles* 20 Oct. 1942, *C2GM*, C 11/228. See also p. 203.

93 Journal de V. Matthys p. 8, *C2GM*.

94 Bulletin des dirigeants 20 May 1941 and *Inspecteur Fédéral* to *Chefs de Cercles* 20 Nov. 1941 and undated, *C2GM*, C 11/99, 181 and 185; P. Delandsheere and A. Ooms *La Belgique sous les Nazis* I, pp. 507–8. Married men were required to contribute 5 per cent and single men 10 per cent to Rexist funds.

95 *Inspecteur Fédéral* to *Chefs de Cercles* 24 Dec. 1941 and 15 Jan. 1942, *C2GM*, C 11/182 and 183; JS Observations sur l'acte d'accusation p. 2, *C2GM*, Fonds José Streel. The minutes of the *cadre politique* of Mons are preserved in *C2GM*, C 11/321.10.

96 *Le PR* 2 Sept. 1941, pp. 1 and 3, 'La nomination de bourgmestres' and 14 Nov. 1941, p. 1, 'Les instituteurs et le personnel'.

97 *Le PR* 1 July 1941, p. 3, 'Le Borinage qui renaît', 7 Feb. 1942, p. 2, 'Le bourgmestre n'admet plus de favoritisme', 9 June 1942, p. 3, 'Des édiles qui sont sans pitié . . .', 19 July 1942, p. 8, 'A Verviers . . .', 26 July 1942, p. 6, 'A Arlon . . .' and 2 Aug. 1942, p. 2, 'Les awirs ont aussi leur maieur rexiste.'

98 *Le PR* 27 May 1942, p. 1, 'La propagande par les actes'; *Vers l'Avenir* 9 Apr. 1946, p. 3, 'Conseil de Guerre de Namur' and 30–1 May 1946, p. 2, 'Au Conseil de Guerre de Namur'; A. Lemaire *Le crime du 18 août* (Couillet, 1947), pp. 41–3.

99 *Le PR* 2 May 1941, p. 3, 'L'arrestation de V. Van Doorne'; *La Meuse* 18 May 1945, p. 2, 'Les usurpateurs du Grand-Liège . . .'; J. Wynants 'Verviers, l'autorité communale . . .', *Cahiers* II (1972), p. 174.

100 Allgemeine Ubersicht 16 Mar. 1942, p. 4219; *Vers l'Avenir* 9 Apr. 1946, p. 1, 'La Gestapo de Dinant . . .'

101 *La Meuse* 18 May 1945, p. 1, 'Les usurpateurs du Grand-Liège . . .', 26 May 1945, pp. 1–2, 'Le Grand-Liège . . .' and 19 July 1946, p. 2, 'Fréson, échevin usurpateur . . .' See also pp. 207–8.

102 Conseil de Guerre de Bruxelles Procès-Verbal de l'audience publique 6 Aug. 1945, *Aud. Gén.*, Doss. JS, Jugement et Appel; JS Observations sur l'acte d'accusation pp. 3–4, *C2GM*, Fonds José Streel.

103 JS *Pro Just.*, 24 May 1945, *Aud. Gén.*, Doss. JS, Info.; JS Notice pour mon défenseur: cinquième suite, *C2GM*, Fonds José Streel.

104 Chanoine Leclef *Le Cardinal Van Roey et l'occupation allemande*, p. 99.

105 *Le PR* 11 Apr. 1942, p. 3, 'In memoriam' and 14 Apr. 1942, pp. 1 and 6, 'Les funérailles de nos héros'; P. Delandsheere and A. Ooms *La Belgique sous les Nazis* II, p. 171. An earlier funeral of a *légionnaire* had apparently passed off without incident: *Cassandre* 1 Feb. 1942, p. 10, 'A la mémoire . . .'

106 *Le PR* 18 Apr. 1942, p. 1, 'La série continue', 21 Apr. 1942, p. 4 and 25 Apr. 1942, p. 3, 'Un service funèbre . . .'; Chanoine Leclef *Op. cit.*, pp. 100–1; *Le diocèse de Tournai*

sous l'occupation allemande, pp. 147–8; C. Chevalier 'La presse francophone et l'église catholique', p. 162.

107 *Le PR* 24 Apr. 1942, p. 4, 'Quand le cardinal Ratti . . .' and 30 Apr. 1942, p. 1, 'Les bénédictions sont réservés à MM. les assassins'. See also Questionnaire addressed by Alain Dantoing to Madame Hepp, widow of Streel, p. 10, *C2GM*, PS 16.

108 *Le PR* 28 Sept. 1941, pp. 1 and 6, 'Mieux vaut la concorde . . .' and 14 May 1942, p. 1, '"Rerum Novarum" . . .'; *Le Soir* 27 Aug. 1942, p. 1, 'La constante catholique en Belgique'.

109 Interview between Jean Vermeire and José Gotovitch 25 Mar. 1971, p. 90, *C2GM*.

110 Chanoine Leclef *Op. cit.*, pp. 101–2; *Le PR* 23 May 1942, pp. 1 and 6, 'Les huit propositions de M. le Chanoine', 4 June 1942, p. 1, 'La paix des consciences . . .' and 12 June 1942, p. 1, 'Illusions, déceptions . . .'

111 *TB* 20, 15 June 1942, p. 2315; Dupont to *Chefs de Cercles* 28 Apr. 1942, *Aud. Gén.*, Doss. Marcel Dupont, Info., Doct. 17.

112 Chanoine Leclef *Op. cit.*, pp. 104–5; *Le diocèse de Tournai sous l'occupation allemande*, pp. 147–8.

113 *Le PR* 28 Aug. 1942, p. 1, 'Y a-t-il sur le plan religieux . . . ?' and 22 Sept. 1942, p. 1, 'Le plus pur des sacrifices'.

114 *Le PR* 8 May 1942, p. 1, 'Hommage solennel . . .' and 15 Sept. 1942, p. 1, 'Le Cercle de Tournai'.

115 *Le PR* 18 July 1942, p. 1, 'Un crime contre le pays' and p. 3, 'Une mise au point . . .' and 2 Aug. 1942, p. 1, 'A la mémoire . . .'; INBEL 29 Oct. 1943, No. 2134, *C2GM*, Fonds INBEL/967.

116 *Le PR* 30 July 1942, p. 4, 'Le Cercle de Tournai . . .'; *Chef de Groupe* of Brussels to *Chefs de Cellules* 13 June 1944, *C2GM*, C 11/323.19. See p. 208.

117 *Le PR* 11 Aug. 1942, p. 3, 'L'inauguration de la permanence J. Demaret'.

118 VM to *Cadres Territoriaux* 5 May 1942, *Aud. Gén.*, Doss. VM. Info., Doct. 138; Constant to *FC* 25 Apr. 1942. *C2GM*, C 11/265 Série I; Documentation Jans 271.

119 See previous note; VM *Pro Just.*, 25 Nov. 1946, *Aud. Gén.*, Doss. LC, Inst., Doct. 210–11.

120 Siméon *Pro Just.*, 15 Dec. 1946, *C2GM*, JB 20; VM to Constant 6 May 1942 and Documentation Jans 52 in *Aud. Gén.*, Doss. VM, Documentation J, Docts. 43 and 47–50.

121 Constant to *FC* 25 Apr. 1942, *C2GM*, C 11/265 Série I; Albert Constant *Pro Just.*, 29 Jan. 1946, *Aud. Gén.*, Doss. Albert Constant, Inst., Doct. 154–5.

122 *TB* 20, 15 June 1942, p. 2384.

123 Mémoire de V. Matthys pp. 91–2, *C2GM*; Albert Constant *Pro Just.*, 2 Oct. 1945 and 18 Apr. 1946, *Aud. Gén.*, Doss. Albert Constant, Inst., Docts. 86–7 and 219–20.

124 Jacobs to *Chefs de Cercles* 30 May and 3 June 1942, *Aud. Gén.*, Doss. Marcel Dupont, Info., Docts. 82–3 and 84.

125 Simar to *Chefs de Groupes* 8 Aug. 1942, *C2GM*, C 11/321.8.

126 Dupont to *Chefs de Cercles* 17 Oct. 1942, *Aud. Gén.*, Doss. Marcel Dupont, Info., Doct. 73.

127 VM to mobilisation candidates [25 Sept. 1942] and Oct. 1942, *Aud. Gén.*, Doss. VM, Documentation J, Doct. 54 and *C2GM*, C 11/149.

128 Documentation Jans 271; Dupont to *Chefs de Cercles* 5 Nov. 1942, *C2GM*, C 11/217.

129 VM *Pro Just.*, 24 Sept. 1945, *Aud Gén.*, Doss. VM, Info., Doct. 205; Militärverwaltungschef Einsatz von Landeseinwohner in unmittelbaren Wehrmachtsdiensten 1 July 1943, GRMA T 175 80 2600715–26; *TB* 24, 1 Aug. 1943, p. 3159; VM to mobilisation candidates Oct. 1942, *C2GM*, C 11/149.

130 Mémoire de V. Matthys pp. 91–2, *C2GM*.

131 *FC* Période d'Instruction 6 Sept. to 3 Oct. 1942, *Aud. Gén.*, Doss. Albert Constant, Documentation Générale II, Farde G, Doct. 3–4; *Sambre et Meuse* 12 July 1946, p. 2, 'Conseil de Guerre de Namur'; *Vers l'Avenir* 12 July 1946, p. 5, 'Conseil de Guerre de Namur'; *La Meuse* 20 June 1947, p. 2, 'Conseil de Guerre'.

132 *Le PR* 14 July 1942, p. 3, 'Onze mille hommes des milices du VNV . . .'

133 *EMF* of *FC* Ordres hebdomadaires [Feb. 1942] and 4 July 1942, *Aud. Gén.*, Doss. Albert Constant, Documentation Générale, Farde A, Doct. 9 and Documentation Jans

14; Constant to *FC* 21 Apr., 29 June and 30 Nov. 1942, *C2GM*, C 11/265, Série I.
134 VM to mobilisation candidates [25 Sept. 1942], *Aud. Gén.*, Doss. VM, Documentation
    J, Doct. 54; *Le PR* 15 Sept. 1942, p. 1, 'Le Cercle de Tournai . . .'
135 See for example 'Périodes d'Instruction' 9 Aug. to 5 Sept. 1942 and 6 Sept. to 3 Oct.
    1942, *Aud. Gén.*, Doss. Albert Constant, Documentation Générale, Farde D, Doct. 18
    and Farde G, Doct. 3–4; VM *Pro Just.*, 3 Oct. 1945, *Aud. Gén.*, Doss. VM, Info.,
    Doct. 206.
136 Albert Constant *Pro Just.*, 2 Oct. 1945 and VM *Pro Just.*, 3 Oct. 1945 and 29 Aug.
    1946, *Aud. Gén.*, Doss. Albert Constant, Inst., Docts. 86–7 and 327 and Doss. VM,
    Info., Doct. 206.
137 Albert Constant *Pro Just.*, 22 July 1945 and Constant to *FC* 27 Feb. 1943, *Aud. Gén.*,
    Doss. Albert Constant, Inst., Doct. 70–1 and Documentation Générale, Farde A,
    Doct. 11.
138 E.g. *TB* 20, 15 June 1942, p. 2314; *TB* 21, 15 Sept. 1942, p. 2507.
139 *Le Drapeau Rouge* Mar. 1942, p. 1, 'Nos "partisans" à l'action'; J. Gotovitch 'Guerre et
    libération, jalons pour une étude' in *Le parti communiste de Belgique (1921–1944)*
    (Brussels, 1980), pp. 70–1.
140 Dupont to *Chefs de Cercles* 24 Feb. 1942 and Secrétariat of *Chef de Rex ad interim* 17
    Apr. 1942, *C2GM*, C 11/220 and C 11/144.
141 P. Delandsheere and A. Ooms *La Belgique sous les Nazis* II, p. 461; Léon Bertrand *Pro
    Just.*, 13 Dec. 1946, *Aud. Gén.*, Doss. VM, Info., Doct. 274–6.
142 *Le Journal de Charleroi* 7 Jan. 1947, p. 2, 'La brigade policière resiste . . .'
143 VM and Albert Constant *Pro Just.*, 12 Feb. 1947, *Aud. Gén.*, Doss. VM, Info., Doct.
    283–4; Simar to *Chefs de Groupes* 18 July 1942, *C2GM*, C 11/321.8; *Vers l'Avenir* 8
    Nov. 1946, p. 2 and 13 Dec. 1946, p. 4, 'Conseil de Guerre de Namur'.
144 *Le PR* 4 July 1942, p. 1, 'Jean Demaret a été assassiné'; VM and Albert Constant *Pro
    Just.*, 27 Dec. 1946 and 12 Feb. 1947, *Aud. Gén.*, Doss. VM, Info., Docts. 280–1 and
    283–4; P. Bodart *Avec l'Armée Belge des Partisans* (Brussels, 1948), pp. 69–70.
145 *Le Journal de Charleroi* 7 July 1942, p. 2, 'Les funérailles de M. J. Demaret'.
146 Documentation Jans 14; A. De Jonghe 'La lutte Himmler-Reeder'. . .', *Cahiers* VIII
    (1984), pp. 88–9.
147 *Le PR* 15 Sept. 1942, p. 1, 'Le Cercle de Tournai . . .' and 24 Sept. 1942, pp. 1 and 4,
    'Après un an de patience'.
148 *EMF* of *FC* Ordres hebdomadaires 26 Sept. 1942 and Gustave Orban and Eugène
    Otten *Pro Just.*, 24 Sept. and 9 and 22 Oct. 1946, *Aud. Gén.*, Doss. Albert Constant,
    Inst., Doct. 339–41 and Pièces entrées après la mise en prévention, Docts. 40, 44 and
    46.
149 See p. 188.
150 P. Struyé *L'évolution du sentiment public*, pp. 101–3; J. Gotovitch 'Guerre et libération'
    in *Le parti communiste de Belgique*, p. 68.
151 P. Delandsheere and A. Ooms *La Belgique sous les Nazis* II, pp. 188–9; P. Struye *Op.
    cit.*, pp. 106–7 and 126.
152 E.g. *Le PR* 8 Apr. 1942, p. 3, 'Plusieurs camarades du Mouvement . . .', 6 Aug. 1942,
    p. 2, 'Un coiffeur rexiste', 11 Aug. 1942, p. 2, 'Les funérailles émouvantes de deux
    Gardes Wallonnes' and 25 Aug. 1942, p. 3, 'Une magnifique réunion . . .'
153 *Le PR* 22 Apr. 1942, p. 1, 'Les brimades dans les écoles' and 7 July 1942, p. 2, 'Le
    martyre de deux vaillantes rexistes'.
154 E.g. *Le PR* 3 Mar. 1942, p. 3, 'Les rexistes dans les Stalags' and 11 Apr. 1942, p. 2,
    'Chronique du Mouvement'; *La Belgique Indépendante* 9 July 1942, cited in *C2GM*,
    Fonds INBEL/980.
155 P. Struye *Op. cit.*, pp. 103–5; *Le Courrier de l'Escaut* 19 July 1946, p. 2, 'Conseil de
    Guerre de Tournai (A)'.
156 *Le PR* 30 Jan. 1942, p. 2, 'Ordres de la Prévôté' and 24 Feb. 1942, p. 1, 'Notre Légion
    de l'Est . . .'
157 *Le PR* 5 and 28 Dec. 1941, p. 2, 'Chronique de la Solidarité Légionnaire'.
158 *Le PR* 13 Feb. 1942, p. 2, 'Chronique de la Solidarité Légionnaire', 25 Aug. 1942,
    p. 3, 'Une magnifique réunion . . .', 1 Sept. 1942, p. 3, 'Journée d'études . . .'; L.
    Degrelle *Feldpost* (Brussels, 1944), pp. 150–1.
159 Constant to *FC* 24 Apr. 1942, *C2GM*, C 11/264.

Chapter Five

1 F. Kupferman *Laval*, pp. 318–71; O.K. Hoidal *Quisling* (Oslo, 1989), pp. 588–98.

2 JS *Pro Just.*, 24 May 1945, *Aud. Gén.*, Doss. JS, Info; Untitled note [19 Sept. 1942] and VM to Daye 23 Sept. 1942, *C2GM*, Papiers Pierre Daye; Mémoire de V. Matthys p. 38, *C2GM*. The new *Conseil* was sometimes referred to as the *Bureau Politique* of Rex.

3 Première séance du nouveau Bureau Politique 25 Sept. 1942, *C2GM*, Papiers Pierre Daye. Degrelle's long-standing lawyer Georges Dubois, a former head of Rex in Brussels Louis Vanderveken, a large-scale economic collaborator René Petit as well as a representative of the *CCW* were also stated to have been members of the *Conseil*: Mémoire de V. Matthys p. 38, *C2GM*; *Le Soir* 1 Dec. 1946 and 12 Jan. 1947, p. 4, 'Les Conseils de Guerre'; *Journal des Tribunaux* 23 Jan. 1949, pp. 53–7, 'Cour Militaire'.

4 P. Struye *L'évolution du sentiment public*, p. 106. See also R. De Becker 'Conférence rédactionnelle au *Soir*' 3 Sept. 1943, *C2GM*, PL 1.

5 P. Dodge *Beyond Marxism*, pp. 206–8; H. De Man *Cahiers de ma montagne* (Brussels-Paris, 1944).

6 R. Poulet 'Prison Diary' 11 July 1946 (Private Collection); *Le PR* 6 Aug. 1942, p. 1, 'Des propositions constructives'.

7 *Le Nouveau Journal* 19 Oct. 1942, p. 1, 'Le point essentiel' and 24–5 Oct. 1942, p. 1, 'Aspiration à la discipline'; *Le Soir* 27 Oct. 1942, p. 1, 'En marche vers l'unité'.

8 Documentation Jans 320; W. Meyers 'Les collaborateurs flamands de France et leurs contacts avec les milieux flamingants belges', *Revue du Nord* LX (1978), pp. 337–46. The post-war trials of collaborators revealed only a few isolated examples of francophone Belgians who had joined Flemish pro-German groups: e.g. *Vers l'Avenir* 26 Mar. and 24 May 1946, p. 2, 'Conseil de Guerre de Namur'.

9 Simar to *Chefs de Groupes* 7 Sept. 1942, *C2GM*, C 11/321.8; *Le PR* 10 Aug. 1941, p. 4, 'A propos de "Wallonie" ' and 4 Jan. 1942, p. 1, 'Les grandes heures de Rex en '41'.

10 *Le PR* 28 July 1942, pp. 1 and 4, 'Le problème de Bruxelles', 5 Aug. 1942, p. 1, 'Manifestations reconfortantes' and 27 Oct. 1942, p. 2, 'Une grande manifestation . . .'

11 J. Willequet *La Belgique sous la botte*, pp. 159–62; A. De Jonghe 'H.J. Elias als leider van het Vlaams Nationaal Verbond', *Revue belge d'histoire contemporaine* VI (1975), pp. 197–238 and VII (1976), pp. 329–423.

12 A. De Jonghe 'La lutte Himmler-Reeder . . .', *Cahiers* IV (1976), pp. 52–81 and 121–34 and V (1978), pp. 82–93.

13 R. De Becker 'La collaboration . . .', *Courrier hebdomadaire du CRISP* No. 497–8 (1970), p. 20; JS 'Note écrite . . .' 27 May 1945 and Conseil de Guerre de Bruxelles Procès-Verbal de l'audience publique 6 Aug. 1945, *Aud. Gén.*, Doss. JS, Info. and Jugement et Appel.

14 *Le PR* 21 Oct. 1942, p. 1, 'Perspectives du parti unique', 7 Nov. 1942, p. 1, 'Jacques Doriot . . .' and 29 Nov. 1942, pp. 1 and 6, 'On ne fait pas la révolution . . .'

15 *Le PR* 30 Sept. 1942, p. 1, 'Besoin de grandeur' and 28 Nov. 1942, p. 1, 'Une belle déclération'.

16 VM to *Chef de Cercle de Virton* 29 Aug. 1942 and Dupont to *Chefs de Cercles* 14 Oct. 1942, *C2GM*, C 11/148 and 217.

17 *Le PR* 27 Oct. 1942, p. 1, 'Une grande manifestation de force et de foi'; P. Struye *L'évolution du sentiment public*, pp. 105–6.

18 *Le PR* 25 July 1942, pp. 1–2, 'Reprenant son commandement au Front de l'Est . . .' and 27 Oct. 1942, p. 1, 'Une grande manifestation . . .'; P. Delandsheere and A. Ooms *La Belgique sous les Nazis* II, pp. 468–9.

19 *Le PR* 27 Oct. 1942, pp. 1–2, 'Une grande manifestation . . .'

20 *Ibid.*

21 *TB* 22, 31 Dec. 1942, p. 2743.

22 *Le PR* 6 Dec. 1942, p. 1, 'Facteurs de mort et de vie'. In his post-war writings, Streel had some difficulty in explaining this politically expedient concession: JS Analyse de l'acte d'accusation: première suite pp. 13–15, *C2GM*, Fonds José Streel.

23 F. Selleslagh 'L'emploi' in *1940–1945 La vie quotidienne en Belgique*, p. 159; P. Struye *L'évolution du sentiment public*, p. 109.

24 Mémoire de V. Matthys p. 69, *C2GM*; Première séance du nouveau Bureau Politique 25 Sept. 1942, *C2GM*, Papiers Pierre Daye.

25 Journal de V. Matthys p. 10, *C2GM*; JS to Daye 3 Oct. 1942, *C2GM*, Papiers Pierre Daye; A. Milward *The New Order and the French Economy* (Oxford, 1970), pp. 113–14.

26 *Le PR* 16 Oct. 1942, p. 2, 'Les "fils à papa" cherchent à échapper . . .'; Mémoire de V. Matthys pp. 70–4, *C2GM*.

27 Dupont to *Chefs de Cercles* 21 Oct. 1942, *C2GM*, C 11/219; *Le PR* 8 Nov. 1942, p. 1, 'Ouste! Au travail!' and 21 Feb. 1943, p. 1, 'Notre jeunesse a aussi des devoirs . . .'

28 Dupont to *Chefs de Cercles* 21 Oct. 1942, *C2GM*, C 11/219; Documentation Jans 53; Journal de V. Matthys pp. 10–11, *C2GM*.

29 Feyaerts to IV Bannière of *FC* 26 Dec. 1942, *C2GM*, C 11/278.

30 Franz Van Moer *Pro Just.*, 19 July 1946, *Aud. Gén.*, Doss. Albert Constant, Inst., Doct. 292; Simar to *Chefs de Groupes* 26 Dec. 1942, *C2GM*, C 11/321.8; *La Meuse* 8 Aug. 1945, p. 1, 'Antoine Dupont . . .'; P. Delandsheere and A. Ooms *La Belgique sous les Nazis* II, p. 467.

31 *TB* 22, 31 Dec. 1942, p. 2731; Dupont and Brunet to *Chefs de Cercles* 3 Mar. 1943 and letter of *Chef des Cadres Politiques Cercle d'Ath*, *C2GM*, C 11/232 and 321.7.

32 J. Culot 'L'exploitation de la main d'oeuvre belge et le problème des réfractaires', *Cahiers* I (1970), pp. 33–66; F. Selleslagh 'L'emploi' in *1940–1945 La vie quotidienne en Belgique*, pp. 159–67.

33 Extraits du Bulletin d'information confidentiel du Ministère de l'Intérieur [1943], *C2GM*, Fonds INBEL/966.

34 *TB* 22, 31 Dec. 1942, p. 2769; Von Craushaar to *Oberfeldkommandanturen* and *Feldkommandanturen* 28 Apr. 1943, GRMA T 501 97 473–81. Streel stated that 140 attacks had been made on Rexists by the end of 1942; JS 'Note écrite . . .' 27 May 1945, *Aud. Gén.*, Doss. JS, Info.

35 *Le PR* 13 Nov. 1942, p. 1, 'Notre camarade Ch. Hénault . . .', 20 Nov. 1942, p. 1, 'Notre camarade Jean Teughels . . .', 19 Dec. 1942, p. 1, 'C'était un saint père . . .' and 22 Dec. 1942, p. 1, 'Le suprême adieu . . .'; J. Wynants *Verviers libéré* (Verviers, 1984), p. 193; P. Delandsheere and A. Ooms *La Belgique sous les Nazis* II, pp. 539–40.

36 Albert Constant *Pro Just.*, 12 Feb. 1947, *Aud. Gén.*, Doss. VM, Info., Doct. 283–4; *TB* 22, 31 Dec. 1942, p. 2743; Informations reçues de Belgique 9 Dec. 1942, *C2GM*, Fonds INBEL/964.

37 *TB* 22, 31 Dec. 1942, p. 2755; *La Meuse* 25 Jan. 1946, p. 2, 'Gérard Willems . . .'

38 JS and VM to *Cadres Politiques* 27 Nov. 1942, *C2GM*, C 11/230; JS *Pro Just.*, 4 Oct. 1945, *Aud. Gén.*, Doss. JS, *Cour Militaire*.

39 JS and VM to *Cadres Politiques* 27 Nov. 1942, *C2GM*, C 11/230; Plaidoyer prononcé par Victor Matthys devant le Conseil de Guerre de Charleroi pp. 3–4, *C2GM*, JP 258; Mémoire de V. Matthys p. 108, *C2GM*.

40 JS to Grauls 19 Nov. 1942 and JS *Pro Just.*, 5 Oct. 1945, *Aud. Gén.*, Doss. JS, *Cour Militaire*; VM to Dr Callies 14 Nov. 1942, Papiers Grauls, *C2GM*, PG 5/245; VM to Reeder (undated) copy in Simar to *Chefs de Groupes* 21 Nov. 1942, *C2GM*, C 11/321.8.

41 See JS and VM to *Cadres Politiques* 27 Nov. 1942, *C2GM*, C 11/230; JS *Pro Just.*, 4 Oct. 1945, *Aud. Gén.*, Doss. JS, *Cour Militaire*.

42 *TB* 22, 31 Dec. 1942, p. 2779; Dupont to *Chefs de Cercles* 22 Nov. 1942, *C2GM*, C 11/289; JS to *Cadre Politique* 4 Dec. 1942, *Aud. Gén.*, Doss. JS [Supplementary File 7, Doct. i].

43 *TB* 22, 31 Dec. 1942, p. 2743; VM to Dr Callies 14 Nov. 1942, Papiers Grauls, *C2GM*, PG 5/245. See also A. De Jonghe 'La lutte Himmler-Reeder . . .', *Cahiers* VIII (1984), p. 84.

44 A. De Jonghe *Op. cit.*, *Cahiers* IV (1976), pp. 96–121 and V (1978), pp. 6–18.

45 *TB* 22, 31 Dec. 1942, p. 2714; E. Reeder *Pro Just.*, 27 Dec. 1949, Procès Von Falkenhausen, Doct. 1749; A. De Jonghe *Op. cit.*, *Cahiers* V (1978), p. 12 and VIII (1984), pp. 54–60.

46 See for example Michel Saussez Curriculum Vitae, *Aud. Gén.*, Doss. Michel Saussez, Inst., Doct. 15; Conseil de Guerre de Bruxelles Exposé des Faits 3 Mar. 1947, pp. 55 and 64, *C2GM*, JB 13.

47 Pièces de Forme, *Aud. Gén.*, Doss. Charles Lambinon; JS Observations sur l'acte d'accusation, pp. 7–8, *C2GM*, Fonds José Streel.

48 JS Observations sur l'acte d'accusation pp. 7–8, *C2GM*, Fonds José Streel; Conseil de Guerre de Bruxelles Exposé des Faits 3 Mar. 1947, p. 4, *C2GM*, JB 13; Henry Marcovitz *Pro Just.*, 4 Nov. 1946, *Aud. Gén.*, Doss. VM, Info., Doct. 152–3; Ordres de l'*EM* des *FC* 12 Dec. 1942 cited in Documentation Jans 53; JS to *Chefs de Cercles* 20 Nov. 1942, *C2GM*, C 11/229; Jean Fontaine *Pro Just.*, 13 Dec. 1946 and Albert Constant *Pro Just.*, 27 Dec. 1946, *Aud. Gén.*, Doss. VM, Info., Docts. 274–6 and 280–1.

49 Michel Saussez to Edouard Saussez 23 Nov. 1942, *Aud. Gén.*, Doss. Michel Saussez, Pièces à Conviction, Doct. 29.

50 JS Mémoire: à partir de ma rupture avec Rex, *C2GM*, Fonds José Streel; [Baumann] to Meyer 22 Jan. 1943, GRMA T 501 175 83; *Le PR* 20 Dec. 1942, p. 1, 'Après une campagne de quinze mois'.

51 JS Mémoire: quelques précisions sur la volte-face de Degrelle, *C2GM*, Fonds José Streel; Légion Belge 'Wallonie' Historique, p. 31, *C2GM*, W 4; *Le PR* 19 Dec. 1942, p. 1, 'Une émouvante exhortation . . .'

52 JS Mémoire: quelques précisions sur la volte-face de Degrelle, *C2GM*, Fonds José Streel. Himmler referred only to the *Chef de Rex* meeting his 'Mitarbeitern' but Degrelle insists that he met Berger: Himmler to Lammers 25 Mar. 1943, *C2GM*, C 11/124bis, Doct. 7; *L'Eventail* 6 June 1980, p. 9, 'Léon Degrelle'.

53 Reeder to *OKH* 26 Jan. 1943, *C2GM*, Procès von Falkenhausen, Doct. 117; Himmler to Lammers 25 Mar. 1943, *C2GM*, C 11/124bis, Doct. 7.

54 JS Mémoire: à partir de ma rupture avec Rex, *C2GM*, Fonds José Streel.

55 A. De Jonghe 'La lutte Himmler-Reeder', *Cahiers* V (1978), pp. 51–60.

56 *Ibid*; *Le Soir* 16 June 1946, p. 2, 'Les Conseils de Guerre'; J.-M. Charlier *Léon Degrelle*, pp. 281–2.

57 A. De Jonghe 'La lutte Himmler-Reeder', *Cahiers* V (1978), p. 59.

58 LD to Dr Bähr 11 May 1942, GRMA T 175 131 2651929; *Le PR* 28 Nov. 1942, p. 1, 'Une belle declération'.

59 Interview with Léon Degrelle 14 July 1988.

60 E.g. J.-M. Charlier *Léon Degrelle*, pp. 302–3.

61 *TB* 22, 31 Dec. 1942, pp. 2721–2.

62 Cited in Comte Capelle *Au Service du Roi* II, p. 131.

63 Reeder to *OKH* 26 Jan. 1943, *C2GM*, Procès von Falkenhausen, Doct. 117.

64 JS Mémoire: quelques précisions sur la volte-face de Degrelle and à partir de ma rupture avec Rex, *C2GM*, Fonds José Streel; R. Poulet 'Prison Diary' 11 July 1946 (Private Collection); *Le PR* 24 Dec. 1942, p. 1, 'La Légion nous indique . . .' and 31 Dec. 1942, p. 1, 'L'unique devoir'.

65 See notes 62 and 64; JS 'Note écrite . . .' 27 May 1945, *Aud. Gén.*, Doss. JS, Info; Berger to Himmler 5 Jan. 1943, Bundesarchiv Koblenz, Doct. NS 19/1541. I am grateful to A. De Jonghe for making a copy of this document available to me.

66 *Le PR* 10 Jan. 1943, p. 1, 'Le Chef de Rex passe en revue . . .'; R. De Becker 'La collaboration . . .', *Courrier hebdomadaire du CRISP* No. 497/8 (1970), p. 50.

67 The phrase was Reeder's: *TB* 23, 15 Apr. 1943, p. 2940.

68 *Ibid*; Reeder to *OKH* 26 Jan. 1943, *C2GM*, Procès von Falkenhausen, Doct. 117; *Le PR* 18 Jan. 1943, p. 1, 'La cérémonie'.

69 *Le PR* 18 Jan. 1943, pp. 1–3, 'Le discours du Chef de Rex'.

70 *Ibid.*

71 E.g. J.-M. Charlier *Léon Degrelle*, p. 306.

72 See JS Mémoire: à partir de ma rupture avec Rex, *C2GM*, Fonds José Streel.

73 J.-M. Charlier *Léon Degrelle*, p. 305; L. Narvaez *Degrelle m'a dit* (Brussels, 1977), p. 306.

74 *L'Eventail* 6 June 1980, p. 9, 'Léon Degrelle'.

Chapter Six

1 *Sipo-SD* 'Meldungen aus Belgien und Nordfrankreich' 3/43, 15 Feb. 1943, p. 26; *TB* 23, 15 Apr. 1943, p. 2941.
2 De Becker to LD 18 Jan. 1943 and De Becker to VM 25 Jan. 1943 in R. De Becker 'La collaboration . . .', *Courrier hebdomadaire du CRISP* No. 497–8 (1970), pp. 68–70; De Ligne to VM 25 Jan. 1943, *C2GM*, Papiers Pierre Daye. Re the continued nominal existence of the *Conseil Politique*, see *Le PR* 6 June 1943, p. 1, 'Le Chef de Rex ad interim . . .'
3 *Le Soir* 16 Feb. 1943, p. 1, 'Pourquoi nous luttons'; *TB* 23, 15 Apr. 1943, p. 2942; R. Poulet 'Histoire du Nouveau Journal' pp. 47–8 and 'Sur un discours politique' (Private Collection); Comte Capelle *Au Service du Roi* II, p. 132.
4 *Cassandre* 24 Jan. 1943, p. 1, 'Dans les marges d'un discours'. See pp. 183–4.
5 JS to La Presse de Rex 1 Feb. 1943, *Aud. Gén.*, Doss. JS [Supplementary File 7, Doct. 11–14]; JS Analyse de l'acte d'accusation: première suite p. 22, *C2GM*, Fonds José Streel.
6 JS Analyse de l'acte d'accusation: première suite p. 22, *C2GM*, Fonds José Streel; Raty to JS 19 Feb. 1943 and Meulenijzer to JS 24 Feb. 1943, *Aud. Gén.*, Doss. JS, [Supplementary File 7, Docts. 9 and 10]; JS Mémoire: à partir de ma rupture avec Rex, *C2GM*, Fonds José Streel.
7 JS to Meulenijzer 25 Feb. 1943, *Aud. Gén.*, Doss. JS [Supplementary File 7, Doct. 7–8].
8 JS to Monseigneur Picard 26 Dec. 1945, *C2GM*, PS 16; JS Mémoire: après mon départ de Rex (suite), *C2GM*, Fonds José Streel.
9 JS to Reeder 25 Feb. 1943, *C2GM*, Fonds José Streel.
10 *National Socialisme* 15 Apr. 1943, p. 12, 'Ordres et Communiqués'; *EMF* of *FC* Ordres hebdomadaires No. 56–7, *Aud. Gén.*, Doss. Albert Constant, Documentation Générale, Farde A, Doct. 10; *Le Soir* 28 Feb. 1945, pp. 2–3, 'Les Conseils de Guerre'.
11 *Sipo-SD* 'Meldungen . . .' 5/43, 15 Mar. 1943, p. 30; Reeder to *OKH* 26 Jan. 1943, *C2GM*, Procès von Falkenhausen, Doct. 117; *Le Soir* 6 Mar. 1946, p. 2, 'Le procès du Grand Bruxelles'.
12 *Informations administratives et politiques* Dec. 1943, p. 40, 'Bilan de fin de l'année'; Extraits du bulletin d'informations confidentiels du Ministère de l'Intérieur INBEL 29 June 1943, *C2GM*, Fonds INBEL/966.
13 LC *Pro Just.*, 27 Nov. 1946 and JS *Pro Just.*, 24 May 1945, *Aud. Gén.*, Doss. VM, Info., Doct. 154–5 and Doss. JS, Info.
14 R. Poulet 'Histoire du Nouveau Journal' p. 46 (Private Collection); P. Delandsheere and A. Ooms *La Belgique sous les Nazis* III, p. 34.
15 LC *Pro Just.*, 27 Nov. 1946, *Aud. Gén.*, Doss. VM, Info., Doct. 154–5; JS Mémoire: à partir de ma rupture avec Rex, *C2GM*, Fonds José Streel.
16 *Le PR* 24 Jan. 1943, p. 1, 'Ni collaborationnistes ni germanophiles', 31 Jan. 1943, p. 1, 'Dans la hiérarchie des peuples . . .', 2 Feb. 1943, p. 1, 'Le destin de notre peuple . . .', 3 Mar. 1943, p. 1, 'L'Etat en face de la communauté populaire' and 5 Mar. 1943, p. 1, 'La Wallonie et l'empire germanique'.
17 *Sipo-SD* 'Meldungen . . .' 5/43, 15 Mar. 1943, p. 30; JS Mémoire: à partir de ma rupture avec Rex, *C2GM*, Fonds José Streel.
18 *Le PR* 6 Apr. 1943, pp. 1–3, 'Le Chef de Rex passe en revue . . .' and 18 Apr. 1943, p. 1, 'Adieu à Paul Colin'; *Sipo-SD* 'Meldungen . . .' 7/43, 15 Apr. 1943, pp. 7 and 38 and 8/43, 1 May 1943, p. 21.
19 H. Philippet *Et mets ta robe de bal* (Privately published), pp. 99–100.
20 Interview between Léon Degrelle and Jean Vanwelkenhuyzen 11–12 Dec. 1977, p. 122.
21 *Sipo-SD* 'Meldungen . . .' 3/43, 15 Feb. 1943, pp. 27–8; *Le PR* 9 Feb. 1943, p. 1, 'Le Chef de Rex parle à nos ouvriers'; [Baumann] to Meyer 22 Jan. 1943, GRMA T 501 175 83; *OKW* WFSt, Qu (Verw.) 13 Feb. 1943, *C2GM*, C 11/124bis, Doct. 3; *TB* 23, 15 Apr. 1943, p. 2942; A. De Jonghe 'La lutte Himmler-Reeder . . .', *Cahiers* V (1978), p. 70.
22 A. De Jonghe *Op. cit.* V (1978), p. 68.

23 H. Trevor-Roper (ed.) *Hitler's Table Talk*, p. 460.
24 *TB* 23, 15 Apr. 1943, p. 2932; Kaltenbrunner to Himmler 24 Mar. 1943 and Jungclaus to [Berger], 25 Mar. 1943, *C2GM*, Berlin Document Center (henceforth BDC) III, Docts. 13 and 14.
25 Politisches Archiv Bonn, Inland II g 487, Namen Degrelle cited in A. De Jonghe 'La lutte Himmler-Reeder . . .', *Cahiers* V (1978), p. 70.
26 A. De Jonghe *Op. cit.* V (1978), pp. 71–2; *OKW* WFSt, Qu (Verw.) 13 Feb. 1943, *C2GM*, C 11/124bis, Doct. 3.
27 Reeder to *OKH* 26 Jan. 1943, *C2GM*, Procès von Falkenhausen, Doct. 117; *National Socialisme* 15 Jan. 1943, p. 12, 'Ordres et Communiqués'; *TB* 23, 15 Apr. 1943, p. 2945.
28 *TB* 23, 15 Apr. 1943, pp. 2932 and 2942; *Sipo-SD* 'Meldungen . . .' 4/43, 1 Mar. 1943, p. 39.
29 E.g. Bericht über die 3 Tagung der germanischen Arbeitgemeinschaft 12 Jan. 1943, Institut für Zeitgeschichte München, Doct. NO 1783, p. 4. I am grateful to A. De Jonghe for providing me with a copy of this document.
30 Himmler to Lammers 25 Mar. 1943, *C2GM*, C 11/124bis, Doct. 7.
31 Journal de V. Matthys p. 14, *C2GM*.
32 *Le PR* 9 Feb. 1943, pp. 1 and 4, 'Le Chef de Rex parle . . .'; L. Degrelle *Lettres à mon Cardinal*, pp. 134–5.
33 Berger to Himmler 5 Jan. 1943, GRMA T 175 80 2600745. After the war, Matthys claimed that it was the SS which proposed the creation of this unit to Rex: Mémoire de V. Matthys p. 51, *C2GM*.
34 'Die Absicht Degrelle's, eine allgemeine wallonische SS zu gründen, ist zurückgestellt worden': Niederschrift über die Besprechung des SS-Ausschusses der Arbeitgemein-schaft für den germanischen Raum 12 Jan. 1943, Institut für Zeitgeschichte München, Doct. PS 705, p. 4. I am obliged to A. De Jonghe for drawing this document to my attention.
35 *TB* 24, 1 Aug. 1943, p. 3147.
36 J. De Launay *Histoires secrètes de la Belgique*, p. 234.
37 JS Au sujet de l'article 115 [p. 12], *C2GM*, Fonds José Streel; *TB* 23, 15 Apr. 1943, p. 2943.
38 Francq to Daye 6 Nov. 1943, *C2GM*, Papiers Pierre Daye; *La Cité Nouvelle* 5 Jan. 1945, p. 1, 'Où se cache la fortune de Degrelle?'
39 R. De Becker 'La collaboration . . .', *Courrier hebdomadaire du CRISP* No. 497–8 (1970), pp. 57–8; E. De Bens 'La presse au temps de l'occupation . . .', *Revue d'histoire de la deuxième guerre mondiale* XX (1970), pp. 11–12; R. Poulet *Ce n'est pas une vie* (Paris, 1976), pp. 152–3; 'Les mémoires de Pierre Daye', *Dossier du mois* No. 12, pp. 28–9; Ch. d'Ydewalle 'In memoriam Paul Colin' in *La Belgique Indépendante* 30 Mar. 1944, cited in *C2GM*, Fonds INBEL/980.
40 JS Analyse de l'acte d'accusation: première suite p. 18, *C2GM*, Fonds José Streel; *Le PR* 9 Apr. 1942, p. 3, 'Le devoir de présence' and 18 July 1942, p. 3, 'L'officier de liaison de la Légion Wallonie . . .'
41 *Le PR* 16 Apr. 1943, p. 1, 'Un soldat'; *Journal des Tribunaux* 23 Jan. 1949, pp. 53–7, 'Cour Militaire'; General Van Overstraeten *Sous le joug*, p. 248; *TB* 23, 15 Apr. 1943, pp. 2941–2.
42 Jean Backx *Pro Just.*, 27 Feb. 1947 and Jacques Peeters *Pro Just.*, 3 Mar. 1947, *Aud. Gén.*, Doss. Joseph Pévenasse, *Cour Militaire*, Doct. 1b; *Le PR* 27 Oct. 1942, p. 1, 'Une grande manifestation . . .'. See also pp. 129 and 205–6.
43 Jean Vermeire *Pro Just.*, 5 Sept. 1945, *Aud. Gén.*, Doss. Jean Denis, Info., Doct. 38; Interview between Jean Vermeire and José Gotovitch 25 Mar. 1971, *C2GM*; J. Mabire *Légion Wallonie*, pp. 120–1.
44 Conseil de Guerre de Bruxelles Exposé des Faits 3 Mar. 1947, p. 55, *C2GM*, JB 13.
45 *National Socialisme* 15 Apr. 1943, p. 12, 'Ordres et Communiqués'. The new depart-ment also assumed responsibility for the work formerly carried out by the *Chef des Cadres Politiques*: *Informations administratives et politiques* Oct. 1943, pp. 1–3, 'Notre tâche'.
46 *Le Soir* 5 Mar. 1946, pp. 1–2, 'Conseil de Guerre de Bruxelles', 6 Mar. 1946, p. 2, 'Le

procès du Grand Bruxelles' and 7 Mar. 1946, p. 2 'Les Conseils de Guerre'; VM to Daye 9 Sept. 1942, *C2GM*, Papiers Pierre Daye; LC to *Auditeur Militaire Général* 30 Apr. 1947, *Aud. Gén.*, Doss. LC, Enquête Complémentaire, Farde C, Doct. 18; P. Delandsheere and A. Ooms *La Belgique sous les Nazis* IV, p. 83.

47 Conseil de Guerre de Bruxelles Exposé des Faits 3 Mar. 1947, p. 55, *C2GM*, JB 13; Charles Peeters 'Organisation interne du mouvement rexiste', *C2GM*, C 11/87; LC *Pro Just.*, 27 Nov. 1946, Collard-[Burtomboy] correspondence, Collard to [German authorities] 30 Dec. 1941 and *Pro Just.*, 13 Nov. 1945, *Aud. Gén.*, Doss. VM, Info., Doct. 154–5 and Doss. LC, Inst., Docts. 14 and 137.

48 JS 'Note écrite . . .' 27 May 1945, *Aud. Gén.*, Doss. JS, Info.; VM and LC *Pro Just.*, 23 and 27 Nov. 1946, *Aud. Gén.*, Doss. LC, Inst., Docts. 209 and 214.

49 *National Socialisme* 15 Apr. 1943, p. 12, 'Ordres et Communiqués'; Louis Shaw *Pro Just.*, 4 Sept. 1946, in Documentation Jans 377; Conseil de Guerre de Bruxelles Exposé des Faits 3 Mar. 1947, p. 4, *C2GM*, JB 13; VM testimony in Documentation Jans 266.

50 *National Socialisme* 15 Apr. 1943, p. 12, 'Ordres et Communiqués'; J. Denis 'Mémoire justificatif d'un condamné à mort' pp. 114–19, *Aud. Gén.*, Doss. Jean Denis. Info., Doct. 53; Charles Peeters 'Organisation interne du mouvement rexiste' *C2GM*, C 11/87.

51 *National Socialisme* 15 Apr. 1943, p. 12, 'Ordres et Communiqués'; Jean Danly to Boveroulle 2 Oct. 1943, *Aud. Gén.*, Doss. Michel Saussez, Pièces à Conviction, Doct. 30; Charles Peeters 'Organisation interne du mouvement rexiste' and Heinesch to *EM*, *C2GM*, C 11/87 and 258; LC and Julien Keutgen *Pro Just.*, 21 Mar. and 13 Sept. 1946, *Aud. Gén.*, Doss. Marcel Dupont, Info., Section 5 and Loose Papers.

52 *Sipo-SD* 'Meldungen . . .' 5/43, 15 Mar. 1943, p. 12; *Le PR* 16 Apr. 1943, p. 1, 'Paul Colin est mort'; P. Delandsheere and A. Ooms *La Belgique sous les Nazis* III, pp. 117–19.

53 INBEL Renseignements reçus de Belgique 21 May 1943 and INBEL Service P No. 512 11 May 1944, *C2GM*, Fonds INBEL/966 and 980; *Le PR* 24 Jan. 1943, p. 6, 'La Camarade Villers lâchement assassinée' and 21 Apr. 1943, p. 1, 'Le camarade Kempeneers . . .'; *National Socialisme* 15 Feb. and 15 Mar. 1943, p. 10, 'In Memoriam'.

54 *Sipo-SD* 'Meldungen . . .' 3/43, 15 Feb. 1943, p. 41; *TB* 24, 1 Aug. 1943, p. 3192.

55 *TB* 23, 15 Apr. 1943, pp. 2914–19; *Sipo-SD* 'Meldungen . . .' 4/43, 1 Mar. 1943, p. 28 and 7/43, 15 Apr. 1943, p. 38.

56 *TB* 23, 15 Apr. 1943, pp. 2936–9; *Sipo-SD* 'Meldungen . . .' 8/43, 1 May 1943, pp. 26–9.

57 Mémoire de V. Matthys p. 93, *C2GM*.

58 *Le PR* 6 Apr. 1943, pp. 1–3, 'Le Chef de Rex passe en revue . . .'; *National Socialisme* 15 May 1943, p. 5, 'Rapport du Chef des Cadres Politiques'; *Sipo-SD* 'Meldungen . . .' 7/43, 15 Apr. 1943, p. 38.

59 *Le PR* 6 Apr. 1943, pp. 1–3, 'Le Chef de Rex passe en revue . . .' and 25 May 1943, pp. 1–4, 'Commémoration de nos héros'.

60 Von Craushaar to *OFKs* and *FKs* 28 Apr. 1943, GRMA T 501 97 473–83. See pp. 227–9. This should not be confused with the *Garde Spéciale* often referred to in the Rexist press at this time. This was the railway guard (*Eisenbahnwachdienst*) which was established at the initiative of the German authorities in early 1943 and which was subsequently integrated into the *Gardes Wallonnes*.

61 Reeder Déposition de Témoin 31 Jan. 1950, *C2GM*, Procès von Falkenhausen, Doct. 2201. See note 60.

62 Questionnaire addressed by Alain Dantoing to Madame Hepp, widow of Streel p. 15, *C2GM*, PS 16; JS Mémoire: Après mon départ de Rex (suite), *C2GM*, Fonds José Streel; Conseil de Guerre de Bruxelles, Procès-Verbal de l'audience publique 6 Aug. 1945, *Aud. Gén.*, Doss. JS, Jugement et Appel.

63 A. De Jonghe 'La lutte Himmler-Reeder . . .', *Cahiers* VIII (1984), pp. 78–82; P. Delandsheere and A. Ooms *La Belgique sous les Nazis* III, pp. 7–8 and 33; Plaidoyer prononcé par Victor Matthys devant le Conseil de Guerre de Charleroi p. 7, *C2GM*, JP 258; *Le Soir* 14 June 1947, p. 5, 'Les Conseils de Guerre'.

64 *Le PR* 25 May 1943, pp. 1–4, 'Commémoration de nos héros'.

65 *Le PR* 18 Apr. 1943, p. 1, 'Adieu à Paul Colin' and 4 May 1943, p. 1, 'Le Chef de Rex

glorifie le travail'.

66 *Le PR* 1 May 1943, p. 1, 'Suprême hommage à un héros'.
67 *Informations administratives et politiques* Dec. 1943, pp. 40–4, 'Bilan de fin de l'année'.
68 Journal de V. Matthys pp. 13–14, *C2GM*; A. De Jonghe 'La lutte Himmler-Reeder . . .', *Cahiers* V (1978), pp. 71–2.
69 See *TB* 25, 15 Nov. 1943, p. 3397.
70 *Informations administratives et politiques* Sept. 1943, pp. 40–8, 'La réunion de septembre 1943'; *Le PR* 25 May 1943, pp. 1 and 4, 'Commémoration de nos héros' and 25 Sept. 1943, p. 3, 'Chronique du Mouvement'; *National Socialisme* 15 Apr. 1943, p. 3, 'Jeunes filles "Foi dans la vie" vous appelle!'
71 *National Socialisme* 15 Apr. 1943, p. 12, 'Ordres et Communiqués'; Région de Bruxelles Ordre du Jour mensuel Jan. 1944, *C2GM*, C 11/323.12; Circular of *Département Politique* 30 Mar. 1943, *C2GM*, Papiers Pierre Daye.
72 *Chef des Cadres Territoriaux* to *militants de base* 30 Oct. 1943, *C2GM*, C 11/221; *Chef de Groupe* 10 Region of Brussels to members, *C2GM*, C 11/323.18; Région de Bruxelles Ordre du Jour mensuel Dec. 1943, *C2GM*, C 11/323.12.
73 E.g. Henry Marcovitz *Pro Just.*, 7 Mar. 1946, *C2GM*, PF 3.
74 Report of Baumann 6 Apr. 1943, Jungclaus to Berger 12 Apr. 1943, Berger to Himmler 15 and 18 Apr. 1943 and Kaltenbrunner to Berger 23 Apr. 1943, GRMA T 175 126 2650990–7.
75 Jungclaus to Berger 12 Apr. 1943, GRMA T 175 126 2650995.
76 A. De Jonghe 'La lutte Himmler-Reeder . . .', *Cahiers* V (1978), pp. 94–6.
77 L. Degrelle *Lettres à mon Cardinal*, pp. 50–2; *Le PR* 27 May 1943, p. 1, 'La Légion Wallonie devient une brigade SS'; *SS Führungshauptamt* 3 July 1943, *C2GM*, W 4 (Loose Papers).
78 Niederschrift über die Übernahme der Wallonischen Legion 24 May 1943, Bundesarchiv Koblenz, Doct. NS 19/neu 27 cited in A. De Jonghe 'La lutte Himmler-Reeder . . .', *Cahiers* V (1978), p. 96. Re attitudes within the *Légion*, see p. 226.
79 This report has survived only in a German translation: 'Übersetzung der Aufzeichnung von Herrn Degrelle' 24 May 1943, *C2GM*, BDC III, Doct. 18.
80 E.g. J. De Launay *Histoires secrètes de la Belgique*, pp. 222–6; J.-M. Charlier *Léon Degrelle*, p. 320.
81 *Le PR* 30 June 1943, p. 1, 'Un important contingent de volontaires wallons . . .' See also *Le PR* 12 Nov. 1943, pp. 1 and 4, 'Le chef a rejoint la Légion'.
82 *Sipo-SD* 'Meldungen . . .' 3/43, 15 Feb. 1943, p. 27.
83 *Le PR* 6 June 1943, p. 1, 'Le Chef de Rex ad interim souligne . . .'
84 *Ibid.*
85 *TB* 24, 1 Aug. 1943, pp. 3117–18; *Sipo-SD* 'Meldungen . . .' 11/43, 15 June 1943, p. 19.
86 P. Delandsheere and A. Ooms *La Belgique sous les Nazis* III, pp. 187–9; R. Poulet 'Histoire du Nouveau Journal' pp. 51–3 (Private Collection).
87 E. De Bens *De Belgische dagbladpers*, pp. 263–5; A. Dantoing *La 'collaboration' du Cardinal*, pp. 259–61 and 393–4. See also p. 181.
88 General Van Overstraeten *Sous le joug*, pp. 243–6.
89 R. De Becker 'Conférence rédactionnelle au *Soir*' 3 Sept. 1943, *C2GM*, PL 1; JS Mémoire: Après mon départ de Rex (suite), *C2GM*, Fonds José Streel.
90 *TB* 23, 15 Apr. 1943, p. 2964.
91 *TB* 24, 1 Aug. 1943, p. 3206; Journal de V. Matthys p. 9, *C2GM*; *Notre Combat* 1 Feb. 1943, p. 2, 'Nos Echos'; Reeder to *OKH* 26 Jan. 1943, *C2GM*, Procès von Falkenhausen, Doct. 117.
92 *Sipo-SD* 'Meldungen . . .' 3/43, 15 Feb. 1943, p. 28 and 8/43, 1 May 1943, pp. 36–7; Mémoire de V. Matthys p. 39, *C2GM*; *TB* 24, 1 Aug. 1943, p. 3149; INBEL 9 Aug. 1943, *C2GM*, Fonds INBEL/1087.
93 This estimate was made in an intelligence report prepared for the Belgian government in London. In July 1942 *AGRA* boasted of having recruited 50 volunteers while in September 1942 Reeder reported the number of such volunteers to be 80: INBEL Service P No. 512 11 May 1944, *C2GM*, Fonds INBEL/980; *L'Ami du Peuple* 18 July 1942, 'Importante réunion de l'AGRA à Charleroi'; *TB* 21, 15 Sept. 1942, p. 2555; *La*

Gazette de Charleroi 12 Oct. 1942, 'Les conditions d'engagement des jeunes wallons dans les Waffen-SS'. Some individual Walloons – amongst them former Rexists – had succeeded in entering the *Waffen-SS* as early as 1941: *Le PR* 7 Nov. 1941, p. 1, 'Des Waffen-SS Wallons . . .' and 23 Dec. 1941, p. 1, 'Solidarité Légionnaire'.

94 P. Dastier 'Degrelle parle', *Dossier du mois* No. 6/7, p. 12; Baumann to Meyer 10 Mar. 1943, GRMA T 501 175 79; Mémoire de V. Matthys pp. 39–40, *C2GM*.

95 *TB* 24, 1 Aug. 1943, p. 3148.

96 *Le PR* 29 June 1943, p. 2, 'Les journées d'études . . .'; *TB* 24, 1 Aug. 1943, p. 3206; Marcovitz to Aumônier de la Prison de St Gilles 22 Feb. 1949 and Pierre Hubermont 'Mémoire à l'intention de M Paul Struye', *C2GM*, W 3/70 and W 3/73.

97 *Le PR* 6 June 1943, p. 1, 'Le Chef de Rex ad interim souligne . . .'

98 See for example *Notre Combat* 9 May 1943, p. 3, 'Quelques précisions nécessaires' and 13 June 1943, p. 1, 'Pour préparer l'avenir'. See also *Le PR* 10 July 1943, p. 4, 'Premier pas vers l'unité'.

99 *Sipo-SD* 'Meldungen . . .' 11/43, 15 June 1943, p. 31; *TB* 24, 1 Aug. 1943, pp. 3149–50.

100 *National Socialisme* 15 July 1943, p. 12, 'Unification wallonne au sein du NSKK'; *Notre Combat* 18 July 1943, p. 1, 'Une méthode qui en vaut bien une autre' and p. 3, 'Au cours d'une impressionnante cérémonie . . .'

101 For example, Céleste Roberti and Désiré Depouhon, both of whom had defected from Rex to *AGRA* in 1941 and held positions of importance in the latter organisation, returned to Rex in 1943 as *chargés de mission* in its *Etat-Major*: Report on *AGRA* meeting of 11 May 1942, *C2GM*, Fonds INBEL/964; *Notre Combat* 1 Oct. 1942, p. 5, 'Dans les Cercles'; *National Socialisme* 15 July 1943, p. 14, 'Ordres et Communiqués'; *La Meuse* 25 July 1945, p. 2, 'Conseil de Guerre' and 2 May 1947, p. 2, 'Conseil de Guerre'.

102 *Sipo-SD* 'Meldungen . . .' 17/43, 15 Sept. 1943, p. 28; *TB* 25, 15 Nov. 1943, pp. 3417–18 and 3452; *TB* 26, 1 Mar. 1944, pp. 3665–6. See also the report of an agent of the *Sûreté* who had infiltrated *AGRA*: Feuillet No. 36 29 Oct. 1943, *C2GM*, C 5/29.

103 *TB* 22, 31 Dec. 1942, pp. 2743–4; *Le Soir* 2 July 1942, 'Un cercle wallon à Berlin', cited in *C2GM*, C 13/13.4; *L'Effort Wallon* 6 Dec. 1942, p. 7, 'Le Cercle Wallon au Pays'.

104 A post-war Belgian police report identified Sommer as the representative of the 'Rasse-und Sippenamt' of the *NSDAP*. No such organisation seems to have existed and it is possible that this is an inaccurate reference to the *RuSHA*. See Documentation Jans 357; H. Krausnick *et al. Anatomy of the SS State* (London, 1968), pp. 233–4, 288 and 296–7; Journal de V. Matthys p. 11, *C2GM*; Pierre Hubermont 'Mémoire à l'intention de M Paul Struye', *C2GM*, W 3/73.

105 Pierre Hubermont 'Mémoire . . .', *C2GM*, W 3/73; *La Gazette de Charleroi* 2 Feb. 1943, 'Les buts et l'activité des Cercles Wallons en Belgique', cited in *C2GM*, C 13/14.3.

106 *L'Effort Wallon* 28 June 1942, p. 1, 'Nous ne sommes pas des convertis . . .' and 25 Oct. 1942, p. 1, 'Politique en vase clos . . .' Hubermont claimed that De Becker, Colin, Matthys and Streel travelled to Berlin with the explicit purpose of bringing about Collard's dismissal. This seems unlikely but an independent source (*Le Journal de Charleroi* 13 Nov. 1942, 'Le Cercle Wallon de Berlin', cited in *C2GM*, C 13/13.4) does indicate that Colin, Matthys, De Becker and Hubermont were in Berlin in the autumn of 1942. It is likely that this visit formed part of the efforts to modify the introduction of German obligatory labour legislation in Belgium (see 'Entretiens de 1940 à 1944', *C2GM*, Papiers Pierre Daye). Collard was not dismissed but a subsequent article by him indicated that he had agreed to refrain from attacking other collaborationist figures: *L'Effort Wallon* 17 Jan. 1943, p. 1, 'La polémique s'achève.

107 *Le Soir* 16 and 18 June 1946, p. 2, 'Les Conseils de Guerre' and 20 Jan. 1948, p. 5, 'Conseil de Guerre de Bruxelles'; P. Jacquet *Brabant Wallon 1940–1944* (Paris–Louvain-la-Neuve, 1989), p. 57.

108 Documentation Jans 201; Journal de V. Matthys p. 11, *C2GM*; P. Hubermont 'Mémoire . . .', *C2GM*, W 3/73.

109 *La Gazette de Charleroi* 22 Jan. 1943, 'Pour nos enfants', cited in *C2GM*, C 13/14.6;

Auditorat Militaire of Charleroi to *Auditorat Militaire* of Brussels 19 Mar. 1945, *C2GM*, C 13/14.1. The first such house was set up in Liège in late 1942 with Antoine Leclercq, the former Rexist and leader of the *MNPW*, as its director. Other houses opened in February and March of 1943: Leclercq to Collard 13 Nov. 1942, *C2GM*, C 13/20.2; *Bulletin des Maisons Wallonnes* 1 Mar. 1944, p. 1, 'Les Maisons Wallonnes'; *La Gazette de Charleroi* 2 Feb. 1943, 'Les buts et l'activité des Cercles Wallons en Belgique' and *Le Journal de Charleroi* 29 Apr. 1943, 'M. Paul Garain parle des Maisons Wallonnes', cited in *C2GM*, C 13/14.3 and 14.4.

110 E.g. Mémoire de V. Matthys pp. 42–3, *C2GM*.

111 *Ibid.* p. 47; VM *Pro Just.*, 5 Sept. 1946 and Rapport de la Police Judiciaire 6 Dec. 1946, *Aud. Gén.*, Doss. VM, Info., Docts. 187–8 and 189–91; Documentation Jans 106.

112 *Notre Combat* 30 May 1943, p. 2, 'F-M Collard rejoint la Waffen SS'; Niederschrift über die Besprechung wegen der Schaffung einer Deutsch-Wallonischen Arbeitgemeinschaft am 13.4.43 (16 Apr. 1943), cited in A. De Jonghe 'La lutte Himmler-Reeder . . .', *Cahiers* V (1978), p. 81.

113 LC *Pro Just.*, 27 Nov. 1946, *Aud. Gén.*, Doss. VM, Info., Doct. 154–5; Mémoire de V. Matthys pp. 52–3, *C2GM*; *TB* 26, 1 Mar. 1944, p. 3666; *Le PR* 4 Mar. 1944, p. 2, 'La Maison Wallonne de Liége'. A Rexist, Hagon, was eventually appointed as administrator of the *Maisons Wallonnes*: Maisons Wallonnes to Westbank 24 Jan. 1944, *C2GM*, C 13/19.5; *Le Soir* 20 Jan. 1948, p. 5, 'Conseil de Guerre de Bruxelles'.

114 Mémoire de V. Matthys p. 54, *C2GM*; Jean Denis 'Mémoire justificatif d'un condamné à mort' p. 154, *Aud. Gén.*, Doss. Jean Denis, Info., Doct. 53. Bank documentation indicates that Sommer probably left Belgium in November or December 1943: *C2GM*, C 13/25.1.

115 A. De Jonghe 'La lutte Himmler-Reeder', *Cahiers* V (1978), p. 81; *TB* 24, 1 Aug. 1943, p. 3150. This was not the first manifestation of *DeWag*. In December 1941, Reeder had reported attempts by an unidentified German *Dienstelle* to create an organisation of the same name: *TB* 18, 21 Dec. 1941, pp. 2119–20.

116 Documentation Jans 357; *Le Soir* 16 June 1946, p. 2, 'Les Conseils de Guerre' and 20 Jan. 1948, p. 5, 'Conseil de Guerre de Bruxelles'; *TB* 24, 1 Aug. 1943, pp. 3150 and 3207. A German officer, *Brigadeführer* Dittmann, was the nominal head of *DeWag*: Peeters to Elias 6 May 1943, *C2GM*, C 13/22. *DeWag* had an office and a bank account in Brussels: Westbank-*DeWag* correspondence, *C2GM*, C 13/25.

117 *L'Effort Wallon* 27 June 1943. Reeder referred to the content of this article in *TB* 24, 1 Aug. 1943, p. 3150.

118 R. De Becker 'La collaboration . . .', *Courrier hebdomadaire du CRISP* No. 497–8 (1970), p. 54; Jean Denis 'Mémoire justificatif d'un condamné à mort' p. 28, *Aud. Gén.*, Doss. Jean Denis, Info., Doct. 53.

119 *Le PR* 11 Sept. 1943, p. 3, 'Chronique du Mouvement'; Jean Vermeire *Pro Just.*, 5 Sept. 1945, *Aud. Gén.*, Doss. Jean Denis, Info., Doct. 38; *L'Effort Wallon* 23 Jan. 1944, p. 6, 'Nos travailleurs en Allemagne'. From May 1944, Vermeire also directed a *Bureau de liaison de Rex* in Berlin: *Le PR* 9 May 1944, p. 1, 'Un bureau de liaison . . .'

120 *Sipo-SD* 'Meldungen . . .' 8/43, 1 May 1943, p. 36.

121 LC to *Chefs de Cercles* 15 July 1943, *C2GM*, C 11/226; LC to *Chef de Cercle* of Virton 2 Oct. 1943, *Aud. Gén.*, Doss. LC, Enquête Complémentaire, Farde E, Doct. 44.

122 VM and LC *Pro Just.*, 14, 21 and 24 May 1947, *Aud. Gén.*, Doss. LC, Enquête Complémentaire, Farde C, Docts. 19 and 20–6. Members of the *cabinet* also attended Rexist rallies and Delvaux was a member of the *Conseil Politique* of Rex.

123 LC to *Chef de Cercle ad interim* of Liège 8 Mar. 1943, *Aud. Gén.*, Doss. LC, Inst., Doct. 114. Lambinon apparently kept a file on Romsée entitled 'Obstruction politique'; Louis Shaw *Pro Just.*, 4 Sept. 1946 in Documentation Jans 377.

124 LC to *Auditeur Militaire Général* 30 Apr. 1947 and *Pro Just.*, 24 May 1947, *Aud. Gén.*, Doss. LC, Enquête Complémentaire, Farde C, Docts. 18 and 20–6; *Le Soir* 28 May 1947, p. 5, 'Les Conseils de Guerre de Bruxelles'. The Rexist headquarters continued nevertheless to issue highly partisan instructions to its militants in central and local government: see p. 254.

125 *TB* 26, 1 Mar. 1944, pp. 3634–5. See also *TB* 25, 15 Nov. 1943, p. 3392. Roughly equivalent figures of Rexists in local government (208 *bourgmestres* and 154 *échevins*)

were provided in a Rexist report of 1944 detailing 'reliable' personnel in local government: Organisation des Forces de Protection Actives 12 Apr. 1944, *C2GM*, C 11/289.9.

126 Mémorandum aux autorités allemandes pp. 16–20, *C2GM*, C 11/324; *TB* 25, 15 Nov. 1943, p. 3395; A. De Jonghe 'La lutte Himmler-Reeder...', *Cahiers* V (1978), pp. 161–7. One of the few well-qualified candidates was the pro-Rexist lawyer, Georges Dubois. In 1943, Rex offered to propose him as *secrétaire-général* of the Ministry of Justice but Dubois prudently declined this offer: *Le Soir* 4 June 1947, p. 5, 'Conseil de Guerre de Bruxelles'; LC and VM *Pro Just.*, 12 and 14 May 1947, *Aud. Gén.*, Doss. LC, Enquête Complémentaire, Farde C, Doct. 19.

127 See *Recensement général de la population de l'industrie et du commerce au 31 janvier 1947* (Brussels, 1949) I, pp. 173–5; H. Hasquin (ed.) *Communes de Belgique* (Brussels, 1980), p. 12.

128 Mémorandum aux autorités allemandes p. 54, *C2GM*, C 11/324; Journal de V. Matthys p. 8, *C2GM*.

129 E.g. *Le PR* 18 Sept. 1943, p. 1, 'Les hutois connaissent des dégrèvements fiscaux'; *Informations administratives et politiques* Sept. 1943, p. 33, 'Activité des Cadres Politiques.'

130 *Secrétaire de l'EM du Chef*, Ordre d'exécution No. 35/4, 13 May 1944, *C2GM*, C 11/159.

131 LC to *Chefs de Cercles* 15 July 1943, *C2GM*, C 11/226; *Informations administratives et politiques* Sept. 1943, p. 1, 'Liminaire' and Oct. 1943, pp. 1–3, 'Notre tâche' and pp. 29–33, 'Activité des Cadres Politiques'.

132 LC to *Chefs de Cercles* 6 July 1943, *C2GM*, C 11/229; INBEL 'Manoeuvres Rexistes' No. 1566, 4 Sept. 1943, *C2GM*, Fonds INBEL/967; VM to *Militärverwaltungsrat* 21 Apr. 1944, *Aud. Gén.*, Doss. VM, Pièces à Conviction, Doct. 20. Degrelle's father, Edouard Degrelle, as a former dignitary of the Catholic party in the province of Luxembourg, had long experience of such political infiltration and took a keen interest in the Rexists' efforts: *L'Avenir du Luxembourg* 31 May 1947, pp. 1–2, 'Au Conseil de Guerre d'Arlon'.

133 E.g. Simar to *Chefs de Groupes* 18 July 1942, *C2GM*, C 11/321.8; Commune de Hornu *Pro Just.*, 23 Nov. 1944, *Aud. Gén.*, Doss. Michel Saussez, Inst., Doct. 10; *Le Courrier de l'Escaut* 20 July and 11 Dec. 1946, p. 2, 'Conseil de Guerre de Tournai (A)'.

134 In Charleroi, the appointment in 1943 of the Rexist *chef de cercle* (Merlot) as an *échevin* reinforced Rexist control over the council while in La Louvière two new Rexist *échevins* (one of whom, Cus, was also the local *chef de cercle*) appointed in 1944 consolidated the Rexist majority there: *Le PR* 7 Feb. 1943, p. 4, 'Un nouvel échevin à Charleroi'; *Le Journal de Charleroi* 5 Sept. 1946, p. 4, 'On va juger Duquesne...!' and 13 Sept. 1946, p. 4, 'Enfin, la Bande Duquesne va payer!'

135 For example, at least seven of the *chefs de districts* of Grand Liège were Rexists, See also *Le Soir* 13 Mar. 1946, p. 2, 'Les Conseils de Guerre'; *Le Journal de Charleroi* 5 June 1947, p. 4, 'Du parti rexiste au Gross La Louvière...'; LC to Froment 27 Dec. 1943, *Aud. Gén.*, Doss. LC, Inst., Doct. 115.

136 *Informations administratives et politiques* Oct. 1943, pp. 29–33, 'Activité des Cadres Politiques'. The expedient of recruiting a *police supplémentaire* had been originally proposed in 1942 but it was some time before they were constituted: *TB* 20, 15 June 1942, p. 2385; *TB* 25, 15 Nov. 1943, p. 3450; Dupont and Brunet to *Chefs de Cercles* 3 Mar. 1943, *C2GM*, C 11/232. In certain localities, the brigades of the Rexist police, the *DSI*, acted as supplementary units of the police.

137 *Le Journal de Charleroi* 23 Jan. 1947, p. 4, 'Le procès des gestapistes de La Louvière.'

138 E.g. Simar to *Chefs de Groupes* 26 Dec. 1942, *C2GM*, C 11/321.8; Procès-Verbal of collège of Grand Liège 2 July 1943 and Post-war Police Report, *C2GM*, C 5/Addenda; *La Meuse* 29 Mar. 1945, p. 2, 'Conseil de Guerre'.

139 *L'Avenir du Luxembourg* 22 May 1946, p. 1, 'Au Conseil de Guerre'; LC to *Chef de Cercle* of Virton 22 July 1943, *Aud. Gén.*, Doss. LC, Enquête Complémentaire, Farde E, Doct. 37; *OFK* 672 to *EM* of Rex 17 Aug. 1944, *C2GM*, C 11/228. Rex also vetted appointments to the *Police Judiciaire*: Brunet to Reusch 1 May 1944, *C2GM*, C 11/226.

140 Mémorandum aux autorités allemandes, *C2GM*, C 11/324.

141 Documentation Jans 373; Statutes of Action Familiale, *Aud. Gén.*, Doss. LC, Inst.,

Doct. 259–60.

142 Documentation Jans 106; Ordres d'*EM* du mouvement aux militants de base Dec. 1943, *Aud. Gén.*, Doss. Marcel Dupont, Loose Papers; VM and LC *Pro Just.*, 5 Sept. and 14 Mar. 1946 and Rapport de la Police Judiciaire 6 Dec. 1946, *Aud. Gén.*, Doss. VM, Info., Docts. 187–8, 189–91 and 214–15; *National Socialisme* 15 Dec. 1943, p. 1, 'Pour le bien-être du peuple'; *Le Soir* 22 May 1947, p. 5, 'Les Conseils de Guerre de Bruxelles'.

143 Further details of the *Volontaires*, are provided in J. Gérard-Libois and J. Gotovitch *L'an 40*, pp. 468–73. Re the *Chantiers*, see R. Austin 'The Chantiers de la Jeunesse in Languedoc 1940–44', *French Historical Studies* XIII (1983), pp. 106–26.

144 *Le PR* 23 Dec. 1942, p. 1, 'Un fier soldat', Membership of the *SVTW* featured in the biographies of a number of *légionnaires* and one former member of the *SVTW* claimed that on arriving at the training camp of the *Légion* he had found 'une bonne quarantaine' of his *SVTW* colleagues: *Le PR* 14 May 1943, p. 1, 'Nos héros de la "Légion Wallonie". . .' and 6 July 1943, p. 1, 'Les VT et la Légion'.

145 *Le PR* 14 Oct. 1941, p. 1, 'Ceux qui "ne font pas de politique"' and 12 May 1942, p. 1, 'Le patriotisme n'est pas un monopole'; Documentation Jans 24.

146 *TB* 23, 15 Apr. 1943, pp. 2933–5; A De Jonghe 'La lutte Himmler-Reeder . . .', *Cahiers* V (1978), pp. 32–9; 'Historique du Service des Volontaires du Travail pour la Wallonie', *C2GM*, W 3/50; *CCW Secrétaire-Général* Circulaire No. 10, *C2GM*, C 4/50.

147 VM *Pro Just.*, 14 May 1947, *Aud. Gén.*, Doss. LC, Enquête Complémentaire, Farde C, Doct. 19; Mémoire de V. Matthys p. 49, *C2GM*; Documentation Jans 24; Jean Denis 'Mémoire justificatif d'un condamné à mort' pp. 147–50, *Aud. Gén.*, Doss. Jean Denis, Info., Doct. 53. Lucien Lippert, the commander of the *Légion*, played a major role in the selection of the trainees: Albert Constant *Pro Just.*, 12 Oct. 1945, Auguste François *Pro Just.*, 17 June 1946 and André Renotte *Pro Just.*, 13 July 1946, *Aud. Gén.*, Doss. Albert Constant, Inst., Doct. 94–5 and Documentation Générale, Docts. 103 and 111–16.

148 'Historique . . .', *C2GM*, W 3/50; *Le PR* 18 May 1943, pp. 1 and 4, 'Les volontaires du travail exagèrent . . .' and 1 June 1943, p. 1, 'Où sont les hommes . . . ?'; Louis De Decker *Pro Just.*, 24 Dec. 1946, *Aud. Gén.*, Doss. LC, Inst., Doct. 250; J. Gérard-Libois and J. Gotovitch *L'an 40*, p. 472.

149 'Historique . . .', *C2GM*, W 3/50.

150 LC *Pro Just.*, 23 Dec. 1946, *Aud. Gén.*, Doss. LC, Inst., Doct. 248; Mémoire de V. Matthys p. 49, *C2GM*.

151 Documentation Jans 24; Pierre Van Craen *Pro Just.*, 4 Oct. 1946, *Aud. Gén.*, Doss. Albert Constant, Documentation Générale, Doct. 130–1; General Van Overstraeten *Sous le joug*, pp. 242 and 251.

152 A. De Jonghe 'La lutte Himmler-Reeder . . .', *Cahiers* V (1978), p. 38; Gérard Romsée *Pro Just.*, 23 Dec. 1946 and 27 Feb. 1947, *Aud. Gén.*, Doss. LC, Inst., Docts. 249 and 309–10.

153 'Historique . . .', *C2GM*, W 3/50; Henry Marcovitz *Pro Just.*, 12 Dec. and 28 Nov. 1946, *Aud. Gén.*, Doss. LC, Inst., Doct. 247 and Doss. VM, Info., Doct. 158–9; Louis De Decker *Pro Just.*, 24 Dec. 1946 and Auguste François *Pro Just.*, 17 June 1946, *Aud. Gén.*, Doss. LC, Inst., Doct. 250 and Doss. Albert Constant, Documentation Générale, Doct. 103.

154 Documentation Jans 24; Pierre Van Craen *Pro Just.*, 12 Oct. 1946 and Gérard Romsée *Pro Just.*, 23 Dec. 1946, *Aud. Gén.*, Doss. Albert Constant, Documentation Générale, Doct. 128–9 and Doss. LC, Inst., Doct. 249.

155 Séance du Comité des Secrétaires-Généraux 1 Oct. 1943, pp. 4–9, *C2GM*.

156 Documentation Jans 72; Brunet and Keutgen to *Chefs de Cercles* 21 Apr. 1944, *C2GM*, C 11/232; *Le PR* 5 May 1944, p. 2, 'Le Service Volontaire du Travail . . .'

157 *TB* 28, 10 May 1944, p. 3927; *TB* 30, 10 July 1944, p. 4105; Siméon *Pro Just.*, 15 Dec. 1946, *C2GM*, JB 20; Ordres d'*EM* du Chef 10 May 1944, *Aud. Gén.*, Doss. LC, Enquête Complémentaire, Farde D, Doct. 30.

158 E.g. LC to *Chef de Cercle* of Namur 13 Aug. 1944, *Aud. Gén.*, Doss. Marcel Dupont, Info., Doct. 64.

159 See also pp. 119–20.
160 Message du *Chef de Rex ad interim* 7 Sept. 1941, *C2GM*, C 11/134.
161 E.g. *Vers l'Avenir* 6 Jan. 1946, p. 3, 'Conseil de Guerre de Namur'; *La Meuse* 2 Apr. 1947, p. 2, 'Conseil de Guerre'. See also p. 147.
162 See p. 257.
163 See the example of Oswald Englebin cited in A. Lemaire *Le crime du 18 août*, p. 41.
164 INBEL No. 2353 20 Nov. 1943, *C2GM*, Fonds INBEL/968; *Vers l'Avenir* 11 July 1946, p. 4, 'Conseil de Guerre de Namur'. See also *L'Avenir du Luxembourg* 6 Feb. 1946, p. 2, 'Au Conseil de Guerre.'
165 E.g. *Vers l'Avenir* 28 Mar. 1947, p. 3, 'Conseil de Guerre de Namur' and 23 Apr. 1947, p. 4, 'A la Cour militaire de Liége'.
166 *L'Avenir du Luxembourg* 21 Jan. 1947, p. 1, 'Au Conseil de Guerre'; *Vers l'Avenir* 19 Mar. 1947, p. 3 and 30 May 1947, p. 4, 'Conseil de Guerre de Namur'.
167 J.-M. Frérotte *Léon Degrelle, le dernier fasciste*, pp. 183–6; *TB* 25, 15 Nov. 1943, pp. 3416–17; P. Delandsheere and A. Ooms *La Belgique sous les Nazis* III, pp. 246–7 and 277–8.
168 Louis Shaw *Pro Just.*, 4 Sept. 1946, Documentation Jans 377; Charles Peeters 'Organisation interne du mouvement rexiste' *C2GM*, C 11/87.
169 See Conseil de Guerre de Bruxelles Exposé des Faits 3 Mar. 1947, *C2GM*, JB 13.
170 Funken's disreputable behaviour and suspected links with the Resistance eventually forced his expulsion from the *DSI*: *SS und Polizeigericht X, Aussenstelle Brüssel* to *SS Richter* 7 Apr. 1944, GRMA T 175 131 2657866–7; Sylvain Jadoul *Pro Just.*, 25 Aug. 1945, *Aud. Gén.*, Doss. VM, Info., Doct. 64–70.
171 Henry Marcovitz *Pro Just.*, 4 Nov. 1946, *Aud. Gén.*, Doss. VM, Info., Doct. 152–3; *SS und Polizeigericht X, Aussenstelle Brüssel* to *SS Richter* 7 Apr. 1944, Bericht über die augenblickliche Lage der *DSI* 11 Apr. 1944 and Report of Gieselmann 13 May 1944, GRMA T 175 131 2657865–6, 2657521 and 2657598.
172 Henry Marcovitz Rapport No. 6, 11 Mar. 1946, *Aud. Gén.*, Doss. VM, Info., Doct. 119–21.
173 Conseil de Guerre de Bruxelles Exposé des Faits 3 Mar. 1947, pp. 59 and 67, *C2GM*, JB 13; Bulletin de Police No. 1, *C2GM*, C 11/288.
174 Conseil de Guerre de Bruxelles Exposé des Faits 3 Mar. 1947, p. 18, *C2GM*, JB 13; *SS und Polizeigericht X, Aussenstelle Brüssel* to *SS Richter* 7 Apr. 1944, GRMA T 175 131 2657866; Henry Marcovitz *Pro Just.*, 4 Nov. 1946, *Aud. Gén.*, Doss. VM, Info., Doct. 152–3; Charles Peeters 'Organisation interne du mouvement rexiste' *C2GM*, C 11/87.
175 Conseil de Guerre de Bruxelles Exposé des Faits 3 Mar. 1947, pp. 18 and 66, *C2GM*, JB 13; Sylvain Jadoul *Pro Just.*, 25 Aug. 1945, *Aud. Gén.*, Doss. VM, Info., Doct. 64–70.
176 Louis Shaw *Pro Just.*, 4 Sept. 1946, Documentation Jans 377.
177 *SS und Polizeigericht X, Aussenstelle Brüssel* to *SS Richter* 7 Apr. 1944, GRMA T 175 131 2657864; Bulletins de Police, *C2GM*, C 11/288. The incidents at Liège are discussed in greater detail on pp. 217–18.
178 Edgard Duquesnes, Léon Lecocq and Jean Gorain *Pro Just.*, 9 Jan. 1946, *C2GM*, JB 20; *Le Journal de Charleroi* 11 July 1945, p. 1, 'Conseil de Guerre de Charleroi', 1 Feb. 1946, p. 3, 'Le chef tueur sous les verrous' and 7 Jan. 1947, p. 2, 'La brigade policière rexiste . . .'
179 Wilhelm Müller *Pro Just.*, 18 Nov. 1946, *Aud. Gén.*, Doss. VM, Info., Doct. 152–3; Bericht über die augenblickliche Lage der *DSI* 11 Apr. 1944, GRMA T 175 131 2657521; Bulletins de Police Nos. 8 and 11, *C2GM*, C 11/288; *Le Journal de Charleroi* 7 Jan. 1947, p. 2, 'La brigade policière rexiste . . .', 8 Jan. 1947, p. 2, 'Le procès des tueurs rexistes . . .' and 9 Jan. 1947, p. 4, 'Les gestapistes de La Louvière . . .'
180 Louis Shaw *Pro Just.*, 4 Sept. 1946, Documentation Jans 377.
181 *Le Journal de Charleroi* 8 Jan. 1947, p. 2, 'Le procès des tueurs rexistes . . .'; *National Socialisme* 15 Dec. 1943, p. 10, 'Ordres et Communiqués'; Jacques Debry *Pro Just.*, 22 Feb. 1947, *Aud. Gén.*, Doss. Charles Lambinon, Inst., Doct. 220; Jacques Debry and Eugène Heuschen *Pro Just.*, 15 June 1946 and Fernand Joly *Pro Just.*, 19 June 1946, *Aud. Gén.*, Doss. VM, Info., Docts. 194–5 and 196.
182 Louis Shaw *Pro Just.*, 4 Sept. 1946, Documentation Jans 377; Bulletin de Police No.

27, *C2GM*, C 11/288.

183 *Le Journal de Charleroi* 25 Oct. 1946, p. 6, 'Conseil de Guerre de Charleroi', 21 Feb. 1947, p. 5, 'Les échevins de l'ex-Grand La Louvière' and 28 Feb. 1947, p. 4, 'Conseil de Guerre de Charleroi'; *Le Soir* 6 Mar. 1948, p. 4, 'Les Conseils de Guerre'.

184 Some limited contact between Brussels Rexists and the *DSI* is described in *Le Soir* 5 Apr. 1946, p. 2, 16 Apr. 1946, p. 3 and 7 June 1947, p. 4, 'Les Conseils de Guerre'.

185 Report of Gieselmann 13 May 1944, GRMA T 175 131 2657599; Charles Peeters *Pro Just.*, 27 May 1946, *Aud. Gén.*, Doss. Marcel Dupont, Info., Section 7.

186 VM *Pro Just.*, 12 and 20 Sept. 1945, Sylvain Jadoul *Pro Just.*, 25 Aug. 1945 and VM and Henri Brichaux *Pro Just.*, 3 and 8 Feb. 1947, *Aud. Gén.*, Doss. VM, Info., Docts. 48–51, 60, 64–70 and 267–70; Mémoire de V. Matthys pp. 97–8, *C2GM*; Bulletins de Police, *C2GM*, C 11/288; *Le Soir* 5 Mar. 1947, p. 5, 'Le procès des tueurs de Rex'.

187 Brunet to VM 17 Aug. 1944, *C2GM*, PG 5, Doct. 190; *Le Soir* 6 Mar. 1946, p. 2, 'Le procès du Grand Bruxelles'. Collard denied that all correspondence with the German authorities had to be signed by him but it was clear from the comments of Matthys and Degrelle that he dominated dealings between Rex and the Germans; Henry Marcovitz *Pro Just.*, 28 Nov. 1946, LC *Pro Just.*, 2 Dec. 1946, VM *Pro Just.*, 21 Dec. 1946 and LD to VM 13 Aug. 1944, *Aud. Gén.*, Doss. VM, Info., Docts. 158–9, 162, 179 and 200–4.

188 LC to *Auditeur Militaire Général* 30 Apr. 1947, *Aud. Gén.*, Doss. LC, Enquête Complémentaire, Farde C, Doct. 18; Conseil de Guerre de Bruxelles, Exposé des Faits 3 Mar. 1947, p. 55, *C2GM*, JB 13.

189 Henry Marcovitz Rapport No. 3, 11 Feb. 1946 and *Pro Just.*, 28 Nov. 1946, *Aud. Gén.*, Doss. LC, Inst., Doct. 168–73 and Doss. VM, Info., Doct. 156–7.

190 VM *Pro Just.*, 29 Nov. 1946 and Jean Chaudoir *Pro Just.*, 12 Oct. 1946, *Aud. Gén.*, Doss. VM, Info., Doct. 160–1 and Doss. LC, Inst., Doct. 303–7; R. De Becker 'La collaboration . . .', *Courrier hebdomadaire du CRISP* No. 497–8 (1970), p. 59. This friendship extended beyond the war. At their trial, Matthys seemed anxious to protect Collard against the more serious accusations made against him: *Le Soir* 5 Mar. 1947, p. 5, 'Le procès des tueurs de Rex'.

191 VM *Pro Just.*, 29 Nov. 1946 and LD to VM, 13 Aug. 1944, *Aud. Gén.*, Doss. VM, Info., Docts. 160–1 and 200–4. Jungclaus' deputy, Moskopff, described Collard as 'ein sehr fähiger und tüchtiger Mann': Rücksprache mit *SS-Hauptsturmführer* Moskopf, 11 May 1944, GRMA T 175 131 2657824.

192 Rapport d'expertise médicomentale 27 May 1947, *Aud. Gén.*, Doss. LC, Enquête Complémentaire, Farde H, Doct. 7.

193 *Le Soir* 5 July 1946, p. 2, 'Les Conseils de Guerre'.

194 *Informations administratives et politiques* Dec. 1943, pp. 40–4, 'Bilan de fin de l'année'.

195 JS Analyse de l'acte d'accusation: première suite p. 17, *C2GM*, Fonds José Streel; LC *Pro Just.*, 27 Nov. 1946, *Aud. Gén.*, Doss. VM, Doct. 154–5; *Informations administratives et politiques* Dec. 1943, pp. 29–30, 'Activité des Cadres Politiques'.

196 Antécédents and Pièces à Conviction, Doct. 7, *Aud. Gén.*, Doss. Jean Colman; Conseil de Guerre de Bruxelles Exposé des Faits 3 Mar. 1947, p. 64, *C2GM*, JB 13.

197 Antécédents, *Aud. Gén.*, Doss. Michel Saussez; Commune de Boussu *Pro Just.*, 9 Dec. 1944; Michel Saussez Curriculum Vitae; Alfred Saussez *Pro Just.*, 14 May 1946; François Boveroulle *Pro Just.*, 24 May 1946; all in *Aud. Gén.*, Doss. Michel Saussez, Inst., Docts. 12, 15, 57 and 64.

198 *Cour Militaire Pro Just.*, 13 Mar. 1947, pp. 6 and 111–12, *C2GM*, JB 12; *Le Soir* 6 July 1946, p. 2, 'Les tueurs de Courcelles'.

199 *Le PR* 27 Jan. 1943, p. 1, 'Replis ordonnés, terrains perdus et vaines illusions', 4 July 1943, p. 1, 'La mort tombera du ciel sur l'Angleterre' and 9 Sept. 1943, p. 1, 'L'Italie capitule sans conditions'.

200 *Le PR* 26 June 1943, p. 1, 'Pourquoi passerions-nous par des intermédiaires?' and 13 Sept. 1943, p. 1, 'Le Chef de Rex exhorte ses militants'.

201 Journal de V. Matthys p. 15, *C2GM*; Letter of Carlos Jacques 9 June 1943, cited in Documentation Jans 373.

202 VM testimony in Documentation Jans 266; *Sipo-SD* 'Meldungen . . .' 11/43, 15 June 1943, pp. 1–2. Few outside of pro-German circles seem to have regarded such an outcome to the war as likely: P. Struye *L'évolution du sentiment public*, p. 138.

203 V. Mastny *Russia's Road to Cold War* (New York, 1979), pp. 73–84.

204 R. De Becker 'La collaboration...', *Courrier hebdomadaire du CRISP* No. 497–8 (1970), p. 52; *Le PR* 15 May 1943, p. 1, 'Les ailes marchantes de la révolution' and 12 Nov. 1943, p. 1, 'Le Chef a rejoint la Légion'.

205 *Le PR* 1 May 1943, p. 1, 'Premier mai...', 22 June 1943, p. 1, 'Pour construire le socialisme' and 13 Sept. 1943, p. 1, 'Le Chef de Rex exhorte ses militants'.

206 V. Mastny *Op. cit.*, pp. 84–5; J. Erickson *The Road to Berlin* (London, 1983), pp. 86–135.

207 *Le PR* 5 Sept. 1943, p. 1, 'Deux balles dans la nuque'; CH MV 926/43 g. pol. 10 Sept. 1943, *C2GM*, Procès von Falkenhausen, Doct. 1751; *TB* 25, 15 Nov. 1943, p. 3384. Reeder stated that 51 Rexists as well as 29 Flemish and Walloon members of military units had been killed. As a number of these were undoubtedly Rexists serving in the *Légion Wallonie* and *Gardes Wallonnes*, the total figure must have been in the region of 60.

208 J. Willequet *La Belgique sous la botte*, pp. 287–8.

209 E.g. *Le Peuple* Jan. 1943, p. 1, 'Tous les traîtres seront punis'.

210 Cited in Radiodiffusion Nationale Belge 9 Aug. 1943, *C2GM*, Fonds INBEL/512. See also J. Willequet *La Belgique sous la botte*, pp. 289–94.

211 *TB* 23, 15 Apr. 1943, pp. 2910–11. See also Speech prepared by José Streel for his trial [1945], p. 1, *C2GM*, Fonds José Streel.

212 *Le PR* 2 Sept. 1943, p. 1, 'Le serment John Hagemans'; Dupont to *Chefs de Cercles* 16 Apr. 1943, *Aud. Gén.*, Doss. Marcel Dupont, Info., Doct. 11; INBEL 1 May 1943 No. 3, *C2GM*, Fonds INBEL/1087; *Vers l'Avenir* 7 Feb. 1947, p. 4, 'Conseil de Guerre de Namur'; P. Delandsheere and A. Ooms *La Belgique sous les Nazis* III, p. 339.

213 Jean Colman to *Geheime Feldpolizei* 13 Dec. 1942 and Commissaire de Forest *Pro Just.*, 6 Nov. 1944, *Aud. Gén.*, Doss. Jean Colman, Inst., Docts. 56 and 3.

214 Mémoire de V. Matthys p. 94, *C2GM*.

215 *SS und Polizeigericht X, Aussenstelle Brüssel* to *Hauptamt SS Gericht* 15 Mar. 1944, GRMA T 175 131 2657869–71. Re the *Ersatzkommando*, see also p. 252.

216 *Ibid.* and *SS und Polizeigericht X, Aussenstelle Brüssel* to *SS Richter* 7 Apr. 1944, GRMA T 175 131 2657873–4 and 2657868; *Le Soir* 25 Sept. 1947, p. 4, 'Conseil de Guerre de Bruxelles'; *Le Peuple* Aug. 1943, p. 3, 'A Namur'. See also the murder in June 1943 apparently by Rexists of a postman in Brussels reported in P. Delandsheere and A. Ooms *La Belgique sous les Nazis* III, p. 180.

217 *Le PR* 8 July 1943, p. 4, 'Les funérailles de notre camarade...'; INBEL Renseignements reçus de Belgique 29 Oct. 1943, *C2GM*, Fonds INBEL/967.

218 Sylvain Jadoul *Pro Just.*, 25 Aug. 1945, *Aud. Gén.*, Doss. VM, Info., Doct. 64–70; *La Meuse* 13 Nov. 1945, pp. 1 and 4, 'La Gestapo de Rex'; *Le PR* 13 Aug. 1943, p. 2, 'La musique de la SS...'

219 *SS und Polizeigericht X, Aussenstelle Brüssel* to *SS Richter* 7 Apr. 1944, GRMA T 175 131 2657864–5; *La Meuse* 13 Nov. 1945, p. 4, and 15 Nov. 1945, p. 1, 'La Gestapo de Rex...'

220 P. Delandsheere and A. Ooms *La Belgique sous les Nazis* III, p. 283; *SS und Polizeigericht X, Aussenstelle Brüssel* to *SS Richter* 7 Apr. 1944, GRMA T 175 131 2657863–4 and 2657868.

221 A. De Jonghe 'La lutte Himmler-Reeder...', *Cahiers* VIII (1984), pp. 18–19; Sylvain Jadoul *Pro Just.*, 25 Aug. 1945, *Aud. Gén.*, Doss. VM, Info., Doct. 64–70; *Vers l'Avenir* 31 Jan. 1946, p. 3, 'Conseil de Guerre de Namur'.

222 *La Meuse* 19 Apr. 1945, p. 2, 'Conseil de Guerre.' A Belgian intelligence report identified his son as one of those who carried out the murders: INBEL Renseignements reçus de Belgique 6 Nov. 1943, *C2GM*, Fonds INBEL/968. Another individual (Fauconnier) cited in a German report as having been involved in a robbery carried out by Pirmolin's group had the same name as the *Chef de l'Organisation* of the *cercle* of Liège: *SS und Polizeigericht X, Aussenstelle Brüssel* to *SS Richter* 7 Apr. 1944, GRMA T 175 131 2657864.

223 *La Meuse* 25 May 1945, p. 2, 'Le Grand-Liège...'; *Gazette de Liége* 27–8 May 1945, p. 1, 'Le procès du Grand Liège'.

224 *SS und Polizeigericht X, Aussenstelle Brüssel* to *SS Richter* 7 Apr. 1944, GRMA T 175

131 2657864; A. De Jonghe 'La lutte Himmler-Reeder . . .', *Cahiers* VIII (1984), p. 123.
225 VM *Pro Just.*, 21 Sept. 1945, *Aud. Gén.*, Doss. VM, Info., Doct. 61–2; *Le PR* 5 Sept. 1943, p. 1, 'Deux balles dans la nuque'; Plaidoyer prononcé par Victor Matthys devant le Conseil de Guerre de Charleroi p. 9, *C2GM*, JP 258; *Le Journal de Charleroi* 14 June 1946, p. 1, 'La Tragédie du 18 août'. Later in 1943, Fauconnier resigned from his post in *Rex-Liége*, indicating that there may have been a purge of those directly implicated in the actions of Pirmolin: *National Socialisme* 15 Nov. 1943, p. 11, 'Ordres et Communiqués'.
226 *Le PR* 5 Sept. 1943, p. 1, 'Deux balles dans la nuque'.
227 *TB* 25, 15 Nov. 1943, p. 3415; INBEL Service P No. 512, 11 May 1944, *C2GM*, Fonds INBEL/980; Félix Spruyt to [*EM* of Rex] 24 Dec. 1943, *Aud. Gén.*, Doss. Marcel Dupont, Info., Doct. 69.
228 E.g. *Le PR* 13 Sept. 1943, p. 1, 'Le Chef de Rex exhorte ses militants'.
229 *Le PR* 24 June 1943, p. 2, 'Journée de foi rexiste'; Région de Bruxelles Ordre du Jour mensuel Oct. 1943, *C2GM*, C 11/323.12. Jean Denis claimed subsequently that all militants were ordered in 1943 to enrol their wives as members: Jean Denis 'Mémoire justificatif d'un condamné à mort' p. 53, *Aud. Gén.*, Doss. Jean Denis, Info., Doct. 53.
230 *TB* 25, 15 Nov. 1943, p. 3415; Constant to [Pévenasse] 13 Jan. 1944 and *Gendarmerie Nationale Pro Just.*, 1 Dec. 1945, *Aud. Gén.*, Doss. Albert Constant, Inst., Docts. 31 and 127; *L'Avenir du Luxembourg* 11 May 1946, p. 1, 'Rexiste notoire'.
231 *National Socialisme* 15 Nov. 1943, p. 11 and 15 Dec. 1943, p. 10, 'Ordres et Communiqués'; Renauld to *Chef des Cadres Territoriaux* 8 Oct. 1943 and *Service administratif et financier des Cercles* to Renauld 29 Nov. 1943, *C2GM*, C 11/321.13 and C 11/221.
232 *National Socialisme* 15 Apr. 1943, p. 12, 'Ordres et Communiqués'; *Le PR* 23 Sept. 1943, p. 3, 'Chronique du Mouvement'; *Secrétaire de l'EM du Chef*, Ordre d'exécution 13 May 1944, *C2GM*, C 11/159.
233 *National Socialisme* 15 Nov. 1943, p. 11, 'Ordres et Communiqués'; *Service administratif et financier* to *Cercle* of Liége 23 Dec. 1943, *Aud. Gén.*, Doss. Marcel Dupont, Info., Doct. 53–4; 'IIIe Bannière des *FC*' 22 Mar. 1943, cited in *C2GM*, Fonds INBEL/965; *Sipo-SD* 'Meldungen . . .' 11/43, 15 June 1943, p. 31.
234 *TB* 24, 1 Aug. 1943, p. 3147.
235 *Sipo-SD* 'Meldungen . . .' 8/43, 1 May 1943, p. 36.
236 The sources upon which this table is based are:

Cercles: See Chapter Six, note 234.

Formations de Combat: VM *Pro Just.*, 3 Oct. 1945, *Aud. Gén.*, Doss. VM, Info., Doct. 206; Siméon *Pro Just.*, 15 Dec. 1946, *C2GM*, JB 20.

Mouvement des Femmes Rexistes: Jean Denis 'Mémoire justificatif d'un condamné à mort' p. 117, *Aud. Gén.*, Doss. Jean Denis, Info., Doct. 53.

Foi dans la Vie: The only assessment of the membership of *Foi dans la Vie* was provided in an article in *Le Pays Réel* (18 July 1943, p. 1, 'En écoutant chanter . . .') which stated that 50 girls were members of its Brussels community in mid-1943. In view of the existence of groups of *Foi dans la Vie* in a number of other towns, the total membership of the organisation was probably in the region of 200.

German Red Cross: A German report noted that 93 Walloon women had joined the organisation from the commencement of recruitment in April 1943 to the end of March 1944; *TB* 27, 10 Apr. 1944, p. 3854. This figure of approximately 100 volunteers is confirmed by a number of other sources: Jean Denis 'Mémoire justificatif . . .' p. 138, *Aud. Gén.*, Doss. Jean Denis, Info., Doct. 53; *TB* 25, 15 Nov. 1943, p. 3424; *TB* 26, 1 Mar. 1944, p. 3671; Documentation Jans 29 and 278.

Légion Wallonie: This was the numerical strength of the *Légion* prior to its entry into combat in November 1943. After the disastrous involvement of the *Légion* in the encirclement at Tcherkassy early in 1944, it numbered only 647 men plus a further 200 in hospital: *Légion Belge 'Wallonie' Historique* pp. 41 and 68, *C2GM*, W 4. New recruits did, however, join the *Légion* throughout 1943 and 1944. For example, 403 volunteers were enrolled from July to September 1943 and a further 335 were recruited between

October 1943 and March 1944; *TB* 25, 15 Nov. 1943, p. 3424; *TB* 26, 1 Mar. 1944, p. 3669; *TB* 27, 10 Apr. 1944, p. 3853. Thus, although the number of volunteers recruited during the last months of the Occupation is not known, it can be estimated with some confidence that in total approximately 2,500 men served in the *Légion Wallonie* at some time during 1943 and 1944.

Gardes Wallonnes: MV Ch. Einsatz von Landeseinwohner in unmittelbaren Wehrmachtsdiensten 1 July 1943, GRMA T 175 80 2600715–26; *TB* 30, 10 July 1944, p. 4105.

NSKK: *Militärverwaltungschef.* Einsatz von Landeseinwohner in unmittelbaren Wehrmachtsdiensten 1 July 1943, GRMA T 175 80 2600715-26

Jeunesse Légionnaire: *TB* 24, 1 Aug. 1943, p. 3152; 'Notes sur le plan de mise en sécurité...', *C2GM*, C 11/259.

SVTW: *TB* 24, 1 Aug. 1943, p. 3152.

Formations B: Initially composed of approximately 300 men in April 1944, the corps was gradually expanded and in June apparently numbered some 460 men: *TB* 27, 10 Apr. 1944, p. 3855; *TB* 29, 10 June 1944, p. 4004.

237 See pp. 240–2.
238 These figures are based on the census carried out in 1947 when the population of the Walloon region was 2,940,085 and that of the Brussels agglomeration (Brussels and the 18 surrounding communes) was 955,929. The total population of the area in which Rex operated at that time was, thus, 3,896,014; *Recensement général* I, pp. 172 and 199.
239 See p. 46.

Chapter Seven

1 *Le PR* 13 Sept. 1943, p. 1, 'Le Chef de Rex...'
2 VM to *Auditeur Militaire* Sasserath 18 Feb. 1947, *Aud. Gén.*, Doss. VM, Info., Doct. 285–7.
3 *Le PR* 10 Aug. 1943, pp. 1 and 4, 'Une émouvante cérémonie d'hommage...', 29 Aug. 1943, p. 1, 'L'état de santé du Chef' and 13 Sept. 1943, p. 1, 'Le Chef de Rex exhorte ses militants'; *TB* 25, 15 Nov. 1943, p. 3415; Daye to Fierens 14 Sept. 1943, *C2GM*, Papiers Pierre Daye.
4 *TB* 25, 15 Nov. 1943, p. 3417; *TB* 26, 1 Mar. 1944, p. 3665; P. Struye *L'évolution du sentiment public*, p. 170; E. De Bens *De Belgische dagbladpers*, pp. 149–51 and 265; *Le Soir* 7 June 1946, p. 3, 'Les Conseils de Guerre'.
5 *TB* 26, 1 Mar. 1944, p. 3631; *Le Soir* 7 June 1946, p. 3 and 9 June 1946, p. 2, 'Les Conseils de Guerre'.
6 *Le PR* 25 June 1944, p. 4, 'Rencontre avec Léon Degrelle'; *La Cité Nouvelle* 5 Jan. 1945, p. 1, 'Où se cache la fortune de Degrelle?'; *Le Soir* 6 Mar. 1946, p. 2, 'Le procès du Grand Bruxelles'; Brunet to Maître Pret 15 May 1943, *C2GM*, Papiers Pierre Daye.
7 E.g. *Le PR* 29 June 1943, p. 1, 'Bruxelles commémore dans la foi...', 1 Sept. 1943, p. 1, 'Deux cent volontaires...' and 1 Dec. 1943, p. 1, 'Nouveau départ de volontaires'. The German authorities reported that 600 new recruits joined the *Légion* from June 1943 to January 1944; *TB* 25, 15 Nov. 1943, pp. 3423–4; *TB* 26, 1 Mar. 1944, p. 3669.
8 Légion Belge 'Wallonie' Historique, pp. 33 and 41, *C2GM*, W 4; Rapport de Mathieu pp. 56–7, *C2GM*, W 4; Raymond Camby Pro Just., 17 July 1945, *Aud. Gén.*, Doss. VM, Info., Doct. 22–36.
9 Souvenirs de Heinz Forsteneichner pp. 2–3, *C2GM*, PF 3; Fierens to Daye 31 Aug. 1943, *C2GM*, Papiers Pierre Daye; H. Philippet *Et mets ta robe de bal*, pp. 101–2; E. De Bruyne *Les Wallons meurent à l'est*, pp. 65–79.
10 A. De Jonghe 'La lutte Himmler-Reeder...', *Cahiers* V (1978), pp. 161–4; Reeder to *Auditeur Général* Wilmart 2 May 1949, *C2GM*, Procès von Falkenhausen, Doct. 351.

11 LD to Reeder 9 Nov. 1943 and Reeder to Keitel 19 Nov. 1943, *C2GM*, C 11/124bis, Docts. 10 and 11.

12 *Ibid*; *TB* 26, 1 Mar. 1944, p. 3665; Légion Belge 'Wallonie' Historique, pp. 39–42, *C2GM*, W 4.

13 *Le PR* 17 Sept. 1943, p. 4, 'Chronique du Mouvement'; *National Socialisme* 15 Nov. 1943, p. 11, 'Ordres et Communiqués'.

14 *Le PR* 5 Nov. 1943, p. 1, 'Cent pour cent ou f . . . ez le camp' and 9 Nov. 1943, p. 11 'A prendre ou à laisser'.

15 Mémorandum aux autorités allemandes, *C2GM*, C 11/324.

16 LC to *Auditeur Militaire Général* 30 Apr. 1947 and VM *Pro Just.*, 20 May 1947, *Aud. Gén.*, Doss. LC, Enquête Complémentaire, Farde C, Docts. 18 and 19.

17 Siméon *Pro Just.*, 15 Dec. 1946 and LC to militants 20 Nov. 1943, *C2GM*, JB 20; Pévenasse and Keutgen to FC and *Chefs de Cercles* 9 Feb. 1944, Pierre Pauly *Pro Just.*, 27 June 1945 and Laisser Passer, *Aud. Gén.*, Doss. Joseph Pévenasse, Doct. 1003 and Doss. Pierre Pauly, Info., Doct. 18 and Courcelles Dossier, *Cour Militaire*, Doct. 1h.

18 *TB* 26, 1 Mar. 1944, p. 3664; A. De Jonghe 'La lutte Himmler-Reeder . . .', *Cahiers* VIII (1984), pp. 20–1; Siméon *Pro Just.*, 15 Dec. 1946, *C2GM*, JB 20.

19 *TB* 26, 1 Mar. 1944, p. 3756; Von Harbou to *OFKs* 29 Nov. 1943 in Documentation Jans 47; VM *Pro Just.*, 25 Nov. 1946, *Aud. Gén.*, Doss. LC, Inst., Doct. 210–11; LC to militants 20 Nov. 1943, *C2GM*, JB 20.

20 See previous note; Documentation Jans 382; LC *Pro Just.*, 3 Jan. 1947, *Aud. Gén.*, Doss. LC, Inst., Doct. 234; *L'Avenir du Luxembourg* 17 Apr. 1946, p. 1, 'Au Conseil de Guerre d'Arlon'; *Le Courrier de l'Escaut* 25 Oct. 1946, p. 3, 'Conseil de Guerre de Tournai (A)'; *Le Soir* 10 June 1947, p. 5, 'Le procès de la Werbestelle'. In addition, the Rexists established a small *Formations C* composed of a handful of men who provided an armed guard for the German-controlled arms factory (the *Fabrique Nationale*) at Herstal near Liège: LC to Rexist officials 28 Dec. 1943 and Pierre Pauly *Pro Just.*, 27 June 1945, *Aud. Gén.*, Doss. LC, Inst., Doct. 149 and Doss. Pierre Pauly, Info., Doct. 18.

21 Pévenasse to *Chefs de Cercles* and FC 14 Jan. 1944, *Aud. Gén.*, Doss. LC, Enquête Complémentaire, Farde E, Doct. 42.

22 LC to militants 20 Nov. 1943, *C2GM*, JB 20; IVe Bannière Réunion des *FC* 23 Dec. 1943 and Charles Peeters 'Organisation interne du mouvement rexiste', *C2GM*, C 11/278 and C 11/87; *Sambre et Meuse* 5 Sept. 1946, p. 2, 'Conseil de Guerre de Namur'; *Le Journal de Charleroi* 17–18 Mar. 1945, p. 1, 'Daumerie a été fusillé . . .'

23 Canaris *Pro Just.*, 25 May 1949, *C2GM*, Procès von Falkenhausen, Doct. 2261.

24 Marcovitz Report No. 3, 11 Feb. 1946, *Aud. Gén.*, Doss. LC, Inst., Doct. 168–73. Re Sommer, see p. 197.

25 These were the figures provided by Moskopff. Matthys stated that the grant was 300,000 to 700,000 BF per month: Rücksprache mit SS-*Hauptsturmführer* Moskopf 11 May 1944, GRMA T 175 131 2657825; Journal de V. Matthys p. 16, *C2GM*.

26 A. De Jonghe 'La lutte Himmler-Reeder . . .', *Cahiers* VIII (1984), pp. 123–5.

27 *Ibid.*, VII (1982), 119–20. This decision was only enacted in July 1944; see p. 268.

28 *Le PR* 1 Jan. 1944; p. 1, 'Message'.

29 *Ibid*. A circular from the *Ersatzkommando* to Brussels newspaper editors stressed the importance of this aspect of Matthys' speech: Documentation Jans 5.

30 LC to *Chefs de Cercles* 19 Jan. 1944, *C2GM*, C 11/103; LC Ordres d'exécution 10 Feb. 1944 and Julien Keutgen *Pro Just.*, 13 Sept. 1946, *Aud. Gén.*, Doss. LC, Pièces à Conviction, Doct. 42 and Doss. Marcel Dupont, Loose Papers.

31 Conseil de Guerre de Bruxelles Exposé des Faits 3 Mar. 1947, p. 64, *C2GM*, JB 13; Pierre Pauly *Pro Just.*, 29 June 1945, Henry Marcovitz *Pro Just.*, 28 Nov. 1946 and LC *Pro Just.*, 2 Dec. 1946, *Aud. Gén.*, Doss. Pierre Pauly, Info., Doct. 18 and Doss. VM, Info., Docts. 158–9 and 162.

32 LC *Pro Just.*, 21 Mar. 1946, VM *Pro Just.*, 27 Aug. 1946 and Julien Keutgen *Pro Just.*, 13 Sept. 1946, *Aud. Gén.*, Doss. Marcel Dupont, Info., Section 5 and Loose Papers.

33 LC to *Chefs de Cercles* 19 Jan. 1944 and 9 Feb. 1944 and VM *Pro Just.*, 19 May 1946, *C2GM*, C 11/103 and *Aud. Gén.*, Doss. LC, Pièces à Conviction, Docts. 37 and 38 and Doss. Jean Denis, Info., Doct. 68.

34 LC to *Chefs de Cercles* 19 Jan. 1944, *C2GM*, C 11/103; Protocole de la réunion du 6 Jan. 1944, *Aud. Gén.*, Doss. Joseph Pévenasse, Doct. 919 II; *TB* 26, 1 Mar. 1944, p. 3638.

35 Constant to Pévenasse 13 Jan. 1944, *Aud. Gén.*, Doss. Albert Constant, Inst., Doct. 31.

36 Mémoire de V. Matthys p. 51, *C2GM*.

37 Protocole de la réunion du 6 Jan. 1944, *Aud. Gén.*, Doss. Joseph Pévenasse, Doct. 919 II.

38 E.g. *Le PR* 9 Jan. 1944, p. 1, 'Bien sûr . . . et après?'

39 Undated speech, *Aud. Gén.*, Doss. Joseph Pévenasse, Doct. 925; *Le PR* 5 Jan. 1944, p. 1, 'Nos belles et dures batailles' and 12 Jan. 1944, p. 1, 'Mais qu'ils débarquent donc!'

40 *Le PR* 29 Feb. 1944, p. 1, 'Nous aurons la victoire . . .'; Région de Bruxelles [Mot d'ordre du mois] 25 Jan. 1944, *C2GM*, C 11/323.3.

41 *Le PR* 7 Mar. 1944, p. 1, 'Le discours du Chef', 17 May 1944, p. 1, Photograph and 20 May 1944, p. 1, 'Résister'.

42 *Le PR* 20 Apr. 1944, p. 1, 'L'anniversaire du Führer'.

43 *Le PR* 21 Mar. 1944, p. 3, 'Région de Bruxelles' and 2 May 1944, pp. 1 and 4, 'Les principes socialistes du Mouvement'; L. Degrelle *Feldpost*.

44 *Le PR* 6 Apr. 1944, p. 2, 'Former des cadres . . .' and 5 June 1944, p. 1, 'Conservation et révolution'; *Informations administratives et politiques* Aug. 1944, p. 1, 'La volonté permanente'.

45 *Le PR* 2 May 1944, pp. 1 and 4, 'Les principes socialistes du Mouvement'.

46 E.g. *Le PR* 6 Apr. 1944, p. 2, 'Des révolutionnaires parlent . . . et agissent' and 13 Apr. 1944, p. 1, 'Camarades, on vous trompe'; *Informations administratives et politiques* Apr. 1944, pp. 38–42, 'La réunion d'avril 1944' and May 1944, p. 1, '*Rex = Ordre = Socialisme*'.

47 *Vers l'Avenir* 18 Nov. 1946, p. 2, 'Conseil de Guerre de Namur'.

48 Keutgen to *Chefs de Cercles* 13 Jan. 1944, *C2GM*, C 11/221; Région de Bruxelles Ordre du jour mensuel Mar. 1944, *C2GM*, C 11/323.12; Gérard Delhalle *Pro Just.*, 3 Aug. 1946 and LC *Pro Just.*, 9 Sept. 1946, *Aud. Gén.*, Doss. LC, Inst., Docts. 194–8 and 201–2.

49 *Le Soir* 21 Mar. 1946, p. 2, 'Les Conseils de Guerre'; Form, *C2GM*, C 11/289.

50 *TB* 26, 1 Mar. 1944, p. 3662; *Le PR* 6 Apr. 1944, p. 1, 'Le Foyer Lucien Lippert'; P. Delandsheere and A. Ooms *La Belgique sous les Nazis* IV, pp. 33–4 and 43.

51 P. Bodart *Avec l'Armée Belge des Partisans*, pp. 201–6; A. De Jonghe 'La lutte Himmler-Reeder . . .', *Cahiers* VIII (1984), pp. 43–4.

52 *Front* Noël 1943, 'Sur le front intérieur' and Jan. 1944, 'Démissionner ou mourir'.

53 *TB* 26, 1 Mar. 1944, p. 3683; *Le PR* 15 Feb. 1944, p. 3, 'Les émouvantes funérailles de nos camarades assassinés'; A. De Jonghe 'La lutte Himmler-Reeder . . .', *Cahiers* VIII (1984), p. 119.

54 *Commandant de Corps* to Units Mar.–Apr. 1944, *Commandant de Corps* of Liége to Units Apr. 1944 and Dossier on Félin Goyen, *C2GM*, PB 3, Doct. 8 and PC 10, Docts. 42 and 50.

55 *National Socialisme* 15 Mar. 1944, p. 8, 'Quelques mesures élémentaires'; LC to *Chef de Cercle* of Liége 28 Jan. 1944, *Aud. Gén.*, Doss. LC, Inst., Doct. 128; *TB* 26, 1 Mar. 1944, p. 3662; *Le PR* 4 Feb. 1944, p. 1, 'Une seule voie . . .'

56 Mémorandum aux autorités allemandes pp. 80–6, *C2GM*, C 11/324; A. De Jonghe 'La lutte Himmler-Reeder . . .', *Cahiers* VIII (1984), p. 43.

57 Mémoire de V. Matthys pp. 109–10, *C2GM*; *Le Soir* 28 May 1946, p. 3, 'Conseil de Guerre de Charleroi'. The accuracy of these Rexist assertions is impossible to establish but A. De Jonghe has suggested that during the post-war trials of Matthys and other Rexists the authorities seemed anxious to avoid any investigation into the comments of De Foy: 'La lutte Himmler-Reeder . . .', *Cahiers* VIII (1984), pp. 91–2.

58 Mémoire de V. Matthys p. 119, *C2GM*.

59 *Le PR* 1 Jan. 1944, p. 1, 'Message'.

60 *Le PR* 1 Feb. 1944, p. 1, 'Edgard Gignot . . .'

61 C. Kesteloot and A. Gavroy *François Bovesse: Pour la défense intégrale de la Wallonie* (Mont-sur-Marchienne, 1990), pp. 3–112; *Le PR* 5 Oct. 1940, p. 8, 'Rex mène

l'action . . .' and 31 Oct. 1940, p. 1, 'Il faut libérer . . .' and 16 Mar. 1941, p. 1, 'Les 95,000 francs de M. Bovesse'.

62 *La Meuse* 24 Oct. 1945, p. 1, 'Deux des assassins . . .' and 25 Oct. 1945, p. 1, 'La mort pour les meurtriers de François Bovesse'; P. Delandsheere and A. Ooms *La Belgique sous les Nazis* IV, pp. 29–31.

63 VM *Pro Just.*, 20 and 21 Sept. 1945, *Aud. Gén.*, Doss. VM, Info., Docts. 61–2 and 81; *La Meuse* 25 Oct. 1945, p. 1, 'La mort pour les meurtriers de François Bovesse'.

64 *Le PR* 4 Feb. 1944, p. 1, 'Les funérailles de nos camarades Edgard et Flora Gignot'.

65 *Le Journal de Charleroi* 29 May 1946, p. 3, 'Le procès des tueurs du 18 août' and 14 June 1946, p. 1, 'La tragédie du 18 août'.

66 *Le Soir* 28 Jan. 1947, p. 5, 'Cour Militaire'; A. De Jonghe 'La lutte Himmler-Reeder . . .', *Cahiers* VIII (1984), pp. 80–1.

67 Jean-Baptiste Bauche *Pro Just.*, 15 Mar. 1946 and Frans and François Boveroulle *Pro Just.*, 19 Dec. 1945, *Aud. Gén.*, Doss. Michel Saussez, Inst., Docts. 55 and 59.

68 *National Socialisme* 15 Mar. 1944, p. 8, 'Ordres et Communiqués'.

69 Lambinon liked to boast that he would soon be the head of the Belgian police: *SS und Polizeigericht X, Aussenstelle Brüssel* to *SS Richter* 7 Apr. 1944, GRMA T 175 131 2657865.

70 Louis Shaw *Pro Just.*, 4 Sept. 1946, Documentation Jans 377.

71 *Ibid*; Marcel Destrain *Pro Just.*, 31 July 1945 and Edgard Duquesne *Pro Just.*, 11 July 1945, *Aud. Gén.*, Doss. LC, Inst., Doct. 91–9 and Doss. Charles Lambinon, Inst., Doct. 122–3; *Le Courrier de l'Escaut* 2 Aug. 1946, p. 3, 'Conseil de Guerre de Tournai (A)'; *La Meuse* 3–4 May 1947, p. 4 and 6 May 1947, p. 2, 'Conseil de Guerre'.

72 *Le Soir* 11 Mar. 1947, p. 5, 'Les tueurs de Rex'; *Le Journal de Charleroi* 8 Jan. 1947, p. 2, 'Le procès des tueurs rexistes . . .' Lambinon tried to exert control by sending members of his Brussels staff to direct local units: Conseil de Guerre de Bruxelles Exposé des Faits 3 Mar. 1947, pp. 37–8 and 43, *C2GM*, JB 13.

73 Conseil de Guerre de Bruxelles Exposé des Faits 3 Mar, 1947, p. 48, *C2GM*, JB 13.

74 *Ibid*. p. 6; Louis Shaw *Pro Just.*, 4 Sept. 1946, Documentation Jans 377. See also p. 209.

75 Rücksprache mit *SS-Hauptsturmführer* Moskopf 11 May 1944, GRMA T 175 131 2657823–4. Other sources suggest that there may have been a number of previous meetings.

76 Henry Marcovitz Report No. 6 11 Mar. 1946, *Aud. Gén.*, Doss. VM, Info., Doct. 119–21; Untitled report of Gieselmann 13 May 1944, GRMA T 175 131 2657598; A. De Jonghe 'La lutte Himmler-Reeder . . .', *Cahiers* VIII (1984), pp. 105–6.

77 Louis Shaw *Pro Just.*, 4 Sept. 1946, Documentation Jans 377; Conseil de Guerre de Bruxelles Exposé des Faits 3 Mar. 1947, pp. 8–53, *C2GM*, JB 13.

78 Sylvain Jadoul *Pro Just.*, 25 Aug. 1945, *Aud. Gén.*, Doss. VM, Info., Doct. 64–70; Henry Marcovitz *Pro Just.*, 4 and 28 Nov. 1946, *Aud. Gén.*, Doss. VM, Info., Docts. 152–3 and 156–7.

79 *Le Journal de Charleroi* 7 Jan. 1947, p. 2, 'La brigade policière rexiste . . .'; Bericht über die augenblickliche Lage der *DSI* 11 Apr. 1944 and Sicherheits und Informations Department 6 May 1944, GRMA T 175 131 2657518 and 2657517; Conseil de Guerre de Bruxelles Exposé des Faits 3 Mar. 1947, p. 7, *C2GM*, JB 13.

80 Albert Constant *Pro Just.*, 5 July 1946, *Aud. Gén.*, Doss. Albert Constant, Inst., Doct. 238; *National Socialisme* 15 Feb. 1944, p. 12, 'L'esprit de la Milice'; *Le PR* 6 Apr. 1944, p. 3, 'Chronique du Mouvement'.

81 A former commander of the *Légion Wallonie*, Pierre Pauly, was in charge of the administration of the corps: Pierre Pauly *Pro Just.*, 27 June 1945 and LC to *Chefs de Cercles* 31 Jan. 1944, *Aud. Gén.*, Doss. Pierre Pauly, Info., Doct. 18 and Doss. LC, Inst., Doct. 130; *National Socialisme* 15 Feb. 1944, p. 10, 'Quelque part en Wallonie . . .'; Untitled report 12 Apr. 1944 and Siméon *Pro Just.*, 15 Dec. 1946, *C2GM*, C 11/289.9 and JB 20.

82 Charles Peeters 'Organisation interne du mouvement rexiste' and De Clerck to *Cdt. de la Bannière* of Brussels 2 June 1944, *C2GM*, C 11/87 and 323.7; *TB* 27, 10 Apr. 1944, p. 3855; *TB* 29, 10 June 1944, p. 4004.

83 Charles Nisolle *Pro Just.*, 18–25 June 1945, *Aud. Gén.*, Doss. Charles Lambinon, Inst., Doct. 47–56; *TB* 21, 15 Sept. 1942, p. 2587; *National Socialisme* 15 Aug. 1944, p. 12,

'Avec nos Gardes Wallonnes'; P. Bodart *Avec l'Armée Belge des Partisans*, pp. 189–91.

84 Protocole de la réunion du 27 mars 1944, *Aud. Gén.*, Doss. Joseph Pévenasse, Doct. 928 I.

85 *Gardes Wallonnes* 25 Oct. 1943, *C2GM*, Fonds INBEL/967; Pévenasse to *Kommandostab Abteilung Z* 15 Mar. 1944, *Aud. Gén.*, Doss Joseph Pévenasse, Doct. 928 II; H. Philippet *Et mets ta robe de bal*, p. 213.

86 Wallonische Verbindungsführung beim Stab der *NSKK*-Gruppe LW to Pévenasse 29 Feb. 1944, *Aud. Gén.*, Doss. Joseph Pévenasse, Doct. 928 III.

87 E.g. *Vers l'Avenir* 22 June 1946, p. 2 and 11 July 1946, p. 4, 'Conseil de Guerre de Namur'.

88 *National Socialisme* 15 Feb. 1944, p. 9, 'La Garde Wallonne'; *La Meuse* 15 Mar. 1945, p. 2, 'Au Conseil de Guerre de Liège' and 20 Nov. 1945, p. 2, 'A la deuxième Chambre...'; *Le Courrier de l'Escaut* 29 Dec. 1946, p. 4, 'Conseil de Guerre de Tournai (A)'.

89 *Le Courrier de l'Escaut* 21 Dec. 1944, p. 1, 'Conseil de Guerre de Tournai (A)'; *La Meuse* 13 Feb. 1945, p. 2, 'Au Conseil de Guerre...', 15–16 Apr. 1945, p. 3, 26 Apr. 1945 and 10 Jan. 1947, p. 2, 'Conseil de Guerre'.

90 *Vers l'Avenir* 7 Nov. 1946, p. 5, 'Conseil de Guerre de Namur'; *Le Soir* 4 Feb. 1947, p. 5, 'Conseil de Guerre de Bruxelles'; *Le Journal de Charleroi* 15–16 and 17 Jan. 1945, p. 2, 'A Namur'; *La Meuse* 12 Apr. 1945, p. 1, 'Au Conseil de Guerre...'

91 E.g. *National Socialisme* 15 Feb. 1944, p. 9, '*NSKK*'.

92 Protocole de la réunion du 27 Mar. 1944 and Marcel Destrain *Pro Just.*, 31 July 1945, *Aud. Gén.*, Doss. Joseph Pévenasse, Doct. 928 and Doss. LC, Inst., Doct. 91–9; *Sambre et Meuse* 12 July 1946, p. 2, 'Conseil de Guerre de Namur'; *Le Soir* 17 June 1945, p. 2, 'Les Conseils de Guerre' and 1 Feb. 1948, p. 5, 'Cour Militaire'.

93 *TB* 30, 10 July 1944, pp. 4104–5; *Sipo-SD* 'Meldungen...' 14/44, 15 July 1944, p. 27; *Le PR* 4 Aug. 1944, p. 2, 'Dans la presse internationale'; *Le Courrier de l'Escaut* 28 Dec. 1944, p. 1, 'Conseil de Guerre de Tournai (A)'; *Vers l'Avenir* 3 Dec. 1946, p. 4, 'Conseil de Guerre de Namur'.

94 Protocole de la réunion du 27 Mar. 1944 and Pévenasse to *Kommandostab Abteilung Z* 15 Mar. 1944, *Aud. Gén.*, Doss. Joseph Pévenasse, Docts. 928 I and II; *TB* 27, 10 Apr. 1944, p. 3850.

95 Undated Speech, *Aud. Gén.*, Doss. Joseph Pévenasse, Doct. 925.

96 Louis Abrassart 'Milice Rexiste' 26 Feb. 1944, *C2GM*, C 11/283.

97 Pierre Pauly *Pro Just.*, 29 June 1945 and Protocole de la réunion du 6 Jan. 1944, *Aud. Gén.*, Doss. Pierre Pauly, Info., Doct. 18 and Doss. Joseph Pévenasse, Doct. 919 I.

98 Pévenasse to *Kommandostab Abteilung Z* 15 Mar. 1944, *Aud. Gén.*, Doss. Joseph Pévenasse, Doct. 928 II.

99 *Le PR* 23 Sept. 1943, p. 1, 'Quand l'attentisme florissant...'; *La Gazette de Charleroi* 19 Jan. 1944, p. 1, 'Ce que nous dit M. Joseph Darnand' and 19–20 Feb. 1944, p. 1, 'La Belgique attend son Darnand'. Re the *Milice*, see J. Delperrié de Bayac *Histoire de la Milice 1918–1945* (Paris, 1969).

100 *Milice Française* file and VM to Darnand 19 Feb. 1944 cited in Siméon *Pro Just.*, 15 Dec. 1946, *C2GM* C 11/293 and JB 20; *Le Peuple* Mar. 1944, p. 3, 'Degrelle: Darnand belge?'

101 E. De Bruyne *Les wallons meurent à l'est*, p. 76; J. Mabire *Légion Wallonie*, pp. 161–2; J. Erickson *The Road to Berlin*, pp. 176–9.

102 *Le PR* 15 Feb. 1944, p. 1, 'Après de durs combats' and 23 Feb. 1944, pp. 1 and 4, 'Triomphe de la vérité'; Légion Belge 'Wallonie' Historique, pp. 64–8, *C2GM*, W 4; *PA Belgien Stimmungsbericht* 1–29 Feb. 1944, GRMA T 175 80 2600688–95.

103 *Le PR* 22 Feb. 1944, p. 1, 'Le Chef reçoit des mains du Fuehrer...'; A. De Jonghe 'La lutte Himmler-Reeder...', *Cahiers* VII (1982), pp. 156–7; J.-M. Frérotte *Léon Degrelle, le dernier fasciste*, pp. 189–90.

104 Radio Bruxelles 22 Feb. 1944, *C2GM*, Fonds INBEL/980; *Le PR* 23 Feb. 1944, p. 1, 'Le Chef est parmi nous' and 28 Feb. 1944, p. 1, 'Le Chef a rendu hommage...', pp. 1 and 2, 'Le discours du Chef' and p. 2, 'Une réception...'; *TB* 26, 1 Mar. 1944, pp. 3628 and 3670; P. Delandsheere and A. Ooms *La Belgique sous les Nazis* IV, pp. 47–50.

105 *TB* 27, 10 Apr. 1944, p. 3850; *Le PR* 3 Mar. 1944, p. 1, 'Le Chef a été reçu...'

106 *TB* 27, 10 Apr. 1944, p. 3850; *Le PR* 7 Mar. 1944, p. 1, 'Le discours du Chef' and 'Devant plusieurs milliers de Français...' and p. 4, 'Le Chef est l'hôte...'; Radio Bruxelles 5 Mar. 1944 and *Les Nouveaux Temps* 8 Mar. 1944 cited in *C2GM*, Fonds INBEL/980; J.-M. Charlier *Léon Degrelle*, pp. 337–8; Institut Hoover *La vie de la France sous l'Occupation (1940–1944)* (Paris, 1957) II, p. 1132. I am grateful to A. De Jonghe for drawing my attention to this reference.

107 A. De Jonghe 'La lutte Himmler-Reeder...' *Cahiers* VII (1982), pp. 156–71.

108 *TB* 27, 10 Apr. 1944, pp. 3841 and 3845; P. Delandsheere and A. Ooms *La Belgique sous les Nazis* IV, p. 73; *Le Peuple* Mar. 1944, p. 3, 'Degrelle: Darnand belge?'

109 *Front* Apr. 1944, 'Visages de la guerre'; P. Delandsheere and A. Ooms *Op. cit.* IV, pp. 83–4; *L'Eventail* 13 June 1980, p. 6, 'Léon Degrelle'; A. De Jonghe 'La lutte Himmler-Reeder...', *Cahiers* VII (1982), p. 163.

110 A. De Jonghe 'La lutte Himmler-Reeder...', *Cahiers* VII (1982), pp. 141–56.

111 Légion Belge 'Wallonie' Historique, p. 75, Keutgen to *cadres* 27 and 29 Mar. 1944 and Henry Marcovitz *Pro Just.*, 7 Mar. 1946, *C2GM*, W 4, C 11/325 and PF 3; *Le PR* 2 Apr. 1944, p. 1, 'Charleroi'.

112 Documentation Jans 28; J. Mabire *Légion Wallonie*, pp. 311–12; *Le PR* 2 Apr. 1944, p. 1, 'Bruxelles'; P. Delandsheere and A. Ooms *La Belgique sous les Nazis* IV, pp. 72 and 75–8; A. De Jonghe 'La lutte Himmler-Reeder...', *Cahiers* VII (1982), pp. 158–9.

113 *PA Belgien Stimmungsbericht* 1–30 Apr. 1944, GRMA T 175 80 2600666; Ch. d'Ydewalle *Degrelle ou la triple imposture*, p. 202; *Le PR* 5 Apr. 1944, p. 2, 'Inoubliable' and 'Un secret bien gardé'. Delegations of *légionnaires* subsequently visited a number of provincial towns including La Louvière, Liège, Tournai and Arlon: *Le PR* 21 Apr. 1944, p. 1, 'La Louvière...' and 23 Apr. 1944, p. 5, 'Le Cercle de Liège...' and 'Le Cercle de Tournai...'; *L'Avenir du Luxembourg* 23 Jan. 1946, p. 1, 'Au Conseil de Guerre'.

114 A. De Jonghe 'La lutte Himmler-Reeder...', *Cahiers* VII (1982), p. 159.

115 *TB* 26, 1 Mar. 1944, p. 3631; *TB* 28, 10 May 1944, p. 3924.

116 *Le PR* 25 June 1944, p. 4, 'Rencontre avec Léon Degrelle'.

117 Souvenirs de Heinz Forsteneichner p. 3, *C2GM*, PF 3; *TB* 24, 1 Aug. 1943, p. 3147; *Sipo-SD* 'Meldungen...' 8/43, 1 May 1943, p. 35.

118 *Het Vlaamsche Land* 29 June 1943, p. 1, 'Tegen het Bolsjewisme'; *TB* 24, 1 Aug. 1943, p. 3138. If the post-war comments of Matthys and Van de Wiele are to be believed, the contacts between Degrelle and the leader of *DeVlag* were matched by an agreement between Rex and *DeVlag*; J. De Launay *Histoires secrètes de la Belgique*, p. 289; Journal de V. Matthys p. 14, *C2GM*.

119 E.g. *Le PR* 2 Apr. 1944, p. 1, 'Bruxelles'.

120 Report by Koch 27 Mar. 1944, GRMA T 175 80 2600672–4; *TB* 27, 10 Apr. 1944, p. 3845; *TB* 28, 10 May 1944, p. 3919.

121 *Le PR* 17 May 1942, p. 1, 'Un rexiste flamand...'; INBEL Informations reçues de Belgique 2 Mar. 1943, *C2GM*, Fonds INBEL/965; *Le Matin* 22 Oct. 1946, p. 1, 'Odiel Daem... devant le Conseil de Guerre'.

122 *Sipo-SD* 'Meldungen...' 8/43, 1 May 1943, p. 36; A. De Jonghe 'La lutte Himmler-Reeder...', *Cahiers* VII (1982), p. 163; Le Gorlais to Constant 23 Mar. 1944, *Aud. Gén.*, Doss. Albert Constant, Farde A, Doct. 23; *Le PR* 25 Apr. 1944, p. 1, 'Jean Azéma et Jean Hérold-Paquis'.

123 *TB* 28, 10 May 1944, p. 3923; *TB* 26, 1 Mar. 1944, pp. 3630–1.

124 J.-M. Charlier *Léon Degrelle*, pp. 243 and 320–1; Institut Hoover *La vie de la France* II, p. 1132.

125 R. Brasillach *Léon Degrelle et l'avenir de Rex* (Paris, 1936) and *Notre Avant-Guerre*, pp. 206–12; P.M. Dioudonnat *Je suis partout*, pp. 143–6.

126 See p. 243. *Le PR* 14 Dec. 1943, p. 3, 'M. Marquès-Rivière...' and 15 Apr. 1944, p. 1, 'Les Chantres de la Joie'; Demande pour un laisser-passer and Antrag auf Erteilung eines Durchlass-Scheines, *Aud. Gén.*, Doss. VM, Info., Doct. 83 and Doss. LC, Pièces à Conviction, Docts. 11–14; *La Gazette de Liège* 25 May 1945, p. 1, 'Le procès du Grand Liège'.

127 *Le PR* 22 Jan. 1944, p. 3, 'Manifestation du CIS' and 8 Feb. 1944, p. 1, 'Jean Hérold-Paquis...'; *La Gazette de Charleroi* 13 Mar. 1944, p. 1, 'Jean Azéma et Jean Hérold

Paquis . . .'; *TB* 26, 1 Mar. 1944, p. 3665; Hérold-Paquis to VM 22 Feb. 1944, *Aud. Gén.*, Doss. VM, Info., Doct. 145–6. See also J. Goueffon 'La guerre des ondes: le cas de Jean Hérold-Paquis', *Revue d'histoire de la deuxième guerre mondiale* XXVII (1977), pp. 27–42; P.M. Dioudonnat *Je suis partout*, p. 443.

128 *Le PR* 21 Apr. 1944, p. 4, 'Engagements à bureau ouvert?' and 27 Apr. 1944, p. 2, 'Réveil de Bourgogne'.

129 *Le PR* 4 Apr. 1944, p. 1, 'Il n'a suffi qu'une liaison dangereuse' and 2 May 1944, p. 3, 'Fêtes rexistes du Travail'; *L'Assaut* 18 June 1944, p. 3, 'Jean Azéma . . .'; W. Tucker *The Fascist Ego: A Political Biography of Robert Brasillach* (Berkeley, 1975), pp. 254–5.

130 G.T. Schillemans *Philippe Pétain, le prisonnier de Sigmaringen* (Paris, 1965), p. 113.

131 J.-M. Charlier *Léon Degrelle*, p. 243; *Le PR* 28 Apr. 1944, p. 1, 'M. Darnand à Bruxelles'.

132 A. Brissaud *Pétain à Sigmaringen (1944–1945)* (Paris, 1960), pp. 347–50; H. Rousso *Un château en Allemagne* (Paris, 1980), pp. 138–40 and 216–17; L. Noguères *La dernière étape Sigmaringen* (Paris, 1956), p. 197.

133 L. Degrelle *Feldpost*, Preface; A. Brissaud *Op. cit.*, pp. 347–8.

134 *L'Effort Wallon* 2 July 1944, p. 2, 'Un autographe de Léon Degrelle' and p. 4, 'Le Commandeur de la *SS*-Division "Wallonie" parle'.

135 Secrétaire de l'*EM du Chef* Ordre d'exécution 13 May 1944, *C2GM*, C 11/159; Documentation Jans 278; *Le PR* 19 Dec. 1943, p. 3, 'Solidarité en action' and 11 Jan. 1944, p. 2, 'Au service . . .'

136 LC *Pro Just.*, 1 Apr. 1946, *C2GM*, JB 20.

137 *Le PR* 28 Feb. 1944, pp. 1–2, 'Le discours du Chef' and 8 Apr. 1944, p. 1, 'Nous sommes le peuple'; Documentation Jans 278; *TB* 24, 1 Aug. 1943, p. 3156; Fierens to Daye 31 Aug. 1943, *C2GM*, Papiers Pierre Daye.

138 *Le Journal de Charleroi* 21 Nov. 1946 and 10 Jan. 1947, p. 4, 'Conseil de Guerre de Charleroi'; *Le Courrier de l'Escaut* 24 July 1946, p. 1, 'Conseil de Guerre de Tournai (A)'.

139 A. Crahay *Les Belges en Corée 1951–1955* (Brussels, 1966), p. 7.

140 *La Meuse* 26 Feb. and 29 Aug. 1946, p. 2, 'Conseil de Guerre'; *L'Avenir du Luxembourg* 9 Jan. 1946, p. 1 and 28 Feb. 1947, p. 2, 'Au Conseil de Guerre'; *Vers l'Avenir* 1 May 1946, p. 2, 'Conseil de Guerre de Dinant' and 20 Dec. 1946, p. 4, 'Conseil de Guerre de Namur'; *Le Soir* 10 June 1947, p. 5, 'Le procès de la Werbestelle'.

141 H. Philippet *Et mets ta robe de bal*, p. 106; *L'Avenir du Luxembourg* 16 Jan. 1946, p. 1, 'Au Conseil de Guerre'.

142 *TB* 28, 10 May 1944, p. 3924; *TB* 29, 10 June 1944, p. 4002; J. Mabire *Légion Wallonie*, p. 311.

143 LD to *Gardes Wallonnes* 5 May 1944, *C2GM*, C 11/274bis.

144 Degrelle made a private visit to Munich early in May possibly in order to meet Himmler or one of his assistants. Louis Collard, however, subsequently denied that German approval for this project had ever been obtained; A. De Jonghe 'La lutte Himmler-Reeder', *Cahiers* VII (1982), p. 166; LC *Pro Just.*, 3 Jan. 1947, *Aud. Gén.*, Doss. LC, Inst., Doct. 234.

145 LC *Pro Just.*, 3 Jan. 1947, *Aud. Gén.*, Doss. LC, Inst., Doct. 234; Mémoire de V. Matthys pp. 76–7, *C2GM*.

146 Secrétaire de l'*EM du Chef* Ordre d'exécution 13 May 1944, *C2GM*, C 11/159; P. Delandsheere and A. Ooms *La Belgique sous les Nazis* IV, pp. 143–4; *Front* 5 July 1944, 'Sur le front intérieur'.

147 P. Delandsheere and A. Ooms *Op. cit.* IV, pp. 143–4; Graide to *Chefs de Cercles* 12 June 1944 and Edouard Joselies *Pro Just.*, 4 Feb. 1947, *Aud. Gén.*, Doss. LC, Enquête Complémentaire, Farde B, Doct. 15 and Doss. VM, Info., Doct. 261–2; Conseil de Guerre de Bruxelles Exposé des Faits 3 Mar. 1947, p. 56, *C2GM*, JB 13.

148 *TB* 30, 10 July 1944, p. 4102; *Le PR* 27 June 1944, p. 1, 'Le Chef exhalte notre révolution', 30 June 1944, p. 1, 'Le Chef Léon Degrelle . . .' and 7 July 1944, p. 1, 'De nombreux ouvriers wallons . . .'

149 See note 147.

150 'Notes sur le plan de mise en sécurité des familles rexistes . . .', *C2GM*, C 11/259; VM testimony in Documentation Jans 266.

151 Folens to Renauld 3 June 1944 and Graide to *Chef de Cercle* of Verviers 10 July 1944, *C2GM*, C 11/321.13 and 259; Secrétaire de l'*EM du Chef* Ordre d'exécution 13 May 1944, *Aud. Gén.*, Doss. LC, Enquête Complémentaire, Farde D, Doct. 31; P. Delandsheere and A. Ooms *La Belgique sous les Nazis* IV, pp. 143–4; *TB* 29, 10 June 1944, pp. 4002–4.
152 E.g. *Front* 5 June 1944, p. 8, 'Visages de la guerre'.
153 *Le PR* 21 Apr. 1944, p. 2, 'Réunions des membres' and 28 Apr. 1944, p. 1, 'Assemblés populaires...'; Région de Bruxelles Ordre du jour mensuel May 1944 in Documentation Jans 74; Keutgen to *Chefs de Cercles* 6 July 1944, *C2GM*, C 11/221.
154 J. Neckers 'La libération' in *1940–1945 La vie quotidienne en Belgique*, p. 283; P. Struye *L'évolution du sentiment public*, pp. 163–4 and 179–81; *Le PR* 23 May 1944, p. 1, 'Les yeux s'ouvrent'.
155 Secrétaire de l'*EM du Chef* Note Générale 13 May 1944, *Aud. Gén.*, Doss. LC, Enquête Complémentaire, Farde E, Doct. 46.
156 *TB* 29, 10 June 1944, p. 3996; *TB* 30, 10 July 1944, pp. 4085–6; *Sipo-SD* 'Meldungen...' 12/44, 15 June 1944, p. 4 and 13/44, 1 July 1944, pp. 1–3; *Le PR* 5 July 1944, p. 1, 'Les armes secrètes de la Reine Bess'.
157 *Le Soir* 5 Mar. 1947, p. 5, 'Le procès des tueurs de Rex'.
158 *Sipo-SD* 'Meldungen...' 14/44, 15 July 1944, p. 6; *Le Soir* 19 June 1946, p. 2, 'Les Conseils de Guerre'; A. Delattre *Mes Souvenirs*, pp. 320–1.
159 *TB* 28, 10 May 1944, p. 3924; *TB* 29, 10 June 1944, p. 4002; P. Struye *L'évolution du sentiment public*, p. 183; Région de Bruxelles Ordre du jour mensuel May 1944 in Documentation Jans 74.
160 *Vers l'Avenir* 8 June 1946, p. 2, 'Au Conseil de Guerre de Namur'; *L'Avenir du Luxembourg* 10 Jan. 1946, p. 1, 'Au Conseil de Guerre'; *La Meuse* 19 Sept. 1946, p. 2, 'Au Conseil de Guerre'.
161 *Le PR* 10 Feb. 1944, p. 1, 'L'éducateur: Chef de la Jeunesse' and 6 Apr. 1944, p. 1, 'Le Foyer Lucien Lippert'; Secrétaire de l'*EM du Chef* Ordre d'exécution 31 Mar. 1944, *C2GM*, C 11/158.
162 *La Meuse* 19 May 1945, p. 2, 'Conseil de Guerre'; *Vers l'Avenir* 11 July 1946, p. 4, 'Conseil de Guerre de Namur'; Paul Piret *Pro Just.*, 7 Oct. 1944, *Aud. Gén.*, Doss. Charles Lambinon, Inst., Doct. 15–16.
163 *TB* 28, 10 May 1944, p. 3929.
164 *Sipo-SD* 'Meldungen...' 14/44, 15 July 1944, p. 5 and 16/44, 15 Aug. 1944, p. 7.
165 P. Struye *L'évolution du sentiment public*, pp. 178–9 and 189.
166 *Front* 5 July 1944, 'Pas de pitié pour les traîtres'; P. Jacquet *Brabant Wallon*, pp. 250–4; *Sipo-SD* 'Meldungen...' 14/44, 15 July 1944, p. 5.
167 *Le PR* 13 Aug. 1944, p. 1, 'Le Cde. Danly...'
168 *Le PR* 15 Apr. 1944, p. 3, 'Notre Camarade Coutelier...', 16 Apr. 1944, p. 4, 'Notre Camarade Blehen...' and 23 May 1944, p. 2, 'Nécrologie'; *L'Assaut* 14 May 1944, p. 3, 'Du sang...' and 18 June 1944, p. 3, 'Encore du sang'.
169 A. De Jonghe 'La lutte Himmler-Reeder...', *Cahiers* VIII (1984), pp. 43 and 120–1; *Sipo-SD* 'Meldungen...' 14/44, 15 July 1944, p. 6; *Le PR* 14 Mar. 1944, p. 3, 'De lâches assassins...', 14 Apr. 1944, p. 3, 'La femme d'un légionnaire...' and 14 May 1944, p. 1, 'Un légionnaire, sa femme et sa mère...'
170 Mémoire de V. Matthys pp. 115–16, *C2GM*.
171 *Ibid*; J.-M. Charlier *Léon Degrelle*, p. 377; C. Suzanne *Commentaires en marge de l'histoire* (Louvain, 1959), p. 30.
172 Jean Binet *Pro Just.*, 25 Nov. 1944, *Aud. Gén.*, Doss. LC, Inst., Doct. 4–8.
173 *TB* 26, 1 Mar. 1944, p. 3634; *L'Avenir du Luxembourg* 3 May 1946, p. 1, 'Trois odieux chasseurs d'hommes...' and 22 May 1946, p. 1, 'Au Conseil de Guerre'.
174 *L'Action Directe* Aug. 1944, *C2GM*, C 11/327.
175 For example at Ciney, see p. 273.
176 *Le Journal de Charleroi* 10 July 1945, p. 1, 'Conseil de Guerre de Charleroi'; *Le Courrier de l'Escaut* 7 July 1946, p. 3, 'Conseil de Guerre de Tournai (A)'; *Vers l'Avenir* 9–10 Mar. 1946, p. 3 and 30 May 1947, p. 4, 'Conseil de Guerre de Namur'.
177 *L'Avenir du Luxembourg* 21 Feb. and 10 May 1946, p. 1, 'Au Conseil de Guerre'.
178 *L'Avenir du Luxembourg* 7 Feb. 1946, p. 4, 'Au Conseil de Guerre'; *Vers l'Avenir* 13

July 1946, p. 2, 'Au Conseil de Guerre de Namur'; Théodat Chantraine *Pro Just.*, 9 Dec. 1944 and Jean Laitat *Pro Just.*, 24 May 1946, *Aud. Gén.*, Doss. Michel Saussez, Inst., Docts, 12 and 64.

179 INBEL 18 Nov. 1943, *C2GM*, Fonds INBEL/968; Henry Marcovitz *Pro Just.*, 28 Nov. 1946 and LC *Pro Just.*, 2 Dec. 1946, *Aud. Gén.*, Doss. VM, Info., Docts. 158–9 and 162.

180 *Le PR* 6 May 1941, p. 2, 'Dans le Mouvement' and 12 July 1944, p. 1, 'Edouard Degrelle...'; V. Marquet 'L'exécution d'Edouard Degrelle. Une bavure?', *Mémo* No. 28 (1989), pp. 4–5.

181 Conseil de Guerre de Namur Exposé des Faits and *Pro Just.*, 20 July 1948, *C2GM*, JB 26.

182 *Ibid*; Heinz Böttcher *Pro Just.*, 11 Apr. 1949, *C2GM*, Procès von Falkenhausen, Doct. 2256.

183 VM *Pro Just.*, 12 Sept. 1945, *Aud. Gén.*, Doss. VM, Info., Doct. 48–51.

184 A. De Jonghe 'La lutte Himmler-Reeder...', *Cahiers* VIII (1984), pp. 140–63; LD to Himmler 14 July 1944 and Himmler to Jungclaus, *C2GM*, BDC III, Doct. 22; V. Marquet 'L'exécution d'Edouard Degrelle...', *Mémo* No. 28 (1989), pp. 8–16.

185 *Le Soir* 26 July 1944, p. 1, 'Le curé d'Ottignies est tué...'; *Front* 21 Aug. 1944, 'Visages de la Guerre'; *Vers l'Avenir* 4 June 1946, p. 2 and 20 June 1946, p. 4, 'Conseil de Guerre de Namur'; *Le Journal de Charleroi* 5 Mar. 1946, p. 3, 'Conseil de Guerre de Mons'.

186 *Le Journal de Charleroi* 27 Feb. 1946, p. 2, 'L'assassinat de M. Hiernaux...'

187 *Le Journal de Charleroi* 7 Feb. 1946, p. 2, 'Les assassinats d'Ham sur Heure'; *Le Soir* 11 Nov. 1947, p. 1, 'Vingt-sept tueurs rexistes...'; *Cour Militaire Pro Just.* 13 Mar. 1947, p. 87, *C2GM*, JB 12; R. De Becker 'La collaboration...', *Courrier hebdomadaire du CRISP* No. 497–8 (1970), pp. 39–42.

188 See note 185; *Le Journal de Charleroi* 12 Oct. 1945, p. 1, 'Du bétail pour l'abattoir...' and 1 Feb. 1946, p. 3, 'Le chef tueur sous les verrous'; *Cour Militaire Pro Just.* 13 Mar. 1947, pp. 84 and 87–8, *C2GM*, JB 12.

189 E.g. Marcel Simon *Pro Just.*, 3 Nov. 1945, *Aud. Gén.*, Doss. VM, Info., Doct. 137.

190 Mémoire de V. Matthys p. 118, *C2GM*; *Le Journal de Charleroi* 4–5 May 1946, p. 1, 'Comment s'y prirent les tueurs rexistes...'

191 Avart, Saussez and Colman of the *Département Politique* were, for example, all directly involved in murders committed in the Hainaut in the summer of 1944; *Le Journal de Charleroi* 13 July 1945, p. 1, 'Conseil de Guerre de Charleroi' and 27 Feb. 1946, p. 2, 'L'assassinat de M. Hiernaux...'; Auguste Scauflaire *Pro Just.*, 15 Feb. 1946 and LC *Pro Just.*, 26 Feb. 1946, *Aud. Gén.*, Doss. Michel Saussez, Inst., Docts. 60 and 61.

192 Jean Binet *Pro Just.*, 5 Nov. 1945 and Ecole de la Haine, *Aud. Gén.*, Doss. VM, Farde B, Doct. 8 and Farde I, Doct. 7–9; A. De Jonghe 'La lutte Himmler-Reeder...', *Cahiers* VIII (1984), p. 180.

193 *L'Action Directe* Aug. 1944, *C2GM*, C 11/327.

194 *TB* 29, 10 June 1944, p. 4002. The exact date of this crisis remains uncertain. Matthys stated that it happened in May or June but the circular announcing the consequent reorganisation is dated 4 August: VM *Pro Just.*, 25 Nov. 1946 and Ordres d'*EM* 4 Aug. 1944, *Aud. Gén.*, Doss. LC, Inst., Doct. 210–11 and Enquête Complémentaire, Farde D, Doct. 32.

195 Ordres d'*EM* 17 and 20 Apr. 1944, *Aud. Gén.*, Doss. LC, Enquête Complémentaire, Farde D, Doct. 29 and Doss. Joseph Pévenasse, Doct. 918.

196 VM *Pro Just.*, 25 Nov. 1946, Doss. LC, Inst., Doct. 210–11; Gesamtbericht des *Wehrmachtsbefehlshabers und Höheren SS- u. Polizeiführers Belgien und Nordfrankreich* 25 Oct. 1944, *C2GM*, BDC II. See also pp. 242–3.

197 LC *Pro Just.*, 18 July 1947, *Aud. Gén.*, Doss. LC, Enquête Complémentaire, Farde G; Mémoire de V. Matthys pp. 51–2, *C2GM*.

198 Interview with Madame R. Meunier 8 Feb. 1988.

199 Ordres d'*EM* 4 Aug. 1944, *Aud. Gén.*, Doss. LC, Enquête Complémentaire, Farde D, Doct. 32.

200 *Sipo-SD* 'Meldungen...' 16/44, 15 Aug. 1944, p. 33.

201 LD to Himmler 14 July 1944, *C2GM*, BDC III, Doct. 22.

202 J.-M. Charlier *Léon Degrelle*, p. 382. But see also A. De Jonghe 'La lutte Himmler-Reeder . . .', *Cahiers* VIII (1984), pp. 157–8.

203 LD to VM 13 Aug. 1944, *Aud. Gén.*, Doss. VM, Info., Doct. 200–4. See also *La Cité Nouvelle* 5 and 6 Jan. 1945, p. 1, 'Où se cache la fortune de Degrelle?' and 17–18 Jan. 1945, p. 1, 'Degrelle avait quelques appréhensions'.

204 *Le PR* 7 July 1944, p. 2, 'Chronique du Mouvement'; Fragebogen für Anträge auf Ausstellung eines Sichtwermerkes, *Aud. Gén.*, Doss. LC, Inst., Docts. 55–64.

205 Rapport d'expertise médico-mentale 27 May 1947, *Aud. Gén.*, Doss. LC, Enquête Complémentaire, Farde H, Doct. 7. In one such incident Collard threatened to kill the cartoonist of *Le Pays Réel*, Paul Jamin, whom he accused of seducing a female member of the Rexist headquarters staff. According to Jamin, Matthys had to intervene to protect him from Collard: *Le Soir* 19 Jan. 1946, p. 2, 'Cour Militaire de Bruxelles'; Interview with Paul Jamin 8 Feb. 1988.

206 *Le Soir* 14 June 1946, p. 2, 'Les Conseils de Guerre'.

207 Police Judiciaire *Pro Just.*, 20 Jan. 1945 and Jean Binet *Pro Just.*, 25 Nov. 1944, *Aud. Gén.*, Doss. VM, Info., Doct. 13 and Doss. LC, Inst., Doct. 4–8.

208 Yvan Demaret *Pro Just.*, 12 Oct. 1946, *Aud. Gén.*, Doss. LC, Inst., Doct. 303–7.

209 Mémoire de V. Matthys p. 83, *C2GM*.

210 E.g. *Le PR* 16 Aug. 1944, p. 4, 'Le discours du Chef ad interim'.

211 Plaidoyer prononcé par Victor Matthys devant le Conseil de Guerre de Charleroi p. 21, *C2GM*, JP 258.

212 P. Delandsheere and A. Ooms *La Belgique sous les Nazis* IV; R. Gobyn 'La vie quotidienne . . .' in *1940–1945 La vie quotidienne en Belgique*, p. 81; *Vers l'Avenir* 26 July 1946, p. 4, 'Au temps où les tueurs rexistes . . .'

213 *L'Assaut* 22 July 1944, p. 1, 'L'aveu de leur impuissance'; *Le PR* 23 July 1944, p. 1, 'Avortement'; *Sipo-SD* 'Meldungen . . .' 15/44, 1 Aug. 1944, p. 1.

214 A. De Jonghe 'L'établissement d'une administration civile en Belgique et le Nord de la France', *Cahiers* I (1970), pp. 67–129. See also pp. 229–30.

215 *Sipo-SD* 'Meldungen . . .' 15/44, 1 Aug. 1944, pp. 5–6; Berger to Himmler 31 July 1944, GRMA T 175 80 2600653–4; *Le Soir* 4 June 1947, p. 5, 'Conseil de Guerre de Bruxelles'.

216 Circular of VM 20 July 1944 cited in Documentation Jans 20.

217 A. De Jonghe 'La lutte Himmler-Reeder . . .', *Cahiers* VII (1982), pp. 171–83 and VIII (1984), pp. 164–72.

218 *Le PR* 17 Aug. 1944, p. 1, 'Sans faiblir'.

219 François Boveroulle, Gabriel Chéron and Auguste Scauflaire, *Pro Just.*, 27 Feb. 1946, *Aud. Gén.*, Doss. Michel Saussez, Inst., Doct. 62.

220 P. Bodart *Avec l'Armée Belge des Partisans,* p. 273; *Front* 21 Aug. 1944, 'Visages de la Guerre'.

221 *Cour Militaire Pro Just.* 13 Mar. 1947, pp. 81–2, *C2GM*, JB 12. Of these, 27 died in reprisals taken after the assassination of the Rexist Mayor of Charleroi: see pp. 271–2.

222 *Vers l'Avenir* 2 Aug. 1946, p. 5, 'De nouveaux forfaits . . .'; *Le Journal de Charleroi* 27 Feb. 1947, p. 4, 'Les représailles rexistes . . .'

223 *Le Journal de Charleroi* 28 and 29 Aug. and 26 Sept. 1945, p. 1, 'Conseil de Guerre de Charleroi'.

224 Alfred Falque *Pro Just.*, 31 July 1945, *C2GM*, JB 20; *L'Action Directe* Aug. 1944, p. 1, 'Vision printanière', *C2GM*, C 11/327; *Le Brabant Wallon* 20 Oct. 1946, pp. 1 and 3, 'Au Conseil de Guerre de Nivelles'; *Le Soir* 6 Nov. 1946, p. 3, 'Les Conseils de Guerre'; R. Goffin *Souvenirs avant l'adieu* (Charleroi, 1980), p. 42.

225 *Le PR* 16 Aug. 1944, p. 1, 'Dans le domaine du terrorisme comme dans celui de la politique . . .'; *Sipo-SD* 'Meldungen . . .' 16/44, 15 Aug. 1944, pp. 31–3.

226 *Le PR* 16 Aug. 1944, pp. 1, 3 and 4, 'Le discours du Chef ad interim'.

227 *Le PR* 17 Aug. 1944, p. 1, 'Sans faiblir'.

228 See note 226.

229 *Le PR* 18 Aug. 1944, p. 1, 'Un crime qui crie vengeance . . .'; *National Socialisme* 15 May 1944, p. 8, 'Oswald Englebin'; A. Lemaire *Le crime du 18 août*, pp. 7–44. See p. 166.

230 *Cour Militaire Pro Just.* 13 Mar. 1947, pp. 84 and 105–6, *C2GM*, JB 12.
231 *Le Journal de Charleroi* 29 May 1946, p. 3, 'Le procès des tueurs . . .'; A. De Jonghe 'La lutte Himmler-Reeder . . .', *Cahiers* VIII (1984), pp. 181–2.
232 Declaration by Camille Felu, copy dated 14 Mar. 1946, François De Keyser *Pro Just.*, 22 May 1946 and Pierre Pauly *Pro Just.*, 4 July 1945, *Aud. Gén.*, Doss. LC, Inst., Doct. 174–5, Doss. Jean Colman, Inst., Doct. 82 and Doss. Pierre Pauly, Info., Doct. 18.
233 See previous note; A. Lemaire *Le crime du 18 août*, pp. 48–81; *Cour Militaire Pro Just.*, 13 Mar. 1947, p. 109, *C2GM*, JB 12.
234 A. Lemaire *Op. cit.*, pp. 85–224; *Le Soir* 29 May 1946, p. 3, 'Conseil de Guerre de Charleroi'; P. Delandsheere and A. Ooms *La Belgique sous les Nazis* IV, p. 237.
235 A. Lemaire *Op. cit.*, pp. 250–360; Declaration by Camille Felu, copy dated 14 Mar. 1946 and Pierre Pauly *Pro Just.*, 4 July 1945, *Aud. Gén.*, Doss. LC, Inst., Doct. 174–5 and Doss. Pierre Pauly, Info., Doct. 18; *Cour Militaire Pro Just.*, 13 Mar. 1947, pp. 114 and 117, *C2GM*, JB 12; *Le Soir* 5 June 1946, p. 3, 'Les Conseils de Guerre'.
236 VM *Pro Just.*, 12 Sept. 1945, *Aud. Gén.*, Doss. VM, Info., Doct. 48–51.
237 'Les mémoires de Pierre Daye', *Dossier du mois* No. 12, p. 35.
238 *Informations administratives et politiques* Aug. 1944, pp. 40–4, 'Réunion d'août 1944'; Région de Bruxelles Ordre du jour mensuel Aug. 1944, *C2GM*, C 11/323.12; *Le PR* 27 Aug. 1944, p. 1, 'Il y a deux ans . . .'; *Le Soir* 7 Mar. 1946, p. 2, 'Les Conseils de Guerre'.
239 E.g. Conseil de Guerre de Bruxelles Exposé des Faits 3 Mar. 1947, p. 35, *C2GM*, JB 13.
240 Louis Jacobs *Pro Just.*, undated, *C2GM*, JB 20; Joseph Kestelyn *Pro Just.*, 23 Apr. 1946 and LC and VM *Pro Just.*, 18 July 1947, *Aud. Gén.*, Doss. LC, Inst., Doct. 188 and Enquête Complémentaire, Farde G.
241 See collection of documents in *C2GM*, JB 20. See also Conseil de Guerre de Bruxelles Exposé des Faits 3 Mar. 1947, pp. 49–51, *C2GM*, JB 13; Guy Nollomont *Pro Just.*, 6 Jan. 1945, *Aud. Gén.*, Doss. Charles Lambinon, Inst., Doct. 21–2.
242 Jean Binet *Pro Just.*, 5 Nov. 1945, *Aud. Gén.*, Doss. VM, Farde B, Doct. 8; P. Delandsheere and A. Ooms *La Belgique sous les Nazis* IV pp. 242–4.
243 Conseil de Guerre de Bruxelles Exposé des Faits 3 Mar. 1947, pp. 13–15, *C2GM*, JB 13; *Journal des Tribunaux* 22 June 1947, pp. 374–6, 'Conseil de Guerre de Bruxelles'; Jean Colman *Pro Just.*, 10 May 1946, *Aud. Gén.*, Doss. Jean Colman, Inst., Doct. 49; *Le Soir* 5 June 1947, p. 5, 'Les Conseils de Guerre'.
244 *Le Soir* 5 Mar. 1947, p. 5, 'Le procès des tueurs de Rex'; VM *Pro Just.*, 12 Sept. 1945 and Lucien Van Uytrecht *Pro Just.*, undated, *Aud. Gén.*, Doss. VM, Info., Doct. 48–51 and Doss. Charles Lambinon, Inst., Doct. 59–60.
245 R. Poulet 'Prison Diary' 13 July 1946 (Private Collection); Paul Piret *Pro Just.*, 7 Oct. 1944, *Aud. Gén.*, Doss. Charles Lambinon, Inst., Doct. 15–16; *Le Soir* 28 Feb. 1945, pp. 2 and 3, 'Les Conseils de Guerre'; *Vers l'Avenir* 9 Apr. 1946, p. 3, 'Conseil de Guerre de Namur'.
246 Interview between Carl Peeters and José Gotovitch 24 Mar. 1972, p. 59, *C2GM*; JS to *M. le Procureur* 31 Aug. 1944, *Aud. Gén.*, Doss. JS [Supplementary File 8].
247 E.g. JS *Pro Just.*, 3 May 1945, *Aud. Gén.*, Doss. JS, Info.
248 Marcel Simon *Pro Just.*, 3 Jan. 1946 and Charles Nisolle *Pro Just.*, 18–25 June 1945, *Aud. Gén.*, Doss. LC, Inst., Doct. 146–7 and Doss. Charles Lambinon, Inst., Doct. 47–56; *La Meuse* 30 Oct. 1946, p. 2, 'Au Conseil de Guerre'.
249 VM *Pro Just.*, 12 Sept. 1945, *Aud. Gén.*, Doss. VM, Info., Doct. 48–51; J. Wynants *Verviers libéré*, p. 9. See the different estimates of numbers in Gesamtbericht des Wehrmachtsbefehlshabers und Höheren SS- u. Polizeiführers Belgien und Nordfrankreich 25 Oct. 1944, *C2GM*, BDC II; Journal de V. Matthys, p. 17, *C2GM*.
250 *Le Soir* 10 Mar. 1946, p. 3, 'Un rexiste meurt . . .' and 28 Mar. 1946, p. 2, 'Les exploits de deux légionnaires'; *L'Avenir du Luxembourg* 21 Jan. 1947, p. 1, 'Au Conseil de Guerre'; P. Delandsheere and A. Ooms *La Belgique sous les Nazis* IV, p. 281.
251 E.g. *L'Avenir du Luxembourg* 30–1 May 1946, p. 1, 'Nos Conseils de Guerre'.
252 *Le Courrier de l'Escaut* 7 Sept. 1944, p. 2, 'Un collaborateur pendu . . .'; F. Maerten 'Aspects de la libération dans le Brabant wallon', *Cahiers* XI (1988), pp. 133–8.

253 Conseil de Guerre de Bruxelles Exposé des Faits 3 Mar. 1947, pp. 16–17, *C2GM*, JB 13; Sylvain Jadoul *Pro Just.*, 21 Sept. 1945, LC *Pro Just.*, 3 Jan. 1947 and Henry Marcovitz Report No. 3, 11 Feb. 1946, *Aud. Gén.*, Doss. VM, Info., Doct. 64–70 and Doss. LC, Inst., Docts. 235 and 168–73; J. Wynants *Verviers libéré*, p. 9.

Conclusion

1 *Le Soir* 22 May 1946, p. 3, 'La tragédie de Courcelles', 23 May 1946, p. 2, and 24 May 1946, p. 3, 'Les Conseils de Guerre', 29 May 1946, p. 3, 'Conseil de Guerre de Charleroi' and 11 Nov. 1947, pp. 1 and 4, 'Vingt-sept tueurs rexistes...'; *Cour Militaire Pro Just.* 13 Mar. 1947, *C2GM*, JB 12.

2 *Le Journal de Charleroi* 26–7 Feb. 1945, p. 1, 'Le *Waffen-SS* Franz Cordier...' and 17–18 Mar. 1945, p. 1, 'Daumerie a été fusillé...'; JS Note politique sur la répression, *C2GM*, Fonds José Streel; 'Entretiens avec un homme libre: Marcel Grégoire', *Revue Générale* Nov. 1985, pp. 12–13.

3 J. Gilissen 'Etude statistique sur la répression de l'incivisme', *Revue de droit pénal et de criminologie* XXXI (1952), pp. 513–628. See also W. Ganshof van der Meersch *Réflexions sur la répression*.

4 See pp. 61–2.

5 E.g. *Vers l'Avenir* 5 Nov. 1946, p. 2, 'Conseil de Guerre de Namur'; *La Meuse* 10 Apr. 1945 and 2 July 1946, p. 2, 'Au Conseil de Guerre'; J.-M. Vanderlinden 'La réinsertion socio-professionnelle des anciens de la 'Légion Wallonie': première approche', *Cahiers* XIV (1991), pp. 217–19.

6 *La Meuse* 10 Feb. 1945, pp. 1–2, 'Audience mouvementée...'; *L'Avenir du Luxembourg* 27 Feb. 1946, p. 1, 'L'épilogue...'; Jean Denis to *Auditeur Militaire* Charles 9 June 1946, *Aud. Gén.*, Doss. Jean Denis, Info., Doct. 80; R. De Becker 'La collaboration...', *Courrier hebdomadaire du CRISP* No. 497–8 (1970), p. 45; R. Poulet *Ce n'est pas une vie*, p. 172.

7 *Le Journal de Charleroi* 4 Mar. 1947, p. 4, 'Conseil de Guerre de Charleroi'; *La Meuse* 21 Sept. 1945, p. 1, 'Conseil de Guerre'.

8 Plaidoyer prononcé par Victor Matthys devant le Conseil de Guerre de Charleroi, *C2GM*, JP 258.

9 *Le Soir* 10 May 1946, p. 2, 'Le Général Chardonne...'

10 1,247 death sentences were passed on collaborators in Belgium after the war. Of these, 241 were carried out of which 14 were in Brussels and 122 in Wallonia. See J. Gilissen 'Etude statistique...', *Revue de droit pénal et de criminologie* XXXI (1952), p. 620.

11 J.-M. Vanderlinden 'La réinsertion des anciens de la "Légion Wallonie"...', *Cahiers* XIV (1991), pp. 203–58; R. Poulet *Ce n'est pas une vie*, pp. 269–83; C. Suzanne *Commentaires en marge de l'histoire*; H. Philippet *Et mets ta robe de bal*, pp. 335–77.

12 Untitled account by VM and Paul Garain *Pro Just.*, 26 Apr. 1945, *Aud. Gén.*, Doss. VM, Info., Docts. 180–5 and 15–17; Henry Marcovitz *Pro Just.*, 7 Mar. 1946, *C2GM*, PF 3.

13 H. Philippet *Et mets ta robe de bal*, pp. 212–13; JS to *Abbé* Lannoy 31 Mar. 1945, *Aud. Gén.*, Doss. JS, Info., Doct. 2.

14 Raymond Camby *Pro Just.*, 14 Nov. 1945, VM *Pro Just.*, 21 Dec. 1946 and LC *Pro Just.*, 3 Jan. 1947, *Aud. Gén.*, Doss. VM, Info., Docts. 106–10 and 179 and Doss. LC, Inst., Doct. 233; Journal de V. Matthys, pp. 18–19, *C2GM*; Documentation Jans 126; L. Degrelle *La Campagne de Russie* (Paris, 1949), pp. 385–400; P. Lévy *Les heures rouges des Ardennes* (Brussels, 1946).

15 Untitled account by VM and Raymond Camby *Pro Just.*, 17 July 1945, *Aud. Gén.*, Doss. VM, Info., Docts. 180–5 and 22–36.

16 *Sûreté de l'Etat Pro Just.*, 7 Sept. 1945, *Aud. Gén.*, Doss. LC, Inst., Doct. 79; Letter of Mathieu 21 Feb. 1986, *C2GM*, JP 722.

17 JS Mémoire pour mon défenseur, suite et fin, *C2GM*, Fonds José Streel; *Le Journal de Charleroi* 7–8 July 1945, p. 1, 'Georges Dubois...est arrêté', 27 Sept. 1945, p. 1, 'Une vingtaine de *Waffen SS*...' and 12 Oct. 1945, p. 1, 'Du bétail pour l'abattoir...'; *Le Soir* 6 Mar. 1948, p. 4, 'Arrestation mouvementée...'

18 VM to wife, Note of arrest of VM 31 July 1945 and *Sûreté de l'Etat Pro Just.*, 7 Sept. 1945 and 2 Feb. 1946, *Aud. Gén.*, Doss. VM, Info., Docts. 41 and 42 and Doss. LC, Inst., Docts. 79 and 163.

19 J. De Launay *Histoires secrètes de la Belgique*, pp. 183–4; L. Degrelle *La Campagne de Russie*, pp. 466–98.

20 J. De Thier 'Pourquoi l'Espagne de Franco n'a pas livré Degrelle', *Revue Générale* Apr. 1983, pp. 3–26.

21 J.-M. Frérotte *Léon Degrelle, le dernier fasciste*, pp. 220–3; J.-M. Charlier *Léon Degrelle*, pp. 395–6.

22 E.g. L. Degrelle *Hitler pour mille ans*; J.-M. Charlier *Léon Degrelle*.

23 Interview with Léon Degrelle 14 July 1988; J.-M. Frérotte *Op. cit.*, p. 223; *Le Monde* 17 Dec. 1987, 'Le jeu de pistes' and 18 Oct. 1991, 'Un "Agenda nationaliste"...'

24 R. Van Doorslaer and E. Verhoeyen *L'assassinat de Julien Lahaut* (Antwerp, 1987); F. Balace and C. Dupont 'Les "anciens" et le Roi: facteurs de cohésion et de divergence 1945–1950', *Cahiers* IX (1985), pp. 123–74.

25 J. Gérard-Libois and J. Gotovitch *Léopold III, de l'an 40 à l'effacement* (Brussels, 1991); P. Theunissen *1950, le dénouement de la question royale* (Brussels, 1986).

26 *Rivarol* 10 Oct. 1953, p. 1, 'A la porte les parlementaires'; 'Nouvelles formes et tendances d'extrême droite en Belgique', *Courrier hebdomadaire du CRISP* Nos. 140–2 (1962); E. Verhoeyen 'L'extrême droite en Belgique (I)', *Courrier hebdomadaire du CRISP* No. 642–3 (1974), pp. 31–3.

27 L. Rowies, J. Moden and J. Sloover 'L'UDRT-RAD', *Courrier hebdomadaire du CRISP* Nos. 924 and 940–2 (1981); P. Brewaeys, V. Dahaut and A. Tolbiac 'L'extrême droite francophone face aux élections', *Courrier hebdomadaire du CRISP* No. 1350 (1992).

28 P. Brewaeys *et al. Op. cit.*

29 E.g. R. De Becker Conférence rédactionnelle au *Soir* 3 Sept. 1943, *C2GM*, PL 1; JS Note politique sur la répression p. 8, *C2GM*, Fonds José Streel.

30 J.-M. Frérotte *Léon Degrelle, le dernier fasciste.*, p. 190.

31 See pp. 18–20.

32 See the remarks of J. Gotovitch in *Le Vif-L'Express* 7–13 Aug. 1992, pp. 30–1, 'Le monde à l'envers'. Re France, see H. Rousso *Le syndrome de Vichy de 1944 à nos jours* (Paris, 1990).

33 For a highly perceptive fictionalised account of the complexities of daily life in pre-war and wartime Belgium, see H. Claus *The Sorrow of Belgium* (New York-London, 1990).

34 See R. Van Doorslaer 'Macht en onmacht in bezettingstijd, het geval België', *Bijdragen en Mededelingen betreffende de Geschiedenis der Nederlanden* CII (1988) No. 4, pp. 610–17.

35 A. Dantoing *La 'collaboration' du Cardinal*; M. Van den Wijngaert 'La politique du moindre mal', *Revue du Nord* Special Number (1987), pp. 63–72; E. Verhoeyen 'Les grands industriels belges', *Cahiers* X (1986), pp. 57–114.

36 G. Warner 'La crise politique belge de novembre 1944: un coup d'état manqué?', *Courrier hebdomadaire du CRISP* No. 798 (1978); E. Witte, J. Burgelman and P. Stouthuysen (eds.) *Tussen restauratie en vernieuwing* (Brussels, 1990), pp. 13–56.

Bibliography

Manuscript Sources

1 *Auditorat Général près la Cour Militaire*, Palais de Justice, Brussels.

Dossiers relating to: Edmond Collard, Louis Collard, Jean Colman, Albert Constant, Jean Denis, Marcel Dupont, Charles Lambinon, Victor Matthys, Pierre Pauly, Joseph Pévenasse, Michel Saussez and José Streel.

2 German Records

a German Records Microfilmed at Alexandria (GRMA)
T 175 80: Berger to Himmler 5 Jan. 1943 and 31 July 1944; Report on military units 1 July 1943; Propaganda Abteilung Belgien 1944.
T 175 131: Correspondence relating to Degrelle and the *DSI*.
T 501 97: Report of Von Craushaar 28 Apr. 1943.
T 501 102–6: *Tätigkeitsberichten* of Reeder 1940–4. The page numbers of these reports cited in the text refer to the photographic copies of the reports preserved in the *C2GM*.
T 501 173: Report of *Sipo-SD* 15 June 1942.
T 501 175: Correspondence relating to the *Légion Wallonie*.

b German records conserved in the *C2GM*, Brussels.
Berlin Document Center Archive: Dossiers II and III.
Sipo-SD: Meldungen aus Belgien und Nordfrankreich 1943 and 1944.
Archive C 11: Miscellaneous correspondence relating to Léon Degrelle.

c Other German records
Bundesarchiv Koblenz: Berger to Himmler 5 Jan. 1943.
Institut für Zeitgeschichte München: Reports relating to the meeting of the *Arbeitsgemeinschaft für den germanischen Raum* 12 Jan. 1943.

3 *Centre de recherches et d'études historiques de la seconde guerre mondiale*, Brussels.

a Official Documents
Séances du comité des secrétaires-généraux 1940–4.
Archives of INBEL.
Archives of *CCW* (C 4).
Archives of *AGRA* (C 5).
Archives of the *Légion Nationale* (C 8).
Archives of Rex (C 11).
Archives of Walloon movements (C 13).
Documents relating to the trial of von Falkenhausen (JB 9).
Cour Militaire Pro Justicia 13 Mar. 1947 (JB 12).
Conseil de Guerre de Bruxelles Exposé des Faits 3 Mar. 1947 (JB 13).

Conseil de Guerre de Bruxelles Exposé des Faits 15 Sept. 1945 (JB 15).
Collection of documents relating to the activities of the *Formations B* (JB 20).
Conseil de Guerre de Namur *Pro Justicia* 20 July 1948 (JB 26).
Henry Marcovitz *Pro Justicia* 7 Mar. 1946 (PF 3).
Collection of documents relating to the *Corporation Nationale de l'Education* (PL 1/332).

b Personal Papers
Journal de Victor Matthys (JB 6).
Mémoire de Victor Matthys (JB 6).
G. Figeys Carnets and Mémoire (JP 093).
Plaidoyer prononcé par Victor Matthys devant le Conseil de Guerre de Charleroi (JP 258).
Documents relating to Mathieu (JP 722).
E. De Bruyne 'Un aspect de la collaboration militaire dans la Belgique francophone 1941–1945' (JP 732).
Papiers Bourguet (PB 3).
Papiers Charlier (PC 4).
Papiers J.-F. Collard (PC 10).
Souvenirs de Heinz Forsteneichner (PF 3).
Papiers Grauls (PG 5).
R. De Becker Conférence rédactionnelle au *Soir* 3 Sept. 1943 (PL 1).
Papiers Del Marmol (PM 14).
Papiers José Streel (PS 16).
Historique du *Service des Volontaires de Travail pour la Wallonie* (W 3/50).
Collection of documents relating to Pierre Hubermont (W 3).
Full text of P. Struye *L'évolution du sentiment public en Belgique sous l'occupation allemande* (W 3).
Collection of documents relating to the *Légion Wallonie* (W 4).
Papiers Pierre Daye (unindexed).

c Interviews in archives of *C2GM*
Jean Vermeire 25 Mar. 1971.
Carl Peeters (Carl Suzanne) 24 Mar. 1972.
Léon Degrelle 11–12 Dec. 1977.

4 Other Unpublished Material

Documentation Jans (Private Collection).
Archives of Robert Poulet (Private Collection).
Telegram from *Chargé d'affaires* at Madrid 10 Feb. 1951, Archives of the Ministry of Foreign Affairs, Brussels (Papers of José Gotovitch).
Anonymous letter relating to Fernand Rouleau 17 Apr. 1987 (Private Collection).

5 Interviews

Paul Jamin 11 Dec. 1987 and 8 Feb. 1988.
Léon Degrelle 14 July 1988.
Other anonymous sources.

Printed Sources

1 Primary Sources

a Rexist Newspapers:
L'Assaut 1944

National Socialisme 1942–4

L' *Avenir* 1943
En Avant 1942
Informations administratives et politiques
1943–4

Le Pays Réel 1940–4
Rex 1936–40.

b Newspapers published during the German Occupation
L'Ami du Peuple 1941–3
Cassandre 1940–4
Le Drapeau Rouge 1940–4
(Underground)
L'Effort Wallon 1942–4
Front 1943–4 (Underground)
La Gazette de Charleroi 1944
Le Journal de Charleroi 1941–2

La Légia 1941–2
Moniteur Belge 1941–2
Notre Combat 1942–4
Le Nouveau Journal 1941–4
Le Peuple 1940–4 (Underground)
Le Rempart 1941–3
Le Soir 1940–4
Het Vlaamsche Land 1943

c Post-war Newspapers
L'Avenir du Luxembourg 1946–7
Le Brabant Wallon 1946
La Cité Nouvelle 1945
Le Courrier de l'Escaut 1944 and 1946–7
Le Drapeau Rouge 1946
L'Echo du Centre 1947
Gazette de Liège 1945–7
Le Journal de Charleroi 1945–7

Journal des Tribunaux 1945–9
La Libre Belgique 1946
Le Matin 1944 and 1946
La Meuse 1945–7
Sambre et Meuse 1946–7
Le Soir 1944–8
Vers l'Avenir 1946–7

d Publications
Annales parlementaires de la Belgique 1936
Akten zur Deutschen Auswärtigen Politik 1918–1945 Serie D Band XI. 1 (Bonn, 1964)
P. Bodart *Avec l'Armée Belge des Partisans* (Brussels, 1948)
R. Brasillach *Léon Degrelle et l'avenir de Rex* (Paris, 1936)
R. Brasillach *Notre Avant-Guerre* (Paris, 1968)
Comte Capelle *Au Service du Roi* (Brussels, 1949)
J.-M. Charlier *Léon Degrelle: persiste et signe* (Paris, 1985)
A. Crahay *Une vie au XXe siècle* (Brussels, 1988)
W. Dannau *Ainsi parla Léon Degrelle* (Strombeek-Bever, 1973)
P. Dastier 'Degrelle parle', *Dossier du mois* Nos. 6/7 (Brussels, 1963)
'Les mémoires de Pierre Daye', *Dossier du mois* No. 12 (Brussels, 1963)
R. De Becker *Le livre des vivants et des morts* (Brussels, 1942)
R. De Becker 'La collaboration en Belgique', *Courrier hebdomadaire du CRISP* No. 497–8 (1970)
L. Degrelle *Les Taudis* (Louvain, 1929)
L. Degrelle *Discours prononcé à Liége le 27 avril 1941* (Liège, No date)
L. Degrelle *Feldpost* (Brussels, 1944)
L. Degrelle *La Campagne de Russie* (Paris, 1949)
L. Degrelle *La Cohue de 1940* (Lausanne, 1949)
L. Degrelle *Hitler pour mille ans* (Paris, 1969)
L. Degrelle *Lettres à mon Cardinal* (Brussels, 1975)
'Léon Degrelle, le procès qui n'a jamais eu lieu', *L'Eventail* 30 May and 6 and 13 June 1980
P. Delandsheere and A. Ooms *La Belgique sous les Nazis* (Brussels, No date)
A. Delattre *Mes Souvenirs* (Cuesmes, 1957)
H. De Man *Cahiers de ma montagne* (Brussels-Paris, 1944)

'Entretiens avec un homme libre: Marcel Grégoire', *Revue Générale* Aug.–Nov. 1985

General von Falkenhausen *Mémoires d'outre-guerre* (Brussels, 1974)

Die Tagebücher von Joseph Goebbels. Sämtliche Fragmente Teil I 1924–1941 (Munich, 1987)

R. Goffin *Souvenirs avant l'adieu* (Charleroi, 1980)

M.-H. Jaspar *Souvenirs sans retouche* (Paris, 1968)

B. de Jouvenal *Un voyageur dans le siècle* (Paris, 1979)

Chanoine Leclef *Le Cardinal Van Roey et l'occupation allemande en Belgique* (Brussels, 1945)

L. Narvaez *Degrelle m'a dit* (Brussels, 1977)

Naval Intelligence Division *Belgium* (No place, 1944)

H. Philippet *Et mets ta robe de bal* (Privately published)

R. Poulet *Ce n'est pas une vie* (Paris, 1976)

Recensement général de la population de l'industrie et du commerce au 31 janvier 1947 (Brussels, 1949)

Recueil de documents établi par le Secrétariat du Roi concernant la période 1936–1949 (No place, 1949)

J.-C. Ricquier 'Les souvenirs politiques d'Etienne de la Vallée Poussin', *Revue Générale* Mar. 1981

J.-C. Ricquier 'Auguste De Schryver: souvenirs politiques et autres', *Revue Générale* May–Sept. 1982

J.-C. Ricquier 'Le Vicomte Eyskens: souvenirs et commentaires', *Revue Générale* Aug.–Sept. 1983

Secrétariat du Roi *Livre Blanc 1936–1946* (No place, 1946)

J. Streel *Les jeunes gens et la politique* (Louvain, 1932)

J. Streel *La Révolution du vingtième siècle* (Brussels, 1942)

P. Struye *L'évolution du sentiment public en Belgique sous l'occupation allemande* (Brussels, 1945)

C. Suzanne *Commentaires en marge de l'histoire* (Louvain, 1959)

General Van Overstraeten *Sous le joug: Léopold III prisonnier* (Brussels, 1986)

R. Verlaine *Sans haine et sans gloire* (Liège, No date)

2 Secondary Sources

R. Austin 'The Chantiers de la Jeunesse in Languedoc 1940–44', *French Historical Studies XIII* (1983)

J.-P. Azéma *De Munich à la Libération* (Paris, 1979)

F. Balace 'Fascisme et catholicisme politique dans la Belgique francophone de l'entre-deux-guerres', *Handelingen van het XXXIIe Vlaams filologencongres* (Leuven, 1979)

F. Balace and C. Dupont 'Les "anciens" et le Roi: facteurs de cohésion et de divergence 1945–1950', *Cahiers d'histoire de la seconde guerre mondiale IX* (1985)

F. Bédarida 'Vichy et la crise de la conscience française', in J.-P. Azéma and F. Bédarida (eds.) *Vichy et les Français* (Paris, 1992)

H. Bernard *La Résistance 1940–1945* (Brussels, 1969)

Biographie Nationale XXXV (Brussels, 1969)

W. Boelcke *Kriegspropaganda 1939–1941* (Stuttgart, 1966)

M. Brelaz *Henri De Man, une autre idée du socialisme* (Geneva, 1985)

M. Brelaz *Léopold III et Henri De Man* (Geneva, 1988)

P. Brewaeys, V. Dahaut and A. Tolbiac 'L'extrême droite francophone face aux élections', *Courrier hebdomadaire du CRISP* No. 1350 (1992)

A. Brissaud *Pétain à Sigmaringen (1944–1945)* (Paris, 1960)

J.-P. Brunet *Jacques Doriot* (No place, 1986)

P. Burrin *La dérive fasciste: Doriot, Déat, Bergery 1933–1945* (Paris, 1986)

G. Carpinelli 'Belgium' in S.J. Woolf (ed.) *Fascism in Europe* (London-New York, 1981)

J.-L. Charles *Les forces armées belges au cours de la deuxième guerre mondiale 1940–1945* (Brussels, 1970)

C. Chevalier 'La presse francophone et l'église catholique en Belgique sous l'occupation allemande (1940–1944)' (Université Catholique de Louvain-la-Neuve Mémoire de licence, 1986)

M. Claeys-Van Haegendoren 'L'Eglise et l'Etat au XXe siècle', *Courrier hebdomadaire du CRISP* No. 542–3 (1971)

H. Claus *The Sorrow of Belgium* (New York-London, 1990)

M. Conway 'Le rexisme de 1940 à 1944: Degrelle et les autres', *Cahiers d'histoire de la seconde guerre mondiale* X (1986)

M. Conway 'Building the Christian City: Catholics and Politics in Inter-War Francophone Belgium', *Past and Present* No. 128 (Aug. 1990)

M. Conway 'Du catholicisme à la collaboration: le cas de José Streel' in *Belgique en 1940: une société en crise, un pays en guerre* (Brussels, 1993)

A. Crahay *Les Belges en Corée 1951–1955* (Brussels, 1966)

J. Culot 'L'exploitation de la main d'oeuvre belge et le problème des réfractaires', *Cahiers d'histoire de la seconde guerre mondiale* I (1970)

A. Dantoing 'La hiérarchie catholique et la Belgique sous l'occupation allemande', *Revue du Nord* LX (1978)

A. Dantoing 'L'épiscopat belge en 1939–1940: De la neutralité à la présence' (Université Catholique de Louvain-la-Neuve Docteur en philosophie et lettres, 1990)

A. Dantoing *La "collaboration" du Cardinal* (Brussels, 1991)

A. Dantoing 'Du fascisme occidental à la politique de présence: Robert Poulet' in *Belgique en 1940: une société en crise, un pays en guerre* (Brussels, 1993)

O.A. Davey 'The Origins of the *Légion des Volontaires Français contre le Bolchevisme*', *Journal of Contemporary History* VI No. 4 (1971)

E. De Bens *De Belgische dagbladpers onder Duitse censuur* (Antwerp-Utrecht, 1973)

E. De Bens 'La presse au temps de l'occupation de la Belgique (1940–1944)', *Revue d'histoire de la deuxième guerre mondiale* XX (1970)

E. De Bruyne *Les Wallons meurent à l'est: la Légion Wallonie et Léon Degrelle sur le Front russe 1941–1945* (Brussels, 1991)

E. Defoort 'Le courant réactionnaire dans le catholicisme francophone belge 1918–1926', *Revue belge d'histoire contemporaine* VIII (1977)

A. De Jonghe 'L'établissement d'une administration civile en Belgique et le Nord de la France', *Cahiers d'histoire de la seconde guerre mondiale* I (1970)

A. De Jonghe *Hitler en het politieke lot van België (1940–1944)* (Antwerp-Utrecht, 1972)

A. De Jonghe 'H.J. Elias als leider van het Vlaams Nationaal Verbond', *Revue belge d'histoire contemporaine* VI (1975) and VII (1976)

A. De Jonghe 'La lutte Himmler-Reeder pour la nomination d'un HSSPF à Bruxelles', *Cahiers d'histoire de la seconde guerre mondiale* III, IV, V, VII and VIII (1974, 1976, 1978, 1982 and 1984)

J. De Launay *Histoires secrètes de la Belgique* (Paris, 1975)

B. Delcord 'A propos de quelques "chapelles" politico-littéraires en Belgique (1919–1945)', *Cahiers d'histoire de la seconde guerre mondiale* X (1986)

J. Delperrié de Bayac *Histoire de la Milice 1918–1945* (Paris, 1969)

R. De Smet, R. Evalenko and W. Fraeys *Atlas des élections belges* (Brussels, 1958)

J. De Thier 'Pourquoi l'Espagne de Franco n'a pas livré Degrelle', *Revue Générale* Apr. 1983

R. Devleeschouwer 'L'opinion politique et les revendications territoriales belges à la fin de la première guerre mondiale 1918–1919' in *Mélanges offerts à G. Jacquemyns* (Brussels, 1968)

Le diocèse de Tournai sous l'occupation allemande (Tournai-Paris, 1946)

P.M. Dioudonnat *Je suis partout: les Maurrassiens devant la tentation fasciste* (Paris, 1973)

P. Dodge *Beyond Marxism: The Faith and Works of Hendrik De Man* (The Hague, 1966)

J. Erickson *The Road to Berlin* (London, 1983)

J.-M. Etienne 'Les origines du rexisme', *Res Publica* IX (1967)

J.-M. Etienne *Le mouvement rexiste jusqu'en 1940* (Paris, 1968)

J.-M. Frérotte *Léon Degrelle, le dernier fasciste* (Brussels, 1987)

W. Ganshof van der Meersch *Réflexions sur la répression des crimes contre la sûreté extérieure de l'état belge* (Brussels, 1946)

E. Gerard *De Katholieke Partij in crisis* (Leuven, 1985)

E. Gerard 'La responsabilité du monde catholique dans la naissance et l'essor du rexisme', *La Revue Nouvelle* (Jan. 1987)

J. Gérard-Libois and J. Gotovitch *L'an 40* (Brussels, 1971)

J. Gérard-Libois 'Rex 1936–1940', *Courrier hebdomadaire du CRISP* No. 1226 (1989)

J. Gérard-Libois and J. Gotovitch *Léopold III, de l'an 40 à l'effacement* (Brussels, 1991)

J. Gilissen 'Etude statistique sur la répression de l'incivisme', *Revue de droit pénal et de criminologie* XXXI (1952)

R. Gobyn 'La vie quotidienne pendant la seconde guerre mondiale: une combinaison étrange d'individualisme et de solidarité' in *1940–1945 La vie quotidienne en Belgique* (Brussels, 1984)

J. Gotovitch 'Photographie de la presse clandestine de 1940', *Cahiers d'histoire de la seconde guerre mondiale* II (1972)

J. Gotovitch 'Guerre et libération, jalons pour une étude' in *Le parti communiste de Belgique (1921–1944)* (Brussels, 1980)

J. Gotovitch 'Du Collectivisme au Plan de Travail' in *1885–1985: Du Parti Ouvrier Belge au Parti Socialiste* (Brussels, 1985)

J. Gotovitch *Du rouge au tricolore: les communistes belges de 1939 à 1944* (Brussels, 1992)

J. Goueffon 'La guerre des ondes: le cas de Jean Hérold-Paquis', *Revue d'histoire de la deuxième guerre mondiale* XXVII (1977)

H. Hasquin (ed.) *Communes de Belgique* (Brussels, 1980)

P. Hayes *Quisling* (Newton Abbot, 1971)

G. Hirschfeld 'Collaboration and Attentisme in the Netherlands', *Journal of Contemporary History* XVI (1981)

O.K. Hoidal *Quisling* (Oslo, 1989)

C.-H. Höjer *Le régime parlementaire belge de 1918 à 1940* (Uppsala, 1946)

J.-L. Hondros *Occupation and Resistance: The Greek Agony* (New York, 1983)

G. Hoyois 'Monseigneur Picard et Léon Degrelle', *Revue générale belge* XCV (Nov. 1959)

G. Hoyois *Aux origines de l'Action Catholique: Monseigneur Picard* (Brussels, 1960)

Institut Hoover *La vie de la France sous l'Occupation (1940–1944)* (Paris, 1957)

E. Jäckel *Frankreich in Hitlers Europa* (Stuttgart, 1966)

P. Jacquet *Brabant Wallon 1940–1944* (Paris-Louvain-la-Neuve, 1989)

P. Janssens 'Les Dinasos wallons 1936–41' (Université de Liège Mémoire de licence, 1982)

Y. Jelinek 'Storm-troopers in Slovakia: the Rodobrana and the Hlinka Guard', *Journal of Contemporary History* VI (1971)

Y. Jelinek *The Parish Republic: Hlinka's Slovak People's Party 1939–1945* (New York-London, 1976)

C. Kesteloot and A. Gavroy *François Bovesse: Pour la défense intégrale de la Wallonie* (Mont-sur-Marchienne, 1990)

H. Krausnick *et al. Anatomy of the SS State* (London, 1968)

E. Krier 'Le rexisme et l'Allemagne 1933–1940', *Cahiers d'histoire de la seconde guerre mondiale* V (1978)

F. Kupferman *Laval* (Paris, 1987)

R. Salas Larrazabal 'La Division "Azul"', *Guerres mondiales et conflits contemporains* XL (1990)

R. Lefebvre 'Dauge et le Daugisme' (Université Libre de Bruxelles Mémoire de licence, 1979)

C. Legein 'Le Parti Socialiste Révolutionnaire (Le Mouvement Trotskyiste en Belgique de 1936 à 1939)' (Université Catholique de Louvain Mémoire de licence, 1982)

A. Lemaire *Le crime du 18 août* (Couillet, 1947)

P. Lévy *Les heures rouges des Ardennes* (Brussels, 1946)

A. Lijphart *The Politics of Accommodation: Pluralism and Democracy in the Netherlands* (Berkeley, 1968)

J.-L. Loubet del Bayle *Les non-conformistes des années 30* (Paris, 1969)

J. Mabire *Légion Wallonie: au Front de l'Est 1941–1944* (Paris, 1987)

F. Maerten 'Aspects de la libération dans le Brabant wallon', *Cahiers d'histoire de la seconde guerre mondiale* XI (1988)

V. Marquet 'L'exécution d'Edouard Degrelle. Une bavure?', *Mémo* No 28 (1989)

V. Mastny *Russia's Road to Cold War* (New York, 1979)

J.M. Mayeur (ed.) *Histoire du Christianisme des origines à nos jours XII Guerres mondiales et totalitarismes 1914–1958* (Paris, 1990)

W. Meyers 'Les collaborateurs flamands de France et leurs contacts avec les milieux flamingants belges', *Revue du Nord* LX (1978)

A. Milward *The New Order and the French Economy* (Oxford, 1970)

J. Neckers 'La libération' in *1940–1945 La vie quotidienne en Belgique* (Brussels, 1984)

L. Noguères *La dernière étape Sigmaringen* (Paris, 1956)

'Nouvelles formes et tendances d'extrême droite en Belgique', *Courrier hebdomadaire du CRISP* Nos. 140–2 (1962)

P. Ory *Les collaborateurs 1940–1945* (Paris, 1976)

R. Paxton *Vichy France: Old Guard and New Order 1940–1944* (London, 1972)

B. Peeters *Le monde d'Hergé* ([Tournai], 1983)

H. Rousso *Un château en Allemagne* (Paris, 1980)

H. Rousso *Le syndrome de Vichy de 1944 à nos jours* (Paris, 1990)

L. Rowies, J. Moden and J. Sloover 'L'UDRT-RAD', *Courrier hebdomadaire du CRISP* Nos. 924 and 940–2 (1981)

L. Schepens 'Fascists and Nationalists in Belgium 1919–40' in S.V. Larsen, B. Hagtvet and J.P. Myklebust *Who were the Fascists* (Bergen, 1980)

L. Schepens 'La mentalité de la population' in *1940–1945 La vie quotidienne en Belgique* (Brussels, 1984)

G.T. Schillemans *Philippe Pétain, le prisonnier de Sigmaringen* (Paris, 1965)

F. Selleslagh 'L'emploi' in *1940–1945 La vie quotidienne en Belgique* (Brussels, 1984)

M. Smith 'Neither Resistance nor Collaboration: Historians and the problem of the Nederlandse Unie', *History* LXXII (1987)

M. Steinberg *L'étoile et le fusil: la question juive 1940–1942* (Brussels, 1983)

J. Stengers 'Belgium' in H. Rogger and E. Weber (eds.) *The European Right: A Historical Profile* (London, 1965)

J. Stengers *Léopold III et le gouvernement: les deux politiques belges de 1940* (Paris-Gembloux, 1980)

J. Stengers 'Paul De Man, a collaborator?' in L. Herman, K. Humbeeck and G. Lernout (eds.) *(Dis)continuities: Essays on Paul De Man* (Amsterdam, 1989)

Z. Sternhell *Ni droite ni gauche: l'idéologie fasciste en France* (Paris, 1983)

P. Theunissen *1950, le dénouement de la question royale* (Brussels, 1986)

J. Touchard 'L'esprit des années 1930' republished in P. Andreu (ed.) *Révoltes de l'esprit: les revues des années 1930* (No place, 1991)

H. Trevor-Roper (ed.) *Hitler's Table Talk* (London, 1953)

W. Tucker *The Fascist Ego: A Political Biography of Robert Brasillach* (Berkeley, 1975)

L. Van Daele 'De Vlaamse Wacht Juni 1941–September 1944' (Rijksuniversiteit Gent Mémoire de licence, 1986)

M. Van den Wijngaert 'La politique du moindre mal: la politique du Comité des Secrétaires-Généraux en Belgique sous l'occupation allemande, 1940–1944', *Revue du Nord* Special Number (1987)

J.-M. Vanderlinden 'La réinsertion socio-professionnelle des anciens de la "Légion Wallonie": première approche', *Cahiers d'histoire de la seconde guerre mondiale* XIV (1991)

R. Van Doorslaer and E. Verhoeyen *L'assassinat de Julien Lahaut* (Antwerp, 1987)

R. Van Doorslaer 'La police belge et le maintien de l'ordre en Belgique occupée', *Revue du Nord* Numéro Spécial (1987)

R. Van Doorslaer 'Macht en onmacht in bezettingstijd, het geval België', *Bijdragen en Mededelingen betreffende de Geschiedenis der Nederlanden* CII (1988) No. 4.

P. Vandromme *Le loup au cou de chien* (Brussels, 1978)

F. Van Langenhove *La Belgique en quête de sécurité 1920–1940* (Brussels, 1969)

J. Vanwelkenhuyzen 'Regards nouveaux sur mai 1940' in *Actes du Colloque d'histoire militaire. belge 1830–1980* (Brussels, 1981)

J. Vanwelkenhuyzen *Les avertissements qui venaient de Berlin* (Gembloux, 1982)

J. Vanwelkenhuyzen and J. Dumont *1940: Le Grand Exode* (Paris-Gembloux, 1983)

E. Verhoeyen 'L'extrême droite en Belgique (I)', *Courrier hebdomadaire du CRISP* No. 642–3 (1974)

E. Verhoeyen 'Les grands industriels belges entre collaboration et résistance: le moindre mal', *Cahiers d'histoire de la seconde guerre mondiale* X (1986)

E. Verhoeyen 'Un groupe de résistants du Nord-Hainaut: la Phalange Blanche', *Cahiers d'histoire de la seconde guerre mondiale* XII (1989)

W. Wagner *Belgien in der deutschen Politik während des Zweiten Weltkrieges* (Boppard, 1974)

G. Warner 'La crise politique belge de novembre 1944: un coup d'état manqué?', *Courrier hebdomadaire du CRISP* No. 798 (1978)

J. Willequet 'Les fascismes belges et la seconde guerre mondiale', *Revue d'histoire de la deuxième guerre mondiale* XVII (1967)

J. Willequet *La Belgique sous la botte: résistances et collaborations 1940–1945* (Paris, 1986)

E. Witte and J. Craeybeckx *La Belgique politique de 1830 à nos jours* (Brussels, 1987)

E. Witte, J. Burgelman and P. Stouthuysen (eds.) *Tussen restauratie en vernieuwing* (Brussels, 1990)

J. Wynants 'Verviers, l'autorité communale en 1940–1941', *Cahiers d'histoire de la seconde guerre mondiale* II (1972)

J. Wynants *Verviers 1940* (No place, 1981)

J. Wynants *Verviers libéré* (Verviers, 1984)

Ch. d'Ydewalle *Degrelle ou la triple imposture* (Brussels, 1968)

Index